Principles of

Macroeconomics

Homework

Black board
submitting quiz
quiz chapter 1 & 2
print complete word
work book 18 - 23

Principles of
Macroeconomics
Sixth Edition

Fred M. Gottheil
University of Illinois

CENGAGE
Learning™

Australia • Brazil • Japan • Korea • Mexico • Singapore • Spain • United Kingdom • United States

CENGAGE
Learning™

Principles of Macroeconomics, 6e
Fred M. Gottheil

V.P. Product Development: Dreis Van Landuyt

Managing Editor: Greg Albert

Custom Production Editor: Kim Fry

Permissions Specialist: Todd Osborne

Marketing Specialist: Lindsay Shapiro

Manufacturing Manager: Donna M. Brown

Sr. Production Coordinator: Robin Richie

Composition House: Macmillan Publishing Solutions

For product information and technology assistance, contact us at
Cengage Learning Customer & Sales Support, 1-800-354-9706
For permission to use material from this text or product,
submit all requests online at **www.cengage.com/permissions**
Further permissions questions can be emailed to
permissionrequest@cengage.com

Library of Congress Control Number: 2009923711

BOOK ISBN 13: 978-1-424-06873-9

BOOK ISBN 10: 1-424-06873-8

South-Western Cengage Learning
5191 Natorp Boulevard
Mason, OH 45040
USA

Cengage Learning is a leading provider of customized learning solutions with office locations around the globe, including Singapore, the United Kingdom, Australia, Mexico, Brazil, and Japan. Locate your local office at:
international.cengage.com/region

Cengage Learning products are represented in Canada by Nelson Education, Ltd.

For your lifelong learning solutions, visit **academic.cengage.com**

Visit our corporate web site at **cengage.com**

Printed in Canada
1 2 3 4 5 6 7 8 09

To my wife, Diane

To my children, Lisa and Joshua,
who grew up together, not just as
sister and brother, but as best friends.

Brief Contents

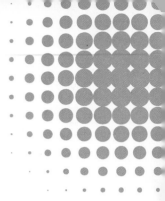

Contents

PART 1 THE BASICS OF ECONOMIC ANALYSIS 1

PART 2 EMPLOYMENT, INFLATION, AND FISCAL POLICY   81

PART 3   MONEY, BANKING, AND MONETARY POLICY   239

PART 4   GOVERNMENT AND THE MACROECONOMY   313

PART 5   THE WORLD ECONOMY   385

In **Every Chapter** You Will Find Features That Make **GOTTHEIL** Even **Greater**

Updated Real Data

Many tables and graphs have been updated with the most recent data available to ensure that information is current and relevant.

on the net

The fifth edition presents an up-to-date collection of the best economic resources on the Internet. The URLs are placed in the context of key economic points to enhance and bring additional understanding.

 perspectives

These updated, socially relevant sidebar features illustrate economic applications in many different contexts—historical, theoretical, global, interdisciplinary—and how they apply to business and daily life.

 ChatEconomics

Introductions to the book's eight parts capture real-life conversations about economics between Gottheil and students. They demonstrate why the content that follows is important.

 check your understanding

Each chapter now presents significant questions at key junctures in the text so that you can assess your comprehension as you read.

 Key Graphs

Updated exhibits emphasize critical graphic concepts in a clear, efficient manner to demonstrate the most helpful graphing principles. "Key Graphs" icons highlight exhibits that demonstrate crucial principles.

Enhanced **End-of-Chapter** Material

Questions and Practice

End-of-chapter questions test your understanding of qualitative concepts covered in each chapter. Practice Problems test your understanding of quantitative or graphical techniques. Both have been updated.

Economic Consultants

This activities feature puts you in the role of the economist for a hypothetical economic research and analysis firm. The work requires economic thinking and analysis as you prepare a report for a client, addressing the fundamental economic issues from the chapter. New Internet links help you with research and analysis.

© Image 100/Royalty-Free/CORBIS

Chapter Review and Key Terms

These features briefly review the principles and new vocabulary introduced in the chapter.

What's Wrong with This Graph?

These Practice Problems help you read and understand graphs by challenging you to identify what's wrong with an incorrect graph or to reproduce a key graphic model from the chapter.

practice**test**

You can quickly assess your understanding of each chapter with eight to ten updated multiple-choice, exam-like problems that address the key principles in the chapter. Answers are available in the back of the book.

Resources for Students

Updated Study Guide

This newly revised feature explains, reviews, and tests the important principles introduced in every chapter. Featured sections include Chapter in a Nutshell, Concept Check, Am I on the Right Track?, Graphing Tutorials, Graphing Pitfalls, True-False Questions, Multiple-Choice Questions, Fill-in-the-Blank Questions, and Discussion Questions. Available in a comprehensive version or in macroeconomics and microeconomics versions.

Gottheil Support Web Site

Access an online study guide, check for updates to the text, take online quizzes and get immediate feedback. You can even communicate with the textbook author, Fred Gottheil. This site also provides links to all the Internet URLs and activities mentioned in the text, downloadable learning support tools, and much more. Visit http://gottheil.swlearning.com/

The Latest Text-Supporting Web Sites

 ## Gottheil Web Resources

The Gottheil Web site provides access to a robust collection of additional online learning tools, including CNN video applications, video clips of the author answering FAQs in Economics, and practice quizzes. Point your Web browser to http://gottheil.swlearning.com/

 ## The Graphing Workshop

The Graphing Workshop is your one-stop learning resource for help in mastering the language of graphs, one of the more difficult aspects of economics. It enables you to explore important economic concepts through a unique learning system made up of tutorials, interactive tools, and exercises that teach how to interpret, reproduce, and explain graphs.

 ## Grasp It!

Java-powered graphs allow you to grasp key economics graphing concepts through hands-on interaction with a live graph.

 ## Economic Applications

EconNews Online, EconDebate Online, EconData Online, and EconLinks Online features help to deepen your understanding of theoretical concepts through hands-on exploration and analysis of the latest economic news stories, policy debates, and data.

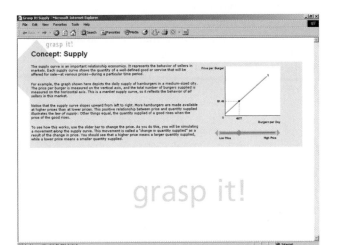

Dear Student,

I may be a little biased, but I honestly believe that the economics course you are about to take will be the most exciting intellectual experience of your college career. When I took economics in college decades ago, it literally blew my mind! It changed the way I saw the world around me. I think that will happen to you.

The study of economics will open up a world of understanding about who you are and how you relate to your community, your country, and the world you live in. It will tell you much about your past, your present, and most important, your future. Economics deals with many real-world issues that you will confront the rest of your life, among them the curse of poverty amid plenty, the problems associated with monopoly and market regulation, the causes of the wealth of nations and why some nations lag behind others, and why our economy repeatedly slips into periods of recession and unemployment. Economics, you will see, is a powerhouse of issues, ideas, and policies.

Many of you may have heardÐthrough the student grapevineÐthat economics is difficult and even esoteric. Not so. Think about it: Most students actually do quite well. There is always a healthy percent of As and Bs. Even C students admit to having learned a lot. If most students can do well in economics, so can you. While the course itself is not difficult, it does require you to give it an honest effort. The keys to your success in economics will be attending classes, listening to your lectures, reading your text, taking notes, checking those notes against the text, working through practice exercises, and asking questions. Asking questions is the best learning experience. Keep asking until the answers make sense.

It has been my experience as a teacher that students are somewhat reluctant to participate in class-room discussion, so when you ask a question in class about material in the lecture or textbook, every-one in class will appreciate it. And the probability is high that most of your classmatesÐand sometimes even your professorÐcould not answer it! It makes you hunt for answers. It makes you think. Everybody gains, especially you.

In fact, you may notice that the economic analysis in this textbook is often built on questions. Check it out. Almost every page asks questions that are followed by answers. I have found that to be the best way to teach and learn. Read this textbook carefully. I think you will enjoy its conversational style and, most important, what it tells you about your world. Good luck!

Fred Gottheil

email: fgotthei@uiuc.edu
phone: 217-333-4591

To the **Instructor**

Working on this sixth edition turned out to be just as exciting as working on each of the earlier ones. Frankly, that didn't surprise me. Because there is always a new idea or a new way of expressing an old idea that makes the telling of the economics story more revealing and perhaps even more appealing to the student. As well, the world around us keeps changing and many of these changes have direct bearing on our economic well being. These changes, too, deserve thoughtful consideration. Remember, Alfred Marshall wrote his *Principles of Economics* in 1891 and, at least for microeconomic theory, is as current today as it was then. After all, the principles are just that: principles. Universal. What we economists have done since is elaborate on them and apply them to the twenty-first century we now inhabit. Marshall would not be shocked that that we still rely on his creative work and would certainly appreciate the fact have we apply it to suit our own circumstances.

That's what I—and other authors of the principles text—have done in the many editions of textbooks that followed the original. The principles remain the bedrock of our analysis, the applications vary to underscore the idea that the principles can be used to explain what is happening in the world about us.

In the fifth edition, the economic consequences of hurricane Katrina, the emergence of China as a superpower, and the war in Iraq became part of our economic analysis. In this sixth edition, the concept of economic bubbles, the sub-prime housing fiasco, immigration in large numbers, and the failed economies of the bottom billion of our world population draw our immediate attention. While these challenging events do not necessarily involve new ideas, they do apply known ideas and analysis to the world we confront.

For example, the role of uncertainty and speculation in economic decision making now becomes a central piece in the analysis of economic bubbles and, as you know, these bubbles have been headline news during our very recent past. This sixth edition weighs in heavily on that kind of analysis. Paul Collier's 2007 volume *The Bottom Billion* is a refreshing descriptive analysis of why several less developed countries have failed to join the many others who managed to perform so well during the past half century. This sixth edition borrows from his analysis and incorporates much of his thinking into the last chapter of the text; on the economic problems of the less developed economies. Immigration from Mexico has always been part of our wage determination analysis, but this sixth addition goes into much more depth on this particular issue. The reason is obvious to you and will be to the student: the subject has become an important piece of our economic lives.

As the editions progressed from the first to this sixth, I have tried to show that the economic principles we teach are imbedded in even the courses students take on American and European literature. In past editions, I have drawn from William Shakespeare, Thomas Hardy, John Steinbeck, Emile Zola, Guy de Maupassant, George Bernard Shaw, Percy Bryce Shelly, and Gertrude Stein. In the fifth edition's chapter on income distribution, I referred back to the poverty-amidst-plenty condition of 18th century England by using both Oliver Goldsmith's poem *The Deserted Village* and George Crabbe's poetic reply in his *The Village*. These are beautiful poems and score the economic points we want to make. In this sixth addition, the students are introduced to Joyce Sutphen poem "Guys Like That" which adds to the discussion of the 2008 financial meltdown.

Fred

A BOOK WRITTEN FOR THE STUDENT

I wrote this textbook with these questions in mind. Although professors, with their own course needs to meet, decide which textbook to adopt, this text was still written *exclusively* for the student. Most of my draft revisions had to do with keeping the focus on the student. Differences between my text and its competitors in style, content, and depth of analysis reflect this focus. A reviewer of several manuscript chapters remarked that they were the most "nonthreatening" principles chapters he had ever read. He got it right! I tried always to keep the analysis within reach of the student. Make the analysis accessible, even personal. Allow the student to appreciate the learning experience, not just to think about the coming exam.

As you know, we absorb ideas in many ways: through our heads, our hearts, and, for lack of better words, our gut reactions. An idea that stirs you emotionally has staying power. If you can feel the importance and relevance of an idea, it becomes more than an academic exercise. The approach I use is intentionally conversational, but the discussion is always serious. I believe economists have something to offer the student. That's what this textbook is about.

Distance Cutting: The Student, the Professor, the Textbook

Think of this text also in terms of distance cutting, that is, narrowing the gap that exists between professor, textbook, and student. Too often that distance creates adversarial roles. Students see themselves as "we," their professors (and their TAs) as "them," and the textbook as "an obstacle to be overcome." How many times have you heard a student ask: "What chapters *do I have to* read for the exam?" Not: "What chapters will *help me understand* the material you covered in class?" Nothing subtle about the differences in language and attitude, is there? You've experienced the difference. I certainly have.

The success of this text, I believe, is *felt* in the converting of "we" and "them" to "us." I wanted the student to feel that he or she, the professor, and the textbook are on the same side. In this academic venture, we're a team. It's important to remember that we're not just teaching economics, we're teaching students. Of course the subject matter is economic principles, but the focus must be on the student.

This textbook makes the student the centerpiece of the analysis. It *talks* to the student. The analysis is built on a series of stories and scenarios that make sense to the student because the stories and scenarios are part of the student's life, or at least familiar to her or him. Recognizing themselves in the analysis matters. It is part of cutting distance.

Questions as a Learning Tool

The text's narrative is built on questions. There is hardly a paragraph in which a question concerning the analysis does not precede discussion. Why questions? Because I believe the best way to understand an idea or concept is to introduce it in the form of a question. Then go to the answer. *The end result is a built-in dialogue* that is conversational, that teaches.

Compare these two modes of communicating an idea: (1) "The child likes chocolate ice cream"; and (2) "What's the child's favorite ice cream?" "Oh, she loves chocolate." Do you hear the dialogue in the second version? When the student reads it, the student is necessarily engaged in the dialogue. It makes it virtually impossible for the student not to participate. Pick a page—*any page*—in this text and see how dialogue dominates the discussion.

And Focusing on the Basics

I love the story of a schoolboy who goes to the public library in search of material on penguins for a school essay. The librarian recommends a book. The child takes it to a reading table but, after three minutes, returns it to the librarian. "What wrong with the book?"she asks. "Nothing really," comes the reply. "It just tells me more about penguins than I wanted to know."

Perhaps one reason students have trouble understanding the principles of economics is that we overload them with esoteric information, which we insist is part of basic economics. To us, it may indeed be basic. To a student looking at economics for the first time, however, it may be anything but basic. *How basic then should basic be*? Admittedly, that's a tough question, but one that ultimately distinguishes a good text from a not-so-good text. In this respect, the difficult decisions that I had to make in writing the textbook were not what to include but what to leave out, and where to find the appropriate level of sophistication that does not shortchange the student or leave him or her mystified and panicked. I often chose to sacrifice new ideas and scores of recent research studies to keep the discussion focused on the basics.

The Approach: Looking at Content

The importance of the $MR = MC$ rule in microeconomics cannot be overstated. It is the key to price determination. In most texts, this idea is developed in the chapter on perfect competition. That is a dreadful mistake! It means students have to cope with many new and complex concepts simultaneously. They must learn about MR, then about $P = MR$ as the horizontal demand curve for the firm, and then about the relationship between that demand curve and industry demand. Finally, they confront long-run equilibrium for both the firm and industry, $P = MR = MC = ATC$. Why start with the most difficult market structure? In this text, I devote a *complete* chapter to the idea of profit maximization, $MR = MC$, *prior to* the analysis of market structure or price determination. The focus is *only* on the $MR = MC$ rule to profit maximization. It allows me—us—to discuss the idea of why marginal analysis lends itself to maximum profit. It affords the opportunity of providing, in an unhurried manner, illustrations and scenarios of how profit maximization evolves. It makes a whale of a difference to the students.

Macroeconomics remains a contentious field of study, and I don't conceal that fact from the student. The text explains what the contention is about and why and how it plays out in the creation of macro theory and policy. While contentious, it is also exciting, and I want the student to know this and be involved in it. A summarizing chapter, "Can Government Really Stabilize the Economy?," brings contending economists into the same space, where the student sees their competing ideas and policy prescriptions.

International trade is no different from any other kind of trade. All that separates international from domestic trade are national borders. That is the message in this text. So the analysis starts with trade between Illinois and Oklahoma. Absolute and comparative advantages are analyzed in this context. Once the student understands the idea, we go to Mexico and beyond. To appreciate this idea—markets are markets everywhere—is to appreciate the one consensus economists believe in: all trade creates win-win outcomes. That's exciting!

Sixth Edition: New and Improved

Textbooks should not be treated like soft drinks and soap detergents. There is no reason to claim a "new and improved" edition every time an edition-cycle year comes around. After all, most textbooks are products of years of experimentation and experience in classroom teaching, of writing and rewriting countless drafts of the text until you think you have it right. How can your text be "new and improved" with every edition? What does it say about the previous ones?

This sixth edition is very much like the fifth. Frankly, I liked the way the first edition turned out. So did the adopters and their students. The style and analysis of the first carried into the second and fourth editions without much change, and this sixth edition is much in the tradition of the earlier ones. The narrative is much the same. The conversational approach is still there. The analysis of principles is still explained in easy-to-understand scenarios. If you liked the earlier editions, rest assured you'll like this sixth. Are there *any* changes? Of course there are! As you would expect, statistical information has been updated so that students have access to the most recent economic data. As well, many boxed perspectives have been revised to reflect the issues that have become center stage in our social, economic, and political life. Critical events and issues over the past three years are used as part of the analysis, not because they are the "big" issues but because they serve as excellent platforms to discuss basic economic principles. For example:

- We don't have to explain to anyone that the housing crisis we now confront has changed the economic fortunes and lives of millions of Americans but we do have to explain *why* a crisis like that could have surfaced in the first place. The analysis on business cycles is expanded in this sixth edition to do just that.
- In 1960, Mexicans, as a percent of foreign born Americans, was 5.9 percent. In 2006, that percent increased to 30.7. What stimuli explain that sharp increase? What impact does that immigration have on the two labor markets of the U.S. and Mexico? This sixth edition looks into these questions.
- In the 1950s, 20 percent of the world's 2.5 billion population was rich while the remaining 80 percent lived in abject poverty. A half century later, one billion of the world's six billion are still rich and growing richer, another four billion have experienced remarkable success in enriching their economic lives, but a billion still remain in deep poverty. Why? Why are there still failed economic societies? This sixth edition addresses these questions, referring much to the recent work done by economist Paul Collier.

The emphasis remains—as it should—on the student. I promise you this: This text is a learning experience. If students read it, it will make your task in the classroom all that much easier and more enjoyable. *And they will read it once they get into it.* That was my goal and I know—after three editions of unsolicited e-mails from students at campuses in almost every state in the country and from their professors as well—that I pretty much achieved that goal. Nothing is perfect and, admittedly, this text is no exception. But it is a fine, student-friendly text. If this claim strikes you as singularly immodest or even downright brash, accept my apologies. But I swear by it!

USE OF PERSONAL NAMES

I believe that economics is about people. As you read through the chapters, you can't help but see many, many names that personalize the discussion. Claudia Preparata buys fish, Diane Pecknold inherits a tobacco farm, Charles Edwards owns a coal mine, Nick Rudd is in the ice cream business. These, along with over 90 more, are real people. They are all friends of my son Joshua, who died in 1989, at age 19, a victim of lymphoma. The text book is my way of honoring Josh and honoring as well the beautiful people who were a part of his life.

Improved **Support** for Instructors

 ### Instructor's Manual

Written and updated by textbook author Fred Gottheil, this indispensable resource gives you ideas on how to approach each chapter, tips on how to present the material, and alternative illustrations for explaining points of theory and policy. It also discusses how to turn student questions into teaching opportunities. Organized for easy reference, the manual also provides detailed answers to the Questions sections that appear at the end of each chapter in the text.

 ### Test Banks

The Test Bank includes multiple-choice, true/false, and essay questions and answers, along with an assignment of difficulty level with each question.

 ### PowerPoint Slides

PowerPoint slides are available for use by students as an aid to note-taking, and by instructors for enhancing their lectures. More than 1,400 slides are included, which consist of key graphs taken from the textbook as well as lecture slides to help the instructor better integrate the material into the classroom presentation.

 ### Instructor's Resource CD-ROM

This easy-to-use CD enables you to review, edit, and copy a huge selection of instructor ancillaries from your desktop in the format you select.

Farewell

Friday, May 12, 1989
The Champaign-Urbana News-Gazette Weekend

"His eyes would light up and he'd talk fast and you couldn't help being
excited about the band or record he'd discovered, too."

P. Gregory Springer

News-Gazette file photo

Part of being young is the feeling of being indestructible.
Josh Gottheil, who died last month after a two-year battle
against leukemia, probably understood that he wouldn't
live forever. But he never stopped working to bring the
music he loved to the world around him. Rock and roll
would carry on.

The punk movement—simultaneously cynical and rea-
list and suicidal and idealistic—tried in a frenzy to wipe
out the commercialism and mass media hallucination
which blurred life's realities, even unpleasant ones like
death. There were bands named Dead Kennedys, Dead
Milkmen, the prototype Dead Boys, and Gottheil's local
band, Dead Relatives.

When he was only a sophomore in high school, Gottheil
became a drummer for the short-lived band, but he was no
angry punk. He heard the message in the music and he set
out, ambitious at a tender age, to deliver it to the community.

At 17, he already had promoted dozens of concerts for
teens in community centers and church foundations. He
was the least pushy music promoter I ever met, enticing
me to see at least one political rock and folk concert
through his complete, quiet reticence.

It was the music that spoke to and through him.

At one concert he arranged, I watched Billy Bragg and
Michelle Shocked get their introductions to the area. And
I saw Josh, standing by the door at Mabel's, anxious to
see that the message and the feeling came across.

His bands rarely disappointed.

Among the many other national bands he brought to
Champaign's clubs were Living Colour, They Might Be
Giants, Soul Asylum, Throwing Muses, Jane's Addiction,
Dead Milkmen, Hüsker Dü, Let's Active, Timbuk 3, Ministry, and the Pixies.

"The scene wouldn't be what it was today without Josh," said Chris Corpora,
an area rock promoter of Trashcan Productions. "He didn't look the part and he
risked his own money. About four years ago he started teen nights when there
was a lull in the scene. I don't want to deify him, but he had an incredible will,
poise, and the wherewithal to get contracts signed and do things he probably
shouldn't have been able to do. When I was 15, I couldn't even read a contract."

Even in the hard-core punk scene, Josh maintained a romantic side, often bringing roses for the girls in his favorite bands, notably Throwing Muses and the Pixies.

"He was always in love with every girl in a band," said Katy Stack, one of many people who considered Josh a best friend.

"He made friends with the Pixies and we flew to California to see them play in San Francisco," Stack said. "They invited him on stage to sing."

For a couple of summers, he worked at the desk at Crystal Lake Pool, announcing the adult swim and checking in bags. After high school, he took some college classes in philosophy and math at Parkland and at the UI, where his father, Fred, is a professor of economics. When he got sick, "it didn't look like he needed to go to college," according to Stack. "He was real busy doing all the music and he always had a lot of money. He was the only 16-year-old that had $2,000 in his checking account."

Another friend, Shara Gingold, actually wrote a book about her crush on Josh.

"He was two years older. The book is called 'I Love You, Josh. Do You Even Know I Exist?'," said Gingold, who lives in Urbana. "I think that it was [the fact that] he was very understanding and caring. We'd meet to play tennis and then we'd just sit and hit the tennis ball against the wall and talk about everything."

Last year, his health started to improve. He gained weight. He was working at Record Swap, surrounding himself in music during the day for the concerts he promoted at night. He had teamed with Chicago promoter Tony Polous, established a limited partnership called Concert One Productions, rented an office in Chicago's Mercantile Building, and developed the financing for big arena shows.

"Josh was destined to be huge," said Polous from the Chicago office. "He was the most effective, easy-going person I ever met. It's not hard to master being pushy and strong. Josh mastered being effective in an unassuming way.

"When he had to go back to the hospital, he never let on how sick he was. Every day I'd call him and he'd ask about what this manager was doing or that agent and he'd make decisions. We never really talked about his health. I never thought he was going to die. I think about him every day."

Despite his illness, Josh moved to Chicago last fall to be immersed in the music business.

"It was a chance, a break, an exciting thing to do. The world was his to conquer," said Fred Gottheil from his UI office. "I remember going up to visit and spend the night. The wind was howling, but he was so proud of the apartment. He was designing tickets on his computer, telling me [about] all the bands he had booked, his new ideas, bubbling with enthusiasm for the possibilities. The move was exhilarating for him. He called home quite frequently, but [Chicago] was where he had to be."

Said former Champaign-Urbana DJ Charlie "The Quaker" Edwards, who shared the Chicago apartment, "He had a real vitality, youth, and infectiousness. His eyes would light up and he'd talk fast and you couldn't help being excited about the band or record he'd discovered, too. Even though there was almost 20 years age difference between us, we'd listen to albums and talk about the bands and share a mutual excitement.

"He was a really good, serious businessman. Much better than I could have been, always dealing with five shows at once. He really loved it, too. He just loved the music."

"Definitely, there are people who are into [punk] because it is a fad," Gottheil said three years ago. "But for the people who really believe in it, it won't die for them."

Josh Gottheil died April 4 at Barnes Hospital in St. Louis, three months short of his 20th birthday. There was a turn-away crowd for his funeral on April 7 at the Sinai Temple in Champaign. Because he did so much to bring a new attitude about music in this area, one of the bands he helped find national prominence, Throwing Muses, has donated its performance at a benefit concert this Sunday at Mabel's, with proceeds going to the Josh Gottheil Memorial Fund for Lymphoma Research.

Author

Illini Studio

Fred M. Gottheil is a professor of economics at the University of Illinois in Urbana-Champaign. He came to Illinois in 1960, planning to spend one year before returning to his native Canada. But he fell in love with the campus, the community, and the Midwest, and he has been at Illinois ever since. He earned his undergraduate degree at McGill University in Montreal, Canada, and his Ph.D. at Duke University. His primary teaching is the principles of economics, and, on occasion, he has taught the history of economic thought, Marxian economics, and the economics of the Middle East. He is the author of *Marx's Economic Predictions* and numerous articles that have appeared in scholarly journals, among them the *American Economic Review*, the *Canadian Journal of Economics,* the *Journal of Post-Keynesian Economics,* and the *Middle East Review.* He has also contributed articles to several edited books on the Middle East. Although he enjoys research, his labor of love is teaching the principles course. His classes have been as large as 1,800 students. He has won a plethora of teaching awards from the university, the college, and the department of economics. Aside from his research and publications as a professor of economics, Professor Gottheil is also on the university's medical faculty, co-teaching the College of Medicine's course on medicine and society. As well, he is director of the University of Illinois's Center for Economic Education. In this capacity, he organizes and team-teaches minicourses and workshops on the principles of economics. He was a White House consultant on the Middle East during the Carter administration and offered expert testimony to several congressional committees. Professor Gottheil was a visiting professor at Northwestern University and at the Hebrew University in Jerusalem, Israel. He has lectured at many universities in the United States, Canada, and abroad, including universities in Syria, Egypt, Israel, and Jordan.

Acknowledgments

I am grateful to many people for help and encouragement throughout the development of this textbook. Many came to the project in a strictly professional capacity; most ended up as good friends. I owe them more than they believe is their due. At the beginning, George Lobell was enthusiastic about the idea of the textbook and believed that it would make a difference in the profession. He read many chapters, stayed in close touch, and still does. I thank this textbook for introducing me to George. David Wishart was a dear friend before we started the project, and working together on this textbook added another dimension to our friendship.

I also wish to thank my colleagues at Cengage who worked with me throughout the development of this fifth edition. Maureen Staudt headed the project and managed a remarkably talented group of professionals. The combined editorial development and production team of Greg Albert, Julie Niesen and Kim Fry ensured the revisions I made to the text—new ideas, current data, and various additional updates—blended into a workable whole. The combined marketing efforts of Rob Bloom and Sara Mercurio brought a fresh and creative approach to getting this sixth edition out to the campuses. I am indebted to this team all for their friendship and expertise. As well, I would like to thank Dreis Van Landuyt, Jack Calhoun, and Kurt Gerdenich at Cengage for their very helpful collaboration on earlier editions. Working with Cengage people has always been a team effort. In the end, the enterprise succeeds or fails depending upon the energies, enthusiasm, and expertise of the sales representatives. They have been particularly supportive and professional, and I thank them for it.

I would also like to thank Frank Hoffman, undergraduate at the University of Illinois, who checked Web sites, searched for new and updated data, and most important, gave me a student's perspective on the chapter narratives. As well, I am much indebted to Susan Jellissen. Although she was writing her doctoral thesis in political science, Susan was my head TA for two years and literally took charge of the principles course. The integration of economics and politics resulted from discussions with her.

I am also grateful to the following people for their valuable contributions and recommendations.

Jessie Martinez
Rochester Community &
Technical College

Ward Hooker
Orangeburg-Calhoun
Technical College

Dr. Ron Smiles
Dallas Baptist University

Nicholas D. Peppes
St. Louis Community
College, Forest Park

Stuart R. Lynn
Assumption College

Cliff Althoff
Joliet Junior College

During this book's long gestation period, I have benefited from the comments and suggestions of many reviewers. My heartfelt thanks go to the following economists. This book is much improved because of their efforts.

Carl J. Austermiller,
Oakland Community College

Michael Bodnar,
Stark Technical College

John Booth,
Stetson University

David Bunting,
Eastern Washington University

Tom Cate,
Northern Kentucky University

Robert Catlett,
Emporia State University

Christopher Colburn,
Old Dominion University

James Cover,
University of Alabama, Tuscaloosa

Jerry Crawford,
Arkansas State

Jane Crouch,
Pittsburgh State University

Susan Davis,
SUNY College at Buffalo

Daniel Fagan,
Daniel Webster College

Abdollah Ferdowsi,
Ferris State University

Eric Fisher,
Ohio State University

Carol Hogan,
University of Michigan, Dearborn

William Holmes,
Temple University

Paul Huszer,
Colorado State University

Bruce K. Johnson,
Centre College

Patrick Kelso,
West Texas State University

Alan Kessler,
Providence College

Joseph Kotaska,
Monroe Community College

Robert Litro,
Mattatuck Community College

Lawrence Mack,
North Dakota State University

Joseph Maddalena,
St. Thomas Aquinas College

Jhon Makrogianis,
Middlesex Community Collage

Gabriel Manrique,
Winona State University

John Marsh,
Montana State University

G. H. Mattersdorff,
Lewis and Clark College

John Merrifield,
University of Texas–San Antonio

James McBearty,
University of Arizona

Henry McCarl,
University of Alabama, Birmingham

James McLain,
University of New Orleans

Lon Mishler,
North Wisconsin Technical College

Norma Morgan,
Curry College

Allan Olsen,
Elgin Community College

Peter Pedroni,
Indiana University

Mitchell Redlo,
Monroe Community College

Terry Riddle,
Central Virginia Community College

Paul Rothstein,
University of Washington at St. Louis

Richard Schiming,
Mankato State University

Jerry Sidwell,
Eastern Illinois University

Phillip Smith,
DeKalb College

Philip Sprunger,
Lycoming College

William Stull,
Temple University

Tapan Thoy,
Eastern Connecticut State University

Doug Wakeman,
Meredith College

Jim Watson,
Jefferson College

Larry Wolfenbarger,
Georgia College

Finally, I want to thank Peter Schran, my colleague and close friend at Illinois, whose advice always made sense although it sometimes took me a while to appreciate it.

Fred Gottheil
University of Illinois

PART 1

The Basics of Economic Analysis

Chat Economics. Tune into the conversation. It's about *your* course. Just change the names, and it's *your* campus, *your* classroom, *your* professor, *your* classmates, and *you.*

Picture the scene. Katy Stack, a freshman planning on majoring in economics, and Professor Gottheil are walking across campus after the first week of class. Katy introduces herself and immediately the conversation gets to the heart of her concerns.

....

GOTTHEIL: Well, good morning, Katy. How do you like the economics course so far?

KATY: Okay, I guess. I'm actually thinking about majoring in it.

GOTTHEIL: Good choice! I think you'll love economics. Not only do I find it intellectually exciting, but it tells us a lot about ourselves. It's about what we do and how we live.

KATY: Frankly, I'm a little uneasy about majoring in it. My friends tell me that economics is difficult.

GOTTHEIL: In what way?

KATY: I think it's just difficult to understand.

GOTTHEIL: Well, Katy, let me tell you an anecdote that addresses your concern. It's an honest-to-goodness story, by the way, told to me by my teaching assistant, Cliff Althoff, who was then working on his Ph.D. in economics here on campus.

KATY: What's he doing now?

GOTTHEIL: He's a professor of economics at Joliet Junior College. Well, here's his story. One day, a number of years ago, he was on his way to visit his then-fiancée, Maureen McGonagle, when, on the sidewalk close by her house, he ran into a small group of 10-year-old girls skipping rope, hopscotching, and playing ball and jacks.

KATY: They weren't economists!

GOTTHEIL: Not exactly, but that's part of the story. One of the girls who had been skipping rope blocked his path to the house and audaciously asked who he was and where he was going. Cliff politely told her who he was, that Maureen was his fiancée, and that he was going to visit her for the day. The girl, still very inquisitive, asked Cliff what he did for a living. Well, he told her he was an economics teacher at the University of Illinois. She then replied, "If you're a teacher of economics, can you teach me something about economics now?"

KATY: Right there on the sidewalk—to a 10-year-old?

GOTTHEIL: You have to know Cliff! He said, "Sure. You were busy hopscotching when I met you, right? But you could have been skipping rope. Now you know that you can't do both at the same time, can you? By choosing to hopscotch, you gave up the opportunity of skipping rope. Economists call that an opportunity cost. You see, the fun you have hopscotching—and it's fun, isn't it—cost you the fun you could have had skipping rope. Make sense? Opportunity cost is a really important economic idea, and now you know it. Well, I really enjoyed talking to you, but I must go."

KATY: That's sort of neat. Teaching opportunity cost to a 10-year-old. Do you think she really understood it?

GOTTHEIL: Well, listen to this: When Cliff walked past the children and was about to enter the house, he heard the girl call back to him, "Hey mister! The opportunity cost of going to see Maureen is not being able to stay here and talk to me. See, I understand economics."

KATY: Awesome!

GOTTHEIL: Not really. Much of what you will learn in economics is like that. It will not be too difficult to understand. Knowing how to use economic principles is another matter. But you'll get to know that as well. Katy, I think you'll enjoy the course, and I certainly will enjoy having you in class.

It is certainly normal to be concerned about how hard any course will be, and economics is no different. Yet, as Cliff showed, the basic concepts in economics are not difficult to understand. As you read through the next few chapters, consider Katy and your own assumptions about your economics course. Who knows, perhaps you will decide to major in economics as well!

ChatEconomics

THIS CHAPTER INTRODUCES YOU
TO THE ECONOMIC PRINCIPLES
ASSOCIATED WITH:

- The earth's renewable and non-renewable resources
- The concept of insatiable wants
- The concepts of scarcity and choice
- The value of economic model building
- Microeconomic and macro-economic analysis
- Positive and normative economics

INTRODUCTION

"In the beginning God created the heaven and the earth" is about as familiar a sentence as any written. The Bible tells us that in the five days that followed the creation of heaven and earth, God separated darkness from light and water from dry land, and brought forth a multiplicity of living plants and creatures to inhabit the newly created land, waters, and skies. And on the sixth day, God created people:

So God created man in his own image, in the image of God created he him; male and female created he them. And God blessed them, and God said unto them, Be fruitful, and multiply, and replenish the earth, and sub-due it: and have dominion over the fish of the sea, and over the fowl of the air, and over every living thing that moveth upon the earth.

And God said, Behold, I have given you every herb bearing seed, which is upon the face of all the earth, and every tree, in the which is the fruit of a tree yielding seed; to you it shall be for meat. And to every beast of the earth, and to every fowl of the air, and to every thing that creepeth upon the earth, wherein there is life, I have given every green herb for meat: and it was so.

Source: NASA and the NSSDC

NO ONE EVER MADE AN OUNCE OF EARTH

What's the lesson we are supposed to draw from this creation narrative? To an economist, the first chapter of Genesis is both a powerful and humbling account of how our **natural resources** came into being. The message is clear. It doesn't even require particular religious conviction. After all, when you think about it, who ever made an ounce of earth? Who ever created a lump of coal or a nugget of gold? It seems that they have always been here for our use. Nobody ever added to nature's bounty.

Although the scientific interpretation of our resource availability differs dramatically from the biblical one, the message is similar. Natural resources have always been here. Physicists express this idea of prior existence and the continuance of matter in the first law of thermodynamics—the conservation principle—which asserts that energy can be neither created nor destroyed.

Economists, too, accept as fact that every resource on the face of this earth is a gift of nature. Resources were here before men and women arrived on the scene. Every ounce of iron, tungsten, nickel, petroleum, copper, zinc, asbestos, gypsum, and the many other metals, minerals, and energy sources, including those yet undiscovered, were here long before we learned how to make cement, gasoline, steel, plastics, and aspirin.

The nutrients attached to every grain of soil were already imbedded in the soil before people even began to think about working the land. The herds of goats, the schools of sea bass, the flocks of geese, the reindeer and rabbits, the forests and grasses, and all our other food resources were there for the taking.

And, of course, we took! We learned how to extract natural resources from the earth, how to fish them out of the waters, and how to harvest them from the lands. Most exciting of all, we learned the tricks of transforming resources from their original states into new ones. We transform iron ore into steel, crude petroleum into plastic, trees into furniture, rays of the sun into energy, coal into nylon, sand into glass, limestone into cement, bauxite into aluminum, and water flow into electricity. We are continually discovering newer techniques for transformation. And we have been doing this for a long, long time.

> **Natural resources**
> The lands, water, metals, minerals, animals, and other gifts of nature that are available for producing goods and services.

Can you describe the finite character of the earth's resources?

Are We Running Out of Natural Resources?

We live in a finite world. No matter how seemingly bountiful the quantity of our natural resources may be or how carefully we try to conserve them, if we keep using them, they eventually are going to run out. It just seems reasonable. Or does it?

Renewable and Nonrenewable Natural Resources

Many natural resources are renewable. Consider, for example, our supply of forests, sea and land animals, water, and grasses. Are not these resources self-renewing? But with rapidly growing human populations, overuse of productive lands can turn them into deserts, and overharvesting of fish and land animals can destroy these living resources. Properly managed conservation, on the other hand, can not only protect these natural resources but even increase their supply.

Admittedly, our metal and mineral resources are not self-renewing. Gold nuggets don't breed. Because the earth contains finite space, its mineral resources exist only in finite quantities. You do not have to be a rocket scientist to figure out that mining one ton of copper ore depletes that resource by one ton. In fact, we have been depleting our copper supply ever since King Solomon began mining copper in the Negev desert. However, before we work our way down to the last ton of copper, it is very possible that we will have already abandoned it as a

What distinguishes renewable from nonrenewable resources?

historical perspective

COAL ... THEN (1865) AND NOW (2004)

In 1865, the celebrated economist Stanley Jevons wrote a very sobering book, *The Coal Question.* Jevons set out to prove that England's economic progress and power were on the verge of collapse. The reason? The energy source that powered England's economic growth—coal—was being rapidly depleted. No alternative energy source seemed likely. Jevons estimated that England's commercially available coal supply would run out in one hundred years. He warned:

...I must point out the painful fact that such a rate of [economic] growth will before long render our consumption of coal comparable with the total supply. In the increasing depth and difficulty of coal mining we shall meet that vague but inevitable boundary that will stop our progress. ... A farm, however far pushed, will under proper cultivation continue to yield for ever a constant crop. But in a mine there is no reproduction, and the produce once pushed to the utmost will soon begin to sink to zero. (pp. 154–155)

Has England run out of coal? England's present coal problem is too much coal! When coal was King, England sent one million coalminers into its pits. In 2004, fewer than 10,000 mine coal. What has happened? The coal's there. *It's the economics that's not in place.* Today, the growth in demand for natural gas is 50 percent higher than that for oil and fully twice that for coal. Unfortunately for the coal industry, coal, oil, and natural gas are competitive. A glut of coal in England and on the world market has sent coal prices plummeting. A far cry from what had been predicted a century ago. As if that's not problem enough, gas-fired power stations produce lower levels of greenhouse gasses than coal-fired ones do, so the environmentally sensitive Brits have been more than eager to switch.

It's not a new story. A decade earlier, the House of Commons energy committee published a report that outlined the bleak future facing the coal industry, despite the fact that productivity in the industry is relatively high. Britain, the committee report stated, still has three centuries' worth of coal at the present rate of consumption. Can you imagine Jevons reading the committee's report? He would be flabbergasted!

MORE ON THE NET

Learn more about Stanley Jevons (http://en.wikipedia.org/wiki/William_Stanley_Jevons). What problems does England face today with coal? Visit the United Kingdom Parliament (http://www.parliament.uk/).

usable resource. In other words, even though copper may not be a renewable resource, we may be well advised to treat it as one.

Does this mean, then, that we will never run out of any natural resource? No such luck. It just means that our knowledge of a resource's relative scarcity, particularly when we consider its availability in the not-too-distant future, is less than exact.

Thousands of years ago, flint was a primary resource used in the production of tools and weapons. Do you know anyone today concerned about our flint supply? We still produce tools and weapons, but we have moved to other technologies that use very different resources. Is copper's future, then, mirrored in flint's past? If so, we may someday regret having conserved our copper supply. We might end up with mountains of unused, useless copper.

Should we conserve the world's oil supply or instead go full speed ahead, using up as much of it as we need to satisfy our current demands? After all, in a generation or two our energy technologies may have already switched to solar and nuclear power, or to some yet unknown technology. What then do we do with oceans of unused, unwanted oil?

How Do You Satisfy Insatiable Wants?

Suppose we had an infinite supply of natural resources. We would still have an insurmountable economic problem. There simply are not enough hours in a day

theoretical perspective

IF NOT THE DEPLETION OF COAL, THEN PERHAPS OIL

In the 1970s, economists and government people looking at the soaring price of oil panicked. What did they see as the cause for rising oil prices? You guessed it! Listen to President Jimmy Carter:

> It is obvious to anyone that looks at it [the oil crisis] that we've got a problem that's serious now. It's going to get more serious in the future. We're going to have less oil. Those are the facts. They are unpleasant facts. (May 25, 1979)

Sound familiar? Perhaps President Carter should have read Stanley Jevons's 1865 book *The Coal Question*. He might have found some reason to be more optimistic about our future and less reason to assert his fears about oil supplies as "unpleasant facts."

In July 2000, the Energy Information Administration (EIA) of the U.S. Department of Energy reported that "data continues to confirm no shortage of crude oil in the open market." And that's no surprise. Why not? Because if we were really running out of oil, we would spend a great deal of time looking for it, wouldn't we? We would be drilling and drilling, using as many drilling rigs as we could employ. But look at the drilling rig data. In July 2003, the U.S. weekly drilling rig count was 1,077. Since 1940, the highest weekly rig count was 4,530, recorded in December 1981. The lowest rig count was recorded in April 1999. The 1,077 rigs in operation tend to confirm the EIA report that nobody is really worried about crude oil supply.

Plenty of oil in the pipeline and oceans more where that came from.

MORE ON THE NET

Visit the U.S. Department of Energy (**http://www.energy.gov/**) and the White House (**http://www.whitehouse.gov/**). What about oil concerns the federal government?

to allow us to transform those resources into all the goods and services we want. That is, the problem ultimately may not be the limited quantity of resources available to us, but rather our limitless, or insatiable, wants.

Let's go back to the biblical story to illustrate the point. Adam and Eve were happy in the Garden of Eden, not because the garden had so much but because they wanted so little. Their problem was eating the fruit from the Tree of Knowledge: One bite and they suddenly realized they had no clothes, no air conditioning, no videocassettes, no quartz watches, no phones, and no Buick. It was a quick trip from the state of ignorant bliss to paradise lost. Their wants became insatiable.

We inherited their genes. Our tastes for goods and services are virtually limitless. There is always something else we want. And once these wants are satisfied, our minds are just as capable of conceiving new wants as they are of conceiving ways of satisfying them. In this respect, we differ from lions and tigers who, after a kill, are prepared to rest until hungry again. Instead, we are perpetually in a state of hunger. Even if we had a never-ending supply of the natural resources required to satisfy our limitless wants, it would take more than 24 hours a day to transform them into all the goods and services we want.

Scarcity Forces Us to Make Choices

If we can't have everything we want today, what do we do? We are forced to make choices. We must choose to produce some goods and services and not others. Sometimes this kind of choosing can be visibly painful. Have you ever watched children in Toys "R" Us with a gift certificate in hand? It can take them all day before they make a choice. And instead of bubbling with excitement over

check your understanding

Why does scarcity force people to make choices?

Scarcity
The perpetual state of insufficiency of resources to satisfy people's unlimited wants.

Economics
The study of how people work together to transform resources into goods and services to satisfy their most pressing wants, and how they distribute these goods and services among themselves.

the toy they bought, they usually appear frustrated over not being able to walk away with everything!

Life is like that. **Scarcity** governs us. Because we cannot have everything all at once, we are forever forced to make choices. We can use our resources to satisfy only some of our wants, leaving many others unsatisfied.

WHAT IS ECONOMICS?

What has **economics** to do with Genesis 1, Adam and Eve, the first law of thermodynamics, scarcities of resources, and infinite wants? Everything! *Economics is the study of how we work together to transform scarce resources into goods and services to satisfy the most pressing of our infinite wants, and how we distribute these goods and services among ourselves.*

The study of economics focuses on four central issues. Who produces what? How? Who consumes what? And who decides? Taken together, these issues form the analysis of how an economy works.

Economics Is Part of Social Science

It is sometimes difficult to separate the study of economics from the study of the other social sciences, such as sociology, anthropology, political science, and psychology. All the social science disciplines, including economics, examine individual and social behavior. While economics concentrates on those aspects of behavior that affect the way we, as individuals and as a society, produce and consume goods and services, our production and consumption are not done in a social vacuum.

What we consume, what we produce, how we produce, and how we go about exchanging resources and products among ourselves is determined, in part, by the character of our political system, by the customs and traditions of our society, and by the set of social institutions and ethical standards we have established.

Consumer sovereignty
The ability of consumers to exercise complete control over what goods and services the economy produces (or doesn't produce) by choosing what goods and services to buy (or not buy).

Our political and economic rights and freedoms stem from the same root. Our right to vote at the ballot box, for example, is not unrelated to **consumer sovereignty** in the marketplace—that is, our freedom to buy or not buy the goods and services offered. This right to choose what we want dictates what producers will ultimately produce, just as our right to choose our political leaders dictates what kind of government policies we ultimately get.

We grow up in a society whose value system, sometimes described as the Protestant ethic, implants in us a belief in the importance of personal frugality, honest labor, and enterprise. To many of us, any alternative value system is considered deviant or antisocial. In this respect, our ethical standards establish the boundaries of permissible economic behavior. We are also taught from childhood to accept a broad set of social responsibilities, many requiring us to share part of our income, through taxes, with people who are less fortunate than us. These accepted social values and responsibilities contribute to the way we select and meet our economic goals and the role we expect our government to play in the economy.

The contributions that economics as a social science discipline makes to the other social sciences are also fundamental. For example, it is difficult to appreciate what federal, state, and local governments do without understanding the economic circumstances underlying their actions. After all, government budgets are economic documents. Taxes and government spending are economic tools used by the political system to meet economic as well as political and social objectives. Political debates on issues such as the national debt, budget deficits, and the welfare system require an understanding of economics.

It is difficult, as well, for sociologists to study the role of the family in society without at the same time studying how the family behaves as an economic unit. To some extent, even when and whom we marry, the number of children we have, and interpersonal relationships within the family are governed by economics.

Using Economic Models

Our real economic world is incredibly complex. Millions of people, making independent economic decisions every day, affect not only their own lives but the lives of everyone around them. In many cases, they influence even the lives of people great distances away. It is one thing to appreciate the fact that we are all mutually interrelating, but quite another to untangle these relationships to draw specific one-to-one, cause-and-effect economic correspondences. It's an imposing intellectual challenge, but economists have been working at it with at least modest success, and in some cases, quite remarkable results.

How do economists start? By abstracting from reality. The purpose of such abstraction is to reduce the complexity of the world we live in to more simplified, manageable dimensions. That is essentially what the economists' models do. The models capture the essence of an economic reality. They try to simplify it without distorting its truth.

In a way, when economists build economic models, they are like children playing house. In both cases, it is essentially reduction and imitation. In child's play, many of the household activities are ignored and many of the real problems are overlooked. However, the central figures are there, the accuracy of their behavior is uncanny, and the issues basic to most households are reflected in the children's mimicry of adult conversation.

Most **economic model** builders insist that while their models exclude many economic activities of the real world, overlook the complexities of how people really behave, and ignore many pressing issues that people confront every day, what they portray in their models is nevertheless the quintessence of how the real economy works.

And that's the point of economic analysis. Economists are not really interested in pure intellectual exercise. Their interest is not the economic model per se but the real world of economics. Their models are designed to serve only as vehicles to a fuller comprehension of what really goes on.

Economic model
An abstraction of an economic reality. It can be expressed pictorially, graphically, algebraically, or in words.

Maslow and Model Building

The eminent psychologist Abraham Maslow once noted that *"if the only tool you have is a hammer, you tend to see every problem as a nail."* What Maslow meant is simply this: There is a gnawing tendency among academic model builders, economists included, to allow the techniques of model building rather than the real world to dictate what kinds of issues, problems, and questions to address. That is to say, rather than applying their talents and energies to investigate the unclear and multifaceted economic issues of the world we live in, many economists are tempted instead to focus only on issues that are solvable within the framework of the models they construct. Maslow goes even further. By being totally and intellectually absorbed in their world of models, some become totally and intellectually unengaged in the world of reality.

Most economists are not unaware of Maslow's critique. And some agree. Cambridge economist Joan Robinson, for example, observed in *Economic Philosophy* that "the function of economic theory is to set up hypotheses that can be tested. But if a hypothesis is framed in terms of the position of equilibrium that would be attained when all parties concerned had correct foresight, there is no point in testing it; we know in advance that it will not prove correct." But Nobel Laureate Milton Friedman offers another interesting view on the realism of assumptions concerning model building: If a model generates predictable outcomes, whatever assumptions it posits, the model, *ipso facto*, has merit and worthiness.

Ceteris Paribus

Ceteris paribus
The Latin phrase meaning "everything else being equal."

One of the most important aids economists use in model building is the assumption of **ceteris paribus**, which translated means "holding constant" or "controlling for the influence of other factors." Ceteris paribus allows economists to develop one-to-one, cause-and-effect relationships in isolation, that is, removed from other potentially influential factors. For example, when the price of filet mignon decreases, economists assert that the quantity of filet mignon demanded increases. But this one-to-one, cause-and-effect relationship between price and quantity demanded holds only if everything else going on in the economy is ignored. If the prices of other foods fall at the same time, then it is questionable whether more filet mignon would be demanded when its price falls. After all, people may be more attracted to the other price-reduced foods than they are to the lower-priced filet.

Or suppose people lost their jobs on the very day the filet prices were cut. Chances are fewer filets would be demanded. When you're out of work, filet mignon at any price is probably out of mind.

How then can economists make definitive statements about any economic relationship when so many economic events, all potentially influencing each other, may be occurring at the same time? They do so by assuming ceteris paribus. It focuses the analysis. That one-to-one, cause-and-effect relationship between price and quantity demanded, however limited by the exclusion of other considerations, is still highly insightful and turns out to be of critical importance to our understanding of price determination.

Ceteris paribus is not confined to economic analysis. When the surgeon general of the United States asserts that smoking causes lung cancer, isn't there a ceteris paribus assumption lurking in the background? After all, the smoking–cancer relationship ignores a host of other factors that may explain the cancer. Consider the science of meteorology. When the weather forecast is rain, isn't there a ceteris paribus assumption made as well? Weather fronts can and often do change direction.

The Circular Flow Model of Goods and Money

Circular flow model
A model of how the economy's resources, money, goods, and services flow between households and firms through resource and product markets.

Let's look now at an honest-to-goodness economic model. Perhaps the simplest model illustrating how an economy works is the **circular flow model** of money, goods, and services shown in Exhibit 1.

In this model, people are both consumers and producers. They live in **households**, where they consume the goods and services they buy on the product market, and they supply their resources—land, labor, capital, and entrepreneurship—on the resource market to **firms** that use the resources to produce the goods and services that appear on the product market.

Household
An economic unit of one or more persons, living under one roof, that has a source of income and uses it in whatever way it deems fit.

In the upper half, the purple arrow depicts the direction of the flow of goods and services from firms, through the product market, to households. Households pay for them with money earned in the resource market. The green arrow depicts the flow of money from households, through the product market, to the firms.

Firm
An economic unit that produces goods and services in the expectation of selling them to households, other firms, or government.

Let's look at households now in their capacity as money earners. They earn money—wages, interest, rent, and profit—by selling or leasing their resources—labor, capital, land, and entrepreneurship—to firms. The yellow arrow in the bottom half depicts the resource flow from households, through the resource market, to firms. Firms transform those resources into goods and services that eventually appear on the product market. The money firms earn selling goods

KEY EXHIBIT 1   The Circular Flow Model

Households supply re-
sources—land, labor, capital, and entrepreneurship—
to firms through the
resource market in return for
money payments—rent,
wages, interest, and profit.
Firms use the resources to
produce goods and services
that they supply on the
product market. There,
households buy those
goods and services with the
incomes received from the
resources they supplied.

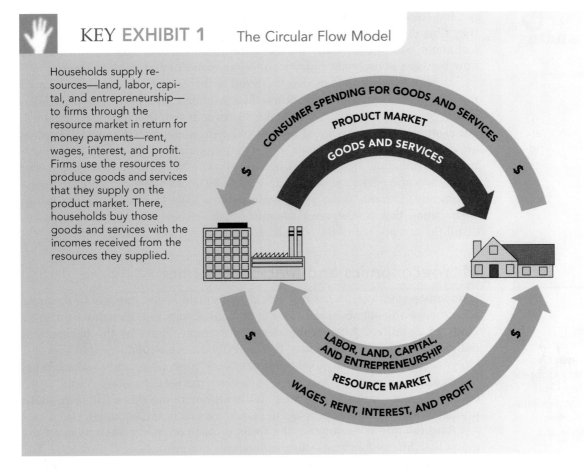

and services pays for the resources they buy. The green arrow depicts the pay-for-resources flow of money from firms, through the resource market, to the households. As you see, for every flow of goods, services, and resources there is a counter flow of money.

How would *you* fit into the circular flow model of Exhibit 1? Suppose you have a summer job making cotton candy at a neighborhood water slide. The job pays $200 weekly. The yellow arrow represents your labor flow to the water slide firm, while the bottom-half green arrow represents the $200 you receive from the firm.

Now let's look at your activity in the upper half of the circular flow model. Using the $200 you earn at the slide—which is now your household income—you go to the product market to buy $200 of goods and services that firms have produced for sale on the market. (Among the goods available is cotton candy.) The purple arrow represents a $200 flow of goods and services to you, while the upper-half green arrow represents the flow of money from you to firms for the goods and services.

Is the circular flow model an accurate reflection of our economic reality? Not really. Where in Exhibit 1's portrayal of that circular flow are the banks? Where is government? Doesn't government, too, consume goods and services? Where are the unemployed? They consume some of the economy's goods and services, but if they are unemployed, they aren't providing resources. Where, then, do they get the money? How does the model account for retired people? They no longer work, but they continue to consume. Where in the model do we find the economy's exports and imports? Where are savings and investments?

Nowhere! The circular flow model of Exhibit 1 isn't designed as a complete picture of our economic reality. In fact, it ignores a host of major economic institutions and activities.

What are some advantages and limitations of the circular flow model?

But these omissions are far from being shortcomings of the model; in fact, they illustrate the model's strength. The model is designed to reflect one basic fact about how the economy works: It shows how money, goods, and services flow between households and firms through resource and product markets.

Most of the economic models analyzed in this text are no more complicated than this circular flow model. Some, like Exhibit 1, are portrayed pictorially, others graphically, and still others take the form of simple algebraic expressions. For example, economists build models of a firm to illustrate how market prices are determined. Other economic models are designed to show how unemployment and inflation arise. Models also illustrate why some nations grow faster than others and why some do not grow at all. Most of these models are expressed graphically. The one thing all of these models have in common is the use of abstraction—that is, the use economists make of simplifying assumptions to distill the essence out of the complicated economic realities they study.

Microeconomics and Macroeconomics

Microeconomics
A subarea of economics that analyzes individuals as consumers and producers, and specific firms and industries. It focuses especially on the market behavior of firms and households.

Read a copy of today's newspaper, such as *USA Today* (**http://www. usatoday.com/**). Can you find articles that address microeconomic and macroeconomic issues?

Macroeconomics
A subarea of economics that analyzes the behavior of the economy as a whole.

What's the difference between positive and normative economics?

Positive economics
A subset of economics that analyzes the way the economy actually operates.

Normative economics
A subset of economics founded on value judgments and leading to assertions of what ought to be.

Economists who look at the real world and create simple models to illustrate what they see do not necessarily look at the same things, nor do they ask the same kinds of questions. **Microeconomics**, for example, looks at the behavior of individual households and firms. It asks, Why do firms produce what they do? How do they price their goods and services? How do markets work? What distinguishes competitive from noncompetitive markets? How are resource prices such as wage rates, interest rates, and rents determined? How do firms make profits? What determines people's demands for goods and services?

As these questions suggest, the focus of microeconomic analysis is on the individual. Microeconomists study individuals as consumers and producers. The economy is regarded as a composite of interacting individual economic units. To understand how the economy functions, then, requires an understanding of how each of these individual units behaves and interacts.

Macroeconomics, on the other hand, tries to explain a different set of facts about the economy. It focuses attention on the behavior of the economy as a whole. To macroeconomists, the economy is more than simply a collection of its individual parts. It has character. It has its own vitality and history. It has an identifiable substance. The macroeconomic unit of analysis, then, is the economy.

The macroeconomic questions concern not the behavior and activities of individual households, firms, or markets, but the behavior and activity of the economy itself. They ask, for example, Why do national economies grow? Why do some grow faster than others? What determines a nation's savings, its investments, or its consumption? Why does it experience inflation? Why does it generate unacceptable unemployment? Why does it fluctuate from periods of economic prosperity to periods of economic recession?

Positive and Normative Economics

It is one thing for economists to explain why our economy grows at 2.6 percent per year and quite another to advocate that it ought to grow faster. It is one thing to explain why the price of corn is $2.10 per bushel and another to advocate that it ought to be higher. It is one thing to explain what happens when firms in certain industries merge and another to advocate that they ought to merge.

You see the differences, don't you? One is a statement of fact (the economy grows at 2.6 percent per year), while the other passes judgment (it ought to grow faster). Economists are typically very careful about differentiating between analysis of *what is* and *what ought to be*. These are not mutually exclusive, but they are different. Economists refer to *what is* analysis as **positive economics** and *what ought to be* analysis as **normative economics**.

theoretical perspective

CONSUMER SOVEREIGNTY AND ADAMS SMITH'S "INVISIBLE HAND"

In 1776, the Scottish moral philosopher and economist Adam Smith, in his *Wealth of Nations*, perhaps the most celebrated book ever written on economics, had this to say about why we end up having precisely the kinds of food we enjoy at our dinner table: "It is not from the benevolence of the butcher, the brewer, or the baker that we expect our dinner, but from their regard to their own self interest." That's a mighty statement! Smith assures us that there's no need to thank the butcher, the baker, nor anyone else who provides us with the goods we consume. These goods are provided only because producers hope to gain by providing them. Concern for your welfare? Don't be silly! But there's no reason to fret about self-centered motivation because working for their own self-interest works to your advantage. Smith explains: "Every individual generally neither intends to promote the public interest, nor knows how much he is promoting it. He intends only his own gain. And he is in this led by an **invisible hand** to promote an end, which was no part of his intention. By pursuing his own interest he frequently promotes that of society more effectually than when he really intends to promote it." In other words, greed can end up promoting munificence. The invisible hand Smith refers to is nothing more (or less) than the market. Anchored in consumer sovereignty, the product market guides producers to produce precisely those goods that consumers want and in this way transforms producers' private interest into our public interest.

How does invisible hand fit into the circular flow model? Unlike the ring on your finger that has no beginning or end, the circular flow of resources, goods, and services begins somewhere. Its starting point is the household.

Why the household? Because that's where consumer sovereignty resides. What you choose to consume dictates what firms will ultimately produce. Feel the power? You really have it! If firms fail to produce precisely what you want, they simply won't be around

very long. For example, if consumers want four-cylinder cars and General Motors ignores consumer preferences by manufacturing eight-cylinder cars, those eight-cylinder monsters will remain clogged in the product market of the circular flow model, never making it through the clockwise flow in Exhibit 1 from the product market to the households. And if those cars don't end up in households, the money that General Motors expects to receive from selling those cars—the counterclockwise flow of dollars from households to firms—never materializes.

The invisible hand—guided by self-interest—put this meal together.

But General Motors does produce four-cylinder cars precisely because your wishes are its command. For the same reason, other firms produce the tens of thousands of other goods and services we demand from the market daily. Firms produce these goods and services not to please us, but because they are interested in pleasing themselves. That is to say, we get the goods we want because firms pursue their own self-interest.

Even though no one actually tells firms in the circular flow model what to produce, the right goods get produced in the right quantities because firms keep their antennae fixed on the product market. That's where consumer sovereignty, originating in the households, is expressed.

Study the circular flow model again. You may not see it, but an invisible hand guides the firms to produce only those goods consumers want. This invisible hand is nothing more (or less) than the combination of consumer sovereignty and firms' self-interest operating on the product market.

There's nothing inherently wrong with advocacy, although these *oughts* are heavily laden with personal and social values. For example, should we have a minimum wage? Should we subsidize farmers? Should we protect our steel industry? Should we tax the rich more than the poor? Should we disallow mergers? Should we regulate bank loans? Should we monitor industrial pollution? Should we control population size?

These are serious economic issues. There is nothing improper about economists applying their own values to economic issues, as long as we know where their value judgments start and their economic analysis ends. It is sometimes difficult to separate the two. Economists, at times, unintentionally disguise advocacy in the language of positive economics. The simple cause-and-effect

Invisible hand
Adam Smith's concept of the market, which, as if it were a hand, guides firms that seek only to satisfy their own self-interest to produce precisely those goods and services that consumers want.

analysis of positive economics is sometimes taken one step further to advocate policy. For example, analyses of market structures are not always separated from the economists' general view that perfect competition is the most socially desirable market form. Most economists share that view, and some will even argue that their analysis of market structures leads inexorably to that view. Their *analysis* of markets may be positive economics, but their *judgment* that competitive markets are more desirable is normative.

WHAT DO ECONOMISTS KNOW?

Does it matter much what policies economists advocate? It matters very much. The White House, for example, has its own Council of Economic Advisers. Congress and the Federal Reserve System have their own cadres of economists. Many corporations, banks, and labor unions have economists on their payrolls. Economists are everywhere in the media, explaining and advising. Still, what do they know?

We listen attentively each morning to the weather forecast, although few of us fully trust what we hear. We know from experience that if the meteorologist predicts sunny skies, we take an umbrella along for insurance. Meteorologists seem to be forever explaining why yesterday's forecast turned out to be inaccurate. Sometimes we feel that they do not know much more about the weather than we do. But, in fact, they do.

The problem is not their forecast, but our reading of it. We expect too much. The forecast is sunny skies *if* the highs and lows behave properly. Remember ceteris paribus? The forecast depends on the fronts moving into our weather region as expected. If they don't, all bets are off. How can meteorologists be held accountable for totally unpredictable changes?

on the **net**

The Council of Economic Advisers (**http://www.whitehouse.gov/cea**) and the Bank of America (**http://www.bankofamerica.com/**) are two examples of organizations that hire economists to predict how the economy will behave.

Nobel Laureates in Economics

There are more than 5,000 academic economists engaged in research and teaching in U.S. universities, colleges, and institutes. Many contribute to the advancement of knowledge, and among them are a select few who have won the Nobel Prize in Economics for having made extraordinary contributions in their particular fields.

YEAR	ECONOMIST	FOR ADVANCING KNOWLEDGE IN THE FIELD OF	UNIVERSITY OR COUNTRY AFFILIATION
1969	Ragnar Frisch, Jan Tinbergen	Dynamic models; analysis of economic processes	University of Oslo; The Netherlands School of Economics
1970	Paul Samuelson	Static and dynamic economic theory	MIT
1971	Simon Kuznets	Economic growth	Harvard
1972	John Hicks, Kenneth Arrow	General economic equilibrium theory and welfare theory	Oxford; Harvard
1973	Wassily Leontief	Input-output analysis	Harvard
1974	Gunnar Myrdal, Friedrich Hayek	Interdependence of economic, social, and institutional phenomena	Sweden; Austria
1975	Leonid Kantorovich, Tjalling Koopmans	Optimum allocation of resources	Academy of Sciences Moscow; Yale
1976	Milton Friedman	Consumption analysis, monetary history and theory	University of Chicago
1977	Bertil Ohlin, James Meade	International trade and international capital movements	Stockholm School of Economics; Cambridge
1978	Herbert Simon	Decision-making process within economic organizations	Carnegie Mellon
1979	Threodore Schultz, Arthur Lewis	Developing economies	University of Chicago; Princeton
1980	Lawrence Klein	Econometric models	University of Pennsylvania
1981	James Tobin	Macroeconomic theory and financial markets	Yale
1982	George Stigler	Industrial structures and regulation	University of Chicago
1983	Gerard Debreu	General equilibrium	University of California
1984	Richard Stone	Systems of national accounts	Cambridge
1985	Franco Modigliani	Financial markets	MIT
1986	James Buchanan, Jr.	Economic and political decision making	Center for Study of Public Choice

YEAR	ECONOMIST	FOR ADVANCING KNOWLEDGE IN THE FIELD OF	UNIVERSITY OR COUNTRY AFFILIATION
1987	Robert Solow	The theory of economic growth	MIT
1988	Maurice Allais	The theory of markets and efficient utilization of resources	École Nationale Supérieur des Mines de Paris
1989	Trygve Haavelmo	Probability theory foundations of econometrics	University of Oslo
1990	Harry Markowitz, Merton Miller, William Sharpe	Financial economics	City University of New York; University of Chicago; Stanford
1991	Ronald Coase	Market failure	University of Chicago
1992	Gary Becker	Microeconomic analysis applied to a wide range of human behavior	University of Chicago
1993	Robert Fogel, Douglass North	Quantitative economic history	University of Chicago; Washington University
1994	John Harsanyi; John Forbes Nash, Jr.; Reinhard Selten	Game theory	University of California, Berkeley; Princeton; Rheinische Friedrich-Willhelms-Universität
1995	Robert Lucas, Jr.	Rational expectations theory	University of Chicago
1996	James Mirrlees, William Vickrey	Economic theory of incentives under asymmetric information	Cambridge; Columbia
1997	Robert Carhart Merton, Myron Scholes	Methods to determine the value of derivatives	Harvard; Long Term Capital Management, Greenwich, CT
1998	Amartya Sen	Welfare economics	Trinity College
1999	Robert Mundell	Monetary and fiscal policy	Columbia
2000	James Heckman, Daniel McFadden	Methods for analyzing selective samples; methods for analyzing discrete choice	University of Chicago; University of California, Berkeley
2001	George Akerlof, A. Michael Spence, Joseph Stiglitz	Markets with asymmetric information	University of California, Berkeley; Stanford; Columbia
2002	Daniel Kahneman, Vernon Smith	Decision making under uncertainty; experimental economics	Princeton; George Mason University
2003	Robert Engle III, Clive Granger	Methods of analyzing time series	New York University; University of California, San Diego
2004	Finn Kydland, Edward Prescott	Dynamic macroeconomics; business cycles	Carnegie Mellon; Arizona State University
2005	Robert Aumann, Thomas Schelling	Game theory	Hebrew University of Jerusalem; University of Maryland
2006	Edmund Phelps	Intertemporal trade-offs in macroeconomic policy	Columbia
2007	Leonid Hurwicz, Eric Maskin, Roger Myerson	Mechanism design	University of Minnesota; Princeton University; University of Chicago

interdisciplinaryperspective

© Royalty-Free/CORBIS

GIFTS OF NATURE

Traveler: Once in a while, if you travel far inland, you will chance upon an old man sitting by a river. This man has a big knife, but he does not intend it for you. Rather, he just sits there and whittles away at pieces of wood. All day and all night he whittles. The chips and splinters fly off and drop into the water, where they become alive. And by the time they reach the sea, they've turned into salmon, char, cod, capelin, lumpsuckers, and halibut. This man is the father of all fish. Do not kill him.

....

CONSIDER

A beautiful story of creation, isn't it? It is an Eskimo tale that appears in a collection of stories gathered and retold by Lawrence Millman in a volume titled *A Kayak Full of Ghosts*. To an economist, it tells not only how the Eskimo people describe Genesis, but also provides information on the supply price of fish, land, and other natural resources. Resources are magical gifts of nature. Cost to society? Zero.

In this respect, economic forecasting is similar to meteorological forecasting. Economic analysis is typically conditioned on the assumption of ceteris paribus, that is, that everything else remains unchanged, but it usually doesn't. The economists' world is one of uncertainty, and economists cannot take into account unforeseen future events that come to bear on their analyses. Explaining why previous economic forecasts were inaccurate doesn't build confidence. Instead, people think twice about whether economists really know more about the economy than anybody else. They do.

In the past fifty years, there has been a continuing, dramatic enrichment of our economic knowledge. New and more sophisticated models have been developed to represent our changing world. Also, the growth of economic data along with the ability to apply modern statistical methods to test models have created a branch of economics called **econometrics**. Econometricians are busy expanding these new and exciting areas of quantitative economic research.

In macroeconomics, for example, we now know more about what determines the levels of national income and employment than ever before. Knowing more doesn't necessarily resolve controversy, however. For example, there is no consensus among economists concerning the role government should play in our economy. Much of the debate is founded upon different readings of the same data.

In microeconomics, quantitative research on international trade, tax incidence, and market and investment behavior is adding more information to an already rich literature. New theories about uncertainty have given economists new insights into microeconomic questions.

Economists can rightfully claim to have covered an impressive intellectual distance in a very short period of time. Economists really do have something to say, but they realize that they must forever be on guard against claiming too much. As in medical research, the more we know, the more complex are the questions we can ask. Today, the task of the economist is no less difficult than fifty years ago, and the problems encountered no easier. The results of our economic research tell us just a little bit more about ourselves and are well worth the effort.

Econometrics
The use of statistics to quantify and test economic models.

on the net
Take a look at econometricians in practice. Visit the econometrics group at the University of Illinois (**http://www.econ.uiuc.edu/**) and the econometrics laboratory at the University of California, Berkeley (**http://www.emlab.berkeley.edu/eml/**).

CHAPTER REVIEW

1. Natural resources are gifts of nature. Our supplies of them are basically finite, fixed by what the earth makes available. Some natural resources are renewable, such as our forests and livestock. Others are nonrenewable, such as our supplies of copper and iron ore.

2. Our wants of goods and services seem to be unlimited and forever expanding. We are able to conjure up new wants just as readily as we have learned how to satisfy others.

3. The problem of economic scarcity is defined by these facts: Our natural resources are limited, while our wants are unlimited. This universal scarcity forces us to make choices concerning which of our unlimited wants we will satisfy and which ones we will not.

4. Economics is the study of how we deal with scarcity. We define economics as the study of how we work together to transform resources into goods and services to satisfy our most

pressing wants, and how we distribute these goods and services among ourselves.

5. Economics is an integral part of the social sciences discipline, which includes sociology, political science, anthropology, and psychology. Each analyzes different aspects of individual and social behavior.

6. Economists use models to describe economic behavior. These models are abstractions of the real world, based on simplifying assumptions about that world, which allow us to focus on basic economic relationships in the model. By understanding cause-and-effect relationships in the model, economists believe they can better understand how the real world works.

7. Microeconomics explains economic relationships at the level of the individual consumer, firm, or industry, addressing such questions as what determines people's demand for goods, why some prices increase while others decrease, and

why some people earn higher incomes than others.

8. Macroeconomics considers the economic behavior of an entire economy, addressing such questions as what determines national economic growth and why unemployment and inflation occur.

9. Positive economic statements are statements of fact. For example, "When the price of popcorn increases, the quantity demanded of popcorn decreases." Normative economic statements are statements expressing value judgments. For example, "The price of popcorn is too high."

KEY TERMS

Natural resources
Scarcity
Economics
Consumer sovereignty
Economic model

Ceteris paribus
Circular flow model
Household
Firm
Microeconomics

Macroeconomics
Positive economics
Normative economics
Invisible hand
Econometrics

QUESTIONS

1. The relationship between choice and scarcity is one of cause-and-effect. Which is cause? Which is effect? Explain.

2. Economists assume that our wants are unlimited. How does that assumption relate to the basic questions relating to economics?

3. What is the difference between renewable and nonrenewable resources?

4. Do you think we should be conserving our oil resources for future generations? After all, there is only so much oil on earth. List the main arguments you can make in favor of conservation. List arguments opposed to conservation.

5. What do you think would happen to our idea of the basic economic problem if we discovered a natural resource that could reproduce itself any number of times and could be transformed by labor into any good or service? Before answering, make sure you understand what the basic economic problem is.

6. What is economics? Why is economics considered one of the social sciences? What are some of the other social sciences? What do social scientists study?

7. What does *ceteris paribus* mean? Why is the concept useful to economists? Cite an example.

8. What defines an economic model? In what way is the circular flow model a simplification of reality? Why would economists want to simplify reality?

9. What is the difference between resource markets and product markets? Cite examples.

10. Reesa Rodier says: "Data show that during the 1990s the price of prescription drugs increased faster than the rate of inflation. These drug prices are simply too high." Are her statements normative or positive, or both?

11. Is an economy malfunctioning when its citizens choose to lunch on unhealthy, fat-ladened fast food instead of choosing healthy, well-balanced meals? Make the case for either side of the argument.

12. Many economists in the spring of 2001 predicted that the recession would end in six months. They were dead wrong. It continued well into 2002. Is it fair to dismiss them as being "less than adequately trained"? Or perhaps "not the brightest economists" in the profession? What arguments can you make in their defense?

13. Identify where each of the following belongs (upper or lower half, flowing in which direction) in the circular flow model in Exhibit 1: automobiles, automobile workers, your purchase of a new automobile, and a $100 rebate payment you receive from General Motors.

14. Consumer sovereignty is an integral part of a democratic society. Why?

PRACTICE PROBLEM

1. Construct a circular flow, and fill in the missing value.

CONSUMER SPENDING FOR GOODS AND SERVICES	$57
WAGES	
INTEREST	$ 6
RENT	$ 4
PROFIT	$ 7

Economic Consultants

Economic Research and Analysis by Students for Professionals

Computer Sell! is a retailer of computers and software. The owners of Computer Sell! are worried that they do not understand the economics of the computer industry or the economic events that affect this industry.

The owners of Computer Sell! have approached Economic Consultants for advice. Prepare a report for Computer Sell! that addresses the following issues:

1. In general, what resources are available?
2. What sources of economic news and analysis, if any, are available for the national economy? For the regional economy where you currently are?
3. What economic resources for the computer industry, if any, are available on the Internet?

You may find the following resources helpful as you prepare this report for Computer Sell!:

© Image 100/Royalty-Free/CORBIS

- **Yahoo!** (http://www.yahoo.com), **Excite** (http://www.excite.com/), and **Lycos** (http://www.lycos.com/)—These popular search engines and directories enable you to get a quick grasp of what is available on the Internet for certain topics, such as economics.
- **Resources for Economists on the Internet** (http://rfe.org) and **WebEc** (http://www.helsinki.fi/WebEc/WebEc.html)—Resources for Economists and WebEc are directories that focus exclusively on economic materials on the Internet.
- ZDN (http://www.zdnet.com/) and **News.Com** (http://www.news.com/)—ZDNet and News.Com, sponsored by CNET, provide news coverage of the technology industry.

1. In our economy, people have the freedom to buy or not buy the goods offered in the marketplace, and this freedom to choose what they want to buy dictates what producers will ultimately produce. The key term defining this condition is
   a. economic power of choice.
   b. consumer sovereignty.
   c. ultimate producer sovereignty.
   d. political economy.
   e. positive economics.

2. JUAN: My potato crop this year is very poor.
   ANNA: Don't worry. Price increases will compensate for the fall in quantity supplied.
   RENE: Climate affects crop yields. Some years are good, others are bad.
   LISA: The government ought to guarantee that our incomes will not fall.
   In this conversation, the normative statement is made by
   a. Juan.
   b. Anna.
   c. Rene.
   d. Lisa.
   e. There are no normative statements.

3. Which of the following describes an economy that has or had no scarcity?
   a. Biblical Israel
   b. Ancient economies of sub-Sahara Africa
   c. A mythical economy where everyone is a billionaire
   d. An economy forever at full employment
   e. None of the above

4. Which of the following is not microeconomics subject matter?
   a. The price of a Dell laptop
   b. The effect of an increase in the supply of international crude oil on the price of international crude oil
   c. The cost in Indonesia of producing a pair of Nike shoes
   d. The demand for airline tickets
   e. The rate of economic growth in Canada

5. Economic models
   a. are designed to explain all aspects of the economy.
   b. never employ assumptions that cannot be tested.
   c. abstract from reality to reduce the complexity of the world we live in to more simplified, manageable dimensions.

   d. provide detailed statistical analysis of the economy.
   e. are more useful in macroeconomic applications than in microeconomic ones.

6. In the circular flow model,
   a. households supply resources to firms through the resource market.
   b. households buy goods and services in the product market.
   c. money flows from firms to households through the resource market.
   d. All of the above
   e. None of the above

7. Apply the idea of a nonrenewable resource to best describe one of the following as nonrenewable:
   a. Eggs used in baking a cake
   b. Corn used to feed hogs
   c. Copper tubing used in residential construction
   d. Hot water used in commercial laundries
   e. Lumber used in industrial construction

8. Which of the following is not one of the four central questions that the study of economics is supposed to answer?
   a. Who produces what?
   b. How are goods produced?
   c. Who consumes what?
   d. When are goods produced?
   e. Who decides what goods to produce?

9. Ceteris paribus is a tool used by economists to
   a. develop one-to-one, cause-and-effect economic relationships.
   b. link resources to goods and services.
   c. promote consumer sovereignty.
   d. distinguish microeconomics from macroeconomics.
   e. perform modern statistical testing of economic data.

10. Econometrics
    a. links positive to normative economics.
    b. applies modern statistical methods to test models.
    c. is an appropriate use of economic models.
    d. is real-world economics as distinguished from economic models.
    e. is the use of ceteris paribus in real-world situations.

Appendix

ON READING GRAPHS

· ·

THE ONLY THING WE HAVE TO FEAR IS FEAR ITSELF

It's happened a zillion times: Students buy their economics textbooks, flip through the pages, spot the dozens of equations and graphs, and fear, before they start, that it's going to be a losing battle. But it hardly ever is, and certainly not because of the graphs or mathematics. There simply isn't enough information in those graphs or equations to confuse or exasperate.

If you can shake the trauma of the graphic and mathematical form of expression, you will do just fine. As President Franklin D. Roosevelt said during his 1933 inaugural speech, "The only thing we have to fear is fear itself!"

A Graphic Language

Graphs and mathematics are simplified languages. Most of what appears in graphics or mathematics can be described in written form—in fact, most ideas are best expressed that way. In *some* circumstances, however, the written exposition becomes so convoluted that graphs and equations can present the idea more clearly.

Suppose, for example, that the simple arithmetic statement

$$(4)(6) + (8/2) - 12 = 16$$

were written as 12 subtracted from the product of 4 multiplied by 6 plus the quotient of 8 divided by 2 equals 16. You lose track of the calculations, don't you? The equation form is easier to read. Graphs are like that, too. They are pictorial representations of ideas that could be expressed otherwise, but not with the same degree of clarity.

Know Your Point of Reference

When you read a map, you typically measure out where you want to go from where you are. The where-you-are position is always your point of reference, putting everything else in place.

If you're sitting in St. Louis, Missouri, then Kansas City, Kansas, is 257 miles due west. If you're searching for Louisville, Kentucky, it's 256 miles due east. Kansas City and Louisville are west and east only because you're looking at them from St. Louis. People in Tallahassee, Florida, see Atlanta as due north, but viewed from St. Louis, Atlanta is southeast. In map reading, everything is measured from a point of reference.

Graphs are read the same way. If you can read a map, you can read a graph. Look at Exhibit A1.

The graph's point of reference is called the **origin**. Using our map example, the origin is the graph's St. Louis. Everything on the graph is measured from it. Points can be viewed as lying to the east of the origin, or to the west, or north, or

Origin
A graph's point of reference.

EXHIBIT A1   The Four Quadrants

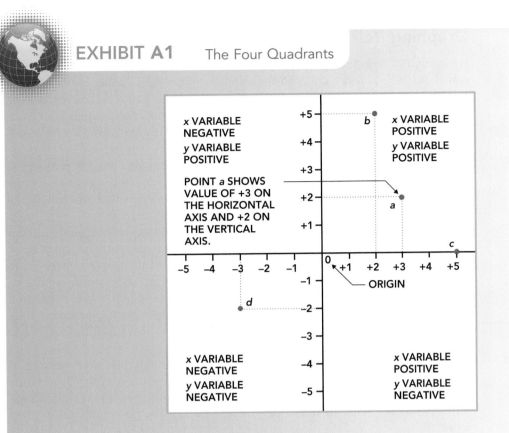

south. More precise readings describe the points as "north by northwest" or "east by southeast." You can see them in your mind's eye.

Note that Exhibit A1 is divided into four quadrants (or parts). The vertical (*y*) axis—running north and south through the origin—and the horizontal (*x*) axis—running east and west through the origin—are its dividers.

Measuring Distances on Graphs

Have you ever seen a NASA space shot countdown? As you know, its point of reference is blastoff. Typically, NASA starts counting before ignition. If you're watching on TV, you'll see the digital readout register −10 seconds, then −9, then −8, counting down to 0. At 0, ignition occurs and the count continues from 0 to +1 seconds, then +2, and so on. The time scale is a continuum, with 0 separating the minuses from the pluses.

Graph scaling is also on a continuum. In Exhibit A1, the vertical scale north of the origin (which is 0) and the horizontal scale east of the origin (which is 0) measure positive values. For example, point *a*, located at (+3, +2), reads +3 units away from the origin horizontally and +2 units away from the origin vertically. It marks the intersection of +3 and +2. Point *b*, located at (+2, +5), reads +2 units away from the origin horizontally and +5 units away from the origin vertically. Look at point *c* (+5, 0). It is +5 units away from the origin horizontally and at 0 on the vertical scale.

The vertical scale south of the origin and the horizontal scale west of the origin measure negative values. For example, point *d*, located at (−3, −2), reads −3 units away from 0 horizontally and −2 units away from the origin vertically. As you see, every point in every quadrant has its own specific numerical bearings.

Graphing Relationships

It's generally true that the more you study, the higher your grade. Suppose somebody who is less convinced than you about the relationship between effort and reward insists on evidence. What can you do to make the point? If logic doesn't work, perhaps a test will. For example, you could experiment with Economics 101 and over the course of the semester, compare your exam scores with the number of hours spent studying for them.

The underlying assumption in such a relationship is that exam scores *depend* on the number of hours of study. By varying the hours studied, you vary the scores obtained. Hours studied is described as the **independent variable** in the relationship, exam scores as the **dependent variable**.

Typically, economists work with relationships that express dependence. For example, the quantity of fish people are willing to buy depends on the price of fish. The price of fish is the independent variable, and the quantity people are willing to buy is the dependent one. The amount of money people spend consuming goods and services depends on their income—again a link between a dependent variable and an independent one. Another such dependent relationship is the number of hours people are willing to work and the wage rate offered.

Suppose you find that with 0 hours of study, you fail miserably, scoring 20 out of a possible 100. With 2 hours per week of study, you score 50. With 5 hours per week, you raise your grade to 70. With 7 hours per week, your grade improves to 80. With 10 hours per week, you top the class with the highest score, 85.

If you experimented with Biology 101 exams, the effort-and-reward relationship would still be positive, but the specific payoffs might be different. For example, with 0 hours, you still fail, this time scoring only 12 out of a possible 100. With 2 hours per week, you score only 35. With 5 hours, you get considerably better, scoring 55; with 7 hours, you score 70; and with 10 hours a week studying biology, you score 75.

That's convincing evidence that increased hours of study produce higher grades, but the written presentation can get confusing, particularly when the number of exams and courses increases. The written form is not always the clearest way to express observations.

Perhaps a clearer presentation of the evidence could be made by converting the information into table form. Look, for example, at the table in Exhibit A2.

Is it any clearer? The information is the same; it's just displayed differently. It is easier to see that the more time spent on study, the higher the score, and comparisons between economics and biology are more readily observed.

Look how the same information is transcribed into graphic form. Exhibit A2, panel *a*, records the same information as the table.

As you see, in panel *a*, hours of study are measured along the horizontal axis. Exam scores are measured along the vertical axis. Both variables in our example are positive. Therefore, the corresponding points in the table—such as 5 hours of study and an exam score of 70 in economics—locate in the upper-right quadrant of the graph. Both graphs in Exhibit A2 show that quadrant.

Connecting Points to Form Curves

The table and graphs in panel *a*, Exhibit A2, are abbreviated displays of evidence. They record only ten pieces of data. The experiment could have been expanded to record an exam score for every hour of study, or even every minute instead of every five hours. That is, if the intervals between the points in panel *a* could be

Independent variable
A variable whose value influences the value of another variable.

Dependent variable
A variable whose value depends on the value of another variable.

EXHIBIT A2   Test Scores for Economics 101 and Biology 101

NUMBER OF HOURS SPENT STUDYING AND TEST SCORES FOR ECONOMICS 101 AND BIOLOGY 101

HOURS	ECONOMICS 101 SCORES	BIOLOGY 101 SCORES
0	20	12
2	50	35
5	70	55
7	80	70
10	85	75

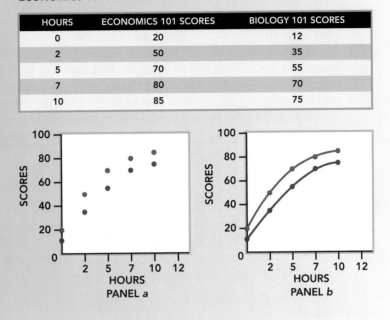

filled in to create a *continuous* series of data points connecting study hours and exam scores (unrealistic, of course, because nobody could take that many exams in one semester), such a completed series would trace a continuous curve on the graph, which is what we see in panel *b*.

But is it necessary to ascertain every point to create a curve? Suppose you want to graph the relationship between income and saving. And suppose the table accompanying Exhibit A3 presents the relevant data.

EXHIBIT A3   Income and Saving

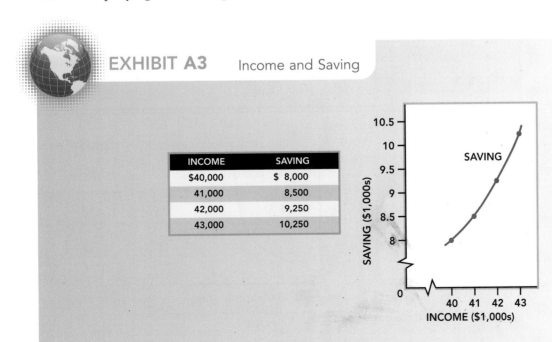

INCOME	SAVING
$40,000	$ 8,000
41,000	8,500
42,000	9,250
43,000	10,250

Note that the data set starts with $40,000 of income. If the graph were to plot *every* income value from $0 at the origin to, say, $43,000 in units of $1,000, 43 units would be marked off on the horizontal axis, but only the last 4 of the 43 units would bear any data. The graph becomes dominated then by empty, dataless space. And to keep the graph within the bounds of the page, it may even be necessary to make each income unit represent $2,000. By doing so, it becomes even more difficult to read on the vertical axis the increases in saving that are associated with the $1,000 increases in income.

Breaking the axes—as shown in Exhibit A3—cuts out the empty, dataless space. The break, introduced after the first units on both the vertical and horizontal axes, allows the graphmaker to magnify the data, making it easier for the reader to focus on the relevant part of the graph. The 40th unit of income follows the break on the horizontal axis, and the 80th unit of saving—each unit representing $1,000 of saving—follows the first unit on the vertical axis. The resulting graph maps out a clear picture of the saving curve.

THE SLOPE OF A CURVE

Consider the law of demand: As the price of a good falls, the quantity of the good demanded increases. The table and graph in panel *a*, Exhibit A4, depict such a relationship between the price of fish and quantity demanded. (The law of demand will be studied more closely in Chapter 3.)

EXHIBIT A4   Price and Quantities Demanded and Supplied of Fish

PRICE AND QUANTITY DEMANDED OF FISH

PRICE	QUANTITY DEMANDED
10	1
9	2
8	3
7	4
6	5
5	6
4	7
3	8
2	9
1	10

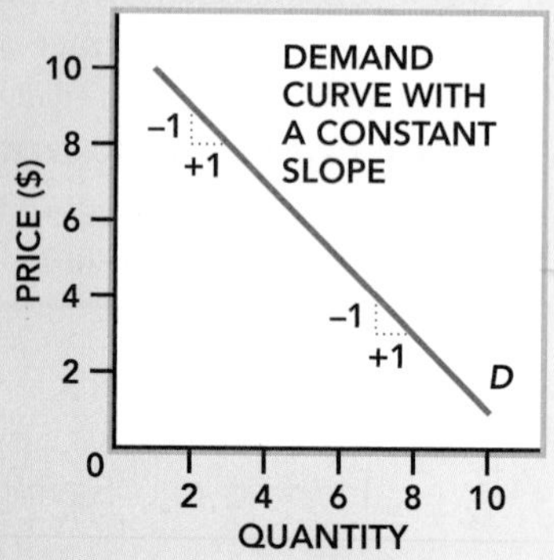

PANEL *a*

PRICE AND QUANTITY SUPPLIED OF FISH

PRICE	QUANTITY SUPPLIED
5	6.5
4	6
3	5
2	3
1	0

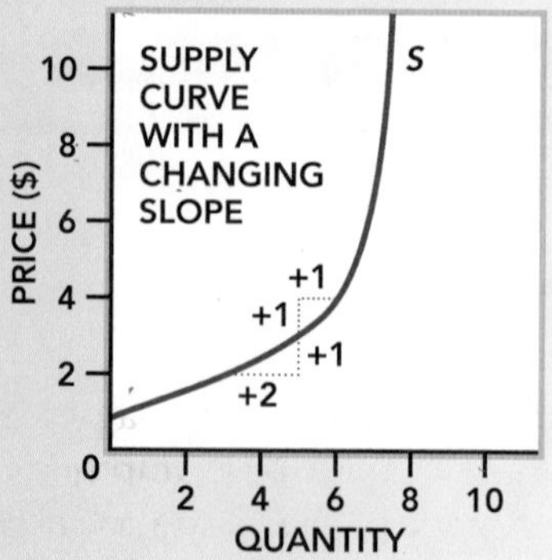

PANEL *b*

Panel *a*, Exhibit A4, connects the discrete data given in the accompanying table to form a solid curve that, as you see, is in the form of a straight line.

The **slope of a curve** measures the ratio of change in the value on the vertical axis to the corresponding change in value on the horizontal axis between two points:

$$\text{slope} = \frac{\text{rise}}{\text{run}} = \frac{\text{change in the value on vertical axis}}{\text{change in the value on horizontal axis}}$$

Slope of a curve
The ratio of the change in the variable measured on the vertical axis to the corresponding change in the variable measured on the horizontal axis, between two points.

Downward-sloping curves—sloping from northwest to southeast—are considered *negatively sloped*; that is, a positive (negative) change in the independent variable is associated with a negative (positive) change in the dependent variable. Upward-sloping curves—sloping from southwest to northeast—are *positively sloped*; that is, a positive (negative) change in the independent variable is associated with a positive (negative) change in the dependent variable.

Look again at Exhibit A4, panel *a*. Every $1 change in price generates a 1-unit change in quantity demanded. For example, when price falls from $10 to $9 (−$1), the quantity demanded increases from 1 to 2 fish (+1). The slope of the curve, within the $10 to $9 price range, then, is

$$-1/+1 = -1$$

The slope is negative. Note that any other price change within any other price range in this example still generates a negative slope of −1. When price increases from $3 to $4 (+$1), the quantity demanded decreases from 7 fish to 6 (−1). The slope +1/−1 remains −1. *Any curve with a constant slope is a straight line.* That's precisely what we see in panel *a*.

Panel *b* represents a typical supply curve. It depicts the willingness of the fishing industry to supply varying quantities of fish at varying prices. The curve slopes upward, indicating that higher prices induce greater quantities supplied. Unlike the demand curve in panel *a*, the supply curve here is not a straight line. It is less steep at low price ranges than at higher ones. Let's calculate the slopes within different price ranges. When price increases from $2 to $3 (+$1), the quantity supplied increases from 3 to 5 fish (+2). The slope of the curve, within the $2 to $3 price range, then, is

$$+1/+2 = +0.5$$

But when the price rises from $3 to $4 (+$1), the quantity supplied increases only from 5 fish to 6 (+1). The slope of the curve within the $3 to $4 price range is

$$+1/+1 = +1$$

There's nothing peculiar or complicated about any curve on any graph or the measurement of its slope. The slope of the curve is only a numerical way of expressing the curve's shape. The numerical value signals the strength of the relationship between changes in the variables measured on the vertical and horizontal axes.

U-Shaped and Hill-Shaped Curves

Some curves that are part of the economists' bag of tools contain both positive- and negative-sloping segments. Look, for example, at Exhibit A5, panels *a* and *b*.

The U-shaped curve in panel *a* shows the relationship between the average cost of producing a good and the quantity of goods produced. Typically, the average cost falls as more units are produced—that's the downward-sloping part

EXHIBIT A5   Cost and Utility Curves

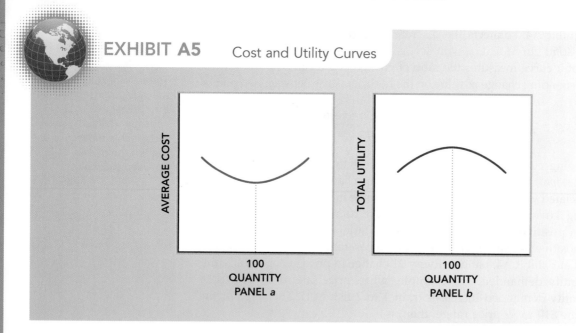

of the curve. Beyond some point, however—100 units in panel *a*—average cost begins to increase with production, which is the upward-sloping part of the curve.

From 0 to 100 units, the slope of the curve, although changing, is always negative. Beyond 100 units, it becomes positive. There's nothing complicated about reading the graph if you consider each point on the curve, one at a time. *Every point on that U-shaped average cost curve represents a specific quantitative relationship between average cost and level of production.* Nothing more!

The hill-shaped curve in panel *b* is much the same. It shows the relationship between the total utility or benefit derived from consuming a good and the quantity of goods consumed. The basic idea is that for some goods—water, for instance—the more consumed, the greater the total enjoyment, but only up to a point. Beyond that point—100 units in panel *b*—the more water, the lower the total enjoyment. Who, for example, enjoys a flood? From 0 to 100 units, the slope of this curve is positive, but it becomes negative thereafter.

Vertical and Horizontal Curves

Economists also work with relationships that, when graphed, trace out as perfectly vertical or horizontal curves. These are represented in Exhibit A6, panels *a* and *b*.

Consider the circumstance where a fisherman returns home after a day's work with 100 fish. Suppose he is willing to supply those fish at whatever price the fish will fetch. After all, a day-old fish isn't something to prize. If the price is $10 per fish, he is willing to sell all 100. If the price is only $9, he is still willing to sell all of them. If the price is $100 per fish, he *still* will supply only 100 fish, because the day's work is done and there are no more fish available. The supply curve, shown in panel *a*, is a vertical line to denote a supply of 100 fish, whatever the price. Its slope is everywhere infinite. That is, when price changes from $10 to $9 (−$1), quantity doesn't change (0). The slope, then, is −1/0. That's infinity.

What about the perfectly horizontal curve? Suppose you are selling tomatoes in an outdoor market, competing against hundreds of other tomato growers. Suppose also that the price is $0.50 per pound, and you can sell as much as you want at that price. If you were to raise your price by just one penny, or even less,

EXHIBIT A6   Vertical Supply Curve and Horizontal Demand Curve

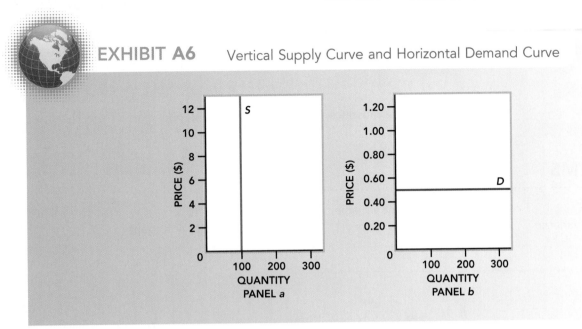

you couldn't sell any tomatoes at all. What a difference a fraction of a penny makes! After all, why would anyone buy your tomatoes when they can buy all they want from your competitors at $0.50?

How would you graph the demand curve you face? It would be a straight horizontal curve, as shown in panel *b*. At $0.50 you could sell 10, 20, or 200 tomatoes. At just an infinitesimally small increase—approaching 0—in price, you sell 0 tomatoes. The slope, then, is 0 divided by any number, which is 0.

Measuring the Slope of a Point on a Curve

Look at the U-shaped curve of Exhibit A7.

To find the slope of any point on the curve, draw a **tangent**—a straight line just touching the curve—at the point where the slope is to be measured. The **slope of the tangent** is the same as the slope of the curve at the point of tangency. What is the slope of the tangent? Look at tangent *td* at point *a* on the curve. Its slope is *ac/cd*, or numerically,

$$-10/+15 = -2/3$$

The minus sign indicates that the point of tangency lies on the downward-sloping part of the curve.

Tangent
A straight line that touches a curve at only one point.

Slope of a tangent
The slope of a curve at its point of tangency.

EXHIBIT A7   Measuring the Slope at a Point on a Curve

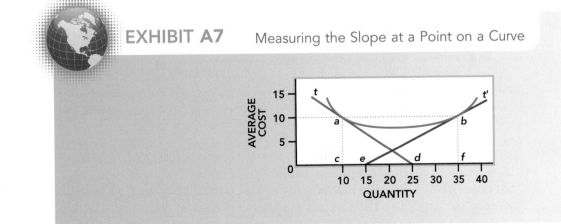

What about the slope at point *b?* Draw the tangent, *et'*. Its slope is *bf/ef*, or numerically,

$$+10/+20 = +1/2$$

Its positive value indicates it is on the upward-sloping part of the U-shaped curve.

KEY TERMS

Origin	Dependent variable	Tangent
Independent variable	Slope of a curve	Slope of a tangent

PRODUCTION POSSIBILITIES AND OPPORTUNITY COSTS

Until recently, natural scientists believed that what distinguished human beings from other animals was our ability to engage in abstract thinking and to fashion tools that could assist us in producing the things we want. It was thought that while many birds fish (think of the swooping pelican), they do so without bird-made fishing tackle. It was also clear that chimps could claw into termite mounds for a delicious snack, but no one thought that they could manufacture tools to make their food gathering more productive.

We, on the other hand, were considered to be very different. We domesticated other animals to do our heavy pulling and pushing. We built myriad kinds of tools to use in all kinds of production processes, from raking leaves to building skyscrapers. We invented tools that made tools. We converted natural resources into forms of energy that light up, heat, and cool just about anything we want to light up, heat,

and cool. We're a clever lot. It was simply inconceivable for these scientists to suggest that members of the "lower species" could do any of that. But they were dead wrong.

Recent discoveries show that hundred of animal species not only can make and master the use of tools but are capable of abstract thought and problem solving.

Let's start with the green heron. To fish for food, it drops a small object onto the surface of the water and waits until fish swim toward it, thinking the object is prey. The heron then snatches the unsuspecting fish. If that's not fishing with bait, nothing is!

Or take the case of the woodpecker finch on the Galapagos Islands. It not only uses tools, but manufactures them. Because its tongue isn't long enough to reach grubs embedded in trees, the finch finds a sizeable cactus spine, puts it in its beak, and uses it to pry grubs out of branches. The finch holds the spine underfoot while eating the grub and even carries the tool from tree to tree to be used again.

Egyptian vultures love ostrich eggs, but these eggs are incredibly tough to crack. While some birds peck away at eggs, this vulture is ingenious. It finds an appropriate rock and uses it as a smashing tool. Although its aim is poor—hitting the target about 50 percent of the time—it is persistent and typically successful.

And then there are Jane Goodall's chimps. They engage in rather sophisticated toolmaking, actually modifying objects to form tools. They break small branches from trees and then strip off leaves and protruding twigs to fashion workable stick tools. They can even join two sticks tools together to make an elongated one to reach otherwise inaccessible places. These tools are used to unearth ants from holes, extract honey from beehives, and haul terminates out of narrow openings.

While animals have yet to manufacture a television set or fly to the moon, the resources they use to do what they do are similar to those we use to do what we do: They and we combine ingenuity, labor, and toolmaking (capital) with gifts of nature. It has worked wonders for them and wonders for us. Let's focus now on what we do with our resources and what choices we make in producing the things we want.

FACTORS OF PRODUCTION

Economists refer to the resources used in the production of goods and services as **factors of production**. The four factors are labor, capital, land, entrepreneurship. Let's elaborate a little on each.

Labor

Labor is the physical and mental exertion of people engaged in the production of goods and services. Labor willingly sells its skills in the resource market for agreed-upon prices. There is no coercion involved, and the agreements or contracts typically specify price per hour, per week, or per year.

Furthermore, the idea that people can choose to offer their labor or not to offer their labor on the resource market indicates that people's labor is, in fact, their own personal asset—their own private property, so to speak—to dispose

Factor of production
Any resource used in a production process. Resources are grouped into labor, land, capital, and entrepreneurship.

Labor
The physical and intellectual effort of people engaged in producing goods and services.

of as they wish. Of course, some labor assets are more valued on the resource market than others. The abilities of a professional basketball player, for example, are an asset richly rewarded. Other abilities, such as those of oncology nurses, are less so, at least as they are appreciated on the market.

Think about the people you know. Some are unrelenting workaholics, aren't they? Others, to put it kindly, are less inclined to spend their day at productive labor. In other words, the qualities and quantities of labor that appear as a factor of production on the resource market are varied and typically highly differentiated.

Capital

What identifies **capital**? Capital is a good used to produce or sell other goods. For example, a hammer is used to produce a house. A textile machine is used to produce a sweater. A blast furnace is used to produce steel. And the steel produced in the blast furnace is used to produce an automobile. The hammer, the textile machine, the blast furnace, and the steel are capital goods. They are used to produce houses, sweaters, and automobiles, which are final goods, that is, consumption goods that end up in our households. We enjoy wearing the sweater. We don't use it to produce another good.

We can identify most capital goods by sight. A shoe factory and the machinery in it are capital goods. So is the leather and stitching material. A farmer's barn and the tractor parked behind it are capital goods. Easy enough, isn't it? Factories, machinery tools, and raw materials are clearly capital goods. But are all capital goods so clearly marked?

What about an automobile used as a taxi? That automobile is a capital good. It is used to produce transportation service. But if you drove the automobile for your own personal use, then that same automobile is a consumption good, not a capital good. As you see, it's not always easy to distinguish between capital and consumption goods by appearances alone.

What about the pairs of shoes piled high on shelves in the back room of a shoe store? They may look like consumption goods but they serve as capital goods. Why? Because the store needs shoes to sell shoes. How else could you choose a pair if the store had no inventory, that is, shoes on display, in varying colors, styles, and sizes? When a pair is sold, another is ordered to replace it. The store needs to maintain that inventory. The inventory is no less a capital good than the machinery that produced it.

Unlike inventory or machinery, some forms of capital are neither physical nor visible. Consider, for example, the capital used by Linda Marshall. Linda is a financial analyst for Smith Barney. Although the brokerage rightfully regards *her* as a valued employee, Linda at work is considerably more than Linda Marshall at work. What are also in play are Linda's professional skills, which she managed to acquire through four years of college. That education is capital to Linda in the same sense that a 2-pound monkey wrench is capital to a plumber. The plumber works with the wrench to produce a functional Jacuzzi. Linda uses her education—now inseparable from Linda—to produce high-quality financial advice. See the comparability? It is capital either way. Economists refer to the special skills acquired through education or training as **human capital**. It is perhaps the most important form of capital in our society and explains, in large measure, our incredibly high economic performance.

Land

Land is a gift of nature. In its natural state, it is the untouched prairies, the expanse of topsoil, the majestic mountains, the oceans of oil beneath the earth's crust, the powerful waterfalls, the coal, copper, iron ore, gold, silver, and other

Capital
Manufactured goods used to make and market other goods and services.

Human capital
The knowledge and skills acquired by labor, principally through education and training.

Land
A natural-state resource such as real estate, grasses and forests, and metals and minerals.

metals and minerals that lie just below the landscape. An uncut diamond is land. A virgin forest is land. The real estate in downtown Dallas is land. So too are the Gobi Desert and the Pacific Ocean.

The problem with the economists' definition of land as a factor of production is that we seldom, if ever, see land in its natural state. A tree that is cut and used in production is no longer strictly a land resource. It becomes capital as well. It was cut down by labor and machines. Lumber, then, is a manufactured good. Irrigated land, too, is not strictly land. The irrigation system is capital. Any improved land is a combination of capital and land.

Entrepreneurship

No good or service is produced by spontaneous combustion. Resources just don't come together on their own. *Somebody* has to conceive of the essential idea of production, decide what factors to use, market the goods and services produced, and accept the uncertainty of making or losing money in the venture. This somebody is the *entrepreneur,* a word that comes from the French, "to undertake." Although **entrepreneurs** who own and operate businesses typically do all these things, economists define their entrepreneurial role only in terms of the uncertainties of business they assume.

After all, entrepreneurs can delegate the buying of land, labor, and capital and the overseeing of production to a hired managerial staff. That's precisely what most modern corporations do. Managerial activity is labor. When entrepreneurs manage the production process, they function as laborers. Entrepreneurs can delegate every other function of production to labor, except the function of assuming risk and uncertainty.

We have briefly surveyed the four factors of production. Now let's put them to work.

ROBINSON CRUSOE'S PRODUCTION POSSIBILITIES

Let's begin our analysis of production by imagining Robinson Crusoe, stranded and alone on an island. The resources at his disposal, while attractive, are limited. And being a person very much like you, he has unlimited wants. In other words, Crusoe, like all of us, faces the unshakable reality of economic scarcity. What can he do in this situation? Let's look at his options.

He can spend part of the day in leisure and part at work. He could pick mangoes right off the trees, or he can fish. He can plant and harvest crops. His principal factors of production are his own labor and the virgin land about him.

Let's suppose he decides to spend his waking hours gathering food for consumption. He climbs trees for mangoes and coconuts and spends the better part of the day trying to pick fish out of the lagoon. He ends each day with six units of consumption. It's enough to keep him going, but, of course, he wants more. How does he get it? Let's suppose he decides to make a fishing spear. That requires finding the right materials and fashioning a spear. He sets aside part of the day to find a young tree that will serve as the shank, a stone that can be sharpened to make a spearhead, and a length of vine to bind the two together.

This takes time. If he takes the time to produce the spear, he can gather only five units of consumption goods. Why then do it? Because with a fishing spear, he expects to catch more fish in the next round of production. It's a risk, of course. There's no guarantee he will catch more fish. Some expectations are never realized. But let's suppose he catches more. The spear is Robinson Crusoe's first unit of capital.

Entrepreneur
A person who alone assumes the risks and uncertainties of a business.

check your understanding

Why do people produce capital goods?

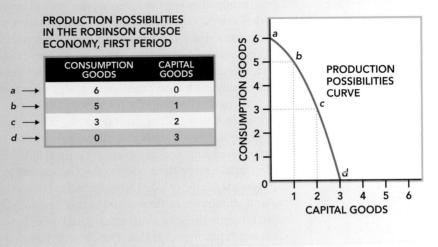

KEY EXHIBIT 1   Production Possibilities Frontier

Robinson Crusoe's economy can produce six consumption goods and zero capital goods, shown at point a. Alternatively, it can produce five consumption goods and one capital good (point b), three consumption goods and two capital goods (point c), zero consumption goods and three capital goods (point d), or any other combination located on this curve. The law of increasing costs accounts for the balloon-like shape of the production possibilities curve.

PRODUCTION POSSIBILITIES IN THE ROBINSON CRUSOE ECONOMY, FIRST PERIOD

	CONSUMPTION GOODS	CAPITAL GOODS
a →	6	0
b →	5	1
c →	3	2
d →	0	3

He decides to make a second spear as well to use as an extension tool so that he can reach the bigger, riper fruit at the top of the trees. He discovers that finding the right material for the second spear takes even more time than it did for the first. Why? He had already used the most available tree for the fishing spear's shank, the most available stone for the spearhead, and the most accessible length of vine to tie them together.

While he is producing both the fishing spear and the extension spear, he can manage to gather only three units of consumption goods. Why then do it? Because with both units of capital, he expects to produce considerably more consumption goods in the next round of production.

The Robinson Crusoe story is incredibly simple, yet it contains all the essential elements of our own modern, busy, and highly sophisticated economy. In our economy, as in all others—including Crusoe's—labor, capital, land, and entrepreneurship combine to produce two sets of possible goods: consumption goods and capital goods.

The components of the set are variable. For example, these factors of production can be combined into any of the **production possibilities** shown in the table in Exhibit 1.

The first possibility, *a*, allows Robinson Crusoe to devote all his time, energies, and talent to the production of six units of consumption goods. That means he produces zero capital goods. But that's a production choice he is free to make. There are other options. He could, if he wishes, shift *some of the resources* he had used to produce the six units of consumption goods into the production of a capital good. We see the result in Exhibit 1, production possibility *b*. Crusoe now ends up producing five units of consumption and one unit of capital. Whatever combination he chooses—there are also possibilities *c* and *d*—he is smart enough to understand that "there is no such thing as a free lunch." Crusoe knows a cost is always involved in adding more of one good. As he sees it—and so do we—the first unit of capital cost him one unit of consumption.

Production possibilities
The various combinations of goods that can be produced in an economy when it uses its available resources and technology efficiently.

Opportunity Cost

What economists mean by cost is **opportunity cost**—that is, the quantity of other goods that must be given up to obtain a good. That's a powerful notion of cost. It applies universally. For example, the opportunity cost of watching the L.A.

Opportunity cost
The quantity of other goods that must be given up to obtain a good.

Lakers play the Boston Celtics the night before an exam is the five points that could have earned an A. The opportunity cost of renovating the high school auditorium is the new biology lab that the school had been thinking about. Opportunity cost applies even where you may least suspect. For example, for a married couple, the opportunity cost of marriage to each partner is the opportunities each gives up that would have been possible had they remained single.

You see the connection, don't you? The thought that goes through Crusoe's mind when contemplating production is the same kind of thinking that you do before studying for an exam. You both think about the opportunities given up. But you make choices. When Crusoe gives up a unit of consumption goods to produce that first unit of capital goods, it's probably because he values that first unit of capital goods more than the consumption good given up. If you spend the evening studying for the exam, it's probably because you value the expected higher grade more than you do the Celtics game.

You may have erred. The game was the season's best and the studying didn't make a difference in your exam score. In hindsight, you find that the studying wasn't worth the cost. But what could you have done otherwise? Opportunity costs are typically subjective. How could you possibly know with certainty what opportunity costs are? Even Robinson Crusoe, making simple choices on the island, must rely on calculating *expected* gains and opportunity costs of choices made.

The Law of Increasing Costs

If Robinson Crusoe decides to produce two units of capital, he ends up with only three units of consumption. Measured in terms of its opportunity cost, that second unit of capital costs Crusoe two units of consumption. That is more than he had to give up for the first unit of capital.

What happens if he decides to produce three units of capital? Look again at the table in Exhibit 1. Their production absorbs all the resources available. He ends up with nothing at all to consume! The opportunity cost of that third unit of capital is the remaining three units of consumption.

Do you notice what's happening? The opportunity cost of producing each additional unit of capital increases as more of the units are produced. Economists refer to this fact of economic life as the **law of increasing costs**. It applies no matter what goods are considered. For example, if Robinson Crusoe had started with three units of capital and began adding consumption, the amount of capital goods he would have to give up to produce each additional unit of consumption would also increase. The graph in Exhibit 1 illustrates the production possibilities of the table in graphic form.

Look at points *a*, *b*, *c*, and *d* in the graph in Exhibit 1. These are precisely the production possibilities shown in the table. Point *a*, for example, represents the choice of devoting all resources to the production of six units of consumption. The curve has a negative slope because any increase in capital goods production comes only at the cost of consumption goods production.

The bowed-out shape to the curve illustrates the law of increasing costs. When Crusoe decides to increase capital goods production from one unit to two, he is forced to use resources less suited to the production of capital goods than the resources employed in producing the first unit. After all, resources are not always of equal quality, and he obviously would use the best first. The result is a movement along the curve from point *b* to point *c* that, when plotted in Exhibit 1, traces out the bowing character of the curve. Suppose Crusoe decides on three units of consumption and two units of capital. He works busily, finishes production, eats the three consumption goods, and has available now what he had not had before—two new units of capital.

Law of increasing costs The opportunity cost of producing a good increases as more of the good is produced. The law is based on the fact that not all resources are suited to the production of all goods and that the order of use of a resource in producing a good goes from the most productive resource unit to the least.

applied perspective

DID YOU EVER FIND A PENNY ON A SIDEWALK?

Some coins yes, some coins no.

How many times, strolling along a sidewalk, have you chanced upon a shiny new penny lying in your path? Picking it up is supposed to bring you good luck. But luck aside it's fun to find it, isn't it? But what about nickels, dimes, and quarters, not to mention Sacagawea dollar coins? When was the last time you saw one of those shiny silver coins lying on the sidewalk? If you're like most people, these silver coins are pretty scarce items on a sidewalk, at least compared to the copper coins we find.

Why? Is it because the supply of pennies is more plentiful than the supply of nickels, dimes, and quarters? It is more plentiful. The U.S. Mint produces about 10 billion pennies a year compared to the approximately 6 billion nickels, dimes, and quarters. But that really doesn't explain why we are more likely to see pennies on the sidewalk than silver coins.

The answer has to do with opportunity cost. If you're walking home and spot a Kennedy half-dollar on the sidewalk, wouldn't you pick it up? You probably wouldn't turn your nose up at a quarter either. Even a dime or nickel is for many people worth the effort of bending down and picking up. A penny? Considerably less so.

The reason why you find so many pennies on the sidewalk relative to silver coins is because it takes time and energy to stop, bend down, and pick them up, and that time and energy are valued more than a penny. That's why pennies on the sidewalk are not an uncommon sight. We simply pass them up. The opportunity cost associated with picking them up is too high. The quarter? most people place a higher value on a quarter they find than on the time and energy it takes to pick up, which explains why you find so few quarters on the street. They are quickly gobbled up. It's all a matter of opportunity cost.

In the next period of production, Crusoe has available the same quantity of resources he used in the earlier period *plus* the two new units of capital that had been produced earlier. With more resources available, Crusoe can produce more goods, which is what we see in the table in Exhibit 2.

Compare this table to the one in Exhibit 1. Working now with two units of capital, Robinson Crusoe can produce more. For example, ten units of consumption can now be produced when Crusoe, using the fishing spear and extension tool, devotes all his labor to consumption. Of course, he may again decide to produce more units of capital goods in order to be able to produce even more units of consumption in the following period. This can go on forever and does in most economies.

Suppose after deliberating over the production possibilities of the table in Exhibit 2, he selects seven units of consumption and two units of capital. This combination means that he not only adds two more units of capital to his resource base but also is still able to produce more consumption goods—seven—than he could have produced in the first period, even had he devoted all the resources exclusively to consumption goods production.

The graph in Exhibit 2 illustrates the change in the Crusoe economy over the two periods.

The production possibilities curve shifts outward to the right. The shift reflects the changing resource base available to Crusoe. In the second period, capital is added to the land and labor resource base of the first. The dashed curves represent later period production possibilities as long as Crusoe continues the strategy of adding units of capital to his resource base.

theoretical perspective

GUNS AND BUTTER

Suppose Robinson Crusoe discovers that he is not alone on the island and that his new neighbors are somewhat less than friendly. Suppose they are down-right threatening. It would be fool-hardy for Crusoe to continue producing only consumption and capital goods. After all, he may wake up one morning to find his uninvited neighbors helping themselves to his consumption and capital goods!

To protect life and property, Robinson Crusoe may have to devote some part of his working day to the pro-duction of defensive weapons. Instead of making a fishing spear, he may make several bows and arrows. Or, per-haps, remembering what the Chinese did, he might build a Great Wall to keep his neighbors out. But Robinson Crusoe knows that every bow, every arrow, and every stone in every defensive wall has an opportunity cost that reflects the quantity of nondefensive goods given up.

Crusoe's guns-versus-butter choices are the same kinds of choices every society has been forced to make from time immemorial. If an economy is operating on its production possibilities frontier, then guns can be produced only at the expense of butter. More guns means less butter.

What are choices in the Robinson Crusoe tale are also real choices for Americans. Dwight D. Eisenhower, the 34th U.S. president, was a five-star general during World War II and also the supreme commander of the Allied forces in Europe. The 1944 invasion of Nazi-occupied Europe under his command and the battles that followed led to Germany's unconditional surren-der. But victory is always bittersweet. No one has expressed the costs of war better than President Eisenhower himself:

> Every gun that is made, every warship launched, every rocket fired signifies, in the final sense, a theft from those who hunger and are not fed, those who

are cold and are not clothed. This world in arms is not spending money alone. It is spending the sweat of its laborers, the genius of its scientists, the hopes of its children.... This is not a way of life at all in any true sense. Under the cloud of threatening war, it is humanity hanging from a cross of iron. (Speech before the American Society of Newspaper Editors, April 16, 1953.)

© Royalty-Free/CORBIS

An economist's image of national security: money buys resources that could have produced other goods.

CONSIDER

Can you imagine a situation in which two people, both agreeing on the opportunity costs of war prepared-ness, would disagree on whether to pursue a policy of preparedness? What other issues do you think they would consider? Do you think nations go to war—or stay out of war—strictly on the basis of economic calculation?

MORE ON THE NET

Visit a few pacifist organizations, such as the American Peace Network (http://www.apn.org/) and the Center for Economic Conversion (http://www.cec.igc.org/cec/). What arguments do these organizations make for decreasing the size of the military? Do these arguments take into account the concept of opportunity cost?

Once Rich, It's Easy to Get Richer

This rather simple way of looking at an economy's production possibilities and growth potential is instructive. Imagine two economies, shown in panels *a* and *b* of Exhibit 3, whose initial production possibilities are described by the table in Exhibit 1. The different selections of consumption and capital these economies make along their identical first-period production possibilities curve trace out their productive growth—or lack of growth—over the course of several production periods.

In the first period, panel *a* people decide to produce three units of con-sumption and two units of capital (point *c*), while those in panel *b* choose six units of consumption and zero capital (point *a*). Comparing themselves to the people in panel *a*, those in panel *b* may think themselves lucky to have twice the consumption goods. But they won't feel that way in the following period.

EXHIBIT 2   Shifts in the Production Possibilities Frontier

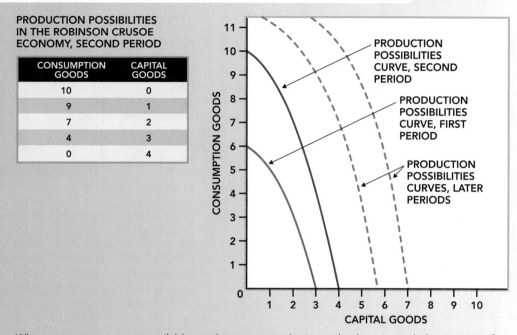

PRODUCTION POSSIBILITIES IN THE ROBINSON CRUSOE ECONOMY, SECOND PERIOD

CONSUMPTION GOODS	CAPITAL GOODS
10	0
9	1
7	2
4	3
0	4

When more resources are available or when more productive technology is used, the quantity of goods and services an economy can produce increases. The increase is depicted by the outward shift to the right of the production possibilities curve.

EXHIBIT 3   Comparative Economic Growth

Initially, the same quantities of resources and technology are available in the economies of panel *a* and panel *b*. Panel *a* chooses to produce three consumption goods and two capital goods, while panel *b* uses all its resources to produce six consumption goods. In succeeding years, the additional capital goods created in panel *a* are added to its resource base, shifting its production possibilities curve outward, while the production possibilities curve in panel *b* remains unchanged. The production gap between the two economies widens over time.

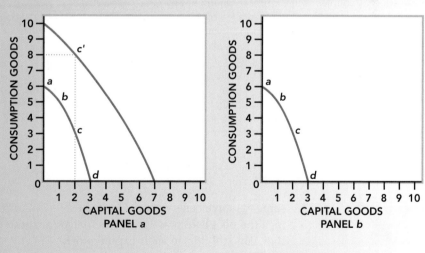

The productive powers of the two economies are no longer the same. Panel *a*'s expanded resource base, now containing the two new capital goods, allows a new and more productive set of production possibilities. Panel *a*'s production possibilities curve shifts outward. Panel *b*, on the other hand, operating on its

applied**perspective**

CHINA'S POPULATION POLICY: ONE COUPLE, ONE CHILD

What do you know about China? Probably that it has the largest population in the world. And you're right. China's 1.26 billion people account for as much as 21 percent of the world's total. That's very many people! In fact, to China's economic and social planners, that's simply too many! It interferes, they believe, with China's ability to create the instrumentalities for rapid economic development. China has been at war with underdevelopment since its 1949 revolution. Its fight to increase standards of living—per capita income—is waged on two fronts: the need to increase GDP and the need to curb population growth.

To deal with its critical demographic concern, the Chinese government in the 1970s introduced an uncompromising family planning policy that confronted China's reality. The policy advocates the practice of "one couple, one child," allowing "a second child only with proper spacing and in accordance with the laws and regulations."

What are these "laws and regulations?" They're excessively harsh by anyone's standards. For example, all pregnancies must be authorized by the government. Menstrual cycles are publicly monitored and pelvic examinations are performed on women suspected of being pregnant. Unauthorized pregnancies are terminated by abortion when detected regardless of the stage of pregnancy. Mandatory IUDs are inserted in women with one child. Removal is difficult and x-ray detection is capriciously applied. There is mandatory sterilization of couples with 2 or more unauthorized children. Women are required to obtain a birth coupon before conceiving a child, the coupon serving as a food rationing device. Without it, family food allotment remains unchanged so that per capita food consumption within the family falls when family size increases without authorization.

These stringent procedures and practices have resulted in a high rate of infanticide and, in particular,

the abandonment of female infants. But the cold facts are that China's population growth, since the initiation of the "one couple, one child" policy, has been brought under effective control. From 1970 to 1999, China's birth rate decreased from 3.34% to 1.53%. The total fertility rate of Chinese women fell below replacement levels.

Focusing on China's future.

The impact of the falling birth rates on family size is notable. Average family size fell from 4.54 members in 1980 to 3.36 members in 1999. Families with 4 or more members fell from 46.3 percent of total families to 23.3 percent. Compared to the developed countries of Europe and North America, China has accomplished these changes in a relatively short period of time.

Chinese planners translate these achievements into movements along and shifts in China's production possibilities curve. By averting the births of an estimated 250 million people and basing the per-child rearing costs from birth to 16 years at 19,000 yuan, China was able to shift resources valued at approximately 4.75 trillion yuan from consumption goods production to investment. That shift contributed to China's "second front" effort to raise standards of living: GDP growth. China's GDP quadrupled since 1980.

Have the high costs been too high? You be the judge.

MORE ON THE NET

Visit the China Population Information and Research Center at http://www.cpirc.org.cn/eindex.htm to find articles and updates on China's population strategy.

same resource base, remains locked on its initial production possibilities curve. In fact, the people in panel *a* now actually consume more than those in panel *b*, and they can still add to their capital stock.

Time is on their side. After several periods, the outward shifts in panel *a*'s production possibilities curve generate a widening gap between this curve and that of panel *b*. In time, the outward shifts in the panel *a* economy become even easier to obtain. Why? Because a solid consumption base is already in place, the opportunity cost of shifting resources to capital goods becomes less painful. Movements along the economy's production possibilities curve further into the *cd* range—more capital, less consumption—push the curve out even further in succeeding periods.

Once Poor, It's Easy to Stay Poor

Catching up is hard to do. If the panel *b* people decide to try, it may take some doing. Obviously, they must choose to move away from position *a* on their production possibilities curve. The further away from *a*, the better. Movements along their curve into the *bc* range—much more capital, much less consumption—may force them to tighten their belts considerably. Where they position themselves along the curve depends upon how well they can tolerate low-level consumption and how quickly they want to catch up.

There are economies with resource bases so underdeveloped that they have little option but to devote all their meager resources to consumption. It is hard enough just to stay alive! Typically, these economies have high rates of population growth, so that it becomes a continuing, dispiriting struggle to feed their own people. The economies simply can't afford to produce the capital needed to shift their production possibilities curves outward. Economists refer to this condition as the **vicious circle of poverty**: The economies are so poor they can't produce capital; without capital, they remain poor. Poverty feeds on itself.

THE PRODUCTIVE POWER OF ADVANCED TECHNOLOGY

Ideas, more so than any factor of production, are the most revolutionizing force able to shift the production possibilities of any economy. Ideas can shift the curve out beyond imagination. Who would have thought just a century ago that we would be walking on the moon? Who would have expected commercial space satellites to beam images from the site of the Super Bowl to an American air base in Turkey in a matter of seconds? Economists describe ideas that eventually take the form of new, applied technology as **innovations**.

Even in the simple economy of Robinson Crusoe, innovation can be shown to cause dramatic leaps forward in the production possibilities available to an economy. The fishing spear Crusoe created was an idea fashioned into a unit of capital. Two fishing spears add more to an economy's productive potential than one, shifting the production possibilities curve out to the right, but the technology is still spears.

Suppose Crusoe hits on an altogether new and creative idea: the fishing net. He sketches out this completely new technology for catching fish that requires a different combination of land and labor. Crusoe uses more vine, less wood, no stone, and more labor. The results of this new technology are dramatic. Exhibit 4 compares the production possibilities of using spear and fishing net technologies.

check your understanding

Why is it that focusing production on capital goods forces consumers to tighten their belts?

Vicious circle of poverty
A country is poor because it does not produce capital goods. It does not produce capital goods because it is poor.

Innovation
An idea that eventually takes the form of new, applied technology.

EXHIBIT 4   Production Possibilities Generated By Spear and Net Technologies

CONSUMPTION	CAPITAL		CONSUMPTION	CAPITAL
10	0		30	0
9	1		26	1
7	2		18	2
4	3		10	3
0	4		0	4

How are technological change and economic growth related?

The net technology yields 30 units of consumption goods compared to the 10 units produced with spears when all resources are devoted to the production of consumption goods. Production possibilities based on net technology make it easier to move down along the curve—producing even more capital goods—and, therefore, shifting the curve in succeeding periods out even further to the right.

Innovations creating even more advanced technology are possible. The exciting conclusion we reach, for the simple Robinson Crusoe economy and for our own, is that there are no impassable limits to the growth potential of our economy. Resource limitations may impose a short-run constraint on what we are able to produce in any period of time, but given enough time and enough minds, new technology reduces the severity of scarcity. Our grandchildren will no doubt regard our technology as rather primitive, but their grandchildren will consider their technology as hardly more advanced.

The Indestructible Nature of Ideas

Capital goods can be destroyed, but ideas are far more durable. Wars can bring havoc to any economy's resource base. People's lives are disrupted. Many do not survive the war. Whole factories, complete with machinery, and roads, bridges, railway networks, electric grids, energy facilities, and any other form of the nation's capital stock can be reduced to rubble. But capital goods can also be replaced quickly. Look at Exhibit 5.

AD represents the economy's prewar production possibilities curve. The destructive effects of war, particularly on its people and capital stock, is shown as an inward shift to the left of the curve, to *A'D'*. Recovery, however, can be whole and swift because people, even with minimal capital stock, don't have to reinvent the wheel. Technological knowledge, once acquired, is virtually indestructible. In time, applying known and more advanced technology, the economy can shift its production possibilities curve back again to *AD* and even beyond to *A"D"*.

The physical devastation of Japan and Europe caused by World War II had some rather paradoxical consequences for these war-torn economies. Because so much of their capital stock in the form of factories and machinery was destroyed, these economies were forced to start over again. But they started over with the most advanced machinery and the most up-to-date factories. The result was an incredible increase in their economies' productivity. Ironically, economies that

✋ **EXHIBIT 5**   Inward and Outward Shifts of the Production Possibilities Curve

With resources destroyed, the economy's production possibilities decrease. The decrease is depicted by the shift to the left of the production possibilities curve, from *AD* to *A'D'*. In time, with the rebuilding of resources and the use of more advanced technology, the economy can recoup and even surpass the levels of production previously attained. This is shown in the shift to the right of the production possibilities curve, from *A'D'* to *A"D"*.

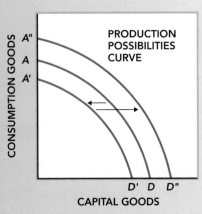

were spared the devastation of the war had their prewar technology still intact and grew less rapidly than those whose capital stocks were destroyed and replaced with the more modern technology.

National Security, Conventional War, and Terrorism in the 21st Century

Let's look more closely at the relationship between a country's national security and its provision for it. It seems reasonable to suppose that by shifting resources from the production of other goods to the production of national security goods, a national security–minded nation acquires more national security. It may also seem reasonable to suppose that the more national security goods it chooses to produce—subject to the law of increasing cost—the more national security it acquires. This is indeed what we see depicted in the move from *a* to *b* along the production possibilities curve of Panel *a* in Exhibit A.

But that may not be the entire story. The production possibilities analysis involving national security is much more complicated than that shown in Panel *a*. Why more complicated? Because a nation's security depends not only on the resources it allocates to the production of security goods but also on the quantity of security goods other nations, particularly worrisome ones, produce. That is, a nation's security is as much contingent upon the sociopolitical and military environments it shares with other nations as it is upon its own military preparedness.

Producing National Security Panel *b* in Exhibit A depicts two nations— an Aggressive one (AGG) and a Defensive one (DEF)—each with identical sets of resources. If the AGG nation's initial move from *a* to *b*—more security goods, less other goods—excites the DEF nation to move from *x* to *y*—more security goods, less other goods—then AGG's national security vis-à-vis DEF remains virtually unchanged. The 200 units of AGG's security goods confronting DEF's 200 units of security goods is the security equivalence of 100 units facing 100 units. In other words, DEF's security response to AGG's security initiative results in both AGG and DEF having less of other goods with no increase in national security.

If AGG opts to do whatever it takes to acquire a national security edge over DEF, say, moving to *c*, and if DEF counters in kind by moving to *z*, a two-nation spiral into a resource-consuming arms race results. Depressing, isn't it? Producing more security goods to acquire more security turns out to be nothing more than an illusion. Is there a way out? Perhaps at some point in the arms race, the opportunity costs associated with the two-nation spiraling becomes prohibitive to one or both nations. Conceivably, a negotiated arms treaty involving on-site inspection and reciprocal reductions in weaponry would reverse the perverse spiral.

On the other hand, if AGG is more willing to accept the increasing opportunity costs of moving further along the production possibilities curve toward more security goods than is DEF, then AGG could end up, in fact, with greater national security. But what AGG gains in security, DEF loses.

Going to War "Strike while the fire's hot!" Can you imagine some circumstance or some moment when a preemptive, first-strike war becomes a preferred option? If moving from *a* to *b* in Panel *c* gives AGG a clear but only temporary national security advantage, AGG may decide to use that advantage to reduce DEF's options. AGG may have correctly calculated that the opportunity cost of going to war is less than the opportunity cost associated with a resource-draining, no-war, no-peace security strategy.

EXHIBIT A

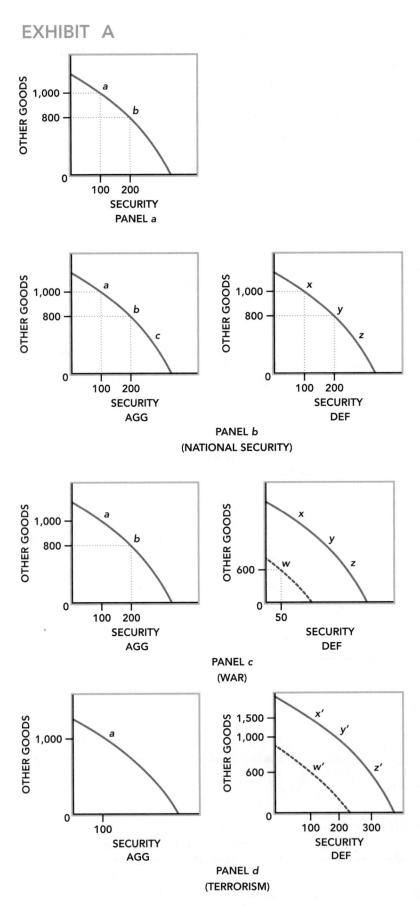

The aim of an AGG first-strike war would be to incapacitate DEF either completely—as in exacting an unconditional surrender—or incompletely—as in a negotiated peace treaty that enhances AGG's security vis-à-vis DEF. In Panel c, AGG's first-strike assault targets DEF's resource base, destroying its military defenses and impairing its ability to produce goods. As a result of the attack, DEF's production possibilities curve shifts inward toward the origin. DEF ends up at w, capable now of producing only 50 units of national security and 600 units of other goods. That is, AGG's first strike pays off: Its national security edge increases by a factor of 4, from a 100-to-100 to a 200-to-50 ratio.

But if DEF retaliates—soldier for soldier, bomb for bomb, missile for missile—the idea of gaining security through war becomes fantasy. In reality, for both AGG and DEF, a war not only involves movements along their production possibilities curves from other goods to security goods but also involves inward shifts of their production possibilities curves. Both end up with considerably less of everything.

If we relax the identical resource base assumption for both AGG and DEF and suppose instead that AGG's base has fewer resources than DEF's—depicted in Panel d—then AGG's appetite for more security or preemptive war may be curbed. After all, security and, in particular, conventional war can be devastatingly expensive. In reality, some wars are not fought or end quickly not because the passion for war subsides but because of the law of increasing opportunity cost.

But what if the techniques and cultures of warfare change quickly and dramatically? What if the opportunity cost to a nation of inflicting considerable human suffering and physical damage on another nation becomes miniscule?

Adopting State-Supported Terrorism

This is precisely what terrorist activity is designed to do: Create massive damage to an economy at bargain prices. A suicide bomber, strapped with explosives, picks a terrorist site and can, if successful, destroy a café and perhaps dozens of people. The act in itself is inconsequential. But its randomness and repetition aren't. Recruiting and training suicide bombers and producing ample supplies of explosive belts are less costly than a company picnic in July. But if repeated often enough, and if left essentially unchecked, terrorist acts can quickly erode a targeted population's confidence in its state's ability to provide personal and national security.

Lack of confidence in the nation's ability to provide security translates into lack of confidence in the nation's future. The targeted nation's economic vitality slackens, and resources—particularly the production of capital goods—contract; all this is depicted in the inward shift of the targeted nation's production possibilities curve. Less of everything is produced.

The conventional soldier-for-soldier response or missile-for-missile response is no longer workable because the terrorist act is produced by neither soldiers nor missiles. That is, the security provided by the targeted nation's production of conventional security goods deteriorates, if not fully, then at least dramatically.

Look again at Panel d. If AGG chooses to become a terrorist-supporting state, it can remain at a—no notable shift of resources to terrorist-mode security goods—yet force DEF to move from x' to y' or z', or even w'. And if DEF rejects the option of itself becoming a terrorist-supporting state, a national security gain, perhaps even security advantage goes to AGG. But that security gain or advantage may ultimately prove to be more illusionary than real. Why illusion?

Because terrorist organizations, although remarkably inexpensive, still require safe havens, a geography that condones and aids the recruiting, training, and equipping of terrorists and that provides logistic support for the terrorist activity. Without a nation's protective shield, it cannot function effectively, if at all. In other words, DEF cannot respond to the terrorism itself, only to the state supporting it. If it does, AGG's own national security becomes once again compromised.

historical perspective

THE DESTRUCTION AND RECONSTRUCTION OF ROTTERDAM

Rotterdam: vibrant and beautiful.

May 14, 1940, is an infamous date in the history of Holland's beautiful city of Rotterdam. It was on that day that Hitler's notorious air force (the Luftwaffe) bombed the city incessantly for 12 hours, until it lay in ashes.

Rotterdam became synonymous with disaster. German bombers, like tractors plowing a field, moved methodically back and forth until all that remained of the city was the shell of the ancient Saint Lawrence Church, the city hall, and a few buildings. Twenty-five thousand homes, 1,200 factories, 69 schools, and 13 hospitals were demolished. Overnight, 75,000 people became homeless and 900 were killed. The seaport, Rotterdam's economic lifeblood, was not spared. Thirty-five percent of the port was later gutted by the German army.

But Rotterdam did not die. The city enjoys a geographical advantage by straddling the delta of the Rhine, which is the main artery of Europe's intricate network of inland waterways. Almost immediately after the war, rebuilding of the harbor began with the most up-to-date cranes, derricks, docks, and cargo-handling technology. By the end of reconstruction, ships were loading and unloading faster and at lower cost than anywhere else in the world. Rotterdam not only rebuilt but also strengthened its economic muscle, funneling a large part of the cargo trade between the prospering Common Market and the rest of the world.

....

MORE ON THE NET

What does Rotterdam look like today? Visit for yourself (http://www.rotterdam.info/uk/).

POSSIBILITIES, IMPOSSIBILITIES, AND LESS THAN POSSIBILITIES

What an economy can produce depends upon the availability of resources and the level of technology applied. If the economy's resources are not fully employed, then obviously it cannot be producing as much as possible. For example, if the economy's labor force is not fully employed or if some of its land and capital resources remain idle, the combination of consumption goods and capital goods that it produces will be less than what is possible.

Such a condition is described by point u in the economy of Exhibit 6. At u, the economy is producing two consumption goods and two capital goods. Its production possibilities curve shows, however, that combination b or c is possible. In each case, more of one good can be produced without having to sacrifice any of the other. For example, it is possible to produce six units of consumption goods and two units of capital, or two units of consumption and six units of capital. Either combination is better than u.

Any point in the interior of the production possibilities curve, such as u, signals either the existence of unemployed or underemployed resources. What are **underemployed resources**? Some people working full time might appear to be fully employed, but in fact they still represent substantial unused resources. How come? They are producing much less than they are really capable of producing.

Imagine, for example, how much more our economy could have produced over the past 200 years if women, blacks, and other minorities had been allowed to exercise their talents fully. How many entrepreneurs have we lost forever? How many innovations were allowed to go undiscovered? How many skilled

Underemployed resources
The less than full utilization of a resource's productive capabilities.

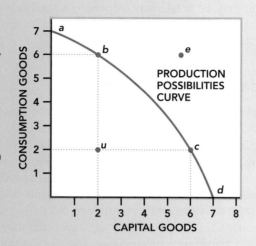

✋ **EXHIBIT 6**   Possible, Impossible, and Less than Possible

Production combinations, located outside and to the right of the production possibilities curve, such as *e*, are unattainable with the resources and technology currently available. Combinations located within the curve, such as *u*, reflect less than full use of available resources and technology. All combinations that fall on the curve, such as *b* and *c*, represent maximum use, or the full employment of the resources and technology available.

craftspeople have wasted their talents? How much further out would our production possibilities curve be if racial, sexual, religious, and ethnic discrimination had been avoided? It staggers the imagination!

Who loses? The underemployed people and the economy. That is, the economy could be producing more, but it isn't. If these underemployed people were allowed to exercise their full productive potential, the economy's production would shift from a position inside the production possibilities curve to a position on it.

Point *u* in Exhibit 6 describes an inefficiently producing economy. **Economic efficiency** refers to the condition in which all factors of production are used in their most productive capacity. In this sense, the only points of production that represent an efficiently run economy are those *on* the production possibilities curve. No one point on the curve is more efficient than any other, since all of them reflect the full employment and maximal use of the economy's available resources.

Any point lying outside the production possibilities curve in the economy of Exhibit 6, such as *e*, is an impossible production combination. After all, points on the curve, such as *a*, *b*, *c*, or *d*, represent production combinations that fully employ the economy's usable resources. How, then, can the economy produce beyond the curve? If the economy is growing, point *e*, impossible now, need not be an impossible dream.

PRODUCTION POSSIBILITIES AND ECONOMIC SPECIALIZATION

The idea that labor productivity is a function of the degree of **labor specialization** goes as far back as 1776 and Adam Smith. In his *The Wealth of Nations*, Adam Smith tells about a visit to a pin factory:

> One man draws out the wire, another straightens it, a third cuts it, a fourth points it, a fifth grinds it at the top for receiving the head; to make the head requires two or three distinct operations; to put it on is a peculiar business, to whiten the pins is another; it is even a trade by itself to put them into the paper....

The reason for such division of labor, he noted, is that these 10 people could make as many as 48,000 pins in a day. If they had each worked separately and independently, they could not have produced more than 200. That's an impressive

check your ✔️
understanding

Why does discrimination create economic inefficiency?

Economic efficiency
The maximum possible production of goods and services generated by the fullest employment of the economy's resources.

Labor specialization
The division of labor into specialized activities that allow individuals to be more productive.

point and certainly one that would not go unnoticed in the economy of Robinson Crusoe. In Crusoe's economy, shown in the table in Exhibit 1, there is no division of labor. Alone, he is forced to produce everything—to fish, hunt, farm, and repair huts. He may be a talented carpenter, a mediocre farmer, and a terrible fisherman, but he is busy doing it all. The production possibilities shown in the table in Exhibit 1 reflect this circumstance.

Specialization on the Island

on the net

The Wealth of Nations in its entirety is available online (**http://www. bibliomania.com/2/1/ frameset.html**).

But suppose Robinson Crusoe was one of thousands stranded on the island. He probably would not have fished a day in his life. The fishing would have been done by people who were good at it. Crusoe would have become the island's carpenter, relieving those who seem only able to hammer their thumbs. Division of labor on that island allows all the castaways to do the specific things each does best.

Labor can be divided and divided again into specialized and even more specialized activities until people are incredibly proficient at doing incredibly minute activities. The result of such specialization and cooperative production can mean enormous production. The production possibility schedule of an economy with 1,000 people, for example, may be 100,000 times more productive than a single-person economy.

Of course, with everyone working at specialized jobs, the people will need to create an exchange system that allows them to exchange the goods produced under conditions of specialization. A shirtmaker, for example, producing 1,000 shirts, may keep only 1 and trade the remaining 999 shirts for goods she needs. After all, working at making shirts all day does not allow her to fish for the evening meal. But her neighbor, fishing all day, would probably want to exchange some of his fish for her shirts. In this way, it is possible for every islander who specializes in production to end up with more of everything.

International Specialization

If specialization among people on the island creates more goods for everyone, then imagine how much more could be produced if there were international specialization and exchange. Suppose contact was made with people on other islands, and the practice of exchanging goods with them became commonplace. Now, even more division of labor and specialization would occur. Instead of producing 1,000 shirts for the local island markets, a shirtmaker may produce 10,000 shirts for the larger islands' markets. More people would be engaged in producing shirts. But instead of every shirtworker making a complete shirt, each would specialize in a specific task in the shirt-making process, such as cutting material, sewing pieces, making buttonholes, and folding.

Perhaps four people working at specialized tasks can produce 10,000 shirts in the time it takes one shirtmaker performing all the tasks alone to produce 1,000 shirts. The more islands that are joined in international specialization and exchange, the greater are the opportunities for division of labor and specialization. Everyone produces more, exchanges more, and consumes more.

The Principle of Comparative Advantage

Let's take this idea of international division of labor and specialization one step further to demonstrate precisely how the advantages of such specialization prevail. Imagine two island economies—Crusoe Island and Yakamaya Island—that each produce fish and shirts. Their production possibilities are shown in Exhibit 7. Look at the top row. Crusoe Islanders, if they choose to devote all their resources to the

EXHIBIT 7   Production of Fish and Shirts Per Eight-Hour Day—
             Absolute Advantage

	PRODUCTION OF FISH	PRODUCTION OF SHIRTS
CRUSOE ISLAND	2	8
YAKAMAYA ISLAND	8	2

production of fish, can produce two fish during an eight-hour day. If they instead decide to devote their resources to the production of shirts, they can produce eight shirts.

The second row shows the production possibilities for Yakamayans. If they devote all their resources to fishing, they end up with eight fish. Alternatively focusing solely on shirtmaking, they can produce two shirts in that eight-hour day.

Because people need both food and clothing, it is most likely that they would choose to produce some of each. And they can. For example, by devoting a half-day to each good, Crusoe Islanders can produce one fish and four shirts while Yakamayans can produce four fish and one shirt. In other words, if they each choose these half-day work shifts for fish and shirts, combined production for both islands would be five fish and five shirts.

But suppose trade routes opened up between the two islands and each specialized in producing goods that required fewer resources than required by the other. Crusoe Islanders would then specialize in shirtmaking—they can produce one shirt in one hour versus the four hours needed by Yakamayans—and Yakamayans would specialize in fishing—they can produce a fish in one hour versus the four hours needed by Crusoe Islanders. Economists refer to Crusoe Islanders as having an **absolute advantage** in the production of shirts while Yakamayans are said to enjoy an absolute advantage in the production of fish.

Exhibit 8 shows combined production under conditions of free trade and specialization.

Note the enormous advantage gained from free trade and specialization. Instead of the two islands producing a total of five fish and five shirts as they did in the scenario of Exhibit 7, they end up producing a total of eight fish and eight shirts in the specialization scenario of Exhibit 8.

Absolute advantage explains not only why Yakamayans produce fish but also why Icelanders produce fish, why Brazilians produce coffee, why Nicaraguans produce bananas, and why the Chinese produce the wares sold in Wal-Mart stores worldwide.

But what if a country has no absolute advantage in producing *anything*? Or what if another country has an absolute advantage in producing *everything*? Does free trade and specialization make sense under these conditions?

Absolute advantage
A country's ability to produce a good using fewer resources than the country it trades with.

EXHIBIT 8   Production Per Eight-Hour Day Under Conditions
             of Free Trade and Specialization

	PRODUCTION OF FISH	PRODUCTION OF SHIRTS
CRUSOE ISLAND	0	8
YAKAMAYA ISLAND	8	0

EXHIBIT 9   Production of Fish and Shirts Per Eight-Hour Day—
Comparative Advantage

	PRODUCTION OF FISH	PRODUCTION OF SHIRTS
CRUSOE ISLAND	8	8
YAKAMAYA ISLAND	8	2

Comparative advantage
A country's ability to produce a good at a lower opportunity cost than the country with which it trades.

You probably anticipated the answer. It is decidedly yes. And here's why. Exhibit 9 shows the production possibilities on the two islands with Yakamayans now having no absolute advantage in producing either fish or shirts. Both islands can produce eight fish in an eight-hour day. But Crusoe Islander shirtmakers can outproduce Yakamaya's shirtmakers 4 to 1. If they work half-day shifts on each good in each island and avoid interisland trade, their combined production is eight fish and five shirts. If they instead specialize and trade, as they do in Exhibit 8, their combined production is eight shirts and eight fish. As you see, specialization still makes them better off. But who produces what?

Crusoe Islanders will give up the opportunity of producing fish even though they are as good at fishing as are Yakamayans. It is a matter of **comparative advantage**. While Crusoe Islanders have every reason to be pleased with their abilities—vis-à-vis Yakamayans—to produce both fish and shirts, they are *exceptionally* impressive—vis-à-vis Yakamayans—in the production of shirts.

Compare the opportunity cost of producing a fish on the Crusoe Island versus on Yakamaya. On Crusoe Island, if they fish the entire day, they can produce eight fish but they give up the opportunity of making eight shirts. The opportunity cost of a fish, then, is one shirt. When Yakamayans fish the entire day, they give up the opportunity of producing two shirts, so the opportunity cost for each of the eight fish they produce is one-fourth of a shirt. That is, the opportunity cost associated with producing fish for Yakamayans is less than it is for Crusoe Islanders. This lower opportunity cost defines Yakamaya's comparative advantage in producing fish. Crusoe Islanders' comparative advantage lies in making shirts. Why? Because the opportunity cost of producing a shirt on the Crusoe Island is only one fish compared with the four fish on the Yakamaya Island.

If the comparative advantage scenario of fish and shirts on Crusoe and Yakamaya islands is less than intuitively obvious, then consider this: The legendary baseball player Babe Ruth was a better hitter *and* a better pitcher than anyone else on the team. But he gave up pitching because his super performance as a hitter vis-à-vis the others was *more outstanding* than his great pitching performance. His comparative advantage was clearly at the plate.

THE UNIVERSALITY OF THE PRODUCTION POSSIBILITIES MODEL

Resource limitations confronting insatiable wants are facts of life that apply to every economic system—large or small, rich or poor, east or west, north or south, capitalist or socialist.

The universality of the production possibilities model and the law of increasing costs create the same kinds of problems and decision making for all economies. Can the economy fully employ its resources? How much of the resources should be allocated to capital goods formation? Who gets what share of the consumption goods produced?

The same questions are asked about peace and war. Just as the production possibilities curve measures out the possibilities of consumption and capital goods production, it can measure out as well the production possibilities of butter and guns. Israeli as well as Egyptian economists knew firsthand the opportunity cost of desert warfare. In no small measure, that knowledge played its part in the countries' historic 1979 peace agreement.

Imagine a couple of Martian economists landing their UFOs undetected on Earth, say, one in Beijing, China, and the other in Dayton, Ohio. If their assignments were to detail how Earthlings behave, they would be struck, upon returning to Mars and comparing notes, not by the differences they observed, but instead by the incredible similarities of our experiences and behavior. They would probably be impressed as well by how similar our economic problems and economic choices are to their own!

CHAPTER REVIEW

1. The economy's resources—or *factors of production*—are labor, land, and entrepreneurship. Labor is what people are willing to offer—their physical and mental abilities—on a resource market in exchange for payment over a period of time. Capital is a good used to produce other goods. Factories, machinery, tools, and raw materials are examples of capital. Human capital is acquired education and experience applied to labor. A degree in medicine is capital. Land, in its natural form, is a gift of nature. Topsoil, water, minerals and metals are part of the land resource. Entrepreneurs undertake risks and uncertainties associated with business enterprise.

2. A production possibilities curve shows the combinations of goods that can be produced with a set of resources. The analysis of a two-goods economy in which consumption and capital goods are produced allows for fruitful discussion of issues associated with economic growth.

3. The opportunity cost of producing a unit of a good—say, a consumption good—is measured by the quantity of the other good—say, a capital good—that must be given up to produce the consumption good.

4. As more and more of a good—say, a consumption good—is produced, the quantity of the other good—say, a capital good—that must be given up to produce each additional consumption good increases. This phenomenon is known as the law of increasing costs.

5. The production of capital goods in one year adds to an economy's resource base, ensuring that the quantities of goods that become possible to produce in subsequent years increase. Rich economies can more easily invest in capital goods production than can poor economies, so that, over years, greater and greater disparities among them may result.

6. New ideas that create innovations in the form of new technology enhance labor productivity and therefore economic growth. For example, when a few tractors replace many horse-driven plows, the production possibilities curve shifts out to the right.

7. An economy producing along its production possibilities curve is both at full employment and producing efficiently. If any factor is unemployed or if any factor is not being used to its fullest capacity (that is, it is underemployed), then the economy is not operating on its production possibilities curve, but somewhere inside it.

8. Division of labor and specialization increase labor productivity and therefore increase what an economy can produce. Absolute and comparative advantage show how nations gain when they specialize and trade among themselves.

KEY TERMS

Factor of production	Production possibilities	Economic efficiency
Labor	Opportunity cost	Labor specialization
Capital	Law of increasing costs	Absolute advantage
Human capital	Vicious circle of poverty	Comparative advantage
Land	Innovation	
Entrepreneur	Underemployed resources	

QUESTIONS

1. What distinguishes entrepreneurship from the other factors of production?
2. Under what conditions would an automobile be a capital good? What about a violin? A tuxedo? Under what conditions would a truck not be a capital good?
3. Why do economists regard a law degree as human capital? Why "capital?" What is "capital" about an educational experience? Can you think of an educational experience that isn't capital?
4. Explain the difference between absolute and comparative advantage.
5. Explain the law of increasing (opportunity) costs. What causes costs to increase?
6. Everybody wants clean air. So why is the air polluted in so many of our cities? (*Hint:* Refer to the law of increasing costs in your answer.)
7. Why are most new technologies considered indestructible?
8. Suppose you were advising the government of Egypt. What policies would you recommend to achieve economic growth? Why should you expect some resistance to your policy suggestions?
9. In the 1990s, China adopted a severe population policy. Using both "carrot and stick" methods, newly formed families were restricted to one child. The policy continues today. Discuss how such a policy affects the position China occupies on its production possibilities curve.
10. What factors or events could cause an inward shift of the production possibilities curve?
11. Why does the production possibilities curve bow out from the origin?
12. The Constitution guarantees the right to free speech. Does the *free* in *free speech* mean that there really is no opportunity cost to free speech? Explain.
13. Professor Kenneth Boulding once noted that Danish butter producers eat very little butter. They use margarine even though they produce some of the best butter in the world. Is this stupid behavior? Or is there a good reason for it?
14. What is meant by the term *vicious circle of poverty*? Draw a graph to illustrate the concept.
15. Immigration is a hot political issue these days. What arguments can an economist make to support a liberal policy of immigration? What arguments can he or she make to oppose immigration? (*Hint:* Think in terms of shifts in the production possibilities curve in the first case, and movements along the curve in the second.)

PRACTICE PROBLEMS

1. Fill in an appropriate number (there can be more than one) for the missing number of bushels of oranges in set C and graph the following sets of production possibilities.

SET	BUSHELS OF GRAPEFRUIT	BUSHELS OF ORANGES
A	200	0
B	150	19
C	100	
D	50	30
E	0	32

2. Graph the following sets of production possibilities and explain why the law of increasing costs is violated.

SET	BUSHELS OF GRAPEFRUIT	BUSHELS OF ORANGES
A	200	0
B	150	19
C	100	40
D	50	80
E	0	130

3. Production costs (in labor hours) of oranges and peaches in Florida and Georgia are shown in the following table.

If the states specialize, what should each produce? Why? (*Hint:* Think in terms of absolute and comparative advantage.)

	ORANGES	PEACHES
FLORIDA	5	5
GEORGIA	2	4

4. Imagine an economy with the following resource base for 2000: 100 units of labor (including entrepreneurs), 100 units of capital, and 100 acres of land. Draw a graph showing the economy's 2000 production possibilities from the following table:

2000	CONSUMPTION	CAPITAL
A	12	0
B	10	2
C	6	4
D	0	6

2001	CONSUMPTION	CAPITAL
A	16	0
B	14	2
C	10	4
D	4	6

On the same graph, draw the economy's production possibilities curve for 2001. Which possibilities in 2000 (among A, B, C, and D) can account for the 2001 curve, and how would such a production possibilities combination affect the economy's resource base for 2001?

WHAT'S WRONG WITH THIS GRAPH?

The Production Possibilities Curve

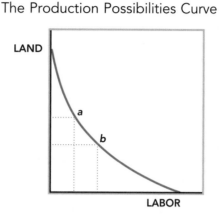

Economic Consultants

Economic Research and Analysis by Students for Professionals

WaterUSA, located in Boise, Idaho, bottles and sells mineral water. This mineral water, drawn from underground springs, offers unparalleled taste and clarity. WaterUSA currently sells its water in the United States, but it is looking to expand its sales into the former Soviet Union, and into Russia in particular.

WaterUSA has approached Economic Consultants for advice on the firm's plans to expand its sales into European markets. Prepare a report for WaterUSA that addresses the following issues:

© Image 100/Royalty-Free/CORBIS

1. Are the conditions favorable in the former Soviet Union for selling mineral water? Are there businesses in Russia selling mineral water?
2. What issues does WaterUSA need to consider with regard to the principle of comparative advantage?

You may find the following resources helpful as you prepare this report for WaterUSA:

- **U.S. Department of Commerce, Business Information Service for the Newly Independent States (BISNIS)** (http://bisnis.doc.gov/bisnis/bisnis.cfm)—BISNIS provides economic information about Russia. In particular, BISNIS publishes market surveys and reports for common U.S. goods.
- **American Chamber of Commerce in Russia** (http://www.amcham.ru/)—The American Chamber of Commerce in Russia provides information for doing business in Russia.
- **Mineral Waters of the World** (http://www.mineralwaters.org/)—Mineral Waters of the World provides directories and ratings for various mineral waters around the globe.

practicetest

1. To economists, the term *capital* refers exclusively to
   a. goods used to produce other goods.
   b. money used to purchase stocks and bonds.
   c. savings accumulated by households to purchase real estate.
   d. money used by capitalists to hire workers.
   e. machinery used by workers to produce goods.
2. If an economy experiences unemployment, it would show up as a point
   a. on the production possibilities curve, but on one of the axes.
   b. outside the production possibilities curve.
   c. inside the production possibilities curve.
   d. on the production possibilities curve.
   e. on a production possibilities curve that is shifting to the right.
3. The weather in the Virgin Islands reminds us of the nursery rhyme "When she was good, she was very, very good, but when she was bad, she was horrid." A hurricane in 1996 was horrid, destroying much of the islands' infrastructure (roads, telephone systems), homes, and factories. An economist describing the effect of the hurricane on the islands' economy would show
   a. an inward shift in the islands' production possibilities curve.
   b. an outward shift in the islands' production possibilities curve.
   c. a movement along the production possibilities curve, from consumption to capital.
   d. a movement along the production possibilities curve, from capital to consumption.
   e. a movement inside the curve, the curve remaining intact.
4. Let's suppose that the day after the hurricane, the governor of the Virgin Islands addresses the population to announce the government's decision to rebuild the economy's infrastructure. Of course, it means higher taxes, which means people will have less income to spend as they please. Ceteris paribus, the tax and rebuilding will create
   a. an inward shift in the islands' production possibilities curve.
   b. an outward shift in the islands' production possibilities curve.
   c. a movement along the production possibilities curve, from consumption to capital.

   d. a movement along the production possibilities curve, from capital to consumption.
   e. a movement inside the curve, the curve remaining intact.
5. Assuming the rebuilding program is successful, in the longer run (in time) you would see
   a. an inward shift in the islands' production possibilities curve.
   b. an outward shift in the islands' production possibilities curve.
   c. a movement along the production possibilities curve, from consumption to capital.
   d. a movement along the production possibilities curve, from capital to consumption.
   e. a movement inside the curve, the curve remaining intact.
6. Which of the following is likely to cause an inward shift in Crusoe's production possibilities curve?
   a. Crusoe invents a fishnet.
   b. A typhoon destroys resources on the island.
   c. Crusoe discovers a forest of trees, perfect for use in making spears.
   d. Crusoe finds a companion, named Friday, to help him fish and make spears.
7. In Adam Smith's illustration of the pin factory, one worker draws out the wire, another straightens it, and a third cuts it. Several others serve the functions of pointing, whitening, and packaging the pins. This process is more productive than if each worker did all the tasks. This illustrates the concept of
   a. opportunity costs.
   b. labor specialization.
   c. economic efficiency.
   d. the law of increasing costs.
8. Gabe Fried is stranded on a Pacific island and realizes that, to survive, he must pick berries. He discovers that he picks more berries in the first hour than he does in the second because it becomes increasingly harder to find berries. Gabe has just discovered
   a. Engel's law.
   b. the law of opportunity cost.
   c. the law of increasing costs.
   d. the law of scarcity.
   e. the law of production possibilities.

9. Among the four factors of production is entrepreneurship. It's the only factor that
   a. does not contract to provide its services for a specific price.
   b. conceives of the essential idea of production.
   c. assumes all the risks and uncertainties involved in production.
   d. earns profit.
   e. All of the above

CHAPTER 3

THIS CHAPTER INTRODUCES YOU TO THE ECONOMIC PRINCIPLES ASSOCIATED WITH:

- Individual and market demand

- Market-day, short-run, and long-run supply

- The determination of equilibrium price and quantity

DEMAND AND SUPPLY

One of the most exciting moments in Shakespearean drama—for economists, at any rate—has to be the final scene in *Richard III* where the king, tired and bloodied at the end of the battle, his horse slain, and standing helplessly alone upon the crest of a hill, sights the enemy about to charge at him. His sword drawn, Richard shouts in desperation: "A horse! A horse! My kingdom for a horse!"

To an economist, that's a dramatic moment, for never has so high a price been placed on a four-legged animal! Not before, and not since. Lassie and Flipper, themselves worth a small fortune, were still well within the reach of any millionaire. The legendary thoroughbred of the 1920s, Man O' War, won every race he ran but one, but even he couldn't command *that* price. Shakespeare was not an economist by profession, yet he understood the market well. In all probability, he picked the right price.

This example raises a more general question about price formation: Why are prices what they are? Why, for example, do oranges sell for 30 cents each? Why not 25 cents? Or 34 cents? Is there something magical about a 30-cent orange? And what about cucumbers? Why are they 49 cents each? Why should they be more expensive than oranges? Why is butter $1.25 per pound? Why is a fresh fish $6?

We can go on identifying thousands of goods that make up our modern economy and ask the same question about each: Why that particular price? From aircraft carriers to salted peanuts, from sweetheart roses to Dell computers, why are the prices what they are?

MEASURING CONSUMER WILLINGNESS

Price formation has to do with people's willingness to buy and sell. There is nothing mysterious about price. It has no life of its own. It has no will. Price simply reflects what people are willing to do.

Suppose that people on a small island are busily engaged each day in some productive activity that affords them a livelihood. The variety of their occupations fills up 40 Yellow Pages in their telephone directory. There are auto mechanics, dentists, farmers, plumbers, computer specialists, business consultants, and especially fishermen. After all, it's an island economy, and we should expect the community to take full advantage of its fishing grounds.

Of course, there's no sense in fishing unless some people like to eat fish. Chances are some prefer fish to filet mignon, although there must be others who wouldn't touch fish under any condition. As the Romans used to say: *De gustibus non est disputandum* (There's no disputing taste). But it would be the height of folly if fishermen went out on the water every day only to discover on returning to dock that nobody showed any interest in the fish they caught. Wouldn't you think that even the dullest of them would give up after a while? Fishermen go out every day because they know from long experience that there are always people willing to buy fish.

MEASURING CONSUMER DEMAND

Fishermen also know that when price falls, people's willingness to buy fish increases—it's so obvious and so sensible a response to price that fishermen regard it as natural. They know, for example, that if the price of fish is outrageously high, say $25 per fish, very few people would be willing to buy. On the other hand, if the price is $10, some people unwilling to buy at $25 now would be willing to buy fish.

If the price falls to $5, more people would be willing to buy even more fish. Some who bought a few at $10 would buy more at $5, and those who had not bought before would now get into the market.

When economists refer to **change in quantity demanded** for a particular good, they always mean people's willingness to buy specific quantities at specific prices. They define the inverse relationship between price and quantity demanded as the **law of demand**. Compare the two statements "I am willing to buy four fish at a price of $6 per fish" and "I am willing to buy fish." There is considerably more information in the first statement.

Measuring Individual Demand

Let's begin by measuring Claudia Preparata's and Chris Stefan's demand for fish. Claudia is the principal labor relations consultant on the island, and Chris is an actress. The tables in Exhibit 1 are **demand schedules** recording their willingness to buy fish at different prices.

You may not know much about these two women, but you do know that if the price of fish was $10, you wouldn't find Claudia Preparata at a fish market!

Chris Stefan, on the other hand, treats herself to a $10 poached salmon. If the price falls to $9, the quantity of fish demanded by both Claudia and Chris increases. Claudia buys one, and the quantity that Chris demands increases to three. If the price keeps falling, the quantity demanded keeps increasing.

The **demand curves** in Exhibit 1 represent Claudia's and Chris's demand for fish at different prices. They contain the same information offered in the tables. It is just a different, more visual way of looking at the information. The demand curves are downward sloping because price and quantity demanded are inversely related. When price falls, the quantity demanded increases.

check your understanding

How does price reflect what buyers are willing to do?

Change in quantity demanded
A change in the quantity demanded of a good that is caused solely by a change in the price of that good.

Law of demand
The inverse relationship between price and quantity demanded of a good or service, *ceteris paribus*.

Demand schedule
A schedule showing the specific quantity of a good or service that people are willing and able to buy at different prices.

Demand curve
A curve that depicts the relationship between price and quantity demanded.

EXHIBIT 1   Individual Demand Curves for Fish

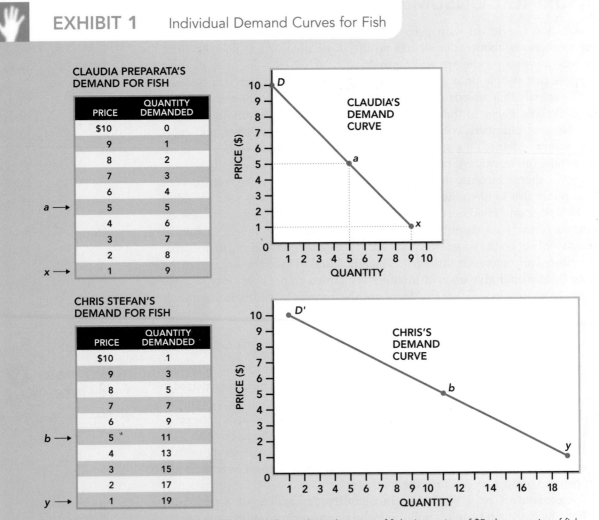

CLAUDIA PREPARATA'S DEMAND FOR FISH

PRICE	QUANTITY DEMANDED
$10	0
9	1
8	2
7	3
6	4
a → 5	5
4	6
3	7
2	8
x → 1	9

CHRIS STEFAN'S DEMAND FOR FISH

PRICE	QUANTITY DEMANDED
$10	1
9	3
8	5
7	7
6	9
b → 5	11
4	13
3	15
2	17
y → 1	19

Ceteris paribus, the quantity of fish demanded depends on the price of fish. At a price of $5, the quantity of fish demanded by Claudia is 5—point *a* on demand curve *D*—and the quantity demanded by Chris is 11—point *b* on demand curve *D'*. At a price of $1, the quantity demanded by Claudia increases to 9—point *x*—and the quantity demanded by Chris increases to 19—point *y*.

Measuring Market Demand

If we were able to record every person's willingness to buy fish at different prices, we would end up with complete information about the community's demand for fish. We can obtain such information only by observing and recording what quantities people actually buy in the market at different prices. Adding up all the individual demands for fish gives us the community demand, or **market demand**. The table and graph in Exhibit 2 represent the market demand for fish.

Market demand
The sum of all individual demands in a market.

MEASURING SUPPLY

On a beautiful April morning we see the fishermen going out in their boats. They live by the weather and by whatever daylight they can manage. At dawn, they head out to the fishing grounds while most people in the community are still

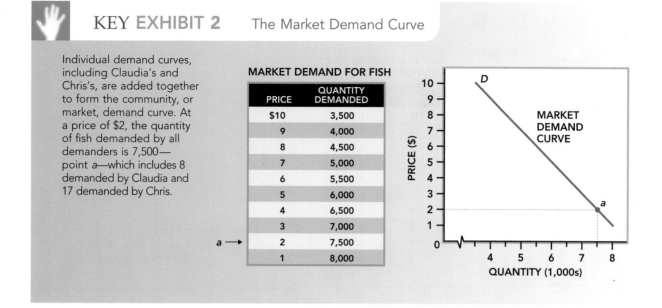

KEY EXHIBIT 2   The Market Demand Curve

Individual demand curves, including Claudia's and Chris's, are added together to form the community, or market, demand curve. At a price of $2, the quantity of fish demanded by all demanders is 7,500—point a—which includes 8 demanded by Claudia and 17 demanded by Chris.

MARKET DEMAND FOR FISH

PRICE	QUANTITY DEMANDED
$10	3,500
9	4,000
8	4,500
7	5,000
6	5,500
5	6,000
4	6,500
3	7,000
2	7,500
1	8,000

asleep. Typically, they move from spot to spot, depending on the season, weather, and time of day. They search, locate, fish, and move on again.

Suppose they return home at the end of this fishing day with 6,000 fish. Imagine the scene: Fishermen unload their catch into their individual stalls, pack the fish in ice, and wash up. They sell them right on the docks. The last thing any fisherman wants to take home is a fish! They want dollars.

Market-Day Supply

Once the fish are in, there's really no decision making concerning what quantity to supply at what price. *Whatever the price,* fishermen are willing to dispose of all 6,000 fish. What else can they do with them? Have you ever handled a day-old fish?

Even if the price was $1 per fish, $P = \$1$, fishermen would be disappointed but still willing to sell all 6,000. Some would probably start thinking about other jobs. On the other hand, if $P = \$10$, the same fishermen would still supply the same 6,000 fish, but this time would be frustrated that they hadn't caught more. But they can't change the quantity supplied once the catch is in. Regardless of price, the quantity supplied is fixed for the market day.

The table and graph in Exhibit 3 represent the **supply schedule** and corresponding supply curve for the **market-day supply**.

Just as the demand curve graphs the relationship between price and quantity demanded, the **supply curve** graphs the relationship between price and quantity supplied. The supply curve for the market day shows that whatever the price, the quantity supplied remains unchanged.

DETERMINING EQUILIBRIUM PRICE

A fish market is a colorful and bustling sight. Suppliers and demanders mill around the fish stalls ready to strike deals. Suppliers busily encourage demanders to buy their fish, and demanders take their time looking for the best price. But fish are fish, and time is short.

Supply schedule
A schedule showing the specific quantity of a good or service that suppliers are willing and able to provide at different prices.

Market-day supply
A market situation in which the quantity of a good supplied is fixed, regardless of price.

Supply curve
A curve that depicts the relationship between price and quantity supplied.

EXHIBIT 3   Market-Day Supply Curve

The market-day supply curve is vertical, reflecting the fact that once the catch is in, fishermen cannot change the quantity they supply. At a price of $9, the quantity supplied is 6,000—point *a* on the supply curve. At a price of $5, the quantity supplied is still 6,000—point *b* on the supply curve.

SUPPLY SCHEDULE FOR FISH FOR THE MARKET DAY

PRICE	QUANTITY SUPPLIED
$10	6,000
9	6,000
8	6,000
7	6,000
6	6,000
5	6,000
4	6,000
3	6,000
2	6,000
1	6,000

a → (price row 9)
b → (price row 5)

Nobody knows what the other's preferences really are until they become expressed on the market through purchase and sale. But Claudia, Chris, and the many other demanders, as well as the fishermen who are the suppliers, know that 6,000 fish are on the docks for sale.

Suppose the Price Is $8

Let's suppose that the asking price, at least at the outset of the market process, is $8 per fish. This already spells trouble. Look at Exhibit 4.

At $P = \$8$, the quantity of fish demanded is 4,500. Of this quantity, Claudia is willing to buy 2, Chris 5. But the fishermen are already nervous about the weakness they sense in the market. There is insufficient demand to absorb the entire 6,000 fish supplied. People are just not picking up fish as the fishermen had hoped. Look at the table in Exhibit 4. At $P = \$8$, there is an **excess supply** of 1,500 fish that will not be sold. Every fisherman is afraid, in the end, of being left holding the bag. Sheila Reed, one of the many fishermen on the docks, knows that the only way to protect herself from this unpleasant eventuality is to cut price. She figures that since all fish are alike, if she is willing to cut her own price to $7, chances are that she will sell out.

Of course, Sheila isn't the only fisherman who thinks this way. Fishermen Lisa Muroga and Shari Zernich had already cut their prices to $7 for the same reason. They draw a crowd. Can you imagine what happens when word spreads among the demanders and suppliers that some fishermen are willing to sell at $7? They make it virtually impossible for other suppliers to maintain the price at $8.

Every supplier, then, has no alternative but to reduce the price to $7. Will that do the trick? Look again at the table in Exhibit 4. At $P = \$7$, quantity demanded increases to 5,000 fish, but that still leaves an excess supply of 1,000. The pressure on suppliers persists.

As long as any excess supply exists on the market, there will always be an incentive for suppliers to cut price. The incentive is self-protection. They really don't enjoy cutting prices, but they enjoy even less the prospect of being caught at the end of the market day with unsold fish.

Excess supply
The difference, at a particular price, between quantity supplied and quantity demanded, quantity supplied being the greater.

check your understanding

What will suppliers do if there's an excess supply on the market?

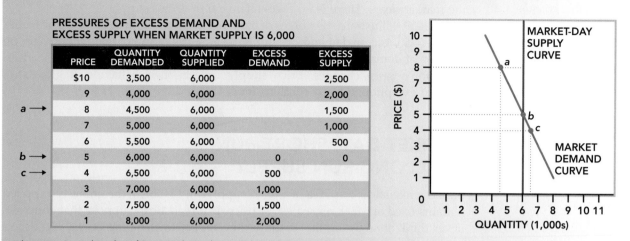

EXHIBIT 4   Excess Demand and Excess Supply

PRESSURES OF EXCESS DEMAND AND EXCESS SUPPLY WHEN MARKET SUPPLY IS 6,000

PRICE	QUANTITY DEMANDED	QUANTITY SUPPLIED	EXCESS DEMAND	EXCESS SUPPLY
$10	3,500	6,000		2,500
9	4,000	6,000		2,000
8	4,500	6,000		1,500
7	5,000	6,000		1,000
6	5,500	6,000		500
5	6,000	6,000	0	0
4	6,500	6,000	500	
3	7,000	6,000	1,000	
2	7,500	6,000	1,500	
1	8,000	6,000	2,000	

(a → row at $8; b → row at $5; c → row at $4)

At any price other than $5, point *b* on the supply and demand curves, excess demand or excess supply will force the price to $5. At $4, point *c* on the demand curve, an excess demand of 500 fish is created, driving up price. At $8, point *a* on the demand curve, an excess supply of 1,500 fish is created, forcing price downward.

How much price cutting will they have to do? From the table in Exhibit 4 it's clear that suppliers will have to cut the price to $5. At P = $5, quantity demanded increases to absorb the entire 6,000 fish supplied. Excess supply is zero.

Suppose the Price Is $4

Suppose, at the beginning of the market process, price is not $8, but $4. What happens now? Market pressure is on the other side of the market. Claudia Preparata, Chris Stefan, and other demanders are the ones who become somewhat nervous.

For example, at P = $4, Claudia is willing to buy 6 and Chris is willing to buy 13 fish. The quantity demanded by the community is 6,500. Both demanders and suppliers now sense that there are insufficient fish to satisfy demand at $4. Fishermen seem less worried about being caught with unsold fish. Now demanders are worried about going home fishless.

As you see in the table in Exhibit 4, **excess demand** at P = $4 is 500 fish. What would you do if you were at the docks and really wanted fish? Afraid of getting caught looking at empty stalls, wouldn't you offer a little more? For example, if you announced that you were willing to pay $5, the chances are that you would draw suppliers' attention. Of course, you're not the only one with fish on your mind; many others are also willing to buy fish at $5.

The $4 price, then, becomes untenable. Demanders, competing among themselves for the limited supply of 6,000 fish, will bid the price up. At P = $5, some buyers drop out. The quantity demanded then falls to 6,000 and the excess demand disappears.

Price Always Tends Toward Equilibrium

In the fish market on this particular day, competition among suppliers to rid themselves of their supply will always force a price greater than $5 down to $5.

Excess demand
The difference, at a particular price, between quantity demanded and quantity supplied, quantity demanded being the greater.

In the same way, competition among demanders will always force a price lower than $5 up to $5. Price is stable only at $5. Economists refer to that price where quantity demanded equals quantity supplied as the **equilibrium price**. At $P = \$5$, the market clears. There is no excess demand or excess supply.

Exhibit 4 illustrates the forces driving price to equilibrium. At any price other than $P = \$5$, excess demand or supply results, triggering bargaining activity on the part of demanders and suppliers to overcome the market's inability to clear. They force price changes. Price simply reflects their behavior. It gravitates, without exception, toward equilibrium.

MARKET-DAY, SHORT-RUN, AND LONG-RUN SUPPLY

But how realistic is this idea of a fixed supply? In Exhibit 4, the quantity supplied remains fixed at 6,000, regardless of price. Is it realistic to suppose that suppliers never think of adjusting the quantity they supply to changing prices? Do fishermen, for example, just keep fishing, day after day, bringing their catch to market without regard to the price their fish fetch on the market? Of course not. A fixed supply makes sense only for the market day. Once the catch is in, today's price cannot affect today's quantity supplied. What is done is done.

But what fishermen will do *tomorrow* depends very much on today's price. A high price today, say $10 per fish, makes fishermen happy and leaves them wishing they had more to supply. While they can't supply more today, they can prepare today to increase the quantity they supply tomorrow. A low price today, on the other hand, say $3 per fish, makes them less happy and less willing to supply fish. While they can't cut supply today—after all, the catch is in—they can prepare today to decrease the quantity they supply tomorrow. Unlike consumers, who can change their quantity demanded instantaneously when prices change, fishermen have to do something to adjust the quantity they supply to price. Doing something takes time.

Let's start with today. Suppose fishermen discover when they get to market that today's price is $10. Are they happy? They're ecstatic! The only regret they have is that their quantity supplied is only 6,000 fish. At that price they wish they had more fish to supply. But they can't undo what is done. What is done is their earlier decision to fish today with a certain amount of boats, crew, and equipment.

Well, what about tomorrow? With a $10 fish in mind, they would love to supply as many as 16,000 if they could. Look at the table in Exhibit 5, column 4.

But how can they possibly increase the quantity of fish supplied from 6,000 to 16,000 *by tomorrow?* They can't. But perhaps the first thing they can do is add more fishermen to their boats. Where would they find them? Well, suppose you are a potato farmer and not particularly happy about the money you are making in the potato business. You may be willing to try something else if that something else paid more; that is, if it met your opportunity cost. With fish now fetching $10, it may be just enough to make you switch from potato farming to fishing.

But there are limits to how many people fishermen can add to their boats. If the boats are designed for crews of six, adding one or two more per boat may bring in more fish, but not the 16,000 fish that fishermen are willing to supply. Anyway, hiring more crew takes time, and the new crew may have very little experience.

What else can fishermen do to increase the quantity supplied? Another option is to stay out on the water for more hours. But staying out longer means

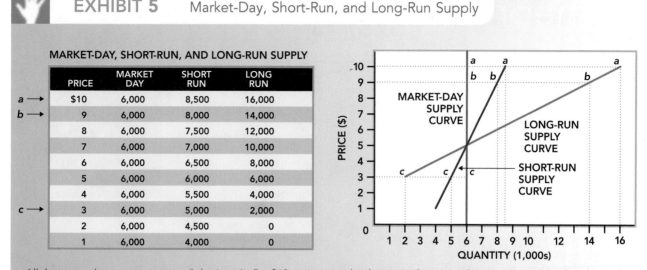

EXHIBIT 5   Market-Day, Short-Run, and Long-Run Supply

MARKET-DAY, SHORT-RUN, AND LONG-RUN SUPPLY

	PRICE	MARKET DAY	SHORT RUN	LONG RUN
a →	$10	6,000	8,500	16,000
b →	9	6,000	8,000	14,000
	8	6,000	7,500	12,000
	7	6,000	7,000	10,000
	6	6,000	6,500	8,000
	5	6,000	6,000	6,000
	4	6,000	5,500	4,000
c →	3	6,000	5,000	2,000
	2	6,000	4,500	0
	1	6,000	4,000	0

All three supply curves are upward sloping. At P = $10, point a on the three supply curves, the quantity supplied on the market day is 6,000, the quantity supplied in the short run is 8,500, and the quantity supplied in the long run is 16,000. At P = $9, point b on the three curves, the quantity supplied on the market day is 6,000, the quantity supplied in the short run is 8,000, and the quantity supplied in the long run is 14,000. At P = $3, point c on the three curves, the quantity supplied on the market day is 6,000, the quantity supplied in the short run is 5,000, and the quantity supplied in the long run is 2,000.

consuming more fuel, more bait, and more ice packaging, all of which may be in short supply.

They do the best they can. Suppose their best effort, given the limitation of boat size, increases the quantity supplied from the market day's 6,000 to 8,500 fish. Look at column 3 in the table in Exhibit 5.

Now, 8,500 fish is more than 6,000 but still considerably less than the 16,000 that fishermen want to supply at P = $10. But to reach 16,000 requires more boats (not just more crew or longer hours), and boat making, let's suppose, takes a full year. In other words, for tomorrow at least, they're stuck at 8,500. Until more or bigger boats are available, their only course of action is to produce as much as they can on the boats they already have. This time interval during which suppliers are able to change the quantity of some but not all the resources they use to produce goods and services is called the **short run**. The 8,500 fish, then, is the quantity supplied in the short run at P = $10.

What about quantity supplied in the **long run**? What distinguishes the long from the short run? In the long run, suppliers have the time to change the quantity of *all* the resources they use to produce goods and services. In the fishing business, the long run is a year—the time it takes to acquire as many boats as fishermen wish. As we see in the table in Exhibit 5, fishermen end up in the long run acquiring enough boats to produce 16,000 fish.

The graph in Exhibit 5 translates the table into graphic form.

The higher the price of fish, the greater the incentive to produce more. As you see for the long run in the table, when the price is $9, fishermen are willing and able to supply 14,000, slightly less than the 16,000 they are willing and able to supply at a price of $10. Why do they supply less? Fishermen will tell you that a $9 fish is not as profitable as a $10 fish. As a result, they hire a smaller crew. As well, fewer potato farmers would be sufficiently motivated to leave potato farming for a $9 fish. Fewer boats are ordered. Still, $9 is a relatively good price for fish. Compare the 8,000 quantity they are willing to supply in the short run to the 14,000 they are willing to and do supply in the long run.

Short run
The time interval during which suppliers are able to change the quantity of some but not all the resources they use to produce goods and services.

Long run
The time interval during which suppliers are able to change the quantity of all the resources they use to produce goods and services.

theoretical perspective

© Image 100/Royalty-Free/CORBIS

After 20 years, it better be good!

HOW LONG DOES IT TAKE TO GET TO THE LONG RUN?

How long does it take to reach the long run? Well, it depends. Focus on the time that elapses between the quantity supplied on a market day and the quantity the suppliers would have been willing to offer at that market-day price.

Consider the babysitting market of panel *a*. If the market-day price was $3 per hour on January 1, 2004, and on that day 100 hours had been supplied, baby-sitters would be less than ecstatic because $3 is a very unattractive price. How long will it take babysitters to find alternative employment? Not long, don't you think? Within a month or so, the quantity supplied of babysitters at $3 would fall from 100 to 30 hours, from point *a* to point *b* on the graph. On the other hand, if the market-day price was $20 per hour, then baby-sitters supplying those 100 hours would be delighted and it wouldn't take long—a month perhaps—for other people to switch from whatever else they were doing to babysitting. The quantity supplied would jump to 400 hours, from point *c* to point *d*.

Now think about Illinois farmers in the corn market of panel *b*. Suppose the price of corn was $20 per bushel and the market-day supply was 100 bushels. Farmers would be ecstatic, not having seen such a high price

before! They would love to produce 400 bushels—but how do you supply more corn when the planting season was last spring? In order to increase the quantity sup-plied, they must wait for the next planting season to adjust their supply to the $20 price. That is, it takes them a full year to move from point *x* to point *y* on the graph.

How long do you suppose it takes California wine producers to increase their quantity supplied of 20-year wine from the market-day 100 bottles to the long-run 400 bottles—from point *r* to point *s* on the graph in panel *c*—when the market-day price is an attractive $20 per bottle? Think about it. How can you produce 20-year wine in less than 20 years? You see the picture, don't you? The length of time it takes to get from market-day supply to long-run supply depends on the character of the good. It takes little time for baby-sitting, and a much, much longer time for aged wine.

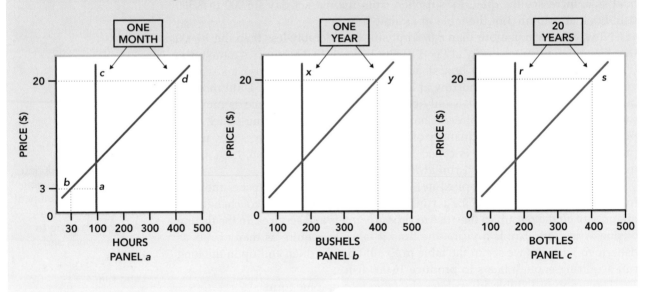

PANEL *a* · PANEL *b* · PANEL *c*

check your understanding

Why don't suppliers shift instantaneously to the long run when prices change?

But look what happens at the relatively low $3 price. The market-day supply is fixed at 6,000. If fishermen have time to adjust supply, they will adjust downward. Some who have good options may quit fishing outright. (Some may end up on a potato farm!) Others may continue to fish but produce less with smaller crews.

It isn't easy to quit outright even if there are job opportunities for fishermen elsewhere. After all, many fishermen have an emotional investment in their business and little experience at other jobs. (Ask anybody going through job retraining today.) Moreover, they have boats and equipment that represent a substantial financial investment. It may pay them to continue fishing even if the prospects are not very attractive, at least until their boats need substantial overhauling. Then the decision to shut down or stay afloat is forced.

As you see in the table in Exhibit 5, at $P = \$3$, fishermen cut back the quantity they supply in the short run to 5,000 and, given time, in the long run will trim back further to 2,000. At the much lower price of $1, very few fishermen go out on the water, cutting back further in the short run and supplying no fish at all in the long run.

All three supply curves are upward sloping, but the slope varies with the suppliers' ability to adjust to the different prices. The market-day supply curve is perfectly vertical, with no adjustment to price variations. The short-run supply curve shows moderate flexibility in adjusting quantity supplied to price, while the long-run supply curve has the most gradual slope, reflecting the fishermen's ability to adjust *fully* to price.

CHANGES IN DEMAND

Let's now look at the fish market of the table in Exhibit 6, whose short-run supply (column 2) is drawn from the table in Exhibit 5 and whose initial demand schedule (column 3) is drawn from the table in Exhibit 4. Now suppose that the demand for fish changes from the schedule shown in column 3 to the one shown in column 4.

Note what happens. At each price, 1,000 more fish are demanded. Prior to the **change in demand**, the quantity demanded at $P = \$10$ was 3,500 fish. It increases now to 4,500. It increases at $P = \$9$ from 4,000 to 5,000, and so on.

The graph in Exhibit 6 depicts the change in demand shown in the table. Demand curve D, graphing the initial demand schedule (column 3), shifts outward to the right to D', graphing the new demand schedule (column 4). Look at the impact on the equilibrium price of fish of the change in demand from D to D'. The old equilibrium price, $P = \$5$, is no longer tenable. Now, at that price, an excess demand of 1,000 fish emerges. The pressure of this excess demand forces the equilibrium price up to $P = \$6$, where the 6,500 quantity of fish demanded equals the 6,500 quantity supplied.

Change in demand
A change in quantity demanded of a good that is caused by factors other than a change in the price of that good.

 EXHIBIT 6   Change in Demand

FISH MARKET WITH CHANGE IN DEMAND

PRICE	QUANTITY SUPPLIED	INITIAL QUANTITY DEMANDED	INCREASE IN QUANTITY DEMANDED	DECREASE IN QUANTITY DEMANDED
$10	8,500	3,500	4,500	2,500
9	8,000	4,000	5,000	3,000
8	7,500	4,500	5,500	3,500
7	7,000	5,000	6,000	4,000
6	6,500	5,500	6,500	4,500
5	6,000	6,000	7,000	5,000
4	5,500	6,500	7,500	5,500
3	5,000	7,000	8,000	6,000
2	4,500	7,500	8,500	6,500
1	4,000	8,000	9,000	7,000

$a \rightarrow$ at row 6, $b \rightarrow$ at row 4

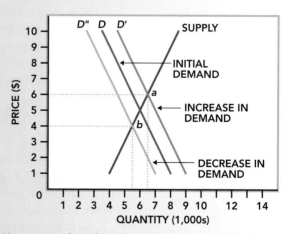

Ceteris paribus, an increase in demand from D to D' raises the equilibrium price from $5 to $6, point a on the graph. The quantity bought and sold increases from 6,000 to 6,500. A decrease in demand from D to D'' lowers the equilibrium price from $5 to $4, point b on the graph, and reduces the quantity bought and sold from 6,000 to 5,500.

What could cause such a change in demand? There are a number of reasons why people change the quantity they demand at the same price. The principal reasons are changes in income, changes in taste, changes in other prices, changes in expectations about future prices, and changes in population size. Let's consider each.

Changes in Income

You don't suppose, do you, that when Madonna dines out in one of New York's finest restaurants, she checks the price of poached salmon to see whether she's willing to make the purchase? Wouldn't you be surprised if she orders the salmon at $P = \$5$ but passes at $P = \$10$?

The more income people have, the more they can afford to buy more of everything. If Claudia Preparata's income were to increase by 25 percent, she might be more willing to buy that first fish at $10. Before, she passed it up. It isn't surprising, then, that when people's incomes increase, the quantity demanded of fish at $P = \$10$ increases from 3,500 to 4,500. It increases as well at every other price level.

On the other hand, what do you suppose happens to the demand for fish when incomes fall? You would expect that the quantity demanded at $P = \$10$ would fall from 3,500 fish to something less and that the quantity demanded at $P = \$9$ would fall from 4,000 to something less, and so on. To economists, fish is a **normal good**—that is, a good whose demand increases (or decreases) when people's incomes increase (or decrease).

Normal good
A good whose demand increases or decreases when people's incomes increase or decrease.

Changes in Taste

Tastes seldom change overnight, but they do change. Suppose that the surgeon general reports that the consumption of red meat is detrimental to health. If enough people worry about the quantity of meat they consume and make a conscious effort to cut down, the demand for fish would increase.

Sometimes, tastes are learned or cultivated. Advertising has much to do with it. Suppose McDonald's came to the island and introduced its filet of fish. Wouldn't *some* people, tasting McDonald's fish for the first time, switch from meat to fish? Can you picture the McDonald's fish commercials? If a McDonald's commercial pushed fish, people on the island would probably end up buying more fish at each price. At $P = \$10$, for example, quantity demanded might increase from 3,500 to 4,500 fish.

You may not sweeten the fish on your plate, but if you have a sweet tooth anyway, your preference now for ingesting "natural products" has resulted in soft-drink, fruit yogurt, cereal, and salad dressing producers switching their sweetening ingredients from high-fructose corn syrup to refined sugar, which is 99 percent sucrose. It's your tastes that made the switch!

Changes in the Prices of Other Goods

You don't have to be frightened by the surgeon general's report to substitute fish for beef. Prices alone can do it. For example, if the price of hamburger jumped suddenly from $1.89 to $2.45 per pound, that might be incentive enough for many people to switch from hamburger to fish. After all, fish and hamburger are **substitute goods**. When the price of one increases, the demand for the other increases.

Suppose people on the island typically eat fish with fries. And suppose, as well, that the price of potatoes increases from $0.75 to $2.75 a pound. What happens to the demand for fish? It falls. People demand less fish at each price because the "fish 'n' fries" combo is more expensive. Fish and fries are **complementary goods**. When the price of one increases, the demand for the other decreases.

Substitute goods
Goods that can replace each other. When the price of one increases, the demand for the other increases.

Complementary goods
Goods that are generally used together. When the price of one increases, the demand for the other decreases.

applied perspective

OUR CHANGING TASTES: THE GALLOPING DEMAND FOR BOTTLED WATER

The future is always uncertain. You know that. But some things are still more predictable than others—like the coming of seasons or the faltering of the Chicago Cubs in late September. Then there are other things, in a class by themselves, whose likelihood of ever happening seems so preposterous that you feel more than confident in saying that, come what may, they simply won't occur.

And then they do! And you're left speechless. One such preposterous idea is that people would be willing to buy water instead of just opening the kitchen faucet and drinking to their heart's content. Paying for tea, coffee, milk, and soft drinks is understandable. After all, the city reservoirs don't stock these beverages. If you want them, you have to buy them. But water? We access the same water supply to drown our thirst as to bathe, to water our lawns, or wash our cars. Why would anyone shell out $2 for a 15-ounce bottle of water when they can get those 15 ounces or even 15 gallons for less than a fraction of a penny?

But facts are facts. There is no denying the galloping demand for bottled water. Our drinking tastes have changed. Just look at college students on campus. There's typically a bottle of water tucked away in the netted pocket of their backpacks. Bottled water has become the beverage of choice. In 2004, the demand for bottled water surpassed that for coffee, tea, beer, and milk to become the second most consumed beverage in the United States. Soft drinks still remain number one, but Michael Bellas, CEO of the Beverage Marketing Corporation, believes that the demand for bottled water will eclipse even soft drinks by 2020.

It's a big business and big players are involved. Perrier is a subsidiary of the multinational conglomerate Nestle S.A. of Switzerland. PepsiCo owns Aquafina and Coca-Cola owns Dasani. Together with smaller players, like Crystal Geyser of California, they make up a U.S. bottled water market whose revenues exceeded $7 billion in 2003. It isn't just an American craze. Bottled water ranks second as well in the European soft drink market and the bottled water industry reaches an overall worldwide market whose annual sales tops $35 billion.

It boggles the imagination. Bottled water, whatever else it is—it's healthy, it's calorie free, it's thirst quenching—is still H_2O.

Refreshing, no doubt—but it's water nonetheless and now kind of pricey.

Think again of the sweetening alternatives facing the soft-drink producers. The price of corn syrup edged higher than the price of sugar in early 2008 which added incentive for producers to make that switch from corn syrup to sugar. Wouldn't you?

Can you think of other complementary goods? How about coffee and milk, milk and cookies, peanut butter and jelly, bagels and cream cheese? Coca-Cola once advertised that "Things go better with Coke." What happens to the demand for Coke when the prices of those "things" increase? It falls.

Changes in Expectations About Future Prices

The demand for fish may change just because people change their expectations about tomorrow's fish price. If you thought that the price of fish would increase tomorrow, you might be willing to buy more fish today; that alone could explain why, at $P = \$10$, the quantity demanded increases from 3,500 to 4,500 (and increases at every price level) in the table in Exhibit 6. Of course, if you had a notion that tomorrow's price would be lower, you might delay consumption by reducing the quantity demanded today. In such a case, the demand for fish decreases.

Changes in Population Size

Suppose an immigration wave increases the island's population by 10 percent. How does such an increase affect the demand for fish? With more mouths to

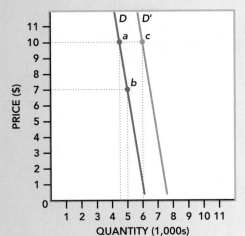

EXHIBIT 7   Distinguishing Changes in Demand from Changes in Quantity Demanded

Movement along the demand curve *D* from a price of $10, at point *a*, to a price of $7, at point *b*, illustrates a *change in quantity demanded* from 4,500 to 5,000. A shift in the demand curve from *D* to *D'* illustrates a *change in demand*. At a price of $10, the quantity increases from 4,500 on demand curve *D* to 6,000 on demand curve *D'*.

feed, the quantity of fish demanded at each price increases. A baby boom on the island would have the same effect.

A Change in Demand or a Change in Quantity Demanded?

Changes in quantity demanded and changes in demand may seem to be two ways of expressing the same idea, but they are not. What's the difference?

Economists define *change in quantity demanded* to mean only the change in quantity demanded of a good that is brought about by a change in the price of that good. They define *change in demand* to mean a shift in the entire demand curve.

Look at demand curve *D* in Exhibit 7. When price falls from *P* = $10 to *P* = $7, the quantity demanded increases from 4,500 to 5,000. Economists describe this increase as "a change in quantity demanded." It traces out a movement *along the demand curve* from point *a* to point *b*.

When demand increases for other reasons, such as population growth, the entire demand curve shifts from *D* to *D'*. Economists call this shift "a change in demand." At the same price, *P* = $10, the quantity demanded increases from 4,500 on *D* to 6,000 on *D'*. The shift in the demand curve from *D* to *D'*—point *a* to point *c* at *P* = $10—occurs because of a determining factor such as a change in people's tastes or income. It is not a result of a change in the price of the good.

What's the difference between a change in demand and a change in quantity demanded?

CHANGES IN SUPPLY

Let us now consider what happens to price when changes in short-run supply occur. Let's suppose that the demand schedule is the same as the one in column 4 of the table in Exhibit 6. The change in short-run supply is 1,000 more fish added (at every price) to the supply schedule of Exhibit 6. The table in Exhibit 8 records this market condition.

The graph in Exhibit 8 depicts the **change in supply** shown in the table.

Supply curve *S*, graphing the initial supply schedule (column 3), shifts outward to the right to *S'*, graphing the new supply schedule (column 4). Look at its

Change in supply
A change in quantity supplied of a good that is caused by factors other than a change in the price of that good.

EXHIBIT 8   Change in Supply

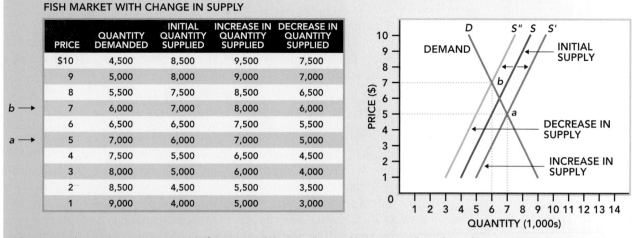

FISH MARKET WITH CHANGE IN SUPPLY

PRICE	QUANTITY DEMANDED	INITIAL QUANTITY SUPPLIED	INCREASE IN QUANTITY SUPPLIED	DECREASE IN QUANTITY SUPPLIED
$10	4,500	8,500	9,500	7,500
9	5,000	8,000	9,000	7,000
8	5,500	7,500	8,500	6,500
7	6,000	7,000	8,000	6,000
6	6,500	6,500	7,500	5,500
5	7,000	6,000	7,000	5,000
4	7,500	5,500	6,500	4,500
3	8,000	5,000	6,000	4,000
2	8,500	4,500	5,500	3,500
1	9,000	4,000	5,000	3,000

Ceteris paribus, an increase in supply from S to S', lowers the equilibrium price from $6 to $5, point a on the graph. The quantity bought and sold increases from 6,500 to 7,000. A decrease in supply from S to S" raises the equilibrium price from $6 to $7, point b on the graph, and reduces the quantity bought and sold from 6,500 to 6,000.

impact on the equilibrium price of fish. The initial equilibrium, $P = \$6$, is no longer tenable. Now, at that price an excess supply of 1,000 fish emerges. The pressure of this excess supply drives the equilibrium price down from $P = \$6$ to $P = \$5$, and the quantities bought and sold up from 6,500 to 7,000 fish.

What could cause such a change in supply? There are a number of reasons why fishermen change the quantity they are willing to supply at every price. The principal reasons are changes in technology, changes in resource prices, changes in the prices of other goods, and changes in the number of suppliers. Let's consider each.

Changes in Technology

Suppose Steve Scariano, an electronics tinkerer on the island, invents a sonar device that allows fishermen to detect the presence of fish at considerable depths. What a bonanza! Imagine JoAnn Weber, one of the island's fishermen, using the same boat and crew but installing Steve's sonar device on her boat. What do you suppose happens to the quantity of fish she is now capable of bringing home? At every price the quantity supplied increases.

Why? New technology, such as Steve's sonar device, typically lowers the cost of producing a good. Each fish is now cheaper to produce. The higher profit makes fishing more attractive and becomes an incentive for fishermen to supply more at every price. And still others switch to fishing.

Changes in Resource Prices

If lower costs raise profit and create incentive to supply more at every price, then any factor that contributes to lowering costs will increase supply. Consider what happens to the supply curve when resource prices associated with fishing fall. For example, suppose the price (wages) of hiring fishing crews falls. Instead of paying a boat pilot $300 a day, fishermen find that pilots are readily available at

$200. Or suppose the prices of bait, fishing gear, fuel, and ice fall. These lower resource prices increase the spread between the market price a fisherman gets for a fish and the costs involved in producing it. That increased spread is greater profit per fish. In other words, lower resource prices increase the quantities of fish supplied at every price in the fish market.

Imagine what happens to the supply curve if resources associated with fish production become more expensive. The reverse occurs. More expensive resources decrease the quantities supplied at every price in the fish market. We see this in S", a new supply curve to the left of S in Exhibit 8.

Changes in the Prices of Other Goods

Many boats, with minor alterations, can serve multiple purposes. For example, a sightseeing boat that transports tourists from island to island can be rigged to fish the same waters. Cargo boats can be scrubbed down and fitted for passengers. Fishing boats can haul cargo.

Suppose faltering island tourism causes the price of sightseeing boat tickets to fall. How long will it take before some of the sightseeing boat operators switch to fishing? And how will that switch affect the supply curve of fish? This change in price of other goods (sightseeing boat tickets) shifts the supply curve of fish out to the right.

Let's digress for a moment. Consider potato farmers. Their fields, too, can serve multiple purposes. If the price of corn skyrockets, many potato farmers may switch from potato to corn farming. How would the switch affect the supply schedule of potatoes? At every price in the potato market, the quantity of potatoes supplied falls. Graphed, it would show the supply curve of potatoes shifting to the left.

Changes in the Number of Suppliers

Perhaps the first thing that comes to mind when trying to explain what could cause the shift from S to S' is simply more suppliers. Somewhat akin to a change in demand occasioned by a change in taste, a change in supply caused by greater numbers of suppliers might reflect changes in people's occupational "taste." More people choosing to fish means more fish at every price.

WHY THE PRICE OF AN ORANGE IS 30 CENTS AT THE SUPERMARKET

The same factors governing the $6 equilibrium price of fish govern as well the 30-cent equilibrium price of oranges. The price of oranges depends upon the supply and demand conditions in the fruit and vegetable market.

If orange imports from Spain, Morocco, and Israel are added to our California and Florida orange supply, the supply curve in the orange market shifts out to the right, forcing the equilibrium price to fall.

Grapefruit and oranges are substitute goods. If the grapefruit harvest in both California and Florida is exceptionally large, resulting in a substantial fall in the price of grapefruit, the demand curve for oranges shifts to the left. The result? The price of oranges falls.

Suppose, on the other hand, that TV commercials sponsored by the orange-growers industry persuade people that orange juice is not only a breakfast drink but an excellent substitute for soft drinks, tea, coffee, or milk at any time of the day. What should the orange growers expect? The demand curve for their oranges shifts to the right, raising both price and quantity.

Exhibit 9 illustrates precisely how changes in demand and supply can generate changes in the equilibrium price and quantity of oranges.

KEY **EXHIBIT 9**   Increases in Demand and Supply

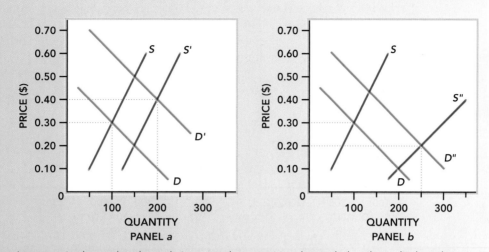

PANEL a

PANEL b

Increases in demand and supply increase the quantities demanded and supplied on the market. In panel *a*, quantity increases to 200 oranges; in panel *b*, to 250 oranges. But the effect of these increases on price depends on the relative size increases in demand and supply. When the demand increase is more sizable than the increase in supply, price rises, as we see in panel *a*, from $0.30 to $0.40. When the supply increase is more sizable than the increase in demand, price falls, as we see in panel *b*, from $0.30 to $0.20.

Suppose both the demand for and the supply of oranges increase simultaneously. For example, health-conscious people switch from consuming soft drinks to consuming orange juice at the same time as orange growers switch to a new harvesting technology that lowers the cost of producing oranges. We see this in panels *a* and *b*, where demand shifts from *D* to *D'* and supply shifts from *S* to *S'*. But note the differences in the size of the shifts. In panel *a*, the demand shift is the more pronounced. In panel *b*, the supply shift dominates. How do these differences affect changes in the price and quantity of oranges?

Let's start with panel *a*. When either demand or supply increases, quantity increases. So when both demand and supply increase at the same time (more orange juice drinkers and newer technology), the combined result increases quantity from 100 to 200 oranges. What about price? Here, the outcome is less clear. An increase in demand, by itself, raises price. But an increase in supply, by itself, decreases price. The combined effect, then, depends on the relative size of the demand and supply increases. In panel *a*, the sizable increase in demand raises price from $0.30 to $0.50, or by $0.20. The less-than-sizable increase in supply lowers price from $0.30 to $0.20, or by $0.10. As you can see, the net effect is an increase in equilibrium price to $0.40. This is because the effect of the change in demand dominates price.

Now look at panel *b*. Here the sizable increase occurs in supply. The increase in orange juice drinkers and new technology shifts the demand and supply curves to *D"* and *S"*, so that the combined effect raises quantity from 100 to 250 oranges. What about price? It falls to $0.20. This is because the effect of the change in supply dominates price.

Exhibit 10 depicts another version of supply and demand changes in the market for oranges. Now the changes move in opposite directions. More orange juice drinkers (increase in demand) combine with a late spring frost that destroys orange groves (decrease in supply). What happens to price under these circumstances? Since both an increase in demand and a decrease in supply raise price, their combined effect unequivocally increases price. This we see in panel *a*, where price

on the
net

Why does Sunkist (http://www.sunkist.com/), a major producer of oranges, provide free orange recipes? To increase the demand for oranges, of course.

KEY EXHIBIT 10   Increases in Demand, Decreases in Supply

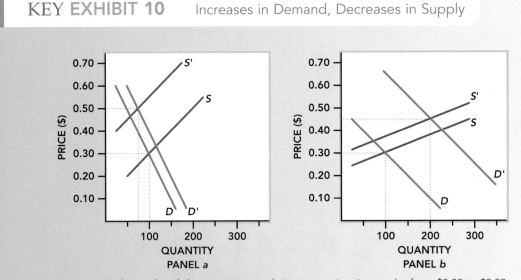

Increases in demand and decreases in supply increase price, in panel *a* from $0.30 to $0.50, and in panel *b* from $0.30 to $0.45. But the effect of the changes in supply and demand on the quantities demanded and supplied depends on the relative size of the increases and decreases in demand and supply. When the demand increase is more sizable than the decrease in supply, quantity decreases from 100 oranges to 75, as we see in panel *a*. When the supply decrease is more sizable than the increase in demand, quantity increases from 100 to 200 oranges, as we see in panel *b*.

increases from $0.30 to $0.50. What about quantity? Here, the combined effect is less clear. The increase in demand increases quantity, while the decrease in supply decreases quantity. Because the decrease in supply is more sizable in panel *a*, the combined effect is a decrease in quantity, from 100 to 75 oranges.

Finally, look at the panel *b* variation, where the increase in demand is more sizable than the decrease in supply. Now price ends up at $0.45 and quantity increases to 200 oranges.

KATRINA AND GASOLINE PRICES

It all happened in less than six hours. On August 29, 2005, Hurricane Katrina charged inland over a 150-mile stretch of the Gulf Coast, at speeds exceeding 175 miles per hour, to thrash, batter, flood, and destroy most everything and everybody in its path. By the time it subsided, more than 1,000 people were dead, many more missing, and over half a million private homes, as well as thousands of businesses, public buildings, streets, parks, underpasses, and overpasses, were despoiled, left submerged in what quickly became a frightening sea of unwholesome water. New Orleans—the *Big Easy* as we knew it—along with entire towns in southeast Louisiana no longer existed. In just those few hours, Katrina produced the largest domestic refugee crisis America experienced since the Civil War.

Katrina also wreaked havoc on the Gulf Coast's vital oil industry. More than 90 percent of the oil production in the Gulf of Mexico was shut down because of damage to its oil rigs and oil refineries. At least 20 rigs or platforms situated in the Gulf were reported battered, listing, sunk, or missing. Nine Gulf Coast oil refineries were closed, and these represented 12 percent of the United States' refining capacity, or about 2 million barrels of oil per day.

Gasoline is a crude oil derivative. The oil is "cooked" to boiling temperatures at the refineries, and at each stage in the boiling process—called fractional

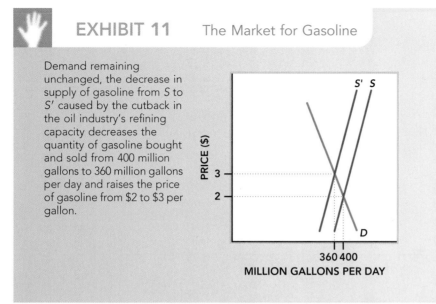

EXHIBIT 11   The Market for Gasoline

Demand remaining unchanged, the decrease in supply of gasoline from S to S' caused by the cutback in the oil industry's refining capacity decreases the quantity of gasoline bought and sold from 400 million gallons to 360 million gallons per day and raises the price of gasoline from $2 to $3 per gallon.

distillation—the evaporation collected forms a differentiated product, among them kerosene, naptha, butane, propane, diesel, lubricating oils, and gasoline.

This dangerous cutback in our refining capacity was an "accident waiting to happen." The oil industry had not built a new refinery in more than 25 years. Already operating near total capacity before Katrina, the aging industry infrastructure left little margin for error. Katrina obliterated that margin and then some.

Exhibit 11 depicts the effects of Katrina at the gasoline pump.

The effects are traced solely to changes in supply, even though Katrina's disruption of life in Louisiana, Mississippi, and Alabama, and to a lesser extent in other states, would certainly have changed demand as well. As you see, the cutback in refinery capacity shifts the supply curve dramatically to the left, from S to S'. Quantity decreases from 400 million gallons to 360 million gallons per day. The average market price for gasoline increases from a pre-Katrina $2 per gallon to a post-Katrina $3.

PRICE AS A RATIONING MECHANISM

Let's step back from gasoline prices and oranges for a moment and return to the fish market again. The demand curve for fish, *D*, depicted in Exhibit 12, panel *a*, is not simply a line drawn on a graph. Each point on that curve represents somebody's willingness to buy fish at some price and, as well, that same person's unwillingness to buy at a higher one. For example, point *a* tells us that Faye Russo will pay $8 for a fish, but will not pay $9. Whether she eats fish or not depends strictly on its price. Point *b* tells us that Jackie Mathews is willing to buy a fish as long as price is no higher than $7. Kim Deal will go as high as $6, Wayne Coyne stops at $3, and Ian Rodier, who likes fish but can't put two pennies together, eats fish only when price is zero. Adding their demand for fish to everyone else's on demand curve *D* generates a total quantity demanded, albeit at different prices, of 250 fish.

Let's now introduce a supply curve, *S*, to the market. As we see in panel *b*, supply and demand create an equilibrium price of $6 and an equilibrium quantity of 100 fish bought and sold on the market.

Consider those 100 fish. How are they rationed among the 250 people who want fish? You already know the answer, don't you? Everybody positioned on the segment of the demand curve above $6 gets a fish; everyone positioned on the

EXHIBIT 12   Rationing Function of Price

Panel *a* identifies specific people's willingness to buy fish at various prices. Altogether, 250 people express a willingness to buy fish. But who gets them? Panel *b* shows the market for fish and its equilibrium price. Only those willing to pay the market price get the fish. All others don't. The demand curve, *D*, and the supply curve, *S*, generate a market price of $6 and a quantity demanded and supplied of 100. It means 100 of the 250 end up with fish, among them Kim Deal. When the supply curve decreases to S', price rises to $7 and quantity falls to 75 fish. It means 75 people end up with fish, and 175 who want fish don't, among them Kim Deal. In this way, price services as a rationing mechanism.

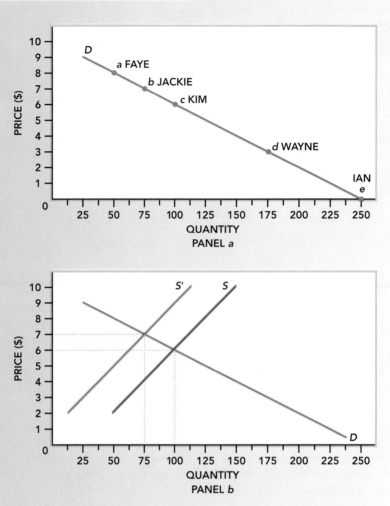

demand curve below $6 doesn't. *The $6 equilibrium price becomes the market's rationing mechanism.* Who are those 100 people? We know they include Faye, Jackie, and Kim. Who are the 150 people who end up without fish? We know they include Wayne and Ian.

If the supply curve shifts to the left to S', the equilibrium price rises to $7 and the equilibrium quantity falls to 75. There are now fewer fish bought and sold. Faye and Jackie still get fish, but Kim, who would buy fish if price were $6, is shut out of the market at $7. She's disappointed. Her income hasn't changed, her taste for fish hasn't changed, but the price she confronts has. She knows, as you do, that price dictates who gets and who doesn't.

CHAPTER REVIEW

1. Consumer demand reflects people's willingness to buy a good. People supply goods on the presumption that there will be a demand for them.

2. The demand for a good represents people's willingness to purchase specific quantities at specific prices. The law of demand is the inverse relationship between price and the quantity demanded. As the price of a good decreases, the quantity demanded increases and vice versa.

3. Graphs translate tabular data for quantities demanded at different prices into individual demand curves. Demand curves have negative slopes because price and quantity demanded are inversely related.

4. Market demand curves represent the sum of individual quantities demanded at different prices.

5. Supply involves production activity over a period of time. The market day is a time period so short that the quantity supplied cannot be changed no matter what price is paid to the supplier. Therefore, quantity supplied is constant during the market day, regardless of price.

6. Market price is determined by the intersection of demand and supply. Because quantity demanded and quantity supplied are equal at the market price, it is also called equilibrium price. If price is above its equilibrium level, an excess supply results and creates competition among suppliers, which drives price down to equilibrium. If price is below its equilibrium level, an excess demand results and creates competition among demanders, which drives price up to equilibrium. There is no excess demand or excess supply in equilibrium. The market clears.

7. In a time period longer than the market day, suppliers can respond to changes in price. The short run is a time period long enough to allow suppliers to make partial adjustments in production in response to price changes. The long run is a time period long enough to allow suppliers to completely adjust their production to changes in price. The longer the time period, the more flexible the response by suppliers to price changes. Thus, as time passes, the supply curve shifts from a vertical line to a flatter, positively sloped line.

8. Changes in demand cause changes in the equilibrium price. When demand increases (shifting the demand curve to the right), excess demand emerges at the original equilibrium, causing price to rise to a new and higher equilibrium where quantity supplied once again equals quantity demanded. When demand decreases (shifting the demand curve to the left), the excess supply at the original equilibrium causes price to fall to a new and lower equilibrium where quantity supplied once again equals quantity demanded.

9. Changes in demand are induced by changes in income, changes in taste, changes in the prices of other goods, changes in expectations about future prices, and changes in population size.

10. Complementary goods have inverse relationships such that an increase in the price of one results in a decrease in the demand for the others (for example, bread and butter). Substitute goods, on the other hand, have direct relationships among themselves such that an increase in the price of one results in an increase in the demand for the others (for example, bread and bagels).

11. Changes in supply cause changes in the equilibrium price. When supply increases (shifting the supply curve to the right), excess supply emerges at the original equilibrium, causing price to fall to a new and lower equilibrium where quantity supplied once again equals quantity demanded. When supply decreases (shifting the supply curve to the left), the excess demand at the original equilibrium causes price to rise to a new and higher equilibrium where quantity supplied once again equals quantity demanded.

12. Changes in supply are induced by changes in technology, changes in resource prices, changes in the prices of other goods, and changes in the number of suppliers.

13. Simultaneous shifts in demand and supply lead to changes in equilibrium price and quantity. Whether price increases or decreases, or whether quantity increases or decreases, depends on the direction and strength of these shifts.

14. Price serves as a rationing mechanism in our economy. As price increases, the available supply of a good is rationed to those who can still afford to buy it. A decrease in price makes a good available to a wider segment of the market because more people are able to buy it.

KEY TERMS

Change in quantity demanded	Market-day supply	Long run
Law of demand	Supply curve	Change in demand
Demand schedule	Excess supply	Normal good
Demand curve	Excess demand	Substitute goods
Market demand	Equilibrium price	Complementary goods
Supply schedule	Short run	Change in supply

QUESTIONS

1. The quantity of CDs demanded by Michael Roux is twice the quantity that Adam Schmidt demands, whatever the price. Does that mean that Michael appreciates music more than Adam? Why or why not?

2. The market price for Cornish hen today is $3.50 or $1.50 above its $2.00 equilibrium price. How does price eventually return to equilibrium?

3. The market price for Cornish hen today is $2.00 or $1.50 below its $3.50 equilibrium price. How does price eventually return to equilibrium?

4. Why is the market-day supply curve for fish drawn as a vertical line? What happens to equilibrium price and quantity when the demand for fish increases in that market?

5. Suppose NAFTA (the U.S. free trade agreement with Canada and Mexico) allows the neighboring economies to enter our slipper market. Draw a graph showing the probable effects of their entry on price and quantity of slippers demanded and supplied in the United States.

6. When the price of hamburger rises, the demand for fish rises. When the price of hamburger rises, the demand for hamburger buns falls. Why?

7. Hans Gienepp is frustrated every year. In March, the price of tomatoes is $1.75 per pound. That is sufficient incentive for him to plant tomatoes in his yard. But in August, when the crop is ready for picking, prices at the grocer have fallen to 25 cents per pound. "I always run into this bad luck," he laments. Why is his problem not a matter of luck?

8. Because there was a rumor in May that the price of compact disc players was going to increase in August, the demand for compact disc players went up in May. Explain.

9. How would each of the following events affect the international price of oil (in each case ceteris paribus): (a) the United States gives economic assistance to oil-rich Ukraine in the form of oil-drilling technology; (b) Iran, in a war against Saudi Arabia, destroys 50 percent of Saudi oil wells; (c) a U.S. invention uses sea-water to fuel automobiles; (d) Western European homes are heated solely by solar power; and (e) the world's population doubles.

10. How do you explain the fact that a single rose at the supermarket florist is $1.49 every day of the year except the week before and during Valentine's Day, when it increases to $3.50?

11. How do you explain the fact that years ago, cheese was considered the poor person's food, selling for less than a quarter of the price of beef? Today, beef and cheese are priced approximately the same.

12. Jeff Foxworthy is a very funny comedian. He always sells out. So how do you explain the fact that when ticket prices are $10, there are lines around the block a mile long for those tickets, and when the price is $40, he sells out, but there are no lines to be seen? Use a graph to aid your discussion.

13. Orange juice producers are dismayed and puzzled. An economist told them that the reason the demand for orange juice fell is that a new technology allows tomato producers to pick ripe tomatoes more quickly, with less damage and at lower cost. Can you make the connection?

14. Professor Carrie Meyer of George Mason University presents her students with the following scenario: "Suppose a frost destroys much of the coffee harvest in Colombia. Show why equilibrium price and quantity change. Suppose, during this period, many coffee drinkers learn to kick the coffee habit. What happens to price and quantity when coffee production returns to normal in the following year?" How would you answer her question?

PRACTICE PROBLEMS

1. Draw a graph depicting the Texas Panhandle market for onions. The Panhandle consists of four counties: El Paso, Hudspeth, Culberson, and Reeves. When price is $2 per 3-pound bag, the quantity demanded in El Paso is 50,000 bags. In Hudspeth, it's 75,000 bags, in Culberson 30,000 bags, and in Reeves 90,000 bags. When price drops to $1 per bag, the quantity demanded in El Paso is 60,000 bags, in Hudspeth 90,000 bags, in Culberson 45,000 bags, and in Reeves 100,000.

2. Draw a graph depicting the Panhandle demand for onions (comparing it to the demand curve you drew in question 1) if the Panhandle's population increases by 20 percent. Draw another graph depicting the Panhandle demand for onions (comparing it as well to the demand curve you drew in question 1) when the price of hamburgers falls by 20 percent. (Hint: People usually order onions with hamburgers.)

3. Supposing you owned a pastry shop, use any numbers you wish to construct a table showing your market-day, short-run, and long-run supply of chocolate éclairs. Explain the differences.

4. Suppose the market for holiday candles was described by the following schedule:

PRICE	QUANTITY DEMANDED	QUANTITY SUPPLIED
$6	1,000	6,000
5	2,000	5,000
4	3,000	4,000
3	4,000	3,000
2	5,000	2,000
1	6,000	1,000

Draw the demand and supply curves and identify the equilibrium price. What effect would a 1,000-unit decrease in demand at every price level have on the demand curve, supply curve, and equilibrium price?

5. The following are the various demand and supply schedules for pizza. Let's start by assuming that the demand and supply on the pizza market are D_2 and S_2. (a) What is the equilibrium price and quantity of pizza? (b) Now suppose people's tastes switch to pizza. What

happens to equilibrium price and quantity? (c) Let's add another change to the market. This time let's assume that, although with that change in taste, the price of pizza ingredients (cheese, onions, and so on) falls. What happens to equilibrium price and quantity? (d) Finally, let's suppose that a new health report reveals that pizza is bad for your health and people's demand for pizza falls dramatically, even below the original D_2 schedule. What happens to equilibrium price and quantity?

PRICE	D_1	D_2	D_3	S_1	S_2	S_3
$5	6	10	14	12	14	18
4	8	12	16	10	12	16
3	10	14	18	8	10	14
2	12	16	20	6	8	12
1	14	18	22	4	6	10

WHAT'S WRONG WITH THIS GRAPH?

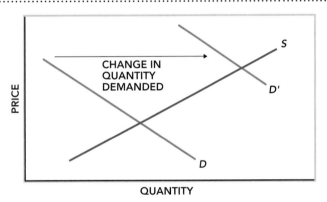

Economic Consultants

Economic Research and Analysis by Students for Professionals

Mort's Ostrich Farm produces high-protein, low-fat ostrich meat for restaurants and consumers. Mort's currently supplies a small number of customers, but the firm believes it can increase the quantity it produces and the price it charges with strategies to increase the demand for ostrich meat.

Mort's has approached Economic Consultants for advice on how to increase the demand. Prepare a report for Mort's that addresses the following issues:

1. What strategies can Mort's implement to increase the demand for ostrich meat?
2. Explain to Mort's the difference between changing the demand for ostrich meat versus changing the quantity demanded. Explain what

strategies will cause a change in demand versus a change in the quantity demanded.

You may find the following resources helpful as you prepare this report for Mort's:
- **Ostrich Central** (http://attra.ncat.org/attra-pub/ratite.html), **Ostrich Growers Meat Company** (http://www.ostrichgrowers.com), and **AZ Ostrich Company, Inc.** (http://www.azostrich.com/)—These suppliers of ostrich meat offer distribution across the United States.
- **The Clio Awards** (http://www.clioawards.com)—The Clio Awards highlight the best advertising campaigns in print, radio, and television.

1. Dog food companies have developed a new technology that makes nutritious dog food out of garbage. We would expect, ceteris paribus, that the
   a. supply curve of dog food would shift to the left.
   b. supply curve of dog food would shift to the right.
   c. demand curve for dog food would shift to the left.
   d. demand curve for dog food would shift to the right.
   e. demand and supply curves would shift to the right.

2. We would also find that the price of dog food would
   a. fall because the supply curve shifted to the right.
   b. fall because the supply curve shifted to the left.
   c. fall because the demand curve shifted to the right.
   d. rise because the demand curve shifted to the right.
   e. rise because the demand curve shifted to the left.

3. When the demand curve for bicycles increases while the supply curve remains unchanged,
   a. the quantity demanded decreases.
   b. the equilibrium price increases and the equilibrium quantity decreases.
   c. the equilibrium price decreases and the equilibrium quantity increases.
   d. quantity supplied increases.
   e. quantity supplied decreases.

4. Which of the following will not shift the market short-run supply of corn?
   a. A change in the price of corn
   b. A change in the price of soybeans
   c. A change in the price of herbicides and pesticides
   d. A change in the storage of technology
   e. A change in the number of acres planted with corn

5. As long as an excess demand for fish exists on the market, there will always be an incentive
   a. for demanders to bid the price up.
   b. for demanders to buy fewer fish.
   c. for fishermen to produce and supply fish.
   d. for fishermen to lower the price of fish.
   e. for demanders and suppliers to seek the equilibrium price.

6. In March, if consumers expect the price of in-line skates to increase as the summer approaches,
   a. the market-day supply of in-line skates in March will shift to the right.
   b. the demand for in-line skates in March will shift to the right.
   c. the demand for in-line skates in March will shift to the left.
   d. the current price of in-line skates will fall.

   e. there will be a movement along the demand curve for in-line skates.

7. Ty manufactures Beanie Baby dolls. The market-day supply curve for Beanie Baby dolls is vertical because
   a. Ty is very responsive to price changes.
   b. the consumer-demand curves are very responsive to even small price changes.
   c. the price will not change as the quantity supplied changes in the market.
   d. the equilibrium price dictates how many Beanie Babies will be sold each day.
   e. Ty cannot increase its supply during a given day in response to price changes.

Supply and Demand for Briefcases

PRICE	QUANTITY SUPPLIED	QUANTITY DEMANDED
$50	100	600
60	200	500
70	300	400
80	350	350
90	400	300

8. The preceding table illustrates the supply and demand schedules for briefcases. The equilibrium price for briefcases in this market
   a. is $50.
   b. is $60.
   c. is $70.
   d. is $80.
   e. cannot be determined without more information.

9. The preceding table illustrates the supply and demand schedule for briefcases. If there is a reduction in the price of leather used to make briefcases, enabling manufacturers to supply 100 additional briefcases at each price, the new equilibrium price
   a. will be the same as the old equilibrium price.
   b. will cause a rightward shift in the market demand curve for briefcases.
   c. will cause a leftward shift in the market demand curve for briefcases.
   d. will be $90.
   e. will be $70.

10. If both the demand and supply curves in the market for oranges shift to the right,
    a. price falls and quantity increases.
    b. price rises and quantity decreases.
    c. price and quantity both decrease.
    d. price increases and it is unclear what happens to quantity.
    e. quantity increases and it is unclear what happens to price.

Appendix

APPLICATIONS OF SUPPLY AND DEMAND

HOW MUCH IS THAT DOGGIE IN THE WINDOW?

The image of a young child's face pushed flush up against the window of a pet shop, watching puppies at play, is a sight that would warm the cockles of anyone's heart. Is it too great a leap from fish markets to the puppy market? Not really. After all, both fish and puppies are produced for and sold on markets. Supply and demand determine the price of puppies just as supply and demand determine the price of fish.

Look at Exhibit A1. In 1993, the supply, *S*, and demand, *D*, for Jack Russell terrier pups generated an equilibrium price of $600 and an equilibrium quantity of 1,000 pups. That was then. This is now. When the sitcom *Frasier* became a sensation on prime-time TV, the market for Jack Russell terriers changed dramatically. Why? Because the sitcom included a Jack Russell terrier named Eddie who was the darling pet of Frasier's dad. The popularity of the TV sitcom increased the popularity of the Jack Russell terrier as a pet dog. As we see in Exhibit A1, the demand curve for Jack Russell terrier pups shifted from *D* to *D'*, which caused the equilibrium price of the puppies to rise from $600 to $900 and quantity to increase from 1,000 to 1,400.

What about the child at the pet shop window? Try as he might—clutching 25 cents in his tiny fist—the Jack Russell terrier pup is far beyond his financial means. He may want that pup as badly as any child wants a puppy, but he confronts the rationing function of price and is just out of luck. The pup goes to someone who is willing and able to pay $900. It's as simple as that. It has nothing to do with love of animals, or love of children, or concern for the pup. It has all to do with willingness and ability to pay the price.

check your understanding

Why can't the child get the puppy?

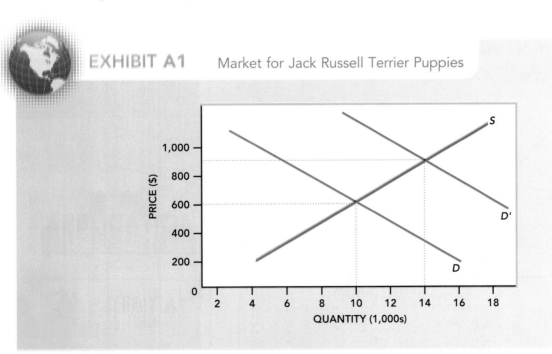

EXHIBIT A1   Market for Jack Russell Terrier Puppies

THE CASE OF THE GUIDE DOG

Let's look at a different dog market, this time for guide dogs, which as you know are indispensable to many blind people. Look at Exhibit A2. The supply curve, *S*, reflects the relatively high cost of training these animals; the demand curve, *D*, reflects the relatively high value sightless people place on having such a dog. Market equilibrium occurs at a price of $25,000 and a quantity of 2,000 dogs. It is pointless to dispute the market's $25,000 equilibrium price. Reasonable or not, it simply records the interaction of supply and demand on the market. Who gets these dogs depends solely on who can afford to pay $25,000.

But is that *really* the way we want to ration those dogs among demanders? Perhaps we can tolerate a child's longing for but not having a Jack Russell terrier puppy, but can we tolerate a sightless person longing for but not having a guide dog? If that's unacceptable, then how do we go about providing these people with guide dogs at affordable prices?

After all, the willingness and ability of suppliers to supply a good depends, as you know, on the opportunity cost of producing the good. Look at the supply curve in the guide dog market of Exhibit A2, panel *a*. What does it tell us? The willingness and ability of suppliers to supply those dogs depends on the opportunity cost of producing them. For example, suppliers' willingness and ability—measured by opportunity cost—to supply 100 dogs is $20,000. It takes $30,000 to create a quantity supplied of 4,000 dogs. How then can suppliers supply *any* quantity of guide dogs at affordable prices?

Look at Exhibit A2, panel *b*. The actual supply curve that functions in the market is the horizontal supply curve, *S'*, which shows that suppliers are willing and able to supply as many as 6,000 guide dogs at $100 each. But how can suppliers supply those dogs at $100 when the opportunity cost of producing them—reflected in supply curve *S*—is considerably higher than $100? The answer is that the suppliers are supported financially by people like yourself. These suppliers solicit donations—by direct mail, collection cans, and boxes at cashier counters—whose sums are sufficient to make up the $30,000 opportunity cost shown on supply curve *S* at the quantity of 4,000. (Have you ever slotted a quarter in their donation card?) Why do these suppliers set their supply curve, *S'*, at $100? It is an arbitrarily picked, very affordable price to indicate to their

EXHIBIT A2   Market for Guide Dogs

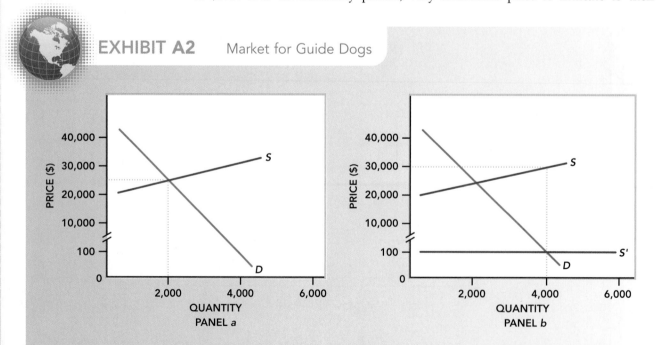

eventual owners that the dogs are not free goods. Can we create a similar donation-supported market for Jack Russell terriers? Of course. But why?

FROM DOGS TO HUMAN BEINGS

If it isn't a great analytical leap from the fish market to the dog market, is it any greater a leap from the pet puppy and guide dog markets to markets for human body parts? Not really. The powerful tools of supply and demand allow us to analyze the highly emotional and ethical issues associated with the buying and selling of human organs. How do we deal with these demands and supplies? Do we put these human body parts on the market as we do fish and puppies? Are their prices market-derived?

The Market for Organ Transplants

Perhaps the most emotionally charged and ethically engaged market we will ever encounter is the market for human organ transplants. At one time—not too many years ago—transplanting a human organ, such as a kidney or lung, from one person to another was strictly science fiction. Today it's a reality. Organ transplantation technology along with genetic engineering has allowed us to defy Mother Nature. How long will it be before we can order through the Internet an upgraded IQ, or a set of lungs, heart, and legs that would allow each of us to break the four-minute mile? Ludicrous? Don't bet on it.

The Market for Human Kidneys That's the good news. The bad news is depicted in Exhibit A3, panel *a*, the market for human kidneys. As you see, demand and supply generate an equilibrium price of $120,000, which is far beyond the financial reach of most who need a kidney. The demand curve, D_a, reflects the urgency and intensity of that demand; the supply curve, S_a, reflects the difficulty people have parting with a nonreplenishable organ of their own—a kidney,

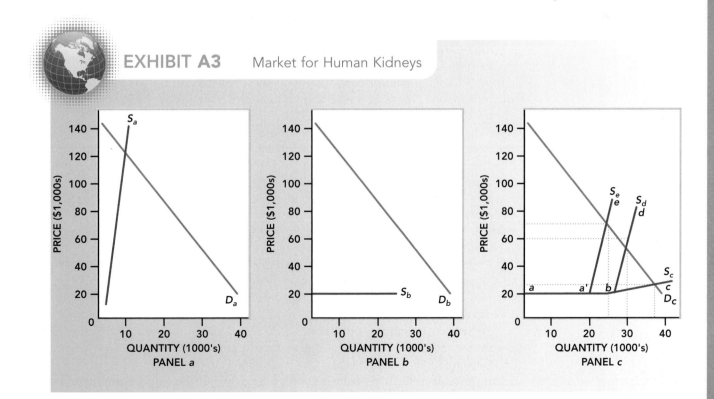

EXHIBIT A3   Market for Human Kidneys

in this case—or even parting with one after death, or with that of a deceased relative.

Is there a problem with that $120,000 price? Theoretically, not any more so than the $900 price tag on a puppy. Price serves as the rationing function in both markets. People willing and able to pay the price get the kidneys and puppies. Others don't. The question is, Should price serve as the rationing function?

The National Transplant Organ Act of 1984

While people may hold strong opinions on this subject, this normative economic issue was resolved, at least legally, with the passage in Congress of the National Transplant Organ Act of 1984. This act disallowed the private sale of organs, making the only legal market for kidneys—and other human organs—the not-for-profit market of Exhibit A3, panel *b*.

Note the difference. Volunteer donors alone provide the entire supply of 25,000 kidneys, *and that supply has nothing to do with price*. The horizontal supply curve, S_b, reflects the willingness of suppliers—in this case, hospitals—to supply any quantity up to 25,000 kidneys at a price of $20,000, a price that simply covers the cost of harvesting the kidney procured from an unpaid donor.

check your understanding

Why is the supply curve horizontal at $20,000?

What about demand? Before the advent of organ transplantation technology, people who suffered an organ failure simply didn't survive. Now, with transplant technology accessible, there is reason to hope—and this hope translates into the Exhibit A3, panel *b*, demand for kidneys, D_b.

Suppliers (hospitals) supply the 25,000 kidneys at $20,000, but at that price, the quantity supplied falls considerably short of the 40,000 quantity demanded, creating a *chronic* excess demand of 15,000 kidneys.

How, then, are the kidneys allocated among demanders? The rationing function of price is not permitted to clear the market. Some other rationing function—such as age, urgency, or geography—must take its place. However reasonable and fair these rationing systems may appear to be, many who need a kidney transplant still end up without one. To these people, and to many others, the outcome generated by the strictly donor-supplied market is simply intolerable. Is there some way to improve the outcome?

Would Organ-for-a-Price Suppliers Help?

Look at the horizontal supply curve, S_b, in Exhibit A3, panel *b*. It shows the willingness of hospitals to supply 25,000 unpaid-donor kidneys at a price of $ 20,000. This reliance on unpaid-donor kidneys acts as a formidable barrier to any increase in quantity supplied.

What incentive scheme motivated these unpaid donors to volunteer one of their two kidneys, or both upon death? For most donors, it is strictly a matter of altruism, touched perhaps by a history of some personal loss or otherwise moved by compassion and social responsibility.

It would be lovely (certainly for those needing kidney transplants) if more people volunteered an organ, extending the supply curve, S_b, to the right. But if that prospect were not immediately forthcoming, then perhaps another way of increasing supply would be to simply pay people for organs supplied.

Organ-for-a-price supply curves are depicted in Exhibit A3, panel *c*. If it takes just a modest payment to induce many people to supply one or more of their kidneys before or after death, then the supply curve of kidneys may very well look like S_c (line *abc*).

At $20,000, quantity supplied is 25,000 kidneys (line *ab*), reflecting the unpaid organ donors' supply. But thereafter, quantity supplied increases as payments kick in (line *bc*). For example, at a payment of $8,000, the equilibrium price for a kidney increases slightly—from $20,000 to $28,000, but the equilibrium quantity increases more than slightly, from $25,000 to $38,000. An attractive option, don't you think?

On the other hand, if the organ-for-a-price supply curve were S_d (line *abd*), it would take a significant payment to induce just a slight increase in quantity supplied. For example, a $40,000 payment to paid donors increases price from $20,000 to $60,000 and quantity supplied by only 3,000—from 25,000 to 28,000.

Consider yet a third organ-for-a-price supply curve possibility, S_e, (line *aa'e*). Here we see a rather perverse outcome. Suppose some unpaid donors are offended by what they consider to be a callous and coldhearted move toward the organ-for-a-price market and respond by reducing their unpaid organ supply by 5,000 so that quantity supplied at a $20,000 price falls from 25,000 to 20,000 kidneys (line *aa'*). If the organ-for-a-price supply curve is S_d-shaped, then S_e becomes the operative supply curve. Now a $50,000 payment for a kidney drives price to $70,000 and quantity supplied to 24,000. That's 1,000 short of the 25,000 kidneys that would have been supplied by unpaid donors in the absence of an organ-for-a-price market.

Which of these organ-for-a-price supply curves reflects the real world we live in? There is no strong consensus among economists on this vital question.

SCALPING TICKETS AT A YANKEES' GAME

Let's end the discussion of supply and demand applications on a less somber note. Suppose you were thinking of going to a Yankee baseball game. Here's the picture. The stadium's capacity is 70,000 seats and when the Yankees are hot, many of their games are sold out. But a sellout doesn't mean you can't buy a ticket! It just means that you will probably have to buy your ticket from a scalper in a **scalper's market**. What does this market look like?

Let's first look at the scalpers' supply curve. People with season tickets or who have bought tickets in advance may be willing to sell their tickets to a scalper instead of attending the game "if the price is right." If the Yankees are playing well, Yankee fans holding tickets may be reluctant to part with them unless they're paid handsomely for them. For example, a scalper could probably buy a few $35 tickets for $50 each. To get more tickets to resell, the scalper would probably have to pay even more than $50 because it would take a higher price to induce the more devoted fans to give them up. As a result, the supply curve for scalpers' tickets is upward sloping.

If the Yankees are having a rough season, losing many of their games, scores of fair-weather fans may be more than willing to sell their tickets for less than the original $35 price. A scalper may get a few $35 tickets for $20 each and more than a few if the supply price is raised to $30.

What about demand? As there are fair-weather suppliers, there are also fair-weather demanders. If the Yankees are doing well, people without tickets would be willing to pay more than $50 for a $35 ticket at a sold-out game. If the scalper lowers price, the quantity demanded increases. You see the outcome, don't you?

The equilibrium price on the scalper's market for a Yankee ticket depends upon supply and demand, as depicted in Exhibit A4; these supply and demand curves reflect the willingness of ticket holders to sell their tickets and the willingness of ticket buyers to pay for those tickets. The scalper is the agent that makes these demands and supplies come to life. If the Yankees are pennant-bound, the demand curve may shift to the right, from D to D', while the supply curve shifts to the left, from S to S', driving the equilibrium price upward from $50 to $90. Is there anything wrong or unethical about a scalper's market? Not really. It actually represents an honest-to-goodness free market for baseball tickets.

Scalper's market
A market in which a good is resold at a price different from the original or officially published price.

What determines the scalper's price?

EXHIBIT A4   Market for Yankees' Tickets

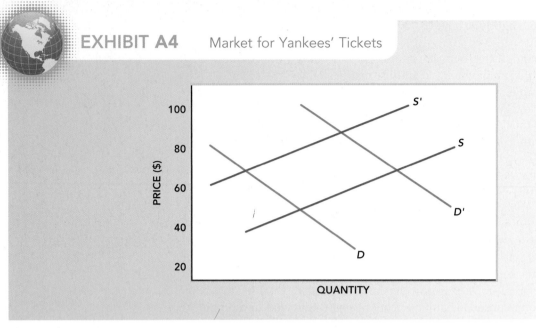

KEY TERM

Scalper's market

QUESTIONS

1. Think about the market for drug-detecting police dogs and the market for pet dogs. Why would their equilibrium prices differ?
2. Make a case for allowing the market to determine the price and quantity of human body parts. Make the countercase that opposes such a pure market determination.

3. Why is the supply curve in the market for kidneys drawn horizontally when the kidneys obtained by the suppliers (hospitals, in this case) are provided by unpaid donors?

PRACTICE PROBLEMS

1. Let's get ready for the Super Bowl! Suppose the game is played in Chicago at Soldier Field, which has a capacity of 105,000 seats. Ticket prices are $75. The game is sold out, which brings the scalper's market to life. The willingness of ticket holders to sell their $75 tickets is shown in the Quantity Supplied column in the following table. The willingness of people to buy those tickets is shown in the Quantity Demanded column. If you were one of those suppliers, how much would you get for your $75 ticket?

2. Now suppose the hype before the game was extraordinary and ticket holders were more reluctant to part with their $75 tickets. At each price level, 1,000 fewer tickets are offered. Fill in this quantity supplied in the following table. At the same time, more people were willing to pay a higher scalper's price. At each price level, 4,000 more tickets are demanded. Fill in this quantity demanded in the table. If you were still one of those suppliers, how much would you get for your $75 ticket?

PRICE	QUANTITY SUPPLIED	QUANTITY DEMANDED
$1,000	7,000	500
800	6,000	1,000
600	5,000	2,000
400	4,000	4,000
200	3,000	6,000

PRICE	QUANTITY SUPPLIED	QUANTITY DEMANDED
$1,000		
800		
600		
400		
200		

PART 2

Employment, Inflation, and Fiscal Policy

Chat Economics. Tune into the conversation. It's about *your* course. Just change the names, and it's *your* campus, *your* classroom, *your* professor, *your* classmates, and *you.*

Professor Gottheil walks into his 9 A.M. Monday class. Everyone is in his or her usual place except Wayne Coyne. He normally sits in the back of the room, but this morning he is seated up front, sporting a rather perplexed look on his face.

WAYNE: (*Waving his hand to draw Professor Gottheil's attention.*) Professor Gottheil, before you start today's lecture, could you explain something that has been puzzling me all weekend?

GOTTHEIL: Fire away!

WAYNE: Well, I was home this weekend and my father asked me what courses I was taking this semester, and I told him about this macroeconomics course. He asked me if I was learning anything.

GOTTHEIL: And what did you say? (*The class laughs.*)

WAYNE: I said I think I was.

GOTTHEIL: Well, I know you are! Your work has been good.

WAYNE: Thank you! My dad quizzed me about something I think I should have known, but I couldn't answer him. I felt pretty dumb. I think he was tricking me.

GOTTHEIL: What did he ask you?

WAYNE: It was sort of a riddle. He said: Suppose someone, let's say Nick Rudd, goes to Bob Diener's Good Vibes shop and buys a $100 CD player, paying for it by check. And Bob later, using the check—he endorses it by signing his name on the back of the check—buys a $100 pair of boots at Lisa Burnett's Leather Shop. And then Lisa, using the same check, endorses it as well—buying $100 groceries at Geoff Merritt's Foods. Geoff also endorses the check, and this goes on through 10 such endorsements. The last person, Louise Gerber, takes the $100 check to her bank, and the bank discovers that Rudd's check is worthless. Louise notes the 10 names signed on the back of the check and invites them to her shop. She tells them that the check they were all passing is worthless and that she is out $100. However, if each gave her $10, half of the $20 profit they made on their sales, she would recoup

the $100. Considering the proposal quite fair, they each contribute $10. Now here's the weird moral to my dad's story: Nick Rudd, the bad-check passer, gets his CD player, and the 10 who endorsed his worthless check come out ahead as well, each making a profit.

GOTTHEIL: So what's the problem?

WAYNE: How can everyone come out a winner when the check was worthless in the first place?

GOTTHEIL: (*Turning to the class, and noticing Jennifer Busey looking away.*) Anyone want to explain it? Jennifer?

JENNIFER: I think Wayne is right. There's a flaw some-`where in the story. It's a trick. It can't really happen.

GOTTHEIL: No flaw, no trick. Wayne's dad tells a good story that makes a very good point. Look at all the $100 sales that the worthless $100 check created. Those sales represent a lot of goods produced and a lot of people employed. If Bob, the first one to get the check, had called the bank to verify it at the very beginning, all those sales the check generated would never have taken place, and all that employment would never have occurred. In a way, you can thank the bad-check writer, Nick Rudd, for stimulating the economy!

WAYNE: But that's cheating. It's like getting something for nothing.

GOTTHEIL: But the nothing actually created something. Wayne, your dad's story is very useful. Remember it when you read the next few chapters. Whether he knew it or not, your dad was describing the mechanics of the income multiplier, something we will study in the next few chapters.

WAYNE: Frankly, I don't think he knew!

Over the next six chapters, you will encounter a number of new economic concepts, such as the income

continued on next page

ChatEconomics

multiplier, the business cycle, the consumption function, aggregate demand, and aggregate supply. These, and others, are concepts we use in economics to describe how our economy works. Read carefully and keep track of each of these new key concepts, and, like Wayne, ask questions when you don't understand. You will be surprised at what you discover.

AGGREGATE DEMAND AND AGGREGATE SUPPLY

Every major league baseball manager knows that no matter how good the team is—even if it ends up winning the World Series year after year—it will go through periods of midyear slumps during which it seems conceivable that any Little League team could beat it. That's an exaggeration, of course, but the point is that for some inexplicable reason, the power hitters who earn $25 million a year couldn't get on base if their lives depended on it and the almost unbeatable pitchers whose sliders never fail to slide and whose fast balls register in the upper 90s become, all of a sudden, very beatable. Typically, managers don't worry too much. At least they try not to. For some other inexplicable reason, the groove comes back. While the team's wins percentage for

THIS CHAPTER INTRODUCES YOU TO THE ECONOMIC PRINCIPLES ASSOCIATED WITH:

- The phases of the business cycle
- Gross domestic product (GDP)
- The CPI and GDP deflator
- Nominal and real GDP
- Aggregate demand and aggregate supply
- Macroeconomic equilibrium
- Demand-pull and cost-push inflation

© Randy Faris/CORBIS

the season may top 60, it's typically a bumpy ride to the coveted championship.

Economies are like that too. A high-performing economy—think of our own—can achieve rates of economic growth for a series of years that are of championship quality. Sustaining, for example, a 4-plus annual rate of growth deserves not only self-applause among the economy's "players" but the respect and admiration from other economies on Earth. But then, for some inexplicable reason—we're still trying to figure it out—the economy dips into a slump that could last for several years. Do we worry? Of course! Because this kind of slump—a **recession**—is not a sporting event but real life, affecting millions of people who rely on the economy's buoyancy to generate life-giving employment, income, consumption, savings, and investment.

As in comedy, timing is crucial. Think of your own situation. You know the economy will perform beautifully in the long run, but suppose the labor market is in one of those nasty slumps when you graduate. Tough luck? Yes, indeed. But to you it's more than tough luck; it's your professional life. You're ready to get out there and do your thing, but you discover that there's no "there" out there. Why?

Economists are racking their brains—that's called economic research—trying to explain just why these things happen. There are a lot of "whys" to answer. We'll try to answer some. Why, for example, are some economies higher performers than others, and why do economies slip into those periodic slumps? That's what we're going to explore in this and the next 10 chapters.

Recession
A phase in the business cycle in which the decline in the economy's real GDP persists for at least a half-year. A recession is marked by relatively high unemployment.

WHY RECESSION? WHY PROSPERITY?

But why recession? Why do so many people who are willing and able to work lose their jobs? Why do people cut back their consumption? What triggers recession, and how does an economy climb out of the economic doldrums?

Depressed enough? Well, picture a different and much more pleasant scenario. Suppose you are working your regular shift at Ford and the plant manager asks you, almost begs you, to work overtime. Apparently, people are buying more automobiles than Ford and the other automakers had anticipated. You also learn that General Motors needs more workers and is offering wages that are higher than you are earning at Ford. You point this out to your plant manager, who immediately matches the General Motors offer. Under these circumstances, morale among management and labor at Ford is understandably high.

Depression
Severe recession.

But suppose that people are not only buying more automobiles, but also trying to buy more of everything. They are demanding more residential housing than is available on the market, so more electricians and carpenters are put to work. More people are flying, so more flight crews are operating. More people are crowding into department stores, as if every day were the day before Christmas. Everywhere in the economy, excess demand for goods and services drives prices up. Trying to take advantage of this robust nationwide consumer demand, producers look for more workers, even hiring workers away from each other. They don't mind paying higher wages under these circumstances.

Producing more is paramount. And suppose more goods and services are produced until all available resources—land, labor, and capital—are fully employed. What happens if the unrelenting demand for goods and services in the now fully employed economy continues? Prices would rise like a hot-air balloon!

Economists define such a period of economic activity as **prosperity**—an economic boom. And an overall increase in prices is called **inflation**.

But why prosperity and inflation? Why do people try to consume more goods and services than producers have planned to produce? Why can people, without much hustle at all, find almost any kind of job at good wages? Sound attractive? Alas, prosperity, like recession, never lasts.

The Business Cycle

Historical experience shows that our economy roller-coasters from periods of prosperity and inflation to periods of recession; then, recovering from recession, it heads back again to prosperity and inflation. Economists describe this roller-coaster pattern of economic activity as the **business cycle**. Exhibit 1 depicts the course an economy takes through such a cycle.

The vertical axis records the economy's production of goods and services, that is, the economy's output. The horizontal axis records time, measured in years.

The first phase of the cycle depicted in Exhibit 1 is recession, that time period when the economy's unemployment rate is greatest and output declines to the cycle's minimum level (or **trough**). The **recovery** phase follows recession. During a recovery, output increases, unemployment decreases, and pressure on the economy's price level begins to build. In time, recovery evolves into the prosperity phase, where output reaches its maximum level (or **peak**), the labor force is fully employed, and increasing pressure on prices is likely to generate inflation. Unable to sustain prosperity, the economy enters its **downturn** phase. Output falls, unemployment once again reappears, and inflation tends to moderate as the downturn becomes recession. The business cycle has run its course and the cyclical process repeats, although no two business cycles are identical. The number of months in any given phase of the cycle, as well as the output levels of peaks and troughs, varies from cycle to cycle.

Prosperity
A phase in the business cycle marked by a relatively high level of real GDP, full employment, and inflation.

Inflation
An increase in the price level.

Business cycle
Alternating periods of growth and decline in an economy's GDP.

Trough
The bottom of a business cycle.

Recovery
A phase in the business cycle, following a recession, in which real GDP increases and unemployment declines.

Peak
The top of a business cycle.

Downturn
A phase in the business cycle in which real GDP declines, inflation moderates, and unemployment emerges.

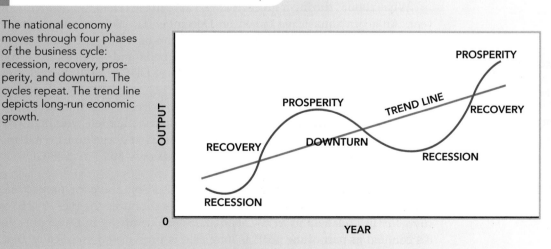

EXHIBIT 1 The Business Cycle

The national economy moves through four phases of the business cycle: recession, recovery, prosperity, and downturn. The cycles repeat. The trend line depicts long-run economic growth.

Economic Growth

Note the upward-sloping trend line cutting through the cycle. It traces the economy's output performance over the course of a business cycle, measured either from recession to recession or from prosperity to prosperity. The upward-sloping character of the trend line signifies economic growth. It shows that the economy's output—production of goods and services—increases, cycle after cycle. The steeper the trend line, the higher the economy's rate of growth. When no growth occurs, the trend line is horizontal.

What causes economic growth? What factors contribute to the increase in the production of goods and services cycle after cycle? Addressing this question (along with questions concerning the economy's cyclical behavior) is what the study of macroeconomics is about.

Understanding why cycles and growth occur is important not just to macroeconomists who study them, but to you and everyone like you who hopes to work for and achieve a growing and reasonable standard of living. Can we harness the disturbing swings in our business cycles? That is to say, can we moderate the inflationary pressures on the economy when it is on the upswing of the business cycle, pressing upon full employment? Can we moderate the inevitable unemployment that occurs when the economy, after reaching its peak, begins its slide into recession? Can we also learn how to engineer an attractive rate of economic growth?

MEASURING THE NATIONAL ECONOMY

Let's look into these questions. Where do we begin? Perhaps the first thing we ought to do is define precisely what we mean by the economy's output and compare the different ways we go about measuring it.

The definition is simple enough: The economy's output, or **gross domestic product (GDP)**, is the *total value, measured in current market prices, of all final goods and services produced in the economy during a given year.*

Let's analyze this definition phrase by phrase. Consider first "final goods and services." This refers to everything produced—from acorn squash to Ziploc bags—that is not itself used to produce other goods. For example, if we produce and eat an acorn squash, it's a final good and counted in GDP. But if we use the acorn squash to make an acorn squash pie, then it's the pie that's counted in GDP, not the acorn squash. After all, we don't want to count the acorn squash twice! The pie is the *final* good, not the acorn squash.

What about "during a given year"? This phrase refers to a specific calendar year. An acorn squash pie baked on December 31, 2007, is counted as part of 2007 GDP. An acorn squash pie produced the next day is counted as part of 2008 GDP. If more pies, along with other goods and services, are produced in 2008 than were produced in 2007, the rate of GDP growth in 2008 is greater than zero.

What about "measured in current market prices"? This phrase refers to the pie's price in the year it was made. If your grandmother tells you that when she was a young lass, acorn squash pies sold for $0.25, it doesn't mean that an acorn squash pie baked in 2008 and priced at $7 adds only $0.25 to 2008 GDP! It's the $7—the current market price—that counts.

What about "produced in the economy"? That's the *domestic* part of gross domestic product. It makes no difference who produces the pie—a U.S.-owned company in Philadelphia or a Canadian-owned company in Davenport, Iowa—it's counted as part of the GDP as long as it is produced domestically, that is, in the United States. On the other hand, a pie made by a U.S.-owned company in

check your understanding

What does macroeconomics attempt to explain?

Gross domestic product (GDP)
Total value of all final goods and services, measured in current market prices, produced in the economy during a year.

on the net

For the latest measure of GDP, visit the Economic Statistics Briefing Room (http://www.whitehouse.gov/fsbr/esbr.html) and the Bureau of Economic Analysis (http://www.bea.gov/).

interdisciplinary perspective

THE PHENOMENON OF CYCLICAL ACTIVITY

© Jeff Vanuga/CORBIS

Again, and again, and again, and . . .

Cyclical activity—the occurrence of recurring events—is an integral part of our world. Things happen, happen again, and happen once again, sometimes with uncanny regularity. At the heart of this cyclical experience are the earth's precise and rhythmic movements. These create our alternating days and nights, our seasons, and the multiplicity of natural occasions, such as ocean tides and spectacular geysers with their mighty rhythmic upheavals—the kind we delight in visiting at our national parks.*

Meteorologists describe the phenomenon of climatic cycles—the skyward rise of earth-warmed air to form rain clouds that subsequently burst upon earth as rain and rise again to re-create the clouds. These climatic cycles nourish and replenish life.

Our biological world is rhythmic and cyclical as well. The seasonal migrations of large animals, birds, and butterflies are never-ending. Observable recurring patterns of activity (and inactivity) are commonplace in the animal kingdom. In winter, bears retreat into a state of hibernation, then reemerge to activity in early spring, year in and year out. Salmon, born in spawning pools, make their way downstream to the ocean, where they live their adult life in the open water and return to complete their life cycle in the very pools in which they were spawned. Even human physiology is replete with rhythms and cycles, and psychologists report the cyclical nature of our moods and behavior.

This phenomenon of cyclical activity is found in the world of economics as well. Economists identify four sequential and recurring phases of economic activity: prosperity, downturn, recession, and recovery. These repeating phases describe the business cycle.

MORE ON THE NET

Find out more about Yellowstone's many geysers by visiting **www.yellowstone.net/geyser**.

* The water at the geyser Old Faithful in Yellowstone National Park is 350 degrees Fahrenheit and is thrust approximately 60 feet into the air for about three or four minutes. It repeats every 35 to 120 minutes, day and night, year after year. Barometric pressure, the moon, the tides, and the earth's tectonic stresses determine the height of the geyser and the time between eruptions.

Halifax, Nova Scotia, is not counted as part of U.S. gross domestic product. It's counted in Canada's gross domestic product.

Suppose the 2008 GDP in the United States adds up to twice the GDP that was produced in 1998. Does this doubling of GDP over a decade indicate that we really doubled our production of goods and services?

Not necessarily. Over time, prices may have drifted upward. That is, it may have been the *prices* of pies and other goods and services, not necessarily the *number* of pies and other goods and services produced, that have increased. Since GDP for any year measures the value—in *current* market prices—of that year's production of final goods and services, price changes alone might have changed the size of GDP over time.

Consider this simple example. Imagine an economy where the only good produced is corn. If total production in 1998 was 100 bushels, and if the 1998 price of corn was $2 per bushel, then GDP in 1998 would be $200.

Now suppose, for some reason, the price of corn a decade later doubled to $4 per bushel, while production remained at 100 bushels. The 2008 GDP, measuring all final goods and services at 2008 market prices, would increase to $400. Even though *real* production in the economy remained unchanged—100 bushels is still 100 bushels—the economy's GDP doubled. Under these conditions, would it make any sense to describe the 2008 economy as being twice as large as the 1998 economy? Not really. After all, eating $4 corn is no more satisfying than eating

check your understanding

Does a $100 increase in GDP indicate a $100 increase in goods and services?

$2 corn. And even though a $400 GDP is twice the $200 GDP, people are still eating only 100 bushels of corn.

Adjusting for Prices

If we want to use GDP as a reliable measure of how well an economy performs—in producing goods and services over time—we must devise some way of eliminating the effect of price changes. To compare GDP in different years, we want to remove the effect of inflation. Economists have created a number of price indexes to do just that. The indexes transform **nominal GDP**—GDP unadjusted for price changes—into **real GDP**—GDP adjusted for price changes. The consumer price index and the GDP deflator are the two indexes most used. How do they work?

The Consumer Price Index (CPI) Let's start with the **consumer price index (CPI)**. Pick a year—any year will do—as a point of reference, or **base year**. Let's pick 2000. Suppose in 2000 we shopped for a basket of goods and services that represented what a typical consumer in an urban household buys. The items we put in the basket probably wouldn't include caviar or yachts but would include clothing, food, fuel, and a variety of household goods and services, such as kitchen appliances, transportation, and health care. Suppose that when we took that basket to the cash register, it cost $350. Using 2000 as our base year, the $350 converts to a price level index of 100.

Now suppose in the following year, 2001, we purchase the same basket of consumer items, and their cost again sums to $350. Some prices may have risen, but just enough to offset those that declined. The 2001 consumer price index, then, is 100.

An unchanging **price level** is a rarity. Let's suppose, instead, that the basket purchased in 2001 adds up to $385. That is, the items in the basket remain unchanged, but the total cost of the items increased by $35. The 2001 CPI, measured against the 2000 base year of 100, is now 110 ($385/$350 × 100). What does a 2001 price level of 110 indicate? It shows that from 2000 to 2001, the cost of the goods and services that consumers typically buy increased by 10 percent.

The CPI for any year is constructed by calculating the ratio between the cost of the basket for that year and its cost in the base year. We can shop for the same basket in 2008, calculate its cost, and draw the comparison to the 2000 cost to derive the 2008 CPI. Or we can go back to 1952, calculate the basket's cost in 1952 prices, then compare it to the 2000 cost to derive the 1952 CPI.

The usefulness of such comparisons, however, diminishes the more distant a year is from the base year. Why? First, new goods and services appear on the market every year. Over time, the consumer basket of a base year becomes increasingly less representative of the things consumers buy. For example, if we used a 1952 base year, we could not have included personal computers, CDs, or DVD players, which are typical consumer purchases today. Second, the quality of the items in the basket changes as well. The automobile in a 1952 basket is not the same as the automobile we drive today. Power steering, power brakes, seat belts, radial tires, and air bags make price comparisons between the two less meaningful. Third, the importance of specific items in the basket changes over time. Food purchases may have accounted for 40 percent of the consumer basket in 1952 but only 25 percent in 2000. If food prices increase more rapidly than other prices in 2000 and if we still count their importance at 40 percent of the basket, then the influence of food prices in 2000 is exaggerated.

That is why the Bureau of Labor Statistics (BLS) of the U.S. Department of Labor, which is charged with the task of composing the CPI, periodically updates

---

Nominal GDP
GDP measured in terms of current market prices—that is, the price level at the time of measurement. (It is not adjusted for inflation.)

Real GDP
GDP adjusted for changes in the price level.

Consumer price index (CPI)
A measure comparing the prices of consumer goods and services that a household typically purchases to the prices of those goods and services purchased in a base year.

Base year
The reference year with which prices in other years are compared in a price index.

Price level
A measure of prices in one year expressed in relation to prices in a base year.

on the net
The Bureau of Labor Statistics publishes the latest consumer price index measurements (http://www.bls.gov/cpi/). The Federal Reserve Bank of Minneapolis publishes historical CPI measurements, with corresponding inflation rates (www.minneapolisfed.org/community_education/teacher/calc/hist1913.cfm).

applied perspective

WHAT'S IN THE 2008 CPI BASKET?

As you know, the consumer price index (CPI) is a measure of the average change over time in the prices paid by urban consumers for a fixed market basket of consumer goods and services. Sounds simple enough, but how do we know what to put in that basket and what prices to use?

Here's how it's done. The basket is derived from detailed information provided by about 7,000 families who are interviewed quarterly by the BLS (Bureau of Labor Statistics). A second source of information is drawn from another 5,000 families who keep diaries listing everything bought during a two-week period. Altogether, about 36,000 individuals and families contribute information to determine what items are bought and the relative importance of each to the basket.

The result is that the thousands of goods and services purchased are classified into 200 categories and these are put into eight major groups, with percentage weights—derived from the data—attached to each. For example, in 2005 the groups were as follows: (1) housing (such as rent of primary residence, owners' equivalent rent, fuel oil, bedroom furniture), weighted at 42.4 percent of the basket; (2) transportation (such as new vehicles, airline fares, gasoline, motor vehicle insurance), weighted at 17.7 percent; (3) food and beverages (such as breakfast cereal, milk, coffee, chicken, wine, full-service meals, snacks), weighted at 14.9 percent; (4) recreation (such as televisions, cable television, pets and pet products, sports equipment, admissions), weighted at 5.6 percent; (5) medical care (such as prescription drugs and medical supplies, physicians' services, eyeglasses and eye care, hospital services), weighted at 6.2 percent; (6) education and communication (such as college tuition, postage, telephone services, computer software and accessories), weighted at 6.0 percent; (7) apparel (such as men's shirts and sweaters, women's dresses, jewelry),

It's everybody's basket.

weighted at 3.7 percent; and (8) other goods and services (such as tobacco and smoking products, haircuts and other personal services, funeral expenses), weighted at 3.3 percent.

How do economists determine the "right" price? Each month, BLS data collectors visit or call thousands of retail stores, service establishments, rental units, and doctors' offices to obtain price information on the 80,000 items used to track and measure price changes. If the item is no longer in use—for example, quart-size glass milk bottles—or there's been a quality change in any usable item, adjustment is made to prevent the change from distorting the CPI measure.

Picking the "right" item is no easy task either. Consider milk. If the BLS selects the specific kind of fresh whole milk that will be priced over time, each kind of whole milk is assigned a probability of selection based on the quantity sold. If vitamin D, homogenized milk in half-gallon containers makes up 70 percent of the sales of whole milk, and the same milk in quart containers accounts for 10 percent of all whole milk sales, then the half-gallon container will be seven times as likely to be chosen as the quart container.

This painstaking method of selection of item and price is absolutely essential if the CPI is to be regarded as a reliable measure. Want a job?

MORE ON THE NET

To look up details on the most recent Consumer Price Indexes, visit the government's CPI site at http:// www.bls.gov/cpi/home.htm#data.

the base year. When it does so, it also revises the specific items and their importance in the consumer basket.

The GDP Deflator The CPI measures the prices of consumer items only. There are other price indexes that include different sets of items. For example, price indexes are constructed for farm goods, producer goods, crude materials, services, capital equipment, and export goods.

The most inclusive of all price indexes is the **GDP deflator**. It contains not only the prices of consumer goods and services, but also the prices of producer goods, investment goods, and exports and imports, as well as goods and services purchased by government. It is the price index generally used to differentiate nominal GDP and real GDP.

GDP deflator
A measure comparing the prices of all goods and services produced in the economy during a given year to the prices of those goods and services purchased in a base year.

From Nominal to Real GDP

The GDP deflator converts nominal GDP, measured in current prices for any year, to real GDP, which is adjusted for price changes. Economists refer to real GDP as GDP expressed in constant dollars.

The conversion formula is

$$\text{real GDP} = \frac{\text{nominal GDP} \times 100}{\text{GDP deflator}}$$

Let's see how it works. Exhibit 2 traces the conversion of nominal GDP into real GDP for the period 2000–2008.

Using 2000 as the base year, 2000 nominal and real GDP are identical. But look at 2001. Nominal GDP increased from $9,817 billion in 2000 to $10,128 billion in 2001, or by $311 billion. Not all of that $311 billion represented an increase in real production of goods and services. Part of it simply reflected the higher prices in 2001. But how much of it?

In 2001, the GDP deflator was 102.4. The formula to convert 2001 nominal GDP to real GDP—measuring 2001 GDP in 2000 prices—is

$$\frac{\$10,128 \times 100}{102.4} = \$9,890.7$$

We can now calculate how much of that $311 billion increase in 2001 GDP represented more real goods and services, and how much simply reflected an increase in prices. The increase attributed to prices alone was $10,128 − $9,890.7, or $237.3 billion. The remaining $73.7 billion represented more real goods and services.

If you were describing the 2000–2001 change in GDP to a friend, which number would you use? Would you say that GDP increased from $9,817 billion to $10,128 billion, or would you choose to compare the $9,817 billion to the $9,890.7 billion? Both are honest-to-goodness changes in GDP. They just represent different evaluations. One set includes changes in both production and prices; the other includes just changes in production. If what you mean to convey to your friend is how much better off people were in 2001 than in 2000, wouldn't changes in real GDP be the appropriate one to use?

Look at Exhibit 2. Again, differences between nominal and real GDP growth rates are rather striking. If we calculate the economy's 2000–2008 performance

EXHIBIT 2   Converting Nominal GDP to Real GDP, 2000–2008
($ billions, 2000 = 100)

	NOMINAL GDP	GDP DEFLATOR	REAL GDP
2000	$ 9,817.0	100.0	$ 9,817.0
2001	10,128.0	102.4	9,890.7
2002	10,469.6	104.2	10,048.8
2003	10,971.2	106.3	10,320.6
2004	11,734.3	109.1	10,755.7
2005	12,479.4	112.1	11,131.1
2006	13,194.7	116.6	11,319.4
2007	13,841.3	121.4	11,566.8
2008	14,201.1	121.4	11,703.6

Source: Survey of Current Business, U.S. Department of Commerce, Washington, D.C., July, 2008.

in nominal GDP, the economy's annual growth rate was 4.7 percent. But if the calculation is made for real GDP, the growth rate was 2.2 percent. Which GDP we choose to express, then, makes a difference.

DERIVING EQUILIBRIUM GDP IN THE AGGREGATE DEMAND AND SUPPLY MODEL

Understanding the difference between nominal and real GDP for 2001 still doesn't tell us why 2001 GDP ended up being what it was. Why was 2001 nominal GDP $10,128.0 billion? Why not $10,000 billion or $7,000 billion? What determines its size?

Several competing theories explain how the equilibrium levels of GDP are derived. We will examine some in detail in later chapters. For now, we focus on one—the aggregate demand and aggregate supply model—to explain how GDP is determined.

The aggregate demand and aggregate supply model is a good place to start. It bears some similarity to the demand and supply model we used to explain equilibrium price and quantity of goods and services. In the case of fish, we saw how the downward-sloping demand curve for fish intersected the upward-sloping supply curve of fish to determine its price and quantity. In what appears to be an analogy, the downward-sloping aggregate demand curve intersects the upward-sloping aggregate supply curve to determine the economy's price level and GDP.

But there the similarity ends. The factors that cause the demand curves in both models to slope downward are quite different. The factors explaining why the supply curves in both models are upward-sloping are different as well.

The demand curve for fish slopes downward because a decrease in the price of fish occurs while all other prices remain unchanged. Fish, then, becomes *relatively* cheaper. As a result, people increase the quantity demanded of fish.

This cause-and-effect analysis cannot explain why the aggregate demand curve slopes downward. After all, the price level reflects all prices, so when it falls, *all* prices are assumed to fall. As a result, the relative prices of fish and everything else remain unchanged. If people demand more of everything, it cannot be because everything becomes relatively cheaper.

What are the forces governing the aggregate demand and supply model? **Aggregate supply** is the total supply of goods and services that all firms in the national economy are willing to offer at varying price levels. **Aggregate demand** is the total quantity demanded of these goods and services by households, firms, foreigners, and government at those varying price levels.

Panel *a* in Exhibit 3 shows the relationship between aggregate supply and the price level. Panel *b* in Exhibit 3 shows the relationship between aggregate demand and the price level.

Explaining Aggregate Supply

Look at the economy's aggregate supply curve in panel *a*. Three distinct segments are apparent. The horizontal segment shows that real GDP can increase up to point *a* without affecting the economy's price level. The upward-sloping segment of the supply curve depicts, from point *a* to point *b*, a positive relationship between real GDP and the price level. The vertical segment marks the full-employment level of real GDP. All resources are fully employed, so that real GDP cannot increase.

The Horizontal Segment
Why the horizontal segment? For any level of GDP in this range—that is, far below full employment—there are ready supplies

Aggregate supply
The total quantity of goods and services that firms in the economy are willing to supply at varying price levels.

Aggregate demand
The total quantity of goods and services demanded by households, firms, foreigners, and government at varying price levels.

EXHIBIT 3   Aggregate Supply and Aggregate Demand

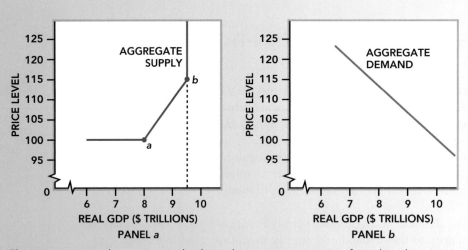

The aggregate supply curve in panel a shows the aggregate quantity of goods and services that firms are willing to supply at varying price levels. For levels of real GDP within the range $0 to $8 trillion, the price level remains unchanged at 100. Beyond $8 trillion, increases in real GDP are accompanied by rising price levels. At real GDP = $9 trillion, P = 110. Full-employment real GDP is $9.5 trillion. The aggregate supply curve becomes vertical at that point. An increase in the price level beyond P = 115 is not accompanied by increases in real GDP.

The downward-sloping aggregate demand curve in panel b shows the aggregate quantity demanded at varying price levels. For example, an increase in the price level from P = 100 to P = 110 is accompanied by a decrease in the aggregate quantity demanded, from $10 trillion to $8.5 trillion.

check your understanding

Why would an increase in real GDP, within some output range, cause the price level to increase?

check your understanding

Why would an increase in the price level, in some instances, lead to an increase in real GDP?

of unused resources. All these idle resources can be put to work before there is any upward pressure on prices. For example, the economy can increase aggregate supply—the production of goods and services—say, from $5 trillion to $6 trillion GDP, without prices going up. Producers can hire more workers without having to raise the wage rate. They can use more capital without having to pay higher interest rates because unused capital in the form of unused plants and machinery is already available. As you see in panel a, any increase in real GDP within the range $0 to $8 trillion can occur with the price level remaining unchanged at 100.

The Upward-Sloping Segment What about aggregate supply beyond $8 trillion? It becomes upward sloping. Increases in output are linked to increases in the price level. Why? Because unused resources become less available at higher levels of real GDP. Faced with the difficulty of finding ready resources, firms resort to offering higher prices for them. For example, to get more labor, firms are willing to pay higher wages. These higher wages increase the cost of production, which in turn raises the prices of goods produced. Beyond $8 trillion GDP, the price level begins to rise above P = 100. The higher the level of GDP—say, $8.5 trillion—the greater is the economy's absorption of the dwindling unused resources, and the more intense the upward pressure on the price level. At a GDP of $9 trillion, the price level is 110.

The upward-sloping relationship between aggregate supply and the price level can be explained in another way. Instead of dwindling unused resources pushing up prices, increasing prices can pull up resource costs. Suppose the price level increases from 110 to 115. As the spread between prices and costs widens, producers earn higher profits. Higher profits attract new firms into production and stimulate existing firms to produce more. The higher production levels tap into unused resource availability, driving resource costs upward.

The Vertical Segment When resources are fully employed, aggregate supply reaches an impassable limit. Full employment is shown in panel *a* of Exhibit 3 at $9.5 trillion GDP. At that level of real GDP, producers may try to hire more workers, but how can they? They can bid away *already* employed workers from each other by offering higher wage rates. But what one producer gains in output by hiring a worker away from another, the other loses. In the end, competition among producers for already employed resources can succeed only in raising the economy's price level. Its aggregate supply remains unchanged. In our example, real GDP stays constant at $9.5 trillion.

Explaining Aggregate Demand

The aggregate demand curve shown in panel *b* is downward sloping. For example, as the price level increases from 100 to 110, aggregate demand of households, firms, foreigners, and government falls from $10 trillion to $8.5 trillion. Why? Because increases in the price level affect people's real wealth, their lending and borrowing activity, and the nation's trade with other nations in such a way that the demand for goods and services produced in the economy declines.

The Real Wealth Effect Consider the effect of a price level increase on the value of people's wealth, and the effect of changes in the value of wealth on aggregate demand. Suppose your own wealth consisted of $100,000 held in the form of cash, bank deposits, and government bonds. You know that, if needed, these holdings can be cashed in, allowing you to buy $100,000 of real goods and services. In fact, that is how you view your wealth: as things it can buy for you.

But suppose while you are holding these financial assets, the economy's price level increases. MP3 players that formerly cost $400 now cost $480. Automobiles that formerly cost $16,000 now cost $18,500. With prices rising everywhere, what happens to the real worth of your $100,000? It can no longer buy the same quantity of goods and services, can it?

That is, the *real* value of your $100,000 wealth decreases. You feel yourself becoming less wealthy. And you're not mistaken! To replenish the value of your real wealth, you would save more and consume less. In other words, when the price level increases, the quantity demanded by most people for goods and services in the economy falls.

The Interest Rate Effect Consider the effect of a higher interest rate on aggregate demand. Few people buy homes with cash. Typically, high-priced items such as homes and automobiles are purchased with borrowed money.

Suppose mortgage rates increase from 10 percent to 15 percent per year. Monthly payments on a home with a $100,000 mortgage, carrying a 20-year loan at 10 percent, are $965.03. At 15 percent, these monthly payments jump to $1,316.79. Wouldn't that difference cut many prospective home buyers out of the market?

Students, too, feel the pinch of higher interest rates. Wouldn't the number of students attending college be affected by higher interest rates on student loans? Even the quantities demanded of restaurant lunches, concert tickets, and designer jeans are linked to the interest rate. Many pay for these items with Visa, MasterCard, or Discover cards. These plastic cards allow people to build up interest-carrying debt. If interest rates on these cards rise, people tend to cut back

on the net

For current wealth and income data, visit the Economic Statistic Briefing Room (http://www.whitehouse.gov/fsbr/income. html) and the Bureau of Economic Analysis (http://www.bea.gov/).

check your understanding

What happens to the value of your wealth when the price level increases?

on the net

The Federal Reserve Board publishes current and historical data on interest rates (http://www.federalreserve.gov/releases/).

global perspective

ECONOMIC SUCCESS? DEPENDS ON WHAT YOU MEASURE

If you want to make the case that Mexico's 1996–2002 economic performance was impressive, just point to the graph depicting the 16-percent-per-year rate of growth of its nominal GDP. But be careful. Why? Because if it's really economic performance you want to measure, the 16 percent rate may be illusory. If you distill out price increases, the rate of Mexico's real GDP growth falls to 3.7 percent! That's the striking difference between nominal and real GDP.

For the six economies depicted in the accompanying graphs, nominal GDP growth over the period 1996–2002 is considerably higher than real GDP growth, indicating—as we always knew—that there's some price bloating embedded in the nominal data. How far nominal GDP diverges from real GDP in each case depends not only on relative price increases, but also on the time lapse between the current and base years. Look at Norway. In 1996, its nominal GDP was only slightly higher than its GDP largely because the base year used was 1995. By 2002, however, the spread between the two GDP measures increased substantially. Norway's 1,521 billion kroner nominal GDP was now over 30 percent higher than its 1,151 billion kroner real GDP. If an earlier base year had been used, such as 1980 = 100, the spread between real and nominal GDP would have been considerably greater. The higher the rate of inflation, the more notable is the difference. Compare the difference between Mexico's nominal and real GDP for 1996, just one year removed from the base year, and its 2002 values. The difference is striking.

Some things are illusionary.

....

MORE ON THE NET

Visit the Organisation for Economic Co-operation and Development (OECD) (http://www.oecd.org/home/) and the *World Factbook* (http://www.odci.gov/cia/publications/factbook/), which both publish macroeconomic data on nations around the world.

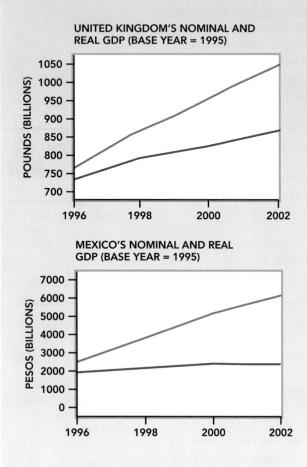

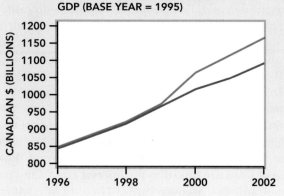

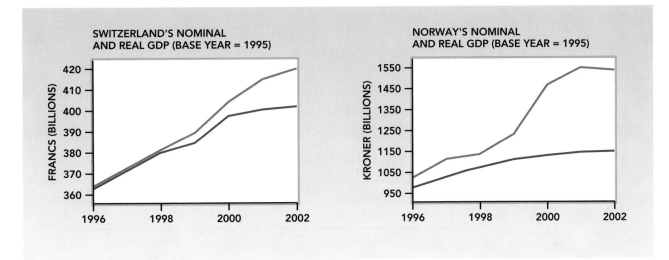

on these purchases, depressing the aggregate quantity of goods and services demanded.

Firms' demands for investment goods are sensitive to the interest rate as well. A firm contemplating an investment in new machinery may calculate making 15 percent profit on the investment. If the interest rate is 10 percent, the 5 percent spread between profit and the interest rate may be sufficient inducement to buy the new machinery. If the interest rate rises to 15 percent, the firm's demand for the new machinery disappears along with the spread, contributing to the decrease in quantity demanded.

The International Trade Effect Suppose the price level in the United States rises while price levels elsewhere in the world remain unchanged. Wouldn't we tend to buy more foreign goods and reduce the demands for our own goods? After all, if prices for domestically produced goods such as wines, lumber, and automobiles increased while other nations' prices remained unchanged, wouldn't French wines, Canadian lumber, and Japanese automobiles become more attractive? Our demand for imports would rise, and our demand for domestic goods would fall.

At the same time, the French, Canadians, and Japanese would find our now higher-priced exports less attractive. Many wouldn't buy them. The quantity demanded of our goods and services, then, would fall.

For current international trade data, visit the Economic Statistics Briefing Room (http://www. whitehouse.gov/fsbr/ international.html) and the Census Bureau (http:// www.census.gov/ftp/ pub/indicator/www/ ustrade.html).

Shifts in the Aggregate Demand and Aggregate Supply Curves

Let's again consider the analogy between the demand and supply model used to explain equilibrium price and quantity of fish that we developed in Chapter 3 and the model of aggregate demand and aggregate supply that we are using to explain equilibrium GDP and price level. In Chapter 3, we distinguished between *changes in quantity demanded* (or *quantity supplied*) of fish—that is, changes along the demand (or supply) curve—and *changes in demand* (or *supply*) of fish—that is, shifts in the demand (or supply) curve.

Let's now draw that same distinction for changes in the aggregate quantity demanded (or supplied) and shifts in the aggregate demand (or aggregate supply) curve.

EXHIBIT 4   Shifts in Aggregate Demand and Aggregate Supply

The aggregate demand curve in panel *a* shifts with changes in government spending, foreign incomes, and consumer or firms' expectations about the future. The aggregate demand curve increases— shifts to the right—when government spending, incomes, and expectations rise. It decreases—shifts to the left—when they fall.

The aggregate supply curve in panel *b* shifts with changes in the availability of resources. More resources shift the aggregate supply curve to the right.

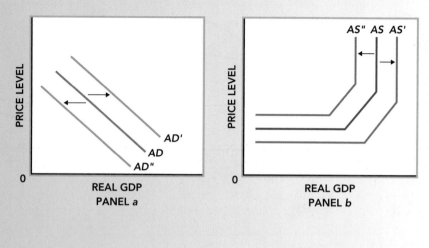

Shifts in the Aggregate Demand Curve
The aggregate demand curve relates the quantity of goods and services demanded in the economy to varying price levels. A change in the quantity of goods and services demanded at a particular price level, however, is represented by a shift in the curve itself. Exhibit 4, panel *a*, maps two shifts in aggregate demand. What could cause such shifts to occur?

Suppose the government decides to overhaul our economy's infrastructure. It initiates programs for major construction on highways, bridges, railroad lines, airports, research hospitals, public housing, and other facilities that are in the public domain. These programs represent new investment demands that shift the aggregate demand curve to the right, from *AD* to *AD'*.

Or consider what would happen to aggregate demand when incomes abroad increase. Canadians, with higher incomes, buy more U.S. imports, shifting our *AD* curve to the right. If we decide to consume more goods and services ourselves—even when prices remain unchanged—aggregate demand increases.

What would cause a change in our consumption behavior? A tax cut could do it, or perhaps changes in our expectations of future income. After all, if we expect to have more money in the future, we may feel more comfortable about buying more today by borrowing more or saving less.

Just reverse the direction of change in these factors, and the aggregate demand curve shifts to the left, from *AD* to *AD"*. For example, a cut in government spending, a decrease in income abroad, an increase in taxes, or an expectation that future income will fall would all tend to lower aggregate quantity demanded at every price level.

check your understanding

What would shift the aggregate supply curve to the right?

Shifts in the Aggregate Supply Curve
One of the principal factors accounting for a shift in the aggregate supply curve from *AS* to *AS'* in panel *b* is an increase in resource availability. Simply put: More workers, more land, more capital, and more entrepreneurial energies—no matter what the price level—result in greater aggregate supply. The prices of these resources affect aggregate supply

as well. If wage rates or interest rates or rents decrease while the economy's price level remains unchanged, profit margins will expand, making producers more willing to supply greater quantities of goods and services.

Anything that reduces resource availability or increases the prices of resources would, of course, have the opposite effect; that is, it would shift the aggregate supply curve from *AS* to *AS"*.

MACROECONOMIC EQUILIBRIUM

Let's bring both aggregate demand and aggregate supply together in a national market for goods and services. This is done in Exhibit 5.

Does it look familiar? As with all markets, Exhibit 5 expresses a relationship between price and quantity. The vertical axis measures the economy's price level. The horizontal axis measures real GDP.

We can now explain—at least according to the aggregate demand and aggregate supply model—why 1997 real GDP was $8,159.5 billion. The quantity of aggregate demand equaled the quantity of aggregate supply at $8,159.5 billion real GDP. The equilibrium price level was 101.95. This **macroequilibrium** position for 1997 persisted only as long as the aggregate demand and aggregate supply curves remained unchanged.

To illustrate why the economy gravitates toward an equilibrium of $8,159.5 billion real GDP and a price level of 101.95, let's suppose the economy was not in equilibrium. Instead, suppose the price level was 110. What happens? With that price level, consumers, firms, government, and foreigners demand fewer goods and services. We see in Exhibit 5 that at a price level of 110, the aggregate quantity demanded falls to $5,000 billion.

What about aggregate supply? How would firms react to the higher price level? At a price level of 110, they are willing to produce more GDP. The aggregate quantity of GDP that firms are willing to supply increases to $9,000 billion.

A problem now emerges. At a price level of 110, the aggregate quantity demanded is insufficient to absorb the aggregate quantity supplied, generating an excess aggregate supply of $9,000 − $5,000 = $4,000 billion GDP. Competition among suppliers will force overall prices downward. That is, given the aggregate demand and aggregate supply curves in Exhibit 5, the economy is unable to sustain a price level of 110.

Macroequilibrium
The level of real GDP and the price level that equate the aggregate quantity demanded and the aggregate quantity supplied.

KEY **EXHIBIT 5**   Achieving Macroeconomic Equilibrium

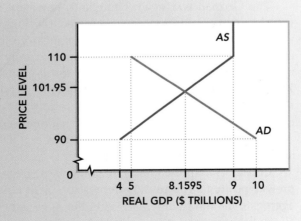

Macroequilibrium is achieved when aggregate supply, *AS*, and aggregate demand, *AD*, intersect at real GDP = $8,159.5 billion and *P* = 101.95. At higher price levels, such as *P* = 110, excess aggregate quantity supplied would emerge, depressing the price level. At lower price levels, excess aggregate quantity demanded would emerge, forcing the price level to increase.

Now suppose the price level is 90. What happens? The aggregate quantity demanded is $9,000 billion and the aggregate quantity of GDP that firms are willing to supply is $4,000 billion. Competition among the demanders—consumers, firms, government, and foreigners—now forces the price level upward.

Where do the price level and GDP come to rest? The aggregate quantity demanded and aggregate quantity supplied equate at $8,159.5 billion GDP and a price level of 101.95. Macroequilibrium is achieved.

TIME LINE ON INFLATION AND UNEMPLOYMENT: 1930–2008

Macroeconomists use this simple aggregate demand and supply model of GDP and price level to show how an economy can move from stable to rising price levels, and from unemployment to full employment. For example, it gives us some understanding of the economic forces that were at work during the depression of the 1930s, during the war-related recovery of the 1940s, during the Vietnam-induced inflation of the 1960s, during the OPEC-induced inflation of the 1970s and early 1980s, during the recession and economic stagnation of the early 1990s, during the 1992–2000 boom and the 2001–2002 recession that followed, and finally, the downturn into recession for the years 2007 and 2008. That's an awful lot of ups and downs—and there's more to come.

The Depression of the 1930s

The 1930s produced one of the poorest GDP performance records in our economic history. For most of the decade, real GDP was either falling or recovering slightly, only to fall once again. It fell by 30 percent in the first four years of the decade, recovered to its 1929 level by 1937, but fell again in 1939. Nobody had any reason to feel optimistic about the future. Unemployment was massive. It rose from 3.2 percent in 1929 to a peak of 25.2 percent in 1933. It fell to 14.3 percent by 1937, only to climb back to 19.1 percent in 1938. How would you have felt about our economic future on New Year's Day 1939?

World War II: Recovery and Much More

By December 1939, however, the fate of the world had changed. Germany invaded Poland in September, bringing Europe to war. Moving swiftly westward, German forces took Holland and Belgium, then overtook an ill-prepared France. Paris fell without a single shot fired.

The German war against England, however, was another matter. German warplanes, in unending waves, crossed the English Channel during the cold winter of 1940 to strike at England's aircraft factories on its eastern coast. English cities, including London, absorbed almost daily bombings. England's prime minister, Winston Churchill, appealed to the United States for material support. We obliged with what he was later to describe as the most generous response any nation afforded another in recorded history. These events of 1939 and 1940 changed the pace and direction of our national economy significantly.

Exhibit 6, panel *a*, illustrates the impact on GDP of the 1930s depression and of our later wartime commitment.

Consider, first, the effects of a shift in aggregate demand on the economy's prewar position. The prewar depression GDP equilibrium is shown where the aggregate demand curve, *AD*, cuts the aggregate supply curve, *AS*, at point *a* along its horizontal range. With double-digit unemployment and substantial

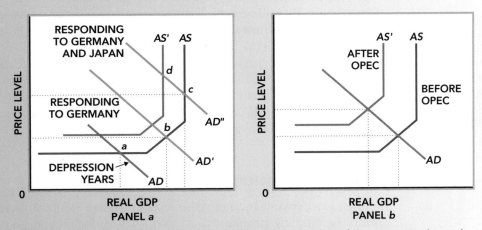

EXHIBIT 6   Aggregate Demand and Aggregate Supply During the Depression and War Period and the Oil Price Increases

The 1930s depression GDP equilibrium occurred at the intersection of the aggregate demand curve, AD, and the aggregate supply curve, AS, in panel a. The demand created by the war in Europe shifted the aggregate demand curve from AD to AD', creating a new macroequilibrium at a higher level of GDP. The extension of the war to the Pacific shifted the aggregate demand curve even further to the right, to AD", creating a new macroequilibrium at a much higher price level.

The transfer of men and women out of civilian employment into the armed forces shifted the aggregate supply curve to the left, from AS to AS', increasing further the pressure on the price level.

The dramatic increase in the price of crude oil during the 1970s and early 1980s pushed overall costs of production upward, which shifted the aggregate supply curve of panel b to the left. A new equilibrium was obtained at a lower level of real GDP and at a higher price level.

plant capacity remaining idle, real GDP could increase considerably without putting any pressure on the price level.

But the war in Europe changed all that. Our idle factories were put to work producing tanks, fighter planes, cannons, armored cars, aircraft carriers, battleships, munitions, and millions of uniforms. Army bases were built overnight, and entirely new military-related factories mushroomed to meet the demands of war. Government's war-related spending shifted the aggregate demand curve outward to the right, to AD', creating a new GDP equilibrium at point b and a higher price level.

The Japanese attack on Pearl Harbor in December 1941 and the subsequent war in the Pacific added even more to the demand for war materials, shifting the aggregate demand curve once again. With the aggregate demand curve at AD", the economy moved to full-employment GDP and exerted substantial upward pressure on the price level (point c).

What about aggregate supply? Millions of men and women volunteered or were drafted into the armed forces, reducing the size of the civilian labor force. With fewer resources available, the aggregate supply curve shifted from AS to AS', increasing further the upward pressure on the price level (point d).

check your ✔ understanding

How does a war affect aggregate demand?

Demand-Pull Inflation: The Vietnam War

That same simple model can be used to describe the effect of the Vietnam War on GDP from 1964 to 1975. Before the war, the economy was relatively vigorous. Aggregate demand intersected aggregate supply on the upward-sloping segment of the aggregate supply curve. In fact, GDP was approaching the impassable limits imposed by full employment, but only moderate pressure was being exerted on the price level.

But in just three years, 1965 to 1968, government spending on defense increased more than 40 percent. The aggregate demand curve shifted to the right, pressing GDP to its limit and forcing the price level upward. In fact, the price level during the 1965–1975 decade rose from 72.8 to 125.8 (1972 = 100). Economists refer to such price inflation as **demand-pull inflation** because the factor contributing most to the rising price level was the increased demand for military goods and the subsequent rightward shift of the aggregate demand curve. This shift *pulled* GDP to full employment and *pulled* the price level up along the vertical segment of the aggregate supply curve.

Cost-Push Inflation: The OPEC Factor

The aggregate demand and aggregate supply model of Exhibit 6, panel *b*, may help explain the puzzling phenomenon of concurrent inflation and unemployment—economists call it **stagflation**—during the 1970s and 1980s. The model illustrates the inflation and unemployment effects generated, in part, by the Organization of Petroleum Exporting Countries (OPEC).

In October 1973, the price of Arabian light crude oil was $2.10 per barrel. By November 1974, OPEC had cut oil production substantially and raised the price to $10.46. While our economy was still trying to adjust to this greater-than-fivefold price increase, a second major oil price shock hit us broadside. By April 1980, OPEC had raised the price to $28, and by January 1982 to $34.

The impact of these OPEC-designed oil price increases on the costs of producing almost everything in our economy—and in the rest of the world—shifted the aggregate supply curve from AS to AS'. As the model illustrates, GDP declined while the price level increased. The OPEC-induced inflation is described as **cost-push inflation** because the factor contributing most to the rising price level was the increase in cost of a basic good and the subsequent shift to the left of the aggregate supply curve.

The Extended Prosperity Phase: 1992–2000

"If winter comes, can spring be far behind?" wrote the English Romantic poet Percy Bysshe Shelly in the early 19th century. The "spring" that followed a 1990–1991 recession turned out to be one of the most remarkable economic recoveries in U.S. history. The boom lasted eight years, from 1992 through 2000, and generated a 50 percent growth in real GDP. By its end, GDP soared beyond $10 trillion to represent fully one quarter of the world's economic output. The rate of unemployment was also cut to 4 percent, registering a 40-year low. Government deficits—government spending minus its tax revenues—vanished during the prosperity, replaced by budgetary surpluses. No one factor explains this lengthy and amazing prosperity. Instead, the boom seemed to reflect a combination of economic ingredients that shifted both the aggregate demand and aggregate supply curves to the right.

Many economists attribute the boom—at least in part—to supply-side factors, principally, the rise in the nation's productivity caused by the maturation and diffusion of computer technology throughout the economy. This diffusion lowered costs of production and widened profit margins. As a result, aggregate supply shifted outward. The incentives were in place to propel aggregate demand out as well.

Demand-pull inflation
Inflation caused primarily by an increase in aggregate demand.

Stagflation
A period of stagnating real GDP, inflation, and relatively high levels of unemployment.

Cost-push inflation
Inflation caused primarily by a decrease in aggregate supply.

The stock market, always sensitive to profit margins and particularly to expectations of future profit margins, reacted favorably. With fevered pitch, the market exploded into a 1992–2000 $14 trillion increase. This "paper wealth" shifted the aggregate demand curve outward. Not only were people buying goods out of income earned and wealth imagined, they took to buying more and more goods out of income yet-to-be earned. Consumer debt doubled during the boom years, from $0.78 trillion in 1992 to $1.53 trillion in 2000. The debt, however, while fueling aggregate demand through the 1992–2000 boom, also contributed to the economic woes that were just ahead.

Nevertheless, what was remarkable about this 1992–2000 economic boom was that it was not accompanied by rising inflation. The outward shift in aggregate supply kept the price level in check. Astonishingly, the rate of inflation fell along with the rate of unemployment.

But as any long-distance runner will tell you, if you set a too-fast pace early in the race, you may run out of gas toward the end. That kind of problem came home to roost in the economy of 2001. The consumer expenditures of the previous decade clogged U.S. households by the turn of the century. The conditions were ripe for economic retrenchment. The 1992–2000 buying spree left consumers without the will or means to keep the spree alive. Much of future income was already committed to paying off old boom-time purchases. The end of the boom came in the late months of 2000. A sluggish aggregate demand—*AD* curve shifting leftward—reflected this consumer expenditures exhaustion.

Buttressing Aggregate Demand: 2003 War in Iraq and Afghanistan

Then came 9/11. It changed the world we live in. Our reaction to it—the war against terrorism—brought the United States into military engagements in Afghanistan and Iraq. Government spending–whether on defense or non-defense items–shifts the aggregate demand curve to the right, increasing both levels of real GDP and employment. And that's precisely what happened. Spending on national security since the eventful 2001 seems to have fueled such a shift, having doubling from $304 billion in 2001 to $607.3 in 2008. The rate of unemployment fell from 5.8 percent during the recessionary 2003 to 4.6 percent in 2006. The tax cut of 2003 nudged the aggregate supply curve out to the right and combined with the outward shift in demand explains the economy's robust 3.5 percent annual increase in real GDP and low-level inflation.

The 'Financial Melt-Down' Induced Recession: 2008

Economists didn't see it coming. A year before the 2008 financial melt-down, economists were worried about a host of problems—deficits, trade balance with China, devaluation of the dollar, the price of oil, even impending inflation—almost everything that might be troublesome, but not the sledge hammer that was about to fall hard on the economy; the collapsed housing market and its pervasive impact on the economy.

Not that the issue of recession was entirely out of mind. After all, most economists understood that business cycles were inherent in our market economy so that at *some time*, a downturn was to be expected. Optimists believed that the 2008 economy was simply facing a mild slowdown, not an honest-to-goodness recession. The formal definition of recession, they argued, is an economy experiencing two consecutive quarters of negative growth, and until the fall of 2008, that did not happen. Pessimists insisted that formal definitions were arbitrary and misleading. The recession was upon us.

Picture yourself in summer of 2008: Slow down or recession? Two events were clear: (1) the oil-price spike—$145 per barrel in July 2008—and (2) a rapidly weakening housing market that produced massive foreclosures and a housing glut. The first event shifted aggregate supply inward to the left shrinking GDP and employment. The second, a glut of unsold homes depressed the value of *all* homes so that people's wealth holdings fell prompting sharp cuts in consumption spending. That shifted aggregate demand inward to the left, further shrinking GDP and employment. Unemployment rose from below five percent in 2006 to over 6.5 percent in 2008. As well, by late fall 2008, the rate of growth turned negative. *We were in recession.* Look again at Exhibit 6's template. The question is: How extensive the shifts in aggregate demand and aggregate supply?

CAN WE AVOID UNEMPLOYMENT AND INFLATION?

If government had a wish list, it would certainly include an economy in equilibrium at full employment with no inflation. In fact, that GDP condition would appear on almost everyone's wish list, wouldn't it? But how realistic are wish lists? Is there anything government can do to make wishes come true? Look at Exhibit 7.

The aggregate supply curve, *AS*, combines with three aggregate demand curve possibilities, *AD*, *AD'*, and *AD''*, each generating different real GDP levels of equilibrium.

You know this: If aggregate demand was *AD*, then real GDP is $10 trillion, or $5 trillion short of the economy's full-employment real GDP. The price level associated with *AD* is 100. On the other hand, if aggregate demand was *AD'*, real GDP equilibrium would be $15 trillion, signaling the economy at full employment with only moderate – a price level of 103 – inflation. If aggregate demand was *AD''*, the level of real GDP equilibrium would be at the $15 trillion full employment mark, but the price level would register at 115.

If *you* had a choice in the matter, which would you prefer? No contest, is it? You would wish for aggregate demand *AD'*. But wishing, as you know, doesn't always make a wish come true! Why suppose that because the *desired* aggregate

---

✋ **EXHIBIT 7**   Obtaining Full-Employment GDP Without Inflation

There is no reason to suppose that the aggregate demand curve will necessarily intersect the aggregate supply curve at a level of real GDP consistent with full employment and no inflation. If the aggregate demand curve is *AD*, unemployment results. On the other hand, if the aggregate demand curve is *AD''*, inflation results. The government can intervene—adding to or cutting its spending and taxes—to shift the aggregate demand to *AD'*, where full employment occurs with moderate inflation—that is, at *P* = 103.

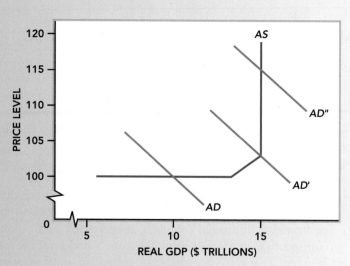

demand curve is *AD'*, the independently derived demands for goods and services by households, firms, foreigners, and government will actually generate an aggregate demand of *AD'*? The unsettling fact is that there is no more reason to expect aggregate demand to be *AD'* than *AD*, *AD''*, or any other aggregate demand curve that can be mapped in Exhibit 7.

Suppose, for example, that aggregate demand is *AD*. Must the economy, saddled with that level of aggregate demand, accept the consequences? Is there any way to move aggregate demand to *AD'*? That's where some economists believe the government should come into the picture. One way the government can shift aggregate demand to *AD'* is by increasing its own spending. And it isn't necessary to start a war to do this! *Any* increase in government spending will do the job. How about increased spending on the economy's infrastructure? Or on health care? Or on education? You can surely think of a few other ways, too. The options are almost unlimited.

Other government policies can influence aggregate demand as well. Reducing income taxes, for example, puts more money in the hands of people who will then spend part of it on more goods and services. That spending shifts the aggregate demand curve to the right. If government cuts the corporate income tax, it leaves corporations with higher after-tax income, which may increase demands for investment goods. That, too, shifts the aggregate demand curve.

Can there be *too much* aggregate demand in the economy? If the aggregate demand curve generated by households, firms, foreigners, and government was *AD''* instead of *AD'*, it would push real GDP to full employment at $15 trillion, but not without pushing the price level up to 115. In other words, the aggregate demand curve *AD''* creates inflation.

What could the government do under these conditions? The appropriate policy would be to reverse gears—to reduce government spending and increase taxes. Either strategy could shift the aggregate demand curve to the left, from *AD''* to *AD'*.

To many, these government actions seem very simple, almost mechanical. Add spending or reduce taxes to increase aggregate demand. Reduce government spending or increase taxes to cut aggregate demand. But the truth is that our real economy isn't nearly as manageable as the aggregate demand and aggregate supply model suggests. Exhibit 7 is about as simple an abstraction of the world we live in as economists can design. In the real world it is difficult enough just to identify full-employment real GDP, let alone create a government policy that puts aggregate demand right on the mark.

Why then bother with the model? Because it is still a useful first approximation of the world we live in. Understanding aggregate demand and aggregate supply gives us a useful handle on understanding the basic movements of the primary factors in our national economy. It allows us to see how problems of unemployment and inflation can emerge, and how the government might intervene to orchestrate change. At least it's a start!

CHAPTER REVIEW

1. The business cycle consists of GDP roller-coasting from periods of prosperity, marked by inflation, to periods of recession, marked by relatively high rates of unemployment. Two intermediate periods, downturn and recovery, describe the cycle's transition from prosperity to recession and from recession to prosperity.

2. Macroeconomics focuses on how the national economy works.

3. The CPI and GDP deflator are the most commonly used indices for converting nominal GDP, measured in current prices, to real GDP, measured in prices associated with a base year.

4. The aggregate demand and aggregate supply model is used to explain how an economy arrives at an equilibrium level of real GDP.

5. The aggregate supply curve—relating the price level to real GDP—has three distinguishing segments. The horizontal segment reflects the availability of unused resources. The upward-sloping segment reflects increasing pressure on the price level as firms bid for resources. The vertical segment reflects the full employment of all resources.

6. The aggregate demand curve relates the price level to aggregate quantity demanded. Its downward-sloping character reflects three principal influences: people's desire to maintain real wealth holdings, the interest rate, and international trade. For example, an increase in the price level decreases people's real wealth. To restore real wealth levels, people increase savings and reduce consumption.

7. Macroeconomic equilibrium occurs at the level of real GDP and at the level of price where aggregate demand intersects aggregate supply. That equilibrium may be associated with either inflation or unemployment and, on occasion, with both simultaneously.

8. Demand-pull inflation occurs when the aggregate demand curve shifts to the right, intersecting the aggregate supply curve on its upward-sloping or vertical segment.

9. Cost-push inflation occurs when the aggregate supply curve shifts to the left while the aggregate demand curve remains unchanged.

10. By manipulating aggregate demand, the government can reduce unemployment and/or inflation.

KEY TERMS

Recession
Depression
Prosperity
Inflation
Business cycle
Trough
Recovery
Peak

Downturn
Gross domestic product (GDP)
Nominal GDP
Real GDP
Consumer price index (CPI)
Base year
Price level
GDP deflator

Aggregate supply
Aggregate demand
Macroequilibrium
Demand-pull inflation
Stagflation
Cost-push inflation

QUESTIONS

1. Suppose someone asked you to explain how an economy's performance is actually measured. What would you say?

2. The 1990s generated for the United States the longest prosperity phase of the twentieth century. What explains it? How did the economy fare in the first years of the twenty-first century?

3. Describe the phases of the business cycle. In what ways is the business cycle illustrated in Exhibit 1 like a roller-coaster ride? In what ways is it different? (*Hint:* What does the trend line look like on a roller-coaster ride?)

4. What is the difference between nominal and real GDP?

5. What is a consumer price index? How is it constructed? Why does the index become increasingly unreliable over time?

6. What is the difference between a consumer price index and a GDP deflator?

7. Which price index is generally used to transform nominal GDP into real GDP? Write the conversion formula.

8. What is aggregate demand? Draw an aggregate demand curve and explain its shape. What factors influence aggregate demand?

9. What is aggregate supply? Draw an aggregate supply curve and explain its shape. What factors influence aggregate supply?

10. What is demand-pull inflation? Draw a diagram illustrating such an inflation. Give an example.

11. What is cost-push inflation? What might cause it?

12. Graph the economy's macroequilibrium position, using the following data.

PRICE LEVEL	AGGREGATE DEMAND	AGGREGATE SUPPLY
160	$1,000	$7,000
150	2,000	7,000
140	3,000	7,000
130	4,000	6,000
120	5,000	5,000
110	6,000	4,000
100	7,000	3,000

13. Suppose aggregate supply shifts to the left by $2,000 at each price level. What happens to the economy's macroequilibrium position?

14. Suppose aggregate demand shifts to the right by $4,000 at each price level. What happens to the economy's macroequilibrium position?

15. If the economy's macroequilibrium position generates too high unemployment, what can the government do?

PRACTICE PROBLEMS

1. Calculate the GDP deflator for the following years for the Canadian economy, using 2001 as the base year.

	NOMINAL GDP ($ BILLIONS)	REAL GDP ($ BILLIONS)	GDP DEFLATOR
2000	$3,052.6	$3,248.8	
2001	3,166.0	3,166.0	
2002	3,405.7	3,279.1	
2003	3,772.2	3,501.4	

2. Calculate the real GDP for the following years for the Australian economy, given data for nominal GDP and the GDP deflator (2001 is the base year).

	NOMINAL GDP ($ BILLIONS)	REAL GDP ($ BILLIONS)	GDP DEFLATOR
2000	$4,268.6	4405.2	96.9
2001	4,539.9		100.0
2002	4,900.4		103.9
2003	5,250.8	4839.4	108.5

3. Compute the percentage change in nominal GDP shown in practice problem 2 over the period 2000–2003, and compare that figure to the percentage change in real GDP over the same period.

WHAT'S WRONG WITH THIS GRAPH?

Aggregate Supply and Aggregate Demand Model

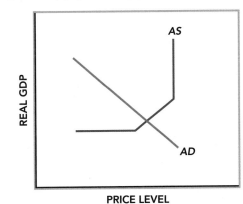

Economic Consultants

Economic Research and Analysis by Students for Professionals

Charles Edwards, a young businessman in Minneapolis, Minnesota, is considering whether to run against the incumbent U.S. senator in his district, who is up for reelection in the next year. Charles hasn't had formal training in economics, but, based on his observations, he thinks that incumbents fare better when the economy is strong and worse when the economy is weak.

Charles wants to know if this is an accurate assessment. He also wants to know how to track the state of Minnesota's economy. For help with these questions, Charles has hired Economic Consultants. Prepare a report for Charles that addresses the following issues:

1. Review real GDP, unemployment, inflation, and business cycle data. Using presidential elections as a point of comparison, have incumbent presidents tended to win reelection if the economy is strong and lose if the economy is weak?
2. What conclusions, if any, can you draw from this analysis? What assumptions are being made in this analysis?
3. What is the current state of the economy in Minnesota? What resources are available for tracking the Minnesota economy?

You may find the following resources helpful as you prepare this report for Charles:

© Image 100/Royalty-Free/CORBIS

- **Bureau of Economic Analysis (BEA)** (http://www.bea.gov/)— The BEA publishes data on the GDP.
- **Bureau of Labor Statistics (BLS)** (http://stats.bls.gov/)— The BLS publishes data on consumer prices and unemployment.
- **The National Bureau of Economic Research (NBER)** (http://www.nber.org/)—The NBER measures U.S. business cycle expansions and contractions.
- **MultiEducator History of Presidential Elections Site** (http://www.multied.com/elections/)—The MultiEducator History of Presidential Elections Site provides presidential election statistics.
- **Federal Reserve Bank of Minneapolis** (http://woodrow.mpls.frb.fed.us/)—The Federal Reserve Bank of Minneapolis publishes regional economic data (www.woodrow.mpls.frb.fed.us/research/data/) and forecasts (www.woodrow.mpls.frb.fed.us/research/data/district).

1. Think business cycles and economic growth. U.S. economic performance during the period 1992–2000 represented
   a. a full cycle that was completed with relatively high spikes of growth and decline.
   b. a full cycle that was completed with relatively low upward and downward movements.
   c. a period of sustained economic stagnation.
   d. a period of sustained high rates of economic growth.
   e. an unusual downward-sloping trend line.

2. A recession can be defined as a period in which
   a. there is an increase in the price level.
   b. the business cycle is at its peak.
   c. inflation and unemployment occur simultaneously.
   d. there is high unemployment.
   e. the business cycle is at its trend line.

3. Which of the following would not be counted as part of the gross domestic product for the United States?
   a. The value of Japanese automobiles sold in the United States and produced in Akron, Ohio
   b. The value of Ford automobiles sold in the United States and produced in Detroit, Michigan
   c. The value of Japanese automobiles sold in foreign markets and produced in Akron, Ohio
   d. The value of Ford automobiles sold in foreign markets and produced in Detroit, Michigan
   e. The value of Ford automobiles sold in the United States and produced in Canada

4. If real GDP in the economy is $8 billion in the current year and nominal GDP is $6 billion in the same year, then
   a. the GDP deflator equals 0.75.
   b. the GDP deflator equals 1.33.
   c. the current year is the base year.
   d. the price level is higher in the current year than in the base year.
   e. the price level in the economy is rising at an increasing rate.

5. One similarity between the aggregate supply and aggregate demand curves is that they both
   a. have positive slopes.
   b. have negative slopes.
   c. shift to the right when prices rise.
   d. are assumed to be linear (straight lines).
   e. relate the price level to real GDP.

6. The price level does not rise along the horizontal section of the aggregate supply curve because
   a. firms do not have to increase wages to hire more workers.
   b. real GDP rises as the aggregate demand curve shifts to the right.
   c. higher wages will not entice any additional individuals to enter the labor force.
   d. the economy is already at full employment along this segment of the aggregate supply curve.
   e. wages and the price level move in opposite directions.

7. Suppose that the economy is producing output at a point along the horizontal segment of its aggregate supply curve. Which of the following strategies would be effective in increasing real GDP?
   a. Decreasing wages paid to workers in the economy
   b. Reducing income taxes
   c. Decreasing government spending
   d. Reducing incomes for foreigners
   e. Increasing the price level in the economy

8. If the aggregate demand and aggregate supply curves intersect at a point along the vertical portion of the aggregate supply curve, then spending increases in the economy will
   a. lead to increases in real GDP.
   b. lead to decreases in real GDP.
   c. shift the aggregate supply curve to the right.
   d. lead to no change in real GDP.
   e. lead to higher levels of employment.

9. If the economy is in macroequilibrium at a point along the positively sloped section of the aggregate supply curve, then an increase in the quantity of resources in the economy will lead to
   a. higher prices and higher real GDP.
   b. lower prices and higher real GDP.
   c. lower prices and lower real GDP.
   d. no change in prices and higher real GDP.
   e. no change in output and lower prices.

10. Inflation created by rightward shifts in the aggregate demand curve is referred to as
    a. cost-push inflation.
    b. hyperinflation.
    c. demand-push inflation.
    d. demand-pull inflation.
    e. cost-pull inflation.

CHAPTER 5

GROSS DOMESTIC PRODUCT ACCOUNTING

Eskimos speaking Inuit, Aivilik, and Igloolik languages are reputed to have 31 names for snow. *Maujaq* refers to deep, soft snow that is difficult to walk in. *Pukak* describes dry snow crystals, like sugar powder. *Niummak* is the hard, driving snow that clings to ice fields. While *masak* is wet, saturated snow, snow in water is called *matsaaq*, and snow layered on the water of a fishing hole is called *mituk*. And if you've ever lived in wintry climates, you would be familiar with *qiqiqralijarnataq*, or hard-packed snow you could walk on.

It makes as much sense for Eskimos to differentiate between the various kinds of snow that impact on their lives in significant ways as it makes sense for economists to differentiate among the varieties of ways of describing a nation's economic performance. Each word or phrase that depicts economic performance means something slightly different, and the difference—like *maujak*, or *pukak*, or *qiqiqralijarnataq*—is important.

© 2007 JupiterImages Corporation

We produce things every day, in every which way, that either satisfy basic needs or are designed to stroke our vanities. We spend the better part of our waking day in pursuit of these things, and in the end, they are used to represent our economic performance.

Among the words or phases that are meant to describe a nation's economic performance are nominal gross domestic product, real gross domestic product, per capita real gross domestic product, gross national product, net national product, national income, personal income, personal disposable income, and per capita income.

Consider, for example, the difference between national income and per capita income. National income refers to the sum of all incomes earned by the nation's population. Per capita income is national income divide by the population. If you're interested in comparing the economic performances of two nations, it may make sense to look at their respective national incomes. But if you want to know how well-off people are in each, perhaps per capita income would be the better guide. If you want to know how many things are produced in the United States, gross domestic product is what you look at. But if you are interested in what Americans produce, look instead at gross national product.

We'll explore what each of these words or phases means, examine how we arrive at their values, and compare nations' performances on the basis of these differing measurements.

TWO APPROACHES TO CALCULATING GDP

As you already know, gross domestic product (GDP) is a measure of the total value of all final goods and services produced in the economy in a given year. One way of calculating GDP for, say, 2006 is to add up the market value of all final goods and services produced in 2006 (Exhibit 1). Another way is to add up the total value of the resources used in producing the 2006 final goods and services (Exhibit 2). The values should be equivalent. After all, goods and services reflect the value of the resources used to make them.

Economists calculate GDP both ways. They add up the total value of all final goods and services produced in the economy in a given year and add up the total value of the resources used in making these goods and services. The former calculation is called the *expenditure approach* to GDP; the latter is called the *income approach* to GDP.

Circular flow of goods, services, and resources
The movement of goods and services from firms to households, and of resources from households to firms.

Circular flow of money
The movement of income in the form of resource payments from firms to households, and of income in the form of revenue from households to firms.

THE EXPENDITURE APPROACH

Counting Final Goods and Services

Let's start with the **expenditure approach**. One of the first concerns you have when adding up the market prices of all final goods and services is to make certain the goods and services whose prices you add are, in fact, *final* goods and services. If you simply add the prices of all goods and services produced in the year, you end up double counting—counting some goods and services more than once. How so? Exhibit 3 illustrates the point.

Expenditure approach
A method of calculating GDP that adds all expenditures made for final goods and services by households, firms, and government.

EXHIBIT 1   The Circular Flow of Goods, Services, and Resources

The circular flow of goods, services, and resources shows the interdependence of households and firms. Households supply their resources—labor, capital, land, entrepreneurship—to the firms in the resource market and, in turn, demand in the product market the goods and services produced by the firms. The firms go to the resource market to demand resources that households supply and, in turn, provide households with the goods and services produced for the product market.

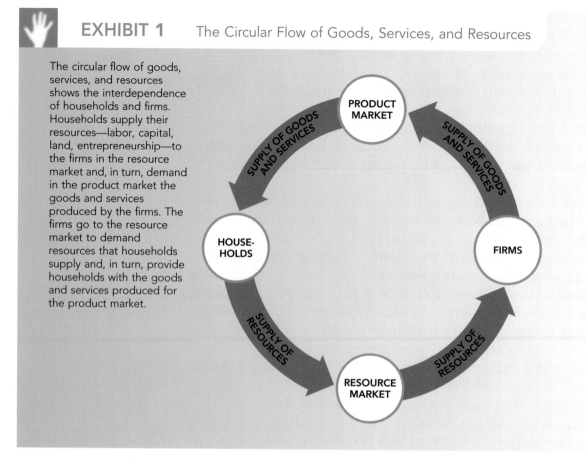

EXHIBIT 2   The Circular Flow of Money

Start with the flow of money—in the form of wages, interest, rent, and profit—that firms in the resource market pay to households for resources supplied. These resource payments are the incomes that enable households to purchase goods and services from firms. The money circuit is completed when the payments flow from households, through the product market, to the firms for the goods and services they supply.

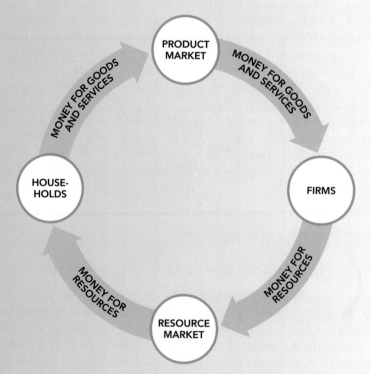

EXHIBIT 3   Market Value and Value Added of Goods Produced

FIRM	GOOD	MARKET VALUE	VALUE ADDED BY FIRM
1. SHEEP RANCH	WOOL ON SHEEP	$ 4	$ 4
2. SHEARING SHEEP	BULK WOOL	7	3
3. KNITTING MILL	WOOL FABRIC	13	6
4. MANUFACTURING	SWEATER	20	7
5. STORE	SWEATER	50	30
TOTAL		$94	$50

How much market value is contributed to GDP in Exhibit 3? As you see, five different firms are involved in producing woolen sweaters. In the first, wool is actually being produced on the sheep. Let's suppose the value of the wool, determined by the market price of wool still on the hoof, is $4. A second firm, producing bulk wool, pays the sheep owner $4—its market price—for the sheep's wool. After shearing, washing, drying, and sizing the wool, the second firm sells it at the $7 bulk wool price.

A knitting mill buys the wool and knits it into a fine wool fabric. At the end of this third stage of economic activity, the market price of the fabric is $13. It is sold to a sweater-making firm that fashions it into a wool sweater, priced at $20.

The firm-to-firm process is finally completed with the sale of the sweater by a clothing store. Here, the sweater is put on display, and a salesperson finally sells it, gift wrapped, for $50.

How do we transfer the information of Exhibit 3 into GDP? We don't simply add up the total values of the goods and services produced by the five firms to get $94. That $94 counts the $4 raw wool five times over. The $4 makes up part of the value of the $7 price of bulk wool and is counted again as part of the value of the $13 price of the fabric, counted once more as part of the $20 price of the manufactured sweater, and counted again as part of the sweater's $50 retail price at the store.

How do we overcome overcounting? By counting only values of **final goods** produced, that is, *goods that are not resold*. The only good not resold in Exhibit 3 is the $50 sweater. What about the raw wool, the bulk wool, the fabric, and the sweater in the sweater factory? These are **intermediate goods**, goods sold by firms to other firms. They are goods used to produce other goods. Their values are accounted for in the value of the final good.

Another way of arriving at the $50 value that is counted as part of GDP is by considering only the **value added** by each of the five firms of Exhibit 3. Look at column 4.

The sheep ranch, where the wool is actually grown, adds $4 to value. The firm producing bulk wool buys the wool for $4 and adds $3 to its value. The knitting mill buys the bulk wool for $7 and adds $6 to its value. The sweater firm buys the $13 fabric and adds $7 to its value. Finally, the store buys the sweater for $20 and adds $30 to its value. The firms' value added sums to $50. That is precisely the market value of the *final* good.

The Four Expenditure Categories of GDP

What kinds of final goods and services are produced in our economy, and who buys them? Economists classify final goods and services according to whether they are produced to satisfy (1) consumption demands by households, (2) investment

on the net

The Bureau of Economic Analysis (BEA) (http://www.bea.gov/national/index.htm#gdp), an agency of the Department of Commerce, is the nation's economic accountant, preparing data on all components of GDP (http://www.bea.doc.gov/bea/glance.htm). The BEA also maintains international data (http://www.bea.doc.gov/bea/di1.htm) and regional data (http://www.bea.doc.gov/bea/regional/data.htm).

Final goods
Goods purchased for final use, not for resale.

Intermediate goods
Goods used to produce other goods.

Value added
The difference between the value of a good that a firm produces and the value of the goods the firm uses to produce it.

Personal consumption expenditures
All goods and services bought by households.

Gross private domestic investment
The purchase by firms of plant, equipment, and inventory goods.

Government purchases
All goods and services bought by government.

Net exports
An economy's exports to other economies, minus its imports from other economies.

Durable goods
Goods expected to last at least a year.

Why is a car considered a durable good?

demands by firms, (3) demands by government, or (4) exports minus imports (net exports)—that is, the demands by foreigners for our goods and services minus our demands for foreign goods and services.

All final goods and services that make up GDP, then, can be expressed in the form

$$GDP = C + I + G + (X - M),$$

where C is **personal consumption expenditures**, I is **gross private domestic investment**, G is **government purchases**, and $(X - M)$ is **net exports**, or exports minus imports.

What did 2008 GDP add up to? Look at Exhibit 4.

GDP equals $14,201.1 billion. Look at the sums and specific character of the goods and services in each of the expenditure categories.

Personal Consumption Expenditures
The $10,053.7 billion personal consumption expenditures make up 70.8 percent of the $14,201.1 billion 2008 GDP. These are the goods and services consumed directly by households. They are grouped into categories of durable goods, nondurable goods, and services.

Durable goods account for $1,065.5 billion. These include familiar household items such as kitchen appliances, television sets, carpeting, personal computers, washing machines, and lawn mowers. Durables include, as well, automobiles, electric saws, and hearing aids.

What sets durables apart from other consumption goods and services? Essentially, their durability. Unlike tuna salad sandwiches, they're not consumed soon after being produced. A refrigerator, for example, once produced, outlasts years of tuna salad sandwiches. Of course, all refrigerators eventually wear out. But it takes time. Economists describe a durable good as one that is expected to last at least a year. For example, a new Ford is *expected* to last more than a year.

EXHIBIT 4   Expenditure Approach to 2008 GDP ($ Billions)

C	**=**	**PERSONAL CONSUMPTION EXPENDITURES**		**$10,053.7**
		DURABLE GOODS	1,065.5	
		NONDURABLE GOODS	2,949.1	
		SERVICES	6,038.2	
I	**=**	**GROSS PRIVATE DOMESTIC INVESTMENT**		**2,038.1**
		NONRESIDENTIAL	1,529.6	
		RESIDENTIAL	505.1	
		CHANGE IN BUSINESS INVENTORY	−30.4	
G	**=**	**GOVERNMENT PURCHASES**		**2,825.5**
		FEDERAL	1,023.3	
		DEFENSE	696.7	
		NONDEFENSE	326.5	
		STATE AND LOCAL	1,802.3	
X – M	**=**	**NET EXPORTS OF GOODS AND SERVICES**		**−717.9**
		EXPORTS	1,798.8	
		IMPORTS	(2,515.0)	
GDP	**=**	**GROSS DOMESTIC PRODUCT**		**14,201.0**

Source: Bureau of Economic Analysis, U.S. Department of Commerce, 2008.

historicalperspective

© Royalty-Free/CORBIS
Taking a bite out of GDP.

THE WEALTH OF NATIONS

Gross domestic product (GDP) is defined as the total value of all final goods and services, measured in current market prices, produced during a year. The only exceptions are illegal goods and services, such as the production of cocaine or the services offered in prostitution. Everything else counts.

The rationale behind such a measure of GDP is consumer sovereignty. If people value a good or service, then regardless of what the good or service is, that value should be considered as contributing to the wealth or well-being of the nation. For example, if people value cotton candy, then despite the fact that it contains no nutritional value and probably rots your teeth, the production of that cotton candy contributes to the wealth of the nation and should be counted as part of its GDP. So too a questionable performance of an off-Broadway production of *Hamlet*.

Classical economists of the 18th and 19th centuries had a very different take on what should be counted in GDP. Adam Smith in his *Wealth of Nations* (1776) argued that only the production of goods that promote economic growth should be regarded as contributing to the wealth of nations. For example, the production of a potato is part of GDP because the potato promotes economic growth. Once planted, it reproduces itself and more. To Smith, all goods that sustain the physical well-being of people are both productive and contributing to the wealth of nations because having and using the goods allow people to reproduce those goods and more.

What kind of production, then, doesn't serve to promote the wealth of nations? Adam Smith is explicit here: All services, *however useful*, fail the economic-growth test. Using his own criterion, Smith would regard himself as unproductive and his services as a professor not contributing to GDP! It's not that Smith underappreciated his place in society. It's simply that he believed his services did not add materially to society. And that's what the wealth of nations was about. He elaborates:

The sovereign with all the officers of both justice and war who serve under him, the whole army and navy are unproductive laborers. Their service, however honorable, produces nothing for which an equal quantity of services can afterwards be procured. In the same class must be ranked some of the most gravest and most important, and some of the most frivolous professions: churchmen, lawyers, physicians, men of letters of all kinds; players, buffoons, musicians, opera-singers, opera dancers, etc. Like the declamation of the actor or the tune of the musician, the work of all of them perishes in the very instant of its production.

It's an interesting way of looking at GDP and perhaps not too surprising for the 18th and 19th centuries. After all, what the "wealth of nations" (or GDP) is, is in truth highly subjective. It depends ultimately on one's conception of value. Does two dollars' worth of cotton candy contribute twice as much to society as a dollar's worth of nursing care? Yes, say 21st-century economists. What say you?

Even if Alice Gorman buys it today and totals it this afternoon on the way home from the dealership, it is still classified as a durable good.

Purchases of durable goods help economists identify the phases of the business cycle. During recessions, consumers tend to hang on to their durables (say, by getting them repaired), so that sales of new durables are relatively weak. As prosperity returns, consumers are more inclined to discard old durables than to repair them. As a result, sales of new durables are relatively strong.

What about **nondurable goods**? These include goods consumed within a relatively short period of time, usually less than a year, such as food, clothing, gasoline, drugs, tobacco, and toiletries. Some things are easy to classify as nondurables—such as bananas—whereas it may take years to consume some spices. Also, many of us wear clothes and shoes for more than a year, yet the U.S. Department of Commerce classifies them as nondurables. Households spend more on nondurables than on durables. In fact, the value of nondurables consumed in 2008 was more than twice the value of durable items.

Nondurable goods
Goods expected to last less than a year.

theoreticalperspective

AN EXPANDED CIRCULAR FLOW

The exhibit on the following page, illustrating the income and expenditure approaches to GDP, is an expanded version of the circular flow models shown in Exhibits 1 and 2. A government sector and international trade have been added.

Let's begin by looking at the resources (labor, capital, land, and entrepreneurship) that flow through the light blue artery from households to the resource market, and then from the resource market to firms that use the resources to produce goods and services. Now follow the flow of these goods and services from firms through the three green arteries on the right side of the figure. The first leads from firms to households through the product market. These represent the households' private consumption. The second artery carries the flow to government. Note that the goods-and-services flow that government buys from firms is passed on to households (as public goods). The third artery carries the flow of goods and services in the form of exports from firms to foreign economies. The foreign economies' contribution is depicted in the flow through the light blue artery from the foreign economies to households. The difference between the import and export flows represents net exports. Finally, some of the firms' output flow is absorbed by the firms

themselves in the form of investment. Combined, these flows of goods and services, all channeled through green arteries, make up the expenditures approach in the circular flow model:

$$C + I + G + (X - M)$$

The circular flow model also depicts a counter-balancing money flow carried through green arteries that represent payments made by households, government, firms, and foreign economies for goods and services received. Note the green arteries that carry money flows from households to firms for the goods and services purchased on the product market, from households to government in the form of taxes, and from households to foreign economies for imports. Households receive money from firms in the form of payments flows for resources provided and from government in the form of transfer payments. Firms pay taxes to government and receive a payments flow from government for goods and services provided. Firms also receive money from foreign economies in the form of a payments flow for exports.

What about saving and investment? The money that households set aside as saving is equal to the value of the goods and services firms set aside for investment.

Services
Productive activities that are instantaneously consumed.

Services are intangible (nonphysical) consumption items consumed as they are being produced. Think about health care. You consume your doctor's service precisely when it is being given. An Economics 101 lecture is consumed as your professor lectures. The St. Louis Symphony is consumed as David Robertson conducts.

Some industries (often those that produce durable goods) produce services as well. AT&T, for example, sells telephones (durable goods) and telephone calls (services). Sears sells washing machines (durable goods) and washing machine repair (service). As you see in Exhibit 4, we spend almost as much on services as we do on durable and nondurable goods combined.

Gross Private Domestic Investment Not all production of final goods and services in 2008 was consumed by households. Some goods and services—$2,038.9 billion of the 14,201.1 billion—were actually purchased by firms themselves in the form of gross private domestic investment. What kinds of goods? The oil rigs produced in 2008 by firms that make oil-drilling equipment were bought by Exxon and Texaco, not by you. The rigs are used by the oil companies to produce energy for households. Construction companies built automobile plants for General Motors and Ford, not for households. These plants turn out the automobiles demanded by households.

The goods that firms buy from each other are classified as new structures (or plants) and equipment. Some plant and equipment purchases merely replace

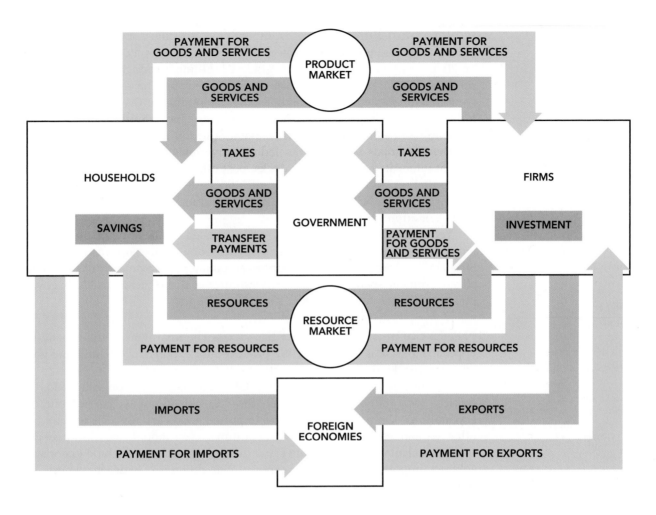

plants and equipment that have worn out producing consumption goods. But some purchases are made to increase the quantity of plants and equipment in use. For example, United Airlines bought aircraft to replace those no longer usable. But it also bought aircraft to expand its fleet.

What about residential investment? Houses and apartment buildings produced in 2008 and used as residences are classified as investment goods, even though a case can be made to classify a homeowner's house—as we do a homeowner's automobile—as a durable consumption good.

Changes in business inventories are counted as **inventory investment**. Why? Inventories are unsold output. Firms keep stocks of finished final goods, as well as stocks of resources used to produce those goods, in reserve in order to promote efficiency in production and sales. How can a clothing store expect to sell sweaters if it doesn't stock a variety of styles, sizes, and colors? How can Goodyear expect to run a smooth production line if it doesn't stock the raw materials used in manufacturing tires?

What does the −$30.4 billion business inventory change in 2008 signify? The goods added to inventory in 2008 were less than the inventory used in production and sales in 2008.

Business inventory changes, positive or negative, are not always intended. Suppose that Rockport Shoes planned to produce and sell $200 million of shoes in 2008, but by year's end was able to sell only $180 million. The remaining unsold $20 million would be recorded as an addition to business inventory, even though Rockport intended the shoes for sale, not inventory. Rockport would end up with more shoes in inventory than it wanted.

Inventory investment
Stocks of finished goods and raw materials that firms keep in reserve to facilitate production and sales.

Why do some goods produced for consumption end up being investment?

Government Purchases Government, too, is a buyer of goods and services. In 2008 federal, state, and local government purchases amounted to $2,825.5 billion, or 20 percent of the economy's $14,201.1 billion production of goods and services. The largest slice of federal government purchases—$696.8 billion—went to national defense. It bought food and clothing for the armed forces, F-15 fighter planes, Bradley tanks, Navy uniforms, and countless other military hardware and software items that make up our military preparedness.

Defense goods were not the federal government's only purchases. It also bought interstate highways, dry docks, post offices, and services such as justice, transportation, and education. It spent money on Amtrak service, for example, and airport construction. Without federal spending on these items, many people could not afford to travel.

Yet, in spite of all the media attention focused on the appetite of the federal government, the biggest government spender doesn't live in Washington, D.C. State and local government expenditures account for approximately 63.8 percent of all government spending. These expenditures and the means used by governments to finance them are described in later chapters.

Net Exports of Goods and Services The final item in the expenditure approach to GDP is net exports. We produced for export $1,798.9 billion of goods and services. How does this item affect our GDP account?

We include exports in calculating GDP because they represent goods and services we produced, even though they do not appear as part of our own expenditures. On the other hand, the imported goods and services we buy from other economies are part of our expenditures even though we didn't produce them. In calculating GDP by the expenditure approach, we include exports and subtract imports. In 2008, net exports—the difference between exports and imports—was negative, a minus $717.0 billion.

THE INCOME APPROACH

Income approach
A method of calculating GDP that adds all the incomes earned in the production of final goods and services.

An alternative approach to calculating GDP is the **income approach**. How does this differ from the expenditure approach? Instead of determining GDP by computing the total value of all final goods and services produced in the economy, the income approach computes the total payments made to households that provide the resources used in producing the final goods and services.

The resources used in production—labor, capital, land, and entrepreneurship—receive income payments in the form of wages and salaries, interest, rent, and profit. These income payments are rearranged in GDP accounting into five categories: (1) the compensation of employees, (2) interest, (3) corporate profit, (4) rental income, and (5) proprietors' income. The sum of these income payments is **national income**.

National income
The sum of all payments made to resource owners for the use of their resources.

National income for 2008 is shown in Exhibit 5.

National income equaled $11,491.7 billion. Look at the sums and specific character of each of the income categories shown in Exhibit 5.

Compensation of Employees

In every morning rush hour, an incredible crush of people head to work. They spend their working life producing the economy's goods and services. Some people work production lines as hourly workers earning wages; others sit behind desks as salaried workers pushing the paper flow that modern production requires. Still others are journalists, teachers, or firefighters.

EXHIBIT 5   2008 National Income ($ Billions)

COMPENSATION OF EMPLOYEES		$8,110.7
WAGES AND SALARIES	6,570.2	
SUPPLEMENTS	1,540.5	
RENTAL INCOME		80.9
CORPORATE PROFIT		1,563.8
NET INTEREST		601.6
PROPRIETORS' INCOME		1,055.9
NONFACTOR CHARGES	1,068.4	
NATIONAL INCOME		12,481.3

Source: Bureau of Economic Analysis, U.S. Department of Commerce, 2008.

In 2008 firms, organizations, and government entities paid out to their employees $6,570.2 billion in wages and salaries, and another $1,540.5 billion in fringe benefits, such as bonuses, paid vacations, and contributions to employees' Social Security. All that compensation of employees was money paid for labor supplied.

No surprise, then, that our national economy appears to be labor generated. After all, the $8,110.7 billion income payment to workers accounts for $64.9 percent of our national income.

Interest

How is capital incorporated into the income approach to GDP? People who provide firms with capital—for example, by buying interest-bearing bonds issued by the firms—receive interest, just as people who provide labor services receive wages and salaries. Firms also borrow capital from banks, which in turn borrow from individual savers. In each case, interest is earned. In 2008, $601.6 billion was received by people in the form of interest.

Corporate Profit

Corporate profit represents the return to owners of incorporated firms. Part of corporate profit is distributed to stockholders as *dividends*, part is retained by the corporation as investment, and a third part ends up with government as corporate taxes. The income approach to GDP includes all of corporate profit, which in 2008 amounted to $1,563.8 billion.

What about the income of corporate managers? These are the people making key corporate decisions. Are their incomes included as part of corporate profit? No. Their incomes, typically salaries, are counted as employee compensation.

Rent

Rent is payment for use of property. The most common property forms are land, housing, and office space. People using their own property typically don't pay themselves rent, but the rent is nonetheless estimated in GDP accounting and counted along with contractual rental leases. Imputed rents associated with owner-occupied dwellings are also counted. In 2008 these rental forms amounted to $80.9 billion.

Proprietors' Income

Although our economy is dominated by large corporations, the largest number of businesses are unincorporated firms. Many people own their own businesses, earning income for the goods and services they produce. How are these incomes classified? They don't fall into the category of corporate profit, because the firms are not corporations. They aren't wages or salaries, because owners don't hire themselves as employees. They obviously aren't rent or interest. They are regarded as proprietors' income.

Imagine an ethnic restaurant in Brooklyn owned and operated by a husband and wife. They work hard, save their pennies, rent the premises, and set up a 12-table restaurant. They prepare the meals, serve, and clean up after a 14-hour workday. They gross $172,000 in 2008. But they must also pay rent and utilities, buy ingredients for meals, and repair wear and tear on their plant and equipment. After paying out all 2008 expenses, they end up with a net income of $44,000. Economists define that net income as proprietors' income. In 2008, unincorporated firms generated $1,055.9 billion for their owners.

BRINGING GDP AND NATIONAL INCOME INTO ACCORD

How do economists reconcile differences between the $14,201.1 billion 2008 GDP and the $12,481.3 billion 2008 national income? First they derive gross domestic product (GDP), then subtract two items from it—depreciation of capital and nonfactor changes.

Nonfactor Charges

Compensation of employees, interest, corporate profit, rent, and proprietors' income are all earning that factors of production acquire in the production process. But there are other items whose values are incorporated in the prices of the final goods they produce, and these items are defined as nonfactor charges. They include indirect business taxes, business transfer payments, nontax liabilities, and government enterprise surpluses less subsidies. In 2008, these nonfactor charges were $1,068.4 billion.

From GDP to GNP

Gross national product (GNP)
The market value of all final goods and services in an economy produced by resources owned by people of that economy, regardless of where the resources are located.

The difference between GDP and **gross national product (GNP)** is ownership and location. Gross domestic product measures location, that is, what is produced and earned *in the domestic economy*. In 2008 GDP equaled $14,201.1 billion. Gross national product, on the other hand, measures ownership, that is, what the *nation's people and their property* produce and earn. In 2008 GNP was $14,321.9 billion. If the nation's entire resources were employed wholly within the economy, then GDP would be exactly the same as GNP.

The reality, however, is that some U.S. workers and other resources are employed outside the country. And some of the resources employed in this country are not owned by U.S. citizens. The value of the automobiles produced by a General Motors plant in Spain is not included in our GDP (it is counted in Spain's GDP). On the other hand, it is included in our GNP. Conversely, a Nissan plant's output in Tennessee is part of our GDP, but not our GNP. In 2008 foreign workers and the property owned by foreigners in the United States created $663.3 billion of income that was included in our GDP but excluded from our GNP. On the other hand, the $784.1 billion of 2008 U.S. assets abroad and income earned by U.S. citizens working in foreign economies was excluded from our GDP but included in our GNP.

If you worked in Japan for an American-owned company, would what you produce be part of American GDP or GNP?

globalperspective

@ Royalty-Free/CORBIS

How they spend them is pretty much the same.

IS THE COMPOSITION OF GDP FOR THE UNITED STATES UNIQUE?

Suppose we hadn't seen the composition of GDP shown in Table A. Could we have guessed it? Probably, if we had access to GDP data for any other year. The consumption expenditures by households, the investment expenditures by firms, the government purchases, and the net exports shares of GDP vary little from year to year, as Table A indicates. In the 43-year period 1960–2008, the consumption share each year varied only slightly from 67 percent of GDP. Investment clustered around 15 percent, and government's share was approximately 20 percent.

These shares not only remain reasonably stable over time, but also are not too dissimilar from the composition shares of GDP for most other market economies. Look at Table B.

The variations, although greater, are still remarkably narrow. For most of the European economies in 2006,

consumption shares vary only slightly around the 60 percent mark. Denmark's 47.9 percent, while relatively low, is counterbalanced by its higher 26.5 percent government share, reflecting Denmark's history of Social Democrat policies.

MORE ON THE NET

Review the *World Factbook* (http://www.odci.gov/cia/publications/factbook/) for GDP measurements and descriptions for nations around the world.

TABLE A: COMPOSITION OF U.S. GDP: 1960–2008

	1960	1970	1980	2008
CONSUMPTION	64.7	64.0	64.6	70.8
INVESTMENT	15.3	14.9	17.3	14.3
GOVERNMENT	19.4	21.0	18.7	19.9
NET EXPORTS	0.5	0.1	–0.5	–5.0
	100.0	100.0	100.0	100.0

Source: *Economic Report of the President, 1997* (Washington, D.C., February 1997); and Bureau of Economic Analysis, U.S. Department of Commerce, 2008.

TABLE B: COMPOSITION OF GDP FOR SELECTED ECONOMIES: 2006

	CONSUMPTION	INVESTMENT	GOVERNMENT	NET EXPORTS
ITALY	58.5	20.6	20.7	–1.0
FRANCE	56.5	19.6	24.1	–0.9
UNITED KINGDOM	65.3	16.6	21.8	–3.9
GERMANY	59.2	17.4	18.6	4.4
CANADA	55.9	20.1	19.3	4.2
JAPAN	56.3	23.4	17.6	2.8
DENMARK	47.9	20.3	26.5	5.0
NETHERLANDS	48.9	19.4	24.3	7.2

Source: *Economist Intelligence Unit*, London, England.

From GDP to National Income

To create the 2008 GDP of $14,201.1 billion, people were busy turning out, day after day, automobiles and computers, corn and health care. They worked in factories and hospitals and on farms. They welded frames, operated tractors, and took X rays. These factories, hospitals, welding machines, tractors, and X-ray

EXHIBIT 6   The Relationship Between Gross Domestic Product, Gross National Product, and National Income: 2008 ($ Billions)

		GROSS DOMESTIC PRODUCT	**$14,201.1**
	MINUS	FACTOR PAYMENTS TO THE REST OF THE WORLD	−663.3
	PLUS	FACTOR PAYMENTS FROM THE REST OF THE WORLD	784.1
	EQUALS	GROSS NATIONAL PRODUCT	14,321.9
	MINUS	CAPITAL DEPRECIATION, NONFACTOR CHARGES	1,840.6
	EQUALS	NATIONAL INCOME	12,481.3

Source: Bureau of Economic Analysis, U.S. Department of Commerce, 2008.

machines—along with other factories and machinery—make up the capital stock in our economy. Wouldn't you think that during 2008 part of this capital stock would be used up producing the economy's 2008 GDP? After all, nothing is forever. Machines in use wear out, as do hospitals and factories.

Shouldn't they be replaced? Typically, they are. During 2008 *new* factories and machinery were produced. New hospitals were built, new tractors manufactured, and new automobile assembly lines constructed.

But if the value of all investment goods produced in 2008 only replaces the value of the capital stock used up in 2008, then 2008 GDP may be giving us an inflated view of our economy's 2008 performance.

Capital depreciation
The value of existing capital stock used up in the process of producing goods and services.

For example, suppose fishermen caught 1,000 pounds of fish, but one used 100 pounds of fish bait to do the catching, the other 500 pounds of fish bait. Wouldn't the difference in their **capital depreciation** influence your evaluation of their performance?

The reduction of GDP to national income involves as well removing indirect business taxes—that is, general sales taxes, excise taxes, customs duties, business property taxes, and license fees—from the GDP accounts. They are called indirect taxes because they are not levied on the firm directly, but on the good or service. For the same reasons, business transfer payments and the difference between government enterprises' surpluses and subsidies are subtracted.

Why bother measuring national income? National income provides us with more specific information. It offers, in some instances, a much sharper picture of the population's economic well-being. After all, national income is what eventually ends up in people's hands.

GDP, GNP, and National Income for 2008

Exhibit 6 summarizes the relationships between GDP, GNP, NNP, and national income for 2008.

PERSONAL INCOME AND PERSONAL DISPOSABLE INCOME

Personal income
National income, plus income received but not earned, minus income earned but not received.

National income is what people earn. **Personal income**, on the other hand, is what they receive. What people receive in any year is not always equal to what they earn. Consider, for example, the income earned and received by corporate shareholders in 2008.

Since shareholders own the corporation, what they earn as shareholders is the profit the corporation makes. But shareholders don't end up with that profit.

First, the corporation is obliged to pay corporate income tax. What it pays out in taxes, its shareholders don't receive. Second, the corporation typically retains some of its after-tax profit for its own internal investment. What it retains for investment, its shareholders don't receive. And third, the corporation is obliged to contribute to Social Security. That represents yet another deduction from corporate earnings that its shareholders don't receive.

What about employees? They don't bring home total employee compensation, either. Employees are obliged to pay Social Security taxes as well. They end up, then, with less than the full measure of their earnings.

On the other hand, some people in 2008 received more income than they earned. How is that possible? People received income from government in the form of retirement benefits, veteran benefits, unemployment insurance benefits, disability payments, Temporary Assistance to Needy Families, and subsidies to farmers. Economists refer to this form of income as **transfer payments** because the government—acting as receiver and dispenser of income—transfers income from taxpayers (who earned the income in the first place by providing resources) to those receiving benefits. These income transfers, prior to the actual transfers, are counted as part of national income because they represent income earned. They are not counted as national income again when they end up in the hands of the benefit recipients.

Transfer payments
Income received but not earned.

Another form of income is the interest people receive on the government savings bonds, notes, and bills they own. This interest is part of their personal income but is not included in national income. Why not? Because the bonds, notes, and bills that government sold to them were primarily incurred to finance *past* recessions and defense, which—however essential they *were*—were not income yielding in 2008. That is, the interest paid out by government in 2008 had no equivalent 2008 income source.

check your ✓
understanding

Why is a $20 lottery win considered part of your personal income, but not part of national income?

In 2008 the economy's $12,012.1 billion of personal income was less than the $12,481.3 billion of national income.

Households, however, were not free to dispose of the entire $12,012.1 billion of personal income as they wished. Why not? Because they were still obligated to pay direct taxes to federal, state, and local governments. What remains after subtracting these taxes out of personal income is **disposable personal income**. In 2008, this disposable personal income was $10,497.4 billion. It is what households have at their disposal to spend on final goods and services or to save.

Disposable personal income
Personal income minus direct taxes.

EVALUATING ECONOMIC PERFORMANCE

How did the U.S. economy fare over the past quarter century? Well, take your pick. Exhibit 7 provides a variety of measures of economic performance, some expressed in current dollars, some in constant dollars (2000 base year), and some that account for changes in population.

By all accounts, the performance is impressive. Whether we look at GDP, national income, personal income, or personal disposable income, the annual rate of growth is slightly over 6 percent. Adjusting for price changes over the 25 years reduces the rate of growth of GDP—real GDP—to 3.1 percent per year. Adjusting further to account for population changes—real GDP per capita—results in a 2.0 percent annual growth rate.

The range, then, runs from 6.2 percent to 2.0 percent and all of them quite legitimate means of measurement. The point is *knowing and understanding* what measure we are using and why we use it. If you were to pick one, which would it be, and why?

EXHIBIT 7   U.S. Economic Performance, 1998–2005 (current and constant $, base year = 2000; and percent)

	1980	1990	2000	2005	ANNUAL RATE OF GROWTH
GDP	$ 2,789.5	$ 5,801.3	$ 9,817.0	$ 12,479.4	6.2
REAL GDP	5,161.7	7,112.5	9,817.0	11,131.1	3.1
NATIONAL INCOME	2,439.3	5,089.1	8,795.2	10,719.6	6.1
PERSONAL INCOME	2,307.9	4,878.6	7,194.0	10,238.2	6.1
PERSONAL DISPOSABLE INCOME	2,009.0	4,285.8	7,194.0	9,031.3	6.2
GDP PER CAPITA	12,249	23,195	34,759	42,047	5.0
REAL GDP PER CAPITA	22,666	28,429	34,759	37,504	2.0
PER CAPITA INCOME	10,712	20,342	31,141	34,622	4.8

Source: *Economic Report of the President*, Washington, D.C., 2006, Statistical Tables. Except for the per capita data, all other data are in billion of U.S. dollars.

HOW COMPREHENSIVE IS GDP?

Does GDP really measure everything produced in the national economy? Is what we produce an adequate measure of our economic well-being? GDP tries to measure everything that *appears on the market*. But not everything produced in the economy gets onto the market. And there are things that contribute to our economic well-being that aren't even produced.

Value of Housework

One of the most glaring exclusions from GDP accounts is the value of housework done by householders. Nobody with any sense at all would argue that housework is any less a productive activity contributing to our economic well-being than, say, manufacturing automobiles. In fact, housework is included in GDP accounts as long as it isn't done by a member of the household. Hired housekeepers, nannies, and cooks working in households are either employees or self-employed persons earning incomes for productive services that are counted in GDP. In most cases, however, the housekeepers, nannies, and cooks are the householders themselves, and because their productive labor is not supplied through a market—they are neither employees nor self-employed—their contributions are not recorded in GDP accounts.

One explanation for the omission is that GDP was never meant to measure all productive activity in the economy, and, anyway, housework is extremely difficult if not impossible to evaluate. On the other hand, economists have found ways to include other forms of nonmarket productive activity in GDP. Is it really more difficult to impute value to housework than to impute value to goods produced and consumed by farm families on family farms? Yet, GDP includes farmers' self-consumed food, but not the value of housework.

The Underground Economy

Some economic activities other than housework also do not get reported—and for good reason. Drug trafficking, money laundering, bribery, prostitution, fraud, illegal gambling, and burglary are activities that aren't negotiated openly in the marketplace. Yet they represent sets of demanders and suppliers, and they generate unreported incomes that can be sizable.

Other activities, legal and mainstream, go unreported by people trying to evade taxes. There is ample opportunity for people who receive payments for service, such as lawyers, physicians, consultants, domestics, tailors, car mechanics, babysitters, and taxi drivers, to understate income earned.

A driving force of the **underground economy** is tax avoidance. If you and a friend swap services (''I'll fix your car if you paint my house''), you both avoid paying taxes. But the car repair and painting are not counted in GDP. Your 9-to-5 economic activity may be counted, but your moonlighting activities are not.

A growing population of legal and illegal immigrants has swelled the not-so-mainstream workforce. Many earn less than minimum wages working in off-the-books entry-level jobs such as sidewalk vendors of electronics, jewelry, and flowers; serving as casual labor in sweatshops and construction; doing illegal piecework at home; and toiling as domestics. Many immigrants apply their entrepreneurial talents in flea markets, greengrocers, and the garment trade. These activities go unreported. Illegal immigrants are sought-after workers by some employers because, typically, they work for lower-than-prevailing market wages, and because the employer makes no contribution to Social Security or unemployment insurance.

How sizable is this unreported underground economy? Exhibit 8 provides a set of estimates for selected countries.

Are you surprised to discover that the United States, at least according to Exhibit 8's reckoning, is the most law-abiding society of the set? The Swedish society, considered to be among the most socially conscious of Europe, nonetheless includes an underground economy that is more than twice our rate. Perhaps it's Sweden's tax structure that creates an irresistible temptation for many to find a way around paying Swedish sales and income taxes. The underground economies of Australia, the United Kingdom, and Japan, by contrast, measure less than 15 percent of their economic activities, and as you see, all pale in comparison to the Argentinean, Mexican, and Peruvian?

> **Underground economy**
> The unreported or illegal production of goods and services in the economy that is not counted in GDP.

 EXHIBIT 8   Underground Economies, Selected Countries (Percent of GDP)

ARGENTINA	28.9
AUSTRALIA	13.5
UNITED KINGDOM	12.2
UNITED STATES	8.4
JAPAN	10.8
MEXICO	33.2
PERU	60.9
SWEDEN	18.3
SWITZERLAND	9.4
FORMER SOVIET BLOC	40.1

Source: The Tax Foundation, Washington, D.C., 2006. Data compiled by Friedrich Schneider, Johannes Kelper University (Linz, Austria).

appliedperspective

UNDERGROUND ECONOMY DOING THRIVING BUSINESS

What does skid row in Nashville tell us about the American economy? Or drug smuggling in Belize, the black market in Cuba, or one of those sleazy traveling carnival games?

A lot, says Bruce Wiegand, a sociologist at the University of Wisconsin at Whitewater, who has made his career the study of what is diplomatically called the underground economy. It is also known as the black market.

According to Wiegand, that shady, off-the-books economy may be one of America's largest and fastest-growing industries.

It includes drug dealers, teenage babysitters, physicians who ask patients to pay in cash, flea market operators, moonlighting carpenters, small business-people who inflate their deductions, and multinational corporations that fudge on the value of goods trans-ferred between their far-flung subsidiaries.

"My guess," says Wiegand, "is that the under-ground economy is about 25 percent the size of the national economy, and that does not include the illegal sector, like drugs and prostitution."

The illicit underground economy—activities such as drugs and loan-sharking that are by their nature illegal—is probably only about a third the size of the legal underground economy, which comprises other-wise legal enterprises that simply cheat on taxes.

The black market really began with Prohibition in 1920, after the 18th Amendment banned booze, and entrepreneurs such as Al Capone began smuggling it to a thirsty public. Prohibition was repealed in 1933, but depression-era shortages of goods and money and then World War II restrictions resulted in a thriving underground economy.

After the war, the big-city ghettos became the reservoir of the underground economy, because for many entrepreneurial blacks, that was the only way to survive, scholars say.

Middle-class whites began to rediscover the black market in the 1970s, and according to Wiegand, it was finally noticed by economists late in that decade.

IRS estimates on tax avoidance give some clues to the nature of the underground economy. Individuals account for an estimated 75 percent of tax cheating and corporations 25 percent, according to the most recent IRS research reports.

If you'll do my taxes, I'll paint your house.

Among individuals who file federal tax returns, almost 57 percent underreport income. The biggest offenders are sole proprietorships (including doctors, lawyers, accountants, sweatshops, and operators of cottage industries), at almost 20 percent of the national total.

Informal suppliers, such as flea market merchants, account for 9 percent, and the underreporting of capital gains by people wealthy enough to claim them accounts for almost 8 percent.

The best compliance, as might be suspected, is by employees who have their income reported to the IRS on their annual W-2 forms. They account for only 1.7 per-cent of the cheating.

MORE ON THE NET

The Internal Revenue Service (http://www.irs.gov/) maintains extensive tax statistics (http://www.irs.gov/taxstats/index.html).

Source: David Young, "Underground Economy Doing Thriving Business," *Chicago Tribune*, July 10, 1992. © Copyrighted Chicago Tribune Company. All rights reserved. Used with permission.

Leisure

What about the economic value of leisure? What about reading a book, or taking a walk, or playing baseball, or visiting friends? The fact that people choose to spend time consuming some quantity of leisure over producing and consuming more final goods and services indicates that adding up the market value of goods and services may not give us the whole picture of a person's or a society's economic well-being. Going to a Detroit Tigers game on Sunday afternoon is purchased entertainment and included in GDP, but playing tennis with friends on that same afternoon is not.

Quality of Goods and Services

People chronically complain about how our goods and services don't live up to their advertised claims. What's the real value of a new automobile, advertised as high quality, when its transmission fails four days after the warranty runs out? How commonplace is that experience? What value should we place on a toaster that cannot be repaired because there are no shops to service the toaster?

Notwithstanding these and tens of thousands more complaints, quality has nevertheless improved dramatically over time. While transmissions do sometimes go out and toasters become instant junk when one part malfunctions, most of the goods and services we consume have increased in quality and serviceability. Radial tires are considerably more durable than the tires available 25 years ago. Automobiles are more reliable, microwave ovens more convenient, and home furnaces more efficient than they ever were. New technologies make health care more accessible and more successful. Higher-quality goods are continually replacing inferior ones even though they do not always meet our more demanding expectations. These quality improvements may not register in our GDP accounts because the prices of the higher-quality goods may actually be less than the prices of the inferior goods they replace.

Costs of Environmental Damage

While firms keep churning out the goods and services that make up our GDP, they churn out pollution that fouls our environment as well. No-deposit bottles and aluminum cans are convenient but litter our physical space. Automobiles provide us with valued mobility but also with rush-hour traffic, noise, and carbon monoxide. We have polluted air, land, and water, and our poor record in cleaning up our atmosphere threatens to damage the ozone layer that protects us from excessive radiation. We have allowed soil erosion to replace forests in parts of our deforested landscape. Destruction of habitat and species follows. How do these negative attributes of our quest for more goods and services fit into our system of GDP accounts? The cleaning-up expenses associated with the pollution we create contribute to GDP, but the actual pollution created is not subtracted.

Although that's precisely how our GDP accounting works, there's something inherently wrong with this system of accounting. After all, if we were to allocate all our resources to producing and cleaning up garbage, we would end up with a GDP and no goods or services!

In the past 25 years, the government has legislated environmental codes and standards that firms are required to observe. Pollution control has been costly. Billions of dollars that could have been invested in new plants and machinery have been spent instead on pollution control devices. On the other hand, ignoring the effects of economic activity on the environment merely postpones payment and increases the damage.

The polluting activities of the recently defunct communist states were nothing short of horrendous. They simply ignored the environmental effects of their polluting factories. After investing almost nothing in pollution control for decades, it is no longer possible for them to postpone the difficult task of cleaning up a costly environmental mess. Perhaps the communist economists should have seen the U.S. television commercial advertising automobile air filters. It showed a mechanic in the foreground holding an air filter to the screen, while in the background we saw an automobile with its hood raised and engine smoking. The mechanic looked straight at the viewer and said: "You can pay me now [the air filter], or pay me later [the engine]."

Do exclusions from GDP measurement of such items as the value of housework, leisure, and the underground economy seriously undermine the usefulness economists ascribe to GDP accounting? Not really. Having a measure of real GDP that can accurately depict recessions and recoveries is worth the exclusion of some economic activities incapable of being accurately measured on a consistent basis. Simply put: The items excluded involve too much guesswork. What we end up with is a measure of GDP sufficiently comprehensive to be a highly reliable indicator of the changes in the overall performance of the economy.

CHAPTER REVIEW

1. The circular flow model illustrates the resource flow from households to firms and the goods and services flow from firms to households. Money flows through the economy in the opposite direction, as resource payments from firms to households and as goods and services purchases from households to firms. The dollar value of the resource flow equals the dollar value of the goods and services flow.

2. The expenditure approach to measuring GDP adds consumption expenditures by households, investment expenditures by firms, government expenditures, and net exports. In 2006, GDP was $13,037.4 billion.

3. The income approach to measuring GDP adds compensation of employees, interest, rent, corporate profit, and proprietors' income.

4. Gross national product, GNP, is GDP plus receipts of factor income from the rest of the world, minus payments to factor income to the rest of the world. Net domestic product, NDP, is GDP minus capital depreciation. Net national product, NNP, is GNP minus capital depreciation. National income is derived by deducting indirect taxes from NNP. National income in 2006 was $11,491.2 billion.

5. Derivative measures calculated from national income include personal income and personal disposable income.

6. GDP fails to include economic activity such as the value of housework performed by householders and the value of production in the underground economy. GDP also fails to account for improvements in the quality of goods and for environmental costs.

KEY TERMS

Circular flow of goods, services, and resources
Circular flow of money
Expenditure approach
Final goods
Intermediate goods
Value added
Personal consumption expenditures

Gross private domestic investment
Government purchases
Net exports
Durable goods
Nondurable goods
Services
Inventory investment
Income approach
National income

Gross national product (GNP)
Capital depreciation
Personal income
Transfer payments
Disposable personal income
Underground economy

QUESTIONS

1. Describe the clockwise and counterclockwise flows that make up the circular flow model of an economy.
2. Contrast the expenditure and income approaches to calculating GDP.
3. How does government fit into GDP accounting?
4. Distinguish between GDP and GNP.
5. How does the problem of double counting arise in calculating GDP, and how is it corrected?
6. Distinguish between intermediate and final goods.
7. Distinguish between durable goods, nondurable goods, and services.
8. What is an investment good? Why are some investment goods unintended?
9. How do economists bring GDP and national income into accord?
10. How does GDP differ from NDP? From national income?

11. In what ways do NDP and national income provide more specific information about an economy's performance than does GDP?
12. What are some of the limitations in using GDP as a measuring rod of our economic well-being?
13. If Madonna married her personal bodyguard, what effect might it have on national income?
14. Professor Kangoh Lee asks his students at Towson State University, "Suppose that in an economy, real consumption, real investment, and real government purchases remain the same from one year to another, while the real trade deficit increases. Can we conclude that real GDP must fall during the same period?" Explain.

PRACTICE PROBLEMS

1. Use the following data to calculate GDP, GNP, NNP, national income, personal income, and personal disposable income.

PERSONAL CONSUMPTION EXPENDITURES	$800
INTEREST	80
CORPORATE PROFIT	120
GOVERNMENT PURCHASES	300
DEPRECIATION	80
RENT	40
GROSS PRIVATE DOMESTIC INVESTMENT	100
COMPENSATION OF EMPLOYEES	750
EXPORTS	100
IMPORTS	60
INDIRECT BUSINESS TAXES	70
PROPRIETORS' INCOME	110
INCOME TAX	100
INCOME EARNED BUT NOT RECEIVED	120
INCOME RECEIVED BUT NOT EARNED	140
RECEIPT OF FACTOR INCOMES FROM THE REST OF THE WORLD	60
PAYMENT OF FACTOR INCOMES TO THE REST OF THE WORLD	50

2. Suppose, in the following year, the changes in economic activity that occur in practice problem 1 are as follows.

DURABLE GOODS	+30
BUSINESS INVENTORY	+10
IMPORTS	+20
INCOME TAX	+10

What effect would these changes have on GDP?

3. Imagine a three-firm, three-stages-of-production economy that produces one final good: a desk. Calculate the value added at each stage of production.

FIRM	GOOD	TOTAL VALUE OF GOOD PRODUCED	VALUE ADDED
LOGGING FIRM	LOG	$40	
LUMBER FIRM	LUMBER	65	
DESK-MAKING FIRM	DESK	150	

Economic Consultants

Economic Research and Analysis by Students for Professionals

Diane Pecknold owns an independent grocery store that has been in operation for 25 years. Over time Diane has enjoyed good and weathered bad economic times, and she has hired and, unfortunately, had to fire dozens of employees. Diane pays taxes and has a savings account. She pays wages to her employees from the money her grocery store brings in, and she buys goods and services for herself and her family from the profits her store makes. Like most people, Diane is worried that the government spends too much money on frivolous programs and not enough on those that matter.

© Image 100/Royalty-Free/CORBIS

Diane read in the paper about the latest measurement for the GDP. While she recognizes that this is an important economic measure, Diane doesn't understand how the GDP relates to her life and her business. Moreover, she knows a number of businesspeople like her who are similarly confused. One of her employees, who works part time while attending college, suggested that she speak with Economic Consultants about conducting a community workshop to explain what the GDP is and what it measures. Diane contacted Economic Consultants, and the firm agreed to conduct this workshop as a service to the community. Prepare a presentation for this community workshop that addresses the following issues:

1. What is the gross domestic product and what does it measure? What components of the economy are included? What components of the economy aren't reflected in the GDP?

2. How does the government measure GDP? How do the actions of someone like Diane affect the GDP?

3. What is the current measure of GDP, and generally, what does it say about the health of the U.S. economy? What resources are available for learning more about the GDP?

You may find the following resources helpful as you prepare this presentation for the community workshop:

- **Bureau of Economic Analysis** (http://www.bea.gov/)—The Bureau of Economic Analysis publishes current GDP measurements along with analysis and commentary.

- **The Dismal Scientist** (http://www.economy. com/dismal)—The Dismal Scientist is an economic news and analysis service, part of which is devoted to the GDP.

1. The 2008 U.S. GDP and GNP are
   a. approximately equal and both approximately $14 trillion.
   b. approximately equal and both approximately $400 trillion.
   c. approximately equal and both approximately $400 billion.
   d. unequal. GDP is approximately $25 trillion and GNP is approximately $14 trillion.
   e. unequal. GDP is approximately $400 billion and GNP is approximately $25 billion.

2. The circular flow of GDP shows the movement of _____ from firms to households.
   a. income
   b. revenue
   c. resources
   d. goods and services
   e. wealth

3. Under the expenditure approach to calculating GDP,
   a. personal consumption expenditures are excluded from the calculation to avoid double counting.
   b. expenditures for all goods and services (intermediate and final) are added together.
   c. exports are not included in the final total.
   d. only intermediate goods are included in the final total.
   e. expenditures on all final goods and services are added together.

4. All of the following are included in the calculation of GDP under the expenditure approach, except one. Which one?
   a. Gross private domestic investment
   b. Net exports
   c. Services
   d. Net interest
   e. Government purchases

5. Changes in inventories would be included in which of the following expenditure categories?
   a. Gross private domestic investment
   b. Net exports
   c. Government purchases
   d. Personal consumption on durable goods
   e. Personal consumption on nondurable goods

6. National income includes all but which of the following components?
   a. Employee compensation
   b. Corporate profits
   c. Gross private domestic investment
   d. Rental income
   e. Net interest

7. Which of the following income payments for the United States represents the smallest proportion of national income?
   a. Net interest
   b. Employee compensation
   c. Proprietors' income
   d. Corporate profit
   e. Rental income

8. The gross national product for Armenia will exceed the gross domestic product for Armenia when
   a. payments to Armenians in other countries exceed payments to foreigners residing in Armenia.
   b. payments to foreigners residing in Armenia exceed payments to Armenians in other countries.
   c. capital depreciation is positive.
   d. capital depreciation is less than indirect business taxes.
   e. capital depreciation exceeds indirect business taxes.

9. National income can be calculated in which of the following ways?
   a. GDP minus indirect business taxes
   b. GNP plus capital depreciation
   c. GNP minus capital depreciation minus non-factors charges
   d. Personal consumption expenditures plus gross private domestic investment, government purchases, and net exports
   e. Personal income minus taxes and transfers

10. GDP calculations have been criticized for omitting all of the following except one. Which one?
    a. The value of housework
    b. The value of leisure
    c. The level of corporate profits
    d. The level of activity in the underground economy
    e. The costs of damage to the environment

CHAPTER

6

CONSUMPTION AND INVESTMENT

....

Ever hear the expression: "Busy as a bee?" Well, they are! They're constantly buzzing around, searching for nectar, dance-communicating with fellow bees about direction, or home at the hive building cells or cleaning house. Whatever their particular assignment, they're busy all the time.

And so are we. We're a hearty set of busy-bodies, as close to the bee as you can get. If we're not busy at work producing goods and services then we're no less busy at the joy of consuming them. And we do that – hundreds of millions of us – all at the same time. And what is interesting – and perhaps troublesome – about this is that the producers who produce and the consumers who consume make their decisions to produce and consume *simultaneously and independent* of each other. In this one respect – there are others – we're quite different from the bees who don't really make independent decisions. They operate on instinct. And

it seems to work in their case. With all their coming and going, building and cleaning, there's synchronization at the hive.

Our 'hive' or economy is a little different. Think about it. If consumers and producers are busy consuming and producing *simultaneously and independently* of each other, how could producers possibly know that what they chose to produce for consumption is what consumers want to consume? See the problem? And if they're off the mark, what happens? For example, suppose Beth Dollins, Inc., decides to produce 1 million pairs of shoes, but when these shoes reach the market, consumers decide to buy only 600,000 pairs. Suppose, at the same time, that Eddie Richard, producer of Richard percussion instruments, produces 8,000 snare drums only to discover later that consumers take fewer than 3,000 off the market. And suppose that their experiences are common among producers. That is, *consumers just aren't buying enough of everything produced.* The most plausible consequence in this scenario is a cutback in overall production (a decrease in real GDP) and an increase in the economy's unemployment. Bees, on the other hand, are never unemployed.

Or suppose also that Dollins's decision to produce 1 million pairs of shoes is still off base, but this time it's because consumers want to buy more than Dollins produced. Suppose also that Richard's 8,000 snare drums are substantially fewer than the number of drums consumers want. And to complete the picture, let's suppose other producers discover that they, too, underproduced for the market. Now the problem is reversed: *Producers are not producing as much as people want to consume.* The most plausible consequence of this scenario is greater overall production (an increase in real GDP) and a decrease in the economy's unemployment.

The uncomplicated fact that production and consumption decisions are made simultaneously and independently of each other is critically important in understanding the forces that determine the level of real GDP, or what goes on in our 'hive.'

WHAT DETERMINES CONSUMPTION SPENDING?

How do people choose their level of consumption spending? What factors are involved in their decisions to increase or decrease the amount of goods and services they consume? Are we just creatures of habit? Or impulse?

If you had to guess the single most important factor influencing a person's consumption spending, you would probably be right on the first try. It's the level of a person's disposable income. (For now, let's assume no government spending or taxes, so that a person's income is the same as his or her disposable income.) You would also be right to suppose that rich people consume more than poor people because rich people have more income. You don't have to be a Nobel laureate in economics to figure that out! Economists refer to this simple, but

check your understanding

What is the principal factor determining the level of a person's consumption spending?

Consumption function
The relationship between consumption and income.

powerful, relationship between consumption and income as the **consumption function**. It is written as

$$C = f(Y),$$

where C represents consumption and Y represents income. It means that consumption is a function of income, or in other words, that the level of consumption depends on the level of income.

Let's use real numbers to illustrate this relationship. Suppose Brenda Nielsen, a manager at Record Swap, enjoys a $1,000 raise in salary. What would happen to her consumption? Does it increase by the $1,000? Or by less? And if by less, by how much less? A number of hypotheses have been offered to explain how changes in an individual's income and, taken collectively, changes in national income affect individual and national consumption.

Absolute Income Hypothesis

John Maynard Keynes, whose 1936 book *The General Theory of Employment, Interest and Money* became the bedrock upon which Keynesian economics was built, advanced the hypothesis that although people who earn high incomes spend more on consumption than people who earn less, they are less inclined to spend as much *out of a given increase in income* than are those earning less. For example, Madonna's consumption spending is greater than Brenda's. Yet, if both were given $1,000, Madonna would likely spend less of the $1,000 on consumption than Brenda.

Why? Keynes believed that consumption behavior reflects a psychological law that links changes in our consumption spending to the absolute levels of our income. He explains:

> The fundamental psychological law, upon which we are entitled to depend with great confidence both *a priori* from our knowledge of human nature and from the detailed facts of experience, is that men are disposed, as a rule and on the average, to increase their consumption as their income increases, but not by as much as their increase in their income.... [A] higher absolute level of income will tend, as a rule, to widen the gap between income and consumption. For the satisfaction of the immediate primary needs of a man and his family is usually a stronger motive than the motives towards accumulation, which only acquire effective sway when the margin of comfort has been attained.

on the net

The Census Bureau (http://www.census.gov/hhes/www/income.html), the Bureau of Economic Analysis (http://www.bea.gov/), and the Bureau of Labor Statistics (http://www.bls.gov/eag/) publish income data for the United States.

Absolute income hypothesis
As national income increases, consumption spending increases, but by diminishing amounts. That is, as national income increases, the *MPC* decreases.

Does this **absolute income hypothesis** seem reasonable to you? Imagine a millionaire receiving a gift of $500. It's unlikely that you would find him running off to buy more food, clothing, or shelter. He would probably just add the $500 to his savings. Why? In Keynes's view, the millionaire's "margin of comfort" is already provided, and the "stronger motive" guiding his behavior, then, becomes "accumulation."

But suppose the $500 were given to an inner-city welfare recipient. What do you suppose he would do? Consult his broker? Do you think he would save a penny? Wouldn't the "immediate primary needs of [him] and his family"—as Keynes aptly put it—lead straight to consumption?

An Individual's Marginal Propensity to Consume Let's pursue Keynes's idea further. If Brenda's income were increased by increments, say, of $1,000—getting richer with every $1,000 added—the amount she would spend on consumption *out of each additional $1,000* would decrease.

EXHIBIT 1   The Individual's Marginal Propensity to Consume

THE MARGINAL PROPENSITY TO CONSUME

TOTAL INCOME (Y)	CHANGE IN INCOME	CONSUMPTION (C)	CHANGE IN CONSUMPTION	MARGINAL PROPENSITY TO CONSUME (MPC)
0		$ 500		
$1,000	$1,000	1,400	$900	0.90
2,000	1,000	2,200	800	0.80
3,000	1,000	2,900	700	0.70
4,000	1,000	3,500	600	0.60
5,000	1,000	4,000	500	0.50

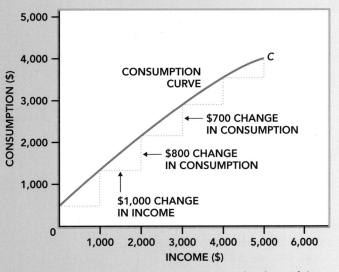

The marginal propensity to consume measures the slope of the consumption function. It is the ratio of the change in consumption to the change in income. When income increases by $1,000—from $1,000 to $2,000—the change in consumption is $2,200 − $1,400 = $800. *MPC* is ($2,200 − $1,400)/($2,000 − $1,000) = 0.80. Note how consumption spending increases by diminishing amounts as the income level increases, tracing out the curvature of the consumption curve, *C*.

Exhibit 1 illustrates this point.

As her income increases in increments of $1,000 from $0 to $5,000, her consumption increases as well. But note the incremental changes. The first $1,000 addition to income—raising income from $0 to $1,000—induces a change in consumption from $500 to $1,400, or by $900. Keynes defines the change in consumption induced by a change in income as the **marginal propensity to consume (MPC)**.

$$MPC = \frac{\text{change in } C}{\text{change in } Y}$$

The marginal propensity to consume, *MPC*, is a quantifiable and behavioral relationship. It measures our inclination, Keynes calls it our propensity, to consume *specific* increases out of *specific* income changes.

At the income level of $1,000, the marginal propensity to consume is ($1,400 − $500)/($1,000 − $0) = 0.90.

Marginal propensity to consume (MPC)
The ratio of the change in consumption spending to a given change in income.

EXHIBIT 2   The Nation's Marginal Propensity to Consume

THE NATION'S MARGINAL PROPENSITY TO CONSUME ($ BILLIONS)

NATIONAL INCOME (Y)	CHANGE IN NATIONAL INCOME	CONSUMPTION (C)	CHANGE IN CONSUMPTION	MARGINAL PROPENSITY TO CONSUME (MPC)
$ 0		$ 60		
100	$100	150	$90	0.90
200	100	230	80	0.80
300	100	300	70	0.70
400	100	360	60	0.60
500	100	410	50	0.50

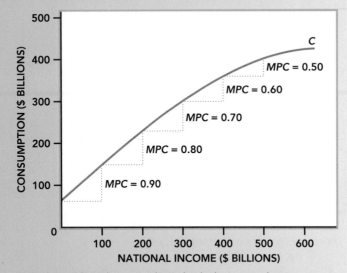

Note the similarity between the individual's marginal propensity to consume of Exhibit 1 and the nation's. When the national income increases, national consumption increases as well, but by diminishing amounts. *MPC* decreases from 0.90 to 0.50 as national income increases from $0 to $500 billion, tracing out the upward-sloping consumption curve, *C*.

What happens to consumption when the second $1,000 of income is added? Consumption increases from $1,400 to $2,200, or by $800. Therefore, at $Y = $2,000$, Brenda's *MPC* is ($2,200 − $1,400)/($2,000 − $1,000) = 0.80. Brenda increases consumption, but by less than she did before. Her *MPC* falls from 0.90 to 0.80.

Note what's going on. As more units of $1,000 are added to Brenda's income, her total consumption continues to increase, but each time by lesser amounts. At $Y = $3,000$, $C = $2,900$ and the corresponding *MPC* = 0.70. At $Y = $4,000$, $C = $3,500$ and *MPC* = 0.60, and so on. MPC *falls as the absolute level of income increases.*

The Nation's Marginal Propensity to Consume To Keynes, national economies behave like individuals. Just as Brenda's *MPC* depends upon the level of her income, so does a nation's *MPC* depend upon its level of national income. Exhibit 2 describes Keynes's view of the nation's consumption behavior.

The nation has its own *MPC*. When national income increases from $300 billion to $400 billion, national consumption increases by $360 − $300 = $60 billion. At $Y = 400 billion, *MPC* = 0.60. Look at the *MPC* column. As the absolute level of national income increases, the nation's *MPC* decreases.

Look at the corresponding graph. Note the step increases along the consumption curve, *C*. They become increasingly smaller as national income increases; the curve flattens out to almost no increase at all at high levels of national income.

The nation's consumption curve reflects Keynes's *absolute* income hypothesis. It shows that the nation's *MPC* depends upon the *absolute* level of national income. Does this make sense? Do you find Keynes's view of consumption spending behavior convincing? Does it reflect reality?

If your intuition tells you Keynes was right, you would be dead wrong! Five years after Keynes's *The General Theory of Employment, Interest and Money* appeared, Simon Kuznets published his *National Income and Its Composition*, which pioneered analysis of national income data. (He won the Nobel Prize in economics in 1971.) Kuznets's findings—as well as the mountains of empirical research that followed—showed that, contrary to intuition, *a nation's MPC tends to remain fairly constant regardless of the absolute level of national income*. Where did Keynes go wrong?

on the net
Review an autobiography of Simon Kuznets (http://www.nobel.se/economics/laureates/1971/index.html).

Relative Income Hypothesis

Every economy, whatever its level of national income, includes people earning different incomes. Knowing someone's absolute income tells us little about that person's income status. For example, Brenda earning $20,000 a year would be considered a low-income person if others in the economy earned more, say $40,000 and $80,000. On the other hand, that same $20,000 makes her a high-income person if others in the economy earn less, say, $5,000 and $10,000.

If Brenda's income doubled to $40,000, but at the same time everybody else's income also doubled—say, from $40,000 to $80,000 and from $80,000 to $160,000—then Brenda, at $40,000 income, would still be regarded as low income.

The distinction between Brenda's relative income (that is, income relative to other incomes) and her absolute income level provided economists with an alternative view of the consumption function. It explains why the marginal propensity to consume in the economy does not decline as national income increases—as Keynes believed it does—but instead remains constant.

According to James Duesenberry, one of the first of the economists to advance the relative income hypothesis, *consumption spending is rooted in status.* High-income people not only consume more goods and services than others, but also set consumption standards for everybody else. They own the most comfortable homes, drive the most expensive cars, enjoy the newest consumer technologies, and read *Architectural Digest* without feeling deprived.

Everybody else takes their cues from the rich. The middle-income people try to stay within reach. Low-income people struggle to keep their consumption within sight of middle-income consumption. For example, if Brenda's *MPC* is 0.80 at an income of $20,000, it remains 0.80 even if her income doubles to $40,000 *as long as her relative income position remains unchanged.* If everybody's income doubles so that their relative income positions remain unchanged, then everybody's *MPC* remains unchanged. That's how Duesenberry, among other economists, explains why, contrary to what Keynes thought, the nation's *MPC* is constant while national income increases.

The logic is compelling and is supported by historical data as well. Keynes's consumption function of Exhibit 2 is modified in Exhibit 3 to reflect the **relative income hypothesis**.

As national income increases by increments of $100 billion, the economy's consumption spending increases by increments of $80 billion so long as

check your understanding
What explains the constant *MPC*?

Relative income hypothesis
As national income increases, consumption spending increases as well, always by the same amount. That is, as national income increases, *MPC* remains constant.

historical perspective

JOHN MAYNARD KEYNES: A NEW MACROECONOMICS

Although he was celebrated for his contributions to economic theory, John Maynard Keynes's creative energies were focused primarily on solving real-world issues. He was interested in changing the world, not simply in understanding it.

In the 1930s the economic world Keynes observed was in turmoil. The reality of a persisting and deepening economic depression seemed to contradict everything economists knew about how an economy works. The conventional wisdom of classical economics argued that depression was only a short-run, temporary departure from full-employment equilibrium and that in the long run the economy would return to it. Keynes's response to this conventional wisdom was that "in the long run, we're all dead."

But Keynes really didn't see the issue—what to do about the depression—as a matter of patience. He was convinced that the economy could not correct itself even in the very long run and explained his reasoning in *The General Theory of Employment, Interest and Money* (1936). *The General Theory* offered an entirely new set of ideas about macroeconomics that, almost instantaneously, became a new school of economic thought. There was ready acceptance of his ideas among the bright young economists in Britain and in the United States, in part because of the collapse of confidence in classical economics during the depression but also because Keynes was already Britain's preeminent economist. Had he proposed that the world was flat, many of his fellow economists would probably have given him the benefit of the doubt and flattened their globes.

Although a rising star at Cambridge, Keynes did not limit himself to academic research. The real world was his natural venue. He divided his time between London and Cambridge, working in London at the Treasury during the week and lecturing at Cambridge on weekends. Quickly establishing a formidable reputation at the Treasury, he became a major participant in international diplomacy, a task he initially relished but later came to dislike. He was the chief economic counsel to the British delegation at Versailles after World War I and there warned against a peace treaty that would impose harsh retribution on defeated Germany, believing that such a policy would ensure the collapse of the European economy. His two-volume work *A Treatise on Money* (1930) established him as the heir apparent to Marshall. During all this time, Keynes was editor of *The Economic Journal*, the premier scholarly research journal in Britain (and, arguably, the world).

John Maynard Keynes changed the way we think about the world of economics.

Keynes also put his financial wizardry to work in stock speculations, which he made in the early morning by phone while still in bed, and which made him a millionaire. While bursar of King's College, he speculated on the college's behalf, increasing its endowment tenfold.

Although new ideas have come to challenge Keynesian economics, many Keynesians still revere him as Shakespeare's Anthony did Caesar: "Here was a Caesar! When comes such another?"

....

MORE ON THE NET

For a sample of Keynes's writing, review his May 1932 *Atlantic Monthly* article, "The World's Economic Outlook", and look at Keynes's *The Economic Consequences of Peace* (http://socserv2.socsci. mcmaster.ca).

everybody's income position remains unchanged. That is, the marginal propensity to consume, *MPC*, is constant at 0.80.

Of course, low-income people have higher incomes when national income is $500 billion than when it is $200 billion. And because they have higher incomes, they spend more on consumption. But because their relative income has not changed—everyone, rich and poor, is richer—their *MPC*, and the economy's, remain unchanged.

Notice the steplike increases in consumption in Exhibit 3. Because *MPC* = 0.80 at every level of income, every dollar increase in income generates an $0.80 increase in consumption—the steps are the same height—so that the consumption curve, *C*, is a straight line.

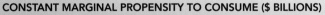

✋   **EXHIBIT 3**   The Marginal Propensity to Consume Remains Constant

CONSTANT MARGINAL PROPENSITY TO CONSUME ($ BILLIONS)

NATIONAL INCOME (Y)	CHANGE IN NATIONAL INCOME	CONSUMPTION (C)	CHANGE IN CONSUMPTION	MARGINAL PROPENSITY TO CONSUME (MPC)
$ 0		$ 60		
100	$100	140	$80	0.80
200	100	220	80	0.80
300	100	300	80	0.80
400	100	380	80	0.80
500	100	460	80	0.80

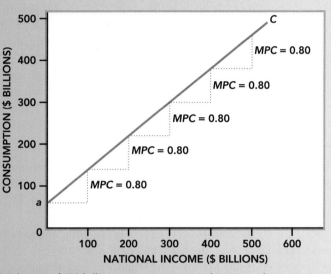

With every $100 billion increase in national income, the nation's consumption spending increases by $80 billion, tracing out a straight-line consumption curve, C. The MPC = 0.80 at every level of national income.

Economists have continued to study the consumption function, providing additional insights into our consumption behavior. Two among the most influential are Milton Friedman's **permanent income hypothesis** and Franco Modigliani's **life-cycle hypothesis**.

Permanent Income Hypothesis

Milton Friedman, who won the Nobel Prize in economics in 1976, believes that people distinguish between their regular income and the income they may happen to make (or lose) in any one year. He refers to regular income as **permanent income**, and to the unanticipated income that adds to (or subtracts from) the permanent income as **transitory income**.

Why make these distinctions? Because, according to Friedman, how much we spend on consumption depends strictly on our permanent income.

Why? Why doesn't transitory income contribute to our consumption spending? Because people don't usually go about changing lifestyles when they suffer a temporary loss of income or even when they enjoy a temporary gain. Consumption spending is generally tied to long-run earning capacity.

Permanent income hypothesis
A person's consumption spending is related to his or her permanent income.

Life-cycle hypothesis
Typically, a person's *MPC* is relatively high during young adulthood, decreases during the middle-age years, and increases when the person is near or in retirement.

Permanent income
Permanent income is the regular income a person expects to earn annually. It may differ by some unexpected gain or loss from the actual income earned.

Review an autobiography of Milton Friedman (http://www.nobel.se/economics/laureates/1976/index.html).

Review an autobiography of Franco Modigliani (http://www.nobel.se/economics/laureates/1985/index.html).

Imagine two people, Natasha Rubel and Peter Holsapple, each earned $50,000 in 2008. Suppose Natasha, a self-employed artist who conducts art-therapy classes for teachers and counselors, had a bad year. A broken leg put her out of work for three months, so that her 2008 income of $50,000 was $15,000 less than the $65,000 she typically earns.

What would Natasha's 2008 consumption look like? The permanent income hypothesis suggests that, assuming $MPC = 0.80$, Natasha's consumption would be $0.80 \times \$65,000 = \$52,000$. The effect of her negative $15,000 transitory income shows up as reduced saving. Her saving in 2008 becomes $\$50,000 - \$52,000 = -\$2,000$. Her negative transitory income creates, then, negative saving, or dissaving. The important point is that she still thinks of herself as a $65,000 person and consumes like one.

What about Peter Holsapple? He's a high school teacher who typically earns $35,000. But in 2008 he received a $15,000 teaching award. Would this $15,000 transitory income affect his $35,000 lifestyle? Not likely. Assuming his $MPC = 0.80$, his 2008 consumption, fixed by his permanent income, is $0.80 \times \$35,000 = \$28,000$. The effect of the $15,000 positive transitory income shows up as saving, which in 2008 becomes $\$50,000 - \$28,000 = \$22,000$.

Friedman's point is simple. To appreciate what influences consumption spending, we must distinguish between transitory and permanent income.

Life-Cycle Hypothesis

Franco Modigliani of MIT, who won the Nobel Prize in economics in 1985, makes his own observation about our consumption behavior. He identifies three consumption phases—young adult, middle age, and near or in retirement—in a person's life cycle. Each specific phase has its specific *MPC*.

The *MPC* for young adults is relatively high. They are busy building families and careers. They buy first homes, first new automobiles, stocks of household durables, sets of clothing for growing children, and streams of services. These items tend to eat quickly into their modest incomes.

When they become middle-aged, enjoying their highest and most rapidly growing incomes, their consumption spending also increases, but modestly, at least compared to earlier years. After all, their homes are virtually mortgage-free, their car payments not nearly so demanding, their children finally graduating from college, and the basics of life already taken care of. They tend to consume more because they earn more, but the ratio of changes in consumption to changes in income tends to fall. That is, their *MPC* falls.

In the third phase, nearing or in retirement, their *MPC* tends to rise. Why? Their retirement incomes don't grow very much, and in many cases, actually decline. But what about their consumption? They become more careful about their spending, but habits are hard to break. People don't change their lifestyles that much.

Modigliani explains why differing *MPC*s over a person's life cycle are still consistent with the observed stability in our national *MPC*. As long as birth and death rates are relatively stable, the percentage of population passing through these three consumption phases at any time remains stable as well.

Autonomous Consumption Spending

The idea that consumption depends primarily on the level of income is so consistent with our experience that very few people have trouble making the connection. But consumption based on income is not the whole story. Look again at Exhibit 3.

When $Y = \$0$, $C = \$60$ billion. Some consumption is autonomous, that is, independent of the level of income. Economists call it **autonomous consumption**.

Why autonomous? Because some consumption spending is simply unavoidable. The spending takes place regardless of the level of income. For example, we might spend less on food, clothing, and shelter when our incomes fall, but there are limits to how deeply we can cut into our consumption of these basics. At some point, we simply cannot consume less and still survive. We make some minimum consumption spending even if we have to borrow, use our savings, or sell off part of our assets. Put simply: If we have no other means of putting food on the table, we may sometimes be forced to sell the table! That explains why in the economy of Exhibit 3, when income is $0, autonomous consumption is positive. The consumption curve, C, in Exhibit 3 begins at a, above the origin on the vertical axis, at $60 billion.

Autonomous consumption Consumption spending that is independent of the level of income.

Shifts in the Consumption Curve

Look at the consumption curve, C, in Exhibit 4. A change in national income from, say, $200 billion to $300 billion induces a change of $80 billion in consumption—from $220 billion to $300 billion. We see this change in consumption as a movement *along* the consumption curve C.

But consumption spending can change even when the level of national income remains unchanged. These changes in consumption are caused by shifts in the consumption curve itself. What factors shift the consumption curve in Exhibit 4 upward from C to C'?

Real Asset and Money Holdings Suppose Sara Cook wins the $190 million Powerball lottery. That's everyone's fantasy! And suppose she decides to keep her $50,000 job at Disney World. It's hard to believe that her lottery winnings would not *eventually* affect her consumption spending. The probability is high that even though she continued to work at her $50,000 job, she would end up consuming more goods and services than before.

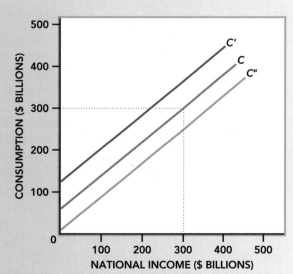

EXHIBIT 4   Shifts in the Consumption Curve

Shifts in the consumption curve are distinguished from movements along the curve. The shifts are unrelated to changes in national income. Among the principal factors causing the shifts in the consumption curve are changes in the economy's asset and money holdings, in people's expectations of price changes, in interest rates, and in taxation. Anything that causes autonomous consumption to change will shift the consumption curve.

check your ✔ understanding

What happens to the consumption curve when people's real asset holdings increase?

Or suppose George Paaswell, who rents a studio apartment in midtown Manhattan, inherits a mortgage-free house on Park Avenue. That's not exactly $12 million, but to George, it's a real asset of considerable value. Wouldn't you think an inheritance like that would affect his consumption spending?

Suppose people's real assets and money holdings in the economy increase. National consumption spending should increase as well. These increases are shown in Exhibit 4 as an upward shift in the consumption curve from C to C'. A decrease in the nation's real assets or money holdings would have the opposite effect, shifting the curve from C to C''.

Expectations of Price Changes People are always anticipating the future. Suppose, for some reason, they expect inflation to increase from 3 to 12 percent in one year and to continue in double digits for the following six years. Wouldn't it be smart for people, *even though they don't expect their income to change*, to increase the level of their consumption spending now, before the expected inflation hits? Such an increase shifts the consumption curve from C to C'.

Credit and Interest Rates People's consumption of relatively costly durables, such as automobiles, houses, and major kitchen appliances, is typically financed by interest-carrying credit. For many, interest payments on these items make up a significant part of their monthly expenditures. If, then, credit is made more available or if the credit terms are made more attractive, say, by a cut in the interest rate, won't people increase their consumption spending even if their incomes haven't changed? The consumption curve would shift upward from C to C'.

Taxation We are all obligated to pay taxes. But how much? Suppose the government decides to cut the income tax rate. Then imagine Meg Weinbaum's delight when she discovers more dollars in her pay envelope at the end of the week, even though her salary remains unchanged. What do you suppose she would do with the extra money? Spend some of it, wouldn't she? She and many millions more would shift the consumption curve from C to C'. If their pay envelopes were lighter because of increased taxes, the consumption curve would shift from C to C''.

on the net

One estimate of future consumption is the consumer confidence index (http://www.conference-board.org/economics/index.cfm). Each month, about 5,000 households respond to questions about expectations for their jobs, their incomes, their careers, and their spending plans. From these responses, economists can gauge whether consumption will likely increase or decrease over the next month.

THE CONSUMPTION EQUATION

As you see, there are two key factors influencing the character of our consumption spending. Keynes's conception of the marginal propensity to consume, and the insightful modifications to the consumption function that followed—by Kuznets, Duesenberry, Friedman, and Modigliani—show that our level of consumption spending is primarily determined by our level of income. Economists refer to this consumption as *induced* consumption, meaning induced by the level of income. A second factor contributing to consumption spending is autonomous consumption.

Adding autonomous consumption to consumption spending induced by income generates a specific form of the consumption function:

$$C = a + bY,$$

where a is autonomous consumption spending, b is marginal propensity to consume, and Y is the level of national income.

Let's see how the equation is used to determine how much consumption spending occurs when $Y = \$800$ billion, $MPC = 0.80$, and $a = \$60$ billion. We simply plug the appropriate values into the equation:

$$C = a + bY$$
$$= \$60 \text{ billion} + 0.8(\$800 \text{ billion})$$
$$= \$60 \text{ billion} + \$640 \text{ billion}$$
$$= \$700 \text{ billion}$$

When national income is $900 billion—assuming *MPC* and autonomous consumption remain unchanged—consumption spending is $780 billion.

WHAT DETERMINES THE LEVEL OF SAVING?

People do two things with their income. They either spend it on consumption or they do *not* spend it on consumption. When people make a decision about one, they automatically make a decision about the other. After all, if you decide to spend 80 percent of your income, you have also made a decision *not* to spend 20 percent, haven't you? The income not spent on consumption is defined as **saving**:

$$S = Y - C$$

That's the economy's saving equation. Moreover, in the same way we derive the marginal propensity to consume, we derive the **marginal propensity to save (MPS)**. The *MPS* measures the change in saving generated by a change in income:

$$MPS = \frac{\text{change in } S}{\text{change in } Y}$$

If *MPC* = 0.80, then *MPS* = 0.20. Why? Because if our marginal propensity to consume is 80 percent of any additional income, then it stands to reason that our marginal propensity to save is the rest. That's the remaining 20 percent.

We could just as well have stated the relationship between *MPC* and *MPS* the other way. That is, if we save 20 percent of any additional income, then our propensity to consume the rest is 80 percent. Either way, the marginal propensities to consume and to save add up to 100 percent:

$$MPC + MPS = 1$$

The equation can be rewritten to focus on the derivation of *MPS*.

$$MPS = 1 - MPC$$

The table in Exhibit 5 shows the relationship between national saving, national consumption, *MPC*, and *MPS*.

As you see, in the unlikely income range of $Y = \$0$ to $Y = \$200$ billion, saving is actually negative. How can people consume more than their income allows? By running down their savings or other forms of accumulated wealth. In this same way, nations can end up with negative saving. As we already noted, economists refer to negative saving as dissaving.

Let's see how the equation is used to determine how much saving occurs when $Y = \$400$ billion and $MPC = 0.8$.

$$S = Y - C$$
$$= \$400 \text{ billion} - (0.8 \times \$400 \text{ billion})$$
$$= \$20 \text{ billion}$$

Saving
That part of national income not spent on consumption.

Marginal propensity to save (MPS)
The change in saving induced by a change in income.

check your understanding

How are *MPC* and *MPS* related?

KEY EXHIBIT 5   The Saving Curve

Saving is defined as income not spent on consumption. When Y is less than $300 billion, C is greater than Y, so that saving is negative, that is, the nation is dissaving. Saving is $0 at $300 billion, and then positive and increasing as national income increases beyond $300 billion. Panel a shows saving as the difference between the income and consumption curves. Panel b depicts the saving curve.

MARGINAL PROPENSITY TO SAVE ($ BILLIONS)

Y	CHANGE IN Y	C	S	MPC	MPS
$ 0		$ 60	$–60		
100	$100	140	–40	0.80	0.20
200	100	220	–20	0.80	0.20
300	100	300	0	0.80	0.20
400	100	380	20	0.80	0.20
500	100	460	40	0.80	0.20

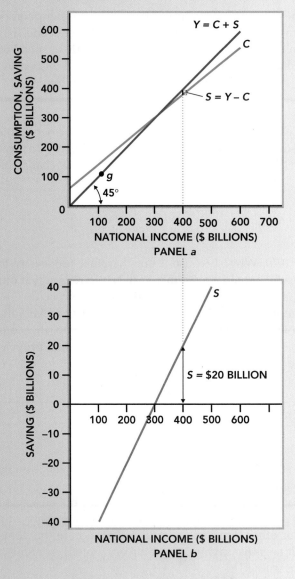

When $Y = \$500$ billion and MPC remains at 0.8 then $S = \$40$ billion. Throughout the income range $Y = \$0$ to $Y = \$500$ billion in the table, saving increases by $20 billion for every $100 billion increase in national income. Afterall, MPS is constant at 0.20.

In panel *a* of Exhibit 5, the 45° diagonal line serves as a point of reference. Since $Y = C + S$, every point on the 45° line equates the level of Y measured on the horizontal axis to the level of $C + S$ measured on the vertical axis. For example, point *g* on the diagonal measures $100 on both axes. The **45° line** measuring $Y = C + S$ is also called the **income curve**.

How do we derive the level of saving in panel *a*? Look, for example, at $Y = \$400$ billion. By using the equation $S = Y - C$, and substituting $(a + bY)$ for C, we derive

$$S = Y - (a + bY)$$
$$= \$400 \text{ billion} - [\$60 \text{ billion} + (0.8 \times \$400 \text{ billion})]$$
$$= \$20 \text{ billion}.$$

Now look at $Y = \$400$ billion in panel *b* of Exhibit 5. Panel *b* is another way of looking at panel *a*, showing only the saving curve, which, as we have seen in panel *a*, is derived from subtracting consumption from national income. At $Y = \$400$ billion, the $20 billion difference between Y and C, shown in panel *a*, shows up as $20 billion in the saving curve of panel *b*.

Because the absolute $(Y - C)$ gap in panel *a* increases as the level of Y increases, the saving curve in panel *b* is upward sloping.

THE INVESTMENT FUNCTION

At the same time that consumers are deciding how much of their income to spend on consumption and how much to save, producers in the economy are deciding how much to spend on investment.

What determines investment? Producers have to decide whether to replace used up or obsolete machinery, whether to expand production, whether to increase raw material or finished goods inventories, and even whether to build completely new facilities for entirely new products.

Each producer makes these investment decisions independently of others. For example, the giant Caterpillar, in Peoria, Illinois, may decide to expand its forklift production line at the same time that a small retail bookstore in Phoenix, Arizona, decides to move into larger space.

Wal-Mart may decide to open another store in Raleigh, North Carolina. The Artistic Headwear Company in Bangor, Maine, protecting itself from inadequate supplies, may decide to increase its raw material inventories.

These and tens of thousands of other investment decisions made by producers make up the **intended investment** for the national economy. As we shall see, intended investment doesn't always end up realized.

WHAT DETERMINES INVESTMENT?

Consider two different levels of national income: Does your intuition tell you that intended investment should be greater when national income is higher? That at $Y = \$800$ billion, producers would tend to invest more than at $Y = \$500$ billion?

Think again. What if the economy at $Y = \$800$ billion is in a downturn phase of a business cycle. Why, then, in a year of declining national income, should producers consider buying more machinery or expanding production lines or building new factories? Why gear up for more production when consumers are not gearing up for more consumption? Shouldn't we expect intended investment, to be relatively weak under these bleak conditions?

What about intended investment at $Y = \$500$ billion? Suppose the economy is in the recovery phase of a business cycle. Wouldn't you expect to find producers busy purchasing new machinery, adding more production lines, and stocking up

Income curve or 45° line
A line, drawn at a 45° angle, showing all points at which the distance to the horizontal axis equals the distance to the vertical axis.

Intended investment
Investment spending that producers intend to undertake.

check your understanding

Why isn't the level of income important in determining investment?

historical perspective

Saving the Buffalo.

PROPENSITY TO SAVE

Why do people save? Seems obvious, doesn't it? Or does it? If you were living in late 19th-century England and attended Cambridge University, you would no doubt have heard Professor Alfred Marshall lecture on the subject. He eventually put his ideas on savings into his celebrated *Principles of Economics* (1891). To Marshall, "... family affection is the main motive for saving." He elaborates:

That men labor chiefly for the sake of their families and not for themselves, is shown by the fact that they seldom spend, after they have retired from work, more than the income that comes in from their savings, preferring to leave their stored-up wealth intact for their families...."

A man can have no stronger stimulus to energy and enterprise than the hope of rising in life, and leaving his family to start from a higher rung of the social ladder than that on which he began.

A lot of economic and social change has occurred since Marshall wrote these lines. Do we still think about family in the same way? Do Marshall's views on our propensity to save make sense in the 21st century?

Professor Christopher Carroll at The Johns Hopkins University has a different take on why we save. It is not to finance our future consumption or that of our heirs, he says, in his paper "Why Do The Rich Save So Much?"* Instead, the reason we save is to create a "flow of services (such as power or social status)." That is, Carroll believes we derive a value from saving as we would from buying any good. In this case, the goods we buy *having savings* are power and social status. It's an interesting and very un-Marshallian idea.

If you haven't thought about it, you will! In the near future, you will become an income earner and a saver and will have to make up your mind about how much of your income you will spend and save. You will eventually have an answer to the question: Why save?

* Carroll's article appears in *Does Atlas Shrug? The Economic Consequences of Taxing the Rich*, ed. Joel Shimrod (Cambridge, Mass.: Harvard University Press, 2000).

on inventories? After all, people with growing incomes are also people whose consumption spending is growing. Intended investment under these spirited conditions would tend to be relatively high.

It would seem then that the level of national income doesn't necessarily play a decisive role in determining investment. Exhibit 6 illustrates this point, showing investment as independent of the level of national income.

The investment curve, I, is a horizontal straight line. If $I = \$75$ billion, it is $\$75$ billion regardless of the level of national income. For example, when $Y = \$100$, $I = \$75$ billion. When $Y = \$200$ billion, $I = \$75$ billion. And so on.

Determinants of Investment

Autonomous investment
Investment that is independent of the level of income.

But why $75 billion? What factors determine the size of the economy's **autonomous investment**? There are four principal determinants of autonomous investment: the level of technology, the rate of interest, expectations of future economic growth, and the rate of capacity utilization.

Technology Level The introduction of new technologies is one of the mainsprings of investment. For example, when the railroad displaced water transport as the principal means of long-distance transportation, it sparked massive investment spending not only in the railroad industry, but in the secondary industries that grew up alongside it. Investments in mining, steel, lumber,

KEY EXHIBIT 6   The Investment Curve

The investment curve is horizontal, independent of the level of national income. Intended investment is $75 billion at every level of national income.

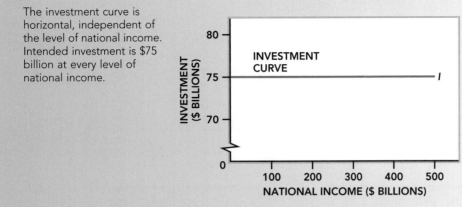

and construction were needed to feed the expanding railroads. But that was only the surface of railroad-led investment. The railroads opened up the West, generating decades of spectacular investment spending in roads and commercial and residential building, as well as in goods that filled these new structures.

Similar technological leaps, such as the automobile, steam power, electricity, the telephone, petrochemicals, television, nuclear energy, drugs, computers, and genetic engineering have produced, in their own times, extensive networks of investment spending.

There is no connection between these technological breakthroughs and the levels of national income they feed, and it is also impossible to fit them into any defined timetable. Like volcanoes, they seem to erupt in their own time and place.

Interest Rate Producers undertake investment when they believe that the rate of return generated by the investment will exceed the interest rate, that is, the cost of borrowing investment funds. For some types of investment, the difference between the expected rate of return and the interest rate is so wide that even a 4 or 5 percent change in the interest rate has no influence on the investment decisions.

There are other investment projects, however, typically large scale and long term, such as housing construction or expansion of automobile assembly lines, for which interest charges are an important cost factor. Slight changes in the rate of interest—even fractions of a point—may be a sufficient incentive or deterrent to such investment spending.

Picture the scene. Michelle Vlasminski, CEO of Michelle Enterprises, asks five of her executives to present investment projects that would cost roughly $1 million each and to estimate their expected rate of return. The following week, Michelle, with the five projects in hand, considers which, if any, to undertake. Their expected rates of return are as follows: project $A = 12$ percent, project $B = 7$ percent, project $C = 10$ percent, project $D = 9$ percent, and project $E = 8$ percent. If the interest rate (what Michelle pays to borrow investment funds) is 15 percent, which, if any, investment project will she accept? None, of course. She would not borrow at a 15 percent interest rate if she can get, at best, only a 12 percent rate of return.

What if the interest rate is 11 percent? Then, project A is feasible. If the interest rate is 9.5 percent, then both projects A and C are advantageous. At 8.5 percent interest, projects A, C, and D increase the profitability of her firm. As you can see,

on the net

While we cannot predict technological break-throughs, we can measure the amount of technological research and development happening in the economy. The National Science Foundation, Division of Science Resources Studies (http://www.nsf.gov/sbe/srs/), does just that.

check your understanding

How is the interest rate related to the level of intended investment?

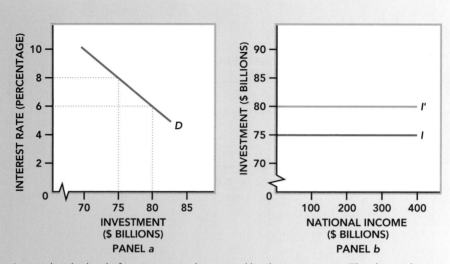

EXHIBIT 7　　The Effect of Changes in the Rate of Interest on the Level of Investment

In panel *a*, the level of investment is determined by the interest rate. The demand curve for investment, *D*, is downward sloping. As the rate of interest decreases from 8 to 6 percent, the level of investment in the economy increases from $75 billion to $80 billion. This increase in investment is depicted in panel *b* as an upward shift in the investment curve, from $75 billion to $80 billion.

a lower interest rate makes more investment projects feasible. In other words, there is an inverse relationship between the rate of interest and the quantity of investment spending.

That's what panel *a* of Exhibit 7 depicts.

The demand curve for investment in the economy as a whole is downward sloping. That is, as the interest rate falls, the quantity demanded of investment increases. For example, when the rate falls from 8 to 6 percent, investment increases from $75 billion to $80 billion. *Note that this increase in investment has nothing to do with changes in national income.* This new level of investment is represented, in panel *b*, by the upward shift of the investment curve from *I* to *I'*, from $75 billion to $80 billion.

Expectations of Future Economic Growth Investment spending reflects how producers view the future. They expand production lines or build entirely new factories if they expect sales to grow. What influences expectations?

Many producers base their expectations of the future on past experience. If the economy grew rapidly in the past, many producers—lacking any contrary information—expect it to continue to grow rapidly in the future. If they expect it to grow, they prepare for the growth by increasing investment spending. On the other hand, if the economy was sluggish in the past, these same producers would expect it to continue being sluggish. Investment may be the furthest thing from their minds. That is to say, investment takes its cue from past performance. It's the changes in national income and the projections of those changes into the future, not the absolute level of national income, that influence producers.

Rate of Capacity Utilization Producers seldom choose to operate at 100 percent capacity. Why not? Because to produce at capacity reduces their ability to expand production on demand. They typically choose a capacity utilization rate that

on the net

One estimate of how producers view the economic future is the Measure of Business Confidence (http://www.conference-board.org/economics/index.cfm). Every quarter, about 150 business leaders from various industries respond to questions about their businesses.

gives them some short-run flexibility. For example, by operating at 85 percent capacity, they can increase production by as much as 15 percent without having to wait for new machinery or raw material inventories. In the highly competitive business world, differences of months, weeks, or even days can make the difference between success and failure.

There is, however, a cost to flexibility. Carrying excess productive capacity can be an expensive way of overcoming short-run production bottlenecks. How much flexibility producers end up choosing, then, influences the economy's level of investment. For producers who choose to operate close to full capacity, a moderate increase in sales may shift them quickly into strong investment spending.

on the
net
The Federal Reserve Board publishes monthly data on capacity utilization and industrial production (http://www.federalreserve.gov/releases/g17/default.htm).

The Volatile Nature of Investment

Any one of the factors just discussed can excite or depress the level of investment. In some years, these factors pull in opposite directions. For example, the interest rate may increase at the same time a new round of technologically induced investments are introduced. One stimulates, the other dampens investment spending.

On the other hand, there are times when, *by chance*, these factors work in unison. A fall in the interest rate combines with an increase in the rate of technological change, with a shift to greater capacity utilization and with impressive economic growth. In such a situation, dramatic upward shifts in the investment curve occur.

The investment curve in Exhibit 8 shows the volatility of investment spending in the U.S. economy.

In some years, a specific combination of factors influencing investment drives the level of investment to new heights, only to be followed by a sharp plunge in investment driven by a reversal in those same factors. Most of the time, the direction—let alone the levels—investment will take is, for everyone, a big unknown.

EXHIBIT 8 The Volatility of Investment

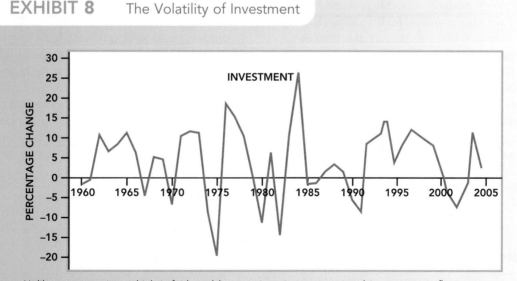

Unlike consumption, which is fairly stable over time, investment is subject to erratic fluctuations even through very short periods of time. The economic and technological factors that influence investment can sometimes create the conditions for rapid expansion of investment and, just as quickly, reverse to cause investment to fall just as rapidly, as we see in the annual rate of change in real investment spending over the years 1960 to 1995.

Source: *Economic Report of the President 2006* (Washington, D.C.: United States Government Printing Office, 2006), p. 285.

COMBINING CONSUMPTION AND INVESTMENT

Let's pause for a moment. The two principal building blocks in the Keynesian model—consumption and investment—have been put in position. What follows is an analysis of the relationship between consumption and investment that explains how the Keynesian model derives national income.

That's the task we assign to the following chapter. It should be viewed as a continuation or second half of this chapter, since both chapters develop the Keynesian model of national income determination.

CHAPTER REVIEW

1. The consumption function relates the level of consumption to the level of income. The relationship is causal: An increase in income increases consumption.
2. Keynes's absolute income hypothesis suggests that as income increases, consumption increases, but at a decreasing rate. Keynes believed that the rich have a lower marginal propensity to consume than do the poor. Extending his theory from individuals to the national economy, Keynes argued that a nation's marginal propensity to consume depends on the absolute level of national income.
3. Empirical work on the national marginal propensity to consume by Simon Kuznets found that contrary to Keynes's hypothesis, the nation's marginal propensity to consume is constant. Duesenberry's relative income hypothesis helps to explain Kuznets's empirical finding. When national income increases and relative incomes remain unchanged, the marginal propensity to consume for the nation is unchanged. Duesenberry's hypothesis suggests a straight-line consumption function.
4. Friedman's permanent income hypothesis distinguishes between permanent income and transitory income. Friedman argues that consumption is dependent on permanent income.
5. Modigliani's life-cycle hypothesis of consumption behavior suggests that a person's marginal propensity to consume changes during one's lifetime. Young people tend to have high marginal propensities to consume. People in middle age have lower marginal propensities to consume. When people are in retirement, the MPC increases again.
6. Autonomous consumption is independent of income. Shifts in the consumption function involve changes in autonomous consumption. The consumption function shifts due to changes in real asset and money holdings, expectations of changes in the price level, changes in interest rates, and changes in taxes.
7. The consumption equation expresses consumption as a function of national income. Consumption is equal to autonomous consumption (a) plus national income (Y) multiplied by the marginal propensity to consume (b): $C = a + bY$.
8. The saving equation is $S = Y - C$. The marginal propensity to save is $1 - MPC$.
9. Changes in investment tend to be unrelated to the level of national income. Investment is regarded as autonomous. Variables that influence investment include technological change, interest rate changes, changes in the rate of growth of national income, and the rate of capacity utilization. Autonomous investment can be quite volatile.

KEY TERMS

Consumption function	Permanent income hypothesis	Saving
Absolute income hypothesis	Life-cycle hypothesis	Marginal propensity to save (MPS)
Marginal propensity to consume (MPC)	Permanent income	Income curve or 45° line
Relative income hypothesis	Transitory income	Intended investment
	Autonomous consumption	Autonomous investment

QUESTIONS

1. What is the *MPC*? The *MPS*? What is the relationship between them?
2. How does autonomous consumption fit into the consumption equation?
3. Accepting the absolute income hypothesis, would you expect the *MPC* in the U.S. economy in 1995 to be higher, lower, or about the same as the *MPC* in the Haitian 1995 economy? Why? How would it compare to the *MPC* in the U.S. economy in 1925?
4. Accepting the relative income hypothesis, would you expect the *MPC* in the U.S. economy in 2003 to be higher, lower, or the same as the *MPC* in the U.S. economy in 1925? Why?
5. Give an example of transitory income. What effect does this income have on the marginal propensity to consume?

6. What is autonomous consumption?
7. Why would a change in asset or money holdings shift the consumption curve?
8. What factor explains movements along the consumption curve?
9. Why is *MPC* + *MPS* always equal to 1?
10. What is dissaving? Describe a situation that would create dissaving in an economy.
11. What factors determine autonomous investment?
12. Consider the variables income, consumption, and investment. One relationship among them is relatively stable, the other quite volatile. Discuss.

PRACTICE PROBLEMS

1. Calculate the marginal propensity to consume, the marginal propensity to save, and the level of saving for each income level in the accompanying table.

Y	C	MPC	MPS	SAVING
$ 0	$ 50			
100	100			
200	150			
300	200			
400	250			
500	300			

2. Calculate consumption for each level of national income, given the accompanying levels of autonomous consumption, C_a, and marginal propensities to consume.

Y	C_a	MPC	C
$100	$50	0.50	
200	60	0.60	
300	70	0.70	
400	80	0.80	
500	90	0.90	

3. Calculate the level of autonomous investment, *I*, for each level of national income.

Y	C	I
$100	$ 50	60
200	100	
300	150	
400	200	
500	250	

4. Accepting Milton Friedman's permanent income hypothesis, calculate the marginal propensities to consume (MPCs) for each of the four scenarios.

PERMANENT INCOME	TRANSITORY INCOME	TOTAL INCOME	CONSUMPTION	MPC
$ 8,000	$ 2,000	$10,000	$ 6,400	
14,000	6,000	20,000	7,000	
25,000	5,000	30,000	19,500	
30,000	10,000	40,000	21,000	

5. For each of the three income levels shown, provide appropriate data to satisfy or be consistent with the absolute and relative income hypotheses.

	CONSUMPTION		MPC	
INCOME	ABSOLUTE INCOME HYPOTHESIS	RELATIVE INCOME HYPOTHESIS	ABSOLUTE INCOME HYPOTHESIS	RELATIVE INCOME HYPOTHESIS
$1,000				
2,000				
3,000				

6. For each of the three income levels shown, provide appropriate data to satisfy or be consistent with the absolute and relative income hypotheses.

	SAVING		MPS	
INCOME	ABSOLUTE INCOME HYPOTHESIS	RELATIVE INCOME HYPOTHESIS	ABSOLUTE INCOME HYPOTHESIS	RELATIVE INCOME HYPOTHESIS
$4,000				
5,000				
6,000				

7. Calculate the 2002 and 2003 MPCs for each of the countries.

	2002			2003	
	ΔY	ΔC	MPC	ΔY	MPC
FRANCE	1,000 EUROS	6,000 EUROS		1,000 EUROS	
ITALY	1,000 EUROS	7,000 EUROS		1,000 EUROS	
BRITAIN	1,000 POUNDS	7,500 POUNDS		1,000 POUNDS	
IRELAND	1,000 EUROS	8,000 EUROS		1,000 EUROS	

8. Calculate the 2002 and 2003 MPCs for each of the countries *when national income falls* by 1,000.

	2002			2003	
	ΔY	ΔC	MPC	ΔY	MPC
FRANCE	–1,000 EUROS	–6,000 EUROS		–1,000 EUROS	
ITALY	–1,000 EUROS	–7,000 EUROS		–1,000 EUROS	
BRITAIN	–1,000 POUNDS	–7,500 POUNDS		–1,000 POUNDS	
IRELAND	–1,000 EUROS	–8,000 EUROS		–1,000 EUROS	

WHAT'S WRONG WITH THIS GRAPH?

The Consumption Curve (Short-Run)

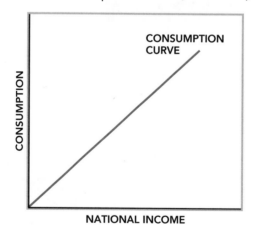

Economic Consultants

Economic Research and Analysis by Students for Professionals

Gary Behrman is regional manager of the Wal-Mart stores in Dallas, Texas. As manager, Gary must decide every month how much inventory to stock and how many people to hire (or fire). He has a layman's understanding that these decisions depend on the state of the national economy and, more specifically, on the economic climate in the Dallas region, but he would like to be better informed about the connection.

One of his part-time employees, a student at Dallas Community College, suggests that he might get the information he seeks by hiring Economic Consultants to show him what specific factors influence people's consumption and how these influences affect the decisions he must make at Wal-Mart concerning its inventory and hiring. Prepare a presentation for Gary that addresses the following issues:

1. What factors (or variables) influence how much consumers spend on consumption goods? What factors influence the amount of consumption goods produced?

2. What resources are available to make short-run forecasts concerning expected consumer sales, wage rates, and production for retail in Texas and in Dallas?

You may find the following resources helpful as you prepare this presentation for Gary:

- **Consumer Confidence Index** and the **Measure of Business Confidence** (http://www.conference-board.org/

© Image 100/Royalty-Free/CORBIS

economics/index.cfm)—The Consumer Confidence Index and the Measure of Business Confidence, released monthly, provide a short-term forecast of consumption and production.

- **Summary of Commentary on Current Economic Conditions by Federal Reserve District (The Beige Book)** (http://www.federalreserve.gov/FOMC/BeigeBook/[type current year])—The Beige Book—so named because the report has a beige cover—is published eight times a year. Each Federal Reserve bank gathers anecdotal information on current economic conditions in its district through reports from bank and branch directors and interviews with key businesspeople, economists, market experts, and other sources. The Beige Book summarizes this information by district and sector (including Dallas, Texas).

- **Federal Reserve Bank of Dallas** (http://www.dallasfed.org/)—The Dallas Fed publishes annual reports (http://www.dallasfed.org/fed/annual/1999p/ar92.html) and publications (http://www.dallasfed.org/pubs/index.html).

- **The *Dallas Morning News*** (http://www.dallasnews.com/)—The *Dallas Morning News* provides business news (http://www.dallasnews.com/business/) for the Dallas area.

1. Comparing investment to the consumption function, we can say that over time
   a. investment is more stable than the marginal propensity to consume.
   b. investment levels are higher than consumption levels.
   c. investment levels are equal to levels of consumption.
   d. investment is more volatile.
   e. marginal propensity to investment is equal to the marginal propensity to consume.

2. According to Keynes's absolute income hypothesis,
   a. individuals have relatively fixed income levels in real (inflation-adjusted) terms over their lifetimes.
   b. wealthy people consume a larger proportion of their wealth then do poor people.
   c. an individual's marginal propensity to consume is constant.
   d. consumption rises as income rises, but at a decreasing rate.
   e. consumption rises proportionately with changes in income.

3. George earns $50,000 per year and spends $40,000 consuming goods and services such as housing and food. Suppose that George receives a lottery prize of $10,000, and he spends $8,000 on a new car and saves the remaining $2,000. Which of the following is true?
   a. George's behavior is consistent with Duesenberry's income hypothesis.
   b. George's marginal propensity to consume is falling.
   c. George reacts differently to marginal changes in income than he does to permanent changes in income.
   d. George's behavior is consistent with Modigliani's income hypothesis.
   e. George's behavior is consistent with Friedman's income hypothesis.

4. The notion that people do not radically alter their consumption patterns due to transitory changes in income is referred to as the
   a. life-cycle hypothesis.
   b. absolute income hypothesis.
   c. transitory income hypothesis.
   d. relative income hypothesis.
   e. permanent income hypothesis.

5. If an individual's income is $0, the consumption level for the individual
   a. must equal 0.
   b. is referred to as transitory consumption.
   c. is referred to as permanent consumption.
   d. is referred to as autonomous consumption.
   e. is negative if the individual has to borrow money to pay for necessities.

6. If there is a fall in interest rates from 8 percent to 7 percent, then
   a. the consumption function will shift downward.
   b. permanent income will rise by 1 percent.
   c. there will be an upward movement along the consumption function.
   d. there will be a downward movement along the consumption function.
   e. the consumption function will shift upward.

7. Suppose that a $6,000 increase in income is accompanied by a $4,500 increase in consumption. The marginal propensity to save
   a. is 0.75.
   b. is 0.25.
   c. is 1.33.
   d. is 0.20.
   e. cannot be determined without knowing the initial levels of income and consumption.

8. If the consumption equation is given to be $C = \$80 + 0.7Y$ and $Y = \$1,000$, then the level of saving in a two-sector economy (saving and consumption)
   a. equals $220.
   b. equals $700.
   c. equals $300.
   d. equals $780.
   e. cannot be determined without information about the savings function.

9. Along the 45° line,
   a. income always equals consumption.
   b. the economy has a declining *MPS*.
   c. the level of saving falls as income rises.
   d. income always equals consumption plus saving.
   e. the consumption function is equal to one.

10. The autonomous investment curve will shift upward when which of the following occurs?
   a. There is a fall in the level of technology.
   b. Interest rates rise.
   c. The level of income rises.
   d. The level of income falls.
   e. There is a rise in capacity utilization in firms.

Appendix

DERIVING THE LONG-RUN CONSUMPTION FUNCTION

. . . .

The consumption function developed in this chapter—and which will be used in others to follow—relates consumption to income under conditions of *ceteris paribus*, that is, "with everything else remaining unchanged." As we saw, the consumption curve shifts upward or downward when "other things happen," such as a changes in people's wealth holding, changes in the government's tax structure, changes in population, or changes in foreign exchange.

The truth of the matter is that these "other things" *always* do change over time. Our wealth holdings are greater today than they were a decade ago and considerably greater than they were a half century ago. Tax reforms are legislated periodically. Population and permanent income increase, and foreign exchange rates continuously shift. These time-related changes, when incorporated into the depiction of the relationship between consumption and income, trace out a consumption curve of a different form. Instead of the curve cutting the vertical axis above the origin, the curve appears to start at the origin. Look at panel *a*.

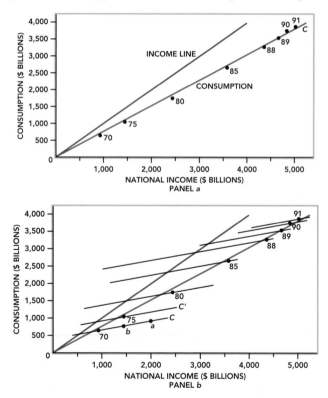

THE LONG AND THE SHORT OF IT

The consumption function or curve in panel *a* lies at every point—whatever the level of national income—below the income line. This different portrayal of the consumption function is *not* a challenge to the familiar relationship between consumption and income that we analyzed in the text. Instead, it depicts the shape of a long-run consumption function that is generated by bringing together a series of short-run consumption curves, the kind analyzed in the text.

To illustrate the derivation of this long-run consumption curve, years 1970 to 1991 are selected—actually any set of years would do—and the accompanying table records for each of these years, levels of national income, and corresponding levels of consumption.

Panel *b* maps the data and sketches a series of short-run consumption curves that match the data points. The link between these short-run curves and the long-run consumption curve is constructed in the following way.

THE CONSUMPTION FUNCTION: 1970

Let's start with the short-run consumption function, *C*. The levels of national income and consumption for 1970 (refer back to the table) are $930 billion and $645 billion. These levels are based on the existence of specific set of wealth holdings, permanent incomes, taxes, population, foreign exchange rates, and so on.

Now follow the logic: *If* in 1970, national income was not $930 billion but, say, $1,440 billion (the national income that was actually realized in 1975), *while the specific set of 1970 wealth holdings, permanent income, taxes, population, and foreign exchange rates remained unchanged*, then according to the 1970 short-run consumption curve *C*, consumption in 1970 at income level $1,440 billion would be approximately $825 billion, position *b* on the curve.

Or, supposing national income in 1970 was not $1,440 but, say, $2,000 billion, then the corresponding consumption in 1970—*again assuming that the specific set of 1970 wealth holdings, permanent income, taxes, population, and foreign exchange rates remained unchanged*—would be approximately $980 billion, at point *a*.

THE CONSUMPTION FUNCTION: 1975

But suppose that after five years of steady economic growth, population increased along with increases in people's wealth holdings and permanent income. Because of these changes, *a new specific and different set of wealth holdings, permanent income, taxes, population, and foreign exchange rates is associated with 1975*. And because there is this new set for 1975, the short-run consumption curve for 1975 shifts to *C'*. In 1975, then, the actual levels of national income and consumption are $1,440 billion and $1,025 billion.

Compare the hypothetical 1970 consumption of $825 billion at the national income level of $1,440 to the actual 1975 consumption of $1,025 billion at the national income level of $1,440. People consume more in 1975 than they would have in 1970 had the same level of national income obtained because in 1975, they had more wealth holding, and so on.

THE CONSUMPTION FUNCTION: 1970–1991

The explanation that derives the two points on the long-run consumption function—1970 and 1975—explains as well how all other points along the long-run curve, 1980 to 1991, are derived.

	NATIONAL INCOME ($ BILLIONS)	CONSUMPTION ($ BILLIONS)
1991	$5,060	$3,900
1990	4,930	3,740
1989	4,675	3,520
1988	4,375	3,295
1985	3,600	2,670
1980	2,430	1,750
1975	1,440	1,025
1970	930	645

EQUILIBRIUM NATIONAL INCOME

THIS CHAPTER INTRODUCES YOU
TO THE ECONOMIC PRINCIPLES
ASSOCIATED WITH:

- Aggregate expenditure

- The equilibrium level of
national income

- The relationship between
saving and investment

- The income multiplier

- The relationship between
aggregate expenditure and
aggregate demand

- The paradox of thrift

Which blade in a pair of scissors cuts the cloth? Silly question? The answer is apparent, isn't it? Both blades do. It is inconceivable to suppose that one blade alone can do the cutting. That's what Alfred Marshall, the celebrated 19th-century economist, said when asked whether demand or costs of production determine price. His reply (*Principles of Economics*, 1891)—using the scissors metaphor—was that both, equally, and in particular, *the interaction of both*, determine price.

© Image 100/Royalty-Free/CORBIS

About a half-century later, a similar question was asked about the determination of the equilibrium level of national income. Which "blade" does the "cutting?" Is it aggregate or aggregate supply? You might think the answer was obvious. But Marshall's most renowned student, J. M. Keynes, while acknowledging that the interaction of aggregate expenditures and aggregate supply determines the equilibrium level of national income, still felt one blade in particular is responsible for most of the cutting. That blade, he was convinced, is aggregate expenditure.

Why he was so convinced is the subject of this chapter. What determines the equilibrium level of national income was an important issue for Keynes then—and is perhaps for us today—because he believed that the economy is always heading toward equilibrium and that its equilibrium level might be a rather troublesome one.

Keynes was trying to explain why the 1930s economy was mired in depression. If he could figure that out, then maybe he could figure out how an economy can get out of it. That is, is it possible to change an equilibrium level?

Let's follow Keynes on this one for now. Let's build a Keynesian-like model to represent an economy heading toward or being in equilibrium. While both aggregate supply and aggregate expenditure will ultimately decide the outcome, *the* key player in this national income determination drama is aggregate expenditure, and in particular, its subcategory, investment.

INTERACTION BETWEEN CONSUMERS AND PRODUCERS

Two very different kinds of people are at work making decisions concerning consumption spending, saving, and investment that affect each other. As we saw in the previous chapter consumers spend part of their income on consumption and save the rest. This is represented as

$$Y = C + S.$$

At the same time, other people, acting as producers, produce both consumption goods and investment goods, partly in response to and partly in anticipation of the demands that consumers make for consumption goods and producers intend to make for investment goods. This is represented as

$$Y = C + I_i.$$

Now suppose, *by chance,* that the investment producers intend to make equals what consumers actually save out of their income. It follows, then, that what producers intend to produce for consumption ($C = Y - I_i$) turns out to be precisely what consumers intend to consume ($C = Y - S$). (The subscript i indicates *intended* as distinct from *actual.*) This perfect match between intended investment and savings is written as

$$I_i = S.$$

Perhaps it is worthwhile to note again that the $I_i = S$ equation is a chance event arrived at, in this illustration, by decision making on the part of producers and consumers that, unbeknownst to both, created the perfect fit. After all, the producers of investment goods do not know *with certainty* what people who do the saving are intending to save. Nor can the people making saving decisions take into consideration what the producers of investment goods, responding to or anticipating investment demand, are intending to produce.

How interesting, then, if this chance event generates for both producers and consumers the condition in which all consumption, investment, and saving intentions in the economy are realized!

The $I_i = S$ equation describes the economy in macroequilibrium. After all, no excess demand or supply exists. All the consumption goods supplied by producers are taken off the market by consumers; **aggregate expenditure** equals aggregate supply.

But what if the intended investment of producers is not equal to the saving people choose to make?

THE ECONOMY MOVES TOWARD EQUILIBRIUM

The national economy, if not already in equilibrium, is always moving toward it. *But not by chance.* Let's suppose the economy is at $Y = \$900$ billion, which is *not* the **equilibrium level of national income**. Suppose as well that autonomous consumption is $60 billion and $MPC = 0.80$. Consumption spending, then, is

$$C = \$60 + (0.80 \times \$900) = \$780.$$

Suppose also that the producers in the economy have decided that of the $900 billion of goods they produced, $100 billion is intended for investment. That's their intended investment demand:

$$I_i = \$100$$

How Consumers and Producers Behave When Y = $900 Billion

Let's focus on how consumers and producers behave under these circumstances. What do consumers do at $Y = \$900$ billion? What do the producers do at $Y = \$900$ billion? These two sets of people make their consumption and investment decisions simultaneously and independently of each other. We can imagine them thinking through their choices and reacting to realized and unrealized outcomes.

Exhibit 1 summarizes their behavior.

Look at the top rows of Exhibit 1. The left-hand side, describing consumers' behavior, simply spells out the fact that consumers divide their income $Y = \$900$ billion into $C + S$. The right-hand side, describing producers' behavior, shows that producers, responding to and anticipating demands for consumption and investment goods, divide their production of $Y = \$900$ billion into $C + I_i$.

But how much of the $Y = C + S$ is in the form of C, and how much of the $Y = C + I_i$ is in the form of C, consumption goods produced. Look at the left-hand side first. At $Y = \$900$ billion, consumers spend [$\$60 + (0.8 \times \$900)$] = $780 billion on consumption. They save, then, $120 billion.

Look now at the right column. Producers intend to invest $100 billion. That means they intend to produce for consumption $800 billion. They immediately run into a vexing problem. How can they sell $800 billion, when consumers are prepared to buy up only $780 billion? They can't.

Aggregate expenditure
Spending by consumers on consumption goods, spending by businesses on investment goods, spending by government, and spending by foreigners on net exports.

Equilibrium level of national income
$C + I_i = C + S$, where saving equals intended investment.

EXHIBIT 1   Consumers' and Producers' Intentions and Activities, by Stages, When $Y = \$900$ Billion

CONSUMERS	PRODUCERS
$Y = \$900$	$Y = \$900$
$Y = C + S$	$Y = C + I_i$
$C = a + bY$	$I_i = \$100$
$C = \$60 + 0.8\,(Y)$	$C = Y - I_i$
$\quad = \$60 + 0.8\,(\$900)$	$\quad = \$900 - \$100$
$\quad = \$780$	$\quad = \$800$
$S = Y - C$	$I_a = \$120$
$\quad = \$900 - \$780$	
$\quad = \$120$	

What happens to the $\$800 - \$780 = \$20$ billion of consumption goods that are produced but remain unsold? Retail stores, unable to move the $20 billion across the counter as final goods, discover they have more inventory than they want. Their shelves are crammed with these unsold goods, many boxed in stockrooms and warehouses. That is to say, *although produced as consumption goods, the $20 billion—by default—becomes investment goods in the form of* **unwanted inventories**. Inventories are investment goods.

In other words, producers intended to invest $100 billion, but their **actual investment**, I_a, turns out to be $120 billion, that is, $20 billion more than the intended investment, I_i:

$$I_a > I_i$$

As you can see, whether producers' investment intentions are realized or not depends on what consumers do. After all, how much people choose to consume out of their income dictates how much of what producers produce for consumption gets sold. This logic underscores Keynes's emphasis on aggregate expenditures.

You can imagine what happens next. Retail stores, saddled with unwanted inventories, scale down their orders for resupply. After all, why reorder when they can't sell what they already have? Producers, in turn, feeling the pinch of fewer reorders, will be unable to maintain production levels.

What follows next? Both retailers and producers lay off workers. And there's nothing employers or workers can do about it. What room is there for compromise? With consumption and investment functions being what they are, the $900 billion level of national income simply cannot support employment for all the workers. Unemployment results. With fewer people working, production and income fall.

How Consumers and Producers Behave When $Y = \$700$ Billion

Now let's suppose national income is not at $Y = \$900$ billion but at $Y = \$700$ billion. What happens to consumer and producer intentions at $Y = \$700$ billion? Look at Exhibit 2.

As you see, the basic consumption and investment functions, $C = \$60 + 0.8Y$ and $I_i = \$100$, remain unchanged. Consumers still spend $60 billion on autonomous consumption and 0.80 of national income. Producers still intend to invest $100 billion.

check your understanding

Why are some inventories unwanted?

Unwanted inventories Goods produced for consumption that remain unsold.

Actual investment Investment spending that producers actually make—that is, intended investment (investment spending that producers intend to undertake), plus or minus unintended changes in inventories.

applied perspective

TELEPHONE CALL TO AUTHOR'S BROTHER, IRVING GOTTHEIL, CEO OF THE ARTISTIC HAT COMPANY, CANADA

Dressed for the occasion.

FRED: Let's talk about business. What's going on this year? Are you doing anything different?

IRVING: We're coming out with new colors and new styles. And producing a lot more hats.

FRED: Who decides how many hats to produce?

IRVING: I do! Come to think about it, it's also the firms I sell to. After all, they retail the hats. You know, the big ones like the Hudson Bay Company, Zeller's Incorporated, Sears, and Wal-Mart. Then there are the hundreds of boutique shops across Canada.

FRED: How do these firms know how many hats to order?

IRVING: Well, when you get right down to it, it's a guessing game. They have to anticipate what consumers want. It's hard. We really can't get into consumers' heads. Of course, we hope to get on their heads.

FRED: Be more specific.

IRVING: Well . . . we make decisions on the basis of what we think people will demand. And what they demand depends upon a lot of things. For example, if it's a cold winter (like last year), they buy. Remember three years ago? It hardly snowed. People didn't need hats. Only Santa Claus wore a hat! We ended up with an overload of unsold inventory. You saw the problem when you were in Montreal that February. Who wore hats? We couldn't give them away. It was a bad year. Some years are really bad for other reasons. Remember when I moved the factory from 124 McGill Street to 5445 de Gaspe Street? I doubled my space expecting a great season. It was a heck of a decision. I was wrong! How did I know the economy was going into a recession. What a recession! I took an awful beating.

FRED: What about Sears and Hudson Bay?

IRVING: They took a beating too! Listen, they're no *mavens* [a maven is a sage]. They were left holding half the hats they ordered. By the way, this is a good year despite the warm weather. It goes to show you. You think you know, and you don't.

FRED: What's in store for next year?

IRVING: I'm optimistic. Not crazy optimistic, but optimistic. The factory is running now at full capacity. I'm even replacing the stamping presses I bought in Milan, Italy, just two years ago. Technology changes so quickly in this business. There's a new press out of Sweden that is top of the line. I figure it will cut my stamping press labor costs by 25 percent. Oh yes, those handmade aluminum molds that come from England . . . a company in Toronto does the same quality work and is much less expensive. I'm going to give them a try.

FRED: Looks like you're banking on a lot of people buying hats.

IRVING: That's right! But you know, Freddie, it's always risky. Someone has to make the decision on how much to produce. And that someone is me. Next year? I need cold weather. I can use an ice age. By the way, why these questions?

FRED: I will use them in the book as an example of firms making decisions concerning production of consumption and investment goods. You're my consumption goods decision-maker.

IRVING: Spell my name right!

FRED: Any message for my students?

IRVING: Yeah. Stay out of the hat business!

FRED: How about giving the student who scores the highest grade in my economics class a hat as a prize?

IRVING: Let's wait until the end of the season, OK? If the season's bad, I could give your entire class hats!

But note what happens now. Consumers spend [$60 + (0.8 × $700)] = $620 billion on consumption goods. Producers, on the other hand, intending to invest $100 billion in new factories, new equipment, new vehicles, and so on, produce only $700 − $100 = $600 billion of consumption goods.

With consumers spending $620 billion on consumption but finding only $600 billion of consumption goods available, retail stores find that inventories they had wanted to hold as investment end up sold as consumption goods.

Picture, for example, David Tietlebaum's Poster and Frame store. Its wall and freestanding shelves are filled with stocks of posters. People can walk into

EXHIBIT 2   Consumers' and Producers' Intentions and Activities, by Stages, When $Y = \$700$ Billion

CONSUMERS	PRODUCERS
$Y = \$700$	$Y = \$700$
$Y = C + S$	$Y = C + I_i$
$C = a + bY$	$I_i = \$100$
$C = \$60 + 0.8\ (Y)$	$C = Y - I_i$
$\quad = \$60 + 0.8\ (\$700)$	$\quad = \$700 - \$100$
$\quad = \$620$	$\quad = \$600$
$S = Y - C$	$I_a = \$80$
$\quad = \$700 - \$620$	
$\quad = \$80$	

the store and choose from among precut Lucite, steel, and wood frames. As you can well imagine, it would be very difficult for David to sell framed posters if he didn't have a ready supply on hand—that is, an inventory—of posters and frames. (Recall, inventories are part of investment.)

How does David fit into the $Y = \$700$ billion scenario? Because consumers spend $620 billion on consumption goods while producers only produced $600 billion of them, David discovers, along with many other producers and retailers, that part of the inventory stocks they wanted to keep on hand — shelves of books at bookstores, new cars in show case windows, new model refrigerators at appliance stores, 64-inch flat screen televisions at Best Buy and Circuit City, you know the list — are taken away by demanding consumers. David's reaction? Happiness, galore. More sales mean more profit. And to replenish the unanticipated draw down of his wanted inventory, he reorders many more posters and frames from his suppliers than he had originally intended to, not only to bring his inventory back to desired levels but to meet this new and unexpected consumer demand. His experience and reaction is shared by other producers and retailers who see their desired inventories decrease. Remember: All this happens because consumers demand $620 billion of consumption goods while only $600 billion of those goods were produced by the producers.

So once again, intended investment will not equal actual investment. But this time, unlike the $Y = \$900$ billion scenario, actual investment is less than intended:

$$I_a < I_i$$

You can hear the telephones ringing off the hooks. You can see the text messages and fax machines working overtime, from retailers to producers: "SOS. We need more goods!" Producers of consumption goods and their retailers are, of course, happy with this shortfall in supply. They're now busy hiring more workers to churn out more consumption goods. New workers earning more income pump national income above $700 billion.

How Consumers and Producers Behave When $Y = \$800$ Billion

Let's now suppose national income is at $Y = \$800$ billion. How would consumers and producers behave? Look at Exhibit 3.

The consumption and investment functions remain unchanged. Look what consumers do now. Consumption spending is $[\$60 + (0.8 \times \$800)] = \$700$ billion.

EXHIBIT 3   Consumers' and Producers' Intentions and Activities, by Stages, When $Y = \$800$ Billion

CONSUMERS	PRODUCERS
$Y = \$800$	$Y = \$800$
$Y = C + S$	$Y = C + I_i$
$C = a + bY$	$I_i = \$100$
$C = \$60 + 0.8\,(Y)$	$C = Y - I_i$
$\quad = \$60 + 0.8\,(\$800)$	$\quad = \$800 - \$100$
$\quad = \$700$	$\quad = \$700$
$S = Y - C$	$I_a = \$100$
$\quad = \$800 - \$700$	
$\quad = \$100$	

Producers, still intending to invest $100 billion, produce $700 billion of consumption goods.

Although producers really didn't know with certainty what consumers intended to do with their incomes, and consumers really didn't know what producers intended to produce, the match is perfect. People's consumption spending turns out to be exactly what producers have produced for consumption. At $Y = \$800$ billion, producers, responding to or anticipating investment demand, intend to invest $100 billion and end up actually investing $100 billion:

$$I_i = I_a$$

Retail stores sell the consumption goods that they had hoped to sell and have left as inventory precisely what they want. What will they do? They will reorder from producers exactly what they had ordered before—no more, no less. Why order more? The market gives no indication that they could sell more than $800 billion. But why order less when experience tells them the market will absorb $800 billion?

Producers, then, will maintain their production level at $800 billion. They will keep in employment precisely that number of workers who produce the $800 billion. At $Y = \$800$ billion, there is no incentive for producers or consumers to change what they do. *The economy is in equilibrium.*

EQUILIBRIUM NATIONAL INCOME

Panels *a* and *b* of Exhibit 4 illustrate what Exhibits 1, 2, and 3 describe. They depict the economy moving to national income equilibrium.

Look at panel *a*. The upward-sloping, straight-line consumption curve, *C*, is a straight line because the marginal propensity to consume is constant, and because autonomous consumption is $60 billion, it intersects the vertical axis at $60 billion. The intended investment curve, $I_i = \$100$ billion is independent of the level of national income and is added to the consumption curve to generate the $C + I_i$ curve, which is the **aggregate expenditure curve (AE)**. (At every level of *Y*, *AE* differs from *C* by the $100 billion of investment.)

The 45° income line (the $C + S$ curve) in panel *a* represents the economy's total production, or aggregate supply. Note that the 45° income (or $C + S$) line intersects the *AE* (or $C + I_i$) curve at *e*, where $Y = \$800$ billion. *The intersection identifies the economy's equilibrium position.*

Aggregate expenditure curve (AE)
A curve that shows the quantity of aggregate expenditures at different levels of national income or GDP.

KEY EXHIBIT 4   The Equilibrium Level of National Income

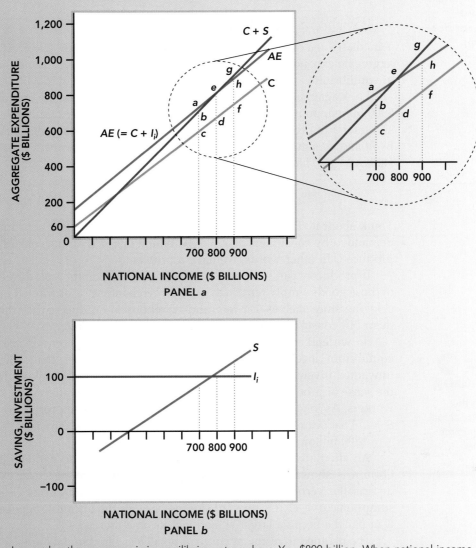

In panel a, the economy is in equilibrium at e, where $Y = \$800$ billion. When national income is below equilibrium, say at $Y = \$700$, aggregate expenditure, that is, people's consumption spending plus producers' intended investment spending, $AE = C + I_i$, is greater than the $700 billion national income, $C + S$. As a result, part of the producers' intended investment, ab, is not realized, driving national income up to $800 billion. When national income is above equilibrium, say at g, where $Y = \$900$, aggregate expenditure, $AE = C + I_i$, at h, is less than the $900 billion national income. The difference, gh, drives national income down to $800 billion.

Panel b focuses on the relationship between saving and intended investment. The inequalities, $S > I_i$ and $I_i > S$, drive national income to its $800 billion equilibrium level.

Suppose the economy is operating at a lower-than-equilibrium income, say, at $Y = \$700$ billion. What happens? At $Y = \$700$ billion, producers still intend to invest $100 billion, which is the distance marked off by ac in panel a, while consumers save $(Y - C)$, or cb, which is $\$700 - [\$60 + (0.80 \times \$700)] = \$80$ billion. That is, the quantity demanded by consumers of consumption goods at $Y = \$700$ billion is greater than the quantity of consumption goods supplied by producers.

The result? Consumers buy up $20 billion of inventory (the purchase by consumers of the inventory converts that inventory from investment goods to

on the
net
The Bureau of Economic Analysis maintains current data on the national income (http://www.bea.gov/bea/dn1.htm).

consumption goods), and producers respond by hiring more workers to replace the $20 billion depleted inventories. More workers means more income. That is to say, national income increases. In a nutshell, when

$$I_i > S,$$

Y increases *and continues to increase until* $I_i = S$. Note where $I_i = S$. At $800 billion, aggregate expenditure, AE, equals aggregate output, $C + S$. The economy arrives at equilibrium.

Look again at Exhibit 4, panel *a* and this time suppose the economy is at $Y = $900 billion, point *g*. What happens now? Remember, we assume that producers still intend to produce $100 billion of investment goods, the distance marked off by *hf* and — simultaneously and independently — consumers save $120 billion, shown as *gf*. That is to say,

$$S > I_i$$

Think about it. This $S > I_i$ inequality must indicate that the consumption goods demanded by consumers at $Y = $900 billion is less than the consumption goods produced. In other words, we have a problem.

If producers can't sell all the consumption goods they produced, then some of those goods simply remain as unsold merchandise — unwanted inventories — clogging store shelves, car lots, and warehouses. Producers *wish* they could sell them but consumers, bent on saving *gf*, don't oblige fully.

So we end up in this situation: When national income is greater than its equilibrium level — in this case $900 billion greater than $800 billion — unwanted inventories build up. If producers can't sell all they produced, what's the sense of producing more? They don't. They have no alternative but to lay off workers. As long as $S > I_i$, national income will fall. The process continues until $S = I_i$. That occurs at point *e* in Exhibit 4. There, the economy is in equilibrium at $Y = $800 billion.

An alternative illustration of the panel *a* approach to national income equilibrium is shown in panel *b*. The upward-sloping saving curve, S, of panel *b* depicts the vertical distance between panel *a*'s income curve, $C + S$, and consumption curve, C. It is upward sloping because the distances between $C + S$ and C in panel *a* become larger as national income increases.

The planned investment curve in panel *b* is a horizontal curve at $100 billion. It intersects the saving curve at $800 billion, the equilibrium level of national income. As panel *b* shows, when national income is below equilibrium, say at $700 billion, $S < I_i$, creating an excess demand for consumption goods that drives national income up to equilibrium. When national income is above equilibrium, say at $900 billion, $S > I_i$, creating an excess supply of consumption goods that drives national income down to equilibrium.

check your ✅
understanding

What happens to the economy when the actual level of national income is greater than the equilibrium level?

CHANGES IN INVESTMENT CHANGE NATIONAL INCOME EQUILIBRIUM

There is no reason to suppose, *as long as the consumption function and the investment demand function remain unchanged*, that the level of national income would move away from equilibrium at $800 billion. As long as aggregate expenditure—that is, consumers' spending on consumption goods and producers' spending on investment goods—exactly matches consumption goods and investment goods production, there is no incentive for producers to increase or decrease their production. Intended inventories would be realized. That's what an equilibrium position implies.

✋ **EXHIBIT 5**   Consumers' and Producers' Intentions and Activities, by Stages, When Investment Increases to $130 Billion and Y = $800 Billion

CONSUMERS	PRODUCERS
$Y = \$800$	$Y = \$800$
$Y = C + S$	$Y = C + I_i$
$C = a + bY$	$I_i = \$130$
$C = \$60 + 0.8\,(Y)$	$C = Y - I_i$
$\quad = \$60 + 0.8\,(\$800)$	$\quad = \$800 - \$130$
$\quad = \$700$	$\quad = \$670$
$S = Y - C$	$I_a = \$100$
$\quad = \$800 - \$700$	
$\quad = \$100$	

But functions do, in fact, change. We noted in the prior chapter how volatile investment can be, and it is not unreasonable to expect that the investment function will shift up or down, perhaps even before the economy reaches an equilibrium position.

Suppose producers decide to take advantage of new technologies and shift $30 billion from consumption production to investment. Intended investment increases, then, from $100 billion to $130 billion.

As we see in Exhibit 5, the $800 billion equilibrium level of national income is no longer tenable.

Intended investment is now $130 billion. How does that affect the equilibrium level of national income? At $Y = \$800$ billion, consumers will still want to spend $700 billion on consumption. But since producers now intend to invest $130 billion of the $800 billion they produce, they supply only $670 billion of consumption goods. That simply isn't enough for consumers.

What will consumers do? What can they do? They will, of course, consume the $670 billion in consumption goods that producers supplied. In addition, they will buy up $30 billion of the inventories that producers had intended to hold as investment. That is to say, consumers convert intended investment into consumption goods. (Imagine the almost empty shelves in retail stores after consumers buy up $30 billion of wanted inventories.) The result is that actual investment ends up being $30 billion less than intended investment.

How will the retailers respond? By faxing producers to replenish their depleted inventories. The producers, excited by this surge in orders, hire more workers. National income increases beyond $800 billion.

Y = $950 Billion: The New Equilibrium

We trace the economy's path to a higher equilibrium level in Exhibit 6.

The consumption and investment spending curve, which is the aggregate expenditure curve, AE, shifts from $C + I_i$ (with $I_i = \$100$ billion) to $C + I_i'$ (with $I_i' = \$130$ billion). How does the shift affect the equilibrium level of national income?

Look at $Y = \$800$ billion. Before the shift, $I_i = S$ (the distance ed). The economy is in equilibrium. After the shift, saving is still ed, but intended investment is jd. In other words, $I_i > S$. The result: Excess demand for consumption goods at $Y = \$800$ billion propels national income upward.

But to where? The new equilibrium level of national income is at $950 billion. Here, both saving and intended investment are $130 billion (this is the distance $e'd'$, which is the same distance as jd). The table in Exhibit 6 lays out the particulars of this new equilibrium position.

EXHIBIT 6   Deriving Equilibrium at $Y = \$950$ Billion

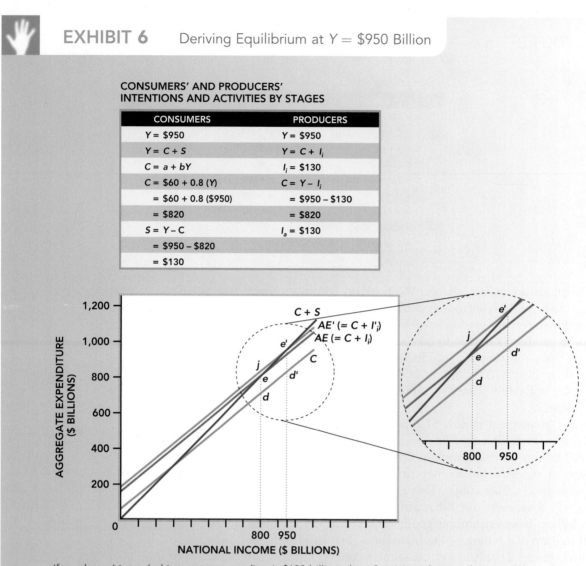

CONSUMERS' AND PRODUCERS' INTENTIONS AND ACTIVITIES BY STAGES

CONSUMERS	PRODUCERS
$Y = \$950$	$Y = \$950$
$Y = C + S$	$Y = C + I_i$
$C = a + bY$	$I_i = \$130$
$C = \$60 + 0.8\,(Y)$	$C = Y - I_i$
$\quad = \$60 + 0.8\,(\$950)$	$\quad = \$950 - \$130$
$\quad = \$820$	$\quad = \$820$
$S = Y - C$	$I_a = \$130$
$\quad = \$950 - \$820$	
$\quad = \$130$	

If producers' intended investment spending is $100 billion, then $S = I_i\ (= ed)$ at e, where equilibrium $Y = \$800$ billion. If producers' intended investment spending increases to $130 billion, then at $Y = \$800$ billion, $I_i > S\ (jd - ed = je)$. National income would increase to e', the new equilibrium level of $950 billion, where $I_i = S = \$130$ billion $(e'd')$.

Look at the left column. At $Y = \$950$ billion, consumers intend to spend $820 billion on consumption goods and save the remaining $130 billion. The right column shows that producers, responding to and anticipating the demand for investment goods, intend to invest $130 billion and produce $820 billion of consumption. The $I_i = S$ equilibrium condition is met:

$$I_i = S = \$130$$

CHANGES IN FOREIGN TRADE CHANGE NATIONAL INCOME EQUILIBRIUM

Although aggregate expenditure includes government and foreign trade expenditures as well as consumption and investment, up to this point in our analysis we deliberately set aside the influences of government and foreign trade

interdisciplinary perspective

A FRACTURED VERSION OF THE EXODUS STORY

"Pyramid-building, earthquakes, and even wars may serve to increase wealth. . . ."*

In the days of the old Pharaoh, many loyal Egyptians were lacking work and those with jobs were earning far less than a livable wage. There was much grumbling among the people. Sensing the possibility of an uprising, Pharaoh's chief economist advised him to open the royal purse to the poor and unemployed.

"Nonsense," said the Pharaoh. "I'm the Pharaoh. They serve me. I don't serve them. I prefer pyramid building. The royal purse will be used to honor me!"

"Where will we find cheap labor?" asked the economist.

"We'll use the cheapest. I have tens of thousands of foreign slaves. Put them to the task."

The Pharaoh's wishes were obeyed. Giant stones were cut from the quarries at Aswan, pulled and rolled to the banks of the Nile and floated down the river to the delta. Slaves were cutting stone, hauling stone, lifting stone, and setting stone upon stone, every day of every week of every month of every year. But they had to be fed. Pharaoh used his royal purse to buy the food. Now Egyptian farmers had to increase their planting and harvesting. As well, toolmakers, rope makers, shipbuilders and road and ramp builders were busier than ever before. Slowly, the pyramid began to take form. And the farmers, toolmakers, rope makers, shipbuilders, and road and ramp builders had more employment and income than they thought possible. They used their newly acquired money to buy more goods for themselves and their families, creating even more income and employment in Egypt.

© Royalty-Free/CORBIS

An ancient symbol of economic prosperity?

During a royal house meeting several years later, the economic adviser confessed to Pharaoh. "You know," he said, "Your idea of a pyramid wasn't such a bad idea after all. No need now to subsidize anybody. Your people have ample jobs and income."

"Good!" said the Pharaoh. "You see, by satisfying me, everybody's satisfied."

"Well, not exactly. There's still the slaves," said the economist.

"I don't think we have to worry about them," replied the Pharaoh.

"Well, maybe not. But there's this fellow Moses . . ."

CONSIDER

How was Egypt's aggregate expenditure increased? What did this increase mean for the national income? How does this story relate to the income multiplier?

*Keynes, J. M., *The General Theory of Employment, Interest, and Money* (London: Macmillan and Co., 1954), p. 129.

expenditures on national income as a matter of expediency. After all, knowing how consumption and investment work on national income was really enough to explain how an economy moves toward its equilibrium. That is, if increases in consumption and investment propel the economy forward, then it stands to reason that increases in exports and government expenditures must work in the same way. And indeed they do.

But the influence of foreign trade on national income determination is less obvious than are the other components of aggregate expenditure because it includes both exports and imports, and these have offsetting effects on the direction a national economy takes. Let's look at each—exports and imports—one at a time, then combined, to see how they affect national income determination.

Changes in Exports

Our exports to other countries create production and incomes in the United States in the same way that production and incomes are created by Americans buying those goods in the United States. For example, a Canadian college student in Montreal buying a *Ratatat* CD on the American label *Excel Recording* creates

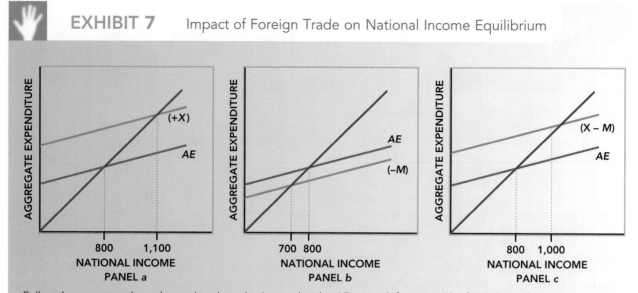

EXHIBIT 7   Impact of Foreign Trade on National Income Equilibrium

Follow the sequence through panels *a*, *b*, and *c*. In panel *a*, the *AE* curve shifts upward by $60 billion of exports, increasing national income to $1,100 billion. In panel *b*, the *AE* curve shifts downward by $20 billion of imports, decreasing national income by $100 billion. In panel *c*, the combined effect of exports and imports shifts the *AE* curve upward by $40 billion ($60 − $20) of foreign trade, increasing national income by $1,000.

production and incomes in the United States in precisely the same way as an American college student in Seattle does buying that same CD. *It makes no difference where the buyers are located.* It's where the CD is produced and where incomes generated from it are earned, not where it ends up. Since the Seattle student's consumption expenditure on the CD is part of U.S. aggregate expenditure, the Canada-bound CD U.S. export must, too, be considered part of U.S. aggregate expenditure.

And what is true for that CD export to Canada is true as well for all American exports. All U.S. exports show up as components of U.S. aggregate expenditure. Let's suppose, for simplicity sake, that total U.S. exports to the rest of the world add up to $60 billion. What effect would those exports have on the U.S. economy's equilibrium? Look at Exhibit 7, panel *a*. The $60 billion of exports is layered onto the economy's aggregate expenditure curve, driving the equilibrium level to $1,100 billion.

Changes in Imports

Let's now consider the impact of imports on aggregate expenditure. Let's suppose the Seattle college student buys not only the American-made CD but a Canadian-made book of poetry. Because both the CD and the book are part of the student's consumption, the book *may appear to be*, like the CD, part of U.S. aggregate expenditure. But it's not.

After all, no American was involved in producing the book. No American worker earned income printing the book. No American entrepreneur earned income publishing the book. No American landlord earned income renting space to the publishing house. All the book-related economic activity—and all the incomes earned as a result—occurred north of the border. But because the book shows up as consumption expenditure in the U.S., its value must be subtracted from U.S. aggregate expenditure. Panel *b* in Exhibit 7 depicts the subtraction of the book and all other imports from U.S. aggregate expenditure. The aggregate expenditure curve shifts downward by $20 billion, driving the national income equilibrium from $800 billion to $700 billion.

Net Impact of Foreign Trade

Panel c in Exhibit 7 depicts the net or combined impact of exports and imports on national income equilibrium. The U.S. aggregate expenditure curve shifts upward or downward depending on the strengths of its exports and imports. In this illustration, the net export component of aggregate expenditure is $40 billion ($60 − $20).

What was once $AE = C + I$ is now $AE = C + I + (X - M)$. As we see in Exhibit 7, panel c, the aggregate expenditure curve, reflecting the combined influences of exports and imports, increases the equilibrium level of national income from $800 billion to $1,000 billion.

AN ALTERNATIVE METHOD OF CALCULATING EQUILIBRIUM

A quick way of calculating the equilibrium level of national income, given specific values for (1) autonomous consumption, (2) *MPC*, and (3) intended investment, is to substitute $(a + bY)$ for C into the aggregate expenditure equation $Y = C + I_i$. For example, since

$$\text{in equilibrium } Y = C + I_i$$
$$\text{and } C = \$60 + 0.8Y$$
$$\text{and } I_i = \$130,$$
$$\text{then } Y = (\$60 + 0.8Y) + \$130.$$

Subtracting $0.8Y$ from both sides reduces the equation to

$$0.2Y = \$60 + \$130 = \$190.$$

Finally, dividing both sides by 0.2 reduces the equation to

$$Y = \$950.$$

Change any of the values for autonomous consumption, *MPC*, or intended investment, and a new equilibrium level of national income results.

THE INCOME MULTIPLIER

If you were told that aggregate expenditure increased by $30 billion last year, you may want to know something more about that particular increase. For example, did consumers demand more consumption goods? After all, consumption expenditure is an integral part of aggregate expenditure. Or perhaps producers, for some reason, decided to invest more? Or the increase in aggregate expenditure could have resulted from an increase in exports.

And if Exhibits 5 and 6 were fresh in your memory, you could visualize that $30 billion increase in aggregate expenditure shifting the AE curve upward by that amount, creating a new and higher level of national income. The question is: How much higher the level? That is to say, by how much would national income increase when aggregate expenditure increases by $30 billion?

Economists define the change in national income that is generated by a change in aggregate expenditure as the **income multiplier**. It is written

$$\text{multiplier} = \frac{\text{change in } Y}{\text{change in } AE}.$$

Income multiplier
The multiple by which income changes as a result of a change in aggregate expenditure.

Deriving the Multiplier

Suppose John Flygare, the owner of a tennis shop in Evanston, Illinois, reads an article in *Sports Illustrated* describing a new machine that restrings tennis rackets in half the time it formerly took. The new technology costs $1,000. Suppose John decides to make the investment.

Let's trace the sequence of events that follow that $1,000 increase in investment. First, a *new* order is placed for the machine. John's decision to invest represents a *new* order for Bradley Hastings, the machinist and inventor of the restringing equipment. He produces the machine, sells it to John, and ends up with a $1,000 increase in income. Of course, John ends up with a new machine.

What do you suppose Bradley does with the additional $1,000 income earned? Since we suppose $MPC = 0.80$, we know, then, that he increases his consumption spending by $800. Let's suppose he spends $800 on a custom-made water bed.

Think about what follows. The carpenter, Jay Malin, makes the bed and earns $800, which represents for him an addition to income. Once again, real output and real income are created simultaneously. And, of course, Jay will do with his new income what Bradley did with his—spend part, and save the rest. With $MPC = 0.80$, $640 of the $800 is put to consumption spending.

The sequence of additions to real output, additions to income, and additions to consumption spending and saving is shown in Exhibit 8.

The initial $1,000 change in investment spending sets in motion a chain of events that creates—in successive rounds of income earning, consumption spending, and saving—a $5,000 change in national income. And, as you see, it creates also water beds, violins, computers, health care, auto repair, space heaters, and a host of other real outputs whose total value is $5,000.

Note that as economic activity progresses through the successive rounds, the additions to national income become smaller and smaller. For at each round, some of the income is set aside as saving. The lower the MPC (or the higher the MPS), the greater is the sum set aside.

check your understanding

How does a change in investment create a larger change in income?

EXHIBIT 8   The Making of the Income Multiplier

ROUND	CHANGE IN I_i	OUTPUT	Y	C	S
1	$1,000	RESTRINGER	$1,000.00	$ 800.00	$ 200.00
2		WATER BED	800.00	640.00	160.00
3		VIOLIN	640.00	512.00	128.00
4		COMPUTER	512.00	409.60	102.40
5		HEALTH CARE	409.60	327.68	81.92
6		AUTO REPAIR	327.68	262.14	65.54
7		SPACE HEATER	262.14	209.71	52.43
.			.	.	.
.			.	.	.
.			.	.	.
n			.	.	.
TOTAL	$1,000	$5,000.00	$5,000.00	$4,000.00	$1,000.00

The Algebra of the Income Multiplier As we see in Exhibit 8, the total income created is the sum of a series of incomes, each one reduced in the succeeding round by the *MPS*, that is, by 0.20. The series is written as

$$1 + MCP + MCP^2 + MCP^3 + \cdots + MCP^n$$

which reduces to

$$\frac{1}{1 - MPC}$$

With *MPC* = 0.80, the income multiplier is

$$\frac{1}{1 - MPC} = \frac{1}{1 - 0.80} = 5$$

so that John Flygare's $1,000 investment ends up creating a $5,000 change in national income.

If ΔAE = $30 billion, then ΔY = $150 billion. Were aggregate expenditure to increase by $100 billion, national income would increase by $500 billion.

What If *MPC* = 0.90?

Suppose *MPC* = 0.90. What would happen to the level of national income if the same $30 billion of aggregate expenditure were added to the economy? The income multiplier now becomes

$$\frac{1}{1 - 0.90} = 10.$$

With $30 billion of aggregate expenditure added, national income increases by $300 billion. In a nutshell, any change in *MPC* changes the income multiplier and consequently the level of national income that the aggregate expenditure would generate.

The Income Multiplier Works in Either Direction

Just as increases in aggregate expenditure stimulate the economy, cuts in aggregate expenditure drag it down. Suppose an increase in the rate of interest shifts the demand curve for investment from $100 billion to $75 billion.

The income multiplier now works in reverse. In the first round of the cutback, national income falls by $25 billion. People whose employment had been supported by the $25 billion investment find themselves with $25 billion less income. But that $25 billion had financed 25 × 0.80 = $20 billion of consumption spending, which was the source of second-round income. That, too, now disappears, creating in turn successive cuts in income and consumption through to the *n*th round. What is the total loss of national income? With a multiplier of 5 (*MPC* = 0.80), the $25 billion investment cutback decreases national income by $25 billion × 5 = $125 billion. National income falls from $800 billion to a new equilibrium level of $675 billion.

Aggregate Expenditure and Aggregate Demand

Up to this point in our analysis, we ignored changes in prices. Movements in the economy toward equilibrium occurred without any change in the price level. We assumed an ample supply of resources available, so that any increase in aggregate expenditure, say, an increase in investment demand, would set off a chain

The White House's Economic Statistics Briefing Room has current data on prices (http://www. whitehouse.gov/fsbr/ prices.html).

EXHIBIT 9   Converting Aggregate Expenditure to Aggregate Demand

Increases in the price level shift the AE curve in panel a downward, creating lower equilibrium levels of national income. Decreases in the price level shift the AE curve upward, creating higher equilibrium levels of national income. This relationship between price levels and aggregate expenditure shifts is depicted in panel b by the downward-sloping AD curve.

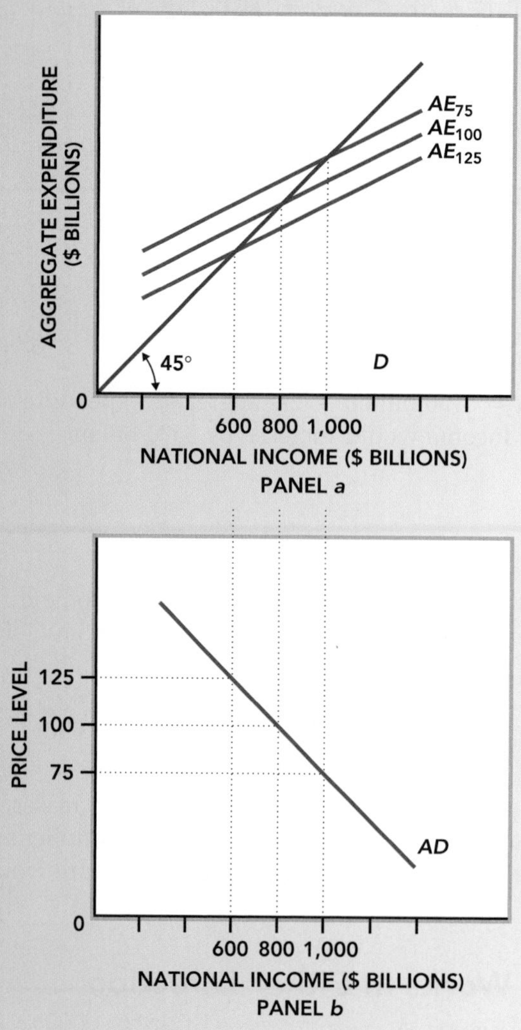

PANEL a

PANEL b

reaction of mutually reinforcing increases in income, production, and consumption, without creating any pressure on the price level.

Let's change that now by relaxing the assumption of fixed prices and considering what happens to aggregate expenditure when prices do change. Let's start by supposing that the economy of Exhibit 9, panel a, is in equilibrium at $800 billion and at a price level of 100.

Suppose a general fall in prices occurs, cutting the price level from 100 to 75. Consumer and investment goods are now cheaper. If you lived in that economy, how would you respond to these lower prices? As a consumer, you would probably buy more consumer goods. As a producer facing lower investment goods prices, you would probably increase investment. And wouldn't you expect other consumers and producers in the economy to respond the same way? In other words, when the price level falls, aggregate expenditure increases. This response is shown in panel a as an upward shift in the aggregate expenditure curve, from AE_{100} to AE_{75}, moving the equilibrium level from $800 billion to $1,000 billion.

If the price level increases, say, from 100 to 125, the opposite responses take place. Now facing higher consumer goods prices, you would probably buy less, and producers, facing higher investment goods prices, would probably invest less. The result: a downward shift in the aggregate expenditure curve, from AE_{100} to AE_{125}, moving the equilibrium level from $800 billion to $600 billion.

Positioning panels *a* and *b* as we do allows us to see the relationship between the price-induced shifts in the aggregate expenditure curve in panel *a* and the formation of the downward-sloping aggregate demand curve in panel *b*. At a price level of 125, aggregate demand is $600 billion. When the price level falls to 100, aggregate demand increases to $800 billion. At a price level of 75, aggregate demand is $1,000 billion.

What about the income multiplier? How can we show it in an economy of changing prices? We saw that in the fixed-price model, a change in aggregate expenditure changes the equilibrium level of national income. Look at Exhibit 10, panel *a*. Assuming the economy is in equilibrium at $800 billion and at a price level of 100, a $40 billion increase in aggregate expenditure creates—if $MPC = 0.80$—a $200 billion increase in the equilibrium level of national income *without changing the price level*. How can we show this multiplier effect in the nonfixed-price model of aggregate demand? By a $200 billion outward shift in the aggregate demand curve in panel *b*, from AD to AD_{+40} *at the same price level of 100*, the +40 signaling the $40 billion increase in investment demand.

EXHIBIT 10   The Multiplier Effect in the *AE* and *AD* Models of Income Determination

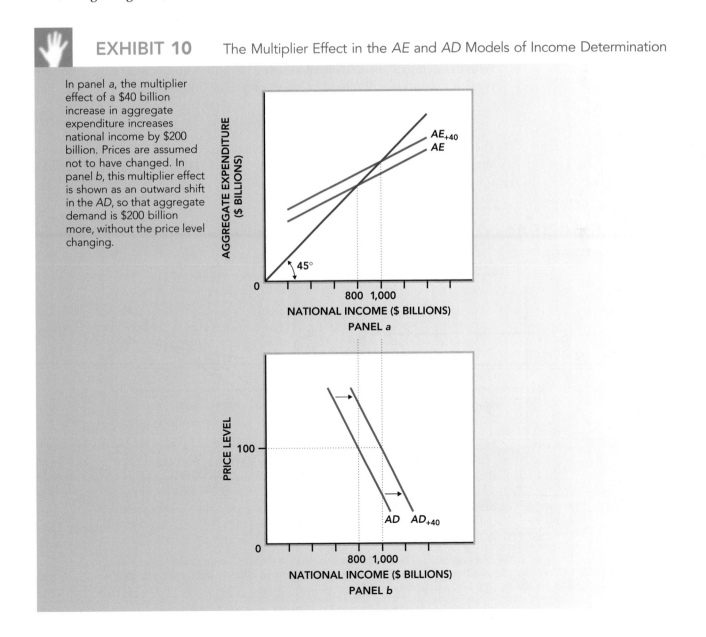

In panel *a*, the multiplier effect of a $40 billion increase in aggregate expenditure increases national income by $200 billion. Prices are assumed not to have changed. In panel *b*, this multiplier effect is shown as an outward shift in the *AD*, so that aggregate demand is $200 billion more, without the price level changing.

THE PARADOX OF THRIFT

Suppose people, afraid that their economic future is not nearly as promising as they once thought, decide to put a higher percentage of their income into saving. Increased saving, they feel, will provide greater economic security. But does their shift out of consumption spending to higher saving really provide them with greater economic security? Do they *really* end up saving more? Not necessarily. In fact, by *trying* to save more, they may actually end up saving less, or at least saving no more. That's what economists call the **paradox of thrift**. But why should trying to save more lead to no greater saving and perhaps even less? The answer depends on how income (and production) responds to a change in saving.

The paradox of thrift
The more people try to save, the more income falls, leaving them with no more and perhaps with even less saving.

Suppose people decide to increase their saving by $30 billion whatever the level of national income. And suppose the economy is in equilibrium at $800 billion. What happens?

Exhibit 11, panel *a*, illustrates the effect of that intention to save on the equilibrium level of national income. The saving curve shifts upward, from S to S', causing the equilibrium level of national income to fall from $800 billion to $650 billion. Follow the logic. Before the saving-curve shift, people intended to save $100 billion, and producers intended to invest $100 billion.

$$S = I_i = \$100$$

With the shift to S', people *intend* to save $130 billion at $Y = \$800$ billion. But can they? If producers still intend to invest only $100 billion, then

$$S > I_i$$

The economy slips into reverse gear. National income falls. The multiplier, when applied to the $30 billion increase in saving ($30 billion cut in consumption),

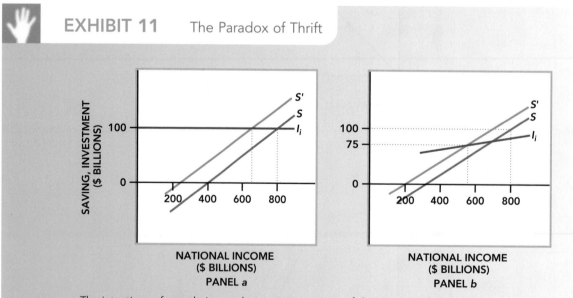

EXHIBIT 11   The Paradox of Thrift

PANEL a / PANEL b — vertical axis: SAVING, INVESTMENT ($ BILLIONS); horizontal axis: NATIONAL INCOME ($ BILLIONS)

The intentions of people in panel *a* to save more out of their income shifts the saving curve to the left, from *S* to *S'*. But their intentions will not be realized because the shift will cause the equilibrium level of national income to fall from $800 billion to $650 billion, leaving saving unchanged and equal to investment spending at $100 billion.

In panel *b*, the investment curve is upward sloping, so that the shift in the saving curve from *S* to *S'* not only causes the equilibrium level of national income to fall from $800 billion to $550 billion but saving to fall from $100 billion to $75 billion.

applied perspective

MOROCCO, COCA-COLA, AND MULTIPLIERS

Coca-Cola is perhaps the most familiar product in the world. Its name, bottle, logo, and, for many, even its taste are known all over the world. In many societies, it has become the symbol of American culture and feared or admired for its commercial reach. And reach it has. It is not only the beverage of choice among consumers everywhere. It is also produced in many of the world's economies, making it also the most recognizable multinational. Its impact on many of the world's people is not simply thirst quenching, but in many cases—and in some more than marginally—it is both income and employment generating. Take the case of Morocco.

Coca-Cola followed the U.S. armed forces overseas during World War II. In 1947, the soft drink was being produced on U.S. ships stationed in the Mediterranean Sea. When U.S. military personnel moved onshore, so did Coca-Cola, setting up a bottling plant in Tangier, Morocco. It wasn't only the American military that drank Coke, however, Moroccans enjoyed Coke as well. Gradually, Coca-Cola's consumer base spread throughout Morocco, from its coasts to its mountains and deserts.

Coca-Cola's impact on the Moroccan economy includes not only its own bottling operations and personnel, but also the upstream and downstream linkages with soft-drink suppliers, distributors, wholesalers, and retailers. These linkage networks span a wide spectrum of Moroccan business—from established corporations, with highly sophisticated technologies, finance, and management, to small entrepreneurs with little capital and small-scale agriculture involved in sugar production.

Coca-Cola's specific bottling and distribution demands that are satisfied principally by domestic production include sugar, soft-drink concentrate, water, coal,

lubricants, electricity, protective clothing, labels, carbon dioxide, chemical detergents, bottle caps, plastic bottles, cartons, and shrink-wrap material.

© CORBIS

It starts here and spreads across the map.

When Coca-Cola expands its scale of production in Morocco—it invested, for example, more than $35 million in 1999 alone—it increases capital expenditures on new machinery, much of it produced domestically rather than having to be imported. Also, when Coca-Cola's expands, it strengthens the construction and real estate industries.

Nevertheless, Coca-Cola Morocco is still only a bottling company. Does it really matter? When the upstream and downstream linkages are added together, Coca-Cola—the largest soft-drink bottler in Morocco—accounted for 0.7 percent of total Moroccan 1999 GDP In other words, it really does matter. Its impact on employment, too, is not insignificant. In 1999, total employment supported by both upstream and downstream linkages was estimated at 65,000. Since Coca-Cola's own employment was less than 5,000, the employment multiplier was approximately 13. That is, for every person employed at one of Coca-Cola's bottlers, the employment of a further 12 persons were supported elsewhere in the Moroccan economy.

· ·

MORE ON THE NET

Visit Coca-Cola Morocco's Web site at http://morocco.coca-cola.com/.

generates a 5 × $30 billion fall in national income. The new equilibrium level of national income is $650 billion. At $650 billion,

$$S = I_i = \$100.$$

Do you see what has happened? Since people's decision to increase saving to $130 billion caused a fall in national income, they cannot save $130 billion! There's the paradox. *The more people try to save, the more they force a fall in national income, which, in spite of their intentions, results in the level of saving remaining unchanged.*

If we relax the assumption that the investment curve is horizontal and instead assume that it is upward sloping, then the consequences of attempting to increase saving are even more severe. Look at panel *b*. Because the investment curve is upward sloping, the shift in the saving curve from *S* to *S'* results not only in a lower equilibrium level of national income but in a fall in the level of investment. And since $S = I_i$ in equilibrium, the paradox now reads: *The more people try to save, the less they end up saving.*

The discovery of this thrift paradox was nothing short of revolutionary, for the paradox of Exhibit 11 challenges the folk wisdom that many of us believe. Benjamin Franklin taught us that a penny saved is a penny earned. We now see how a penny saved may cause national income to fall! Thrift is no longer an unqualified virtue.

Is increased saving *always* detrimental to our economic health? Not by a long shot. If accompanied by increased investment, increased saving is both inevitable and desirable. After all, if intended investment increases to $130 billion along with intended saving, national income increases to $950 billion. The increased saving that people intended to make is actually made. And we're all the better for it. But if saving increases unattended by a complementary increase in intended investment, some economists—notably Keynesians—see economic trouble.

CHAPTER REVIEW

1. Because consumers and producers make their consumption and production decisions independently and simultaneously, it is only by chance that what consumers purchase for consumption is equal to what producers produce for consumption. If consumers purchase just as much as producers produce for consumption, then the investment that producers intend to make will equal the saving consumers make. The economy is in equilibrium when producers' intended investment equals consumers' saving.

2. When producers intend to invest more than consumers save, there are more consumption goods demanded by consumers than producers have produced. Wanted inventories (investment goods) are converted into consumption goods, so that actual investment ends up being less than intended. Producers hire more workers to replenish their inventory stock. National income and employment increase.

3. When producers intend to invest less than consumers save, there are fewer consumption goods demanded by consumers than producers have produced. Unwanted inventories (investment goods) accumulate, so that actual investment ends up being more than intended. Producers lay off workers to decrease actual investment to intended levels. National income and employment decrease.

4. The size of the income multiplier depends on the size of the marginal propensity to consume. The higher the *MPC*, the larger the income multiplier. The income multiplier is the result of an initial change in aggregate expenditure that creates income for some people who spend part of it on consumption, which then becomes income for other people. These people, too, spend part of their income on consumption, which generates income for still other people. This income/consumption-generating process continues, each round of income created being less than that of the previous round. (The shrinkage is accounted for by the marginal propensity to save.)

5. A fall in the price level creates an upward shift in aggregate expenditure, which results in an increase in the equilibrium level of national income. The aggregate demand curve traces the relationship between changes in aggregate expenditure (corresponding to changing equilibrium levels of national income) brought about by changes in the price level.

6. The paradox of thrift contends that the more people try to save, the more income falls, leaving them with no more, and perhaps with even less, saving.

KEY TERMS

Aggregate expenditure
Equilibrium level of national
   income

Unwanted inventories
Actual investment
Aggregate expenditure curve (AE)

Income multiplier
The paradox of thrift

QUESTIONS

1. "I cut production not because costs were too high, but because demand was too weak." "I cut production not because demand was too weak, but because costs were too high." Which statement best reflects the Keynesian view of national income determination?
2. If you live in Morocco, you don't have to love soft drinks to appreciate Coca-Cola's contribution to the Moroccan economy. Explain.
3. The chapter emphasizes that two different groups of people in the economy operate simultaneously and independently of each other. Who are these groups, and why is it important to emphasize that they operate in this way?
4. What happens to the level of national income when intended investment is greater than actual investment?
5. What happens to the level of national income when intended investment is greater than saving?

6. The creation of unwanted inventories or the depletion of wanted inventories signals coming changes in the level of national income. Explain.
7. What effect would an upward shift in the investment curve have on the equilibrium level of national income?
8. Describe how the income multiplier works.
9. What is the numerical value of the income multiplier when $MPC = 0$? When $MPC = 1$? Describe what happens to national income in each case.
10. What is paradoxical about the paradox of thrift?
11. Professor Arvind Jaggi asks his students at Franklin and Marshall College: "Building schools is not only good for students but for many nonstudents as well." Who are these nonstudents? Explain why they benefit.
12. Explain the relationship between aggregate expenditure and aggregate demand.

PRACTICE PROBLEMS

1. Fill in the missing cells for C, S, and I_a in the following table, given that autonomous consumption = $100, $MPC = 0.50$, and intended investment = $200. Indicate whether the economy is in equilibrium.

CONSUMERS	PRODUCERS
Y = $600	Y = $600
C =	C =
S =	I_a =

2. Fill in the missing cells for C, S, and I in the following table, given that autonomous consumption = $100, $MPC = 0.50$, and intended investment = $150. Indicate whether the economy is in equilibrium.

CONSUMERS	PRODUCERS
Y = $600	Y = $600
C =	C =
S =	I_a =

3. Fill in the missing cells in the following table.

MPC	MPS	INCOME MULTIPLIER
0.40		
0.60	0.25	
	0.10	

4. Suppose investment spending increases by $200 and $MPC = 0.90$. Calculate the effect of that increase on the first five rounds of changes in income, changes in consumption, and changes in saving. Illustrate these changes by describing the changes in real output (use your imagination).

ROUND	Y	C	S	OUTPUT
1				
2				
3				
4				
5				

5. Imagine an economy with the consumption function $C = \$100 + 0.90Y$. Now consider four scenarios of intended investment: (1) $I_i = \$100$, (2) $I_i = \$150$, (3) $I_i = 250$, and (4) $I_i = 350$. Calculate the equilibrium levels of national income under these four scenarios.

INTENDED INVESTMENT	NATIONAL INCOME
$100	
$150	
$250	
$350	

6. Use your imagination to create the first five rounds of a $1,000 change in aggregate expenditure. Show the final effect on national income when MPS = 0.10.

ROUND	GOOD	Δ Y ($)	Δ C ($)
1			
2			
3			
4			
5			
			TOTAL =

WHAT'S WRONG WITH THIS GRAPH?

Deriving Equilibrium National Income (EQ Y)

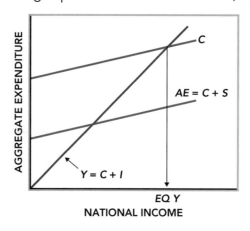

Economic Consultants

Economic Research and Analysis by Students for Professionals

Beth Dollins, mayor of New Orleans, LA, is trying to secure a new NHL franchise that will involve both private and city financing. Beth knows that although the franchise has many supporters, there are still many people who oppose the idea principally because they anticipate increases in their city taxes. There has been much discussion in the media about the projected costs, job and income creation, and the taxes associated with the creation of the franchise, but no reliable data have been presented. Beth is convinced that if accurate estimates of costs and benefits were given, the proposed franchise would win overwhelming support in New Orleans.

To make her case, Beth has hired Economic Consultants to prepare a report for Beth that addresses the following issues:

© Image 100/Royalty-Free/CORBIS

1. How much annual income would the hockey franchise create in the New Orleans downtown region—increased revenues for restaurants, retail stores, hotels, and the like—and what impact would this new income have on the surrounding areas?

2. How would the proposed franchise contribute to job creation in the New Orleans region?

3. What kinds of arguments have been made by other cities that have used public funding to help finance new professional sport franchises?

4. What strategies should Beth pursue to convince the citizens of New Orleans that a professional hockey team in the city is in each citizen's own self-interest?

You may find the following resources helpful as you prepare this presentation for Beth:

- **NHL.COM** (http://www.nhl.com/)—NHL.com is the official site of the National Hockey League.

- **Progressive Minnesota** (http://www.progressivemn.org/)—This site gives the background on one group that opposes public financing for stadiums.

1. If the marginal propensity to consume is 0.80 and the marginal propensity to save is 0.20, then the income multiplier is
   a. 1.00.
   b. 0.60.
   c. 5.
   d. 8.
   e. 2.
2. John Maynard Keynes believed that
   a. aggregate supply was most responsible for determining national income.
   b. both aggregate expenditure and supply contribute equally to determining the rate of inflation.
   c. aggregate expenditure is most responsible for determining national income.
   d. both aggregate expenditure and supply contribute equally to determining national income.
   e. aggregate expenditure has no effect on national income.
3. Suppose that the consumption function is $C = 110 + 0.7Y$, and national income is $800 billion. If producers intend to invest $100 billion, then
   a. the economy will be in macroequilibrium.
   b. savings will equal $100 billion.
   c. national income will fall because actual investment exceeds intended investment.
   d. national income will rise because actual investment is less than intended investment.
   e. savings exceeds actual investment in equilibrium.
4. Unwanted inventories arise when
   a. intended investment is less than savings.
   b. intended investment exceeds savings.
   c. the economy is in macroequilibrium.
   d. actual investment is $0.
   e. the aggregate expenditure curve lies below the consumption curve.
5. National income rises when intended investment exceeds actual investment because
   a. interest rates rise so that additional income can be generated.
   b. additional workers are hired to produce more output.
   c. workers are laid off in response to lower demand for goods and services.
   d. planned consumption is less than planned savings.

e. the economy is moving upward along its aggregate demand curve.
6. The Keynesian $C + I = C + S$ model assumes that prices
   a. rise when the aggregate expenditure curve shifts upward.
   b. rise when the aggregate supply curve shifts upward.
   c. are determined by aggregate demand and aggregate supply.
   d. are constant because the economy always tends toward equilibrium.
   e. are constant because there is an excess supply of resources that can be drawn upon to increase real GDP.
7. Consider the relationship between aggregate demand and aggregate expenditure. A fall in the price level in the AD model will, in the AE model,
   a. shift the AE curve upward.
   b. shift the AE curve downward.
   c. leave the AE curve unchanged, but increase the level of AE.
   d. leave the AE curve unchanged, but decrease the level of AE.
   e. leave the AE curve and the level of AE unchanged.
8. If the consumption function for an economy is $C = 180 + 0.75Y$, and intended investment rises by $800, then the resulting change in national income is
   a. +$2,400.
   b. −$3,200.
   c. +$3,200.
   d. −$800.
   e. +$1,133.
9. If the marginal propensity to save decreases, then
   a. changes in intended investment would have larger effects on national income.
   b. the marginal propensity to consume would fall by the same amount.
   c. changes in intended investment would have smaller effects on national income.
   d. the economy cannot attain macroequilibrium.
   e. the income multiplier will fall.
10. According to the paradox of thrift,
   a. as national income falls, consumption rises, thereby offsetting any change in planned saving.

b. if individuals try to save more, they may actually save less, because national income will increase.

c. when the aggregate expenditure curve shifts upward, it is exactly offset by the change in saving in the economy.

d. if individuals try to save more, they end up saving no more and may actually save less, because national income will decrease.

e. the multiplier effect makes it impossible for the level of saving in the economy to exceed national income in equilibrium.

FISCAL POLICY: COPING WITH INFLATION AND UNEMPLOYMENT

....

What is so great about being in equilibrium? After all, a prizefighter who is knocked out is in his own equilibrium position lying motionless on the canvass. But there's nothing joyous about ending up in that position, is there? Being in an equilibrium position simply means that no forces are at work tending to change that position.

So what's so great about an economy being in equilibrium? What's really so great about people consuming and investing what they intended to consume and invest? Perhaps their intentions, given their circumstances, weren't very promising in the first place! After all, poor people intend to consume very little because they are poor and, because they are poor, actually do consume very little. Do you suppose they're happy about the fact that their intentions were realized? When the economy is in equilibrium, it can sometimes be distressful.

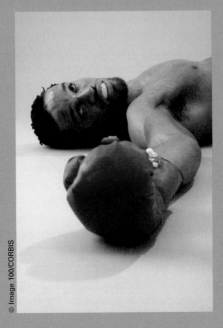

© Image 100/CORBIS

In the preceding chapter, we assumed that the economy was in equilibrium at $800 billion. Consumers chose to spend $700 billion on consumption, precisely the amount that producers, acting independently, chose to produce for consumption. As a result, the actual investment producers made was exactly what they intended to make.

But is $800 billion, itself, particularly attractive? Were people, in fact, satisfied with their lot? *Equilibrium tells us nothing about satisfaction* or the general state of the economy.

EQUILIBRIUM AND FULL EMPLOYMENT

Let's consider the relationship between the economy's equilibrium position and the level of national income that would support full employment. After all, the equilibrium position is determined by the consumers' and producers' specific consumption and investment decisions, and these have little to do with how large the labor force is or how many of those in the labor force are actually working.

The economy can be in equilibrium and at the same time still be unable to provide employment to those wanting jobs. In fact, that's precisely what Keynes saw in the 1930s. He and millions of other people who experienced unemployment or who had to live under its threat didn't think that kind of national income equilibrium was anything to celebrate.

on the net

The Bureau of Labor Statistics provides current data (http://stats.bls.gov/) on unemployment.

Identifying Unemployment

When is an economy at full employment? When everybody is working? Although this sounds like a reasonable enough criterion, it's far from useful. Why? Because there are always some people who, at prevailing wage rates, *choose* not to work. Suppose, for example, that Brian Vargo, an auto repair mechanic, refuses to work unless he is paid $1,000 per hour. Who would hire him at that wage? It would be silly, then, to count him among the unemployed. In defining full employment, therefore, we need to look at the reasons why people may not have jobs.

The Frictionally Unemployed What about people who voluntarily quit a job to spend time looking for a better one? Most people, particularly in the early years of their working life, are relatively mobile. They are always thinking about the possibilities of an upward move. They may have read about the prospects in Alaska, or heard about the new Japanese auto plant being built in Tennessee. Their antennas are always up, searching for new and better employment.

Many times, they do more than think about changing jobs. They actually do it. A real lead or a passed-over promotion could trigger their decision to quit. They gamble on improvement. For a short period—days, weeks, or perhaps even months—they explore their opportunities. It takes energy and patience. Some may decide to return to school to complete a degree or develop new technical skills.

Or consider the construction worker who has just finished a project and is not yet hired for another. He *expects* to work at his craft, but moving from a job completed to a new one is not always instantaneous. That's also the case for men and women in the world of entertainment. You may be on the Broadway stage one day and sitting anxiously in your agent's office the next. And chances are that if you see Mariano Rivera, the ace reliever for the New York Yankees, dining in a fashionable restaurant in November, he would be out of work—at least until spring training. His profession, as it is with so many others, is seasonal.

How would you classify these between-jobs people or people entering the labor force for the first time and looking for their first job? Economists use the term **frictional unemployment** to convey the idea that initial job hunting or job switching for improvement is seldom smooth or instantaneous, but quite natural in a dynamic economy.

The Structurally Unemployed

It is quite another matter when workers wake up one morning to find their jobs gone because of a technological change in the production process or because of a change in demand for the goods they were producing. And it is hardly a comfort to them to know that both technological change and changes in demand are quite natural phenomena in a dynamic economy. Economists describe such a loss of jobs as **structural unemployment**.

When a new technology displaces an old one, it typically displaces the old technology's operators as well. For example, when the steam-driven locomotive was the principal mode of moving passengers and freight across the country, railroad firemen were needed to fuel the engines. But when the railroads switched from steam to diesel, these formerly indispensable firemen became technologically obsolete.

The firemen soon discovered they weren't alone. As rail transportation gave way to trucks and airplanes, many locomotive engineers, porters, stationmasters, switch operators, rail repairmen, and others employed in the manufacture of rails, locomotives, boxcars, refrigerator cars, and railway stations found themselves out of work. What could they do? Not every ex–railway worker can pilot a Boeing 747.

Changes in consumer tastes, too, destroy jobs. Wisconsin dairy farmers lost their farms and employment when consumer preferences shifted from butter to margarine. When people switched from reading newspapers to watching television, a stream of editors, columnists, reporters, printing press workers, and newspaper vendors found themselves out of work. Should we not watch television because editors need jobs?

What do you suppose will happen to fur trappers, traders, tanners, and fur-coat makers if activists struggling for animal rights succeed in convincing millions of consumers? What happens to tobacco workers when people stop smoking? When people in France switch from wine to Coke—and they seem to be doing so in increasing numbers—vineyard workers in southern France join the ranks of the structurally unemployed.

Unemployment-creating changes in technology and consumer taste strike workers indiscriminately—no industry or worker is immune—but the impact of such change falls particularly hard on older workers. After all, they acquired years of on-the-job experience to match a specific technology. When the technology changes, their work experience and skills often count for zero. What can they do? It is difficult for them to start over again. They find themselves competing for lower-paying jobs against the preferred younger workers.

Can we avoid structural unemployment? Only by avoiding the modern conveniences of life such as central heating, paved streets, electric lights, personal computers, and vacuum cleaners. That is to say, if people are to enjoy the benefits that advanced technology affords, then the pain of structural unemployment has to be paid. But for those who pay it, the question always is: Why me?

The Cyclically Unemployed

Why me? is the same question asked by people who lose their jobs not to technological change but because the economy

Frictional unemployment Relatively brief periods of unemployment caused by people deciding to voluntarily quit work in order to seek more attractive employment.

Structural unemployment Unemployment that results from fundamental technological changes in production, or from the substitution of new goods for customary ones.

happens to be languishing in a downturn or recession phase of a business cycle. In these economically depressed phases, many businesses are forced to cut back on production and consequently cut back as well on the number of workers they are able to employ.

Cyclical unemployment
Unemployment associated with the downturn and recession phases of the business cycle.

Economists define this kind of joblessness as **cyclical unemployment** because it is governed by the rhythms of the business cycle—increasing as the cycle moves into its recession phase and decreasing as it moves out.

If you're among the unfortunate workers who are cyclically unemployed during some part of the recession, you would probably find it difficult to get a new job. After all, who is hiring during a recession? You may be eager to work, but eagerness is not the issue.

The Discouraged Worker How long can you search for a job without becoming totally discouraged and give up? Many of the unemployed do just that. Perhaps you would too if, day after day, week after week, you confront only rejection. You become increasingly disheartened not only because you can't find employment but also because the skills that have served you well become, during the extended search for work, ''rusty'' or obsolete. In the worst case, you accumulate overwhelming debt, default on the mortgage, lose not only the house but family and friends, and end up, like so many thousands of others, in the abyss of homelessness. After a while you may no longer even think of yourself as a worker or as part of the labor force. Many **discouraged workers** end up in a nonwork culture and remain permanently separated from the productive society. And once in that culture, it may take more than the availability of jobs to get them back into productive life.

Discouraged workers
Unemployed people who give up looking for work after experiencing persistent rejection in their attempts to find work.

The Underemployed Worker Take the case of Nancy Krasnow, an aeronautical engineer who once earned $60,000 working for Lockheed in Los Angeles. In the midst of a recession, Lockheed laid her off, along with 2,000 of her coworkers. After months of fruitless job searching, and with savings close to zero, Nancy's only viable prospect (other than slipping into the world of the discouraged worker) was flipping hamburgers at McDonald's, which earns her slightly more than minimum wage. Reluctantly, she sets aside her talents and experience and takes the job. But what is she now, an aeronautical engineer or a hamburger flipper?

If she were asked whether she was unemployed and looking for a job, how would she answer? The fact is that she *is* employed. But how would *you* define her status? In periods of recession, the number of people who end up as discouraged workers or among the **underemployed workers** can be rather significant.

Underemployed workers
Workers employed in jobs that do not utilize their productive talents or experience.

COUNTERFEIT UNEMPLOYMENT

Not everybody who's unemployed is really unemployed. There are ne'er-do-wells that can offer more excuses for not working than you would think possible. Yet, they insist that they are actively seeking employment and consider themselves part of the labor force. They know how to turn a job down as deftly as they know how to cash their unemployment insurance checks. They are right about one thing: *They are not working.*

There are other folks who make no pretense at all about looking for work. They are *waiting* for the ''right'' opportunity to come their way, and it is always ''just around the corner.'' In the meantime, they, too, are not working.

interdisciplinary perspective

FROM JOHN STEINBECK'S *CANNERY ROW*

It was a lazy day. Willard was going to have to work hard to get up any excitement. "I think you're a coward, too. You want to make something of that?" Joey didn't answer. Willard changed his tactics. "Where's your old man now?" he asked in a conversational tone.

"He's dead," said Joey.

"Oh yeah? I didn't hear. What'd he die of?"

For a moment Joey was silent. He knew Willard knew but he couldn't let on he knew, not without fighting Willard, and Joey was afraid of Willard.

"He committed—he killed himself."

"Yeah?" Willard put on a long face. "How'd he do it?"

"He took rat poison."

Willard's voice shrieked with laughter. "What'd he think—he was a rat?"

Joey chuckled a little at the joke, just enough, that is.

"He must of thought he was a rat," Willard cried. "Did he go crawling around like this—look, Joey—like this? Did he wrinkle up his nose like this? Did he have a big old long tail?" Willard was helpless with laughter. "Why'n't he just get a rat trap and put his head in it?" They laughed themselves out on that one, Willard really wore it out. Then he probed for another joke. "What'd he look like when he took it—like this?" He crossed his eyes and opened his mouth and stuck out his tongue.

"He was sick all day," said Joey. "He didn't die 'til the middle of the night. It hurt him."

Willard said, "What'd he do it for?"

"He couldn't get a job," said Joey. "Nearly a year he couldn't get a job. And you know a funny thing? The next morning a guy come around to give him a job."

John Steinbeck: His muse was the suffering poor; his genius was conveying their pathos.

···

CONSIDER

Judging from that snippet of conversation, would you describe Joey's father as having been a discouraged worker? Why or why not?

Source: From *Cannery Row* by John Steinbeck. Copyright 1945 by John Steinbeck. Renewed © 1973 by Elaine Steinbeck, John Steinbeck IV, and Thom Steinbeck. Used by permission of Viking Penguin, a division of Penguin Putnam, Inc.

Then there are others who never seem to hold onto a job. It's an in-and-out kind of thing with them. You would swear that they are earnest about employment, but for some reason or another, they are let go over and over again after short spells at work or they quit on their own because "office politics" or an "unfriendly environment" made life at the job too unpleasant to continue. This sort of thing then continues job after job.

None of these people are discouraged or underemployed, and certainly none are victims of the business cycle or a technological change. Nor is there anything frictional about their state of unemployment. It is for all a counterfeit unemployment.

Calculating an Economy's Rate of Unemployment

Imagine an economy with the employment/unemployment characteristics shown in Exhibit 1.

How would you go about determining the economy's rate of unemployment? Do you simply sum up the unemployed—that is, the $150 + 200 + 500 = 850$ and divide by the total number of workers? That reckoning would generate an unemployment rate of $850/10{,}250 = 8.3$ percent.

EXHIBIT 1   Number of Workers and Types of Unemployment

NUMBER OF WORKERS	10,250
FRICTIONAL UNEMPLOYMENT	150
STRUCTURAL UNEMPLOYMENT	200
CYCLICAL UNEMPLOYMENT	500
DISCOURAGED WORKERS	250
UNDEREMPLOYED WORKERS	300

But what about the 300 underemployed workers? A tough call, isn't it? After all, is an aeronautical engineer flipping hamburgers at McDonald's really employed? If you're inclined to answer no and count such workers among the unemployed, the economy's unemployment rate increases to 1,150/10,250 = 11.2 percent.

But look again at Exhibit 1. There are 250 discouraged workers who have no jobs. Are you prepared to write them off the list of unemployed because they have given up looking? If you include them, the rate of unemployment increases to 1,400/10,250 = 13.7 percent. As you see, the unemployment rate for the Exhibit 1 economy depends on your decision about who belongs in the unemployment pool.

The Bureau of Labor Statistics Definition of Unemployment

How does the rate of unemployment you choose as being appropriate compare to the rate chosen by the Bureau of Labor Statistics (BLS) of the U.S. Department of Labor? Each month, the bureau conducts a nationwide employment survey of 60,000 households. The critical question asked is: *Are you presently gainfully employed or actively seeking employment?* Only those answering yes are counted in the labor force. That is, according to the BLS, the **labor force** consists of working people plus the unemployed who are looking for work.

Suppose, for example, that Elisa Kilhafer, a homemaker in St. Louis, Missouri, is surveyed by the BLS and reports that she is neither gainfully employed nor looking for work. According to the BLS, Elisa is neither unemployed nor a part of the labor force. On the other hand, if she had said that she was looking for work but couldn't find any, she would be counted not only among the unemployed but also as a member of the labor force.

How does the BLS treat the underemployed? As long as the underemployed are working somewhere at some job, they are counted as employed and in the labor force. Discouraged workers, on the other hand, are viewed differently. Why? Because it makes no difference to the BLS *why* discouraged workers have no jobs. The fact that they are not actively looking is reason enough to exclude them from the labor force and from the lists of the unemployed.

According to the BLS, then, the labor force in Exhibit 1 is 10,250 – 250 discouraged workers = 10,000. The number of workers unemployed—now excluding discouraged and underemployed workers—is 150 + 200 + 500 = 850. The BLS-derived rate of unemployment is 8.5 percent.

The Natural Rate of Unemployment

Does an 8.5 percent unemployment rate signal that the economy is 850 jobs short of full employment? Not exactly. Economists recognize that some of that

Labor force
People who are gainfully employed or actively seeking employment.

on the net
The Bureau of Labor Statistics maintains statistics and information from its monthly report of households, called the Current Population Survey (http://stats.bls.gov/cps). Included is a Labor Department report on how the government measures unemployment (http://stats.bls.gov/cps/cps_htgm.htm).

unemployment is natural, that is, it does not necessarily reflect an economy unable to absorb its unemployment. After all, they argue, even if the economy of Exhibit 1 were bursting with energy and the demand for workers outstripped the supply, there would still be workers looking for better positions, and others displaced from their jobs because of technological improvements. If we accept the fact that these forms of unemployment are both natural and inevitable, then—setting that unemployment aside—if all other workers are employed, the economy is at full employment.

The 350 frictionally and structurally unemployed of Exhibit 1 make up what economists describe as the economy's 3.5 percent **natural rate of unemployment**. What remains are the 500 cyclically unemployed, accounting for 5.0 percent of the labor force.

Economists distinguish between the 8.5 percent actual rate of unemployment, the 3.5 percent natural rate, and the 5.0 percent rate of cyclical unemployment. *To economists, the economy is at full employment when the actual rate of unemployment equals the natural rate.* Put differently, the economy is considered to be at **full employment** when the rate of cyclical unemployment is zero.

Natural rate of unemployment
The rate of unemployment caused by frictional plus structural unemployment in the economy.

Full employment
An employment level at which the actual rate of employment in the economy is equal to the economy's natural rate of unemployment.

Full-Employment Level

Let's apply the concept of full employment to the aggregate supply curve developed in the aggregate demand and aggregate supply chapter and redrawn here in panel *a* of Exhibit 2.

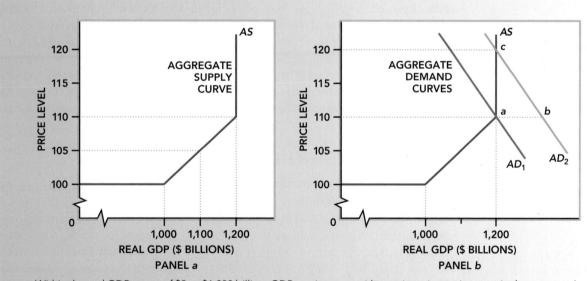

EXHIBIT 2   The Full-Employment Level of the Aggregate Supply Curve and the Effects of an Increase in Aggregate Demand

Within the real GDP range of $0 to $1,000 billion, GDP can increase without triggering an increase in the economy's price level. This is depicted in panel *a* by the horizontal segment of the aggregate supply curve at $P = 100$.

Beyond that point, producers must offer higher wage rates to induce more people into the labor force. Higher wages cause higher price levels, shown in the upward-sloping segment of the aggregate supply curve. At $GDP = \$1,200$ billion, everyone who is capable of working at *any* wage rate is working. No further increase in the price level can generate more real GDP. That is why the aggregate supply curve becomes perfectly vertical at $1,200 billion.

The shift in aggregate demand from AD_1 (point *a*) to AD_2 creates excess aggregate demand—aggregate quantity demanded minus aggregate quantity supplied—at $P = 110$ (point *b*). Since output and income at $Y = \$1,200$ billion are already at full-employment level, the pressures of excess aggregate demand force prices upward to $P = 120$ (point *c*).

The shape of the aggregate supply curve reflects the view (expressed in the preceding chapter) that the price level is constant at low levels of employment. Output and income can increase anywhere along the horizontal segment without any upward pressure on the price level because there is a ready pool of unemployed workers to draw upon at current wage rates.

The price level is constant only up to a level of $1,000 billion. From $1,000 billion to $1,200 billion, the price level rises from 100 to 110. At a *GDP* of $1,000 billion, everyone willing to work at the current wage rate is employed. There are others in the economy who are not working but would be willing to work—but only at wage rates higher than the current rate. If they can't get the higher rates, they prefer not to be members of the labor force.

How, then, can the economy get beyond $1,000 billion to, say, $1,100 billion? By inducing more people into employment with higher wage rates. But higher wage rates raise the cost of producing goods, and producers pass these higher costs on to consumers, with varying degrees of success, by raising prices. In the end, higher wage rates are accompanied by higher prices. Note that at $1,100 billion, the price level is 105. In other words, real GDP and employment both increase, *but only under conditions of price level increases.*

That's why the aggregate supply curve slopes upward within the GDP range $1,000 billion to $1,200 billion. Increases in both GDP and employment occur, but only with increasing doses of inflation.

What happens beyond $1,200 billion? *There is no beyond $1,200 billion.* At $1,200 billion, the aggregate supply curve becomes vertical. The economy's employment potential is *fully* exhausted. There are no more workers available at any wage rate to increase real GDP. The only increase that occurs at $1,200 billion is in prices. This is illustrated in panel *b* of Exhibit 2. The combination of the aggregate demand curve, AD_1, and the aggregate supply curve, *AS*, creates an equilibrium of real GDP of $1,200 billion at a price level of 110, point *a*. But look what happens to real GDP and the price level when the aggregate demand curve shifts upward to AD_2. At the price level of 110, the quantity of output demanded—point *b* on AD_2—is now greater than the quantity supplied.

Although production of goods and services cannot increase beyond $1,200 (the economy's maximum output is depicted by the vertical segment of the aggregate supply curve), the prices of the goods and services can. Excess aggregate demand at the price level 110 drives the price level up along the AD_2 curve from point *b* to point *c*, where a new equilibrium occurs at $1,200 billion and a price level of 120.

UNDERSTANDING INFLATION

Suppose you were living in the economy of Exhibit 2, panel *b*, and could choose between a GDP of $900 billion and a price level of 100 (moderate unemployment with no inflation) and GDP of $1,200 billion and a price level of 110 (full employment with inflation). Which would you choose? If you are like most people, you would probably choose the second option because you can more easily identify with the pain associated with being out of a job than you can with the pain associated with inflation. Unlike unemployment, whose victims are personal and recognizable, inflation covers the economy like a fog, affecting everything and everybody, making it sometimes difficult to distinguish inflation's victims from its nonvictims. In fact, there are many in the economy who actually benefit from inflation.

Winners and Losers from Inflation

Inflation affects people's real incomes differently. Who wins when inflation occurs? Who loses?

Who Loses from Inflation? Perhaps more than any other single group, people living on fixed incomes, such as retirees, have reason to worry about inflation. Why? Listen to Tina Eckstrom's sad story. Back in 1960, she and her husband bought a deferred annuity that cost them $100 monthly. In 2003, it started to pay them $700 a month in retirement benefits. They were excited about the prospect of living comfortably in retirement on the $700 monthly check, along with the savings they had accumulated. After all, back in 1960 when they put their retirement plans together, their rent was $125 per month, a new automobile was $1,500, milk was $0.25 a quart, and a first-run movie was $0.35. What they didn't factor into their plans was inflation.

When they retired in 2003, they began to receive their $700 each month. But their retirement dreams were shattered. Why? The $700 doesn't come close to covering their condominium rent, and a new car—now at $20,000—is simply out of the question. They, along with millions of other people who live on fixed incomes, are big losers from inflation.

For the same reason, landlords worry about inflation, especially those whose incomes are tied to long-term rental leases. So too do workers who accepted union-negotiated, multiyear, fixed-wage contracts. Imagine how you would feel if you were working for minimum wage during the 1990s. The annual inflation rate was 2.2 percent, and the minimum wage was fixed at $5.15. If you bought $100 worth of groceries in 1990, by 2000 you could buy only $75.07 worth of groceries (assuming the price of groceries went up at the same rate as the price level).

Savers can lose as well. How? Suppose you saved $100 last year, giving up the option of buying a $100 pair of Nike cross-training shoes. This year, you decide to use the savings to buy the shoes. You withdraw $105 from the bank—your savings earned 5 percent interest—only to discover that the shoes now cost $110. While your money was in the bank, inflation was 10 percent. You're in a relatively worse position. Imagine if you had saved $10,000, not $100.

Remember Benjamin Franklin's comment: A penny saved is a penny earned. Think about it. In inflationary times, it simply isn't true.

Why are savers sometimes losers from inflation?

Who Gains from Inflation? Not everyone loses from inflation. Borrowers, for example, are among those who benefit. Let's consider those shoes again. Suppose that last year you borrowed $100 at 5 percent interest to buy the shoes. This year, you repay the bank with interest, $105, and come away a winner. Why? *Inflation!* Had you waited until this year to buy the shoes, with inflation at 10 percent, it would have cost you $110. Of course, if inflation works in favor of borrowers, it works against lenders. What you won through inflation, the bank lost. The $105 that the bank now holds buys less goods and services for the bank than the $100 it held (and loaned you) last year.

Let's paint another scenario. Suppose you considered buying a beautiful brick ranch house sitting on a ¼-acre lot. It had three bedrooms, two baths, a sunken living room with fireplace, a large study, wood-floored dining room, and a two-car garage. The owner, eager to sell, will accept $140,000. The bank offers you a 30-year fixed-rate mortgage at 6½ percent. Your monthly payments amount to $850. That's $300 more than the two-bedroom apartment you now rent, but the difference in comfort is so striking that you decide to buy the house. Six years later you drive by your old apartment building and notice a For Rent sign sitting on the front lawn. What shocks you is the advertised rent: $885 per month! More than your present monthly mortgage payments. You may have made silly purchases in your lifetime, but the house, thanks to 10-percent-per-year-inflation, was not one of them. You come away a winner.

What ends up as gains from inflation to borrowers like you also works for government. After all, government is the largest single borrower. Interest payments every year on its more than $4 trillion national debt exceed $200 billion.

historicalperspective

© Perry Mastrovito/CORBIS

Getting up so high can be damaging to your health.

INFLATION AND HYPERINFLATION

Suppose you earned $70,000 a year as a mechanic. You planned to spend $56,000 on a shopping list of marvelous things. Good idea? Sounds great.

But then it happens. A 10 percent inflation descends on the economy. What had cost $20 before, say a toaster oven, now costs $22. The new fully equipped Saturn was once $17,000; it's now $18,700. The rent on your apartment jumps from $700 per month to $770. The $56,000 you commit to consumption still buys $56,000 of consumption goods. But because prices rose, it buys fewer goods.

Let's bump that inflation rate up to 100 percent. Wow! That $34,000 Saturn alone eats away most of your $56,000 consumption. You're hardly able to toast your bread!

Rates of inflation are measured in percentages, which may seem somewhat esoteric until you consider the things inflation prevents you from buying.

While there is no specific percentage that economists use to differentiate inflation from very high inflation, economists will grant that any rate in the 50 percent to 100 percent range is mighty high inflation!

When economists think of hyperinflation, they think 50 percent or higher *per month*. Imagine: A toaster in January costs $20; in February, $30; and if you're thinking about a Christmas gift, think $1,730. Crazy, isn't it? People have actually lived through months and years of hyperinflation. Look at the accompanying table of hyperinflations.

German workers, during Germany's hyperinflation, insisted on being paid twice a day so they could buy their groceries during lunch break. If they waited until the end of the workday, they could not have afforded the food! It was ridiculous to save because their savings would lose its value overnight.

Yugoslavia's 5 quadrillion percent inflation—from October 1993 to January 24, 1995—represents the worst episode of hyperinflation in recorded history. The average daily rate was nearly 100 percent. Money became virtually useless. One story suffices: Postmen collected telephone bills. One postman found that by the time he collected the 780 bills on his route, their value was virtually zero. So he decided to stay home and pay the bills himself, which cost him the equivalent of a few U.S. pennies!

How safe would you feel if you had to cope with hyperinflation? There would be no anchor to your economic life. How could you plan for your family's future? Could you feel any sense of security?

It's no surprise, then, that economists worry about inflation. Moderate inflation can escalate into high inflation and high inflation may end up being a ticking time bomb that explodes into that dreaded twilight zone of hyperinflation.

GERMANY	1922	5,000%
HUNGARY	1946	20,000%
BOLIVIA	1985	10,000%
PERU	1990	7,500%
UKRAINE	1993	5,000%
YUGOSLAVIA	1993–95	5,000,000,000,000,000%
ZIMBABWE	2006	1,200%

on the net

Changes in the consumer price index (CPI)—a measure of the average change in prices paid by urban consumers for a fixed market basket of goods and services—is a standard measure of inflation. The Bureau of Labor Statistics provides current and historical data on the CPI (http://stats.bls.gov/cpi).

And just as your $850 mortgage payments every month became less and less burdensome through inflation, so too does inflation, with time, reduce the *real* cost to government of carrying the national debt.

Inflation could help the government in yet another way. If prices of goods and services increase at about the same rate as wage rates and other sources of income, you end up paying more income tax. Why? Because a higher money income may put you in a higher tax bracket. Suppose, for example, that 10 years ago, your income was $40,000 and the last $1,000 of it was taxed at 20 percent; you paid $200 tax on it. Now, after 10 years of inflation, you earn $75,000, and the last $1,000 of it is taxed at 31 percent. You now pay $310 tax on that $1,000. You have been bumped into a higher tax bracket, even though the $75,000 buys the same groceries now as the $40,000 did 10 years ago. In other words, even though your real income remains the same, your disposable income decreases because government collects more.

Moderating the Wins and Losses Wouldn't you think that habitual losers of inflation would get tired of losing and try to do something about it? Many do, and succeed. For example, many banks offer home mortgages whose rates vary directly with the rate of inflation. Instead of charging 6½ percent on a 30-year mortgage, they may charge 5 percent *plus the inflation rate*. In this way, they check the loss of future income through inflation. Unions understand as well that they could end up being big losers if they sign multiyear fixed-wage contracts. Most union contracts now include a built-in cost-of-living adjustment (COLA) that covers the rate of inflation. Even taxpayers now can get some relief from "bracket creep" because the federal government recently adjusted the income levels associated with tax brackets to the rate of inflation.

LIVING IN A WORLD OF INFLATION AND UNEMPLOYMENT

Look at the economy of Exhibit 3, panel *a*. It's in equilibrium at $800 billion, where aggregate expenditure, AE_2, intersects the 45-degree line. But note: that's $400 billion below the economy's $1,200 billion full-employment level.

At $800 billion, firms responding to or anticipating demands for consumption and investment goods continue to produce $700 billion of consumption goods and $100 billion of investment goods, and if at the same time consumers continue to spend $700 billion on consumption and save $100 billion, then the number of people employed in the economy remains stuck at less than full employment. Moreover, there is no reason for those unemployed to expect to find employment, no matter how hard they may try.

Wouldn't it be cruel, under these circumstances, to accuse people willing to work but unable to find a job of being lazy or listless? If they can persuade an employer to hire them, it likely means that they have displaced other workers in a game of employment musical chairs. After all, at $Y = \$800$ billion, only so many workers will be employed.

Identifying the Recessionary Gap

A $400 billion national income deficiency separates the $800 billion equilibrium level from the $1,200 billion full-employment level. What it takes to drive the equilibrium level of national income up to full employment is more aggregate expenditure; how much more depends principally on the marginal propensity to consume. For example, if $MPC = 0.80$ and generates an income multiplier of 5, then it would take an additional spending of $80 billion—which is the amount represented by the distance hg—to shift the equilibrium level of national income up from $800 billion to $1,200 billion. This $80 billion deficiency in aggregate expenditure is called the **recessionary gap**.

In Exhibit 3, the recessionary gap reflects the difference between the $100 billion that producers invest (investment being part of aggregate expenditures) and the $180 billion total investment demand required to bring equilibrium to full employment.

The fact that many people are jobless when producers invest only $100 billion is unfortunate, not only for the unemployed but for producers as well. After all, they would love to produce more. But they confront the economy's consumption and investment spending, which tells them that producing more would be

Recessionary gap
The amount by which aggregate expenditure falls short of the level needed to generate equilibrium national income at full employment without inflation.

KEY EXHIBIT 3 Recessionary and Inflationary Gaps

The $800 billion equilibrium level of national income in panel a is $400 billion short of the economy's $1,200 billion full-employment national income level. To achieve full-employment equilibrium, aggregate expenditures must increase by $80 billion (the income multiplier is 5), from AE_2 to AE_1, which defines the recessionary gap hg. The $1,600 billion equilibrium level of national income is $400 billion above the zero-inflation full-employment level. To eliminate the inflationary gap, ef, aggregate expenditures must be cut $80 billion, from AE_3 to AE_1. In the real GDP version of the economy, panel b, gh defines the $80 billion recessionary gap and fg defines the $80 billion inflationary gap.

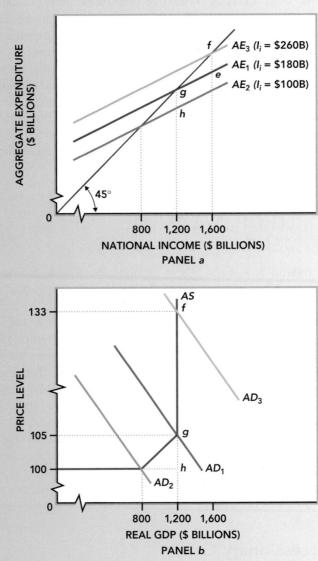

PANEL a

PANEL b

check your understanding

Why don't producers simply increase their investment to close a recessionary gap?

foolhardy. They can't be expected to increase investment when there's no evidence that demand exists for the investment goods. That is to say, neither the unemployed nor the producers can be faulted for the economy's recessionary gap.

This recessionary gap can also be illustrated in the aggregate demand and aggregate supply model of real GDP shown in Exhibit 3, panel b. If aggregate demand is AD_2, then the economy comes to equilibrium at $800 billion real GDP, when $AD_2 = AS$. What would it take to bring panel b's economy to its $1,200 billion full-employment equilibrium? An increase in investment demand from $100 billion to $180 billion, which would shift the aggregate demand curve from AD_2 to AD_1. This distance hg marks the recessionary gap. But note: The move to full employment creates in this version of the economy a moderate inflation, shown in panel b as a price level increase from 100 to 105.

Identifying the Inflationary Gap

Let's go back to panel *a* in Exhibit 3 for a moment. Let's now suppose that the aggregate expenditures curve is AE_3. The economy is then propelled to an equilibrium level of $1,600 billion. But is that possible?

Think about it. How can an economy be in equilibrium at $1,600 billion when the full-employment level is $1,200 billion? That is to say, how can the economy create more goods and services when all its resources are fully engaged producing $1,200 billion? The answer: It can't. What then explains the difference between the $1,200 billion full-employment level and the $1,600 billion equilibrium level? Inflation. National income above the $1,200 billion level reflects only price increases.

What would it take to bring the economy to equilibrium at full employment without inflation? Assuming again that $MPC = 0.80$ and the income multiplier is 5, an $80 billion cut in aggregate expenditure would draw the equilibrium level of national income down by $400 billion to the $1,200 billion full-employment level. This need for an $80 billion aggregate expenditure cutback defines the economy's **inflationary gap**.

The inflationary gap can be illustrated as well in the aggregate demand and aggregate supply model of panel *b*. If investment demand increases from $180 billion to $260 billion, shifting the aggregate demand curve upward to AE_3, the economy achieves equilibrium at full employment, at $1,200 real GDP, but with a matching price level of 133. (The $1,200 billion real GDP multiplied by the 133 price level creates a nominal GDP of $1,600 billion, corresponding to the inflationary $1,600 billion national income equilibrium of panel *a*.) The distance *fg* in panel *b* identifies the inflationary gap.

Inflationary gap
The amount by which aggregate expenditure exceeds the aggregate expenditure level needed to generate equilibrium national income at full employment without inflation.

CLOSING RECESSIONARY AND INFLATIONARY GAPS

Suppose the president of the United States asks for your advice. The economy he confronts is the recessionary one of Exhibit 3, and his goal is to bring the economy to equilibrium at full employment. What do you tell him?

How about presidential persuasion? You could advise the president to invite the economy's most influential producers to a White House breakfast and there explain the importance of increasing aggregate expenditure.

It would be marvelous if all it took was a little presidential sweet talk to get producers to add another $80 billion to investment. But even producers who voted twice for the president couldn't justify a penny more investment when the economy is already in equilibrium at $800 billion. Where, then, do you find the $80 billion?

Enter Government

If nobody else will do it, government can. How does government get into an $80 billion investment business? It designs a public investment package that totals $80 billion. In ten minutes the president can probably come up with projects that would completely close the recessionary gap.

There are always more interstates to build, more public housing to construct, more pollution control facilities to finance, more space missions to undertake, more health care schemes to fund, and more defense to procure. In fact, the least of his problems would seem to be finding suitable projects to absorb the $80 billion.

What about Congress? Would it go along? Members of Congress have to be sensitive to voters' concerns back home, and among their concerns in times of recession are jobs.

on the net
For a detailed account of how much the federal government spends on what, review the federal budget of the United States (http://www.gpo.gov/usbudget/index.html).

historical perspective

© 2007 JupiterImages Corporation

Bad news for the economy?

A MAN MUST BE PERFECTLY CRAZY . . .

Perfectly crazy? What's this all about? Well, it's actually about the core issue of this chapter. It's about the relationship—or lack thereof—between saving and investment. The core issue is: When a person decides to save a dollar, does it mean that the saved dollar will automatically become a dollar's worth of investment? That is, does a person's intention to save guarantee that there is an accompanying intention to put that saving into some form of investment?

Read Adam Smith, *The Wealth of Nations* (1776), on this topic: "a man must be perfectly crazy who, where there is tolerable security, does not employ all of the stock which he commands whether it be his own or borrowed of other people. . . ." What he means by "employing all his stock" is that a person "employs" or uses some part of his or her "stock" of income to buy consumption goods and "employs" or uses the rest to engage in some form of investment. Whatever the proportions, it's all used up. The idea that someone would save without the thought of investing was, to Smith, just perfectly crazy.

If Smith is right, then the idea of a recessionary gap goes out the window. Insufficient aggregate demand is, in this mind-set, conceptually impossible.

It seemed then, in the late 18th, and early 19th centuries, that only a perfectly crazy economist would challenge Adam Smith's view on this and there weren't too many of them. On this core issue of saving and invesment, Smith's view became conventional wisdom. David Ricardo's *On the Principles of Political Economy and Taxation* (1817) restates it: "No man produces but with a view to consume or sell, and he never

sells, but with the intention to purchase some other commodity." In other words, perfect alignment always between saving and investment. Jean Baptiste Say's *A Treatise on Political Economy* (1803) put the idea in the form of a celebrated law: "supply creates its own demand."

But there were dissenters. In the backwaters of the conventional wisdom, Thomas Malthus argued that the idea was both counterintuitive and counterfactual. In *Principles of Political Economy* (1820), he writes: "This doctrine, however, as generally applied, appears to me to be utterly unfounded, and completely to contradict the great principles which regulate supply and demand."

A nation's economic woes can be attributed, he thought, to our saving behavior, or to "parsimony," as he put it. The question he raises is: Why would anyone invest in producing more goods when no one's buying and no one's buying because everyone's saving. Malthus recognized the possibility and importance of insufficent aggregate demand: ". . . a country such as our own, which had been rich and populous, would, with too parsimonious habits, infallibly become poor and comparatively unpeopled."

Who's "perfectly crazy"? Is it crazy to think that people will save without necessarily intending to invest? Whatever the answer, the question is absolutely core to the analysis of macroeconomics.

The government now becomes an integral part of the economy's aggregate expenditures. What was once AE_2 is now AE_1 = the $80 billion increase representing government purchases of goods and services.

Suppose the president asks you to brief the White House staff on your $80 billion recommendation. You prepare Exhibit 3, panels *a* and *b*, which shows the economy struggling along without the $80 billion of government spending on goods and services, and how the economy fares with the government spending.

They would see the difference immediately.

One critic of government spending is the Cato Institute (http://www.cato.org/), a nonpartisan public policy research foundation.

Government Spending Is Not Problem-Free

Simple? Perhaps too simple. Critics of this view of closing a recessionary gap offer a series of objections. First, they warn that once the $80 billion of government spending is introduced into the economy, it takes on a life force of its own. *Once in, always in.* Whether or not it is needed to close recessionary gaps in subsequent years, the politics of the spending—such as defense and road

appliedperspective

ARE DEFICIT BUDGETS STRICTLY TOOLS OF COUNTERCYCLICAL FISCAL POLICY?

Back in 1980, economist Irwin Kellner, writing about Keynes and deficits, said: "Those who have written about Keynes in an effort to interpret his writings have drawn the conclusion that budget deficits are quite acceptable during periods of economic slack. I would agree. Some authors believe that Keynes had a cavalier attitude toward budget deficits, pointing to the views of many of his disciples who assert that deficits do not matter. With this I would disagree. If Keynes did not place great emphasis on the implications of a budget deficit beyond that of stimulating the economy, it is simply because he believed that deficits should not be used as a main tool of economic policy, and when they were, they were to be used during periods of slack. It is Keynes's followers and the politicians whom they educated that are to blame for the 'cavalier' attitude toward budget deficits that subsequently developed in the 1950s and 1960s."

Whether Kellner is right or wrong about Keynes, the record on deficits and surpluses tells the story.

During the 1940s, 1950s, and 1960s, 22 of the 30 years had deficit budgets. Since then, from 1970 through 1997, *every year* was a deficit year. In other words, only 8 of the 57 years since 1940 had surplus budgets. Obviously, in the many years of robust economic growth during that period, the budget was still generating deficits. Even though the 1998–2000 period generated surpluses, as Kellner noted, the data do not support the idea that deficits necessarily reflect countercyclical fiscal policy.

© CORBIS

Plunging into deficits year after year.

···

MORE ON THE NET

The Bureau of the Public Debt (http://www.publicdebt.treas.gov/) and the Concord Coalition (http://www.concordcoalition.org/) publish data and information about federal budget deficits and the public debt.

Sources: Adapted from Irwin L. Kellner, *Economic Report* (New York: Manufactures Hanover Trust Company, November 1980); and *Statistical Abstract of the United States, 1994* (Washington, D.C.: U.S. Department of Commerce, 1994).

building—guarantees its continuity. In addition, *once in, always grows.* That is, $80 billion of government spending today, because of the vested political interests it creates, might push to $500 billion in a decade.

Second, they insist that advocates of government intervention fail to appreciate the self-correcting nature of the economy. Given sufficient time, market forces will shift private-sector investment upward to the right, narrowing the recessionary gap. For example, changes in prices and wage rates may make investment more attractive to producers. Time also takes its toll on the economy's machinery and physical plants. Eventually, they must be replaced, and thus they contribute also to the upsurge in demand for investment.

Third, the critics note the obvious: Government spending is not cost-free. The funding for $80 billion in government spending must come from somewhere, and, too often, it is debt financed. Apart from the other objections to spending, this debt financing—the national debt—places a new burden on the economy that can sap the vitality of the economy's future.

Closing the Inflationary Gap

What about closing the inflationary gap? Do you simply reverse the process that closes the recessionary gap? That's just about it. The idea is to bring AE_3 down to AE_1 in panel *a* of Exhibit 3 (or AD_3 down to AD_1 in panel *b*). How do you do that? By cutting $80 billion out of investment demand. Either government spending gets chopped or private-sector investment shrinks, or both. If consumers won't cut their spending on consumption and producers won't cut their demand for investment goods, then the president must cut government spending. It means, of course, less highway construction, less public housing, and less defense spending. You can imagine, can't you, some strong resistance back home! If it's your highway, your public housing, or your defense factory that gets cut, then your voice will get heard in Congress. For this reason, Congress may be less willing to go along with curbing inflation than promoting full employment.

How much cutting is necessary? The $80 billion cut multiplied by 5 (the income multiplier) creates the $400 billion cut needed to bring the economy down from $1,600 billion to $1,200 billion.

MAKING FISCAL POLICY

Let's again consider the recessionary gap of Exhibit 3. Knowing that government spending of $80 billion will drive national income from $800 billion to the desired $1,200 billion is an important initial step in the formation of fiscal policy. But that information doesn't tell us where the government *gets* the $80 billion. It doesn't materialize out of nowhere.

Perhaps the first thing the president considers is taxation. If the government needs $1, it can raise taxes by $1. If it needs $80 billion, then it simply taxes the people $80 billion. Of course, the people always have the final say. If taxes become too burdensome, it may be the last time the president sees the inside of the White House.

Suppose the president shows a strong reluctance to tax. Is it hopeless? Not yet. The government can borrow the $80 billion. From whom? From people like you who are willing to lend the government money in exchange for its interest-bearing IOUs. These IOUs take the form of government securities, such as Treasury bills, notes, and bonds. As long as the interest rate the government offers on these securities is competitive with the rate in the private market, the government should be able to finance the $80 billion of government spending.

The use of government spending and taxation to make changes in the level of national income is what economists call **fiscal policy**.

Fiscal policy
Government spending and taxation policy to achieve macroeconomic goals of full employment without inflation.

Choosing the Tax Option

Let's suppose the government decides against borrowing and instead chooses the tax option. For every dollar the government decides to spend, it gets that dollar by taxing the people one dollar. This one-to-one correspondence between government spending, G, and tax revenue, T, results in a **balanced budget**:

Balanced budget
Government spending equals tax revenues.

$$G = T$$

Of course, balanced budgets come in all sizes. The government can program a $100 billion, or even a $500 billion, recession-fighting balanced budget. As long as it collects in taxes what it spends on programs, that is, if $G = T$, the budget is balanced.

Full Employment, Zero Inflation, and a Balanced Budget

If the president insists on a balanced budget, he cannot simply inject $80 billion of government spending into the economy and allow the income multiplier to shift the equilibrium level of national income from $800 billion to $1,200 billion. He now has to worry about the effects of financing the $80 billion spending with taxes.

If government imposes a tax, most people would be scrambling about trying to come up with the money to pay it. Where would they find it? Obviously, right at home. To pay the tax, people will have to consume less and save less. But consuming less during recession adversely affects the level of national income. And that's a new problem.

Does the negative impact of higher taxes on national income simply cancel out the positive impact of government spending? Not at all. Any increase in the government's balanced budget—that is, government spending and taxes increase by the same amount—actually adds to the level of national income. Why is this so?

Deriving the Tax Multiplier The answer is linked to the relationship between the income multiplier and the tax multiplier. Like the income multiplier, which magnifies the effect of government spending on the level of national income, the **tax multiplier** magnifies the effect of taxes on the level of national income. *But income magnification from taxes is the weaker of the two.* Why?

Suppose Bob Diener, an attorney working for the FBI in Santa Fe, earns $50,000 annually. And suppose that he spent $40,500 of that income on consumption and put the remaining $9,500 into savings.

Now suppose Congress agrees with the president and imposes a 20 percent income tax. Come April 15, Bob is obligated to transfer $50,000 × 0.20 = $10,000 of his income to the government. Where would he get it? Would he take it all from savings? Or all from consumption? Neither is likely.

In fact, we know precisely how much he will draw from each source. Since his $MPC = 0.80$ and $MPS = 0.20$, he will give up $8,000 of what would have been consumption spending and $2,000 of what would have been saved.

That $8,000 cutback in consumption sends shock waves through the economy. After all, what Bob no longer spends on consumption, others no longer earn as income.

Picture the scene. Unaccustomed to being frugal, Bob must nonetheless cut back. But where? Suppose that among the consumption items he picks to trim are his catered parties. Prior to the tax, he had spent $1,000 annually on catering. He now cuts that out completely.

The first to feel the effect of his consumption cut is, of course, his caterer, Ayala Donchin. Ayala now discovers she has $1,000 less income, and with less income she consumes less herself. How much less? With $MPC = 0.80$, she cuts her consumption by $0.80 × $1,000 = 800. That, in turn, means $800 less income for some other person. And so this shock wave, initiated by a $1,000 cut in catering, continues.

You should see a *tax-induced multiplier* at work. But note what triggers the rollback in income. It is Bob's $8,000 cutback in consumption, not the entire $10,000 tax. After all, $2,000 of the $10,000 tax came from his would-be savings. Only $8,000 would have gone through the income stream. The multiplying factor associated with such a tax multiplier when $MPC = 0.80$ is

$$\frac{-MPC}{1 - MPC} = \frac{-0.80}{1 - 0.80} = \frac{\text{change in } Y}{\text{change in } T} = -4.$$

The $10,000 tax, then, generates a $10,000 × −4 = $40,000 decline in national income.

Government Uses the $10,000 Tax for $10,000 of Spending The government now has Bob's $10,000 in tax revenue. What does it do with the tax? If it were to save $2,000 and spend the remaining $8,000 on, say, sewage repair, then the income multiplier effect of that spending would exactly offset the

Tax multiplier
The multiple by which the equilibrium level of national income changes when a dollar change in taxes occurs. The multiple depends upon the marginal propensity to consume. The equation for the tax multiplier is $-MPC/(1 - MPC)$.

check your understanding

Why isn't the tax multiplier equal to the income multiplier?

$40,000 cut in national income induced by the tax. That is, if the government saved $2,000, the net effect on national income of a $10,000 increase in taxes and spending, $G = T$, would be $0.

But the government doesn't save. It spends the entire $10,000 of Bob's taxes. The income multiplier effect is not on $8,000, but on the entire $10,000. The income multiplier on that $10,000, with $MPC = 0.80$, is 5:

$$\frac{1}{1 - MPC} = \frac{1}{1 - 0.80} = \frac{\text{change in } Y}{\text{change in } G} = 5$$

The increase in national income that government creates by spending the $10,000 is $10,000 \times 5 = $50,000.

The Balanced Budget Multiplier

In brief, things aren't always what they seem. When the government levies a $10,000 tax on people's income and puts the $10,000 back into the economy, national income does not remain the same. It expands. For example, a $10,000 increase in both G and T generates a $50,000 − $40,000 = $10,000 expansion of national income. We get this result from

$$\frac{1}{1 - MPC} + \frac{-MPC}{1 - MPC} = \frac{1}{0.2} + \frac{-0.8}{0.2} = 5 - 4 = 1,$$

Balanced budget multiplier
The effect on the equilibrium level of national income of an equal change in government spending and taxes. The balanced budget multiplier is 1.

subtracting the government's tax multiplier of 4, operating on T, from the income multiplier of 5, operating on G. This gives us a **balanced budget multiplier** of $5 - 4 = 1$. *No matter what the specific income multiplier and tax multiplier may be, the balanced budget multiplier always equals 1.*

How to Get to Full-Employment and Balance the Budget

The only way to drive the recessionary economy of Exhibit 3 out of its equilibrium position at $Y = $800 billion to a $Y = $1,200 billion equilibrium at full employment, *and balance the budget at the same time,* is to generate a government budget of $400 billion—that is, $400 billion of taxes and $400 billion of government spending. This budget produces the desired $400 billion increase in national income.

But that's strong fiscal policy! You can see why the president, bent on full employment, might think twice about balancing the budget. What would you advise?

PURSUING BUDGET DEFICIT OPTIONS

It's worth exploring other ways to bring the economy out of Exhibit 3's recession. Why not relax the balanced budget constraint slightly. Or perhaps even more than slightly. The government has several fiscal policy options. Look at Exhibit 4.

Every fiscal policy option in Exhibit 4 produces the same results. In each, national income increases by the targeted $400 billion. That is, each budget option completely closes the $400 billion recessionary gap.

The first option balances the budget. If the target is $400 billion of national income, then $G = T = $400 billion does the job. We know that because the balanced-budget multiplier is one. But that $400 billion tax bite may be more than Congress or the president is prepared to impose.

Consider the second option that combines $G = $160 billion with $T = $100 billion. Applying the income multiplier of 5 to the $160 billion of government spending will raise national income by $800 billion. However, the tax multiplier of -4

EXHIBIT 4   Sample Budget Options to Close a Recessionary Gap ($ Billions)

OPTION	GOVERNMENT SPENDING	TAX REVENUE	BUDGET DEFICIT	TARGET CHANGE IN INCOME
1	$400	$400	$ 0	$400
2	160	100	60	400
3	120	50	70	400
4	80	0	80	400

applied to the $100 billion of taxes will reduce national income by $400 billion so that the net effect is the $400 billion target increase in national income. But note: It creates a **budget deficit** G>T, of $60 billion.

A third option reduces the nasty tax bite from $100 billion to $50 billion and combines that tax with $120 billion of government spending to achieve the $400 billion national income target. But this option increases the deficit to $70 billion. The fourth option is entirely tax free—"read my lips, no new taxes"—but it saddles the economy with the even higher deficit of $80 billion.

Budget deficit
Government spending exceeds tax revenues.

How Mixed Is the Mixed Economy?

Although all the fiscal policy budget options of Exhibit 4 lead to a national income of $1,200 billion at full employment, they don't all produce the same mix of government and private sector economic activity.

For example, if the president chooses the first option from Exhibit 4—the balanced budget option at G = T = $400 billion—government becomes a major participant in the national economy. This is an important consideration that the president and Congress must address. As you know, much of the political debate in the United States and other countries focuses on this one issue: How much government is the right amount of government?

check your understanding

Why is it sometimes inappropriate to rely on the balanced budget multiplier to close a recessionary gap?

WHEN SURPLUS BUDGETS ARE APPROPRIATE

Look again at Exhibit 3. With aggregate expenditures at AE_3, an inflationary gap of $80 billion emerges creating an equilibrium level of national income of $1,600 billion or $400 billion higher than the non-inflationary full employment level of $1,200 billion. What fiscal policy measures are appropriate now? The government has several options. Look at Exhibit 5.

Note that the target is now negative. The government wants to *cut* national income by $400 billion. Raising taxes will take income away from people which will reduce aggregate expenditure in the economy. That's a move in the right direction. A cut in government spending will accomplish the same. If the goal is to maintain a balanced budget while cutting national income to its target level of $1,200 billion, then the first option G = T = −$400 billion will work.

While cutting taxes by $400 billion would be a treat for most people, cutting $400 billion out of government spending could be painful. Less Medicare, less education funding, less interstate repair, less national security, less support for troubled industries, less aid to dependent children, less funding for health and hospitals, less protection of our environment, and perhaps less exploration of space.

A less drastic cut in government spending is possible. But note that each of the three remaining options of Exhibit 5 generates a **budget surplus**, T>G. Apply

Budget surplus
Tax revenues exceed government spending.

EXHIBIT 5   Sample Budget Options to Close an Inflationary Gap ($ Billions)

OPTION	GOVERNMENT SPENDING	TAX REVENUE	SURPLUS BUDGET	TARGET Δ Y
1	–$400	–$400	$ 0	–$400
2	–160	–100	60	–400
3	–40	50	10	–400
4	–80	0	80	–400

the income multiplier of 5 to cuts in government spending with the tax multiplier of −4 applied to the corresponding tax and the $400 billion target change in national income is obtained.

Are our fiscal policy options really that simple? Does the president really face recessionary gaps and inflationary gaps that emerge when equilibrium levels of national income deviate from no-inflation full-employment levels?

Many economists believe that this model of national income determination and the fiscal policy prescriptions (to close recessionary and inflationary gaps) that follow from it are accurate enough reflections of our economic reality to make them useful.

COUNTERCYCLICAL FISCAL POLICY

Useful, perhaps, but with some reservation. Why reservation? Because the problem with this fixed target-driven fiscal policy is that the national income target the president pursues becomes almost immediately out of date *while the policy to pursue it is in play*! It's not unlike trying to hit a constantly moving target. Most difficult.

And the reason the target keeping moving is because the economy's performance itself is always in a constant state of motion. Exhibit 6 portrays this motion, shown as year-to-year deviations from a horizontal trend, covering the years 1860–2003.

These deviations seem to trace a series of recurring cycles, with some years of rapid economic growth followed by others of economic decline. Some cycles appear to be quite moderate, while others seem severe. It isn't hard to pick out the depression of the 1930s and the sharp recovery during World War II, is it?

In other words, locking on to a static or stationary target of national income equilibrium *as if it exists* might seem somewhat pointless to a policy adviser. What, then, need government do? In brief, to engage in **countercyclical fiscal policy**, that is, to introduce ever-changing fiscal policy prescriptions in order to temper the always recurring cycles.

Countercyclical fiscal policy
Fiscal policy designed to moderate the severity of the business cycle.

on the
net
Learn more about William Stanley Jevons (http:// en.wikipedia.org/wiki/ William_Stanley_Jevons).

What Causes Business Cycles?

What causes cycles in the first place? Some are thought to be triggered by *external*, random events, such as wars, population booms, housing starts, clustering of innovations, and tech-stock or credit bubbles. Other cycles are thought be *internal*, that is, self-generating by and within the economy.

Let's examine some of these cycles to see if any fit the historical record mapped in Exhibit 6.

War-Induced Cycles Are we destined always to go to war? From time immemorial, wars have been viewed as innate to the human experience. Admittedly,

KEY **EXHIBIT 6**   The U.S. Business Cycle Record: 1860–2003

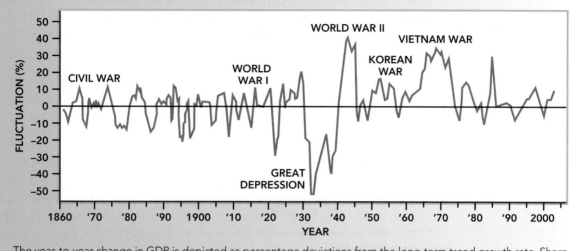

The year-to-year change in GDP is depicted as percentage deviations from the long-term trend growth rate. Sharp upturns are clearly marked by the Civil War, World War II, the Korean War, and the Vietnam War. The Great Depression of the 1930s and the sharp economic recovery following World War II dominate the picture.

Source: Ameritrust Company, Cleveland, Ohio and Economic Report, The President, 2006.

the evidence is frightfully confirming. Regardless of whether wars can be avoided, economists have long observed a link between wars and business cycles.

Does such a link make sense? Think about it. Armies need to be staffed, fed, clothed, housed, transported, equipped, and mended.

War requires considerable spending. You can see the income multiplier working overtime. In each of our major wars—the 1861–65 Civil War, the 1914–18 World War I, the 1939–45 World War II, the 1950–53 Korean War, the 1964–74 Vietnam War, the 2003 to present Iraq War—military production spurred the economy. And in at least some, if not all, of them, the end of war brought an end to the economy's war-induced prosperity.

Look again at Exhibit 6. Note the link between wars and economic upturns. For World War I, World War II, and the Korean War, the war-induced expansion came *when the economy was in the downswing or trough phase of an already existing cycle.* We were still in the throes of the Great Depression when Japan attacked Pearl Harbor in 1941. These war-induced cycles are random shocks to an economy already in continuous cyclical motion.

The Housing Cycle   Another externally induced cycle is the 15- to 20-year housing cycle, also known as the Kuznets cycle, named for Nobel Laureate Simon Kuznets, who pioneered research on the relationship between cycles and housing construction.

How do housing cycles originate? What could touch off an extraordinarily large investment in housing within a relatively short period of time? Imagine what would happen to the demand for housing if a wicked series of hurricanes tore away much of south Florida. Think of Katrina Midwest floods and California brushfires, too, come to mind as cycle triggers, but such calamities of nature are not the only causes of housing cycles.

For example, if interest rates are unusually high for an unusually long period of time, housing construction suffers. If people don't buy houses, they tend also not to buy a vast array of house furnishings. Picture the income multiplier at work. When interest rates finally fall, mortgage payments once again become

on the
net
Review an autobiography of Simon Kuznets (http:// www.nobel.se/economics/ laureates/1971/kuznets-autobio.html).

affordable. Housing investment booms to satisfy the backlog of housing and housing-related demands.

But at some point housing investments slow down and the cycle's downturn phase begins. The housing cycle reappears with far less intensity. After all, not all housing depreciates at once. Some houses seem to last forever; others, poorly built or maintained, are torn down much sooner. Typically, a first-wave housing cycle lasts 15 to 20 years.

The Innovation Cycle Joseph Schumpeter explained innovation clustering by identifying specific innovations that create major breakthroughs in technology. These pioneering innovations not only require massive investment themselves but promote a host of supporting innovations that together create an economic upswing that could last as long as 30 years.

What do these innovations look like? We live in their shadow. The railroad, the automobile, petrochemicals, television, nuclear energy, computers, genetic engineering, and space technologies are innovations that changed the character of our economy, society and culture. Each, in its time, stimulated the development of entirely new industries that dictated for generations the specific pace and direction of our economic life.

Consider, for example, the railroad. It extended the size of our markets and, therefore, almost everything marketable. It created industries where none could have existed before, bringing millions of previously remote land into the productive economy.

Yet even the mighty railroad ultimately exhausted its potential. What happens to the economy when the massive investment momentum subsides? The income multiplier effect of reduced demand and employment triggers the downturn phase of this long-wave innovation cycle.

The automobile and the myriad industries it fostered created its own long-wave cycle. Petrochemicals and television followed, creating superstructures of investments that revolutionized the way we live. Are space and genetic engineering innovations now about to revolutionize our economic life? What kinds of earthbound investments will outer space inspire?

What factors contribute to internally induced cycles?

BUBBLES AND CYCLES

Some new technologies come charging onto the economy in very big ways and end up breeding their own variety of the business cycle. They take on the character of bubbles, and like bubbles often get pumped and puffed up very quickly to a size much beyond their ability to self-sustain. Eventually, inevitably, and even suddenly, they burst.

Economic bubbles are like that. They materialize when producers, venture capitalists, and stock traders passionately disagree about the future prospects of a new product—typically but not always representing a new technology—that appears on the market.

How does a bubble form? Initially, there is a mad scramble on the part of many investors to get on board whatever-it-is in the hope that whatever-it-is will be the next 'electric light' or the next 'sliced bread.' *The key ingredient that distinguishes this new product or innovation from others is the excitement it elicits in the market and the excitement is contagious.*

A rush of people believe or want to believe that it's their chance of a lifetime and plunge into either ownership of the companies making this what-ever-it-is or into the purchase of the product itself. Prices in this hyped market begin to reflect their buying frenzy and companies' stock prices soar in tandem. With investors expectations confirmed, resistance to the lure of 'almost guaranteed' record-breaking profits breaks down completely.

applied perspective

THE MAKING OF A BUBBLE: THE MOVIE

Speculators may do no harm as bubbles on a steady stream of enterprise. But the position is serious when enterprise becomes a bubble on a whirlpool of speculation. When the capital development of a country becomes a by-product of the activities of a casino, the job is likely to be ill-done.

John Maynard Keynes, 1936

The cast

a ne'er-do-well, penniless, unemployed, prospective homeowner
a sleazy broker employed at We'll Do Anything Mortgage House
an even shadier banker at the First National Bank of Anything Goes
marketing wizard at the First National Bank of Anything Goes
investment manager at the New York Firemen's Pension Fund
investment banker at Trust Me Investment Bank

Opening Scene: at the *We'll Do Anything Mortgage House*

Ne'er-do-well: I saw your commercial on television last night which said you will provide a mortgage to anybody who breathes. Well, I do. But that's about it. I have no money, no job. I can offer no down payment. Do I qualify?
Sleazy broker: Absolutely! Since the value of your house will always increase, we need no down payment. And we can give you a very low mortgage rate right now. Of course, we may have to increase it later. It will depend on the mortgage lending market. Sounds fair?
Ne'er-do-well: Sounds fantastic! You people really care about folks like me. Gosh, lending me all that money even though my credit worthiness is zero.
Sleazy broker: Well, let me make it clear. We don't actually lend you the money. What we do is find a bank that will. Of course, we get our deserved commission.

Scene II: boardroom at *First National Bank of Anything Goes*

Shadier banker (musing): Wow! I'm loaded down with these worthless mortgage loans that I picked up from sleazy brokers. Now, to get rid of them at a profit.
Marketing wizard at the bank: I have an idea. Let's create a new security and use these worthless mortgages as its collateral. We can market these new securities to investors with the promise to pay them back when the mortgages are paid off.
Shadier banker: But look at the ne'er-do-wells who are mortgaged up to their teeth. Those mortgages will never ever be paid off.
Marketing wizards: Probably not, but don't forget that housing always increases in value so even if we

foreclose on the ne'er-do-wells, we can repossess their houses and profit again on their resale.
Shadier banker: Brilliant! Comb your hair, shine your shoes and let's pay a visit to investment banks that specialize in marketing these kinds of securities.

Scene III: boardroom *at Trust Me Investment Bank*

Investment banker: "Let's see. I bought these "First National Bank of Anything Goes" securities. Now to sell them at a handsome profit. Who would buy them? Let's look at my client list. How about the New York Firemen's Pension Fund. Those funds represent the payments firemen make to finance their future pensions. The firemen should be interested, particularly if these securities are sold at a high enough interest rate.

Scene IV: [Two years later] *Urgent telephone call from NY Firemen's Pension Fund to Trust Me Investment Bank*

NY Firemen Fund manager: Excuse me, but I'm rather nervous. I'm not getting the interest payments on the securities you sold me.
Investment banker: Gosh, I meant to tell you. We have a problem here. It seems that many of the ne'er-do-wells who took out the housing mortgage loans that back your securities are unable to pay them off.
NY Firemen Fund manager: But you told me these securities were solid, backed by housing collateral.
Investment banker: Caught me by surprise too. The mortgage loans, it appears, were far riskier than I thought.
NY Firemen Fund manager: How can that be? You told me that housing prices always go up and that being the case borrowers can always refinance their home mortgages!
Investment banker: You're right. I did say that. But it turns out that housing prices have fallen and are still falling and mortgage rates have increased. As a result, borrowers can only sell their houses at substantial losses and with so many foreclosures, the housing market is glutted. Nor do they have the money to refinance at the now higher mortgage rates.
NY Firemen Fund manager: But I have hundred of millions of dollars—our firemen's future pensions - tied up in the securities you sold me.
Investment banker: I'm sorry. By the way, you're not the only serious loser. Hundreds of thousands of home-owners—decent folk as well as those ne'er-do-wells—were caught in falling housing values and rising mortgage rates, many of them losing their homes and savings.
NY Firemen Fund manager: Being sorry is not an acceptable answer!
Click.
NY Firemen Fund manager: Hello . . . hello . . . Are you there?

The mania—skyrocketing product and stock prices—continues even though most of the knowledgeable market players realize that these prices are totally at variance with market fundamentals.

But the variance is ignored because the issue is no longer estimating the worth of the product or company as much as it is estimating what others might believe the product or company is worth and will be worth tomorrow. Reality gives way to sheer speculative activity.

The bubble's burst? The first sign of any hesitancy among a critical mass of buyers may do the trick. If the hesitancy is sufficient to just dampen the increase, that dampening may convince others that the outrageous product and stock prices have finally come to an end and that the smart thing to do is to get out of the market immediately and completely before the onset of the now expected collapse. That thinking alone brings it on.

The collapse is not only financial. Many, if not most of the companies that produce the whatever-it-is end up bankrupted taking down with them their own employees and a host of supporting industries. The multiplier process, working in reverse, exacerbates the downturn in the real economy.

The housing or real estate bubble of 2001–2008 is the most recent of U.S. bubble history, coming upon the heels of the dot-com bubble of 1995–2000 that had created Silicon Valley and in its collapse, weeded out much of that creation. The real-estate bubble played havoc with homebuyers, both the scrupulous and unscrupulous. Its sharp decline, which began in 2006, had a direct and depressing impact not only on real wealth holdings of homeowners but on mortgage markets, the construction industries, the home furnishing industries, and home supply retail outlets.

MULTIPLIER AND ACCELERATOR CYCLE

The interaction of the multiplier and accelerator alone can induce cycles. The multiplier explains how a specific change in investment ends up generating a specific change in national income.

$$m = \frac{\Delta Y}{\Delta I}$$

And as we saw, it plays an important role in designing fiscal policy. But the multiplier effect on the economy has consequences far greater than moving national income from one level to another. Partnered with the accelerator, it explains as well why business cycles occur.

Think about it. When national income increases as a consequence, producers see the reasonableness of engaging in even more investment spending. After all, they know that people having more income will increase their demand for consumption goods. To prepare for the production of those goods, producers would need to build inventories, buy new machinery, and perhaps expand physical plant. That requires a fresh round of investment. The **accelerator** spells out the relationship between the new level of investment that is induced by changes in national income.

Accelerator
The relationship between the level of investment and the change in the level of national income.

$$a = \frac{\Delta I}{\Delta Y}$$

There is an interaction going on here. Changes in investment and changes in national income become mutually reinforcing. An initial change in investment generates, via the multiplier, a change in national income that induces, via the

interdisciplinaryperspective

THE FINANCIAL MELTDOWN: 2008

What kind of mental exercise is involved in someone deciding to sell you the Brooklyn Bridge? And what kind of mentality is needed to buy the bridge! Amazingly, that bridge has been bought and sold a million times over. Maybe nobody in the past went broke buying it and perhaps few really got rich selling it, but if you were to add a string of zeros—say, six or nine of them—to the price, then we're talking not necessarily about that bridge but a score of "bridge-like" assets and we're talking about modern day Fannie Mae, Freddie Mac, Lehman Bros, AIG, and their friends. These guys really made a gigantic killing on these financial "bridge-like" markets and, of course, there were millions of non-suspecting folks who were taken to the cleaners by them. Which begs the question: Is that what 21st century investment finance has become?

It also raises the question: What kind of people are seemingly comfortable poisoning our economic well that way? Joyce Sutphen takes a stab at it, addressing the question in her perceptive poem *Guys Like That.*

Guys Like That

Drive very nice cars, and from
where you sit in your dented
Last-century version of the
most ordinary car in America, they

look dark-suited and neat and fast.
Guys like that look as if they were thinking
about wine and marble floors, but
really they were thinking about TiVo

and ESPN. Women think that guys
like that are different from the guys
driving the trucks that bring cattle
to slaughter, but guys like that are

planning worse things than the death
of a cow. Guys who look like that—
so clean and cool—are quietly moving
money across the border, cooking books,

making deals that make some people
rich and some people poorer
than they were before guys like that
robbed them at the pump and on

their electricity bills, and even
now, guys like that are planning how
to divide up that little farm they just
passed, the one you used to call home.

accelerator, a higher level of investment that generates, via the multiplier, yet another change in national income, and so on.

This mutually reinforcing phenomenon may explain why the economy, once triggered by investment, steamrolls onward. But why does this growth take on a cyclical character?

Consider this: Suppose a college had to build 10 new classrooms to accommodate increased enrollment. It hires masons, carpenters, electricians, plasterers, painters, and plumbers to do the job. These people, now earning incomes, increase the demands for consumption goods in the college community. The economy flourishes.

But to keep these masons, carpenters, electricians, plasterers, painters, and plumbers employed, the college must continue to build 10 new classrooms each year. Otherwise many of those classroom building workers would lose their jobs. Without jobs, they're without income and without income they're unable to continue to buy the goods they previously did. So the interaction of the multiplier and accelerator now works in reverse.

The point is that it isn't enough that college enrollment increases and stays at that increased level or even that it continues to increase but at a slower pace,. *It must continue to increase at that heightened pace just to keep employment and income from falling.* Herein lays the origins of what may become the cycle.

Depending on the values of the multiplier and accelerator, the growth path taken by an economy may be cyclical, either increasing in intensity or dampening over time. The appendix provides an illustration of a cycle with increasing intensity.

This kind of cycle—reflecting the interaction of the multiplier and accelerator—is regarded as an internally-induced cycle, that is, one that is self-generated and self propelled.

REAL BUSINESS CYCLE THEORY

check your ✔
understanding
Why is the real business cycle theory not a cycle theory?

on the
net
For more about real business cycle theory, visit the Quantitative Macroeconomics and Real Business Cycle Home Page (http://dge.repec.org/).

Some economists challenge the idea that internal or external cycles exist (even though their own theory is called the real business cycle). They believe that the idea of an economy actually moving through regular and distinct phases of a business cycle is a misreading of our economic reality. They argue that the economy is highly dynamic and competitive, operating close to if not at full employment, and that what other economists diagnose as cycles are in fact variations in the rate of growth of a full-employment economy. (Imagine a production possibilities curve shifting outward year after year but with a different-sized shift each year.) These variations—tracing out an uneven growth path of twists and turns or, more appropriately, robust spurts, not-so-robust spurts, and, very occasionally, short, moderate dips in real GDP—are misconceived of as the business cycle.

The principal factor shaping the unevenness (not cycles) in the economy's growth path, they argue, is the random injection by firms of individually minor but still large numbers of unconnected technological changes that cumulatively raise the level of productivity in the economy. They emphasize both the *large numbers of minor, unconnected technological changes* and their *randomness*.

Consider first their idea that technological change in the economy is the result of numerous minor innovations that occur regularly in all industries. This characterization of technological change is consistent with their view that the economy is both dynamic and competitive. The key to success and to ultimate survival for the great numbers of firms that compete is to develop or at least adopt new technology. *New technology raises real productivity*, which allows for lower costs and prices. Firms that don't adopt new technology cannot be price competitive with those that do. In the end, they drop out of the market. The real productivity increases that occur in this competitive environment make up the increase in the economy's real GDP.

Second, the randomness of these technological changes accounts for the variations in year-to-year increases in real productivity. For example, one year may bring in a host of technological changes, followed by a year with relatively few changes. These changes are independent of one another. Their frequency and numbers are randomly distributed over time and space.

The difference between theories of the business cycle—from the external cycles, such as the housing or war-induced cycles, to the internal cycles, such as the interaction between the multiplier and accelerator—and the real business cycle theory is the role assigned to government. While economists associated with business cycle theories, in particular with the internally generated theories, see cycles as a problem and government as an instrument to correct the problem, real business cycle theorists see the unevenness in the economy's growth path not as a problem but as a natural, anticipated, and positive outcome of technological change and increased productivity. That is, in the one case, government is viewed as a contributor to the economy's long-run growth and stability, while in the other it is viewed as a long-run economic growth obstructionist. (A more complete analysis of the competing theories and ideas concerning the proper role of government awaits us in the chapter "Can Government Really Stabilize the Economy?")

CHAPTER REVIEW

1. The types of unemployment that can exist include frictional unemployment, structural unemployment, cyclical unemployment, discouraged workers, and the underemployed.

2. The natural rate of unemployment consists of workers who are frictionally and structurally unemployed. Full employment exists when the unemployment rate is equal to the natural rate.

3. Inflation hurts people living on fixed incomes, landlords, and savers. Those who gain from inflation include borrowers and the government. Bankers have developed ways to moderate their losses from inflation. Unions bargain for cost-of-living allowances in their wage contracts to protect themselves from the erosion of real wages.

4. A recessionary gap exists when the equilibrium level of national income is below the full-employment level. The amount by which aggregate expenditure must increase to achieve full employment is the recessionary gap. An inflationary gap exists when the equilibrium level of national income is above the full-employment level. The inflationary gap is the amount by which aggregate expenditure must decrease to achieve full employment.

5. A recessionary gap can be closed by government spending. When the government spends, a multiple expansion in national income arises. Government spending is not without its problems. It may raise the deficit.

6. Cuts in government spending are the means by which inflationary gaps can be closed. The problem with cuts in government spending is that those who are hurt by the cuts will oppose them, so that Congress and the president are less likely to follow through.

7. Fiscal policy involves choosing both the level of government spending and the level of taxation. A variety of fiscal policy options to close recessionary gaps exists. Gaps can be closed in such a way as to leave the deficit unchanged, or they can be closed with various-sized budget deficits. Closing an inflationary gap involves the creation of a surplus budget where tax revenues exceed government spending.

8. Theories explaining the causes of business cycles can be viewed as belonging to one of two sets: (1) external theories, such as the sunspot cycle theory, the war-induced cycle theory, the housing cycle theory, and the innovation cycle theory; and (2) the internal cycle theory, triggered by the interaction of the multiplier and accelerator.

9. Real business cycle theorists reject the idea of the business cycle, believing instead that the economy is highly dynamic, operating close to, if not at, full employment. What explains variability in the economy's year-to-year real GDP is the variability and highly random nature of the year-to-year changes in new technology.

10. Countercyclical fiscal policy, as its name implies, is fiscal policy (such as changing taxes, government spending, or both) used to counter or moderate the inflationary or recessionary phases of the business cycle. Its effectiveness depends on its proper use at the appropriate time.

KEY TERMS

Frictional unemployment
Structural unemployment
Cyclical unemployment
Discouraged workers
Underemployed workers
Labor force
Natural rate of unemployment

Full employment
Recessionary gap
Inflationary gap
Fiscal policy
Balanced budget
Tax multiplier
Balanced budget multiplier

Budget deficit
Budget surplus
Countercyclical fiscal policy
Accelerator

QUESTIONS

1. "The economy's in equilibrium!" Is that good? Bad? Or what?
2. What is frictional unemployment? Why is it not regarded as a serious economic problem?
3. Who are discouraged workers? Underemployed workers? Are they counted as part of the labor force? As part of the unemployed?
4. What is the relationship between the full-employment level in an economy and the economy's natural rate of unemployment?
5. Who are the winners and losers from inflation?
6. Draw graphs showing recessionary and inflationary gaps and explain how these gaps emerge.
7. What fiscal policy measures can the government employ to close a recessionary gap? An inflationary gap?
8. What is a tax multiplier? How does it differ from the income multiplier?
9. Why is the balanced budget multiplier always equal to 1?
10. Why shouldn't the government *always* program a balanced budget?
11. What causes an innovation cycle?
12. What is the acceleration principle? How does it differ from the income multiplier?
13. Explain how interactions of the multiplier and accelerator generate cycles of national income.
14. Real business cycle theory is not a theory about cycles. Explain.

PRACTICE PROBLEMS

1. Calculate the following rates of unemployment and size of the labor force from the following data: frictional unemployment = 20; structural = 30; cyclical = 40; discouraged workers = 10; underemployed = 25; employed workers = 375.

SIZE OF LABOR FORCE	
NATURAL RATE OF UNEMPLOYMENT	
ACTUAL RATE OF UNEMPLOYMENT	
BLS'S RATE OF UNEMPLOYMENT	

2. Fill in the missing cells in the following table.

MPC	MPS	TAX MULTIPLIER
0.50		
	0.50	
0.75		
	0.40	

3. Fill in the missing cells to raise national income by $100, assuming *MPC* = 0.80.

TAX	GOVERNMENT SPENDING	CHANGE IN NATIONAL INCOME
$25		$100
	$60	$100
$30		$100
	$50	$100

4. Calculate the values for the recessionary or inflationary gaps for each of the four cases in the following table.

MPC	EQUILIBRIUM Y	FULL EMPLOYMENT Y	RECESSIONARY GAP	INFLATIONARY GAP
0.60	$400	$300		
0.70	400	900		
0.80	500	900		
0.90	500	200		

5. Calculate both the tax revenue required to generate the surplus budget shown and the change in national income that will result in each of the three cases in the following table.

MPC	SURPLUS BUDGET	GOVERNMENT SPENDING	TAX REVENUE	CHANGE IN NATIONAL INCOME
0.70	$100	$50		
0.80	200	60		
0.90	300	70		

WHAT'S WRONG WITH THIS GRAPH?

The Recessionary Gap

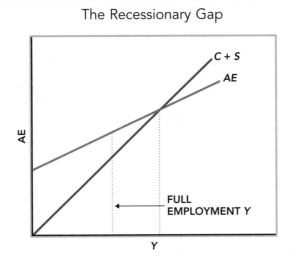

Economic Consultants

Economic Research and Analysis by Students for Professionals

Jobs for Everyone (JFE) is a private, not-for-profit corporation in Chicago, Illinois, that helps people find new or better jobs. For several years, JFE has been assisting people in the Chicago area, but Gordon Kay, its director, now finds that the number of people seeking JFE's assistance far exceeds JFE's ability to accommodate them. Strapped by its limited resources, Gordon is convinced that the only way to provide adequate assistance is to encourage government to become more actively involved in job creation. He believes government has the potential to help thousands of job-needing people in Chicago and, given a broader focus, can even address the job-related concerns of millions of Americans nationwide. Thus, Gordon has decided to use some of JFE's time and energy to lobby government agencies to do more to create jobs. Before JFE can do this, it needs to get a better understanding of the issues associated with unemployment in Chicago and nationwide, and what the government is currently doing about the problem.

© Image 100/Royalty-Free/CORBIS

Economic Consultants, aware of JFE's good work and success, has offered its services to the organization, and Gordon has accepted. Prepare a report for JFE that addresses the following issues:

1. What is the current rate of unemployment in the United States, as defined by the Bureau of Labor Statistics? What is that rate for Chicago? What other kinds of information concerning unemployment would you want to consider?

2. What does government currently do to provide jobs for people or to help people find jobs?

3. JFE believes everyone should have a job. What are the possible costs and benefits of full employment?

You may find the following resources helpful as you prepare this report for JFE:

- **Department of Labor** (http://www.dol.gov/)—The Department of Labor provides a number of employment-related programs, such as America's Job Bank (http://www.ajb.dni.us/) and Welfare to Work (http://www.doleta.gov/).
- **Bureau of Labor Statistics (BLS)** (http://stats.bls.gov/)—The BLS is the primary source for labor data for the federal government. The BLS also publishes the *Occupational Outlook Handbook* (http://www.bls.gov/oco/), which provides job descriptions, working conditions, training and educational requirements, and similar information on various jobs.
- **Bureau of the Census** (http://www.census.gov/)—The Census Bureau maintains labor data (http://www.census.gov/hhes/www/laborfor.html).
- ***Chicago Fact Book*** (http://www.cityofchicago.org/plan/ChgoFacts/index.html)—The *Chicago Fact Book*, maintained by the city of Chicago, provides extensive labor and demographic information.

practicetest

1. Suppose there are 1,100 people in the economy. Of these, 700 are employed, 100 are under-employed, 200 are looking for work, and the remaining 100 are either retired or in school. According to the BLS, the unemployment rate is
   a. 20 percent.
   b. 18 percent.
   c. 29 percent.
   d. 27 percent.
   e. 36 percent.
2. The natural rate of unemployment refers to the rate(s) of
   a. cyclical unemployment.
   b. frictional and structural unemployment.
   c. underemployed and discouraged workers.
   d. actual unemployment.
   e. cyclical, frictional, and structural unemployment.

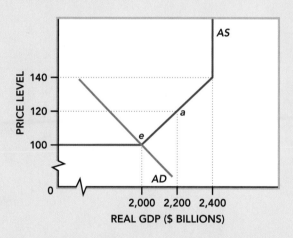

3. The graph shows the economy in equilibrium at $2,000 billion real GDP. Which of the following explains how the equilibrium-level real GDP increases to $2,200 billion?
   a. A shift in the aggregate demand curve to the left
   b. A shift in the aggregate demand curve to the right
   c. A shift in the aggregate supply curve to the left
   d. Movement along the supply curve from point *e* to point *a*
   e. A fall in price level
4. If an increase in aggregate demand does not lead to inflation, we can assume that

a. there are sufficient resources available at prevailing prices.
b. the full-employment level of real GDP has been reached.
c. the economy's equilibrium level of real GDP is positioned along the vertical segment of the aggregate supply curve.
d. the aggregate supply curve must have decreased, offsetting the increase in aggregate demand.
e. wages fell as real GDP increased.
5. During periods of high inflation,
   a. people on fixed incomes, such as retirees, benefit.
   b. money lenders who earn fixed rates of interest on their loans benefit.
   c. landlords who negotiated long-term rental leases benefit.
   d. people who borrowed money at fixed rates of interest benefit.
   e. people who pay fixed mortgage rates on their purchased homes lose.
6. Suppose the full-employment level of national income is $2 billion and the equilibrium level of national income is $1.4 billion. If $MPS = 0.25$, then there is a(n) _____ gap that can be closed by
   a. recessionary/increasing aggregate expenditure by $600 million.
   b. inflationary/increasing aggregate expenditure by $600 million.
   c. recessionary/decreasing aggregate expenditure by $600 million.
   d. inflationary/decreasing aggregate expenditure by $150 million.
   e. recessionary/increasing aggregate expenditure by $150 million.
7. The tax multiplier is
   a. positive and smaller than the income multiplier.
   b. negative and smaller than the income multiplier.
   c. positive and larger than the income multiplier.
   d. the same as the income multiplier.
   e. positive and equal to the income multiplier.
8. Which business cycle theory suggests that spurts of technological innovations are a major cause of business cycle fluctuations?
   a. The innovation cycle
   b. The sunspot theory

c. The housing cycle

d. The high-technology cycle

e. The accelerator principle

9. The accelerator is used to show that

a. wars increase the speed at which national income changes over time.

b. there is no such thing as a regular business cycle.

c. business cycles are created by the multiplier effect relating induced investment to changes in national income.

d. countercyclical fiscal policy can be an effective tool in reducing the magnitude of the business cycle in the economy.

e. administrative lags reduce the effectiveness of countercyclical fiscal policy.

10. Real business cycle theorists

a. argue that business cycles are actually variations in the growth rate of the economy.

b. believe that natural phenomena such as sunspots can create business cycles.

c. advocate strong countercyclical policy to reduce the effects of the business cycle on the economy.

d. believe that clusters of innovations in the economy lead to the appearance of business cycles.

e. argue that the accelerator is the primary cause of the business cycle.

Appendix

THE BUSINESS CYCLE: ACCELERATOR-STYLE

How does the interaction of the multiplier and accelerator actually create economic booms and bottoms? What triggers the turnabouts? To answer these questions, let's create a simple economic model and apply to it six assumptions about quantitative relationships between national income, consumption, autonomous investments, and values for the multiplier and accelerator. The assumptions are:

1. The economy is in equilibrium in year 1. National income is $1,500 billion, consumption is $1,200 billion, and autonomous investment is $300 billion.
2. MPC equals 0.80; the income multiplier is 5.
3. Refer to the accelerator analysis in the appendix. If $Y_{t-1} = \$1,000$; $Y_{t-2} = 1,200$; $I_t = a(Y_{t-2} - Y_{t-1})$; and $MPC = 0.80$, calculate Y_t and Y_{t+1}.
4. Autonomous investment, I_t, is $300 billion in years 0 and 1, and $310 billion every year thereafter.
5. Induced investment, $I'_t = \alpha(Y_{t-1} - Y_{t-2})$. Aside from autonomous investment that occurs each year, an additional investment induced by changes that occurred in national income during the previous year occurs.
6. The accelerator, is α, 1.1. Applied to the equation for induced investment, it shows that producers, looking to past performance as an investment guide, make investments equivalent to 110 percent of the change in national income that occurred in the previous year.

Table A1 tracks national income over 25 years.

Look at national income, Y_t. *There's the business cycle.* It increases from $1,500 billion in the initial year to $1,621.43 billion in year 8, falls to $1,448.61 billion in year 15, and peaks again at $1,692.98 in year 22. What triggers the cycle? A $10 billion increase in autonomous investment in year 2. That's it!

Look at the behavior of producers and consumers during the second year. Consumption is $1,200 billion. What about induced investment? It is equal to 110 percent of the change in national income that occurred in the previous year—that is, in year 1. Since there was no change in national income from year 0 to year 1, induced investment, $\alpha(Y_1 - Y_0) = 0$. As a result, national income in this second year is $1,200 + $310 + 0 = $1,510 billion.

The seeds of the cycle have been planted. That $10 billion increase in national income in year 2 generates a $\alpha(Y_2 - Y_1) = \$11$ billion increase in induced investment in year 3. Note that consumption increases as well. After all, it is 0.8 of last year's income, which increased from $1,500 billion to $1,510 billion. Autonomous investment remains at $310 billion. As a result, national income in year 3 is $1,208 + $310 + $11 = $1,529 billion.

The $19 billion increase in national income during year 3 excites producers to add $\alpha(Y_3 - Y_2) = \$20.90$ billion of induced investment in year 4. The $19 billion increase in income also fuels greater consumption. As a result, national income in year 4 is $1,223.20 + $310 + $20.90 = $1,554.10 billion.

Do the interrelationships between consumption, induced investment, and national income create rising national incomes forever? Not so. The signal of trouble ahead occurs in year 6. Although national income did increase by $23.29 billion, that was less than the $26.79 billion increase of the year before.

Table A1

YEAR	I_t	C_t	I'_t	Y_t	CHANGE IN Y
0	300	1,200.00	0.00	1,500.00	
1	300	1,200.00	0.00	1,500.00	
2	310	1,200.00	0.00	1,510.00	
3	310	1,208.00	11.00	1,529.00	19.00
4	310	1,223.20	20.90	1,554.10	25.10
5	310	1,243.28	27.61	1,580.89	26.79
6	310	1,264.71	29.47	1,604.18	23.29
7	310	1,283.34	25.62	1,618.96	14.78
8	310	1,295.17	16.26	1,621.43	2.47
9	310	1,297.15	2.72	1,609.86	−11.57
10	310	1,287.89	−12.73	1,585.16	−24.70
11	310	1,268.13	−27.17	1,550.96	−34.20
12	310	1,240.77	−37.62	1,513.14	−37.82
13	310	1,210.52	−41.60	1,478.92	−34.23
14	310	1,183.14	−37.65	1,455.49	−23.43
15	310	1,164.39	−25.78	1,448.61	−6.87
16	310	1,158.89	−7.56	1,461.33	12.72
17	310	1,169.06	13.99	1,493.05	31.72
18	310	1,194.44	34.89	1,539.34	46.28
19	310	1,231.47	50.91	1,592.38	53.05
20	310	1,273.91	58.35	1,642.26	49.87
21	310	1,313.80	54.86	1,678.67	36.41
22	310	1,342.93	40.05	1,692.98	14.32
23	310	1,354.39	15.75	1,680.13	−12.85
24	310	1,344.11	−14.13	1,639.98	−40.16
25	310	1,311.98	−44.18	1,577.80	−62.17

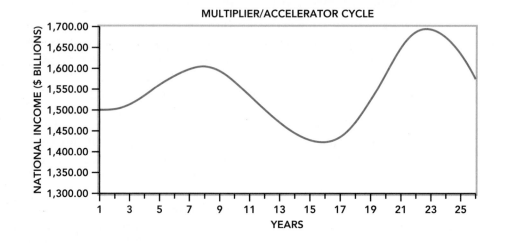

In other words, the *source that fuels induced investment was beginning to weaken.* That weakening dampens increases in income which further weakens induced investment.

By year 9, induced investment shrinks to $2.72 billion, causing national income in that year to actually fall. The slide in national income continues until year 15, which marks the recovery phase.

LONG-RUN ECONOMIC GROWTH

Imagine yourself a passenger on an aircraft that's about to take off from New York City's La Guardia airport. The runway stretches 7,000 feet. The pilot gets clearance from the control tower, opens the throttles fully, and releases the break. The plane bolts from the head of the runway and for a spell of time—it may seem like an eternity—the plane hardly lifts. With 6,000 feet of runway behind you, you're still pretty much on the concrete. Another 500 feet covered and the plane is still hugging mother earth. Even with only 300 feet of runway ahead, the plane still hasn't made any noticeable surge. And then, with barely 200 feet of the 7,000 foot runway left, the plane suddenly jerks upright to an almost vertical position, and like a Cape Canaveral rocket, climbs skyward.

Perhaps it's an exaggeration. But not by much. Economic historians can tell pretty much the same story describing the trajectory of world GDP over the course of 2,000 years or more. Their story is depicted in Exhibit 1.

THIS CHAPTER INTRODUCES YOU TO THE ECONOMIC PRINCIPLES ASSOCIATED WITH:

- Capital-labor and capital-output ratios
- Technology and labor productivity
- Labor productivity and economic growth
- Saving, investment, and economic growth

© MedioImages/CORBIS

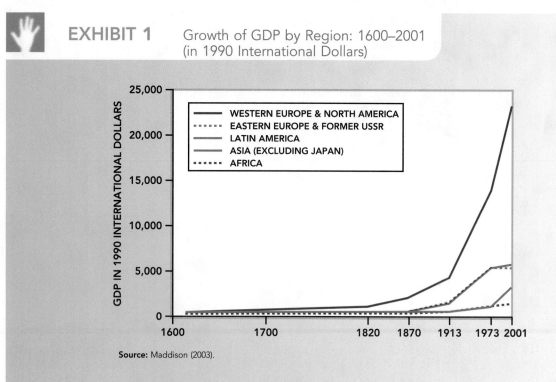

EXHIBIT 1   Growth of GDP by Region: 1600–2001
(in 1990 International Dollars)

Source: Maddison (2003).

The distance in Exhibit 1 is 400 years, not 7,000 feet, but the 'flight' path is familiar. A long stretch of time without much lift and then suddenly, a skyward bolt. As you see, it's more pronounced for the Western European and North American economies than for the other regions, but with the possible exception of Africa, there is still that dramatic lift for the other regions as well.

REACHING BACK

Look, for example, at the estimates offered in Exhibit 2 and 3 made chiefly by economic historian Angus Maddison for the years 100 to1998. Professor Maddison's 'runway,' so to speak, is pushed back much beyond the 400 years of Exhibit 1, but the results he derives are still much the same. The last few centuries of world GDP stand in sharp contrast to the millennia of GDPs that preceded them. While long-run economic growth has always been part of our experience, *the change in the annual rate of change*, particularly during the last two centuries, has been unique and phenomenal.

Over the course of 900 years, from year 100 to 1000, world GDP increased from $100 billion to $120 billion, although not without experiencing some intervals of decline. It took another 500 years, from 1000 to 1500, for world GDP to double. Compare this 500-year doubling to the doubling of world GDP during the 25-year span from 1973 to 1998. It's impressive.

Who the world's economic superpowers were over a goodly stretch of this time may surprise you. Exhibit 3 shows the country (or regional) share of world GDP over the roughly two millennia.

India and China, until as late as the eighteenth century, were economic superpowers, accounting for as much as 40 percent of world economic production. To economic historians, the relative strengths of their economies come as no surprise. For centuries, the Chinese were the world's technological innovators.

EXHIBIT 2   Estimates of World GDP: Years 100–1998 (Bills of International PPP Dollars)

YEAR	WORLD GDP	YEAR	WORLD GDP
1998	34,000	1700	375
1973	16,000	1600	330
1950	5,400	1500	250
1913	2,700	1000	120
1820	700	100	100

EXHIBIT 3   Share of World GDP, by Selected Country or Region: 100–1998 (in percentage)

	INDIA	CHINA	WESTERN EUROPE	EASTERN EUROPE	AFRICA	WEST ASIA	FAR EAST	RUSSIA	USA	JAPAN	LATIN AMERICA
100	33	26	11	2	7	9	7	2	<1	1	2
1000	29	23	9	2	12	11	7	2	<1	3	4
1500	25	25	19	3	7	4	8	3	<1	3	3
1700	25	22	22	3	7	3	8	4	<1	4	1
1820	16	33	23	3	5	3	5	5	2	3	2
1913	8	9	33	5	3	1	5	9	19	3	5
1950	4	5	36	4	4	2	5	10	27	3	8
1973	3	5	25	3	3	5	14	9	22	8	9
1998	5	12	20	2	3	5	9	3	22	8	9

They began printing with carved wood blocks 600 years before Gutenberg's bible. They built the first chain drive 700 years before the Europeans. And they had the magnetic compass at least a century before it appeared elsewhere. They developed the ship's rudder, invented the wheelbarrow, gun powder, porcelain, and the multiplication table. Somewhere in the middle of the fifteenth century this advanced civilization suddenly ceased its spectacular leadership in innovation and economic progress. As you see in Exhibit 3, its decline from preeminence continued into the twentieth century but has very recently reversed.

The West European share of world GDP rose until the mid-twentieth century then fell from approximately a third of world GDP to a still sizable fifth. The 'new kid on the block,' so to speak, who rises to superpower status, at least from the twentieth century onward, is—no surprise, is it?—United States. In terms of economic superpowers, Europe and the USA today are the China and India of yesterday.

Look again at Exhibit 1. What is there about Western Europe and North America that allowed them, after so many centuries of quite modest economic progress to suddenly develop a breakaway GDP growth rate that separates them so completely from the other regions of the world? Is this divergence likely to continue through the twenty-first century?

And the economies of modern Eastern Europe, Latin America, Asia, and even Africa have, too, achieved considerable success. What economic fortunes await them? How would *or how should* these regions read Exhibits 1, 2, and 3?

If long-run GDP growth is considered an indicator of economic progress, then economic progress is what world societies have experienced from time immemorial. Measured in terms of production, size of the labor force, capital employed per worker, productivity per worker, technology adopted in the workplace, or the standards of living these indicators afford, the economies of the modern world dwarf the accomplishments of the economies of ancient Rome, Greece, China, and India.

We live better, longer, and have far greater opportunities than our ancestors ever had. Consider this: During the hot summer months of 1638–1715, even despotic Louis XIV, King of France, suffered the heat as did the lowly French peasant. None of the rooms at his magnificent palace at Versailles was air-conditioned. And while he may have traveled in the luxury of gilded coaches, the roads were uneven, often impassable, and the time required to cover even short distances irritatingly long. Louis never enjoyed the simple pleasure of flying Air France from Paris to New York or to wherever modern international airlines schedules take us. Makes you think, doesn't it? Would you really trade places with the King of France, let alone the lowly French peasant?

Think about Alexander the Great? While he conquered a good part of his ancient world, he still died in Babylon before his thirty-third birthday from what historians believed were either complications of the flu or malaria. Had he access to a modern clinic dispensing modern pharmaceuticals, he could have gone on to a ripe old age conquering and killing.

And think about Hollywood's epic movies depicting the lives and times of biblical Samson, Solomon, David, and Jesus. If we traded places with a typical Israeli then, the comforts of life we would enjoy would be something less than epic. The diet was monotonous. Wheat and barley bread—more barley than wheat—was, along with some olive oil, the staples of the two meals eaten daily. And even though the Scriptures tell us that Methuselah lived 900 years, most others at the time hardly made it past 40.

Do you suppose, for example, that former economic superpowers China and India look back to the year 1600 with any kind of nostalgia? Not if GDP is the criterion. China's GDP in 1600 was $96 billion and that compares to the $740 billion GDP China produced in 1998.

Think of a pizza pie and its slices. The world's GDP pie today is incredibly larger than the pies baked a thousand or so years ago so that even if a region's slice becomes smaller over time, as it does for Africa, there may be still considerably more pie on its plate.

But is there more pie per person? While a country's or region's GDP may increase, its population may increase as well so that the GDP each person ends up with may actually be less. After all,

$$GDP \ per \ capita = \frac{GDP}{population}$$

What does the record show? What you probably have guessed. We've fared pretty well even in terms of GDP per capita, although some countries and regions fared better than others. Look at Exhibits 4 and 5.

During the first 1,700 years of the 2,000 years of Exhibit 4, GDP per capita increased but slightly. But it wasn't without interruptions. The fall of the Roman Empire led to a big decline in European living standards and population. As well, the bubonic plague in the fourteenth century reduced population and living standards in medieval Europe and Asia. But setting these events aside, the long-run rate of population growth doggedly matched the long-run growth in world GDP. As a result, the standard of living—measured by GDP per capita—remained virtually unchanged during the first millennium and increased, albeit

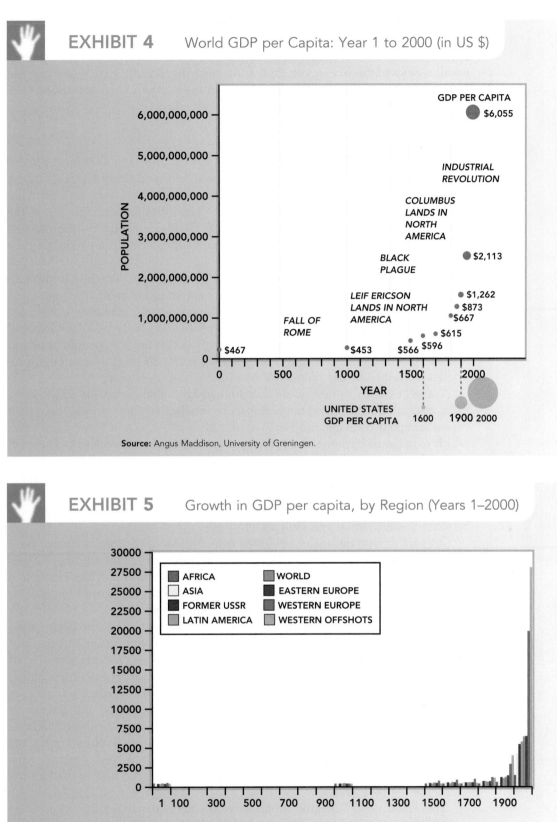

EXHIBIT 4   World GDP per Capita: Year 1 to 2000 (in US $)

Source: Angus Maddison, University of Greningen.

EXHIBIT 5   Growth in GDP per capita, by Region (Years 1–2000)

Legend: AFRICA, WORLD, ASIA, EASTERN EUROPE, FORMER USSR, WESTERN EUROPE, LATIN AMERICA, WESTERN OFFSHOTS

Source: Angus Maddison, The World Economy: A Millennial Perspective (OECD, 2001).

unevenly, from $453 to $566 during the next 500 years. But that kind of performance was about to change. During the twentieth century, while world population soared from less than 3 billion to approximately 6 billion, world GDP grew so robustly that per capita GDP shot up from $1,252 to $6,055.

Roughly speaking, the world's standard of living increased five-fold in just that one century. But not everyone in the world shared equally in that abundance. Look at the bar graph of Exhibit 5. While the standards of life improved for all regions of the world, you can't really miss the incredible successes enjoyed by the few economies of Western Europe and the Western Offshoots of the U.S., Canada, Australia, and New Zealand.

What Caused the Upsurge?

The story goes that when President Lincoln was informed about General Grant's excessive drinking, he replied: "Find out what brand of whiskey he's drinking and send a barrel of it to my other generals." The question we might ask of the remarkable achievement in world GDP and GDP per capita during the last 150 years is: What brand of economics made it happen? And can we distribute it to all regions?

Many economists believe that if there is a brand name attached to the economic progress made, it could well be labeled enlightenment. For what distinguished the economic environments of these past two centuries from those before it was the dawning of an enlightenment—essentially an overwhelming sweep of new ideas and knowledge—whose impact on the way people lived and worked as well as on how and what they were able to produce can be appropriately described as the progenitor of an industrial revolution.

These "essentially new ideas and knowledge" challenged virtually everything associated with conventional European intellectual and spiritual thought. It erased accepted doctrine and replaced it with a *tabula rasa*, a blank slate upon which experience becomes the primary source of human knowledge. This new approach to acquiring knowledge was based on acceptance of unfettered criticism, universal tolerance, and experimentation to derive empirically-tested truths. These precepts allowed for the irreversible change in the way people viewed causation, the possibility of material progress, and the relationships between the individual and civil society.

As part of this European enlightenment, the ideas of Francis Bacon, Isaac Newton, Edward Gibbons, Rene Descartes, Thomas Hobbes, John Locke, Jacques Turgot, Francois Quesnay, David Hume, and Adam Smith—all belonging to a new breed of philosophers, mathematicians, and historians—cleared the way for the belief in, and the development of the scientific method.

Freed from the shackles of mysticism and unquestioned obedience, individual pursuit of mind and fortune became a mass phenomenon and the idea that the means of production should be anchored in private property served as its catalyst. Among the many new insights, findings, and explorations: James Bradley discovered the aberration of light, William Herschel revised the calendar, Joseph Priestly discovered oxygen, James Hutton discovered the science of geology, and John Pringle investigated the causes of scurvy, the use of vaccination, and the development of pathology. Eighteenth century explorers made the world even smaller. James Cook was the first European to New Zealand, Australia, Hawaii, and British Columbia and James Bruce, the first to explore the sources of the Blue Nile.

These and other scientific events were an integral part of the onset of an industrial revolution. At the heart of this revolution was the invention of steam power and the combustion engine. These eventually transformed agriculture, mining, textile making, transportation, metallurgy, machine tooling, and chemistry. They increased productivity—output per worker—in every branch of enterprise to heights unimagined before. The population explosion that accompanied the industrial revolution—a dramatic surge compared to the population growth of earlier centuries—was both a stimulant to and a consequence of that revolution. In short, these events remade the European economic world and our thinking about it.

MODERN ECONOMIC GROWTH

The industrial revolution's legacy is our modern economic world. It is an economic world now secured in the widespread use of computers, nuclear energy, information technologies and other innovations inconceivable just a short time ago. Our experience with innovations and sustained economic progress—the business cycles notwithstanding—is central to the way we think about our economic future and what we understand are factors contributing to it.

There's no misreading it: Economic growth is second nature to us. Countries that don't grow are considered exceptions to the rule. We expect growth to happen just as we expect the sun to rise every morning. But how do we account for, say, changes in our real GDP year after year? For example, how do we explain, looking at Exhibit 6, panel b, how that economy moves from point b on AS_1 to point c on AS_2, to point d on AS_3, and so on. That is to say, what factors contribute to the outward shifts in aggregate supply?

Creating the Environment for Long Run Growth

Let's start by looking at environment. Understanding why some nations grow—by experiencing outward shifts in aggregate supply—and others don't, or why some grow quite robustly and others less so, has as much to do with an appreciation for the sociopolitical environment that nurtures economic growth, as with the economic factors governing the growth process itself.

"In the state of nature," says philosopher Thomas Hobbes, "life is nasty, brutish, and short." If you've seen any television program about animals in their

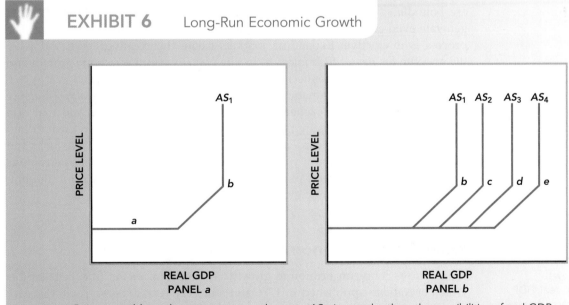

EXHIBIT 6   Long-Run Economic Growth

Points a and b on the aggregate supply curve, AS_1, in panel a show the possibilities of real GDP positioning, given a fixed set of resources. Points b, c, d, and e on aggregate supply curves AS_1, AS_2, AS_3, and AS_4 in panel b show the possibilities of attaining higher levels of real GDP with changing levels of the economy's resources. Panel a reflects policy consideration for the short run; panel b reflects policy considerations affecting the long run.

natural habitat, you get the picture. It's not fun being a yearling with a pride of lions hanging around.

Imagine living in a world where no laws prevail and where protection and respect for personal property are entirely absent. Not much sense planting an apple tree, is there? After all, as soon as apples appear, you can bet they will disappear! And if, by chance, you catch the culprit in the act of "acquiring" the fruit of your labor, who ends up with the fruit becomes strictly a matter of who's the lion and who's the yearling. Then why bother planting? Why bother investing in any productive enterprise when the fruits of enterprise are so insecure?

That's the question Thomas Malthus addressed in his *Principles of Political Economy* (1820). In the first page of Chapter One, Book II, titled *On the Progress of Wealth,* he writes: "Among the primary and most important causes which influence the wealth of nations, must unquestionably be placed, those which come under the head of politics and morals. Security of property, without a certain degree of which, there can be no encouragement to individual industry, depends mainly upon the political constitution of a country, the excellence of its laws and the manner in which they are administered."

How comfortable would you be living in a society where the laws governing property and rights to property change at the whim of those holding political power? What expectations about the future can you make when laws and constitution become means to political ends? The absence of confidence in the dependability of laws must dull the creative edge.

It's a matter of linking effort and reward. Legitimate rights to personal property and having a sense of security concerning those rights create the incentive for personal effort and expected reward. It is inconceivable to think of economic progress without such a linkage.

Most economists would also insist that the market system—the freedom and ability to exchange goods, resources, and money for each other—is an indispensable agent of economic growth. It allows individuals to engage with each other as producer and consumer, to specialize and trade, and to save and invest. The productiveness of these activities is limited only by the size of the market. In the long run, market size is virtually boundless because people's imaginations are boundless, creating always newer and more productive technologies that generate even greater specialization, more trade, and increased market size. The process is interactive: Expanding markets excite the creative nerve and whet the appetite for newer technologies. In this way, long-run economic growth and markets are inexorably connected.

This connection is dramatically illustrated in Adam Smith's *Wealth of Nations.* You can almost feel his excitement: "The discovery of America, and that of a passage to the East Indies by the Cape of Good Hope, are the two greatest and most important events recorded in the history of mankind." That's as bold and assertive a statement as any you will ever read and also incredibly perceptive! Smith saw these two events as creating the global market, and with it, the limitless potential for economic growth.

What Causes Economic Growth?

Economic growth
An increase in real GDP, typically expressed as an annual rate of real GDP growth.

What causes long-run **economic growth**? If you look at the title page of *The Wealth of Nations*—published in 1776 and still very readable—you will discover that its complete title is *An Enquiry into the Nature and Causes of the Wealth of Nations.* Smith struggled with the same question we ask about our economy today, and, interestingly, what economists today know about the causes of long-run economic growth is not terribly dissimilar from the insightful observations Smith made more than 200 years ago.

interdisciplinary perspective

POLITICAL RISK AND ECONOMIC GROWTH

Climb into the shoes of a developing country's prime minister in, say, south Asia. Suppose you were facing—as so many do in developing countries—a shortage of capital goods that thwarts economic growth. How do you generate capital goods when your own economy is not able to produce capital in quantities that would trigger economic growth? What are your options? Do you beg, borrow, or steal? Or perhaps invite others to create capital formation.

Now climb into the shoes of the prime minister of a developed economy in western Europe. Suppose you're sympathetic to the economic plight of the south Asian country. How do you express it? If it "begs," do you grant economic aid—a gift—in the form of capital goods? If it asks to "borrow," do you loan the funds at market interest rates? What about its "stealing" option? How do you protect against theft?

Typically, it's the developing country that invites foreign corporations in to participate in its economy's capital formation. This is called *foreign direct investment*. The corporations build factories, hire labor to work those factories, and produce goods. In this way, the corporations earn a profit and contribute to the host country's economic growth.

Yet there is always a lingering worry. It's the nagging concern about theft. How secure is the corporation's foreign direct investment? After all, it sits on foreign soil and is subject to foreign laws. Some of the governments that invite foreign direct investments have low credibility, high corruption, and political instability. But which ones? With profit margins in mind, how do the corporations calculate the political risk associated with such foreign direct investment?

Economists distinguish between two kinds of political risk: catastrophic and creeping expropriation. The catastrophic is the less likely, but may involve the loss of the corporation's entire investment. The concern is that the host government may expropriate the corporations' capital or renege on its contract. In the case of government-to-government debt payments, it may simply default. Foreign corporations and the lending governments typically have no legal recourse.

All investments are risky. But the degree of risk and its consequences can vary considerably.

The creeping expropriation kind of political risk involves being subject to new and adverse rules and regulations, more layers of red tape, and higher degrees of corruption, all of which erode profit margins and the value of the corporation's investment.

A paradox then looms in this political risk environment. Many poor-performing countries, desperately in need of foreign direct investment, are precisely the ones most bogged down by political instability, corruption, and bureaucracy. Their political character contributes to poor performance and high political risk—and that combination dissuades foreign direct investment.

Adam Smith identified four principal factors that contribute to a nation's economic growth: (1) the size of its labor force, (2) the degree of labor specialization (or the division of labor), (3) the size of its capital stock, and (4) the level of its technology.

That is to say, if more people are employed, more goods and services are produced. If people are better educated, they can produce more goods and services. If they use more capital, the goods and services they produce increase even more. And the more advanced the level of technology, the higher their productivity.

Now fast forward 230 years to read what *The Economic Report of the President, 2007* says in its first chapter dealing with "Growth in GDP over the Long Term." It's Adam Smith in tone and content. Among the primary factors cited in *The Report* as contributing to the growth of **labor productivity**—goods produced per hour of work—are restatements of Smith's four factors, described in *The Report* as capital deepening, labor skill, efficiency gains, and entrepreneurship. What do they mean?

Labor productivity
The quantity of GDP produced per worker, typically measured in quantity of GDP per hour of labor.

Capital deepening
A rise in the ratio of capital to labor.

Consider **capital deepening**. Deepening means providing *each* worker with more and better equipment and machinery so that each ends up producing more goods or services during his or her work day. Think about it. In our modern world, almost every economic activity has a history of such deepening. Imagine how much more lawn you can cut in an hour riding on a John Deere three rotary-bladed mower compared to its single rotary-bladed one? Or consider how many more sales are handled by a single worker at Amazon.com compared to the sales handled by a bookstore sales person just decades earlier. What about the number of tickets processed at a Delta Airlines reservations desk using modern computer systems compared to the tickets processed in a pre-computer day? The farm industry is no exception. It took a 1830s farmer over 250 hours to produce 100 bushels of wheat. By 1890, with horse-drawn machinery, the hours were cut to below 50 and with tractors and combines today, the hours needed are less than four. It's a safe bet to make: The deeper the capital—that is, the **rise in the ratio of capital to labor**—the more productive is the worker.

Labor skills
The proficiency to perform actual tasks and technical functions required in specific occupational fields. These skills reflect the laborer's natural ability, experience-on-job, and education.

And there's nothing really complicated either about the idea that labor productivity is associated with the quality of **labor skills**. Simply put: Skilled workers out-produce unskilled workers. What matters here are natural ability, experience-on-the-job, specific job-training, and education. Adam Smith associated increasing labor specialization with increasing labor skills—he called it labor dexterity—and with increasing labor productivity. "Jack-of-all-trades, master-of-none" becomes "Jack-of-one-trade, heck-of-a-producer." Nowadays, education has become the key to improved labor productivity and success. An office worker at Aetna Insurance, for example, can sharpen his or her skills and move more quickly up the administrative ladder by taking college courses in actuarial and computer sciences. Many engineers, after several years in the field, go back to campus for an MBA. The combination—engineering and business degrees—is their new and more productive skill.

Efficiency gains
The increase in productivity associated with adoption of new technology and the reorganization of the workplace to accommodate the technology.

You may have heard the expression "a cluttered desk is a sign of a cluttered mind." That may or may not be true but what is true is that greater labor productivity can be achieved by devising better ways of organizing the workplace. Economists refer to the increases in productivity generated by such reorganization as **efficiency gains**. Go back to the desk illustration. Often, just reorganizing your desk can cut considerable time off getting things done. You know that. And what is Google if not the reorganization of information delivery on the Internet. Think of the time required to access specific information on Google compared to the time it took in pre-Google days. It boggles the imagination!

Entrepreneurship
A person who alone assumes the risks and uncertainties of business.

The 2007 Report uses the term **entrepreneurship** as a companion or complementary piece to capital deepening, efficiency gains, and technological change. After all, neither capital deepening nor technological change occurs spontaneously. They require someone or some people to make them happen; someone willing to bear the risks and uncertainties of enterprise and to engage the competition. Whether research and development (R&D) investments that generate the technological change occur at large, corporate facilities or at small-scale plants, they are both entrepreneurial driven.

The Capital Deepening Model of Economic Growth

Let's take these ideas that Adam Smith had originally identified as contributing to economic growth—updated in the 2007 *Economic Report of the President*—and explain how they actually generate growth. To begin, let's construct a model, shown in Exhibit 7, to show how capital deepening alone generates the growth—using a lumber-producing economy as illustration—and later expand our analysis to include the influences of technological change and changes in the labor force.

✋ **EXHIBIT 7**   The Labor Productivity Curve

The curve Q shows the relationship between labor productivity and capital deepening. The more capital per laborer, the greater the laborer's productivity. For example, at point a, a laborer working with $200 of capital produces an output of $50. Raising the capital-labor ratio to $220 raises the laborer's output to 54, point b. New technology can increase the laborer's productivity. This is shown as an upward shift in the labor productivity curve, from Q to Q^T. At $K/L = \$200$, the new technology raises output per laborer from $50 to $60.

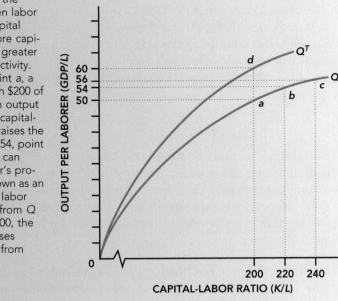

Let's start by imagining a labor supply, L, of 100 laborers working with a capital stock, K, of $20,000 so that the capital deepening or the **capital-labor ratio**—the capital available for each worker—is

$$K/L = \$20{,}000/100 = \$200$$

Suppose that each of the 100 lumberjacks, equipped with the $200 worth of gear and tools, are able to fell four trees per year. If the price per tree were $12.50, then each of the lumberjack's labor productivity, GDP/L, is

$$GDP/L = \$12.50 \times 4 = \$50$$

We have all the information needed to derive GDP. Simply multiply the $50 labor productivity of each lumberjack, GDP/L, by the 100 workers, L, in the economy.

$$\$50 \times 100 = \$5{,}000$$

Look at point *a* in Exhibit 7. It depicts the unique relationship between K/L and the resulting GDP/L. If K/L remains unchanged at point *a*, and if capital, labor, and the price of trees remain unchanged, GDP = $5,000 and is reproduced year after year. *There is no economic growth.*

But let's change that scenario. Suppose now that capital stock increases from $20,000 to $22,000—the mechanics of the increase is described in Exhibit 8—so that the capital-labor ratio rises from $200 to $220, shown at point *b* in Exhibit 7. Each of the lumberjacks now works with *more* gear and tools although the basic technology—the reliance on axe and saw, for example—remains unchanged.

With capital so deepened, GDP/L or labor productivity increases from $50 to $54. And with the same 100 workers employed, GDP increases from $5,000 to $5,400 or by eight percent. *Where once there wasn't, there is now economic growth, g.*

$$g = \frac{\$5{,}400}{\$5{,}000} - 1 = 8 \quad \text{percent}$$

Capital-labor ratio
The ratio of capital to labor, reflecting the quantity of capital used by each laborer in production.

Let's push this growth scenario further. Let's suppose capital stock keeps increasing year after year while the economy's labor supply remains at 100 workers. That is to say, capital deepening becomes an ongoing process. What happens to workers' labor productivity? Look at the shape—flattening curvature—of the Q function in Exhibit 7.

It indicates that as capital deepens, *labor productivity increases but at a decreasing rate*. Why the decreasing rate? The law of diminishing returns is the culprit. For example, when K/L reaches $240, GDP/L increases but to only $56, point c, so that GDP becomes $5,600 and the rate of economic growth

$$g = \frac{\$5,600}{\$5,400} - 1 = 3.7 \text{ percent}$$

That is to say, as capital deepens, the law of diminishing returns translates into the diminishing rate of economic growth. Some, if not most, nineteenth century economists predicted—on the strength of this law of diminishing returns—that, capital deepening notwithstanding, economic growth will eventually fizzle to zero. But they were wrong, of course. The reason has much to do with technological change.

The Role of New Technology

Look at Exhibit 7 again. If the $200 of capital per worker represented not the axe-and- saw technology of point *a*, but instead a new power-driven chain-saw technology, GDP/K or the labor productivity per worker increases to $60, point *d* on Q^T. The curve Q shifts upward to become Q^T, (subscript T indicating advanced technology) reflecting at each level of capital deepening higher levels of labor productivity compared to the levels associated with workers operating with older technology.

And if you were to chance on the History Channel's Modern Marvels hour-long feature 'Ax Men,' which traces lumbering technology from ancient times to the modern mega-mills, you may well buy into the idea that there is virtually no limit to increasing labor productivities nor, then, to rates of economic growth that combinations of capital deepening and technological change are able to generate.

The Role of Changing Labor Supply

To the extent that increases in the size of the labor force allow for greater specialization and upgraded skills in the workplace, labor productivity, for that reason alone, would shift the Q curve upward, enhancing economic growth.

As well, any increases in the labor force—assuming capital deepening and technology remain unchanged—will directly affect economic growth. Since GDP = GDP/L × L, if the labor force increases from, say, 100 to 105, then the rate of economic growth resulting from that labor force increase alone is 1.5 percent.

$$g = \frac{(\$50)(105)}{(\$50)(100)} = \frac{\$5,750}{\$5,000} - 1 = 1.5 \text{ percent}$$

The Role of Saving

How does saving fit into this economic growth scenario? According to Adam Smith and many economists today, saving automatically converts to investment, so that investment-induced growth is dependent on saving.

Exhibit 8 illustrates the saving-investment link to economic growth. Look at the left-hand side of the exhibit. In year 1, capital stock = $20,000, L = 100, K/L = $200, and *GDP* = $5,000. Economists define the relationship between capital stock and GDP as the **capital-output ratio**, in this case, $20,000/$5,000 = 4.

What do people do with the $5,000 income earned producing the $5,000 GDP? They spend some and save the rest. Look at the *C* + *S* rectangle. Of the

Capital-output ratio
The ratio of capital stock to GDP.

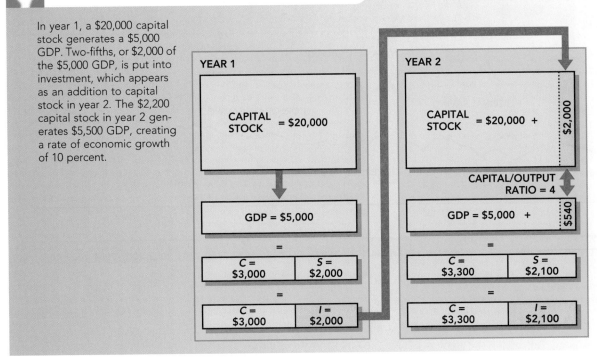

KEY **EXHIBIT 8**   The Growth Process

In year 1, a $20,000 capital stock generates a $5,000 GDP. Two-fifths, or $2,000 of the $5,000 GDP, is put into investment, which appears as an addition to capital stock in year 2. The $2,200 capital stock in year 2 generates $5,500 GDP, creating a rate of economic growth of 10 percent.

YEAR 1

CAPITAL STOCK = $20,000

GDP = $5,000

=

| C = $3,000 | S = $2,000 |

=

| C = $3,000 | I = $2,000 |

YEAR 2

CAPITAL STOCK = $20,000 + $2,000

CAPITAL/OUTPUT RATIO = 4

GDP = $5,000 + $540

=

| C = $3,300 | S = $2,100 |

=

| C = $3,300 | I = $2,100 |

$5,000 income, $3,000 is consumed and $2,000 is saved. Look at the saving conversion to investment in the $C + I$ rectangle. The $2,000 saving becomes a $2,000 investment.

Follow the red arrow from year 1 to year 2, shown on the right-hand side of Exhibit 8. The $2,000 of year 1 investment adds to capital stock in year 2, which grows to $22,000. Because capital deepens to $220 per laborer, labor productivity increases to $54, so that GDP in year 2 is $5,400. The growth rate over the period year 1 to year 2, then, is 8 percent.

Applying the saving-rectangle analysis of economic growth to the U.S. economy, Exhibit 9 traces the ratios of saving to GDP for the United States over the years 1975 to 2007.

Slightly above 20 percent during the early 1960s, the ratio of national (or gross) saving to GDP took an erratic but plodding slide to approximately 16 percent by 2000 and continued downward to 13 percent by 2007. With domestic investment equivalent to 20 percent of GDP, the relatively low U.S. saving ratio means that the United States must draw on foreign saving to fund part of its domestic investment.

In the context of the growth model depicted in Exhibit 8, it is clear why the Council of Economic Advisers, who authored the *Report,* believes, as most economists do, that saving matters.

U.S. Productivity Growth: 1990–2005

Whatever else can be said of U.S. economic performance in recent years, it is clear that compared to the performances of other industrial economies and tracked over time, the United States' record is rather impressive. That's what we see in Exhibit 10. If awards were to be given for 'best improvement' and 'best performance,' the U.S. would walk away with both.

Except for Japan, where average annual productivity growth remained fairly stable over the 15 years of Exhibit 10, the productivity rates of the other economies 'turned south.'

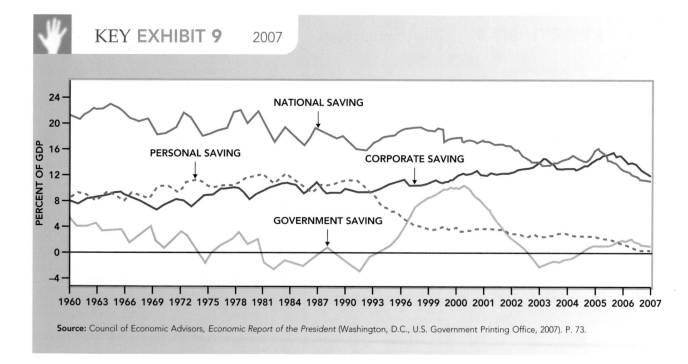

Source: Council of Economic Advisors, *Economic Report of the President* (Washington, D.C., U.S. Government Printing Office, 2007). P. 73.

EXHIBIT 10   Average Annual Productivity Growth, Selected Countries 1990–2005

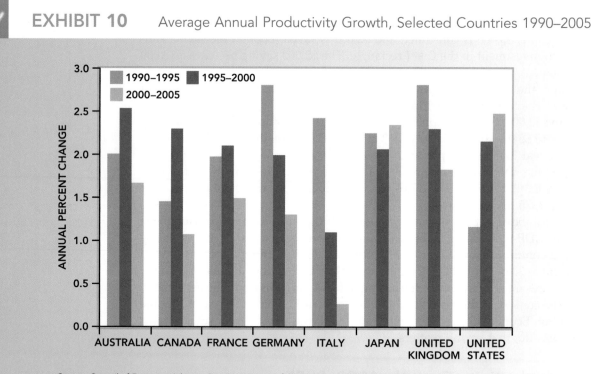

Source: Council of Economic Advisers, *Economic Report of the President*, 2007 (Washington, D.C.: U.S. Government Printing Office, 2007).

While Italy's nosedive is particular, the United Kingdom and Germany show the same pattern. Of the group, only the United States heads in the right direction. And the climb is noteworthy. Reaching back over 30 years, the 1995–2005 period of U.S. annual productivity growth averaged 2.5 percent which compares favorably to the 1.4 percent registered for the preceding 20 years.

theoretical perspective

A VIEW FROM THE PAST: ZERO LONG-RUN ECONOMIC GROWTH

The classical economists of the 19th century had a pretty grim vision of where the economy was heading. In their view, the economy's growth rate will steadily drop to zero and remain at zero thereafter. No ifs and no buts. Zero. As if that weren't enough to wipe the smile off anyone's face, it gets worse! Not only will the economy cease to grow, but its performance level will sustain only minimal subsistence for the majority of its population. Grim may be too sanguine a description of what 19th-century economists saw as our economic future.

Of course they were wrong. In hindsight, we may be puzzled at how mind-bogglingly mistaken these brilliant minds were. What they never fully appreciated was the impact that technology and capital deepening could have on labor productivity. The idea of a computerized world was as alien to their thinking as UFOs are to ours. They would likely have dismissed Exhibit 3 as highly improbable.

What they saw instead is the world depicted in the accompanying graph. The production function, Q, represents the quantity of GDP generated by a specific population size. Its curvature reflects the law of diminishing returns: As population grows, GDP grows but by smaller and smaller additions.

Line M represents the GDP per person needed for minimal subsistence. If minimal subsistence is $50 and population is 500, then $25,000 GDP is needed just to keep the population alive.

How do we get to zero long-run economic growth? Start with a population of 1,000 that generates $100,000, or $50,000 GDP greater than needed for subsistence. This over-subsistence GDP is put into investment. The economy grows, the demand for labor grows, wages are ($100,000/1,000) = $100 or $50 above subsistence, and with the higher than subsistence wages, *people have more children.* Suppose population grows to 1,500. The GDP generated is $110,000. The over-subsistence GDP falls to $35,000, slowing the economy's rate of growth.

GDP per person falls to ($110,000/1,500) = $73.34. Because it's still above $50 minimal subsistence, population continues to grow.

This process continues until population reaches 2,400, generating a GDP of $120,000. Wages equal the $50 minimal subsistence. There is now no above-subsistence GDP, no investment, and no economic growth.

The difference between their rather dismal forecast of our future and the one we have come to experience and enjoy is the incredible impact on productivity of capital deepening and technology. Amen to them both!

••

CONSIDER

What are some recent technologies besides the computer that have increased economic growth? Are there any that you think will come along in the future?

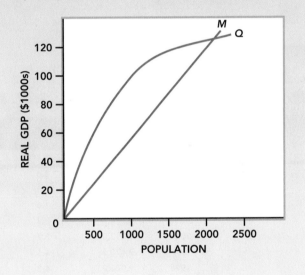

How did this happen? What explains its recent success? The clues are offered in Exhibit 11.

Increases in labor skills, efficiency gains, and capital deepening all played a role. In each of the three sub-periods, the leading factor of productivity growth is the efficiency gains associated with technological change, new methods of production, new products, and major investments in key industries, such as information technology. It explains 56 percent of the 2000–2005 growth, up from 40 and 48 percents for the earlier sub-periods. But in many ways, the initial shock of productivity increase can be attributed to capital deepening which was then followed by further productivity gains as firms became more efficient at using the new technology.

EXHIBIT 11   Sources of Labor Productivity Growth 1990–2005

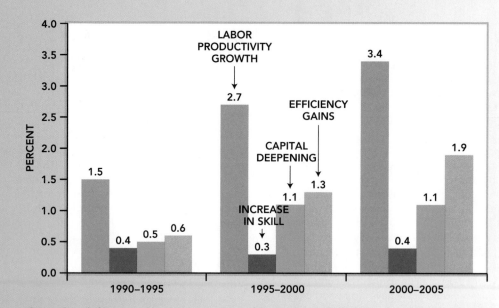

Source: Council of Economic Advisers, *Economic Report of the President,* 2007 (Washington, D.C.: U.S. Government Printing Office, 2007).

EXHIBIT 12   Real GDP and Annual Rate of GDP Growth: 1990–2005 (billions 2000 $ and percent)

	REAL GDP	RATE OF GROWTH		REAL GDP	RATE OF GROWTH
2005	11,003.4	3.1	1997	8,703.5	4.5
2004	10,675.8	3.6	1996	8,328.9	3.7
2003	10,301.0	2.5	1995	8,031.7	2.5
2002	10,048.8	1.6	1994	7,835.5	4.0
2001	9,890.7	0.8	1993	7,532.7	2.7
2000	9,817.0	3.7	1992	7,336.6	3.3
1999	9,470.3	4.5	1991	7,100.5	−0.2
1998	9,066.9	4.2	1990	7,112.5	1.9

Source: Council of Economic Advisers, *Economic Report of the President* (Washington, D.C.: U.S. Government Printing Office, 2008).

Although less prominent as a contributing factor to labor productivity growth, the increase in labor skills, as you see, matters. The increase in skill levels is attributed primarily to increased rates of college attendance.

U.S. Economic Growth: 1990–2005

As we saw in our analysis of the capital deepening model of a lumber-producing economy, changes in labor productivity are at the core in explaining changes in real GDP. Exhibit 12 records the successes—and the few less successes—of U.S. economic performance over the years 1990–2005.

For eight of the 16 years of Exhibit 12, the annual rate of real economic growth was greater than 3 percent and for half those years, the rate exceeded four

globalperspective

I'VE GOT TO ADMIT IT'S GETTING BETTER, A LITTLE BETTER ALL THE TIME

© Hulton-Deutsch Collection/CORBIS

Tangerine trees and marmalade skies.

The incredible Beatles album *Sgt. Pepper's Lonely Hearts Club Band* has, among its list of enduring hits, the optimistic song *Getting Better*. The lyric "I've got to admit it's getting better, a little better all the time" came to Beatle Paul McCartney during a walk on Primrose Hill in London, on the first sunny day of spring in 1967. Remarking on the weather, Paul commented offhand to journalist Hunter Davies that it was "getting better." It struck him then as a good idea to work on. It also reflected the cheerfulness he felt then because the weight of a stressful tour had been lifted.

Economists, too, could tell the same story, although perhaps not with the poetry of a Paul McCartney lyric or the loveliness of a John Lennon musical composition. Still, economists know that there is good reason to feel optimistic about our economic future if you look back at data on long-run growth of real GDP from, say, 1967—the year of the Beatles song—to 2003, as shown in the accompanying table.

There are no negatives in any of the 14 economies in the table. All experienced some degree of economic growth, although it was more than "a little better" for some. Ten of the 14, including the United States, achieved average annual rates of growth of 2.5 percent or more. Small economies such as Ireland, as well as major leaguers such as Japan, France, and the United States, enjoyed that "little better all the time" year after year and, along with most economies of the world, have reason to expect that the 21st century will be even a little better.

Long-Run Growth of Real GDP for 14 Selected Economies: 1967–2003 (Billion $US, 1995)

	1967 GDP	1998 GDP	AVERAGE ANNUAL GROWTH RATE, 1967–2003
AUSTRALIA	$139	$410	3.6%
BELGIUM	130	294	2.7
CANADA	234	620	3.4
DENMARK	94	199	2.4
FRANCE	705	1,646	2.7
GREECE	46	127	3.3
IRELAND	18	87	5.4
ITALY	487	1,127	2.7
JAPAN	1,487	5,319	4.0
NETHERLANDS	181	442	2.7
SPAIN	227	616	3.2
SWEDEN	132	245	2.0
UNITED KINGDOM	606	1,195	1.8
UNITED STATES	3,458	8,023	3.0

percent. By all accounts, a remarkable achievement. In only four years did the annual rate fall below 2.5 percent. Business cycles notwithstanding, the U.S. economy in the latter part of the twentieth century and into the early years of the twenty-first was exemplary.

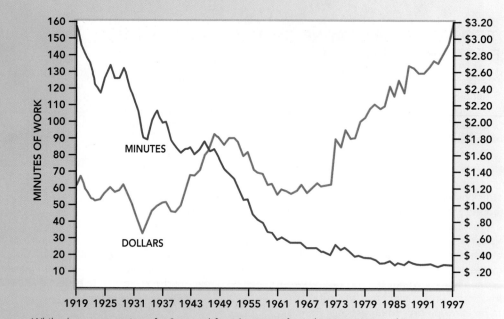

KEY EXHIBIT 13   Costs of Acquiring a 3-Pound Chicken

While the money price of a 3-pound fryer has risen from $1.23 in 1919 to $3.15 today, its real price—work time—has fallen from 2 hours 37 minutes to just 14 minutes.

check your understanding

What factor is the most significant contributor to economic growth?

HOW ECONOMIC GROWTH AFFECTS YOUR LIFE

While it is clear that a 3.5 percent annual rate of growth is higher than a 2.5 percent annual rate of growth and that differences in technology along with differences in the size of a nation's capital stock and its labor force has much to do with it, the question can still be asked: *What does all this mean to you?* What tangible benefits, if any, have years of economic growth brought to *your* life?

One way of measuring the gains you personally derive from years of previous economic growth is to compare the cost your grandparents or perhaps great-grandparents had to pay to acquire things to the cost you pay now.

Take the case of the 3-pound chicken, shown in Exhibit 13. In terms of dollar cost, your great-grandparents in 1919 bought that chicken for $1.13. You paid $3.15 for it in 1997. Have costs really tripled? Were your great-grandparents that much better off? What happened to the so-called gains of economic growth?

It's there, but it's masked by the use of "dollar value" as the yardstick. If instead of dollars, you calculate the number of minutes of a day's work it takes to buy that chicken, the comparison between what you "pay" and what your great-grandparents "paid" changes dramatically. It took about 2½ hours of your great-grandparents day to get that chicken. It takes you only 14 minutes. Now who's better off? Who has it easier?

Exhibit 14 displays a series of goods and work-time costs comparisons that tell the same story: how much easier your life has been made by years of economic growth.

Just look at the time it took your great-grandparents to acquire the goods that make up our standard of life and how relatively cheap it is for us to load up on these things. Milk was expensive back then. Refrigerators were well beyond the reach of common folk. But note some exceptions. Women's haircuts are actually more expensive today than they were in 1920 and new homes are only slightly less costly today than they were a half century ago. The explanation has to do with the labor intensity of their productions. While barbering, too, has taken advantage of technological advances, it's *still* a barber and a pair of scissors and a

EXHIBIT 14 Selected Goods, in Minutes or Hours of Work Time: Then and Now

	THEN	WORK TIME (MINUTES)	NOW	WORK TIME (MINUTES)
NONDURABLES				
GROUND BEEF (1 lb)	1919	30	1997	6
BREAD (1 lb)	1919	13	1997	4
MILK (½ gal)	1919	39	1997	7
BIG MAC	1940	27	1997	9
WOMAN'S HAIRCUT	1920	27	1997	46
DURABLES		(HOURS)		(HOURS)
DISHWASHER	1913	463	1997	28
REFRIGERATOR	1916	1,132	1997	68
COLOR TV	1954	562	1997	23
COAST-TO-COAST FLIGHT	1930	71	1997	16
NEW HOME (sq ft)	1920	7.8	1997	5.6

Source: W. Michael Cox and Richard Alm, *Time Well Spent*, Federal Reserve Bank of Dallas, Annual Report, 1997, pp. 2–14.

EXHIBIT 15 Percentage of Households Enjoying the Bounty of Economic Growth

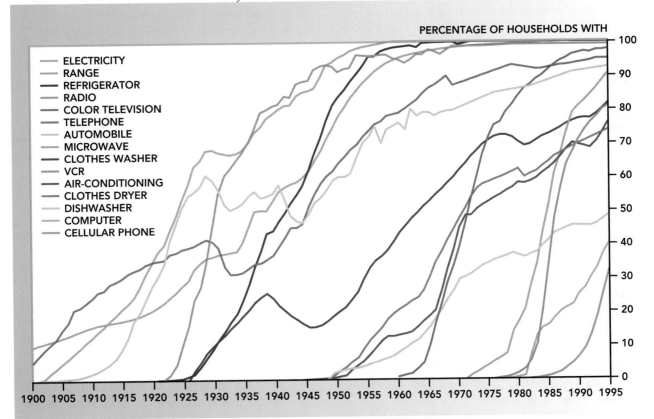

PERCENTAGE OF HOUSEHOLDS WITH

- ELECTRICITY
- RANGE
- REFRIGERATOR
- RADIO
- COLOR TELEVISION
- TELEPHONE
- AUTOMOBILE
- MICROWAVE
- CLOTHES WASHER
- VCR
- AIR-CONDITIONING
- CLOTHES DRYER
- DISHWASHER
- COMPUTER
- CELLULAR PHONE

same size head! Building a home? Brick-laying, carpentry, plumbing, electrical installation, and roofing are still very labor intensive as well.

Exhibit 15 is about as dramatic a display of the enormous bounty associated with our nation's growth over the better part of the 20th century. The goods that make your life so comfortable are also making comfortable the lives of almost everyone in your community.

CHAPTER REVIEW

1. World economic performance, dating back several millennia, records minimal and uneven economic growth until the eighteenth century. During the two centuries—1800–2000—world GDP grew at a comparatively dramatic annual rate.

2. Until the eighteenth century, China and India were the world's two economic superpowers, accounting for more than 40 percent of world GDP. Today, Europe and the United States replace China and India as the world's leading producers.

3. Economic historians attribute the spectacular increase in world economic performance since the eighteenth century, particularly in Europe and North America, to the European enlightenment which introduced a new approach to acquiring knowledge, the scientific method. Based on acceptance of criticism, tolerance, and experimentation, it allowed for the irreversible change in the way people viewed causation, the possibility of material progress, and the relationship between the individual and civil society.

4. The four factors identified in Adam Smith's *The Wealth of Nations* (1776) as principal contributors to economic growth—that are still relevant today—are the size of the economy's labor force, the degree of its labor specialization, the size of its capital stock, and the level of its technology.

5. The 2007 *Economic Report of the President* redefined the factors Adam Smith identified as contributors to economic growth. The Report describes capital deepening, labor skills, efficiency gains, and entrepreneurship as factors contributing to increases in labor productivity. They are, in large measure, restatements of Smith's four factors.

6. Over the period 1990–2005, U.S. labor productivity, propelled by capital deepening and technological change, increased steadily, outpacing the labor productivity achievements during that period scored by European economies.

7. Modern economic growth depends upon a favorable set of prerequisites, among them laws governing rights to property. These laws foster the sense of security and help reduce political risk, both important in entrepreneurial decision making.

8. The capital-deepening modern of economic growth explains how increases in the economy's capital stock increase labor productivity; that increase subject to the law of diminishing returns. The roles of saving, technological change, changes in workers' skills and the size of the labor force shift the labor productivity curve upward so that long-run economic growth is sustainable.

KEY TERMS

Economic growth	Labor skills	Capital-labor ratio
Labor productivity	Efficiency gains	Capital-output ratio
Capital deepening	Entrepreneurship	

QUESTIONS

1. The metaphor used to describe the trajectory of long-run world GDP growth over the past two millennia is an aircraft taking off from New York's La Guardia airport. Why does the metaphor make sense?

2. Think in terms of world superpowers, today and centuries ago. Who were they then? Who are they now? When did the change occur?

3. Economic historians refer to the age of European enlightenment and the resultant industrial revolution it created as factors contributing to the remarkable change in the rate of change in world economic growth. Discuss.

4. What is/are the difference(s) between changes in real GDP and changes in real per capital GDP? How has world real per capita GDP changed over the past two millennia? Compare the per capita growth achievements by region.

5. You have to have a workable investment project to make a profit. That's under your control. But political risk, which affects profitability of any project, is not under your control. Explain.

6. Classical economists had a grim view of the future. Why?
7. What is meant by capital deepening? How does it affect labor productivity? Give an example. How does the law of diminishing returns come into play?
8. What is meant by technological change? How does it affect labor productivity? Give an example.
9. What is meant by efficiency gains? How does it affect labor productivity? Give an example.
10. How do increases in labor skills affect labor productivity? Give an example.

PRACTICE PROBLEM

1. In 2007, the economy's resource base consists of 10 laborers and a capital stock of $50. Its capital-output ratio is 2. In 2008, its capital stock increases to $75, while the number of laborers and capital-output ratio remain unchanged. Calculate (1) the 2007–2008 rate of economic growth, (2) the capital-labor ratio in 2007, (3) the GDP in 2007, and (4) the 2007–2008 capital deepening.

WHAT'S WRONG WITH THIS GRAPH?

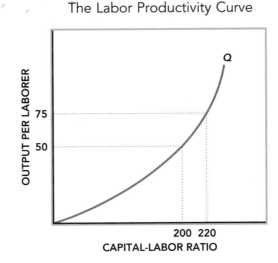

The Labor Productivity Curve

Economic Consultants

Economic Research and Analysis by Students for Professionals

Future Now! is an organization of business leaders in both the biotechnology industry and the computer industry. It is actively involved in educating the public—business and government people, in particular—about the economic benefits to society of having a cutting-edge biotechnology industry. In this way, it hopes to create an economic environment to its business interests. Future Now! has been invited to testify before the Senate Subcommittee on Science, Technology, and Space about a congressional proposal to downsize government spending on technology research and development.

Alice Gorman is the public relations director of Future Now! Having interned with Economic Consultants while at college, she is familiar with its expertise and has hired the firm to help her prepare her statement before the Senate subcommittee. You are assigned the project and asked to work with her on the following issues:

© Image 100/Royalty-Free/CORBIS

1. What has government done in the past to promote technological development in the economy and in the biotechnology industry in particular?
2. What effects might new advancements in biotechnology have on the economic growth of the industry and the economy in general?
3. What effects would a cut in government spending on biotechnology research have on the industry and the economy in general?
4. What existing government programs fund biotechnology research?

You may find the following resources useful as you prepare your report for Future Now!:

- **House Committee on Technology and Innovation (** www.science.house.gov/subcommittee/tech.aspx**)—This committee** has jurisdiction over federal research and development funding, among other areas.
- **National Science Foundation (NSF)** (http://www.nsf.gov/)—The NSF is an independent U.S. government agency responsible for promoting science and engineering through programs that invest over $3.3 billion per year in almost 20,000 research and education projects in science and engineering. Biotechnology research is handled through the Directorate for Biological Sciences (http://www.nsf.gov/bio/start.htm).
- **Biotechnology Information Resource** (www.nal.usda.gov/bic/)—The Department of Agriculture sponsors the Biotechnology Information Resource, a library of resources for biotechnology.
- **National Institute of Standards and Technology** (http://www.nist.gov/public_affairs/nandyou.htm)—This is an agency of the U.S. Department of Commerce (http://www.doc.gov/) that works with industry to develop and apply technology.

1. Looking back over the past two millennia of long-run world economic growth, the "take-off" century of the world's GDP growth occurred during the
   a. tenth century
   b. fifteenth century
   c. eighteenth century
   d. nineteenth century
   e. twentieth century

2. Prior to the seventeenth century, the world's economic superpowers were
   a. Europe and the United States
   b. Egypt and Israel
   c. Europe and Japan
   d. Latin America and Africa
   e. China and India

3. The European enlightenment is regarded by economic historians as having been the principal agent in bringing about the world GDP "take-off." This enlightenment refers to ideas associated with
   a. the expansion of international trade
   b. laws governing national security
   c. the scientific approach to the creation of knowledge
   d. the standardization and measurement of GDP
   e. the technology of printing

4. The 2007 *Economic Report of the President* refers to capital deepening and efficiency gains as contributors to increasing labor productivity. Efficiency gains refers to
   a. the better way of organizing the workplace or the better use of a known technology
   b. the increased value of capital
   c. the substitution of capital for labor
   d. the gains derived from labor specialization
   e. the gains derived from switching from smaller to larger plants

5. Although labor productivity derived from capital deepening is subject to the law of diminishing returns, economic growth does not necessarily approach zero because
   a. the price of the good produced will increase to compensate for the decreasing labor productivity
   b. new and more advanced technology will increase the labor productivity associated with a given level of capital deepening
   c. capital will eventually substitute for labor which will increase labor productivity
   d. higher levels of labor skills will eventually substitute for low levels of capital deepening which will increase labor productivity
   e. the economy will reach the stationary state before economic growth falls to zero

6. In the three periods 1990-1995, 1995-2000, and 2000–2005, productivity growth in the U.S. increased by a(n) _____ percent and in each, _____ was the leading factor contributing to its growth.
   a. increasing; increase in labor skills
   b. decreasing; increase in efficiency gains
   c. increasing; increase in efficiency gains
   d. increasing; capital deepening
   e. decreasing; capital deepening

7. All of the following inhibit (or dampen) an economy's rate of economic growth except:
   a. political risk
   b. decreases in the rate of investment
   c. a declining rate of technological change
   d. immigration
   e. higher levels of economic uncertainty

8. Suppose that the capital-output ratio in the economy is equal to 5. If GDP is equal to $200 billion, then the capital stock
   a. must equal $1 trillion.
   b. must equal $40 billion.
   c. is also equal to $200 billion.
   d. must be falling.
   e. cannot be determined without more information.

9. Suppose that an economy consists of 200 workers (*L*) and a capital stock of $50,000 (*K*). Assume that each worker can contribute $100 to GDP. Given this information,
   a. labor productivity is $2,500.
   b. the capital-output ratio is 2.5.
   c. the capital-labor ratio is 4.
   d. the capital-output ratio is 4.
   e. the capital-labor ratio is $2,500.

10. Capital deepening is said to occur when
    a. the capital-labor ratio increases.
    b. decreases in the capital stock increase the quantity of labor in the economy.
    c. labor productivity decreases.
    d. workers can produce more output per unit of labor than before.
    e. the capital-output ratio moves in the same direction as the capital-labor ratio.

PART 3
Money, Banking, and Monetary Policy

Chat Economics. Tune into the conversation. It's about *your* course. Just change the names, and it's *your* campus, *your* classroom, *your* professor, *your* classmates, and *you.*

Before beginning the morning lecture, Professor Gottheil asks for questions. Two hands shoot up. The first belongs to Gen Clark, a freshman who hopes to major in fine arts. The second belongs to Chris Stefan, also a freshman, who has philosophy in mind.

GOTTHEIL: Gen, you have your hand up. What's the problem?

GEN: Well, I think I have an intuitive feeling about real GDP. I mean, I can understand the idea that people produce things—and that's real GDP, right?—and they consume things and save. I can see them actually doing these things. But I'm having trouble visualizing how money—you know, dollar bills—fits into the picture. After all, it's just paper.

GOTTHEIL: OK. Let's talk about it. In fact, that's what our next few lectures are about, anyway. Let's see if we can grasp the vital connection between the real world of GDP and the world of money, even before we sink our teeth into the money chapters. We'll get to your question next, Chris.

CHRIS: It's really the same question! I was thinking about banks and money. They don't seem to have much to do with the real things that make up our GDP, like the food we eat or the house we live in.

GOTTHEIL: OK. Let's pick up on the idea of the house we live in. Chris, do you know what scaffolding is?

CHRIS: You mean the scaffolding used in construction?

GOTTHEIL: That's right. Describe to the class what scaffolding is.

CHRIS: Well, it's everywhere you see buildings going up. It's a wood-and-piping, skeleton-like structure that frames the outside of the building site. It's actually a series of temporary platforms used to support construction workers who are building a building. Is that what you mean?

GOTTHEIL: That's a fairly accurate description. It is not actually part of the building, is it, but it is what the building must have if it's going to be built at all. OK, now, what happens when the building is completed?

CHRIS: They remove the scaffolding.

GOTTHEIL: Right. And what do they do with it?

CHRIS: I guess they can use it again to construct another building.

GOTTHEIL: But suppose only 80 percent of the scaffolding is usable. Some of it can get pretty well banged up in construction. So if they had put up a five-story building before, what remains of the scaffolding limits them to a four-story second building. Right? And when that's done, the scaffolding is disassembled and removed to a third site, where there would be only enough scaffolding to support a three-story building. Got the idea?

CHRIS: Makes sense. I guess if you told me what the initial scaffolding was and its rate of wear and tear, I could figure out the total number of stories that could be built.

GOTTHEIL: I'm glad you said *could* be built, not *would* be built. Because suppose after the five-story building is up, nobody wants another building. You disassemble the scaffolding and it just lies there. All you have, then, is a total of five stories.

CHRIS: That's right. I got a strong feeling that you're about to make a connection between the use of scaffolding in building a house and the use of money in making real things.

GEN: Chris, I think I know where Professor Gottheil's going with this. Suppose you want to build a $100,000 house. You go to the bank to get a $100,000 loan—that's the scaffolding—and use the money to buy the materials and labor. In other words, the money supports

continued on next page

ChatEconomics

the building of the house, although it's not part of the actual house. When you sell the house, the money is returned to the bank, just as scaffolding is disassembled to be used again.

CHRIS: OK. Loans are equivalent to scaffolding. But where's the wear and tear on money?

GOTTHEIL: Good question. There's no wear and tear on money, but suppose we insist that banks must retire a certain percentage of the money, say, 20 percent, from active duty after each loan is completed. That is, every time the bank receives $100 in money, it can loan out only $80. When the $80 is repaid, it can lend out $64, and so on.

GEN: Got it! Money isn't the real things built, but to get the real things built, you need the support system of money. The scaffolding analogy makes sense.

Keep this scaffolding analogy in mind when you review the chapters on banks and money creation. And always remember, it's producing real things, like houses, that matters. Money is only the scaffolding to get there.

MONEY

Indulge yourself! Imagine that you are on an island loaded with fruits, berries, rabbits, and exotic fowl, and teeming with a wide variety of fish always accessible in the shallows of the island's crystal-clear lagoons. All at your disposal.

Sounds marvelous, doesn't it? Now suppose, during the late hours of a summer afternoon, while leisurely digging for truffles with your pet pig, you chance upon a treasure chest filled with 1,000 gold coins. Each bears the imprint of an ancient Spanish realm.

An exciting find? Well, perhaps. What would you do with the coins? You couldn't eat them, wear them, or sleep on or under them, could you? They may be beautiful to look at, but so too are clouds! You may end up deciding that a sensible thing to do with the find is to bury it again.

THIS CHAPTER INTRODUCES YOU TO THE ECONOMIC PRINCIPLES ASSOCIATED WITH:

- Barter exchange
- The characteristics of money
- Gold-backed and fiat money
- Liquidity
- The equation of exchange
- The quantity theory of money
- The classical view of money
- The Keynesian view of money
- Monetarism

© Andrew Dernie/Getty Images

Suppose, months later, another person arrives on the island. Nature's abundance is now shared. You both agree to divide the daily chores: You pick berries, he does the hunting and fishing. At the end of each day, you exchange the rewards of your specialized labor. For example, one bowl of berries for one fish. Or one egg for two pieces of fruit, depending, say, on the time required to produce these goods.

If one of you were an economist, you would know straightaway that this kind of direct goods-for-goods exchange is defined as **barter**.

Now suppose a third person appears. This situation creates even more possibilities for specialization, doesn't it? The chores are now divided among three. One specializes in fishing, another in berry and fruit picking, while the third hunts. You set up a flourishing three-way barter exchange.

Let's add a fourth person. And a fifth. Berry and fruit picking are divided, and egg gathering, once handled by the person raising fowls, becomes a specialized activity. Barter exchange now becomes a little more complex, and exchange-matching problems are bound to occur.

For example, suppose the egg gatherer wants to exchange eggs for berries, but the berry picker, worried about cholesterol, is not an egg eater. Or suppose the berry picker wants rabbit for dinner, but the hunter has no taste for berries, preferring eggs instead. You can see the problems.

If they all got together in one place at one time they could probably straighten out this no-match exchange mess. But it would still involve some degree of risk taking. After all, the hunter would have to accept unwanted eggs in exchange for rabbit in the hope of later exchanging those eggs for berries. He would like to have prior knowledge, however, that the berry picker will really want eggs. That's a lot of indirect arranging to do.

As you see, barter can be an excellent means of exchanging goods as long as the people and goods involved are few and simple. But it breaks down quickly when the numbers increase. To function effectively, barter requires *the double coincidence* of each party to the exchange wanting precisely what the other has to offer. That's difficult to achieve among five people, impossible among five thousand.

THE INVENTION OF MONEY

If you find yourself stuck in a barter situation, what can you do? One solution—common to all societies—is to pick one of the available goods as a medium of exchange, that is, as **money**. All other goods are measured in units of the one selected. Suppose the choice is eggs. By common consent, eggs are the accepted currency. A rabbit exchanges for 14 eggs, a peahen exchanges for 10, a basket of berries for 2, and a banana for 1.

This wouldn't last very long. People will quickly discover that eggs are a poor money form. They are too fragile. If the hunter sells 3 rabbits and receives in exchange 42 eggs, most likely many would break before the day is out. There goes the money! How would you feel walking about with 42 eggs in your pocket?

Barter
The exchange of one good for another, without the use of money.

Money
Any commonly accepted good that acts as a medium of exchange, a measure of value, and a store of value.

Money must be *durable* and *portable*. Eggs are out on both counts. What about fish? They are too perishable. You wouldn't want to keep that money form in your pocket for very long, would you?

Rabbits? They are more durable than eggs or fish, but how would you buy an egg with a unit of rabbit? How could you measure out one-fourteenth of a rabbit? And what would you do with the remaining thirteen-fourteenths? You see the problem: money must be *divisible* as well.

Another problem with rabbits as a money form is that some rabbits are big and fluffy, others are not. Some are cute, others less so. As long as some are preferred to others, people will tend to hoard preferred rabbits and use only the less preferred ones as money. In such cases, then, not all of the money form actually serves as money. To overcome this problem, the units of any money form selected must be *identical,* or homogeneous.

There's still another problem with rabbits. They breed like rabbits! If rabbits are money, it becomes impossible to control the money supply. The supply of fish and eggs, too, can be expanded without much effort. If money is to serve as a reliable store of value, its supply, at least in the short run, must be fairly *stable*.

As you can see, almost any choice on the island creates a problem. But we all do the best we can. Some Native Americans, before Europeans arrived, used wampum, strings of beads made of shells, as money. During the colonial period, fish, furs, corn, cattle, whiskey, and, at various times, even gunpowder were used as money.

Elsewhere, other goods served as the medium of exchange. In the South Pacific, the tiny island of Yap came to use large stone wheels, one of them 12 feet in diameter, as its money form. In Homer's day, cattle were used as money. The ancient Egyptians used necklaces, hatchets, and daggers. U.S. prisoners of war during World War II used cigarettes. In fact, most common goods, including beans, fishhooks, pearls, cocoa seeds, nails, rum, tea, pepper, sheep, pigs, dates, salt, rice, sugar, skins, silk, reindeer, and whale teeth have served somewhere at some time as money.

Gold as Money

Economies tend to select whatever goods they have that come closest to satisfying the prerequisites for perfect money. What money form would *you* choose if you were on the island? Think about it. If homogeneity, divisibility, portability, durability, and unchanging supply count, what about that gold buried among the truffles? Before exchange, it was useless. Now it appears to satisfy all five prerequisites:

- Its supply—the 1,000 coins—is fixed. In the real world, supplies of gold are hard to come by. People have searched the globe for gold, but whatever the discovery, even the San Francisco Gold Rush of 1849, year-to-year additions to total stock have been less than dramatic. Gold is just hard to find.
- It's perfectly homogeneous. Gold is gold. One ounce is identical to any other. No ounce is preferred to another.
- It's incredibly durable. Just try destroying a nugget of gold. It doesn't rot, rust, fade, overripen, or dry up. Its luster withstands the elements of time.
- It's perfectly divisible. Gold can be melted down and remolded into any shape or size. Think of gold jewelry. Gold nuggets can be reduced to standard-sized ounces, and ounces cut to minute fractions. Gold dust is still gold.
- It's portable. It can be held, pocketed, or carried about. There's a limit, of course, to the quantity a person could carry, but for most people, the quantities required are quite manageable.

Because gold has these marvelous physical properties, it satisfies the primary functions of money. That is, it serves as (1) a *medium of exchange* (a payment for any

historical perspective

BEAVER-SKIN BASED PRICE LIST

(goods sold to the Indians were priced in beaver skins)

July 14th. 1703.

Prices of Goods

Supplyed to the

Eastern Indians,

By the several Truckmasters ; and of the Peltry received
by the Truckmasters of the said *Indians*.

ONe yard Broad Cloth, *three* Beaver skins, *in season*.
One yard & half Gingerline, *one* Beaver skin, *in season*
One yard Red or Blew Kersey, *two* Beaver skins, *in season*.
One yard good Duffels, *one* Beaver skin, *in season*
One yard & half broad fine Cotton, *one* Beaver skin, *in season*
Two yards of Cotton, *one* Beaver skin, *in season*.
One yard & half of half thicks, *one* Beaver skin, *in season*.
Five Pecks Indian Corn, *one* Beaver skin, *in season*
Five Pecks Indian Meal, *one* Beaver skin, *in season*.
Four Pecks Pease, *one* Beaver skin, *in season*.
Two Pints of Powder, *one* Beaver skin, *in season*.
One Pint of Shot, *one* Beaver skin, *in season*.
Six Fathom of Tobacco, *one* Beaver skin, *in season*.
Forty Biskets, *one* Beaver skin, *in season*.
Ten Pound of Pork, *one* Beaver skin, *in season*.
Six Knives, *one* Beaver skin, *in season*.
Six Combes, *one* Beaver skin, *in season*.
Twenty Scaines Thread, *one* Beaver skin, *in season*.
One Hat, *two* Beaver skins, *in season*.
One Hat with Hatband, *three* Beaver skins, *in season*.
Two Pound of large Kettles, *one* Beaver skin, *in season*.
One Pound & half of small Kettles, *one* Beaver skin, *in season*
One Shirt, *one* Beaver skin, *in season*.
One Shirt with Ruffels, *two* Beaver skins, *in season*.
Two Small Axes, *one* Beaver skin, *in season*.
Two Small Hoes, *one* Beaver skin, *in season*.
Three Dozen middling Hooks, *one* Beaver skin, *in season*.
One Sword Blade, *one* & *half* Beaver skin, *in season*.

What shall be accounted in Value equal
One Beaver in season : *Viz.*

ONe Otter skin in season, is *one* Beaver
One Bear skin in season, is *one* Beaver,
Two Half skins in season. is *one* Beaver
Four Pappcote skins in season, is *one* Beaver
Two Foxes in season, is *one* Beaver.
Two Woodchocks in season, is *one* Beaver.
Four Martins in season, is *one* Beaver.
Eight Muncks in season, is *one* Beaver.
Five Pounds of Feathers, is *one* Beaver.
Four Raccoones in season, is *one* Beaver.
Four Sell skins large, is *one* Beaver.
One Moose Hide, is *two* Beavers.
One Pound of Castorum, is *one* Beaver.

purchase), (2) a *measure of value* (a yardstick for measuring the value of other goods), and (3) a *store of value* (a means of holding wealth from one time period to another).

Its divisibility, portability, and homogeneity make gold a perfect medium of exchange and measure of value. Its durability and relative scarcity make it an excellent store of value. People feel confident that they can store it away knowing that when they choose to spend it, it will buy as much as it would today. In this sense, money transfers goods from our past to the present and from our present into the future.

Gold-Backed Paper as Money

If the island switched its money form to gold, it would not be the first economy to do so. In fact, gold coinage dates back to the eighth century B.C.E., when coins were issued by the Kingdom of Lydia, by the Greek coastal cities, and by the Persian Empire.

Exchanging rabbits for gold, eggs for gold, and fish for gold works very well. In time, gold becomes the most recognizable good in the economy. Even children know how it works. It is carried about, stored away, traded for real goods, borrowed, and loaned. It represents the power to purchase any good at any time.

But somebody comes up with a new idea. Why not print paper money to represent the gold? It's more convenient than carrying the physical gold around. It can be easily tucked away in a pocket or purse, and simply by printing higher numbers on the paper, it can be made to represent great quantities of gold. Of course, a unit of paper money would be backed by a specific quantity of gold, so that paper money could always be cashed—converted back—for gold.

It's a revolutionary idea, almost as revolutionary as gold money itself. If it works, why not? What, then, should we do with the physical gold? Bury it once more! As long as people have confidence that paper money will serve the functions of money, then it's as good as gold.

Fiat, or Paper, Money

One good idea leads to another. Suppose a violent storm washes away the entire supply of gold. Does the island lose its money? Not at all. Why couldn't the paper money, or **fiat money**, still continue to serve as the medium of exchange? Is the gold backing really necessary? As long as everyone continues, as before, to accept the paper as money—why worry?

Fiat money
Paper money that is not backed by or convertible into any good.

Still, there is reason for concern. If we no longer link the quantity of paper money to a specific quantity of gold, then what's to limit the supply of paper money? Nothing. It seems reasonable to suppose that people, knowing that money serves as a store of value only if its supply is relatively stable, would be careful about overprinting paper money. But sometimes reason is of no avail. There is a temptation for economies to print more money. If a society chooses fiat money as its money form, then it must be particularly vigilant about controlling the quantity of money.

MONEY IN A MODERN ECONOMY

When was the last time you saw a gold coin, let alone bought anything with it? What, then, do we use as our money form? For a start, look in your pocket.

Coins and dollar bills are money in the form of **currency**. Look closely at the dollar bill. Although it says in bold and large print: "The United States of America," it is not government-issued currency. It is, instead, issued by our central bank, the Federal Reserve System (commonly referred to as the Fed). The dollar bill is a Federal Reserve Note. In your pocket, it represents the Fed's IOU. Why do we hold it? Read the fine print. It says: "This note is legal tender for all debts, public and private." That is to say, the Fed assures you that the dollar (its note) can be used by you or by anyone else as a medium of exchange and as payment for debts. Nowhere on the bill does it say anything about gold, because there is no gold backing it. The dollar bill is fiat money.

Currency
Coins and paper money.

It works. No one hesitates to accept the dollar bill as payment for pizza, popcorn, or photographic equipment. We can even buy other nations' currencies with it. Canadians gladly accept our dollars in exchange for theirs. Japanese accept our dollar for their yen. Russians would be thrilled to exchange rubles for dollar bills.

on the net
The Federal Reserve (http://www.federalreserve.gov/) issues the money we use to buy our favorite goods and services.

U.S. Losing Money When It Makes Money

If you were in charge of the United States Mint, you would be facing a rather perplexing problem that you probably never had anticipated. Your job is to produce coins—pennies, nickels, dimes and quarters—but the cost of producing pennies and nickels is now more than the pennies or nickels are worth. It's a losing proposition. Consider this: The prices of copper, zinc, and nickel more than tripled since 2003. A penny, which consists of 97.5 percent zinc and 2.5 percent copper, will cost you 1.26 cents to make. The nickel, which is 75 percent copper and 25 percent nickel, will cost you 7.7 cents. Do these fractions of a penny differences in cost and face-value matter? You better believe it. The Department of the Treasury lost $100 million in 2007 minting these coins.

What can you do? You have no control over the market price of metals. Congress came in on the issue and directed the Treasury secretary to "prescribe"—suggest—a new more economical composition of the nickel and penny. But Treasury balked, insisting that the constitution does not delegate it the power to decide on coinage composition. Any ideas? How about abolishing the penny? Or, how about creating a two-penny coin? Or, perhaps do nothing. It's hard to imagine Abe Lincoln on any coin but the penny.

Money and Liquidity

Liquidity
The degree to which an asset can easily be exchanged for money.

If you were to play a word-association game with economists and say "money," chances are they would all respond with "liquidity." **Liquidity** is what distinguishes money from any other asset form. Liquidity is the ease with which an asset can be converted into a medium of exchange. Look around your room. What assets do you have that can be readily converted into a medium of exchange? How about that dollar bill on your desk? That's instant. The dollar is a perfectly liquid form of asset. That is to say, the dollar, *in its present form*, can be used as a medium of exchange. A pizza maker, for example, will accept your dollar *as is* in exchange for pizza. A physician will accept it as payment for services.

What about your other assets? Consider, for example, your ticket to next week's basketball game. Can you use it now, *in its present form*, to buy a pizza? Not likely. Even if the ticket is refundable, you still must go to the refund office to convert it back into dollars. The ticket, *in its present form*, is not a perfectly liquid form of money. What about your stereo? It's worth something, isn't it? But *in its present form*, it is highly illiquid. What about the U.S. savings bond in your top drawer? It's more liquid than your stereo, but not nearly as liquid as your dollar bill.

As you see, each one of those assets in your room—the financial as well as the real goods—can be ordered according to liquidity. Some assets are perfectly liquid, that is, can serve immediately as money. Others are less liquid, representing a less-than-perfect money form. Most are highly illiquid, that is, far removed from a money form.

How much money we have, then, depends on how much (or how little) liquidity we accept for a money form. Let's consider the various qualities of money that make up our **money supply**.

Money supply
Typically, M1 money. The supply of currency, demand deposits, and traveler's checks used in transactions.

The Liquidity Character of Our Money Supply

Do we just add up the dollar bills and coins issued by the Fed to compute our money supply? That is to say, is our money supply simply all currency?

Not quite, although currency is part of our money supply. Consider the other money forms we use as a medium of exchange. If you saw a T-shirt you liked, what kind of money would you use to make the purchase? Most likely, currency. But how do you pay your rent? If you're like most people, you write a check on your checking account. The landlord accepts it as payment. As far as the landlord is concerned, your check is money.

**on the
net**
The Federal Reserve (http://www.federalreserve.gov/) maintains current and historical data on M1 and M2 money.

The M1 Money Supply In fact, the check is the most commonly used money form. Most working people receive their wages and salaries in the form of checks. Corporations pay out dividends by check. Most large-ticket items are bought by

applied perspective

Maria, you look better on the ten thaler than on the one.

WHY THE DOLLAR IS CALLED A DOLLAR

What's in a name? Have you ever wondered why we call our paper money the dollar? The origin of the name is not American. In fact, it predates America by well over two centuries.

Its origin, as a currency name, traces back to a silver mining town in Bohemia called Joachimsthal. (The town exists today as Jachymov and lies within the borders of the Czech Republic.) There, in 1519, silver coins were minted, and because of its location, the coins were called Joachimsthaler. That's a mouthful. Later, a much shortened version—*thaler*—became common. The dollar is the Anglicized form of *thaler*.

The *thaler*, as coin and name, traveled far and wide. It was called the *tolar* in Slovenia; the *daalder* in the Netherlands; the *daler* in Sweden, Denmark, and Norway; and the *thaler* in Prussia and Germany. Coins known as the *thaler* were also used in Scotland during the 17th century. And the use of the term *dollar*, as a currency form, shows up in early 17th-century England as well. It even appears as currency in William Shakespeare's *Macbeth* (act 1, scene 2). Ross, a nobleman from Scotland, speaks to Duncan, King of Scotland, and to Duncan's eldest son Malcolm at a camp near Forres:

"That now Sweno,
The Norway's King craves composition;
Nor would we deign him burial of his men
Till he disbursed at Saint Colme's Inch
Ten thousand dollars to our general use."

Macbeth was performed as early as 1611, so people then in the audience must have known that "ten thousand dollars" was a kingly sum. Shakespeare refers to the dollar as well in *The Tempest* (act 3, scene 1), and it, too, was performed in 1611.

Among the common currencies in use in early colonial America were the English pound sterling—so called because the coin weighed 1 Troy pound of sterling silver—the Spanish piastre, and the most recognized *thaler*—the Maria Theresa *thaler*—minted during the reign of Queen Maria Theresa of Hungary and Austria.

When America broke from the English crown to become a sovereign state, an American currency had to be invented. The founding fathers could have created some form of the pound sterling or the piaster but chose instead the dollar. In 1786, Thomas Jefferson proposed it as the unit of American currency, and in 1794, it became official legal tender.

The dollar sign, $, is another matter. There are many versions or tales concerning how that came about. One explanation is that it is a construct of the plural form of the piastre; symbol "P" with a small "s" above it. Eventually, the loop on the "P" disappeared, leaving the upper stroke to cut through the "s." The most widely accepted version is that it is the U.S. monogram, and the "U" (bottom loop removed) and the "S" superimposed. The two strokes were later reduced to one.

---

check. How do you pay your telephone bill? How did you pay your college tuition? Next time you're in line at the supermarket, watch the cashier. Three-bag purchases are often paid for by check.

How many checks you can write depends, of course, on the size of your checking account. That is, your checking account balance represents your money supply.

After all, if you were asked to add up your own money supply, wouldn't you count the dollars and cents you have in your pocket, and then add the money you have on deposit in your checking account?

Economists describe these money forms as **M1 money**. M1 money is highly liquid (immediately available) money. Currency is about as liquid as money could be. Checking accounts? Banks are legally obligated to give you any fraction or all of your deposit immediately *upon demand*. That's pretty liquid, and that is why economists describe checking account balances as demand deposits.

Traveler's checks, too, are M1 money. Think about it. There are times when traveler's checks are more convenient and even more liquid than checks drawn on local banks. They are particularly useful when we're away from home. If you

M1 money
The most immediate form of money. It includes currency, demand deposits, and traveler's checks.

were in Italy, for example, you would probably find it easier to buy a leather jacket with a traveler's check than with a check drawn on your local bank. The Italian merchant may not know much about your bank balance at home but has confidence that the traveler's check you offer can be readily converted into Italian lire.

The M2 Money Supply A broader definition of money is **M2 money**. M2 money includes M1 money and more. How much more? What about your savings deposits? What about your time deposits (or certificates of deposit, commonly referred to as CDs)? Are they money? Yes, indeed. But they are not nearly as liquid a form of money as M1. Why not?

Consider your savings deposit. It may come as a surprise to you, but banks are not obligated to release all or any part of that deposit to you without you first giving them 30 days' notice. That's pretty illiquid, isn't it? Still, as you have probably experienced, banks seldom exercise that 30-day notice privilege. A savings deposit is a less perfect form of money than M1 for yet another reason: It isn't a medium of exchange. For example, you can't pay your rent with a check drawn on your savings account.

What about your time deposit? As its name implies, you are committed to leave your money with the bank for a specified period of time. If you want to convert the time deposit into M1 money—think of cashing in a CD prior to its maturity date—you pay a penalty. The CD's not quite as handy as your checking account, is it? But you think of it as money, don't you?

Why, then, bother with savings and time deposits? Because they typically yield higher rates of interest to depositors than do checking accounts.

Money and "Near" Money

If you received a $100 U.S. savings bond as a birthday gift, would you regard it as a money gift? Would you treat it the same way you would a gift of $100? Have you ever sold a U.S. savings bond before its maturity date? If you have, you know why it isn't a perfectly reliable money form or store of value. Although you can sell the bond anytime at *some* price, the price it will fetch on the bond market will be less than the stated maturity value.

What about corporate bonds? Is an AT&T bond any more reliable a money form than a U.S. savings bond? It too is marketable (and therefore convertible into cash), but at what price? There is even greater risk attached to the corporate bond. Economists refer to these financial assets as near money.

What Isn't Money?

When you think about it, what isn't money? After all, can't you really convert any asset you own into money? Couldn't you sell your wristwatch at *some* price? That's why pawnshops are in business. They allow you to convert your belongings (or someone else's!) into money by purchasing them from you. But do you really think of your watch as a form of money?

Unquestionably, people regard their checking accounts as money. That's what they look at when they worry about making it through the month. They know they can always dip into savings, but savings is something they prefer to protect. It was never really intended as a medium of exchange. Few people think of their homes as money, even though second mortgages are a common way of financing expenditures.

Nevertheless, every asset we own is potential money. At some price, it can be converted into money. Still, we make distinctions between our money, near

on the net
Think about the credit card applications you receive in the mail, or visit Visa (http://www.visa.com/) and MasterCard (http://www.mastercard.com/). Is it clear from these advertisements that credit cards aren't money?

historical perspective

EXPLAINING THE IMPRESSIVE GROWTH OF M2 MONEY

Bank robber Willie Sutton was once asked why he robbed banks. He replied, "Because that's where the money is." And, indeed, that's where it was. But since the late 1970s, and particularly since the deregulation of the banking industry in the early 1980s, money deposits in the form of M2 money found a haven in financial institutions such as credit unions, savings and loan associations, and investment companies that competed directly with banks. How did the competition come about?

Let's start with investment companies. They got into the banking business in the late 1970s by creating money market mutual funds (or MMMFs). These funds were preferred by many depositors over the traditional savings accounts or time deposits of banks because they paid higher rates of interest. (Using the deposits, the investment companies bought government securities and business debt, which yielded even higher rates of return.)

But the MMMFs had a downside. They were a much less convenient form of M2 money for depositors. Originally, the investment companies placed severe restrictions on the number of withdrawals allowed each month on an MMMF and on the minimum size—$500 to $1,000—allowable for each withdrawal. Although many of these restrictions have since been relaxed, restrictions are still imposed.

How did the banks react? In the 1970s, they couldn't. Banks were unable to compete with the MMMFs because they were prohibited by state law from paying comparable interest rates on savings deposits. As a result, money market mutual funds became a preferred M2 money form. But in 1980, when the state-imposed interest rate ceilings were lifted, banks created their own version of the MMMF called the money market deposit account, MMDA.

The competition between the MMMFs and the MMDAs made these money forms more and more accessible—providing depositors greater and greater liquidity—so that the old distinctions between M1 and M2 forms of money became increasingly blurred.

Adding to this blurring process was an innovation of the savings and loan associations (S&Ls)—the NOW account, or negotiable order of withdrawal. This allowed depositors to use S&L savings accounts as honest-to-goodness checking accounts. Not to be left behind, credit unions created the share-draft account, their own version of NOW.

Banks didn't sit idly by. They met the NOW competition by creating the ATS account, or automatic transfer of savings, which allowed depositors to automatically transfer funds from savings to checking when their checking accounts were depleted.

This intense competition for depositors between banks and other financial intermediaries since the 1970s resulted in depositors moving energetically into these many forms of M2 money deposits, creating an impressive rate of M2 growth.

money, and nonmoney assets, don't we? These distinctions, however problematical, depend not only upon how liquid these assets are, but also upon the intended purpose we ascribe to them.

What about your Visa and MasterCard? Are they money? Not at all. They may be accepted as readily as money, but the reason these cards are honored at shops, restaurants, and hotels is because merchants expect to be paid by the financial institution that issued the card. Eventually, you pay off your bill by writing a check to the financial institution or bank that issued the card. But without an adequate checking account, Visa would soon discover that the credit receipt it received with your signature on it was virtually worthless.

Using credit cards is often more convenient than writing checks. Because we travel farther and more frequently than we ever did, these plastic cards have become indispensable. They are readily accepted in other cities and even in other countries by people who would otherwise refuse a check on an unknown bank. And the best part of all is that every time you use a credit card, you receive an interest-free loan for a month or two. You don't need to have money in hand (or in your checking account) until the time comes to pay the bill.

check your understanding

Are your credit cards a form of money?

EXHIBIT 1   U.S. Money Supply: 2008 ($ Billions)

M1		$1,374.8
CURRENCY	$761.8	
TRAVELER'S CHECKS	6.2	
DEMAND DEPOSITS	297.0	
OTHER CHECKABLE DEPOSITS	309.7	
M2		$7,664.3
M1	$1,374.8	
SAVINGS DEPOSITS, MMDAs	4,007.8	
SMALL TIME DEPOSITS	1,215.6	
MMMFs	1,066.1	

Source: *Federal Reserve Bulletin* (Washington, D.C.: Federal Reserve, March, 2008), p. A13, table 1.21.

Adding Up Our Money Supply

Exhibit 1 totals the M1 and M2 money supply for the 2008 U.S. economy.

Look at currency, the money form most people would describe as money. It amounts to about 8.4 percent of the M2 money supply.

Much of the M2 money supply growth since the 1960s, and particularly through the 1970s, can be explained by the introduction of money market mutual funds and deposit accounts into the banking system. They were the right money form at the right time. People favored an asset that could perform both as investment and as reasonably accessible money. As you can see in Exhibit 2, M2 has grown considerably faster since 1970 than any other money form.

Another factor that contributed to the rapid growth of M2 during the 1970s was the sluggish stock market. High-interest-yielding accounts looked good compared to the stock market performance. People shifted out of the stock market into these M2 money forms.

Unless otherwise specified, *economists mean M1 when they refer to money.* It is what people and businesses use in their day-to-day market transactions.

check your understanding

What specific money form do economists have in mind when they refer to *money?*

THE QUANTITY THEORY OF MONEY

How does the money supply affect prices? To show the money-price connection, imagine an economy consisting exclusively of 100 apple trees producing a real GDP of 5,000 apples. Suppose also that the economy's money supply is $10,000. Under these conditions, the price of apples is $2. The total value of the apples (or nominal GDP) is $5,000 \times \$2 = \$10,000$.

The equation of exchange relating the economy's price level, P, the quantity of goods, Q, and the money supply, M, is written as

$$P = \frac{M}{Q}.$$

If the money supply doubles to $20,000 and Q doesn't change, the price level doubles to $20,000/5,000 = \$4$. If the money supply falls to $5,000 and Q is still unchanged, the price level falls to $5,000/5,000 = \$1$.

EXHIBIT 2   Growth of the Money Supply: 1970–2008

DATE	M1	M2
1970	214	419
1975	295	663
1980	415	1,651
1985	627	2,566
1990	825	3,328
1997	1,065	3,904
2000	1,095	4,861
2008	1,374.8	7,664.3

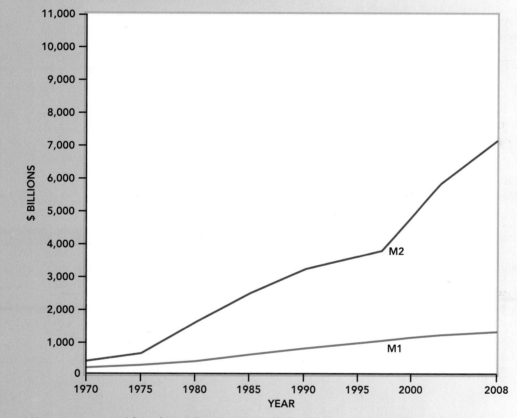

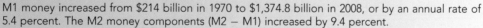

M1 money increased from $214 billion in 1970 to $1,374.8 billion in 2008, or by an annual rate of 5.4 percent. The M2 money components (M2 − M1) increased by 9.4 percent.

Look at the other correspondences in the equation of exchange. If Q (real GDP) doubles from 5,000 to 10,000 apples and M doesn't change, the price level falls to $10,000/10,000 = 1. Simple enough?

The Velocity of Money

Actually, it's too simple. The equation of exchange shown in our apple illustration does not take into account the **velocity of money**. The price level depends not only on Q (real GDP) and M (the quantity of money), but also on velocity—that is, on the number of times a dollar is used during a year transacting Q.

Velocity of money
The average number of times per year each dollar is used to transact an exchange.

global perspective

© Royalty-Free/CORBIS

MONEY AIN'T WHAT IT USED TO BE

Scene: Midnight. Lisa Beth gets out of a Yellow Cab on New York's East 19th Street and Park Ave and heads for home, a few yards away. Before she reaches her destination, she is stopped by two young men who seem to be as uncomfortable and unsure as they are threatening.

First Man: "Lady, just give us your money and nobody gets hurt. OK? We'll walk away."

Lisa: "I can't help you because I have no money."

(*The second man takes her purse, opens her wallet, and sure enough, finds no money.*)

Second Man: "She's right. There's no money here. How did you pay the cab fare?"

Lisa: "With a credit card. I always do."

First man: "Then we'll escort you home. You must have some money there."

Lisa: "You can come home with me, but you'll be wasting your time. You won't find money there either."

First Man: "How then do you buy food and clothes and stuff like that?"

Lisa: "All bought with credit cards."

Second Man: "What about the money you make?"

Lisa: "Well, I do make money—as you put it—but I never actually see it. The firm I work for deposits my earnings each month in my personal account at Chase Manhattan. Come to think about it, I haven't seen a dollar bill in ages. I hear they redesigned them and added multiple colors."

Second Man: "Is she putting us on?"

First Man: "Lady, are you telling us that you *never* use money?"

Lisa: "That's right. I used to, like everybody else. But over time, I discovered that it's more convenient to use credit and debit cards. And in some cases, it's even simpler. My utility bills go directly to the bank, and I've authorized the bank to pay them. I'm completely out of the loop. So is my connection to hands-on money."

Second Man: "Lady, if this catches on, we're out of business."

Lisa: "I'm sorry to tell you, but it's catching on. Look at the table on this page."

First Man: "What you're telling us is pretty depressing. There go promising careers."

Lisa: "Look, you guys don't look like you enjoy this kind of thing. You're young and healthy. Go back to school or get an honest job."

Second Man: "You *really* don't use money?"

Lisa: "Nope."

Deserving of kisses galore.

CREDIT CARDS: HOLDERS, NUMBERS, AND SPENDING: 2000–2008* (*PROJECTED)

	2000	2003	2008*
CARDHOLDERS (MILLIONS)	$ 159	164	176
NUMBER OF CARDS (MILLIONS)	$1,425	1,460	1,513
CREDIT CARD SPENDING (BILLIONS)	$1,458	1,735	2,604

Source: U.S. Census Bureau, *Statistical Abstract of the United States: 2006,* p. 766.

D. H. Robertson illustrates the importance of money velocity in a rather amusing story:

> On Kentucky Derby day, Bob and Joe invested in a barrel of beer and set off to Louisville with the intention of selling at the racetrack at a dollar a pint. On the way, Bob, who had one dollar left in the world, began to feel a great thirst, and drank a pint of beer, paying Joe the dollar. A little later, Joe yielded to the same desire, and drank a pint of beer, returning the dollar to Bob. The day was hot, and before long Bob was thirsty again, and so, a little later, was Joe. When they arrived at the track, the dollar was back in Bob's pocket, but the beer was all gone. One single dollar had performed a volume of transactions which would have required many dollars if the beer had been sold to the public in accordance with the original intention.[1]

---

[1] D. H. Robertson, *Money* (New York: Harcourt, 1922), p. 35. The original text referred to the famous Derby at Epsom, in England, not the Kentucky Derby, and to shillings, not dollars. The derby and currency were changed here to make the illustration more familiar to the reader.

A busy dollar working 50 times a year can do the same money-work as 50 one-dollar bills that work only once a year. In one case, the velocity of money, V, is 50; in the other, it is 1.

Adding the velocity of money completes the **equation of exchange**:

$$MV = PQ$$

Consider once more the apple economy. If $Q = 5,000$ apples, $M = \$10,000$, and V increases from 1 to 8, then the price level P increases from \$2 to \$16. The velocity of money, as you see, can be important.

Although the equation of exchange seems to be a matter of simple arithmetic, economists are nowhere near agreeing on how changes in M, for example, *really* affect P. Some economists, notably Keynesians, believe that if a change in M occurs, it may not affect only P, as we see in the equation of exchange, but also and at the same time Q. If that happens, then the one-to-one correspondence between M and P in the equation of exchange is lost. They also see an interdependence between changes in M and changes in V; that is, changes in M cause changes in V. But other economists—classical economists, in particular—disagree, arguing that the velocity of money is not at all affected by changes in M, P, or Q.

These opposing views on the interdependence of the variables V, Q, M, and P in the equation of exchange lead to differing theories concerning the relationship between money and prices.

The Classical View

The classical view of the relationships among money, real GDP, money velocity, and prices fits into the broader picture that classical economists present of an economy in equilibrium at full-employment GDP. Real GDP—Q in the equation of exchange—depends upon the amount of resources available in the economy. If the amount of resources does not change—a condition supposed by classical economists for short-run equilibrium—Q does not change. Prices, on the other hand, are flexible in the classical world, adjusting the value of the goods produced, Q, to the money supply.

What about the velocity of money? According to classical economists, the velocity of money is constant. After all, they argue, people tend not to change the way they use money.

Think about it. How much money we need to purchase the goods and services we buy in a year depends, in part, on how often we get paid during the year. Suppose Kirsten Gentry earns \$52,000 annually and is paid that \$52,000 in one lump sum, say, on December 31. That is, there is only one payday per year. She would use that \$52,000 a dollar at a time throughout the year to buy goods and services. On the other hand, suppose there were 52 paydays per year so that she received \$1,000 weekly. In that case, the same \$1,000, used over and over in each of the 52 weeks, could buy the same \$52,000 worth of goods and services. That is to say, \$1,000 M, with $V = 52$, can transact as many goods and services as \$52,000 M with $V = 1$. As long as the number of paydays is an established practice in the economy, velocity remains fairly stable.

Our spending and saving behavior is habitual as well. As impulsive as we think we are, the truth of the matter is that we use approximately the same quantity of money week after week to buy our goods and services, and even on exceptional occasions such as vacations and holidays, our spending is fairly conventional.

Classical economists convert the equation of exchange into a **quantity theory of money**. Since they believe that both V and Q are constants for an economy in short-run equilibrium, the equation of exchange becomes a theory in which the *quantity of money explains prices:*

$$P = \frac{MV}{Q}$$

interdisciplinary perspective

VELOCITY OF ANOTHER KIND

Suppose you're one of 100 students taking Economics 101 and every student, including yourself, is fully aware that having *and reading* the assigned economics textbook is essential to a good grade. The 100 students, then, would buy 100 books. Make sense?

But suppose these students didn't take the class in the same semester. Suppose, instead, class size was limited to 20 students so that the 100 students were forced to take the course over 5 semesters. The first semester's class of 20 students would need only 20 textbooks.

And suppose, after finals, these first 20 students sold their 20 textbooks back to the campus bookstore, which resold them as used books to the second set of 20 students enrolled in next semester's class. At the end of the second semester, those students resold their texts to the same bookstore, which resold them again as used books to the third-semester class, and so on.

Sound familiar? It should on two counts. First, that's probably what you will end up doing with your textbook. Second, the *idea* of velocity of textbooks is identical to the *idea* of velocity of money in a money economy. Each of the 20 textbooks over the course of 5 semesters "worked" 5 times as hard—or 5 times as much—as 100 textbooks used in the class of 100 students taking the course in one semester. The equivalence? Twenty texts working 5 times equals 100 texts working once.

© Brooklyn Production/CORBIS

Look! this is Lisa's old book.

Causality is clear and mechanical. If *M* increases, then because *V* and *Q* are constants, the price level, *P*, increases.

For the sake of argument, even if the economy tends to be at full employment, there is nothing that compels us to believe that *Q* must remain constant *in the long run*. In fact, there's good reason to suppose it doesn't. Why not? Because in the long run, the supply of resources available, such as labor and capital, increases. And since classical economists believe that the economy operates at full employment (always using its available resources and the most advanced technology), then with more resources used, more *Q* is produced.

To illustrate the classical view of the relationship between money and prices in the long run, let's suppose that the economy's resource supply increases by 5 percent every year.

The simple proportionality between money and prices supposed in short-run equilibrium breaks down. With more resources available every year, full-employment *Q* increases every year by 5 percent. How does that full-employment *Q* growth affect prices? If the money supply *M* grows by 5 percent every year as well, then with velocity constant, the price level remains unchanged year after year. If, on the other hand, *M* grows at 7 percent while *Q* grows at 5 percent, then the price level, *P*, increases by 2 percent (inflation) every year. And if *M*'s growth is lower than *Q*'s—say, 3 percent compared to *Q*'s 5 percent—then *P* falls (deflation) by 2 percent. Classical economists saw the quantity theory of money as proof that money cannot influence how much we produce but that it does influence the prices of the goods we produce.

Monetarism: A Modification of the Classical View

The idea that money velocity is constant was challenged in the 1970s by economists *within the classical tradition*. Their reformulation of the classical view on money became known as monetarism.

In a sense, the monetarist view of money was an attempt to rescue the classical view from the onslaught of empirical evidence that showed that M1 money velocity was anything but constant. Look at Exhibit 3.

As you see, M1 money velocity is quite erratic. Its long-run trend was downward until the 1950s, when it reversed and rose steadily until the mid-1980s. Since then, it has been even more erratic.

Monetarists accept the idea that velocity is not constant; nonetheless, they believe that it is still highly predictable, well behaved, and independent of money supply.

They explain the steady increase in money velocity since the 1950s by pointing to the technological changes associated with the transactions demand for money. For example, the use of computers speeds up the banking process. Also, the widespread use of credit cards allows people to buy and sell goods and services with less cash and lower bank balances relative to nominal GDP. The result: higher money velocity. Since technologies in money and banking are still developing and pay periods are becoming more frequent, monetarists believe it is reasonable to predict increases in velocity over time, and for the short run at least, they believe the increases will be well behaved.

If money velocity is known—that is, relatively stable and highly predictable—and if Q is at full-employment real GDP, then the quantity theory of money—expressing the relationship between money and prices—remains intact. In the end the monetarist version of the quantity theory of money still leads to the same classical conclusion: Although money cannot influence how much we produce, it does influence the prices of the goods and services we produce. Look again at Exhibit 3. If you were an economist looking at M1 velocity during the mid-1950s until well into the 1970s, you couldn't be faulted for believing that money velocity is, indeed, fairly predictable. There's an almost steady growth path. But from the mid-1980s onward, confidence in its predictability quickly evaporated, along with many believers in monetarist ideas.

check your understanding

According to classical economists and monetarists, what does a change in the money supply affect? What can it not affect?

EXHIBIT 3   Historical Record of Money Velocity

Until World War II, the velocity of money drifted downward, with some short-run upward swings, from approximately 4.0 in the 1920s to 2.0 in 1945. The trend reversed dramatically thereafter, increasing, with some short-run downturns, from 2.0 in 1945 to 9.1 in 2005.

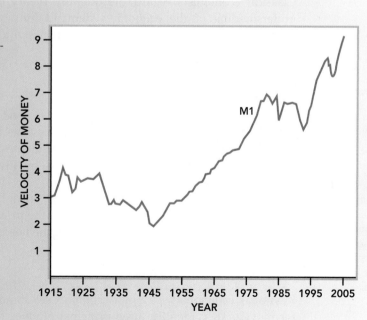

The Keynesian View

Keynesians offer a different view of the quantity theory of money. They reject the idea that V is either stable or predictable and that Q always reflects full-employment GDP. If they're right—that is, if V is neither stable nor predictable and if Q is not necessarily at full employment—then changes in the supply of money may end up affecting more than prices. They may affect Q as well.

Consider how Keynesians view the velocity of money. They do not challenge the classical or monetarist view that payment schedules and patterns of spending and saving are basically stable. What they do challenge, however, is that these are the principal determinants of money velocity.

What is missing? To Keynesians, velocity is also affected by changes in people's *expectations*. A price increase, for example, may lead to an increase in money velocity. Why? Because people typically expect past performance to continue into the future. If prices increase, people will expect them to increase again; that is, they expect future prices will be higher. In that case, people will buy more now to avoid the higher future prices. In other words, price increases today can change spending habits today. To accommodate the increase in spending, the velocity of money increases.

What reduces velocity? The same logic is applied. This time, if prices decrease, people expect lower future prices, so they decrease present consumption in order to buy cheaper later. The decrease in spending today decreases the velocity of money.

Setting aside the issue of whether money velocity is stable or predictable or unpredictably variable, the idea that Q always reflects full-employment real GDP is totally unacceptable to the Keynesians because it contradicts their central argument that an economy can be in equilibrium at less than full employment. If we really don't live in a world characterized by full-employment real GDP, then the tight relationship between money and prices that classical economists supposed existed comes completely unglued. (The Keynesian idea that changes in the money supply can affect real GDP is developed in the next section.)

THE DEMAND FOR MONEY

The Classical View

Classical economists regard the quantity theory of money as the key to our understanding of the economy's demand for liquidity, that is, money. The quantity theory of money equation is transposed to

$$M = \frac{PQ}{V}.$$

Since PQ is nominal GDP (the quantity of goods produced multiplied by the price level) and since classical economists assume V is constant, the quantity of money demanded by households and businesses to transact the buying and selling of the goods produced is derived by dividing nominal GDP by the velocity of money. That's it!

Transactions demand for money
The quantity of money demanded by households and businesses to transact their buying and selling of goods and services.

This **transactions demand for money** is the only motive classical economists see for anyone demanding money. If either the price level or real GDP increases, more money would be demanded to meet the needs of increasing nominal GDP.

The Keynesian View

Keynesian economists see a more complex set of motives influencing the demand for money. They identify three principal motives for demanding money. These are the transactions motive (which classical and monetarist economists accept as the only motive), the precautionary motive, and the speculative motive.

The Transactions Motive People hold money (liquid assets) to transact purchases they expect to make. This notion is fairly classical. People prefer to avoid the inconvenience of having to convert their nonmoney assets into money every time they decide to buy something. Can you imagine the headache converting nonmoney assets into money every time you buy a tuna sandwich? People learn, then, to hold a specific quantity of money for the groceries, movie tickets, gasoline, clothes, audio CDs, and other items they habitually purchase. The quantity of money demanded to satisfy transactions needs increases with the level of nominal GDP. The more people buy, the more money they need to make the purchases.

The Precautionary Motive People also hold money as insurance against *unexpected* needs. Let's suppose Joel Spencer plans a trip that he estimates will cost $1,000. Is that the quantity of money he will take along? Most unlikely. Joel will probably add another $100 *just in case.* More-cautious people may add more. The motive? Precautionary.

And what about unexpected problems? A dented fender. A broken furnace. A slipped disc that keeps you out of work for three weeks. A pink slip in your pay envelope. All is possible and, at *some* time, most probable. People hold money, giving up interest-bearing accounts, just to cover these eventualities.

The Speculative Motive Another major consideration for demanding money is the speculative motive. People have the choice of holding their assets in the form of either money or other financial assets, such as interest-bearing certificates of deposit (CDs). How much they choose to hold of each depends on the interest rate. Look at Exhibit 4.

Why is the speculative demand curve for money downward sloping? If the rate of interest is high, say, i_1, people will choose to hold only M_1 and use the rest of their money to buy interest-bearing assets. After all, the opportunity cost of holding more than M_1 is the relatively high i_1 interest rate.

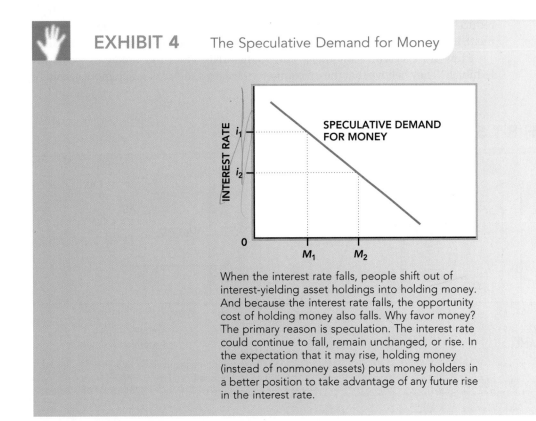

EXHIBIT 4   The Speculative Demand for Money

When the interest rate falls, people shift out of interest-yielding asset holdings into holding money. And because the interest rate falls, the opportunity cost of holding money also falls. Why favor money? The primary reason is speculation. The interest rate could continue to fall, remain unchanged, or rise. In the expectation that it may rise, holding money (instead of nonmoney assets) puts money holders in a better position to take advantage of any future rise in the interest rate.

But if the interest rate falls to i_2, people will most likely shift out of holding interest-bearing assets into holding money. Why? Because the opportunity costs associated with holding money and holding interest-paying assets have changed. In Exhibit 4, the quantity of money demanded increases to M_2. Holding money now costs less because the interest is less. Holding the now lower-interest-yielding assets increases the cost of not having the money immediately available to take advantage of any unforeseen good prospect that may arise suddenly. That is to say, when interest rates fall, people feel more inclined to *speculate*. According to Keynesians, then, the demand for money is not just to satisfy people's transactions and precautionary needs, but to satisfy their speculative proclivities as well.

Money Affects Real GDP We are now prepared to explain why Keynesians believe money affects real GDP. Look at Exhibit 5.

Suppose the money supply increases from S_1 to S_2. (The demand curve is assumed to be D_1.) The effect of that increase lowers the equilibrium interest rate from i_1 to i_2, as shown in panel *a*. The fall in the interest rate increases the investment spending from I_1 to I_2, which is shown in panel *b*. (Note the steepness of the investment curve. It reflects the Keynesian view that changes in investment are relatively insensitive to changes in the interest rate.) Since investment is an integral part of aggregate demand, the increase in investment shifts the aggregate demand curve to the right, from AD_1 to AD_2, shown in panel *c*. And because Keynesians believe that the economy typically operates below the full employment level, the shift in aggregate demand raises real GDP from GDP_1 to GDP_2.

What about the price level? If the shift in aggregate demand and the consequent change in real GDP occur along the horizontal segment of the aggregate supply curve—and that's how Keynesians view the world—then the price level remains unaffected by changes in money supply. A different outcome would occur, however, if the economy were operating along the upward-sloping segment of the aggregate supply curve. In this situation, an increase in the money supply that raises aggregate demand to AD_3 raises both real GDP and prices.

The cause-and-effect sequence depicted in panels *a*, *b*, and *c* can be made to show what happens when the money supply falls. Interest rates (in panel *b*) increase, which reduces the quantity of investment undertaken in the economy. The fall in investment, in turn, shifts the aggregate demand curve to the left, thus decreasing real GDP.

How do classical economists and monetarists view the linkages shown in Exhibit 5? They believe that the investment curve (in panel *b*) is much more sensitive

check your understanding

Why do Keynesians believe that an increase in the money supply raises GDP and not price?

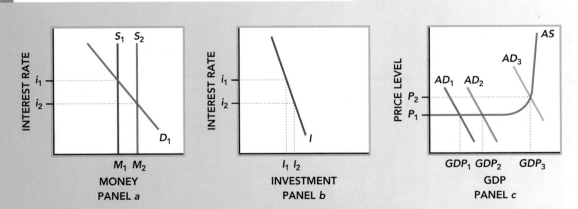

KEY EXHIBIT 5   Money Affects Real GDP

Follow the sequence of events through panels *a*, *b*, and *c*. When the money supply increases from S_1 to S_2, the interest rate falls from i_1 to i_2, which increases the quantity demanded of investment goods from I_1 to I_2. This increase in investment shifts aggregate demand from AD_1 to AD_2. The result is an increase in real GDP from GDP_1 to GDP_2.

to changes in the interest rate than Keynesians suppose. Since they also believe that the economy operates at full-employment real GDP—that is, along the vertical segment of *AS*—any increase in the money supply (which lowers the interest rate and raises the quantity of investment and consequently aggregate demand) can only end up raising the price level. Nominal GDP increases, but real GDP does not.

CHAPTER REVIEW

1. Barter exchange requires a double coincidence of wants. As the number of people and the number of goods increase, barter becomes increasingly more difficult. One good then becomes chosen as the money form. The characteristics of a good money form are durability, portability, divisibility, homogeneity, and stability. Gold is an exemplary money form.

2. Money serves three functions: It is a medium of exchange, a measure of value, and a store of value. Paper (or fiat) money can substitute for gold as long as it is universally accepted as the medium of exchange.

3. The different measures of our money supply depend upon the degree of liquidity we use. M1, the most liquid form of money, is essentially currency and checkable deposits, such as NOW and ATS accounts. M2 includes M1 plus small-denomination time deposits, such as MMDAs, and savings accounts.

4. The equation of exchange is written as $MV = PQ$. Classical economists believe that because output, Q, is constant at full-employment equilibrium, and because the velocity of money, V, is constant, then the price level in the economy, P, varies directly with the money supply, M.

5. Monetarists accept the classical idea that the economy operates at full-employment equilibrium, but unlike the classicists, they believe that the velocity of money is not constant but nonetheless stable and predictable enough to ensure the usefulness of the equation of exchange linking prices to the money supply.

6. Keynesians believe that because output and velocity are neither constant nor stable and predictable, changes in the money supply can affect real GDP as well as prices.

7. According to classical economists, the demand for money is strictly a transactions demand. Keynesians, on the other hand, use the transactions, precautionary, and speculative motives as determinants of money demand.

KEY TERMS

Barter	Liquidity	Velocity of money
Money	Money supply	Equation of exchange
Fiat money	M1 money	Quantity theory of money
Currency	M2 money	Transactions demand for money

QUESTIONS

1. Why do we need money?
2. H'ow much currency is there in our M1 money supply? What's the story behind the "missing currency"?
3. Why does barter exchange become increasingly less useful as the number of people engaged in exchange increases?
4. What are the essential properties of money?
5. What are the principal components of M1 and M2 money?
6. What is the relationship between money and liquidity?
7. What is "near" money?
8. Are Visa and MasterCard balances part of M1? Why or why not?
9. What is money velocity?
10. How do the classical and Keynesian views of money velocity differ?
11. Compare the classical and Keynesian views concerning the demand for money.
12. The demand for money is inversely related to the interest rate. Explain.
13. Explain how changes in the money supply can result in changes in real GDP.

WHAT'S WRONG WITH THIS GRAPH?

The Speculative Demand for Money

Economic Consultants

Economic Research and Analysis by Students for Professionals

JoAnn Weber is an economics teacher at Washington High School in Miami, Florida. For her honors economics class, JoAnn has decided to include a section on the history, uses, and quantity of money in the United States.

As part of an arrangement with school districts in the Miami area, Economic Consultants helps economics teachers create their curricula. JoAnn has contacted Economic Consultants to prepare background materials on money. You are assigned to the project and asked to prepare a report for JoAnn that addresses the following issues:

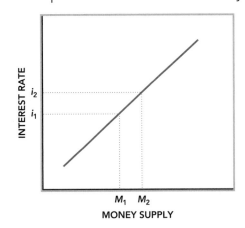

© Image 100/Royalty-Free/CORBIS

1. Why and in what ways do we use money?
2. What economic institutions have been instrumental in the histori-cal development of money in the United States?
3. What is meant by liquidity and how is it used to distinguish different money forms? Who actually produces the money we commonly use?
4. What resources are available for students interested in learning more about money?

You may find the following resources helpful as you prepare this report for JoAnn:

- **Fundamental Facts about U.S. Money** (http://www.frbatlanta.org/publica/brochure/fundfac/money.htm)—The Atlanta Federal Reserve pub-lishes an online brochure about U.S. money.
- **Monetary Museum** (http://www.frbatlanta.org/atlantafed/tours_museum/tour/tour_atlanta.cfm)—The Atlanta Federal Reserve maintains a physical and virtual museum devoted to money.

- **Our Money** (http://www.minneapolisfed.org/community_education/teacher/money.cfm/)—The Minneapolis Federal Reserve provides informa-tion on U.S. currency and new designs, counterfeit pro-tections, and the history of money.
- **Your Money Matters** (http://www.moneyfactory.gov/)—The U.S. Treasury Department publishes information on every denomination of U.S. paper money.
- **The U.S. Mint** (http://www.usmint.gov/)—The U.S. Mint provides exten-sive information about the composition, production, and history of coins.
- **Bureau of Engraving and Printing (BEP)** (http://www.moneyfactory.gov/)—The BEP designs and manu-factures paper money, among other securities. The BEP has extensive information about paper money, including videos that show how currency is printed and information on what happens to mutilated money.
- **Currency Facts** (http://www.moneyfactory.gov/document.cfm/18/94)—The Bureau of Printing and Engraving has dozens of facts and trivia about currency.
- **Know Your Money** (http://www.treas.gov/usss/index.shtml)—The U.S. Secret Service, which, in addition to protecting the president, protects against counterfeiting, provides information for spotting fake money.

1. In 2008, the M2 money in the United States was approximately
   a. $750 billion.
   b. $7.5 billion.
   c. $ 7.5 trillion.
   d. $750 trillion.
   e. $20 trillion.

2. Barter becomes difficult to implement in a large economy because
   a. individuals are less willing to trade in large economies.
   b. individuals have fewer wants in large economies.
   c. it becomes more difficult to find a double coincidence of wants in large economies.
   d. fiat is usually not available in large economies.
   e. there are many places that individuals in large economies can gather to find double coincidences of wants.

3. Which of the following assets is the most liquid form of money?
   a. Currency
   b. U.S. savings bonds
   c. Commercial water
   d. An automobile
   e. Gold

4. All of the following are components of the M1 money supply except one. Which one?
   a. Coins
   b. Savings accounts
   c. Checking accounts
   d. Dollar bills
   e. Traveler's checks

5. Small-denomination time deposits are included in which the following definitions of the money supply?
   a. M1 only
   b. M3 only
   c. M2 only
   d. Both M1 and M3
   e. Both M1 and M2

6. The velocity of money represents
   a. whether individuals are increasing or decreasing the quantity of money spent in the economy.
   b. the quantity of money available in the economy.
   c. the level of prices determined by the equation of exchange.
   d. how often money is used in a specific period of time.
   e. whether currency is accepted as a medium of exchange in the economy.

7. According to the quantity theory of money,
   a. increases in the money supply, ceteris paribus, will lead to inflation.
   b. the level of inflation is independent of the money supply.
   c. the money supply times velocity is equal to real GDP.
   d. when real GDP rises, the money supply must fall by the same proportion.
   e. the velocity of money is assumed to fluctuate wildly over time.

8. Monetarists differ from classical economists in their view of money in that monetarists believe that
   a. the velocity of money is relatively constant over time.
   b. prices are not influenced by real GDP.
   c. prices are not influenced by the money supply.
   d. the level of unemployment is directly related to the money supply.
   e. the velocity of money varies over time.

9. According to classical economists,
   a. individuals desire to hold money only because of the precautionary demand for money.
   b. individuals do not hold money for either precautionary or speculative reasons.
   c. the velocity of money is not constant but is predictable.
   d. the velocity of money is not constant and cannot be predicted with any degree of certainty.
   e. individuals have no reason for wanting to hold onto money.

10. The speculative demand for money suggests that
    a. individuals hold onto money for the purpose of engaging in transactions.
    b. as the rate of interest rises, the demand for money will rise.
    c. when the economy becomes more uncertain, people are more likely to hold onto money.
    d. the velocity of money is constant.
    e. as the rate of interest falls, the demand for money will rise.

MONEY CREATION AND THE BANKING SYSTEM

If you don't believe in magic, this chapter may make you change your mind. The magic performed is the creation of money. Like pulling a rabbit out of a hat, money seemingly appears from nowhere. Not only does the magician make money appear, but the money created ends up in the hands of those who have reason to use it.

Let's start our analysis of money creation with a simple tale. Imagine a premodern economy where gold is used to satisfy the people's transactions and precautionary money needs. But here, life can be quite nasty, brutish, and short, particularly for those holding large quantities of gold. People in this economy without banks have a problem. Where do they put their gold for safekeeping?

Amar Bazazz is the answer. Why him? He owns a deep cave and an enormous, unfriendly dog. He uses the cave as a depository where people can keep their gold. With the dog pacing the cave's entrance, nobody would dare try their luck.

Amar charges depositors 10 percent per year for guarding the gold they deposit in his cave. They regard that percentage as an insurance premium.

Sounds uneventful so far, but the plot thickens. What people don't know is that Amar is addicted to gambling. Every night, he takes some of the deposited gold to the casino in the next town and loses it all in a matter of hours. In fact, he gambles away fully 80 percent of the deposits in the cave.

But what he discovers, to his shock, is that it doesn't really matter. Everybody thinks their gold is in the cave, and when they come to withdraw some of it—few withdraw all, and certainly not everyone at once—*enough* is always there. Gold is gold. Perfectly homogeneous. That's the way Amar Bazazz makes his living, earning 10 percent per year on gold that isn't there.

Let's now suppose that in the twilight of his life, Amar confesses his gambling to his only son who, although shocked at the disclosure, is quick enough to see the possibilities. Inheriting the cave and the dog's ferocious pups, he goes into his father's gold-keeping business.

Amar's son doesn't gamble in casinos. Instead, he takes the deposited gold to other towns and gambles there on what he thinks are sound investments. In this way he earns money both by safe-keeping the gold *and* on the investments. To get his hands on more gold, he lowers the security rate he charges to 5 percent. People are so moved by his generosity, they elect him mayor.

He is a smart businessman. He holds to a sound fractional reserve rule. He always keeps 20 percent of the deposited gold in reserve to handle the transactions demands of the depositors. That, of course, still leaves 80 percent free for investments. He even hires people to locate good investment projects for him.

To encourage growth in his investment business, he not only cuts the security rate to 0 percent but offers to pay his depositors a small percentage to deposit their gold in his cave. For fear they would think him insane, he comes clean. He tells them about his father's gambling, his own investments, and explains how the security of their deposits is guaranteed in a **fractional reserve system**.

Should the depositors panic? Should they be concerned that only 20 percent of their gold deposits are in reserve? Not at all. They accept his assurance that they can get their entire deposit returned upon demand. Some even refer to their deposits as *demand deposits*. It works. Now they actually draw interest on their entire deposit although only a fraction of their gold is being safely kept in the cave.

Who said life can't be wonderful? The tale may be simple, *but this is essentially the basis of all modern banking.*

Fractional reserve system
A banking system that provides people immediate access to their deposits but allows banks to hold only a fraction of those deposits in reserve.

HOW BANKS CREATE MONEY

Let's update the story to a modern economy. Suppose we want to go into the banking business. What would it take? What would we do? Why do it?

The last question is easy. The reason people go into banking is to earn profit. Bankers are like barbers, automobile makers, and coal mining entrepreneurs. These others cut hair, make automobiles, and dig coal because that's how they make a profit. Bankers hope to make a profit by borrowing your money at low prices and lending it to others at higher prices. That's all there is to it. Nothing really complicated.

Well, let's do it! Let's set up the Paris First National Bank (PFN) in downtown Paris, Texas. We pick out an imposing, gray stone building. We hire cashiers, loan officers, and other personnel. We're ready.

Attracting Depositors

We run a series of radio and television commercials inviting depositors to bank at PFN. The commercials also invite people looking for bank loans to come by.

Let's suppose Jeff Kaufman decides to bank with PFN. He opens a checking account by depositing $1,000. He knows, of course, that he can withdraw that sum of M1 money any time he pleases. It is, after all, a demand deposit.

PFN's **balance sheet**—a summary of the bank's assets (what it has) and liabilities (what it owes)—after this initial $1,000 demand deposit is

Balance sheet
The bank's statement of liabilities (what it owes) and assets (what it owns).

Paris First National Bank

Assets		Liabilities	
Reserves	$1,000	Demand Deposits	$1,000

Look at PFN's assets and liabilities. Its assets, held by the bank as reserves in its vaults, are $1,000. What does that mean? Simply that it has Jeff Kaufman's $1,000 in cash. Is the bank, then, $1,000 richer than it was before Kaufman came in? No. Although it has the $1,000, it also has a $1,000 obligation to give the money back to Kaufman. In fact, Kaufman can demand the money back any time he pleases. The bank may *use* the money, but it's not the bank's. It's Jeff Kaufman's. In fact, if you ask Kaufman how much money he has, he would tell you. It's $1,000.

Making Loans

Demand deposits are only half of PFN's business. Loans are the other. PFN makes a profit only on the loans it provides, not on its deposits. So PFN is now willing and able to lend money, but it can do so only if borrowers show up. And they do. Some borrow to finance consumption purchases, such as automobiles and houses; others borrow to finance business investments.

Let's suppose Matt Taylor approaches the bank with an idea of setting up a Japanese food carryout. His presentation to the bank is impressive. He explains that there are many pizza, taco, hot dog, and hamburger places in town, as well as Chinese restaurants. But no one offers Japanese food. He has also done his homework. He shows that he could renovate a vacated Pizza Hut for $800 and make a 25 percent profit in the first year. What he needs is an $800 loan.

PFN likes the idea and loans Matt $800 at an interest rate of 10 percent. In fact, $800 is the maximum it can loan because, by law, banks are required to keep 20 percent of their demand deposits on reserve, either in their own vaults or at the Federal Reserve Bank. The Federal Reserve decides what the **legal reserve requirement** will be. The 20 percent legal reserve requirement in this story is only hypothetical. In fact, the legal reserve requirement that the Fed actually picks for our economy is typically less than 10 percent. (We'll say more about the Federal Reserve later.)

Legal reserve requirement
The percentage of demand deposits banks and other financial intermediaries are required to keep in cash reserves.

Let's look at PFN's balance sheet after the loan is made:

Paris First National Bank

Assets		Liabilities	
Reserves	$1,000	Demand Deposits	$1,800
Loans	800		

theoretical perspective

CYBERSPACE BANKING

Ask your grandparents. They probably know what the expression "banker's hours" used to mean These hours were relatively short—as though bankers had it easy or so it seemed—typically 10 A.M. to 3 P.M. But the fact is that when banks locked their doors at 3 P.M., their employees were still inside busy at work posting the banking transactions that occurred during that day. The day's deposits, withdrawals, and loan entries had to be recorded, and they were often written into bank ledgers by hand. This took time. Seldom did bank employees leave the building before others left their workplace, and often much later.

Computer technology, spreadsheet software, and the Internet revolutionized, among most other things in our lives, commercial banking. Entries are now made on computers. New information is instantaneously recorded and bank accounts updated at the same time. Retrieval of that information is done in matters of seconds. When people accessed computers to make their deposits and withdrawals, the idea of banking hours—*any* hours—became technologically obsolete. Banks were virtually "open" 24 hours a day.

But why stop there! Access to the Internet propelled modern banking into cyberspace. People choose to have their wages and salaries automatically deposited. They never see or touch their earnings. They can choose to pay their monthly telephone and utility bills, for example, without personal intervention. Funds are withdrawn automatically. There is little reason to be in their bank—ever. It's all cyberspace.

The savings to customer and bank alike can be substantial. For example, customers may enjoy no-fee

checking accounts, zero cost use of the bank's ATMs, and with online bill payments, may end up savings as much as $100 a year on stamps. Banks are big winners. (The post office, of course, is not.) They need considerably less physical space and fewer employees. Consider: The cost of processing a paper check averages $1.20 and each credit card payment ranges from $0.40 to $0.60. Done electronically, these banking transactions cost less than $0.01.

What's the downside to cyberspace banking? The two major concerns are Web reliability and security of information. If people have trouble logging on to a cyberspace site, and if the trouble is habitual, cyberspace may have to wait on technology improvements. The bigger concern, however, is security. If cyberspace banks cannot guarantee security of information, the attractiveness of the new technology may quickly disappear. Can people break the 128-bit encryption code? Is password protection secure? The issue is so important that many banks will automatically log you off after a short period of inactivity to protect whatever personal banking information is on your screen.

But the future is here. Cyberspace banking, like electricity, is fast becoming something we take for granted when transacting our financial accounts. This can't be said for the meaning of "banker's hours." Technology—with few exceptions—dictates what we do and how we do it.

You may never need to know what money looks like.

Note what happens to the bank's assets. They change from $1,000 in reserves to $1,800 in reserves and loans. By agreeing to loan Matt $800, PFN has a new asset in the form of Matt's signed $800 IOU to the bank (shown as the $800 loan in the asset column of the balance sheet). What does PFN give Matt Taylor in return? The bank opens an $800 demand deposit for him. Note what's happened. *The loan creates the demand deposit.* There is now $1,800 in demand deposits, up from $1,000 before the loan. That is, loans create money.

Does the bank give Matt the $800 in currency? Not likely. Instead, it gives Matt a checkbook—like yours—and the right to write checks up to the amount of the $800 demand deposit. It really makes no difference to Matt whether he has checking privileges or currency. It's still M1 money. He can just as easily write checks as use currency to buy labor and materials needed for the carryout.

The Interaction of Deposits and Loans

Suppose Matt Taylor hires Charlie Dold, a skilled carpenter, who can do the work for $800. Dold completes the project in a week. Taylor, satisfied with the job, writes out a check to Dold for $800. Dold accepts the check as his week's income and deposits it in *his* bank, Paris Second National (PSN).

Let's see what happens to the balance sheet at the Paris First National Bank after the check clears:

Paris First National Bank

Assets		Liabilities	
Reserves	$200	Demand Deposits	$1,000
Loans	800		

The $800 check to Charlie Dold wipes out Matt's $800 demand deposit at PFN. The bank's total demand deposits fall from $1,800 to $1,000. At the same time, PFN's cash reserves fall from $1,000 to $200. After all, PFN paid out $800 to the Paris Second National Bank.

Let's now look at PSN's balance sheet:

Paris Second National Bank

Assets		Liabilities	
Reserves	$800	Demand Deposits	$800

Dold's $800 demand deposit creates an $800 asset and an $800 liability for PSN. Imagine a conversation between Jeff Kaufman and Charlie Dold. Dold could ask, "How much money do you have?" Jeff would respond, "$1,000 in Paris First National. What about you?" Charlie would reply, "$800, in Paris Second National." They are both right. *What was once $1,000 in Kaufman's pocket now becomes, through the banking process, $1,800 of money in the form of demand deposits.*

Of course, PSN doesn't sit on Dold's $800 demand deposit. It is eager to loan. Let's now suppose Laura Spears, a city park district director, wants to refinish her old 1965 Mustang. She plans to sell it on the antique car market and needs a loan of $640 to rebuild the engine and transmission. She's sure she can make a 50 percent profit on the car, and after checking out her car and the market, PSN agrees. Laura Spears gets the loan. Let's look at PSN's revised balance sheet, right after the loan has been credited to Laura's checking account:

Paris Second National Bank

Assets		Liabilities	
Reserves	$800	Demand Deposits	$1,440
Loans	640		

The two depositors in PSN are Charlie Dold (with $800) and now Laura Spears (with a new account set up in her name for $640, which is the amount of her loan). *Remember, the loan creates the new demand deposit.* Let's suppose Spears hires Balty Deley, a mechanic with a passion for classic automobiles, to rebuild the engine and transmission for the agreed $640. He is paid with a PSN check, which he promptly deposits in his bank, the Paris Third National (PTN).

Once Laura writes a check to Balty for $640 and the check clears PSN, her demand deposit at PSN is wiped out. The bank's new balance sheet looks like this:

Paris Second National Bank

Assets		Liabilities	
Reserves	$160	Demand Deposits	$800
Loans	640		

Look at its assets. Cash reserves are reduced from $800 to $160 (it paid out $640, the amount of Laura's check) and it has $640 in loans. Its $160 in reserves is 20 percent of its $800 demand deposit. In other words, PSN is also completely loaned out. That's precisely what PSN had hoped for. It makes profit on the $640 loan.

What about PTN after Balty deposited Laura's $640 check? Look at its balance sheet:

Paris Third National Bank

Assets		Liabilities	
Reserves	$640	Demand Deposits	$640

PTN, too, is now ready and able to loan money. Like other banks, it is obligated to keep at least 20 percent of its demand deposits in reserve, which entitles it to loan out a maximum of $512.

Do you see what's happening throughout the banking system? Kaufman's original $1,000 demand deposit in PFN set in motion a chain reaction of loans and demand deposits that created not only a series of new money but also bank loans that make the creation of real goods, such as carry-out restaurants and rebuilt cars, possible.

What does it take to create money? There are three prerequisites.

First, there must be a fractional reserve system operating within **financial intermediaries**, such as banks, savings and loan associations, or credit unions, that are able to loan out some fraction of their deposits.

Second, there must be people willing to make demand deposits.

Third, there must be borrowers prepared to take out consumption loans or loans to finance investment projects.

Without borrowers like Matt Taylor, Jeff Kaufman's original $1,000 demand deposit in the PFN would remain completely sterile.

How Much Money Can the Banking System Potentially Create?

Let's add up the creation of money that takes place in the first 10 rounds of our example, from the initial deposit made in the Paris First National Bank through to one placed in the Paris Tenth National Bank:

Financial intermediaries
Firms that accept deposits from savers and use those deposits to make loans to borrowers.

check your understanding

What three factors are needed for a banking system to create money?

Total Demand Deposits in the Banking System after 10 Rounds of Deposits and Loans

Bank	Demand Deposits
Paris First National	$1,000.00
Paris Second National	800.00
Paris Third National	640.00
Paris Fourth National	512.00
Paris Fifth National	409.60
Paris Sixth National	327.68
Paris Seventh National	262.14
Paris Eighth National	209.72
Paris Ninth National	167.77
Paris Tenth National	134.22
Total M1	$4,463.13

After 10 rounds, the initial $1,000 deposited by Jeff Kaufman has triggered a series of financial transactions that creates an additional $3,463.13 of M1 money. But the process continues. With a new demand deposit of $134.22, the Paris Tenth National can loan out $107.38. As long as there is a sufficient number of people willing to borrow, each demand deposit created by a preceding loan creates the reserves for the succeeding one. With the legal reserve requirement, LRR, set at 20 percent, the *total* amount of money—the initial $1,000 plus all the money potentially created by the banking system—is

$$M = \frac{ID}{LRR},$$

where M is the total demand deposits in the banking system, ID is the initial deposit, and LRR is the legal reserve requirement. When $ID = \$1,000$ and $LRR = 20$ percent, M is $5,000.

$$M = \frac{ID}{LRR} = \frac{\$1,000}{.20} = \$5,000$$

It's a pretty neat system, isn't it? That's why economists marvel at its performance. When you think about it, it's almost magical.

Let's sum up. How is money created? Borrowing creates it, automatically, when the borrower's checking account at a bank is credited as a result of a loan. Why do borrowers demand money? To produce goods and services. So there we have it. The banking system is perfectly synchronized with real-world production. As more goods and services are produced, the banking system automatically creates the equivalent money.

The Potential Money Multiplier

Of course, the amount of money created depends on the legal reserve requirement and on borrowers *actually* utilizing the maximum permissible loans. If $LRR = 10$ percent, a demand deposit of $1,000 will generate—assuming willing borrowers—a money supply of $10,000. If LRR increases to 50 percent, the money supply is only $2,000.

Another way of describing this process of money creation is by developing the concept of the banking system's **potential money multiplier**, m. It is simply

$$m = \frac{1}{LRR}.$$

Potential money multiplier
The increase in the money supply that is potentially generated by a change in demand deposits.

When $LRR = 20$ percent, the potential money multiplier is $1/0.2 = 5$. That is, a new demand deposit of $1,000 placed in any bank can potentially support $5,000 of demand deposits.

Why are there excess reserves?

Living with Excess Reserves

Why do we call it a *potential* money multiplier? Because we can't assume that there will always be sufficient borrowers to take advantage of the available loanable reserves. Suppose Jeff Kaufman deposits $1,000 in PFN, but only $400 is demanded by Matt Taylor. Although PFN is willing and able to loan twice that sum, the potential simply isn't realized. What happens?

Look at PFN's revised balance sheet:

Paris First National Bank

Assets		Liabilities	
Required Reserves	$200	Demand Deposits	$1,000
Excess Reserves	400		
Loans	400		

Excess reserves
The quantity of reserves held by a bank in excess of the legally required amount.

Kaufman's $1,000 shows up, as before, as the PFN bank's liability. But look at its assets' composition. Although the legally required reserve remains $200, PFN's *actual* reserves are $600. It holds, then, **excess reserves**, reserves in excess of those legally required, of $400.

The presence of excess reserves changes how much money the banking system *actually* creates. With PFN now loaning out only $400, the second-round demand deposits in PSN fall to $400. Even if every other bank in the series loans out the maximum permissible, the money created by Kaufman's initial $1,000 deposit shrinks from $4,000 to 400/0.20 = $2,000. Adding Kaufman's own $1,000, the total demand deposits in the banking system are $3,000 instead of $5,000.

But this $3,000 assumes that no other bank aside from PFN holds excess reserves. That's a strong assumption. If other banks, too, do not loan out the maximum permissible, then the actual demand deposits created in the economy by Kaufman's original $1,000 deposit could be most any sum less than $5,000.

The role played by the borrower in money creation cannot be overstated. Without someone actually coming into the bank to demand a loan, there is no process of money creation.

REVERSING THE MONEY CREATION PROCESS

In our example, we have focused on Kaufman's initial $1,000 demand deposit, and for good reason. We were interested in understanding the mechanics of creation, and the simplicity of the example was useful.

Obviously, Jeff Kaufman cannot be PFN's only depositor. Let's add 2,000 more depositors. Now look at PFN's new, fully expanded balance sheet:

Paris First National Bank

Assets		Liabilities	
Required Reserves	$ 4,000,000	Demand Deposits	$20,000,000
Loans	16,000,000		

PFN is a thriving bank. Deposits are $20 million. Look at its asset position. With the legal reserve requirement at 20 percent, PFN is fully loaned out. The bank has $4 million in required reserves and the remaining $16 million of its assets in outstanding loans.

Why 20 percent? Because, in our illustrative scenario, that's what the Federal Reserve instructs. Let's change the instruction. Let's now suppose that the Federal Reserve increases the legal reserve requirement from 20 to 40 percent. All financial intermediaries—commercial banks, savings and loan associations, and credit unions—are obliged to comply. How would PFN react?

It knows what it has to do. It must raise its reserves from $4 million to $8 million. But how? By converting loans back into reserves. Perhaps the least painful way of converting loans into reserves is to wait until some of them are paid off—every day some of them are being paid off—and instead of loaning them out again, keep them in reserves.

Imagine the bank's loan department at work loaning money and then recovering loans that come due. By redirecting some of this flow, the bank can pull in the reins. In the end, its balance sheet is revised:

Paris First National Bank

Assets		Liabilities	
Required Reserves	$ 8,000,000	Demand Deposits	$20,000,000
Loans	12,000,000		

Nothing, of course, changes in the PFN bank's liabilities. Demand deposits remain at $20 million. But look at its asset position. The bank shifted $4 million out of loans into reserves to comply with Federal Reserve instructions. Its loan position contracted from $16 million to $12 million.

check your understanding

What happens to bank loans when the Fed raises the reserve requirement?

interdisciplinary perspective

IF WILLIAM SHAKESPEARE RAN THE FED

Suppose William Shakespeare gave up his job as playwright to become the chair of the Federal Reserve System. In all likelihood, both the principles and practices of the Fed and of the banking system would be dramatically different.

Imagine Shakespeare writing his first position paper. His instruction to all banks would probably begin with: "Neither a borrower nor a lender be, for loan oft loses both itself and friend and borrowing dulleth the edge of husbandry."[1] Doesn't leave banks much room for creating loans, does it?

The reserve requirement consistent with such an instruction is 100 percent. If you deposited $1,000 in the Stratford-upon-Avon Bank, the bank would have $1,000 in the form of liabilities and $1,000 in the form of assets. Its balance sheet would be as follows:

Stratford-upon-Avon Bank

Assets	Liabilities
$1,000 cash reserve	$1,000

With a reserve requirement of 100 percent, the bank has no excess reserves. It can make no loans. Without the ability to make loans on the strength of its deposits, the banking system's money creation process grinds to a halt. And that's precisely what Shakespeare intended.

Shakespeare's 100 percent reserve requirement idea would probably not be the most popular idea to hit the banking community. After all, banks would lose their most profitable activity. Would-be borrowers would not be entirely happy either. Without access to

bank loans, they would have to find an alternative source of financing.

What would a Shakespeare-run Fed advise? Probably that would-be-borrowers should rely on their *own* savings, because using other people's money—borrowing from banks—to finance enterprise "dulleth the edge of husbandry." Does such a Fed opinion sound reasonable to you? Are people more inclined to take risks if the money involved is not theirs?

And even if most business people are prudent, regardless of whose money is involved, borrowing can end up being riskier than imagined. Shakespeare tells the story[2] about Antonio, a Venetian merchant, who borrowed 3,000 ducats for three months from the moneylender Shylock. Unable to repay the loan because his own business ventures went awry—four laden ships were lost at sea—Antonio would have forfeited his life were it not for a prejudicial court that, violating the spirit of the loan contract, ruled in his favor against Shylock.

While no financial institution, including the Fed, can protect either borrower or lender *completely* against the uncertainties associated with enterprise, a 100 percent reserve requirement minimizes the possibility of any set of failed investments triggering a negative, spiral reaction throughout the money economy. Shakespeare's Fed presented the trade-off: Monetary stability versus money creation—or in real terms, less GDP but less fluctuation in GDP as well.

[1] *Hamlet*, Act I, Scene 3.
[2] *The Merchant of Venice*, Act I, Scene 3.

With a potential money multiplier of 5, that's an awful lot of money shrinkage. That is, the Fed's effect on PFN alone reduced the economy's money by $4 million × 5 = $20 million. With 15,000 banks operating in the United States, that's an awful lot of play in the money supply. It makes you appreciate the Fed's awesome power.

WHY BANKS SOMETIMES FAIL

Suppose Matt Taylor's Japanese carryout restaurant is less than a great success. Because people still prefer hamburgers to Matt's sushi, he is in a mess of trouble. But so, too, is the PFN bank. What seemed at first like a great idea to both Taylor and PFN just didn't work out.

What, then, happens to PFN's $800 loan to Taylor? As much as Taylor would like to, he simply can't repay it. He used the bank's money in an honest effort but ended up with a lot of unsold sushi and little money. When the carryout finally closes, the bank can claim its used equipment. And that's about it.

Most likely, the bank survives the Taylor folly. After all, PFN has a diversified loan portfolio and can absorb a loss here and there. In fact, it probably expected something, somewhere, to go afoul. If you were the bank, wouldn't you? Not *everything* works out as planned. That's life.

But what if Taylor's failure was the bank's usual experience—the rule, not the exception? What if too many of PFN's loans to promising business ventures turn out to be not so promising? How many loan defaults can PFN absorb without running into problems of survival itself? On occasion, banks do fail.

Any business failure is an unhappy event. Everyone associated with the enterprise suffers. Some never recover. But when a bank fails, not only do bank owners and bank staff lose the money they invested in the bank and their jobs, but the people who deposited money in the bank discover they no longer have deposits.

Unfair, isn't it? People who deposit money in banks don't regard themselves as being in the banking business. That was not the intent of their deposit. Yet, *unless they are protected in some way*, they become unsuspecting partners in the bank's financial losses.

Moreover, any bank failure can undermine an entire banking system. Imagine a rumor spreading that a bank just failed completely, wiping out its depositors' money. How secure would you feel about your own bank deposit? After all, what happens to one bank could happen to any other. Could yours be next? How could you protect yourself? You would probably do what everyone else was doing. Run quickly to withdraw your money.

Such a run on the bank creates the very problem it tries to avoid. Obviously, no bank, including your own, can expect to satisfy all deposit withdrawal requests at once, even though it is legally obligated to do so. It keeps less than 100 percent in reserve. The entire banking system could collapse if people lose confidence in its ability to function.

The United States has had bank runs brought about by numerous bank failures. It happened in 1907 and triggered an economic downturn. Then, in March 1933, people panicked and set off a run on the banks that forced President Roosevelt to declare an unprecedented week-long "bank holiday." The bank shutdown was meant to calm the troubled financial waters and to signal that government would come to the people's rescue.

check your understanding

Why does bank failure represent a potentially destabilizing threat to the economy?

SAFEGUARDING THE SYSTEM

When banks fail and people panic, how can the banking system protect itself from its inherently explosive vulnerability? Is there no way to protect depositors from the frightening consequences of bank failure?

The Federal Deposit Insurance Corporation

Why not an insurance policy? Why can't banks insure demand deposits just as you insure your automobile? If your automobile disappears, you're covered. Well, if a bank fails and your demand deposits disappear, you're covered as well.

That's precisely what the **FDIC—Federal Deposit Insurance Corporation**—does. It insures all demand deposit accounts up to $100,000 in banks choosing FDIC protection. The protection costs the participating bank an insurance premium that represents only a small percentage of its deposits. It makes sense for depositors and banks. Most everyone, including Jeff Kaufman, can now relax. If PFN goes under, no small depositor is hurt.

Federal Deposit Insurance Corporation (FDIC)
A government insurance agency that provides depositors in FDIC-participating banks 100 percent coverage on their first $100,000 of deposits.

theoretical perspective

© Paul Edmondson/CORBIS

FEDERAL DEPOSIT INSURANCE AND MORAL HAZARD

Why do banks fail? One reason, ironically enough, has to do with the very mechanism that protects depositors in case a bank should fail: deposit insurance. The Federal Deposit Insurance Corporation (FDIC), created by Congress in 1933, protects depositors from incurring losses in the event of a bank failure. Prior to the creation of the FDIC, banks had been plagued by capricious, rumor-fed, panicked runs on deposits. Congress believed that federal deposit insurance would prevent this from happening. Once people understood that their deposits were safe even if the bank failed, fear of bank failure would no longer lead inexorably to panicked withdrawals and bank runs.

There is a problem, however, with the FDIC. Fully insuring deposits leads to a costly side effect known as moral hazard. Once a person is insured, the insured has an incentive to take on more risk than he or she otherwise would. This is why, for example, fire and auto insurance policies have deductibles. With deductibles, the insured has more incentive to pick up old paint cans and drive cars more carefully. Deposit insurance in most cases doesn't require a "deductible" of banks and depositors, thereby providing incentive to profit-maximizing banks and depositors to assume an immoderate amount of risk. And, as the numerous bank failures in the 1980s and early 1990s demonstrated, the taxpayers were left to pay the hefty bill for bailing out the failed banks.

What can be done to counteract the effects of moral hazard? Two primary alternatives to the current system have been offered. The first is to privatize the deposit insurance system. The second is to reduce the scope of the current system and thus rely more on the markets to discipline the banking system. But Ricki Helfer, one-time chairman of the FDIC, argued that any change in the current deposit insurance system would be itself risky: "We know federal deposit insurance works to stabilize the banking system in times of great stress. Can we be sure that another approach will work as well?"

The Japanese banking crisis of 1997–98 was, in part, a matter of moral hazard. The big banks relied on the longstanding Japanese banking policy of *too-big-to-fail*—the belief that the Japanese government would always rescue the big ones. As a result, they were less inclined to deny loans to their traditional corporate borrowers, even though the loans financed unsound investments. The inevitable happened. Hokkaido Takushoku, Toyo Shinkin, Hyogo, and Hanwa, among 14 other large banks in Japan failed, triggering the largest financial collapse in Japan since 1945.

Hey, that's my money in there. Is it safe?

CONSIDER

Why is it that deposit insurance, created to reduce the risks of banking, actually may increase that risk? In your opinion, is it the role of government, the free market, or both to regulate how banks operate?

The FDIC, which is a government-owned corporation, was created in 1933, too late for the tens of thousands of people who had been financially wiped out by bank failures in the Great Depression. Today, bank failures still occur, but their sting has been localized and most of the depositors are compensated.

Bank Audits and Examinations

But why close the barn door *after* the horse escapes? While the FDIC is the insuring institution that protects depositors against bank failure, why allow a financially unsound bank to get into trouble in the first place?

Bank audits and examinations are designed to prevent bank failure. The task of auditing and examining falls upon the FDIC, which regularly evaluates bank performance to detect weaknesses in operations. Recognized early enough, serious damage can be avoided.

Still, Banks Do Go Under

Bank failures used to be rare events, as we see in Exhibit 1. Only 43 of approximately 14,000 banks failed in the 1950s. That is less than 5 failures per year. The number per decade increased during the 1960s to 63, and to 83 during the 1970s. Still, there were less than 10 failures per year. Bank failures fell to zero in 2005, the first time since 1962.

In the early 1980s, however, bank failures became somewhat more visible. In 1981 alone, 48 banks went under. Many were small, located in rural communities, but a few were large banks involving substantial sums of money and numbers of people. Why the increase?

The Bank Debacle of the 1980s and 1990s
These bank failures reflected the severe shocks that troubled specific sectors of our real economy, such as agriculture. High farm prices in the 1970s misled many farmers. As land values rose to reflect these higher prices, farmers brought more land under cultivation, bought more machinery, and expanded production. They financed these activities with loans extended to them by accommodating banks that accepted the price-inflated land as collateral for the loans.

The honeymoon ended abruptly when farm prices and land values collapsed in the early 1980s. Many farmers, caught between falling farm prices and rising costs, went bankrupt and defaulted on their bank loans. Some unfortunate banks, whose loan portfolios were heavily involved in these farm ventures, could not survive.

What about the large urban banks? A few, with heavy international loan commitments, were hit as well. The circumstance that led to their problems was the unexpected slide in oil prices. Anticipating that oil prices in the 1980s would remain as high as or even higher than they were in the 1970s, major U.S. banks loaned billions to oil export economies such as Mexico and Venezuela. The banks anticipated that the oil economies would have no problems meeting their interest and loan obligations.

EXHIBIT 1 Bank Failures: 1930–2005

For years after the Great Depression the number of bank failures was insignificant. All that changed in the 1980s. With the recession of 1982, bank failures increased dramatically. In 1988 alone there were more bank failures than the combined total for the previous 25 years.

But they guessed wrong. The dramatic fall in oil prices during the 1980s sent many of the oil exporters, even Saudi Arabia, into deficit. Mexico alone incurred a $100 billion bank debt, and after the first shock of falling oil prices, it was forced to seek new terms on its loan repayments. To press its need for loan restructuring, Mexico even threatened default.

Mexico was not alone among the less-developed economies seeking relief from excessive loan obligations. Brazil, for example, had to borrow extensively during the 1970s to finance its trade deficit—the difference between its imports and exports. Here, too, oil was at the heart of the problem. OPEC's ability to increase the price of oil tenfold during the 1970s accounted for the dramatic rise in Brazil's oil import bill and, consequently, in its trade deficit.

The connection between the plight of agriculture and the oil industry and bank failures shows up clearly in the numbers of bank failures by state for the latter part of the 1980s. Look at Exhibit 2.

Note the large number of failures in the oil-based economies of Texas, Oklahoma, and Louisiana. Look also at bank failures in the farm states of Iowa, Kansas, Florida, California, and Minnesota. The disproportionality is striking, isn't it?

Even the Mighty Fall Perhaps the most dramatic bank failure of the 1980s was the demise of Chicago's Continental Illinois Bank. The cause of its death: overdosing on high-risk loans. In one dramatic but fatal move, Continental enhanced its loan portfolio by buying up more than $1 billion in loans from the Penn Square Bank of Oklahoma City. Continental believed it was acquiring high-performing assets. In fact, the Penn Square loans were basically unsound. The loss was more than Continental could digest.

The FDIC took Continental over and, to everyone's surprise and the depositors' delight, announced it would cover *every* deposit, not just accounts under $100,000. It then tried to sell Continental to another bank. But even at bargain prices, no bank showed any interest. In the end, the FDIC invested billions of its own money to make the bank solvent once again.

Why didn't the FDIC just allow Continental to fold, as it did the smaller rural banks? Size was the difference. The FDIC's decision to keep Continental alive was made to protect the confidence people place in our banking system. In the view of the FDIC, Continental was simply too important a bank to be allowed to go under.

EXHIBIT 2   Bank Failures, Selected States: 1987–89

TEXAS	296	NEBRASKA	8	OHIO	2
OKLAHOMA	66	ARIZONA	7	ALABAMA	2
LOUISIANA	46	MISSOURI	7	IDAHO	1
COLORADO	30	ILLINOIS	6	KENTUCKY	1
KANSAS	19	MONTANA	6	MICHIGAN	1
MINNESOTA	19	ALASKA	5	MISSISSIPPI	1
CALIFORNIA	12	ARKANSAS	5	PENNSYLVANIA	1
IOWA	12	NEW YORK	5	OREGON	1
FLORIDA	11	UTAH	5	WYOMING	1

Source: Federal Deposit Insurance Corporation, Annual Report, 1989 (Washington, D.C., 1989), p. 11.

globalperspective

DEPOSIT INSURANCE, ASSURANCE-DÉPÔTS, TUTELA DEI DEPOSITI, PROTECCIÓN AL AHORRO BANCARIO, ETC., ETC.

It is no great surprise that the first deposit insurance scheme was born in the United States during the Great Depression of the 1930s. Necessity, an old adage goes, is the mother of invention. What *is* perhaps surprising is that for the following two decades, the United States remained the only country with such deposit protection. But the idea finally spread. Germany, Finland, and Canada introduced their own systems in 1966–67. Japan followed in 1971, followed by Belgium and Sweden in 1974. France and the Netherlands created their deposit insurance schemes in 1979–80 and Italy, a latecomer, followed in 1987. By 1995, all countries within the European Union were expected to have deposit guarantee schemes that met the minimum conditions with respect to types of coverage and eligible deposits. And more recently, many European countries that aspire to join the European Union—among them Hungary, Poland, Slovenia, and the Czech Republic—have adopted deposit insurance schemes of their own.

Many countries in Asia, Africa, and Latin America provide deposit guarantees. India adopted its system as early as 1962, long before most European countries. In the mid-1980s, countries such as Mexico, Chile, Venezuela, and Kenya introduced theirs.

The accompanying table compares the coverage provided to depositors in a randomly selected set of developed and developing countries.

Comparison of Selected Deposit Insurance Schemes

COUNTRY	TYPE OF DEPOSITS COVERED	COVERAGE (MEASURED IN $US)
BELGIUM	ALL DEPOSITS EXCEPT FOREIGN AND INTERBANK	$11,750
CANADA	DEMAND AND TIME DEPOSITS, PENSIONS	$40,000
FINLAND	ALL DEPOSITS	100%
FRANCE	DOMESTIC CURRENCY, INCLUDING INTERBANK	$57,840
GERMANY	MOST DEPOSITS EXCEPT INTERBANK	90%
HUNGARY	ALL DEPOSITS EXCEPT INTERBANK	$3,580
INDIA	ALL DEPOSITS EXCEPT INTERBANK	$640
IRELAND	DOMESTIC CURRENCY	80% OF 1ST $6,000
		70% OF 2ND $6,000
		50% OF 3RD $6,000
ITALY	ALL DEPOSITS EXCEPT INTERBANK	100% OF 1ST $100,000
		80% OF NEXT $400,000
JAPAN	DEMAND AND TIME DEPOSITS	$86,000
MEXICO	MOST DEPOSITS, INCLUDING FOREIGN CURRENCY	100%
NETHERLANDS	ALL DEPOSITS	$17,200
NORWAY	ALL DEPOSITS	NO LIMIT
PHILIPPINES	ALL DEPOSITS EXCEPT INTERBANK	$1,960
UNITED STATES	ALL DEPOSITS	$100,000

The Savings and Loan Debacle of the 1980s and 1990s What about savings and loan associations (S&Ls)? They, too, felt the sting of financial bankruptcy. Look at Exhibit 3.

Why the dramatic growth in S&L failures in the 1980s? Prior to the 1980s, S&Ls were busy providing long-term (20- to 30-year) mortgages to private homeowners. They had a virtual monopoly in the home mortgage market because government regulations prohibited banks from competing in that market and prohibited S&Ls from competing in any other. And because government also set ceilings on the

EXHIBIT 3   Thrift Failures: 1980–91

The combination in the late 1980s of banking deregulation, higher-risk loans made by the S&Ls, and outright S&L banking fraud led to the collapse of the S&L industry and the extraordinary number of S&L failures in the 1988–91 years.

interest rates that banks and S&Ls were allowed to pay depositors (Regulation Q), S&Ls enjoyed the spin-off effect of competing with banks for depositors at relatively low rates of interest, while making loans to homeowners at much higher mortgage rates. In other words, long-term private residential mortgage loans not only were fairly safe investments for the S&Ls, but were quite lucrative as well.

But deregulation of economic activity became the new focus of government policy during the 1980s and the undoing of the S&Ls. Among the industries affected by deregulation was banking. The deregulation created an open-season banking environment. Investment houses, such as Merrill Lynch, were allowed to compete with banks and S&Ls for depositors. They offered money market mutual funds at rates higher than those offered by banks and S&Ls. These funds gave depositors the best of two worlds: sound investments at attractive interest rates and the privilege of using these funds as checking accounts. To create a level playing field for banks and S&Ls, the government discarded Regulation Q so that banks and S&Ls now had the opportunity to raise interest rates to keep their depositors from switching to the competing investment houses. These events sealed the fate of many S&Ls.

Why? Because the S&Ls were locked into fixed long-term mortgage loans at rates that were often lower than the rates they now had to pay depositors. To recoup losses, they moved into new loan markets, such as speculative land development, that earned more, *but were much riskier* than the private residential home mortgage market they had once dominated.

Another factor contributing to the S&Ls' demise was the substantial fraud that crept into their deregulated banking environment. "Loans" were made to S&L management friends and families that, upon later investigation, amounted to outright theft. In the end, as Exhibit 3 shows, disaster struck. By 1987 a third of S&Ls had gone bankrupt.

What about their depositors? They were protected by the government-created FSLIC—Federal Savings and Loan Insurance Corporation—the S&L counterpart to the FDIC. But the extraordinary number of S&L failures during the 1980s and 1990s was too much for the FSLIC to absorb. The FSLIC itself was driven into financial crisis, forcing the government to enact the Financial Institutions Reform,

Recovery and Enforcement Act in 1989. The act established the Resolution Trust Corporation, which handles the disposal of all failed S&Ls. The act also transferred the defunct FSLIC's insuring functions to the FDIC.

Although the FSLIC (like the FDIC) was set up to provide depositors with some measure of security against S&L (or bank) failure, it is somewhat paradoxical that the FSLIC may have actually contributed to the S&L demise. Why? Because the S&Ls, having that FSLIC-backed security, had less incentive to prevent failure from occurring. That is, having the FSLIC insurance as a guaranteed safety net, they were more inclined to venture into high-risk loans that would not have been considered loanworthy otherwise.

CONTROLLING THE FINANCIAL INSTITUTIONS THAT CONTROL THE MONEY SUPPLY

Georges Clemenceau, the French statesman who served as war minister during the First World War, once remarked: "War is too important to be left to the generals." Had he looked at the banking system, he might well have added: "And the money supply is too important to be left to the banks."

Few economists would disagree. We have seen how the banking system, almost by magic, creates money.

But the relationship between the money that financial institutions are willing and able to create and the economy's need for the money is *not always* one-to-one.

Paradoxical as it may seem, it is when the economy most needs injections of money that the financial institutions are most reluctant to supply it. And only when the economy least needs it do they show a willingness—sometimes an eagerness—to offer money.

And that's a problem. In periods of prosperity—when prices, wage rates, interest rates, employment, and consumer spending are relatively high—banks, S&Ls, and credit unions feel confident in the economy's future and, therefore, in borrowers' ability to repay loans. Under these conditions, most bankers are eager to lend the maximum permissible. Such loan behavior, coupled to the money multiplier, creates maximum permissible supplies of money. But it is precisely in the heady times of prosperity, with the economy already at full employment, that maximum permissible money can push the economy into unintended inflation.

On the other hand, in periods of recession—when prices, wage rates, interest rates, employment, and consumer spending are relatively low—the financial institutions' expectations of the economy's future change from confidence to caution. Their loan policies, reflecting this change, become increasingly hesitant. Their concern now is to minimize loan defaults. They are more willing, then, to hold greater excess reserves. In other words, precisely when the economy could use more investment money, banks and other financial institutions are more inclined to forego the opportunities of creating money.

Frustrating, isn't it? The marvelous invention of modern banking allows us to create the money supply to promote maximum real goods production. Sometimes, however, it overindulges, and at other times it denies that supply and exacerbates the economy's bouts with inflation and unemployment.

If the financial institutions cannot be counted upon to create the proper money flows to foster economic activity with minimal inflation and unemployment, then perhaps *some* control over their control of the money supply is needed. That's where the Federal Reserve System comes in.

CHAPTER REVIEW

1. Fractional reserve banking is based on the idea that a bank need not keep all of its deposits on hand as reserves. Loans can be made based on deposits, with only a fraction of the deposits held as reserves. In this way, a bank can earn interest on loans while paying depositors interest for their deposits.

2. A fractional reserve banking system is able to create money. When a bank receives a new deposit, it can loan a portion of this deposit, leaving enough of the deposit on hand to satisfy the reserve requirement. The borrower spends the proceeds from the loan. These expenditures end up as a new deposit in a second bank. The second bank is able to loan a fraction of its new deposit. And in this way, a sequence of events occurs that causes the money supply to expand by a multiple of the original deposit.

3. The banking system can create new deposits equal to the initial demand deposit divided by the legal reserve requirement. The potential money multiplier is calculated by dividing 1 by the legal reserve requirement. The money supply may not expand to the extent determined by the potential money multiplier, because banks may elect to hold some of their excess reserves, people may not want to borrow, and not all the loans made find their way back into bank deposits.

4. The money creation process can run in reverse. When loans are paid back, checks are written on bank accounts, which decreases deposits and forces banks holding loans up to their legal reserve requirements to reduce their loans. The potential money multiplier can be used to calculate the extent to which the money supply will shrink as deposits decrease.

5. Banks sometimes fail when a large portion of the loans they have made are not repaid. When people learn of bank failures, they tend to become nervous about their own deposits and withdraw them. As deposits are withdrawn, loans must be called in, and the money supply shrinks. Serious bank failures can trigger waves of failures and drastic reductions in the money supply.

6. Federal deposit insurance is intended to assure depositors of the safety of their deposits, so they won't be easily inclined to withdraw their funds. Bank audits and examinations help improve faith in the banking system by making certain that banks operate according to sound principles and legislated regulations.

7. In spite of the FDIC and bank auditing on a regular basis, banks do fail sometimes. During the 1980s and the first years of the 1990s, bank failure rates rose significantly. Savings and loan associations also went through a difficult period during the 1980s as banks began to compete with them for customers in the home mortgage market. S&L failures were so extensive in the 1980s that a special government-sponsored corporation, the Resolution Trust Corporation, had to be established to dispose of the failed S&Ls.

8. If left to their own devices, financial intermediaries would tend to make downturns in the business cycle more pronounced and upturns more extreme. During a downturn, a bank or other intermediary is less likely to lend, for fear of not being repaid. The money supply shrinks as outstanding loans are repaid, causing the interest rate to rise and investment to fall. Thus, the downturn is made more severe. During an economic expansion, banks are more inclined to lend, which causes the money supply to grow more rapidly than it would otherwise, resulting in lower interest rates and more borrowing. As the economy approaches full employment, there is upward pressure on the price level.

KEY TERMS

Fractional reserve system	Financial intermediaries	Federal Deposit Insurance
Balance sheet	Potential money multiplier	Corporation (FDIC)
Legal reserve requirement	Excess reserves	

QUESTIONS

1. What is meant by the fractional reserve system? Why is it fundamental to modern banking?
2. Explain why the United States has a legal reserve requirement.
3. Explain why Canada gets by without a legal reserve requirement.
4. What is the potential money multiplier? Why is it called *potential?*
5. What are the three principal requirements for the banking system to create money?
6. What is the significance of calling the deposits you make in your checking account *demand deposits?*
7. Explain how a new demand deposit of $100 can potentially create $500 of new money if the legal reserve requirement is 20 percent.

8. If the legal reserve requirement is 50 percent, how much new money could the $100 deposit create?
9. How does a bank end up with excess reserves?
10. Suppose your neighborhood bank has no excess reserves and the legal reserve requirement is raised from 20 percent to 50 percent. What must it do to conform to the new requirement?
11. What can cause a bank to fail?
12. What has been the record of bank failures in the United States over the past 4 decades?
13. Which states have been hardest hit by bank failures? Why?
14. What role does the FDIC play in our banking system?

PRACTICE PROBLEMS

1. Suppose you land your first job with Columbia Records in New York City and, after your first week at work, you deposit $100 in your checking account at Chase Manhattan Bank. If the reserve requirement is 10 percent, show how your $100 deposit can create money. Illustrate the process by filling in the missing data for the cells through 5 stages in the following table.

BANK	DEMAND DEPOSIT	LOANS
CHASE MANHATTAN	$100	
CHEMICAL BANK		
HANOVER TRUST		
CITIBANK		
1ST NATIONAL BANK OF NY		

2. Suppose the Federal Reserve raised the reserve requirement to 50 percent. Show how that would affect the value of money creation through the first 5 stages of deposit and loan in practice problem 1.

BANK	DEMAND DEPOSIT	LOANS
CHASE MANHATTAN	$100	
CHEMICAL BANK		
HANOVER TRUST		
CITIBANK		
1ST NATIONAL BANK OF NY		

3. Using the potential money multiplier equation and the values in the following table, show what the initial deposit, the total money supply created (that is, initial deposit plus subsequent deposits), and the reserve requirement must be in each of 5 situations.

INITIAL DEPOSIT	RESERVE REQUIREMENT	TOTAL MONEY CREATED
$ 100	40 PERCENT	
	10 PERCENT	$1,000
$ 200		$1,000
$1,000		$1,000
$ 0	50 PERCENT	

Economic Consultants

Economic Research and Analysis by Students for Professionals

Steve Scariano graduated from the University of Toronto with a degree in journalism. After a brief stint with CJAD radio in Montreal, Steve was hired by CNN as a researcher in its news department. His first project is to write a primer for the network's business correspondents on banks and the banking system in the United States.

While Steve, a native Canadian, studied economics in college, he is unfamiliar with the intricacies of the U.S. banking system. He can write succinctly, but he desperately needs a refresher course on money and banking if he is to do the job well. He has heard great things about Economic Consultants, and he asked CNN to hire the firm to assist him. CNN has agreed. You are assigned the task of preparing a report for Steve that addresses the following issues:

© Image 100/Royalty-Free/CORBIS

1. What do banks do with the money deposited in their accounts, and how are banks interrelated?
2. Why are banks sometimes in financial trouble? Are such troubles inherent in the banking system? What safeguards can prevent banks from getting into trouble?
3. What role does government play in the banking system?
4. What sources are available to provide readers with up-to-date information on banking news?

You may find the following resources helpful as you prepare this report for Steve:

- **FDIC's Learning Bank** (http://www.fdic.gov/about/learn/learning/index.html)—The Federal Deposit Insurance Corporation (FDIC) educates the public about banks, banking, and the FDIC.

- **The Federal Reserve** (http://www.federalreserve.gov/)—The Federal Reserve provides a detailed description of its operations (http://www.federalreserve.gov/general.htm).

- **The Federal Reserve System's National Information Center (NIC)** (http://www.ffiec.gov/nic/)—The NIC has news, data, and information about banks.

- **The Fed: Our Central Bank** (http://www.chicagofed.org/publications/index.cfm)—The Chicago Federal Reserve bank publishes this pamphlet on the workings of the Federal Reserve.

- *American Banker* (http://www.americanbanker.com/)—*American Banker* is a journal providing banking and financial services information.

- *ABA Banking Journal* (http://www.ababj.com/)—*ABA Banking Journal* is an online magazine devoted to the banking industry.

- **Thomson Reuters** (http://www.thomsonreuters.com)—Thomson Reuters is now the publisher of Faulkner & Gray's line of banking journals and newsletters, many of which are available online.

- **Bankrate.com** (http://www.bankrate.com/brm/default.asp)—Bankrate.com regularly surveys 4,000 institutions in 50 states to provide current interest rates.

1. The three principal requisites for money expansion are
   a. FDIC, a fractional reserve system, and lenders.
   b. fractional reserve system, initial deposits, and borrowers.
   c. FDIC, initial borrowers, and the interest rate.
   d. fractional reserve system, interest rate, and lenders.
   e. assets, liabilities, and interest rate.

2. Suppose that the Gamehendge First National Bank has initial reserves of $4,000. If the legal reserve requirement is 15 percent, then the initial level of liabilities that the bank must have had is equal to
   a. $4,000.
   b. $600.
   c. $4,600.
   d. $3,400.
   e. $7,400.

3. If Betty secured a $5,000 loan from the First National Bank and then deposited the money in the Second National Bank,
   a. it would be listed as an asset with only the First National Bank.
   b. it would be listed as an asset with only the Second National Bank.
   c. it would be listed as an asset with both the First and Second National Banks.
   d. it would lead to a reduction in the money supply, since the same money is held in two separate locations.
   e. she would make a profit when the Second National Bank pays interest on all deposits.

4. What is the maximum amount by which the money supply can increase due to an initial deposit of $20,000 when the legal reserve requirement equals 25 percent?
   a. $60,000
   b. $25,000
   c. $20,000
   d. $65,000
   e. $100,000

5. Banks hold excess reserves
   a. when the rate of inflation is low.
   b. when the amount they loan out is less than they are permitted to loan out.

   c. to earn more money on their loans to customers.
   d. to put pressure on the Federal Reserve to raise the legal reserve requirement.
   e. so that the potential money multiplier will rise.

6. The government agency that protects deposits up to $100,000 in member banks is known as the
   a. federal government.
   b. Federal Deposit Insurance Corporation.
   c. Federal Savings and Loan Insurance Corporation.
   d. fractional reserve system.
   e. World Bank.

7. All of the following except one contributed in part to the large number of bank failures that occurred during the 1980s. Which one?
   a. Risky investments by banks
   b. Loans to oil-exporting countries
   c. Loans to developing countries
   d. Falling farm prices
   e. High interest rates

8. When deregulation of the banking industry occurred in the 1980s, savings and loan associations
   a. became more profitable due to less competition from the banking industry.
   b. faced more competition and thus underwrote riskier investments.
   c. chose to reduce the number of loans made to customers.
   d. increased interest rates and increased their excess reserves.
   e. chose to invest their funds in banks.

9. The bank's balance sheet is divided into
   a. assets and liabilities.
   b. currency and demand deposits.
   c. M1, M2, and M3 money.
   d. savings and loans.
   e. required reserves and excess reserves.

10. If the reserve ratio is 10 percent, the potential money multiplier is
    a. 1/10.
    b. 1.
    c. 9.
    d. 10.
    e. 100.

CHAPTER 12

THIS CHAPTER INTRODUCES YOU TO THE ECONOMIC PRINCIPLES ASSOCIATED WITH:

- The Federal Reserve System as a central bank

- Reserve requirements as a tool of monetary policy

- The discount rate as a tool of monetary policy

- Open market operations as a tool of monetary policy

- Money supply versus interest rate targets

- Countercyclical monetary policy

THE FEDERAL RESERVE SYSTEM AND MONETARY POLICY

If there is anything you've learned in school, in your home, and in your daily life, it is that we are a society that jealously cherishes individual freedom. Freedom to travel around. Freedom to say what we please. Freedom to take any job we like or none at all. Only *very* reluctantly do we agree to compromise our personal freedoms.

We resisted the regulation of our money system. We allowed private banks guided by the profit motive to determine their own reserve requirements, and we allowed interest rates, which govern the quantity of money demanded and supplied in our economy, to be determined in an unregulated market by an unregulated banking system.

© John Foxx/Getty Images

American resistance to control over our monetary system finally broke down in the early part of the 20th century. It had become unmistakably clear that unregulated banking had too often triggered financial panics that endangered the economic well-being of nearly everyone.

The core problem until the 20th century seemed to be the money system itself. From the very beginning of our republic through the 19th century, the overriding and chronic money problem we faced was the banks' *inclination to overissue currency*. The early and hesitant attempts by Congress to curb the banks' tendency to overissue repeatedly ended in failure and finally led to the enactment of the more assertive Federal Reserve Act of 1913. We need to consider the principal historical events that led to the creation of the Federal Reserve.

A GLIMPSE AT HISTORY

In colonial times, before banks printed their own **bank notes**, our money was simply a collection of foreign currencies. The French guinea, the Spanish pistole, and the English crown, among many others, circulated as money on the streets of New York, Baltimore, Philadelphia, and Boston. They were exchanged readily for each other. The nation had no currency of its own. But the system worked.

Bank note
A promissory note, issued by a bank, pledging to redeem the note for a specific amount of gold or silver. The terms of redemption are specified on the note.

Continental Notes

Then came the American Revolution. It transformed our money system as well as our political system. It took a great deal of money to recruit, equip, feed, and pay a growing army. The Continental Congress, pressed for funds, turned to the states. But little help was forthcoming. With no real alternative, the Continental Congress took to the printing presses.

Between 1775 and 1780, $242 million of Continental Notes, our first real money, were printed. Since Congress had no taxing authority, it turned to the printing press for money. As the quantity of Continentals multiplied, their value depreciated. In 1777 they traded 2 for 1 against silver. By 1779, as more and more of these notes came on the market, the exchange rate jumped to 20 to 1. By 1781, with printing presses still churning them out, the notes traded 1,000 to 1 against silver. Continentals were rapidly becoming worthless.

To create some semblance of monetary order, Thomas Jefferson proposed a new money, based on the Spanish dollar, metrically divisible, and *backed by gold and silver*. His recommendations were accepted by the Continental Congress, and in 1786, the government established the dollar as the country's unit of account.

The Chartering of State Banks

But who was to supply the dollars, and how many of them? In those pre-banking years, this simple money system became increasingly incapable of providing adequate supplies to satisfy our monetary needs. Farmers pushing westward needed credit to finance their homesteads. Businesspeople back east sought credit to expand their growing manufacturing operations. Some form of banking system that could offer credit was not only desirable but imperative.

In 1781 the Bank of North America, chartered by the State of Pennsylvania, was formed. It was the first bank in the United States to accept deposits and issue

State-chartered bank
A commercial bank that receives its charter or license to function from a state government and is subject to the laws of that state.

bank notes. Soon, other **state-chartered banks** sprang up—the Bank of New York and the Massachusetts Bank in 1784—each printing and issuing its own bank notes. Exhibit 1 traces the growth of state-chartered banks.

With each new bank issuing its own bank notes, with no established rule on specie backing, and with little discipline on what should be acceptable collateral, was there any way the government could have controlled the banks' control of the money supply? Should it have tried?

There were opposing views on this issue. Some felt that the states had the right to charter banks and that banks should have the right to issue notes unimpeded by the federal government. They were very reluctant to interfere with a bank's freedom to give or not give credit. They did not like the idea of creating a government monitor over the money supply. But others, no less supportive of a banking system, were still worried about the unconstrained behavior of the banks. They were fearful that these profit-making, state-chartered banks would end up overissuing bank notes, which would undermine the stability of the monetary system.

The First Bank of the United States

The worriers prevailed. In 1790, Congress proposed that the Bank of North America take on the functions of a central bank. Its primary function would be to control the economy's money supply. It would have the power to dictate what banks could and could not do. The idea of central banking was anything but novel. Central banks were already functioning in Sweden, England, and Holland.

An alternative proposal was put forward by Alexander Hamilton. Instead of the state-chartered Bank of North America acting as the country's central bank, he proposed the creation of a **nationally chartered bank** that would exercise control over the nation's money supply *and* be authorized to extend credit to the government.

Nationally chartered bank
A commercial bank that receives its charter from the comptroller of the currency and is subject to federal law as well as the laws of the state in which it operates.

Thomas Jefferson and James Madison opposed the idea of a central bank altogether because, in their view, establishing a central bank exceeded the powers of the federal government under the strict interpretation of the Constitution. Moreover, they were convinced that central bank activity would favor the already powerful northern merchant class.

Congress bought the Hamilton plan. In 1791, it set up the First Bank of the United States. The bank's charter was designed to expire after 20 years but could be renewed by Congress.

EXHIBIT 1   Growth of State Banks: 1784–1860 ($ Millions)

	NUMBER OF BANKS	CAPITAL
1784	3	$ 2.1
1801	31	22.4
1805	75	40.4
1811	88	42.6
1816	246	89.8
1829	329	110.1
1839	840	327.1
1859	1,476	402.9

Source: U.S. Bureau of the Census, *Historical Statistics of the United States, 1789–1945* (Washington, D.C.: U.S. Government Printing Office, 1949), pp. 261–263.

Actually, the First Bank of the United States performed reasonably well. It served as the government's fiscal agent and even succeeded in dampening the inclination of the state-chartered banks to overissue notes. How? Since many of the state bank notes found their way to the First Bank, the bank could present the notes to the state banks for payment in gold or silver. Aware of this prospect, the state banks became more careful about issuing bank notes in excess of their gold and silver.

The Second Bank of the United States

And yet in 1811, when the time came to renew the First Bank's charter, Congress declined to do so. The advocates of states' rights won out. Over the next five years, the number of state-chartered banks almost tripled, from 88 in 1811 to 246 in 1816. Left without a central bank's restraining influence on the issuance of bank notes, bank note depreciation and fraud became commonplace. By 1814, most banks had suspended specie payment; that is, they would no longer convert paper bank notes into gold and silver. Would you put your gold into such a bank?

It didn't take Congress long to regret having disposed of the First Bank. It became painfully clear that something had to be done to stabilize the money supply. The answer, just five years after the demise of the First Bank, was to establish the Second Bank of the United States. This time, Congress gave the national bank the right to issue its own notes. These soon became the most widely accepted currency in the nation, preferred to the less-trusted notes of the state-chartered banks.

When the Second Bank took on the task of making specie payment in exchange for its notes, it confronted strong regional resistance. Many state banks in the West and South catered to the unrestrained money demands of farmers, merchants, and land speculators. Many banks ended up holding excessive quantities of overvalued real estate collateral that they, in turn, used to fuel their bank note issues.

Recognizing the weakness of these issues, the Second Bank pressed for sounder specie backing. The southern and western banks balked, viewing this pressure as discriminatory. Animosity toward the Second Bank intensified when it instructed northern banks not to accept bank notes from the southern and western banks that could not back their currency with gold and silver.

Like the First Bank, the Second Bank had a laudable performance record. And like the First, it was abandoned. When Andrew Jackson, an opponent of central banking, was reelected to the presidency in 1832, the Second Bank's constitutionality was an election issue, and its fate was virtually sealed. Jackson shifted Treasury funds from the Second Bank back to state banks, which undermined the Second Bank's ability to control the issuance of notes by state banks. By 1836 it had become just another bank in Pennsylvania.

From the demise of the Second Bank as a central bank until Congress passed the National Banking Act in 1864, the economy's money supply was once again left in the hands of the state banks. And once again, unsound loans and overissuing of notes led to an unhealthy climate of unreliable money. The Civil War pressured Congress to rediscover central banking.

The National Bank Act

The cost of the Civil War pushed Congress far beyond its financial capabilities. The steady outflow of specie from the Treasury made it impossible for it to continue buying back its notes. Congress reluctantly allowed the Treasury to begin to print money. The Treasury printed Greenbacks, so called because of the ink used on the back side of the notes. They became the economy's most common, but rapidly depreciating, currency.

on the net

Review the National Bank Act (http://www.law.cornell.edu/uscode/12/38.shtml).

Once again, the government faced two classic problems: how to provide itself with the financial resources it needed to carry on the affairs of government and, at the same time, stabilize the monetary system. This time, it came up with a novel idea that ultimately was legislated in 1864 as the National Bank Act.

The idea was to develop a national banking *system*. The act created a new office, comptroller of the currency, housed in the Treasury, which chartered national banks. A national bank had to buy Treasury bonds equal to one-third of its capital, and could issue notes only in proportion to its Treasury bond holdings.

Now how do you reestablish people's confidence in the banking system? Banks were no longer allowed to accept real estate as collateral for loans, nor lend more than 10 percent of the value of their capital stock to any single borrower. Also, each bank was required to provide financial reports to the comptroller of the currency and was subject to periodic bank audits.

To encourage state banks to switch over to the national system, the comptroller levied a 10 percent annual tax on state-chartered bank note issues. This was a steep tax, but there wasn't a rush to conversion. For one thing, not all state-chartered banks could afford the minimal capital required to obtain a national charter. As a result, state-chartered and nationally chartered banks coexisted within the banking industry.

The National Bank Act did tighten the money supply, but it was by no means the banking industry's panacea. It could not stem the credit expansion that banks generated by holding each other's deposits. This practice of credit expansion heightened the banking system's volatility.

For example, in winter, when farmers' demands for funds were relatively weak, country banks would deposit some of their reserves in the larger city banks to earn interest. Counting these deposits as their own reserves, the city banks would create new loans.

Then came spring. Farmers, now ready to get back into the fields, needed money for seed and equipment. The country banks, ready to service farmers, withdrew their winter deposits from city banks, leaving them with much-depleted reserves. There was nothing city banks could do but call in outstanding loans. At times, these wholesale shifts of deposits touched off financial panics and recessions.

The Knickerbocker Trust Disaster

The 1907 Knickerbocker disaster was the straw that broke the camel's back. Both state and national banks, along with mushrooming financial trusts, were caught up in a whirlwind of speculative loans. In October, frightened depositors looked in horror at the collapse of the Knickerbocker Trust Company, a highly reputable and seemingly sound financial institution. The thought in everyone's mind—as it would have been in yours—was, Who's next? Panic spread. People ran to their banks to withdraw their deposits, and hard-pressed banks in turn scrambled for liquidity by calling in outstanding loans. Investment projects, in various stages of incompletion, were suspended. Sound businesses, drained dry of credit, were forced into bankruptcy. The result was almost instant recession.

Once again, Congress was forced to intervene. This time, with Knickerbocker still fresh in mind, Congress broadened its concerns from simply coping with the chronic problems of overissue of bank notes and inadequate collateral to addressing a newly perceived menace, the overreach of powerful financial trusts. The response came in the form of the Federal Reserve Act of 1913.

THE FEDERAL RESERVE SYSTEM

The Federal Reserve Act of 1913 created the **Federal Reserve System**, commonly referred to as **the Fed**. Why the Federal Reserve *System* and not the Federal Reserve *Bank?* The Fed was designed as a system because Congress wanted a decentralized central bank. The decentralization was essentially geographic, reflecting people's desire for regional monetary independence.

The need for such regional autonomy has since dissipated, but the structure remains intact. The Fed's structure is simple. It consists of 12 district Federal Reserve banks, each serving a region of the country. The larger district Federal Reserve banks have smaller branches. Under this arrangement, a bank in a specific district would use its own district Federal Reserve bank as its central bank. In this way, banks in Omaha, Nebraska, or Ocala, Florida, would not have to depend upon banking decisions made in New York. Exhibit 2 maps the geographic domain of the 12 district Federal Reserve banks and their locations.

Who Owns the Fed?

Unlike the Bank of Canada, the Bank of France, the Bank of England, and other central banks in democratic market economies, the Federal Reserve System is not owned by the government. Although created by and responsible to Congress, the Fed pursues an independent monetary policy that at times can conflict with government's economic policy. For example, the government may be pursuing a stimulative fiscal policy (lower taxes, increased government spending), while the Fed may be more interested in controlling inflation.

Who owns the Fed, then, if not the government? Each district Federal Reserve bank is owned by its member banks. Each member bank contributes 3 percent of

Federal Reserve System (the Fed)
The central bank of the United States.

check your ✓ **understanding**

Why was the Fed designed as a decentralized central bank?

EXHIBIT 2   The Geography of the Federal Reserve System

— DISTRICT BOUNDARIES
— STATE BOUNDARIES

NOTE: ALASKA AND HAWAII
ARE IN THE TWELFTH DISTRICT

● RESERVE BANK CITIES
★ BOARD OF GOVERNORS OF THE
   FEDERAL RESERVE SYSTEM

its capital stock to the Federal Reserve bank in its district, and another 3 percent is subject to call by the Fed.

Of the 9,988 banks in the country, fewer than 3,000 are chartered nationally; the rest remain state chartered. You can identify some national banks just by name. The Chicago First *National*, the First *National* of Toledo, the First *National* of Fresno, and so on. Look at Exhibit 3.

All nationally chartered banks must be members of the Fed. The state-chartered banks can choose to be members. Even though less than 17 percent of the state-chartered banks are members of the Federal Reserve System—1,003 out of 6,133 banks in 2000—they, along with nationally chartered banks, hold more than 50 percent of all deposits in our economy.

The Fed's Purpose and Organization

The Federal Reserve System's main charge is to safeguard the proper functioning of our money system. It is the watchdog of our money supply, our interest rates, and the economy's price level.

Obviously, if it's going to do that job at all, it has to monitor the activities of the nation's financial institutions, anticipate what they will do, prevent them from doing some things, and encourage them to do others, and all this without interfering too much in the conduct of private business. Impossible? Some people think so. But these same people are unable to imagine a modern economy operating without a central bank.

The Fed's organizational structure is not very complicated. Look at Exhibit 4.

The nucleus of the Federal Reserve System is its Board of Governors, which meets in Washington, D.C. The board consists of seven members, appointed by the president and confirmed by the Senate. Each serves a 14-year term. Appointments are staggered, one every other year, so that no president or Senate session can manipulate the composition of the board. This also ensures continuity. The chairman is a board member appointed by the president to a 4-year term. Chairmen may be reappointed, but they cannot serve longer than their 14 years on the board.

Typically, chairmen are reappointed for lengthy periods that overlap Republican and Democratic presidents. Paul Volcker, who preceded chairman Alan Greenspan, was appointed by Jimmy Carter and twice reappointed by Ronald Reagan. Greenspan continued into the George W. Bush administration and retired in February 2006. Ben S. Bernanke succeeded him as the current Federal chairman. Much earlier, William McChesney Martin chaired through the Eisenhower, Kennedy, and Johnson administrations and even into the early Nixon years.

EXHIBIT 3   National Banks, State Banks, and Total Deposits ($ Billions)

	NUMBER OF BANKS	ASSETS
TOTAL	9,988	$7,268
COMMERCIAL BANKS	8,375	6,064
NATIONAL	2,242	3,363
STATE (FED MEMBER)	1,003	1,573
STATE (NONFED MEMBER)	5,130	1,126
SAVINGS INSTITUTIONS	1,613	1,204

Source: Federal Deposit Insurance Corporation, *Statistics on Banking, 2000* (Washington, D.C.: FDIC, 2000).

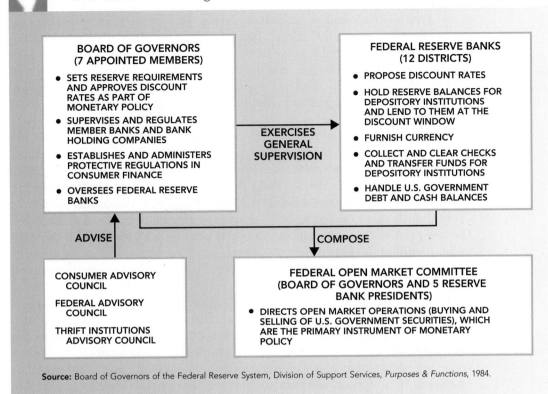

EXHIBIT 4   Organizational Structure of the Federal Reserve System

> **BOARD OF GOVERNORS**
> **(7 APPOINTED MEMBERS)**
> - SETS RESERVE REQUIREMENTS AND APPROVES DISCOUNT RATES AS PART OF MONETARY POLICY
> - SUPERVISES AND REGULATES MEMBER BANKS AND BANK HOLDING COMPANIES
> - ESTABLISHES AND ADMINISTERS PROTECTIVE REGULATIONS IN CONSUMER FINANCE
> - OVERSEES FEDERAL RESERVE BANKS

EXERCISES GENERAL SUPERVISION

> **FEDERAL RESERVE BANKS**
> **(12 DISTRICTS)**
> - PROPOSE DISCOUNT RATES
> - HOLD RESERVE BALANCES FOR DEPOSITORY INSTITUTIONS AND LEND TO THEM AT THE DISCOUNT WINDOW
> - FURNISH CURRENCY
> - COLLECT AND CLEAR CHECKS AND TRANSFER FUNDS FOR DEPOSITORY INSTITUTIONS
> - HANDLE U.S. GOVERNMENT DEBT AND CASH BALANCES

ADVISE   **COMPOSE**

> **CONSUMER ADVISORY COUNCIL**
>
> **FEDERAL ADVISORY COUNCIL**
>
> **THRIFT INSTITUTIONS ADVISORY COUNCIL**

> **FEDERAL OPEN MARKET COMMITTEE**
> **(BOARD OF GOVERNORS AND 5 RESERVE BANK PRESIDENTS)**
> - DIRECTS OPEN MARKET OPERATIONS (BUYING AND SELLING OF U.S. GOVERNMENT SECURITIES), WHICH ARE THE PRIMARY INSTRUMENT OF MONETARY POLICY

Source: Board of Governors of the Federal Reserve System, Division of Support Services, *Purposes & Functions*, 1984.

More often than not, board members are drawn from within the banking industry, either from commercial banks or from the Fed's district banks. Volcker, for example, came from the New York Fed. Such ties to banking experience can be both helpful and problematic. While members must understand the complexities of banking, their strong connection to the industry seems to compromise, for some people, their role as guardians of the public trust. But not all come from banking. Arthur Burns, for example, left his professorship at Columbia University to serve as chairman during the late Nixon years. And in 2006, Ben Bernanke, a Princeton professor, succeeded Alan Greenspan as chair of the Fed.

District Federal Reserve Banks   The 12 district banks make up the second tier of the Fed's structure. Each is managed by a board of nine directors, six chosen by the member banks of the district, the other three appointed by the Board of Governors. The president of each district bank is selected by its nine directors.

Federal Open Market Committee   The nerve center of the Fed is its **Federal Open Market Committee**. Here, the Fed exercises monetary control over the economy through its open market operations (discussed next). The 12-person committee is composed of all seven members of the Board of Governors, the president of the New York Fed, and four district presidents who rotate voting on the Committee. Each member has one vote. Its composition reflects the power of the board, the unique position held by the New York Fed, and the Fed's commitment to regional representation.

Federal Open Market Committee
The Fed's principal decision-making body, charged with executing the Fed's open market operations.

The Fed as Money Printer

The Fed has a monopoly on printing our paper currency. Occasionally, others try it, but typically they end up in federal prison. The actual printing presses are located in Washington, D.C. There, the U.S. Bureau of Engraving and Printing prints up stocks of Federal Reserve bank notes in various denominations for each district bank. These are stored until the district banks call for specific quantities.

Until they are actually used by the district Federal Reserve banks, the notes are just so much printed paper (actually, cloth—75 percent cotton and 25 percent linen). They are not counted as part of the money supply. But once the district Feds put the printed paper into circulation by transferring it to their member banks, the printed paper becomes currency. How much currency we have at any one time, then, is determined by the wishes of commercial banks and especially by the public.

We all know what currency looks like. All dollar bills are Federal Reserve notes, representing the Fed's liability. Each bears a seal—placed to the left of George Washington on the $1 bill—identifying the district bank that issued it. The fine print on the seal spells out the particular district bank, but a large letter makes identification easier.

Exhibit 5 matches the letter markings on the seal to specific district Federal Reserve banks.

Check the seals on your own dollar bills. How many different district Federal Reserve bank notes do you have? Chances are that out of five notes in your wallet, two or three will be different bank issues. How do you suppose the San Francisco Fed's note ends up in a Boston wallet? Or a Kansas City Fed's ends up in Dallas? We are an open, active, and wide-ranging economy. When you can fly from Los Angeles to New York in less than six hours, it doesn't take long for currency to travel across the country.

The Fed as the Bankers' Bank

The Federal Reserve System is often called the bankers' bank because it provides specific services to its member banks that in some respects are like the services banks provide to us. For example, member banks can create their own accounts at the Fed, allowing them to deposit and withdraw their funds on demand. They

EXHIBIT 5   Identifying Letters and District Banks

LETTER	FEDERAL RESERVE BANK OF
A	BOSTON
B	NEW YORK
C	PHILADELPHIA
D	CLEVELAND
E	RICHMOND
F	ATLANTA
G	CHICAGO
H	ST. LOUIS
I	MINNEAPOLIS
J	KANSAS CITY
K	DALLAS
L	SAN FRANCISCO

can even borrow from the Fed, just as we borrow from banks. The Fed provides them with check-clearing services and, of course, with currency.

Holding Reserves

As you know, banks are obligated to keep some fraction of their demand deposits in reserve. But they can also hold reserves in excess of the reserve requirement set by the Fed. Suppose that the Paris First National Bank (PFN), a member of the Federal Reserve System, with $1,000,000 in demand deposits, holds $300,000 in reserve, $200,000 more than the 10 percent legal reserve requirement.

What does it do with the $300,000? Some of it, say $75,000, stays in Paris in PFN's vaults. The remaining $225,000 is sent to Dallas, where it is deposited in PFN's account at the Dallas Fed, just as you deposit money in your account at your own bank. PFN can always add to or subtract from its account at the Dallas Fed.

Providing Banks with Currency and Loans

Suppose PFN finds that its depositors are demanding much more currency than it has available in Paris. What does it do? It simply calls the district Federal Reserve bank in Dallas. The Dallas Fed ships the currency in an armored car (or mails it—insured, of course!) to PFN and deducts that amount from PFN's deposits at the Dallas Fed.

If, on the other hand, PFN discovers that the amount of currency it has on hand is abnormally large, it can transfer some of it to the Dallas Fed. The Fed then simply credits PFN's account with that amount. This is the same process you go through with your bank.

Now suppose the PFN wants to make a loan to Shara Gingold but has no excess reserves it can draw upon. It holds only the legally required reserves. Are PFN and Shara out of luck? Not necessarily. PFN can borrow from the Dallas Fed just as we can borrow from banks. If the Dallas Fed decides to make the loan to PFN, it charges PFN an interest rate on the loan—called the **discount rate**—just as we are charged an interest rate on bank loans. Obviously, the discount rate charged to PFN is lower than the rate of interest PFN charges Shara if Shara is to get the loan.

Why is the Fed so generous? These Fed loans to member banks provide the Fed not only with a means to service member banks, but also with a means to control what banks do.

Discount rate
The interest rate the Fed charges banks that borrow reserves from it.

Clearing Banks' Checks

Suppose Brian Mosley, watching David Letterman on TV one night, sees a Rock Classics commercial for five Billy Bragg CDs and decides to get them. He writes a check for $49.95 on his bank, the First National of Cincinnati, FNC, and mails the check to Rock Classics in Athens, Georgia. He expects the CDs in six weeks.

Exhibit 6 traces the sequence of bank transactions that Brian triggers with his $49.95 check. Two days after it is mailed, Brian's check arrives in Athens. Rock Classics deposits the check in its account at the First National Bank of Athens, FNA. Rock Classics's account at FNA is richer by $49.95.

It never occurs to Rock Classics that FNA would refuse Brian's check. But why not? Why should an Athens bank accept a check drawn on a bank in Cincinnati? How does the Athens bank collect the $49.95 from Cincinnati?

Here's where the Federal Reserve System comes in. FNA transfers the check to its district Federal Reserve bank, the Atlanta Fed, for deposit. FNA now has an additional $49.95 on deposit at the Atlanta Fed, and the Atlanta Fed now has Brian's check. What does the Atlanta Fed do? It wants to be reimbursed. After all, its liabilities to FNA just increased by $49.95.

The Atlanta Fed transfers the check to the Cleveland Fed and informs the Interdistrict Settlement Fund in Washington about the transfer. The fund credits the Atlanta Fed's account at the fund by $49.95—the Atlanta Fed is now reimbursed—and debits the Cleveland Fed's account at the fund by $49.95.

EXHIBIT 6   Bank Transactions Triggered by Brian's Purchase

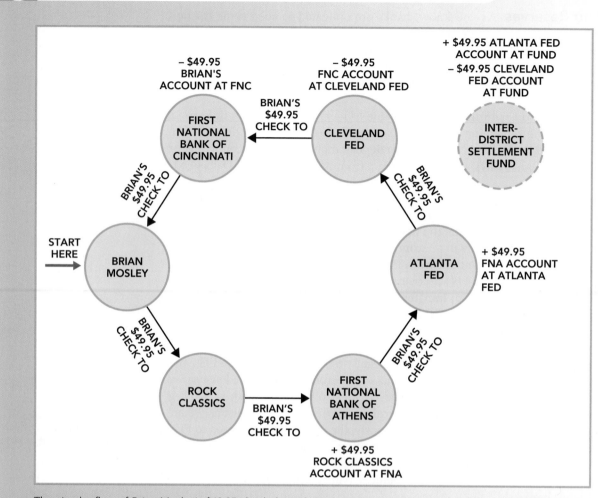

The circular flow of Brian Mosley's $49.95 check through Rock Classics, the First National Bank of Athens, the Atlanta Fed, the Cleveland Fed, and the First National Bank of Cincinnati.

on the net

Browse the New York Fed's Fedpoints (http://www.newyorkfed.org/aboutthefed/fedpoints.html), in particular those that address how the Federal Reserve controls the money supply: "Reserve Requirements" (http://www.newyorkfed.org/aboutthefed/fedpoint/fed45.html), "Discount Rate" (http://www.newyorkfed.org/aboutthefed/fedpoint/fed18.html), and "Open Market Operations" (http://www.newyorkfed.org/aboutthefed/fedpoint/fed32.html).

What does the Cleveland Fed do? It deducts $49.95 from the First National Bank of Cincinnati's account with it. The FNC, in turn, gets reimbursed by reducing Brian Mosley's account by $49.95. The trail ends with the cancelled check sent back to Brian.

Imagine how busy the banks, the district Feds, and the fund must be on any banking day. Millions of accounts in banks, at the district Feds, and at the fund are in a state of constant change. The Fed processes over 30 billion of these migrating checks each year, serving millions of people and businesses. It is hard to imagine how our economy could survive without such an arrangement.

CONTROLLING THE MONEY SUPPLY

As we noted earlier, a primary function of the Fed is to control the money supply. Focusing on the flow of money in the economy allows the Fed to exercise some control over the economy's price level, interest rates, and level of employment. What the Fed hopes to achieve by all this control activity is the promotion of the

global perspective

CANADA CHOOSES A ZERO RESERVE RATIO

Zero reserve requirement.

Do we really need speed limits in school zones? After all, don't you think drivers can gauge for themselves what a safe speed is and adjust their speed accordingly? Do we really need the speed zones, police surveillance, and the court system to administer child safety?

Think about your own behavior. Would you race through a school zone at 70 MPH? What about 40 MPH? What about 30 MPH? Feeling uncomfortable? Many do speed by at 30 MPH, confident that they are in control. But, unfortunately, some are not. Many have never experienced the fright of having to brake quickly to avoid hitting a child chasing another in traffic or coming upon a young teenager darting out between two parked cars to fetch a ball. The difference between 20 MPH and the 30 MPH that some drivers think reasonable may end up being the difference between life and death.

Why, then, do people drive through schools zones at 30 MPH? Most are anxious to get to where they're going as quickly and safely as possible. It's a judgment call, and sometimes, safety gets compromised.

What have speed limits to do with the banking industry's reserve ratios? Everything. The reason central banks impose reserve requirements on the industry is pretty much the reason we impose speed limits in school zones. Even though most bankers are reasonable people and appreciate the seriousness of ending a banking day with negative balances, many push their luck too far by holding insufficient cash reserves. It's hard to resist. After all, every dollar held in cash reserve means a dollar less of loans, and it is the loan not the cash reserve that generates profit for the bank. The higher the reserve ratio, the more opportunities for profit making are lost. You see the problem, don't you? Bankers know, as you do, the necessity to safeguard against negative balances but, like old mother Hubbard, at times their cupboards are bare.

How do we overcome that problem? Is there a "perfect" or "correct" reserve ratio? What about imposing a 100 percent reserve ratio? It would certainly create the most effective safeguard against incurring negative balances. But a 100 percent ratio completely undermines the banking system's ability to create loans and deposits that fuel the economy's real growth. What's "correct" about that? If a 100 percent ratio is less than preferred, what specific ratio is preferred? The fact that ratios vary from country to country suggests that the preferred ratio is a matter of central bank judgment and judgments of commercial banks in the industry, as well. Some prudent banks may actually choose to hold more reserves than the minimum

required by the central bank. But many other banks in the same economy would squeeze their cash reserves to the legal minimum and whine about having to hold that much.

What would be the banking industry's preferred minimum? Zero, of course, and some countries—Canada, United Kingdom, Switzerland, Australia, and New Zealand—have actually moved to a zero reserve requirement. Their zeros contrast with the rather broad range of reserve ratios shown in the economies of Exhibit A.

The ratio differences in Exhibit A reflect, in part, the past experiences of different countries with varying ratios as well as their differing views on monetary prudence versus sympathy for banking industry's profit margins. In some cases, such as Canada's, its history of ratios reflects a series of its central bank's ratio changes. Look at Exhibit B.

At one time, the Canadian reserve ratio was as high as 50 percent, but since the mid-1950s, its ratios were more akin to those of other industrial economies and not too dissimilar from those in the United States. Its high was 12 percent in 1968, and its low hit zero in 1994. As Exhibit B shows, the variability in the Canadian ratio over time also reflects shifts in direction, increasing in some years and decreasing in others.

Why did Canada opt for zero in the 1990s? Because, its central bank and the Canadian commercial banking industry contend, cash reserve requirements are really

Exhibit A: Reserve Ratios for Selected Monetary Systems (1998)

COUNTRY	REQUIRED MINIMUM RESERVE RATIO (%)
UNITED STATES	3 TO 10
GERMANY	1.5 TO 2
FRANCE	1
ITALY	15
RUSSIA	9 TO 14
ARGENTINA	10 TO 20
BRAZIL	55
INDIA	8.5
ISRAEL	8
SINGAPORE	3

Continued

Exhibit B: History of Canada's Reserve Ratio from 1954 to 1994

BEGINNING PERIOD	PERIOD ENDING	RESERVE RATIO (%)
	JULY 1954	5
AUG. 1954	JUNE 1967	8
JULY 1967	JAN. 1968	0.5 INCREASE PER MONTH TO 12
FEB. 1968	FEB. 1981	12
MAR. 1981	AUG. 1984	0.25 REDUCTION EVERY 6 MONTHS
SEPT. 1984	JUNE 1992	10
JULY 1992	JAN. 1994	REDUCE AT MONTHLY INTERVALS TO 0
JAN. 1994		0

unnecessary and actually detrimental to the health of the banking industry, the borrowing firms, and Canadian economic performance.

Unnecessary? What about safeguards against ending days with negative balances? How do banks deal with the financial embarrassment of not having sufficient reserves to transact daily banking business? In cases of end-of-day negative balances, the Bank of Canada comes to the commercial banks' rescue. It lends overnight reserves at a predetermined rate—aligned with prevailing short-term money market rates—to the reserve-starved bank. As far as the banks

are concerned, holding either positive or negative balances always entails some cost; interest they are obliged to pay to the Bank of Canada in the case of negatives, and interest forfeited in the case of positives. But these costs, they argue, are preferred to those associated with having to meet greater-than-zero reserve requirements. Canadian banks try to come as close as possible to zero daily balances. A tough chore in a world of uncertainty, but having the Bank of Canada available as their "reserve source of last resort" makes it the lesser of the two evils.

economy's stability and growth. Look at Exhibit 7. It depicts the way the Fed can influence real GDP, that is, engage in countercyclical policy.

Look at the sequence of events that occurs when money supply increases. First, an increase in the money supply from M_1 to M_2 causes the interest rate to

EXHIBIT 7   From Changes in the Money Supply to Changes in Real GDP

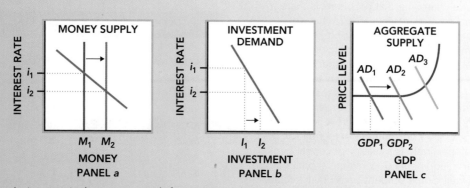

An increase in the money supply from M_1 to M_2 lowers the interest rate from i_1 to i_2. This fall in the interest rate raises investment spending from I_1 to I_2, which shifts the aggregate demand curve from AD_1 to AD_2. As a result, real GDP increases from GDP_1 to GDP_2.

fall from i_1 to i_2. That fall in the interest rate causes the quantity demanded of investment to increase from I_1 to I_2. Finally, the increase in investment spending shifts the aggregate demand curve from AD_1 to AD_2, which increases the level of real GDP in this illustration.

Of course, what goes up can come down. By reversing policy on the money supply, the Fed can engineer a decrease in the price level. How? Imagine aggregate demand at AD_3. By decreasing the money supply, the interest rate rises, investment falls, and aggregate demand falls, causing the price level to fall. As you see, the Fed's key to controlling GDP and the price level—the heart and soul of **countercyclical monetary policy**—is controlling the money supply.

How does the Fed control the money supply? It relies upon three instruments: reserve requirements, the discount rate, and open market operations.

Changing the Legal Reserve Requirement

By lowering the **reserve requirement**, the Fed can trigger a new series of additional loans and deposits throughout the banking system. For example, lowering the reserve requirement allows banks to make more loans. More borrowers mean greater real production in the economy.

If the Fed wants to curb production, it can increase the reserve requirement and restrict loans and thereby decrease the money supply. In this way, the economy's money supply can be expanded or contracted at the Fed's discretion. In times of recession, the Fed can lower the reserve requirement. In times of full employment and inflation, it can raise it. But there's a hitch to its effectiveness. Even if the Fed lowers the reserve requirement to increase the money supply, there is no guarantee that the money supply will increase. Why not? Because it depends upon whether borrowers are willing to take up the new loans that the Fed now makes available. If borrowers, for their own reasons, choose not to borrow, then the Fed can lower the legal reserve requirement all it wants without changing the money supply by one penny.

The legal reserve requirement set by the Fed applies not only to banks, but also, since the enactment of the Depository Institutions Deregulation and Monetary Control Act of 1980, to savings and loan associations and credit unions, whether or not they are state or nationally chartered or members of the Fed.

Exhibit 8 shows that the reserve requirement imposed on banks by the Fed depends on the size of a bank's total deposits.

Although the Fed's ability to change the reserve requirement would seem to be an effective tool to control money supply, it is rarely used. Why not? Because it creates uncertainty that banks prefer to avoid. For example, every time the Fed

Countercyclical monetary policy
Policy directives used by the Fed to moderate swings in the business cycle.

Reserve requirement
The minimum amount of reserves the Fed requires a bank to hold, based on a percentage of the bank's total deposit liabilities.

on the

The Federal Reserve maintains current and historical data on aggregate reserves for banks (**http://www.federalreserve.gov/releases/H3/**) and interest rates (**http://www.federalreserve.gov/releases/H15/update/**).

check your ✔ understanding

Why isn't the reserve requirement a preferred tool of monetary power?

✋ **EXHIBIT 8** Reserve Requirements (July 2006)

BANKS WITH CHECKING ACCOUNT BALANCES	PERCENTAGE OF CHECKING ACCOUNT DEPOSITS
$0 TO $7.8 MILLION	0
$7.8 TO $42.8 MILLION	3
MORE THAN $42.8 MILLION	10

Source: Board of Governors of the Federal Reserve System, *Federal Reserve Bulletin* (Washington, D.C., July 2006).

applied perspective

HOW THE INTEREST RATE ON GOVERNMENT SECURITIES IS DETERMINED

Suppose one of your friends wanted to borrow $1,000 from you. Admittedly, that's a lot of money and you probably have dozens of other ideas concerning the disposition of the $1,000. Lending it to a friend—even a good friend—would probably not rank very high. But suppose your friend offered to pay you a 10 percent rate of interest. You quickly calculate the interest payment at $100 per year. Not bad at all. And why not help a friend. You agree. Your friend writes an IOU, stipulating the rate of interest and the date when the $1,000 loan will be repaid. It's signed and delivered. You hold the IOU (your friend's security), and he gets the $1,000.

Suppose the borrower is not a friend but the United States government. It comes to you with the following proposition: If you lend me $1,000, you will receive a 10 percent rate of interest each year. The government may not be your buddy, but its $100 interest payment each year is as good as anyone's $100.

Good idea? Many people think so, which is why many people—perhaps yourself included—hold government IOUs or securities. Have you ever wondered who in the government actually borrows the money and how the rate of interest—5 percent, 10 percent, or whatever percent—is determined?

The government borrower is the Department of the Treasury. That department actually offers a variety of federal government IOUs or securities, which include T-bills (the T stands for Treasury), which are offered with 3-, 6-, or 12-month maturities, T-notes with maturities ranging from 2 to 10 years, and T-bonds whose maturities exceed 10 years.

The interest rate? Government offers these securities hoping to pay as low an interest rate as possible. Makes sense, doesn't it? If you borrowed money by offering your own IOUs, wouldn't you want to pay as little as possible? The lenders to government (that is, the buyers of government securities), on the other hand, hope to collect as high an interest rate as possible. That makes sense too.

Well, what rate of interest does the government actually end up paying, and how is that rate determined? Here's where the securities auction comes into play. The government's T-bills, T-notes, and T-bonds are offered for sale at auctions conducted by the Federal Reserve Banks. How does that work? Consider the weekly auctions of 3- and 6-month T-bills.

Buyers of these T-bills are ordinary people like yourself, large financial institutions, and dealers who specialize in government securities. To accommodate these different types of buyers, the government permits two different kinds of bids—or offers to purchase—called competitive and noncompetitive tenders.

- *Competitive tenders:* These bidders, principally the professional dealers in government securities, will buy T-bills only if the T-bills yield an interest rate at least as attractive as a rate they can obtain elsewhere in the securities market. These dealers make their competitive bids specifying how many T-bills they want to buy and the interest rate they wish to receive. These are closed and secret bids. The government, seeking to pay the lowest possible rate, will first accept bids from those dealers willing to buy the T-bills at the lowest interest rate submitted, then the next lowest, and so on until the government has sold the amount of T-bills it wants to sell that week. Competitive bidders who tendered a bid at a comparatively too-high rate will end up with no T-bills. That's the nature of competition.
- *Noncompetitive tenders:* People who want to buy T-bills without the hassle of competitive bidding can submit noncompetitive bids, indicating how many they want to buy at the average rate of interest determined by the competitive bidders. These noncompetitive bids typically account for no more than 5 percent of the total dollar value of T-bill sales, but they make up a large majority of the buyers. They are the nonprofessional buyers, much like you.

raises the requirement, it forces banks to contract outstanding loans. This can be highly disruptive to both banks and borrowers.

Changing the Discount Rate

The Fed can change the discount rate it charges banks who borrow from the Fed. For example, if Paris First National's excess reserves are exhausted, it can approach the Dallas Fed for a loan. Suppose the Dallas Fed agrees. It charges PFN a discount rate, determined by the Fed. PFN will borrow from the Fed only if the

EXHIBIT 9   Change in the Dallas Fed's Accounts after Providing a $5,000 Loan to PFN

ASSETS	LIABILITIES
LOAN TO PFN +$5,000	RESERVE DEPOSIT OF PFN +$5,000

discount rate it is obliged to pay is less than the interest rate it charges its borrowers. The spread between these two rates determines the banks' eagerness to borrow from the Fed.

If there is a recession and the Fed wants to encourage banks to provide loans in the economy, it lowers its discount rate. On the other hand, if the economy is inflationary, the Fed wants to restrict bank lending. It does so by raising the discount rate.

How are the Fed's loans to banks transacted? See, in Exhibit 9, how the accounts of both the Dallas Fed and PFN change after a $5,000 Fed loan is made to PFN.

In making the loan to PFN, the Dallas Fed simply creates a $5,000 deposit in PFN's account. That's potentially *new* money that never existed before. *The Fed brought it into being by simply changing its assets and liabilities.* The PFN, with $5,000 added to its total reserves, can now make additional loans, the amount depending upon the reserve requirement. Exhibit 10 shows how the Dallas Fed's loan affects PFN's account.

If the reserve requirement is 20 percent, then PFN's new $5,000 reserve allows PFN to loan out $4,000. That *may* trigger a series of deposits and loans throughout the banking system that could potentially raise the economy's money supply by

$$\$5,000 \times \frac{1}{.20} = \$25,000.$$

What do discount rates look like in the real world? How frequently do they change? Look at Exhibit 11.

As you see, the Fed is very much disposed to change its discount rate. Changes are sometimes as frequent as weekly. These changes not only affect the percentage spread that banks earn on a Fed loan, but also, no less important, reflect the Fed's thinking about the money supply. That's important information to banks, perhaps enough to make them reconsider their own loan behavior.

Engaging in Open Market Operations

The most effective and frequently used tool the Fed has at its disposal to change the economy's money supply is its **open market operations**—that is, its buying and

Open market operations
The buying and selling of government bonds by the Federal Open Market Committee.

EXHIBIT 10   Change in PFN's Accounts after Receiving a $5,000 Loan from the Dallas Fed

ASSETS	LIABILITIES
RESERVES AT THE FED +$5,000	BORROWING FROM THE FED +$5,000

EXHIBIT 11   Federal Reserve Bank of New York Discount Rates, 1990–2008
(Selected Dates)

Rates for short-term adjustment credit. For rates applicable to other types of discount window credit, see source. See also Historical Statistics, Colonial Times to 1970, series X, pp. 454–455.

DATE	RATE	DATE	RATE
MAY 1, 2008	2.25	NOV. 16, 1999	5.00
JUNE 29, 2006	6.25	NOV. 17, 1998	4.25
JUNE 30, 2004	2.25	JAN. 31, 1996	5.00
JUNE 25, 2003	2.00	FEB. 1, 1995	5.25
NOV. 6, 2002	0.75	NOV. 15, 1994	4.75
NOV. 6, 2001	1.50	JULY 2, 1992	3.00
MAY 19, 2000	6.00	DEC. 18, 1990	6.25

Source: Federal Reserve Bank, New York, July 2008.

selling operations in the government securities market. The Fed's operating rule is simple: It buys government securities on the open market when it wants to increase the money supply and sells some of its government securities when it wants to reduce the economy's money supply.

The nerve center of the Fed's securities buying and selling activity is located in its Federal Open Market Committee (FOMC), which issues directives to the securities trading desk at the Federal Reserve Bank of New York. Suppose the FOMC wants to increase the money supply and decides to buy $10 million of government securities. Where would it find the security sellers? Who are they?

If you owned government securities, wouldn't you be willing to sell them if the Fed met your price? Suppose you owned a $1,000 government bond and discovered that the Fed was willing to pay $1,100 for it. Would you sell? You may not be the only one who would take the deal. Many corporations and most banks own government securities for the same reason you do; they pay interest. And like you, they will sell their interest-bearing securities if the price is right.

The market price of government securities is determined, like the price of most goods, by buyers and sellers operating in the market. The securities market is described as *open* because securities holders and would-be securities holders freely negotiate the prices of all securities.

The FOMC enters the securities market to purchase $10 million of securities. Suppose the Paris First National Bank decides to sell $10 million of the securities it owns. Exhibits 12 and 13 trace the effect of the sale on the Fed's and PFN's accounts.

PFN transfers $10 million of its securities to the Fed. The Fed now owns them. Look at the Fed's new asset position. It has increased by $10 million. However, the securities are hardly a gift. The Fed pays for the securities by adding $10 million to PFN's reserves at the Fed. This appears as a $10 million increase in the Fed's liabilities to PFN.

What about PFN? Exhibit 13 describes the change in its accounts.

EXHIBIT 12   Change in the Fed's Accounts after Buying $10 Million
of Securities from PFN ($ Millions)

ASSETS	LIABILITIES
GOVERNMENT SECURITIES +$10	PFN'S RESERVE +$10

EXHIBIT 13 Change in PFN's Accounts after Selling $10 Million of Securities to the Fed ($ Millions)

ASSETS	LIABILITIES
GOVERNMENT SECURITIES −$10	NO CHANGE
RESERVES AT FED +$10	

Note the change in PFN's asset position. Before, it held $10 million in interest-bearing government securities. It now holds, instead, $10 million in excess reserves at the Fed. *These new excess reserves can be used by PFN to support $10 million in additional loans.*

That's precisely why the Fed went on the open market to buy the securities. It wanted to increase the economy's money supply. If sufficient numbers of borrowers can be found, the $10 million of increased reserves at PFN will trigger ($10 million × 1/0.20) = $50 million more in deposits throughout the banking system. That's a $50 million increase in the economy's money supply. And that's precisely what the Fed had in mind.

But suppose the Fed bought the $10 million of securities from individuals, not from PFN. Would it change the results? Yes, but only slightly. Let's trace the sale of these securities by supposing, for simplicity's sake, that only one person, Maria Snarski, sold the securities to the Fed.

What happens now? Maria sells her $10 million of securities on the open market. The Fed buys them. She receives a check, made out by the Fed, for $10 million. She deposits the check in her account at PFN.

What does PFN do with it? Look at Exhibit 14.

Maria's $10 million deposit increases PFN's assets and liabilities by $10 million. PFN sends the $10 million check to the Fed for collection. The Fed credits PFN's account at the Fed by $10 million. We see this recorded in Exhibit 15.

The increase of $10 million in reserves allows PFN to loan out $8 million—rather than $10 million as in the previous example—and begin the process of money creation throughout the banking system. As you see, that process occurs whether the Fed buys securities from the bank directly or from individuals like Maria.

check your understanding

Why does the Fed buy government securities?

EXHIBIT 14 Change in PFN's Accounts after Maria Sells $10 Million of Securities ($ Millions)

ASSETS	LIABILITIES
CASH RESERVES +$10	DEMAND DEPOSITS +$10

EXHIBIT 15 Change in the Fed's Accounts after Buying $10 Million of Securities from Maria ($ Millions)

ASSETS	LIABILITIES
GOVERNMENT SECURITIES +$10	PFN'S RESERVES +$10

EXHIBIT 16 Change in PFN's Accounts after Buying $10 Million of Securities ($ Millions)

ASSETS	LIABILITIES
RESERVES AT FED −$10	NO CHANGE
GOVERNMENT SECURITIES +$10	

Now suppose the economy is in an inflationary phase and the Fed decides to reduce the money supply. How would it do it? It just reverses its open market operations. It *sells* securities instead of buying them. Banks, corporations, and individuals buy them from the Fed if the price is right. Let's suppose again that PFN gets into the act. This time it decides to buy securities from the Fed. What would it do? Look at Exhibit 16.

PFN writes out a $10 million check to the Fed. PFN pays for these additional securities out of its reserves (i.e., the Fed reduces PFN's reserves by $10 million). So far, the only change has been in the composition of assets PFN holds. With $10 million fewer reserves, PFN is not in a position to loan $10 million. This eliminates a series of loans and deposits that might have taken place throughout the banking system. The reduction in credit available to consumers and businesses is likely to reduce spending. Not a bad outcome if the economy is in an inflationary phase.

The results would be the same if Maria Snarski, Merrill Lynch, or Nike Corporation did the buying.

CONTROLLING THE INTEREST RATE BY MANAGING THE FEDERAL FUNDS RATE

While traditional tools of monetary policy—reserve requirement, discount rate, and open market operations—give the Fed considerable flexibility with respect to managing the economy's money supply, it has yet another monetary tool option at its disposal that allows it to exercise direct influence over the economy's interest rate and through it the economy's level of economic activity.

The Federal Funds Market

Its field of operation is the federal funds market, and the tool at the Fed's disposal is the federal funds rate. Here's how it works.

Suppose PFN, at the close of a brisk banking day, discovers that it is $100,000 short of the reserves the Fed requires it to hold. And suppose at the close of that same day, Paris Second National discovers that it holds $100,000 in excess reserves at the Dallas Fed.

Now PFN is legally bound to cover that deficit, and PSN is none too happy to have its $100,000 of excess reserves earning no interest. You know what PFN must be thinking. It must borrow to cover its $100,000 reserve deficit, but where does it find a lender? Paris Second National is thinking as well. Where does it find a borrower?

Obvious, isn't it? There are a lot of late-in-the-day, last-minute transactions going on at the Dallas Fed, where banks that need funds find banks that have excess funds, and vice versa. It's an awfully busy market when you consider—aside from PFN and PSN—the number of lending and borrowing banks that must be involved. That market is called—no surprise—the **federal funds market**, since these transactions take place at the Fed.

Federal funds market
The market in which banks lend and borrow reserves from each other for very short periods of time, usually overnight.

Here's what happens: A transaction is initiated by either a lender or borrower. The most common practice is for the lender bank with excess reserves at the Fed to authorize the Fed to debit its own reserve account at the Fed and to credit the reserve account of the borrowing bank. In this case, PSN authorizes the Dallas Fed to debit its account at the Fed by $100,000 and to credit PFN's account at the Dallas Fed by that same amount.

Of course, there's no charity involved here. Borrowers and lenders negotiate the price of the lending and borrowing in much the same way as any price is determined on any market. The price on this federal funds market is called the **federal funds rate**. The table below records selected changes in the rate from 1997 to 2008.

Federal funds rate
The interest rate on loans made by banks in the federal funds market.

Federal Funds Rate, 1997–2008

YEAR	RATE	YEAR	RATE
2008	3.25	2001	2.00
2006	5.25	2000	6.50
2004	1.25	1999	5.25
2003	1.00	1998	4.75
2002	1.25	1997	5.50

Source: New York Federal Reserve.

How the Fed Manages the Rate

Since the federal funds rate is determined by the many bank borrowers and bank lenders who make up this very competitive federal funds market, how can the Fed influence the rate at which these borrowers and lenders trade? It influences the rate by adding to or drawing down deposits held in the banks' accounts at the Fed. The operative tool is the Fed's open market operations.

Example: To lower the federal funds rate, the Fed will buy government securities on the open market. Its success will depend on the price it offers. The higher the price, the more willing will owners of securities be willing to sell. Among the owners are banks themselves. When banks sell securities to the Fed, the Fed pays for them by crediting their accounts at the Fed. In this way, the banks' deposits at the Fed increase, easing the demand pressure on the federal funds market. As a result, the federal funds rate falls.

To raise the federal funds rate, the Fed will sell government securities on the open market. Banks, among other purchasers, pay for them by drawing down their deposits at the Fed. In this way, fewer funds are supplied or made available on the federal funds market. As a result, the federal funds rate increases.

Why Manage the Rate?

The Fed ends up being a very significant but *indirect* player on the federal funds market. As it turns out, the federal funds rate is highly sensitive to the Fed's open market operations. But it still begs the question: Why would the Fed want to influence the federal funds rate?

The answer, as always, has to do with the larger economy. The Federal Reserve Act specifies that the Federal Open Market Committee should seek "to promote effectively the goals of maximum employment, stable prices, and moderate long-term interest rates." Movements in the federal funds rate have important implications for these goals. A fall in the federal funds rate stimulates economic growth. A rise in the rate curbs both growth and inflation.

This happens because banks take their signals from the federal funds market. Banks' loan and investment policies are guided by the federal funds rate. Interest rates that banks charge their clients—from small firms to large corporations—move in sync with the federal funds rate. After all, bank decision makers compare the federal funds rate with rates that are yielded in other investment markets.

THE FED'S ALTERNATIVE TARGET OPTIONS

Suppose you were chairing a Federal Reserve Open Market Committee meeting and the discussion turned to the high probability of undesirable increases in the price level. What becomes your line of attack? Do you focus on the money supply in order to control the interest rate or, instead, focus on the interest rate in order to control the money supply?

Both are workable strategies, but they are "either-or" options. They cannot be pursued at the same time. Which, then, is preferred? The Fed, by the way, has switched from one to the other, then back again. The limitations associated with each of the Fed's options are depicted in Exhibit 17.

Choosing the Money Supply Option

Look first at panel *a*. Suppose the Fed decides to target the money supply at S_1. It uses its tools—the federal funds rate, the reserve requirement, the discount rate, and open market operations—to create S_1. If the Fed believes that the demand curve for money is D_1, then it knows that the interest rate will be i_1. But the truth of the matter is that the Fed lives, as we all do, in a world of uncertainty. It doesn't *really* know the position of the demand curve for money, in which direction it may shift, or how often it shifts, even for the short run. For example, if after fixing the money supply at S_1, the money demand curve turns out to be D_2 or D_3 and not the D_1 curve the Fed anticipated, then the interest rate that results could vary between i_2 and i_3. That variation could create a new set of problems for the Fed. At, say, i_2, producers may want to invest more than the Fed anticipated or considers desirable. Simply put: *If the Fed chooses to target the money supply, it cannot at the same time control the interest rate.*

EXHIBIT 17   The Fed's Target Options

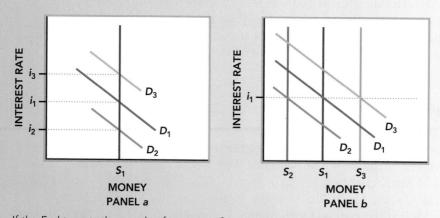

If the Fed targets the supply of money at S_1, as we see in panel *a*, then it cannot control the interest rate, for that depends on the positioning of the demand curve for money. If, on the other hand, it targets the interest rate at i_1, and if the demand curve for money is D_1, as we see in panel *b*, then the Fed loses control over the supply of money.

appliedperspective

THE U.S. BANKING SYSTEM IN A NUTSHELL

The following tables show the financial positions of all commercial banks in the United States and the Federal Reserve.

Loans represent more than 60 percent of the commercial banks' assets. Their holding of government securities adds another 13 percent, and their cash reserves of $667.3 billion are their third most important asset.

Deposits of $3,762.2 represent the single most important liabilities item. These consist of checking, savings, and large time deposits. Of the $1,220.3 billion bank borrowing, $372.5 billion are borrowings from banks in the United States.

U.S. Treasury securities represent the Fed's most important asset holding. When it engages in open market operations, it either adds to or sells off some of these securities. Loans to banks are related to its discount rate policy. Its gold holdings are holdovers from the 1930s, bought from the U.S. Treasury. Gold plays no role in monetary policy, nor does it have anything to do with the money supply. The Fed's own notes—Federal Reserve Notes, that is, our dollar bills in various denominations—represent more than 85 percent of its liabilities. The commercial banks' deposits with the Fed amount to $17.6 billion.

MORE ON THE NET

For more information about what the Fed offers to financial institutions, visit Federal Reserve Financial Services at http://www.frbservices.org/.

Consolidated Balance Sheet of U.S. Commercial Banks: September 2000 ($US Billions)

ASSETS		LIABILITIES	
CASH	$ 667.3	DEPOSITS	$3,762.2
LOANS	3,836.3	BORROWING	1,220.3
GOVERNMENT SECURITIES	807.3	OTHER	1,022.1
OTHER SECURITIES	518.5		
OTHER	175.2		
TOTAL	$6,004.6	TOTAL	$6,004.6

Balance Sheet of the Federal Reserve: September 2000 ($US Billions)

ASSETS		LIABILITIES	
GOLD	$ 11,046	FEDERAL RESERVE NOTES	$538,816
COIN	831	BANK DEPOSITS (RESERVES)	17,624
LOANS TO BANKS	372	U.S. TREASURY DEPOSITS	8,459
U.S. TREASURY SECURITIES	511,413	OTHER LIABILITIES AND	
OTHER ASSETS	61,963	NET WORTH	20,726
TOTAL	$585,625	TOTAL	$585,625

Choosing the Interest Rate Option

The Fed, instead, can choose to target the interest rate, allowing the money supply to take its course. We see the consequences of this option in Exhibit 17, panel *b*.

Suppose the Fed, using the federal funds rate, reserve requirements, discount rates, and open market operations, wishes to fix the interest rate at i_1. If the demand curve for money is D_1, then the money supply must be set at S_1 (quantity of money demanded equals quantity of money supplied in equilibrium). But what if the Fed guesses incorrectly and the demand curve for money is not D_1, but, say, D_2 or D_3? Now the money supply, to keep the interest rate fixed at i_1, must be S_2 or S_3. Once again, the Fed may confront problems it didn't anticipate; that is, it may end up with a money supply it really doesn't want. But it has no alternative. *By choosing to target the interest rate, it loses control over the money supply.*

Is There Really a Preferred Target Option?

You see the Fed's dilemma, don't you? *It faces an opportunity cost no matter which option it chooses.* But is the opportunity cost really debilitating? After all, even though the Fed loses some control over the interest rate once it targets money supply, *the interest rate still moves in the appropriate direction.* That is, any increase in the money supply, whatever the demand for money may be, lowers the interest rate. Conversely, any decrease in the target interest rate, whatever the demand for money may be, increases the money supply. *Correct directional movement counts!*

In other words, the Fed's countercyclical monetary policy works, whether it targets money supply or interest rates. And since the Fed is not entirely blind to the demand for money, the actual opportunity cost associated with either target may, except in very volatile times, be rather minimal.

What the Fed Ended Up Choosing

Over the years, the Fed has vacillated from fixing on one target to fixing on another. Through the decades of the 1950s, 1960s, and 1970s, the Fed kept an anxious eye on both but favored the interest rate target. That is, it used its discretionary powers over reserve requirements, discount rates, open market operations, and federal funds rate to make the money supply conform to a targeted interest rate. The linkages were understood and expected. GDP depends upon aggregate demand, which depends upon investment, which depends upon the interest rate.

But by 1980, with Paul Volcker as chairman of the Fed, the Fed's focus shifted to the money supply. Worried about persisting high inflation, the Fed's plan was to target money supply to bring inflation under control. It understood that the unavoidable consequence of lowering the money supply was rising interest rates. But in the 1980s, imbued with the ideas of monetarism, the Fed felt that higher interest rates were not only tolerable but desirable. After all, higher rates would reduce investment and aggregate demand, easing pressure on inflation.

The Fed's monetary target shifted once again in the 1990s. Chairman Alan Greenspan sought to bring interest rates down, ignoring the swing it might create in the money supply. The Fed hoped that lower interest rates would stimulate investment, aggregate demand, and real GDP. Inflation? It was now the lesser of the problems.

Ancillary Tools Available to the Fed

Aside from the big four—the reserve requirement, the discount rate, open market operations, and the federal funds rate—the Fed can exercise some additional control over the money market by controlling margin requirements on the financing of stock market purchases and by exercising moral suasion. But these are strictly the Fed's utility players in the major league game of money control.

Controlling Stock Market Margin Requirements
You've heard stories, haven't you, about the killings people make on the stock market? Sometimes, the lure of the market can be downright intoxicating, blurring our vision of reality. In truth, playing the stock market is about as reliable a way of getting rich quickly as playing the tables at Las Vegas or betting on the horses at Churchill Downs.

Here's how it's supposed to work. If you have real inside information (as many people suppose they do) or a strong sense of the market's moods (as many

applied perspective

PAST FED GOVERNOR MARTHA SEGER DESCRIBES HOW THE FOMC WORKS

QUESTION: You taught about the Fed in the classroom before joining it. Were there any differences between the Fed of economic textbooks and what you found when you actually became a member of the board?
SEGER: The biggest difference between the Fed as the textbook writers describe it and how it actually works is that it's just about a hundred times more tough to make the decisions. There isn't some cute little formula to use, even though the Fed has a tremendous computer system and 350 or so researchers with all sorts of Ph.D.'s in finance, economics, math, and econometrics. You can't just run some econometric model and have the policy answer pop out.

Making monetary policy is much more an art than a science—it's not a science at all.
QUESTION: Could you give us a little of the flavor of an FOMC meeting? Are the discussions heated or is there an air of calm deliberation? What goes on?
SEGER: At the beginning of the meeting, you have a report from Fed staffers on what's been happening to monetary policy since the last FOMC meeting. You get a chance to compare what the FOMC had told the staff to do with the actions it actually carried out.

Then there is a staff presentation on their view of the economic outlook. Then they would go around the table and everyone who is at the meeting—the seven members of the Board of Governors plus all 12 district bank presidents—gets a chance to ask a question of the staff about their forecast. During this period some of the participants may challenge the staff forecast. It's not heated, but I would say it's an open discussion, an open exchange of views, questions, comments. Then after that's done, they go around the table and people can give a little spiel on how they see the economy.

In addition to the discussions at the meeting, members are also given two books of materials, called the "Green Books," prior to the meeting with reports and analyses about the economy. They also receive the "Blue Book," which outlines monetary policy options.

© Royalty-Free/CORBIS

The only quiet moment at the Fed.

The "Blue Book" usually spells out three options: option A, option B, option C. Then one of the staffers in the monetary affairs section would make the presentation on those options and what you might get in terms of monetary growth and what would happen to the federal funds rate and other interest rates if you chose A, or you chose B, or C. Again, that's information, not always accurate, but still it was presented. And then there would be a discussion after that presentation by the members about the options and about the assumptions, and people would express their views about which ones they thought were most reasonable. And then we would have a break and go for coffee and doughnuts.

While we were relaxing, the chairman would go off with this staffer who was basically in charge of the "Blue Book," and they would prepare a proposed Directive for the group to consider. The Directive gives instructions to the Fed's staff for how to conduct open market operations until the next FOMC meeting. They would draft the Directive based on what they thought they were hearing from everybody. Then everybody else could talk about his or her views and then finally we would have an up or down vote on it. So that's basically what goes on.

MORE ON THE NET

Experience a Federal Open Market Committee meeting through a simulation (http://www.newyorkfed.org/education/fomcsim.html) created by the New York Fed.

Source: *The Margin,* Spring 1992.

more people feel they have), then speculating on the market is a nice, clean way of making money. For example, if you believe that the price of Xerox stock, now at $50 per share on the New York Stock Exchange, will reach $60 by this time next year, it pays to buy Xerox. If you bought $50,000 worth of Xerox, you would end up netting $10,000.

But how do you get your hands on $50,000? Here's the trick. Just go to Paris First National and borrow $40,000. Why would PFN loan you $40,000? Because you can offer the $50,000 Xerox stock as collateral on the $40,000 loan. All you have to put up of your own money, then, is $10,000.

If you have speculated correctly, you end up making $10,000 on a $10,000 personal investment. That's a cool 100 percent. Even adjusting for the interest on the $40,000 loan, that's a mighty fine percentage.

Where's the catch? Everybody in the stock market business knows that what goes up can come down. Suppose Xerox falls from $50 to $30 two months after your purchase. Your stock is now worth $30,000. Not only has your $10,000 expected profit evaporated, but PFN realizes it can recover only $30,000 of its $40,000 loan.

What does it do? PFN may choose to take the $30,000 rather than chance waiting for an upswing in prices. A speculative loss of $10,000, or even more, may not trouble a bank whose loan portfolios are basically sound. But if the bank's assets are dominated by an array of loans to stock market speculators, then even moderate downward movements in stock prices can do the bank in.

And if the banking system itself is heavily into loans supported by stock market collateral, then any downward movement in stock prices that frightens banks enough to sell off their stock collateral will drive stock prices down even further. It may not take much to trigger a stock market panic. That's precisely what happened in the stock market crash of 1929. When the dust clouds of that infamous October cleared, it was obvious that loans made on stock market collateral were as uncontrollable as a runaway locomotive on the downside of a mountain. As J. M. Keynes so aptly noted just a few years after the crash:

> Speculators may do no harm as bubbles on a steady stream of enterprise. But the position is serious when enterprise becomes the bubble on a whirlpool of speculation.

If it didn't make sense before, it certainly made sense after the crash that some control over the banking system's holding of stock market collateral was required. The Federal Reserve seemed to be the logical choice. The Fed was called upon to establish stock market **margin requirements**, the fraction of the stock's price that must be put up by the person buying the stock.

Margin requirement
The maximum percentage of the cost of a stock that can be borrowed from a bank or any other financial institution, with the stock offered as collateral.

The Fed reacted to the inflationary pressures built up during the war years of the 1940s by raising the margin requirement from 50 to 100 percent. In this way it dampened the enthusiasm of stock buyers who were bent on loan speculation. After all, by restraining bank loans, the Fed could deflate the pressures on inflation.

At other times — for example during the recessions of 1949 and again in 1953 — the Fed cut the margin to 50 percent to help bolster a lackluster economy. The reduced margin gave banks the green light to grant stock-supported loans. The Fed expected such loans to create new deposits, new money, and new jobs. Using margin requirements as a counter cyclical tool, the Fed raised and lowered the percentage several times, from a high of 90 percent in 1958 back to 50 percent in 1974. In 1984, the margins were set at 50 percent by Regulation T, which governs the credit extended to security brokers and by Regulation U, which governs credit to banks set the margin at 50 percent.

Moral Suasion
We have all used some form of moral suasion on friends and foes to promote a particular idea. How many times did you hear your high school teacher say before an exam: "No copying from your neighbor." Sometimes, this admonition would be followed by a threat: "Those found cheating will be suspended from school."

Did it work? Sometimes, on some people. The problem with relying on moral suasion is that in the final analysis it relies entirely on morality and persuasion. But that's what the Fed sometimes uses to encourage or discourage bank loans.

For example, the chairman of the Board of Governors may explain in a television interview that the Fed hopes banks show more restraint in providing consumer credit, because inflation is a problem. Sometimes these expressions of concern take the form of official Fed policy statements or direct appeals by way of letters to thousands of bank presidents.

Whatever its form, these pronouncements rely on voluntary compliance. They may seem weak as instruments of policy, but they are always supported by the unspoken threat that if moral suasion doesn't work, the Fed can always resort to more reliable instruments. Moral suasion, then, can be viewed as an omen of things to come. And banks take note.

THE FED'S COUNTERCYCLICAL MONETARY POLICY

Let's put the analysis of the Fed's operating tools into the context of the Fed's countercyclical monetary policy. When you think about it, the Fed and the government can be described as partners in a shock-absorbing business, protecting us against the bumps of unemployment and inflation. The government manages its activity through its budget, adding or cutting taxes and spending as the occasion warrants. The Fed works either directly through the banking system or indirectly through its open market operations.

Typically, the Fed and government work in unison, pursuing common goals. For example, when a recession hits, we would expect the government to run a budget deficit by raising the level of its spending or by cutting taxes, or perhaps both. At the same time and for the same reason, we would expect the Fed to reduce the reserve requirements, reduce the discount rate, and buy securities on the open market. All three activities are engineered to promote bank loans. After all, loans create jobs.

What about Fed and government policies during periods of full employment and inflation? Both have the tools to reverse their lines of attack. We would now expect government to create a surplus budget by cutting its own spending and raising taxes. At the same time and for the same reason, we would expect the Fed to raise the reserve requirements, raise the discount rate, and sell securities on the open market. In this way, banks would find it more difficult to loan, easing the inflationary pressures on the economy.

Exhibit 18 depicts the Fed's countercyclical monetary operations. Although there appears to be symmetry in the Fed's policies during the upswing and downswing phases of the cycle, in fact, there isn't. The Fed is more effective in curbing inflation in periods of prosperity than it is in promoting employment during a recession. Why? Because the Fed can prevent banks from loaning, but it can't force people to borrow.

check your ✔
understanding

Why is the Fed more effective controlling inflation than stimulating the economy?

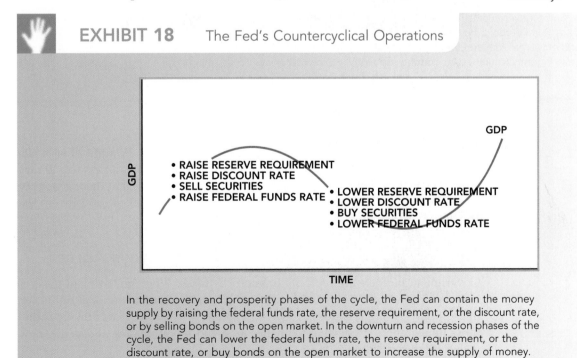

✋ **EXHIBIT 18**   The Fed's Countercyclical Operations

In the recovery and prosperity phases of the cycle, the Fed can contain the money supply by raising the federal funds rate, the reserve requirement, or the discount rate, or by selling bonds on the open market. In the downturn and recession phases of the cycle, the Fed can lower the federal funds rate, the reserve requirement, or the discount rate, or buy bonds on the open market to increase the supply of money.

interdisciplinary perspective

THE CASE OF THE MISSING CURRENCY

Interested in mysteries? According to the Federal Reserve, the quantity of currency in our 2003 M1 money supply is $646.4 billion. That's our dollar bills and coins. It's supposedly in our wallets, in our purses, in our pockets, in the glove compartments of our cars, in wall safes, in a hundred other places that we tend to keep (or misplace) currency. But it's not *all* there.

If we searched those places and added up the total currency found, it would turn out to be less than 25 percent of that $646.4 billion! That is to say, we can't account for approximately $500 billion of the $646.4 billion. It's like losing the Grand Canyon. So the mystery is: Where's the missing currency?

Economist Case Sprenkle of the University of Illinois went looking for it and his answer might surprise you. It's gone! It left the country! Our missing currency is in Argentina, in Russia, in the Middle East, in the Balkans, and in many of the developing countries. The Federal Reserve estimates that approximately 70 percent of our $100s and 45 percent of our $50s are held abroad.

How did it get there? And why is it there? Detectives look for motives in missing case files and so did Professor Sprenkle. *Why,* he asked, would foreigners want to hold our currency? Don't they have enough of their own? And if they need more, can't their central banks just print it? Why in the world would they want ours?

Here's a clue. Money is a medium of exchange, a standard of value, and a store of value. It's principally the store-of-value function that explains why U.S. currency is a preferred currency even in countries far removed from our borders.

Life is full of uncertainties. Some countries have histories of chronic economic, social, and political upheavals. Some governments have a history of printing money. A Russian ruble may buy a loaf of bread one day and only a half loaf the next. Why? Perhaps the Russian government succumbed to printing rubles by the bushel—inflation erodes the value of the ruble—or perhaps a radical and unexpected change of government threw Russian society into an abyss of uncertainty that undermined people's faith in Russia's future. Here's the point: Faith in any currency rests upon people's faith in the country's political and economic future.

It's sometimes hard for Americans to appreciate just how stable our currency is and the respect people everywhere have for it. Our political and economic institutions are founded in tradition and laws. Our Federal Reserve has a deserved reputation for safeguarding our currency. Also, the last time we had a revolution was in 1776. The dollar is a recognized safe haven.

If you lived in Argentina through its calamitous economic crises of the 1980s, 1990s, and in 2001, wouldn't you prefer to keep your wealth in U.S. dollars rather than in unstable Argentinean pesos? Or if you lived in war-ravaged 1990s Serbia, wouldn't you feel more secure holding dollars than Serbian dinars? The 1990–91 Gulf war had Iraqis and other Middle Easterners scrambling for U.S. dollars. The U.S. Treasury estimates that Saddam Hussein in 2003 had approximately $900 million in U.S. currency! If you travel abroad, rest assured that you can buy most anything with your dollars as with local currencies and that each of your dollars will be warmly received and most likely stored away.

© Image 100/Royalty-Free/CORBIS

One Benjamin Franklin to another: Where are we? What language are they speaking? It's not English.

Does it make sense? Imagine a college without a library. Wouldn't that make it difficult for students to learn? Suppose a library is built. Does access to a library guarantee that students will learn? The facilities may be there, but there is no way to ensure that students will use them. In the same way, the Fed can prevent the creation of loans, but it can't force loan creation.

The Fed and the Government Don't Always Agree

Government budgets are typically financed by taxes. When government decides to spend more, it can simply tax more. It enjoys that as a constitutional right. Yet, interestingly enough, it doesn't always exercise it. Instead, government sometimes finds it more convenient to finance its spending by creating and selling new government securities.

In the past decade, government has financed its $200 billion annual budget deficits principally by creating government securities and selling them, that is, by borrowing. The interest rate it must offer to attract securities buyers is no minor issue. As you would suspect, the government would much rather pay lower than higher interest rates.

But that's not how the Fed views ideal interest rates. It supports high interest rates when it wants to curb inflation, and it switches to supporting lower interest rates when it promotes employment.

There are times, then, when the Fed's interest rate policy clashes with the government's. During recession, the Fed may be working to lower interest rates so that borrowers will find it more attractive to take up bank loans, while the government, financing a deficit, may find it necessary to offer higher interest rates to sell its securities. Sometimes, their conflicting interests require a series of summit meetings to negotiate an acceptable interest rate strategy. In such cases, it is generally the pressing needs of government that win out.

A New Role for the Fed: 'Reluctant' Regulator

The desperate cry for financial help by major brokerage houses in 2007–08 — the collapsing Bear Stearns, for one—and by the two largest home mortgage lenders, Fannie Mae and Freddie Mac—who, together, owned or backed $5 trillion in mortgages, roughly half the nation's $12 trillion mortgage market — brought the Congress and the Fed into this housing-related turmoil.

Both Fannie and Freddie are government sponsored enterprises (GSE), meaning that government considers them so vital to our economic health that it *may* lend support financially if circumstances merit. The circumstances became ripe with peril during the housing crisis of 2007–08. The questions facing government and the Fed then were: How to handle this immediate crisis and how to guarantee that such a crisis did not recur.

Fannie and Freddie buy mortgages on the secondary market from banks and other financial institutions, pool them, and sell them as mortgage-backed securities to investors on the open market, The investors think they know a pretty good deal when they see it. And the deal seemed even sweeter because government was *thought* to back the securities. But it was a *thought* without substance. GSEs are private enterprises, not government owned or government guaranteed.

But to allow Fannie and Freddie to collapse in this downward spiraling housing market would be ruinous to the economy and for that reason alone, the government and the Fed decided not let them (and their investors) 'walk the plank.' The Fed announced in 2008 that it would bail out these giants by allowing them access to the Fed's enormous credit line in amounts needed to provide stability in the housing and financial markets.

This was a Fed venture never practiced before. And to make sure it won't be practiced again, the Fed insisted that it monitor the financial positions of the major investment banks, including Fannie and Freddie. That introduced a new and rather 'thick' layer of regulation, self-imposed on the Fed by the Fed with the consent of Congress. Not to insist on these regulatory powers would have been sheer folly for the Fed and for the taxpayers who ultimately pay for the bail out.

on the n e t

To ensure that Congress knows what the Federal Reserve is doing, the chairman of the Federal Reserve must make a semiannual report on economic conditions and the conduct of monetary policy (**http://www.federalreserve.gov/boarddocs/hh/**). This report is commonly known as the Humphrey-Hawkins testimony, named for the federal statute that requires it.

CHAPTER REVIEW

1. Colonial America's money was a mixed bag of foreign currencies. The Continental Note—the first authentic U.S. currency—was introduced during the American Revolution and, tied to the silver standard, become quickly devalued by overprinting. The first banks in the post-independence United States were state chartered, and their bank notes—serving as our new currencies—were also plagued by overprinting. The First Bank of the United States was

established to overcome the chronic instability in the supply and value of U.S. money.

2. Bowing to opposition from southern and western states, Congress did not renew the First Bank's charter, even though the bank was relatively successful in stabilizing the economy's monetary system. Its demise was followed by the rapid growth in state banks and a return to the undisciplined growth in the money supply. As a result of the ensuing monetary instability, the Second Bank of the United States was established. Like the First Bank, the Second Bank successfully promoted a stable financial environment and, again like the First Bank, was short-lived. The third attempt at bringing some form of control over the economy's monetary system came during the Civil War with the National Bank Act. This act was in place until the eve of World War I. The history of banking in the United States up to that time was marked by growing economic power without the direction of a central bank.

3. The Federal Reserve Act of 1913 created the Federal Reserve System, a decentralized central bank. It is composed of 12 district Federal Reserve banks, each owned by member banks in the district. Its main purpose is to provide the economy with an appropriate money supply consistent with a stable price level. It also issues the nation's currency and serves as the banker's bank.

4. To achieve its goals, the Fed uses 3 principal tools: the reserve requirement, the discount rate, and open market operations. To stimulate the economy, it can lower the reserve requirement, lower the discount rate, buy government securities on the open market, or use some combination of these actions. To check inflation, it can reduce the nation's money supply by raising the reserve requirement, raising the discount rate, selling government securities on the open market, or combining these actions in some way. By manipulating these money-supply-affecting tools, it can engage in countercyclical monetary policy during the different phases of a business cycle. The Fed also uses 2 minor tools to promote its monetary policy: stock market margin requirements and moral suasion.

5. The Fed recognizes that changes in the money supply affect the interest rate and, through the interest rate, the level of investment and the level of real GDP. If the Fed chooses to target money supply, it cannot, at the same time, target an interest rate, because it has no control over the demand for money. For the same reason, if it chooses to target an interest rate, it cannot, at the same time, target the money supply. At times, the Fed has focused on money supply targets, allowing the interest rate to vary according to its market-determined level, and at other times, it has focused on interest rate targets, allowing the money supply to vary.

6. The Fed tends to be more effective in controlling inflation during periods of inflation than in combating unemployment during periods of recession. On occasion, the Fed's monetary policy to control inflation has conflicted with the government's fiscal policy to combat unemployment.

KEY TERMS

Bank note
State-chartered bank
Nationally chartered bank
Federal Reserve System (the Fed)
Federal Open Market Committee

Discount rate
Countercyclical monetary policy
Reserve requirement
Open market operations
Federal funds market

Federal funds rate
Margin requirement

QUESTIONS

1. What were "Continental Notes" and "Greenbacks," and what did they—unfortunately—have in common?

2. The Federal Reserve System was designed as a decentralized central bank. Why?

3. When the Fed sells government bonds, the nation's money supply decreases. Explain how this works. To illustrate, you can construct your own bank transactions and changes in the assets and liabilities of the Fed and of banks.

4. What is the discount rate, and how can the Fed use it to control the nation's supply of money?

5. One way the Fed can increase the nation's money supply is by reducing the reserve requirement. Explain how this works. To illustrate, you can

construct your own bank transactions and changes in the assets and liabilities of banks.

6. Why is the Fed more effective in preventing the money supply from increasing than in increasing the money supply?

7. Suppose your bill for a seafood dinner in San Francisco came to $100 and you paid it with a check drawn on your bank, the First National Bank of Boston. Describe the circuit the check would take through banks and district Feds.

8. Who prints currency for whom? How does the currency finally make its way to the thousands of banks operating in the economy?

9. How does a bank's borrowing reserves on the federal funds market differ from borrowing from the Fed? Which interest rates are typically higher?

10. What has happened to the discount rate during the 2001–2003 period? What explains the change?

Economic Consultants

Economic Research and Analysis by Students for Professionals

Hans Gienepp runs one of the largest real estate agencies in Los Angeles, California. He recognizes, from his own practical experience, that changes in the interest rate and in the rate of inflation have affected his agency's sales. He also knows that the Federal Reserve is a major player in controlling interest rates and the price level, and even though he took a course in economics at college, he doesn't really understand how the Fed can exercise such influence.

He has decided that knowledge is money and has hired Economic Consultants to counsel him and his agents about the economics of the real estate industry. As a new member of the Economic Consultants team, you are assigned the task of preparing the report on the relationship between the Fed, the money system, and the real estate market. Hans specifically asked that your report include the following issues:

© Image 100/Royalty-Free/CORBIS

1. What is the Federal Reserve System, and what is its relationship to the commercial banking system? Is it a government agency?

2. How does the Fed influence interest rates and the economy's price level? Can Hans use this information to predict how interest rates and prices will behave in the short run? What kind of data would he need, and how accessible is it?

3. What kinds of materials are published by the Fed to address these issues, and how can Hans learn more about them?

You may find the following resources helpful as you prepare your report for Hans:

- *U.S. Monetary Policy: An Introduction* (http://www.frbsf.org/publications/ federalreserve/monetary/index.html)—The San Francisco Fed publishes this online booklet on how the Federal Reserve conducts monetary policy.

- *The Structure of the Federal Reserve System* (http:// www.federalreserve.gov/ pubs/frseries/frseri.htm)—This online pamphlet, created by the Federal Reserve, provides an introduction to the workings of the Board of Governors, the Federal Open Market Committee, district Federal Reserve banks, and the Board of Directors of the Federal Reserve.

- *The Federal Reserve System: Purposes and Functions* (http:// www.federalreserve.gov/pf/ pf.htm)—The Federal Reserve publishes this detailed description of what the Fed is and how it operates.

- *The Fed: Our Central Bank* (http://www.chicagofed.org/ publications/fedcentralbank/ fedcentralbank.pdf)—The Chicago Fed publishes this online pamphlet on how the Federal Reserve operates.

- **Fedpoints** (http://www. newyorkfed.org/aboutthefed/fed points. html)—Fedpoints, published by the New York Fed, provides discussion for over 40 aspects of the Fed's operations.

- **Federal Reserve Statistical Releases** (http:// www.federalreserve.gov/releases/)—The Federal Reserve releases daily economic statistics on interest rates, among others.

- **Fed Ed on the Web** (http://www.kc.frb.org/ fed101/)—Fed Ed is a directory of educational resources provided by the various district Federal Reserve banks.

1. Commercial banks, like the Paris First National in the text, have bank accounts as you do and make demand deposits as you do. Where are their accounts and where do they make those deposits?
   a. Not to keep their "eggs in one basket," they each make deposits in each other's bank.
   b. The banks have accounts (and deposits) with the government.
   c. The banks have accounts (and deposits) at the Fed.
   d. The banks have accounts at the Fed and deposits at the FDIC.
   e. The banks have accounts at the FDIC and deposits at the Fed.

2. When state-chartered banks first came into being, they
   a. all issued the same Continental Notes.
   b. were designed to coordinate and control the nation's money supply.
   c. were not permitted to earn profits.
   d. were originally backed by the Federal Reserve System.
   e. issued their own bank notes.

3. The most effective and frequently used tool the Fed has at its disposal is
   a. open market operations.
   b. the discount rate.
   c. the federal funds rate.
   d. the money supply.
   e. the legal reserve requirement.

4. The federal funds market is the market in which
   a. the government can finance its deficit budgets.
   b. banks can borrow from the Fed by paying the discount rate.
   c. district Federal Reserve banks can borrow from the central Federal Reserve bank.
   d. banks lend and borrow from each other for short periods of time.
   e. open market operations occur.

5. The Canadian banking system differs from ours in this respect:
   a. Canada has no central bank, the equivalent of our Fed.
   b. The Canadian Fed has ten district banks, that is, one in each Canadian province's capital.
   c. The Canadian Fed owns the Canadian commercial banks.
   d. There are no Canadian government bonds, so there is no open market operations in Canada.

   e. The Bank of Canada imposes no reserve requirement.

6. The membership of the Federal Open Market Committee consists of
   a. only the Board of Governors.
   b. only the 12 presidents of the Federal Reserve banks.
   c. the Board of Governors and five Federal Reserve bank presidents.
   d. the chairman of the Federal Reserve System and the 12 Federal Reserve bank presidents.
   e. five members of the Board of Governors and five presidents of Federal Reserve banks.

7. Responsibility for proposing discount rates
   a. does not fall under the jurisdiction of the Federal Reserve System.
   b. rests with the Board of Governors.
   c. rests with the Federal Advisory Committee.
   d. rests with the Federal Reserve banks.
   e. rests with the Federal Open Market Committee.

8. Which of the following actions by the Federal Reserve would lead to an increase in the money supply?
   a. Raising the legal reserve requirement
   b. Raising the discount rate
   c. Selling government securities on the open market
   d. Reducing the number of loans made to member banks
   e. Lowering the legal reserve requirement

9. When there is an increase in the discount rate,
   a. banks have less incentive to borrow from the Fed.
   b. the legal reserve requirement rises by the same percentage.
   c. the money supply increases.
   d. banks must keep on hand a greater percentage of their assets.
   e. interest rates fall.

10. If the Fed's policy is to target the money supply, then
    a. it cannot also control the rate of interest.
    b. the rate of interest is also held constant.
    c. it cannot do so through engaging in open market operations.
    d. it cannot do so through changing the legal reserve requirement.
    e. it cannot do so through changing the discount rate.

PART 4

Government and the Macroeconomy

Chat Economics. Tune into the conversation. It's about *your* course. Just change the names, and it's *your* campus, *your* classroom, *your* professor, *your* classmates, and *you.*

Carrying his lunch tray into the cafeteria dining area, Professor Gottheil spies a number of his students at a table, among them Claudia Preparata, Kim Deal, Charlie Dold, and Jon Kaufman, engaged in what seems to be a rather heated discussion. He joins them and listens.

....

CLAUDIA: So you think the government has no right to raise the tax on cigarettes?

CHARLIE: That's right. Why should smokers pay such an exorbitant tax on cigarettes? If they want to smoke, that's their business. If they want to eat candy, that's their business as well. But along comes government, poking its nose into our business. It interferes with our choices. It taxes us only a little on candy, but a heck of a lot on cigarettes. Why? I mean, why should government dictate what we do?

CLAUDIA: Are you saying that there are no occasions whatsoever in which society's choices should dominate the individual's?

CHARLIE: Stick to the issue of cigarettes. And I say: Yes, keep government out of my business.

CLAUDIA: What about speed limits? Should government not impose them? If I choose to drive 100 miles per hour through my neighborhood, should I have the right to do so?

CHARLIE: Now that's stupid! Who in their right mind would do that?

CLAUDIA: You're quibbling about numbers. Okay, let's try 50 miles per hour. If you think I'm so stupid, ask the police how many tickets they write for over-50-miles-per-hour speeding violations in 30-miles-per-hour zones. And remember, every speed zone and every ticket is government's way of controlling behavior. If you think police should write those tickets, I don't see how you could object to an exorbitant cigarette tax.

KIM: Look, you guys are arguing about whether the government has the right to discriminate when taxing. That's only one side of the government-interfering-in-my-life coin. How about its spending? Why should government provide billions in welfare?

CLAUDIA: Are you against space exploration?

KIM: No, I think it's legitimate. I just don't want government passing my money around to other people. Let them work for it like I do.

CLAUDIA: Well, some people don't want government passing their money around for space shots. Heck, I'm one of them!

KIM: It's not the same.

JON: I think she has a point. It *is* the same. Look, I happen to be in favor of space exploration and unhappy about welfare payments, but that's just my tastes. Different people want different things from government, and they also want government to tax in different ways. I don't think there's anything *intrinsically* right about anyone's taste. I bet we all agree, though, that we want government to do *some* things and want it to tax in *some* way. True, some want government to do more, and some less. But, let's face it, it's not an all-or-nothing proposition, right?

GOTTHEIL: I don't think I could have said it better. Almost all of this interesting discussion is normative economics. You've been talking about what government should or shouldn't do. Now, that's OK, as long as we understand that it reflects our own personal judgments and biases. We'll soon get around to discussing what government actually does. That's positive economics. It describes *what is* as distinct from *what ought to be.* OK, finish up and get ready for class.

Consider the difference between what you think government should do—normative economics—and what government actually does—positive economics. This will help you as you read the next few chapters.

ChatEconomics

THIS CHAPTER INTRODUCES YOU
TO THE ECONOMIC PRINCIPLES
ASSOCIATED WITH:

- The classical school of employment and inflation

- The Keynesian school of employment and inflation

- The neo-Keynesian school of employment and inflation

- The rational-expectations school of employment and inflation

- The supply-side school of employment and inflation

- Phillips curve analysis

- Automatic stabilizers

CAN GOVERNMENT REALLY STABILIZE THE ECONOMY?

Most physicians will tell you that in cases they consider life threatening, they will advise the patient as a matter of course to get a second opinion. They do so not because they feel uncomfortable with their own diagnosis, but rather because they know we all live in a world of imperfect information. They realize that their understanding of the human body, however expert, is still subject to error.

A second opinion may confirm the first. But not always. If the first physician consulted advises radical surgery and the second suggests that the medical problem will correct itself, what should the patient do? Consult a third? What if the third physician prescribes a different remedy altogether? Should the patient seek a fourth opinion? How many are enough? Do additional opinions really add to the patient's stock of knowledge? Sometimes, the opinion offered reflects the temperament or set of values of the attending physician. Some physicians are known to be aggressive, immediately recommending a maximalist approach, such as strong drugs or surgery. Other physicians belong to a more conservative school and typically advise a number of approaches, from the least interfering to more interventionist treatments, before even thinking about surgery.

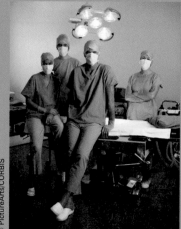

© PictureArts/CORBIS

THE NATURE OF ECONOMIC ADVICE

Economists, too, live in a world of limited information and have a less-than-perfect understanding of how the economy they study really works. They will readily confess that even after centuries of systematic observation of their subject matter, of data collecting, theory building, empirical testing, and amassing historically relevant material, they still arrive at different and sometimes even highly conflicting conclusions and recommendations.

Their opinions reflect a wide array of temperaments and ideologies. Some schools of economic thinking are interventionist by design. These economists are quick to advocate that government and the Fed, sometimes in massive doses, correct what they believe ails the economy. Other economists, looking at the same situation and reflecting a more conservative ideology, advocate much less interference in the private sector.

It is reasonable to ask whether ideology dictates economic policy, or whether economic policy is the logical derivative of an ideology-free understanding of how the system works. For example, do conservative economists advocate conservative policy because they are ideologically conservative, or do they become ideologically conservative because they see and accept a particular understanding of how the economy behaves? The same question, of course, is asked of interventionist economists. Do their liberal policies simply reflect a preconceived ideology, or is their ideology spun out of a particular understanding of the economy's behavior?

How should we view appointments to the president's Council of Economic Advisers? Economists picked by the more conservative presidents have been known advocates of conservative economic policy. For example, it was not surprising that President George W. Bush chose Edward Lazear to head his council—or that his father had chosen Michael Boskin—all known and respected conservatives. Nor was it surprising that President Clinton called upon Laura Tyson, Janet Yellen, Joseph Stiglitz, and Martin Bailey to head his councils through his two terms in office. They were all known and respected liberals. Isn't that precisely why they were chosen? But how should we read their appointments? Is the expert economic advice that presidents receive from the council, then, rigged from the start?

WHY DOES THE ECONOMY GENERATE INFLATION AND UNEMPLOYMENT?

Some people, listening to expert opinion on economic policy over the years, are convinced there are more views held by economists than there are economists. Admittedly, there's some truth to that conviction, particularly when the focus of discussion is macroeconomic policy. After all, every macroeconomist sees the economic world through a unique lens. Some views are similar to others, but even among these there are important shades of differences.

Yet just as we have come to know schools of painters—French impressionists, surrealists, cubists, postmodernists—so too do we find schools of thinking on matters of economic policy. Most economists agree that the most demanding macroeconomic issue is economic stability: *Why do unemployment and inflation exist, and what should be done about them?*

Exhibit 1 details the years of moderate successes (some, perhaps, less moderate) in keeping rates of unemployment and inflation in the United States within tolerable ranges. If the comparison is made with the depressing economic performances of the 1930s—when unemployment soared to 25 percent of the labor force—the record of Exhibit 1 deserves some commendation. But is the Depression the yardstick we ought to use? Many economists hold different views, some

EXHIBIT 1   U.S. Rates of Unemployment and Inflation, 1975–2007 (percent)

DATE	RATE OF UNEMPLOYMENT	RATE OF INFLATION	DATE	RATE OF UNEMPLOYMENT	RATE OF INFLATION	DATE	RATE OF UNEMPLOYMENT	RATE OF INFLATION
2007	4.6	2.9	1996	5.4	2.9	1985	7.2	3.6
2006	4.6	3.2	1995	5.6	2.8	1984	7.5	4.3
2005	5.1	3.4	1994	6.1	2.6	1983	9.6	3.2
2004	5.5	2.7	1993	6.9	3.0	1982	9.7	6.2
2003	6.0	2.7	1992	7.5	3.0	1981	7.6	10.4
2002	5.8	1.6	1991	6.8	4.3	1980	7.1	13.6
2001	4.7	2.8	1990	5.6	5.4	1979	5.8	11.2
2000	4.0	3.4	1989	5.3	4.3	1978	6.1	7.6
1999	4.2	2.2	1988	5.5	4.1	1977	7.1	6.5
1998	4.5	1.6	1987	6.2	3.7	1976	7.7	5.8
1997	4.9	2.3	1986	7.0	1.9	1975	8.5	9.2

Source: Economic Report of the President, Washington, D.C., 2008. Inflationdata.com, http://inflatiodata.com/inflation/Inflation_Rate/HistoricalInflation. aspx?dsInflation_curre.

Stabilization policy
The use of countercyclical monetary and fiscal policy by the government and the Fed to stabilize the economy.

strikingly so, on this issue and have different ideas about the usefulness and even futility of pursuing **stabilization policy**.

Over the course of the past century, ideas associated with the causes of and policies related to inflation and unemployment could be grouped into five mainstream schools of economic thought: Classical, Keynesian, Neo-Keynesian, Rational Expectations, and Supply-Side economics. Their advocates, with respect to stabilization policy, are all very much alive in the worlds of academe and government, each having acquired a considerable following over some stretch of time.

Classical economics, for example, was the dominant school until the 1930s depression when Keynesian economics successfully challenged its authority to become the prevailing conventional wisdom. The Keynesian grip on the academic mind was firm well into the 1970s—even President Nixon once quipped: "We are all Keynesians"—until its policy prescriptions just didn't seem to jibe with our new economic reality. It was quickly eclipsed by a group of economists who modified Keynesian analysis into a new school that became identified as Neo-Keynesian. Classical economic thinking, never really abandoned by some, became re-invented into schools of Rational Expectations and Supply-Side economics.

In a real sense, their co-existence as contending ideas isn't so much warfare as it is (or they are) mutually enriching. While challenging each other, they have also borrowed from each other. The Keynesian paradigm is still a rather pervasive one; its language—the lexicon developed by Keynes—still very much on everyone's tongue.

You're familiar with the Keynesian approach to income determination and stabilization policy. You know something about the classical view of economics. And in this chapter, you will be introduced to the Neo-Keynesian, Rational Expectations, and Supply-Side schools of economic thought. Pay attention to the logic of their arguments and to the assumptions they make in their models that allow them to believe in the worthiness of their stabilization policies.

THE CLASSICAL SCHOOL

Classical economics
The school of thought that emphasizes the natural tendency for an economy to move toward equilibrium at full employment without inflation. It argues against government intervention.

The **classical economics** view of how our economy behaves is this: *If the economy were left on its own—without the interference of government or the Fed—it would move toward an equilibrium rate of growth that would produce, with only minor interruptions, full employment without inflation.*

There's something refreshing about this approach to handling inflation and unemployment, isn't there? After all, what it really argues is that the problems of inflation and unemployment disappear by just doing nothing! That's as simple a policy as you could find.

Moreover, it doesn't make too many demands on our limited skills. Doing nothing is what most of us do well! But if it's all that simple, why then do we find ourselves continually plagued by inflation and unemployment? Because, the classical economists argue, in spite of all their advice to the contrary, we still insist upon tampering with the machinery.

This hands-off view rests upon two simple propositions about markets: (1) all markets are basically competitive, and (2) as a result, all prices are flexible upward and downward, approaching equilibrium, if they are not already there.

Why Unemployment?

How do classical economists, then, explain unemployment? In their view, unemployment is only a temporary condition, caused by wage rates climbing above the equilibrium rate. In the long run, these above-equilibrium wage rates cannot last. The excess labor supply—the unemployed—competes with those who have jobs, driving the wage rates down to equilibrium and employment levels to full employment. The graphics of the classical view are shown in Exhibit 2.

Suppose the wage rate lies above the $6 equilibrium, say at $10. The supply curve shows that at $10, 16,000 people are willing to work but only 12,000 people actually find employment. The 4,000 who would be willing to work are out of luck. What happens? The 4,000 compete with those already working, driving the wage rate down. As the wage rate falls toward $6, more people get hired.

How many more? At the $6 equilibrium wage rate, 14,000 people are willing to work and 14,000 are hired. That is, *everyone who is willing to work at the equilibrium wage rate will eventually find employment.* Unemployment disappears.

If classical economists insist that unemployment is only temporary, why do we find unemployment stubbornly persisting in the real world? Because, they argue, people interfere with the competitive process, preventing wage rates from reaching equilibrium. The interference creates the unemployment.

Who interferes? Labor unions, for example, might use their market power to push wage rates above equilibrium levels, but they can do so only at the expense of employment. In other words, unions might end up being their own worst enemy.

on the
net
For each of the last several months, review the level of unemployment in the United States and the current consumer price index and employment cost index, which both measure inflation (http://stats.bls. gov/). Next, review interest rates over the same months, as published by the Federal Reserve (http:// www.federalreserve.gov/ Release/H15/). Does the natural-rate-of-employment hypothesis seem to hold? Has the Federal Reserve raised or lowered interest rates in line with this hypothesis?

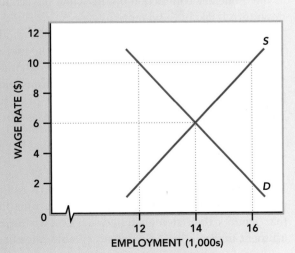

EXHIBIT 2   Classical Determination of Unemployment

The demand curve for labor and the supply curve of labor create employment for 14,000 workers at a wage rate of $6. If the wage rate is above $6, say at $10, the quantity of labor supplied is 16,000 while the quantity of labor demanded is 12,000, creating an excess labor supply (or unemployment) of 4,000. Competition among the employed and unemployed will force the wage rate to $6, erasing the unemployment.

Congress, too, gets into the act. It creates unemployment by imposing minimum wage laws that necessarily cut people out of jobs they otherwise would have taken at less than the minimum wage. The unintended result is painfully clear. The unskilled, teenagers, minorities, and women are big losers. What, then, should government do? The most appropriate countercyclical policy, or stabilization policy, in times of unemployment, according to classical economists, is for the *government to do nothing*. The competitive market should be allowed to work its way to equilibrium.

Why Inflation?

How do classical economists explain inflation? Just as unfettered competition in the labor market will always generate full employment, unfettered competition in the market for capital generates the full employment of capital.

With labor and capital busy at work, the economy produces full-employment real GDP, or Q, as shown in the quantity theory of money equation:

$$P = \frac{MV}{Q}$$

Recall that P is the price level, M is money supply, V is money velocity, and Q is the quantity of goods and services produced. If resources are fully employed and if money velocity is constant, then the price level, P, depends on the quantity of money, M.

According to classical economists—in a view shared by monetarists—if the growth rate of M equals the Q growth rate, the price level remains unchanged. *Inflation occurs when the annual rate of growth in the money supply exceeds the annual rate of growth of full-employment real GDP.*

But the growth rate of our money supply, they remind us, is not a matter of chance. The Fed controls the money supply, they argue. The Fed is typically busy with countercyclical monetary policy, which more often than not ends up causing more damage to price-level stability than ensuring that stability. Attempting to curb the growth of money in periods of economic expansion and stimulate monetary growth during periods of recession, the Fed often worsens the problem of inflation.

After all, the Fed can only estimate how much money is needed. These estimates could overshoot or undershoot the appropriate money supply. Inflation is likely to be a serious problem if the Fed has increased the money supply so that the impact of the monetary expansion coincides with an economic climate already near full employment. If the Fed has restricted the money supply so that the impact of the monetary contraction occurs when the economy is entering a recession, the downturn is likely to be more intense.

What would classical economists or the modern-day monetarists suggest? The Fed should set the rate of increase in the money supply to be approximately equal to the economy's long-run full-employment rate of growth (i.e., about 3 percent) and let it be. This noninterventionist policy would tend to reduce the intensity of recessions and promote greater price stability. In other words, *the best countercyclical policy is no countercyclical policy.*

Yet, Another Consideration...

The classical school not only advocates for a government-free style of economic policy but sends out warning signals concerning the dangers inherent in a policy that ignores their demonstrated classical virtues and relies instead upon government intervention to shape acceptable rates of inflation and unemployment.

The classical view insists that, economists' and policy makers' intentions aside, such shaping, allegedly to promote stabilization, inevitably promotes government pork-barrel expenditures and that these often have less to do with stabilization than with serving "special interests." That is, classical economists have a healthy disrespect for not only what interventionists say they can do but also for what they actually end up doing, given the opportunity.

THE KEYNESIAN SCHOOL

Keynesian economics rejects the classical economists' basic premise concerning competitive markets and flexible prices and, therefore, rejects the stream of classical policy implications that follow from it. To Keynesians, monopolies and unions tend to be permanent fixtures in our economy, and the prices they create tend to be inflexible, at least downward. The classical idea of flexible prices, they argue, is a figment of the imagination.

Exhibit 3 depicts the Keynesian view of how changes in demand for goods affect production.

Note that prices are inflexible at $30. What *is* flexible is the firm's production level. If the demand curve for swimsuits is *D* in Exhibit 3, the quantity produced is 100,000. If demand falls to *D'*, production falls to 80,000. Price remains fixed at $30, whether production is 100,000 or 80,000. What happens to employment in the swimsuit industry? It depends on production levels. The firms employ more workers at 100,000 than at 80,000.

Keynesian economics
The school of thought that emphasizes the possibility that an economy can be in equilibrium at less than full employment (or with inflation). It argues that with government intervention, equilibrium at full employment without inflation can be achieved by managing aggregate demand.

Why Unemployment?

This downward inflexibility of price in individual markets is built into any Keynesian macroeconomic analysis. Aggregate demand determines the level of GDP and therefore the level of employment in the economy.

Aggregate Demand and Aggregate Supply   Panels *a* and *b* in Exhibit 4

summarize the Keynesian view.

Aggregate demand in panel *a* is *AD*. The right-angled aggregate supply depicted by *AS* reflects the early Keynesian view that the price level does not rise as long as there is any unemployment. Equilibrium real GDP is $900 billion, and the price level is *P* = 100.

The same equilibrium condition results in the more familiar Keynesian model of panel *b*. Aggregate demand, *AD*, in panel *a* is depicted as aggregate expenditure

EXHIBIT 3   Keynesian View of Demand and Prices in the Swimsuit Market

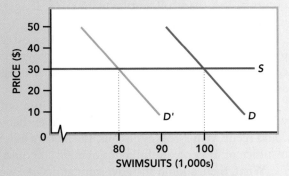

The $30 price curve for swimsuits remains unchanged over the firm's production range. If the demand curve the firm faces is *D*, it produces 100,000 swimsuits. If the demand curve falls to *D'*, price remains at $30, but production falls to 80,000.

EXHIBIT 4   Aggregate Demand, GDP, and Employment

Given the right-angled aggregate supply, AS, if aggregate demand is AD, the economy in panel a is in equilibrium at $900 billion real GDP and price level P = 100. This equilibrium condition is depicted also in panel b. Aggregate expenditure AE = C + I intersects aggregate supply, C + S, at $900 billion *nominal* GDP.

If full-employment real GDP is $1,000 billion, then in both panel a and panel b the economy is in equilibrium at less than full employment. To achieve full employment without inflation, aggregate demand in panel a must shift to the right to AD', and aggregate expenditure in panel b must shift to AE' = (C + I)'.

If aggregate demand instead shifts to AD", real GDP stays at $1,000 billion full-employment level, but the price level rises to P = 110. In panel b, if C + I shifts to (C + I)", an inflationary gap of ab emerges at nominal GDP equilibrium of $1,100 billion, which is equivalent to panel a's $1,000 real GDP at a price level of 110.

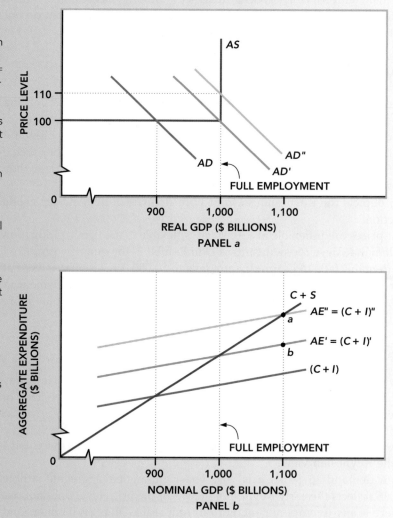

AE = C + I, and aggregate supply, AS, is depicted as C + S. The economy is at equilibrium where the C + I curve intersects the C + S curve, that is, at $900 billion. In panel b, the price level, which is not explicitly shown, is assumed to be fixed.

Note that in both versions of the Keynesian model, with aggregate demand drawn as AD in panel a and aggregate expenditure as AE in panel b, equilibrium occurs at less than full-employment GDP. If aggregate demand doesn't change, unemployment is chronic.

That's why Keynesians reject the classical view that competitive markets ultimately drive the economy to full-employment equilibrium and dismiss the countercyclical policy of doing nothing—that is, allowing market forces to work—as totally inappropriate.

An economy bogged down at equilibrium with less than full employment is what Keynesians saw in the 1930s, and they believed that depressing condition could recur. Why? To Keynesians, the level of aggregate demand in the 1930s was insufficient to generate full employment. It could happen again.

What, then, should the government do? As we have already shown in earlier chapters dealing with Keynesian fiscal policy, the Keynesians focus on aggregate demand. In the model of Exhibit 4, fiscal policy should shift aggregate demand from AD to AD' (which is the equivalent shift of aggregate expenditure from AE to AE').

The Full Employment Act of 1946 In the midst of the 1930s Depression, Keynes was invited to the White House to explain his theory of employment to President Franklin D. Roosevelt. After the meeting, Keynes was asked by fellow economists whether Roosevelt understood the theory. Keynes replied that although the president didn't understand it, the president would "do the right thing" because he seemed ideologically prepared to accept its policy prescriptions.

Keynes was right about Roosevelt's willingness to use the government as a vehicle to shift aggregate demand. The president seemed undisturbed about the new and expanded role that government would play in our economic lives. Although it is unclear whether Roosevelt believed that government spending to create jobs should be a permanent feature in stabilizing the economy, it was clear that he was prepared to create deficit budgets for that purpose. The president called this commitment to full employment a New Deal for the nation.

The economic pain caused by the Depression made the New Deal ideology more digestible for many people. In 1946, Congress officially recognized its role as the economy's stabilizer by enacting the epoch-making Full Employment Act:

> The Congress hereby declares that it is the continuing policy and responsibility of the Federal Government to use all practical means... to foster... conditions under which there will be afforded useful employment for those able, willing, and seeking to work, and to promote maximum employment, production, and purchasing power.

This act, a somewhat milder version of an earlier bill that had referred to the people's "right" to employment, indicates the extent to which government had become legitimized as an agency of economic stabilization.

Why Inflation?

What about inflation? When a house is burning, do you suppose firefighters are bothered by a little rainfall? In the 1930s, when unemployment rates climbed as high as 25 percent of the labor force, Keynesians were little troubled by the prospects of inflation.

Look at Exhibit 4, panel *a*, again. Inflation doesn't occur until aggregate demand shifts to the right, beyond AD', say to AD''. The economy's real GDP cannot increase beyond $1,000 billion, but the price level rises from 100 to 110. That is, a shift in aggregate demand to the right of AD' causes inflation. The same phenomenon is shown in panel *b*. If aggregate expenditures shift to AE'', an inflationary gap, *ab*, results.

In other words, as long as aggregate demand is less than AD' or AE', equilibrium GDP falls short of full employment, and inflation is of no concern. In fact, fiscal policy can push the economy to full-employment real GDP—where the actual unemployment rate equals the natural rate—without worrying at all about inflation. That is to say, *it never occurred to Keynesians that they would ever have to choose between policies to control unemployment and policies to control inflation.*

The Economics of Fine-Tuning

Countercyclical policy is rather uncomplicated for Keynesian economists. In periods of recession, government creates deficit budgets, and the Fed expands the money supply to increase economic activity and decrease the rate of unemployment. In periods of prosperity, government works with surplus budgets, and the Fed contracts the money supply to slow the economy and decrease the rate of inflation.

During the Kennedy and Johnson administrations in the 1960s, there was broad consensus among members of the Council of Economic Advisers with respect to which stabilization policy to pursue. It was mostly a matter of how well the policy could be pursued. Keynesian economists such as Arthur Okun and Nobel laureates Robert Solow, Paul Samuelson, James Tobin, and Lawrence Klein worked at perfecting techniques of economic stabilization. It was, they insisted, a matter of *fine-tuning* the economy.

But these fine-tuners, and the entire school of Keynesian fine-tuning economists, were ill-prepared for the events that beset the U.S. economy in the 1970s and 1980s: high rates of unemployment concurrent with high rates of inflation.

THE NEO-KEYNESIAN SCHOOL

That had to be a puzzlement for Keynesian economists. After all, they see unemployment and inflation as either/or problems, not as concurrent ones. Keynesian countercyclical policy is a one-problem-at-a-time policy. How do you manage two at a time when each problem requires diametrically opposite prescriptions? Wouldn't you think the presence of high rates of unemployment *and* high rates of inflation would have undermined the confidence Keynesians placed in their understanding of how the economy works?

A new term, stagflation, came into vogue in the early 1970s to describe this unusual combination of inflation and unemployment. It was an uncomfortable mix of low rates of economic growth, high rates of unemployment, and high inflation.

What had Keynesians gotten wrong in their view of the economy? Why had inflation become a problem long before the economy approached full employment? Was stagflation an exception to the rule, or was the Keynesian view of the economy simply dead wrong?

In retrospect, it appears that the coexistence of inflation and unemployment never was a secret, not even to Keynesians. It was perhaps a situation that caused the Keynesians, still traumatized by the extraordinary unemployment of the Great Depression, to push the issue into the background.

But in 1958, New Zealand economist A. W. Phillips, after studying employment and inflation data for 1861–1957 in Britain, published his findings, which showed the inverse relationship between rates of inflation and unemployment. Historically, inflation rose when unemployment fell. The graphic expression of this inverse relationship became quickly accepted and is known as the **Phillips curve**.

Phillips's findings, illustrated in Exhibit 5, forced Keynesians to modify their Exhibit 4 view of the economy.

Phillips curve
A graph showing the inverse relationship between the economy's rate of unemployment and rate of inflation.

Phillips Curve Trade-Offs

Keynesians began to see the world in terms of Exhibit 5 and faced a dilemma they had not before considered. If government and the Fed succeed in reducing unemployment, they exacerbate the problem of inflation. One cure creates the other disease. In Exhibit 5, you accept either 8 percent unemployment with 4 percent inflation, or 3 percent unemployment with 9 percent inflation. There is no option of 0 percent unemployment (that is, 0 percent cyclical unemployment) and 0 percent inflation, as Keynesians had believed possible.

EXHIBIT 5   The Phillips Curve

The Phillips curve traces a set of combinations of rates of unemployment and inflation. Because these rates are inversely related, the government cannot use fiscal policy to reduce both at the same time. If government chooses to cut the rate of unemployment, it must accept higher inflation. If it chooses to cut inflation, it must accept higher rates of unemployment.

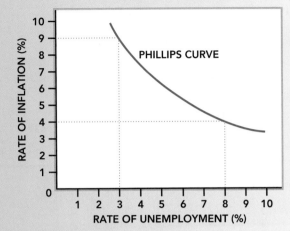

EXHIBIT 6   The Neo-Keynesian Aggregate Supply Curve

The Phillips curve reflects the intermediate, upward-sloping segment of the Keynesian aggregate supply curve of Exhibit 4. It shows that increases in real GDP create pressures on the price level before reaching full-employment real GDP.

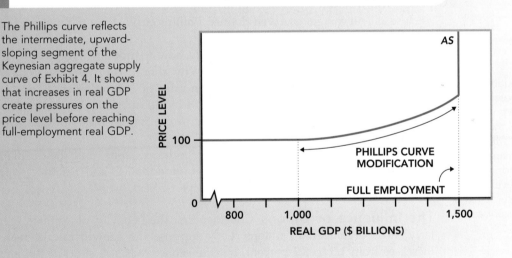

Incorporating the Phillips curve into the Keynesian aggregate supply curve of Exhibit 4 produces the neo-Keynesian aggregate supply curve of Exhibit 6. This is the aggregate supply curve we have been using throughout most of our study of macroeconomics.

The horizontal and vertical segments of the aggregate supply curve, shown also in Exhibit 4, are separated by an intermediate segment that represents the Phillips curve trade-offs. For example, an increase in real GDP within the range $1,000 billion to $1,500 billion can be achieved only at the expense of price stability. And there's the connection between Exhibits 5 and 6. If government is intent on lowering the rate of unemployment within that GDP range, it must accept a higher rate of inflation.

As the Phillips curve of Exhibit 7 shows, the inflation and unemployment rates experienced during the decade of the 1960s seemed to indicate that the economy was operating on the intermediate segment of the aggregate supply curve.

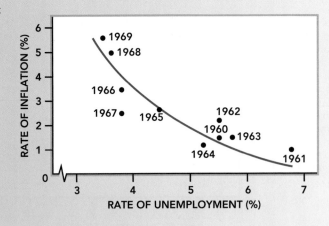

EXHIBIT 7   The Phillips Curve During the 1960s

The rates of unemployment and inflation in the 1960s map out a well-behaved Phillips curve. Stabilization policy during the 1960s centered on the trade-offs reflected in the Phillips curve.

Note the year-to-year changes in rates of unemployment and inflation. The fall in inflation from 1960 to 1961 was matched with a rise in unemployment. The fall in unemployment from 1965 to 1966 was matched with a rise in inflation. If you were a 1960s economist concerned about the possibilities of stabilization policy, you would have been mightily impressed with Exhibit 7. That fit is about as close as you can get to a well-defined Phillips curve. It would make you a true believer.

But putting the statistical evidence aside, how do proponents of **neo-Keynesian economics** explain the Phillips curve? Why should the economy behave this way? Is the inverse relationship between rates of unemployment and rates of inflation *causal*? That is to say, does a fall in the unemployment rate *cause* the rate of inflation to increase? Does a rise in the rate of inflation *cause* the rate of unemployment to decrease?

The neo-Keynesian answer is yes to both questions, and they explain the causality. The market power that unions, monopolies, and resource suppliers exercise in their markets creates the Phillips curve.

The Influence of Unions
Consider first the behavior of workers, particularly those organized in unions. Let's suppose the growth rate of real GDP increases from 1.5 to 3.7 percent, but the economy is still short of full employment. How do firms and workers in that economic growth environment react?

With the economy growing, firms attempt to increase production by hiring more workers. Unemployment rates fall. How do workers react to falling unemployment rates? Feeling somewhat more secure about their jobs, they shift their focus away from job protection, which made sense when unemployment was high, to wage demands. The firms respond positively to their higher wage demands. Why not? With the economy growing more rapidly, their main concern is retaining workers. After all, other firms are expanding production as well and are competing aggressively for workers by raising wage rates.

Firms' resistance to strong wage pressure weakens for still another reason. During periods of rapid economic growth, they find it easier to pass along higher wage rates in the form of higher prices without having to worry about losing markets. In other words, a decline in the rate of unemployment *causes* higher rates of inflation, either or both the rough cost-push or demand-pull pressures.

Neo-Keynesian economics
The school of thought that emphasizes the possibility that an economy can be in equilibrium at less than full employment with inflation. It argues that by managing aggregate demand, government can achieve the most acceptable combination of unemployment and inflation.

What factors create the Phillips curve?

Why does a fall in the rate of unemployment cause the rate of inflation to rise?

What happens during a recession? When growth rates of GDP fall, say, from 3.7 percent to −1.5 percent, the rate of unemployment rises. Many workers are now more concerned about protecting their jobs than protecting their wage rates, so they accept smaller wage increases.

They're no dummies. They know that when the economy is sluggish, many firms have difficulty keeping production at the same levels. If workers insist on high wage increases, then the high-wage-paying firms become disadvantaged in competition. Everybody loses. Workers must choose, then, between jobs and wage rates.

When workers accept smaller wage rate increases, they may make it possible for firms to moderate price increases. That is, higher rates of unemployment that accompany declining GDP may slow the economy's rate of inflation.

The Influence of Supply Shocks Unusual events may sometimes trigger a resource supply shock that jolts the economy from one position on the Phillips curve to another. For example, in October 1973 OPEC—the petroleum exporting countries—drastically cut the supply of oil to the rest of the world. The result was a tripling of oil prices by January 1974. (The tight control on supply by OPEC continued throughout the 1970s, tripling the price from $6 a barrel to $18 a barrel by 1979, and almost doubling it again to $34 a barrel in 1982.) The effect on the economic performance of the rest of the world from this oil price increase alone was immediate and devastating. Many economists attribute the prolonged worldwide stagflation of the 1970s to the supply shock caused by OPEC. The cost of producing and delivering almost all goods and services in the oil-importing economies soared, shifting their aggregate supply curves to the left. The outcome: Price levels increased and real GDP decreased.

The Phillips Curve and Countercyclical Policy

What do Keynesians do now? Is it back to the drawing board? The countercyclical monetary and fiscal policies that were supposed to produce full employment without inflation don't work in economies characterized by the Phillips curve. How do you avoid raising the rate of inflation when pursuing a countercyclical policy aimed at reducing the rate of unemployment during recession?

The Humphrey-Hawkins Act of 1978

Many economists saw the futility of trying to hammer both inflation and unemployment to zero. If we can't engineer full employment without inflation, then we must learn to live with *some* inflation and *some* unemployment (unemployment above the natural rate). That is, reality forced economists to accept the new stabilization policy of choosing the *most livable point on the Phillips curve.*

To Congress, the most livable point on the Phillips curve was spelled out in its 1978 enactment of the Full Employment and Balanced Growth Act, commonly referred to as the Humphrey-Hawkins Act. This act, a modified version of Congress's 1946 Full Employment Act, initially identified a 4 percent rate of unemployment and a 3 percent rate of inflation as acceptable and reasonable targets. But few economists took it seriously. Why? Because, for the decades of the 1970s and 1980s, these target rates proved to be hopelessly unrealistic. Look again at Exhibit 1.

Almost as soon as neo-Keynesians accepted the Phillips curve as the starting point of stabilization policy, they confronted a new problem. They discovered

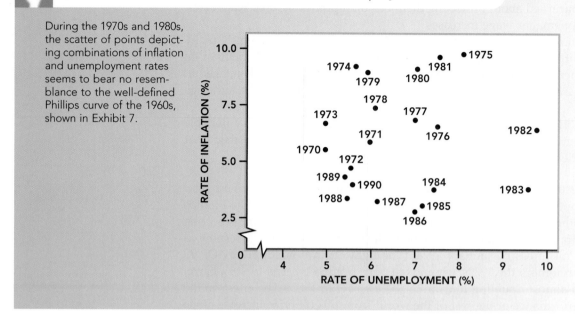

EXHIBIT 8   Rates of Inflation and Unemployment: 1970–90

During the 1970s and 1980s, the scatter of points depicting combinations of inflation and unemployment rates seems to bear no resemblance to the well-defined Phillips curve of the 1960s, shown in Exhibit 7.

that the rates of inflation and unemployment in the 1970s and early 1980s seemed to have run completely amok. By no stretch of the imagination could the 1970s and early 1980s data be fitted into the Phillips curve of Exhibit 7, or into any downward-sloping Phillips curve for that matter. Look at Exhibit 8.

How do you draw a Phillips curve in Exhibit 8? It seems at first glance that the scatter of annual inflation and unemployment rates for the 1970s and 1980s has little in common with the well-behaved Phillips curve of the 1960s. What's left, then, of neo-Keynesian Phillips curve analysis if the data contradict the Phillips curve? Was the 1960s fit simply an accident?

Long-Run Phillips Curves

Neo-Keynesians took a hard look at the 1970s and 1980s scatter of inflation and unemployment rates and found a Phillips curve hidden among them. Only what they discovered was not a single Phillips curve, but *a set of Phillips curves*. The neo-Keynesian idea that an economy can choose only between a limited set of inflation and unemployment options still holds, except that the set of options shifts over time. Exhibit 9 illustrates the point.

What had been a set of scatter points in Exhibit 8 is now points in a set of Phillips curves. But what explains the set? The analysis has to do with the way workers and firms react once a movement along a Phillips curve takes place. For example, when government tries to lower the rate of unemployment, it triggers a movement to a new and different position along the Phillips curve. But that's not the end of the story. Workers and firms, now at that new position, are forced to assess their new situation. Their reaction is illustrated in Exhibit 10.

The effect of the follow-up reaction is illustrated in Exhibit 10. Suppose the economy in Exhibit 10 is at point *A*, with an unemployment rate of 6 percent and an inflation rate of 4 percent. The government regards 6 percent unemployment as unacceptable. What can it do? If it insists on reducing the rate of

check your understanding

What causes the Phillips curve to shift?

EXHIBIT 9 Shifting Phillips Curves

Neo-Keynesians revised their understanding of how people react to government policy to explain why the data of the 1970s and 1980s can be fitted into a *set* of Phillips curves.

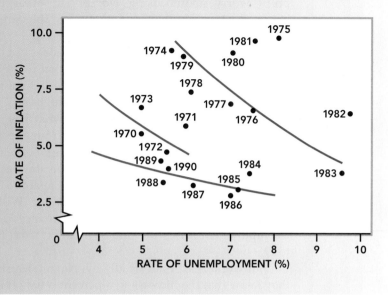

KEY EXHIBIT 10 Shifting Phillips Curves

Beginning at point A on the Phillips curve PC, government policy cuts the rate of unemployment from 6 percent to 4 percent, which causes the rate of inflation to rise from 4 percent to 6 percent. This result is shown as a movement from point A to point B along the Phillips curve PC.

The inflation raises costs and lowers profit, causing firms to cut production and employment, shown as a new combination point C (the rate of unemployment is again 6 percent, while inflation remains at 6 percent). Point C lies on the new Phillips curve PC'.

Frustrated, the government tries to restore the 4 percent rate of unemployment, causing the economy to move first to point D on PC', then to E on PC", where the rate of unemployment is back to 6 percent but the rate of inflation has increased to 8 percent. As long as government tries to cut the rate of unemployment below 6 percent, the rate of unemployment will eventually return to 9 percent, but the rate of inflation will increase.

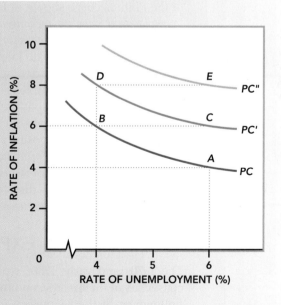

unemployment to 4 percent, it must accept an increase in the rate of inflation to 6 percent, shown at point B on the Phillips curve PC.

But the economy doesn't stay at B for long. Why? Because workers learn that their real wages have been eroded by the higher prices they now pay for goods and services. Should they be upset? Wouldn't you be? How do they recover lost ground? By bargaining for wages high enough to make up what they lost through increased inflation.

Typically, they succeed. Why? Because firms enjoying higher prices and profit worry about losing workers to other firms that are also expanding production. Under these conditions, they are inclined to concede to wage demands.

But the workers' success is only short-lived. The higher wages raise production costs and lower profits. Production is cut back and workers are laid off. In other words, in the long run the higher rate of inflation causes the unemployment rate to climb again to, say, 6 percent, point C in Exhibit 10.

Good intentions notwithstanding, what has government accomplished by trying to lower the unemployment rate from 6 to 4 percent? The economy shifts from A on Phillips curve PC to C on Phillips curve PC'. The unemployment rate is back to 6 percent, but the rate of inflation stays at 6 percent.

Frustrated, the government may try again to cut the rate of unemployment to 4 percent with even stronger fiscal policy. Will it work? As we saw, only in the short run. Movement along Phillips curve PC' from 6 percent to 4 percent unemployment raises the rate of inflation from 6 to 8 percent, that is, from C to D.

But workers will not sit idly by. Having learned their painful lesson earlier, they know that the increase to 8 percent inflation reduces their real wages. They again press to recover lost ground. They succeed, but firms suffer the higher costs and cut production. The rate of unemployment rises again, creating the new position E on Phillips curve PC".

If the government insists on reducing the rate of unemployment to 4 percent, the rate of inflation will continue to increase while the rate of unemployment stays at 6 percent. This scenario is illustrated in the repeated shifting to the right of the Phillips curve shown in Exhibit 10. That is to say, *in the long run the rate of unemployment remains unchanged in spite of government stabilization policy, but the dynamics of the economic activity that the government sets in motion generates accelerating rates of inflation.* The long-run Phillips curve is effectively vertical.

That's pretty disheartening, isn't it? These short-run employment policy victories disappear in the long run, producing in their wake accelerating inflation. The policy implications are clear. Neo-Keynesians show the futility of trying to reduce rates of unemployment and inflation simultaneously. All that's left of stabilization policy is choosing a set of monetary and fiscal policies that achieve a desired position on the Phillips curve. Unless workers, industry, and government resist temptations to improve upon it, any attempt to manipulate a better outcome invites inflationary disaster.

THE RATIONAL-EXPECTATIONS SCHOOL

The 1970s and early 1980s world of stagflation basically broke the Keynesian consensus of the macroeconomic world. Many young macroeconomists saw the hollowness of the Keynesian view when they looked at the decade of exceptionally high inflation and high unemployment. Again, look at the 1974–84 data in Exhibit 1.

As we noted earlier, classical economists believe that government should abstain from activist fiscal and monetary policies. Their policy prescription is clear and simple: Set money supply growth equal to the economy's real growth rate. That's it! But classical economics and monetarism had a decidedly low profile back in the 1970s.

historical perspective

DISPUTING THE ONCE-INDISPUTABLE 6 PERCENT NAIRU

Some ideas, at least for some period of time, appear to be as indestructible as they seem to be obvious and totally defensible. The idea that the world was flat has to be one of them. The social sciences as well as the natural sciences are replete with such "indisputable facts of life" that were, at one time or another, beyond reasonable doubt.

Among the more recent of the economic "facts of life"—*circa* the 1980s and early 1990s—was an idea associated with the rate of unemployment. The idea that there exists in the United States a natural rate of unemployment of approximately 6 percent—give or take a half percent—was universally accepted by economists as a more or less indisputable, inarguable "fact of life." The natural rate is the lowest rate of unemployment that can be sustained in an economy without triggering inflationary pressures.

Economists refer to this rate as the *non-accelerating inflation rate of unemployment,* or by its acronym, NAIRU.

Not only did most academic economists during the 1980s and early 1990s buy into the 6 percent idea, but the 6 percent rate, with its academic imprimatur, also became the benchmark for both Federal Reserve and government policies. The 1978 Humphrey-Hawkins Act had mandated Congress to achieve a no-higher-than-4-percent rate of unemployment. But how could Congress be expected to act on that mandate when the academic profession—liberal and conservative wings alike—was telling Congress that such a mandated goal was impossible to achieve without creating troublesome inflation? Congress, almost without debate, accepted the 6 percent barrier and legislated employment policy accordingly. The Federal Reserve, too, accepted the rate without reservation.

Among the notable dissenters was Northwestern's Robert Eisner, who argued that inflation might actually be lower when the unemployment rate is lower. Although it may be true that high unemployment reduces inflation, it does not follow, he said, that low unemployment raises inflation. The post-1980s data seem to support his view.

During the years 1995–2000, the 6 percent natural rate "fact of life" became anything but a fact of life. The rate of unemployment in the United States fell below the once-thought-impossible 4 percent, and instead of the falling rate triggering troublesome inflation as it was supposed to do, the rate of inflation fell as well.

What about the naturalness of the 6 percent natural rate? Despite the evidence to the contrary, some economists still kept the faith. Others were less sure about it. Then-Fed Chairman Alan Greenspan confessed at one time that he just didn't know what was going on. In economics, as in many of the other sciences, "indisputable facts of life" may turn out to be more disputable than we'd like to believe.

Some things are easier to measure than others.

© Royalty-Free/CORBIS

However, when the economy seemed to be stuck in the rut of stagflation and Keynesians no longer seemed to have all the answers, new and challenging conservative ideas quickly emerged. By far the most important set of conservative ideas to blossom and to draw many young adherents was **rational expectations**.

Rational-expectations economists challenge the neo-Keynesian view that stabilization policy can have some short-run success, even if it disappears in the long run. They offer a different interpretation of how workers and industry respond to government's fiscal policy. The implications of their view are striking: *There is absolutely nothing government can do, even in the short run, to reduce the economy's unemployment rate.* Compare this view of government's role in the economy to the view held by classical economists. Ends up being pretty much the same, doesn't it? Both advocate a hands-off policy. That's not quite the view held

Rational expectations
The school of thought that emphasizes the impossibility of government reducing the economy's rate of unemployment by managing aggregate demand. It argues that because people anticipate the consequences of announced government policy and incorporate these anticipated consequences into their present decision making, they end up undermining the policy.

by Keynesians or even neo-Keynesians, is it? But why do rational-expectations economists believe there is nothing government can do to alleviate unemployment in the short or long run?

Anticipating Fiscal Policy Undermines the Policy

They start with a view, quite different from the neo-Keynesian one, of how people react to the inflationary effects of government job-creating fiscal policy. Rational-expectations economists believe that workers are not only rational but also smart enough to learn from experience how best to overcome the effects of the government's fiscal policy. Workers understand that a Phillips curve exists, even if they don't know what a Phillips curve is. Their experience tells them that the government's attempt to lower rates of unemployment is linked to higher rates of inflation. They therefore not only respond to the past inflation that has eroded real wages, but also, expecting rates of inflation to increase again because of government policy, incorporate that expectation into their future wage demands. That is, their wage demands include anticipated inflation.

This anticipating factor transforms Exhibit 10 into Exhibit 11.

Suppose the economy is at *A*, where the unemployment rate is 6 percent and the rate of inflation is 4 percent. Workers demand a 4 percent wage increase to keep their real wages from eroding.

Suppose government tries to cut unemployment to 4 percent. The economy moves along the Phillips curve to *B*. Inflation is at 6 percent. Now trouble begins. Workers catch on quickly. They don't just try to make up for past inflation losses but try to *prevent a repeat* of the short-run erosion of real wages.

How do they do that? Because they have seen inflation increase from 4 to 6 percent, they *expect it will continue to increase at that rate*. After all, government's

KEY **EXHIBIT 11**   Rational-Expectations Model

Correctly anticipating the increase in the rate of inflation that is generated by the government's policy to cut the rate of unemployment, workers make wage demands that cover the anticipated inflation, thereby erasing any short-run gains in profit that firms would have made. As a result, the unemployment rate remains unchanged, but the rate of inflation increases. If the government keeps trying to cut the rate of unemployment, the rate of inflation keeps increasing along the vertical path of the Phillips curve.

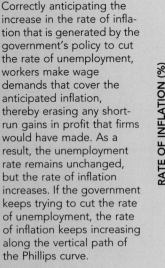

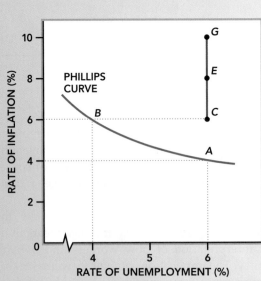

announced policy is to drive unemployment to 4 percent, and workers, being rational, know from experience that such a policy causes inflation. So, anticipating that their real wage will fall because of the government's policy, they ask not for 6 but for 8 percent. That is, they try to stay one step ahead of losing out, to preempt any short-run loss.

But firms, too, are rational and incorporate expectations into their decision making. They, too, learn to read the effects of government's fiscal policy on inflation. They also know that workers' demands will *instantaneously* eliminate the short-run price-cost gap, cutting out that source of short-run profit. Losing the incentive to expand production, they don't hire more workers. The unemployment rate, therefore, remains unchanged—frustrating the government's efforts—while the rate of inflation keeps increasing at the expected rate.

This scenario is played out in Exhibit 11. The economy moves from *B* to *C;* then from *C* directly to *E;* from *E* directly to *G;* and so on. Look at the shape of the Phillips curve these points map out. It becomes a vertical line at 6 percent unemployment.

Policy Goal: NAIRU   What then becomes the policy goal of rational-expectations economists? It is to discover the **non-accelerating inflation rate of unemployment (NAIRU)** and make sure that the actual unemployment rate in the economy doesn't fall below it. As we already noted, a lower rate—say, a rate less than 6 percent in Exhibit 11—will trigger accelerating inflation. There's nothing complicated about the idea of NAIRU. It is simply the familiar natural rate of unemployment—structural and frictional unemployment—that is consistent with a non-increasing rate of inflation.

Non-accelerating inflation rate of unemployment (NAIRU)
Any rate equal to or higher than this rate will not cause the inflation rate to increase. Any rate lower than this rate will cause the inflation rate to increase.

Anticipating Monetary Policy Undermines the Policy

Suppose the Fed, worried about a prolonged recession, decides to increase GDP and employment by increasing the money supply. To do this, it announces a cut in its discount rate. How do people react? Past experience tells them that the Fed's expansionary policy typically is linked to higher rates of inflation. Incorporating that expectation into their plans, workers demand wages that will cover the anticipated inflation. Firms, expecting the rise in inflation, raise their own prices. Banks react to the expected inflation by raising interest rates. The result? Aggregate demand falls because consumer spending declines, especially for big-ticket items that normally involve some borrowing, and because business investment spending declines due to higher interest rates charged by banks.

Firms, facing decreasing aggregate demand, cut back production; anticipating inflation, they raise prices, which feeds inflation and further depresses the demand for goods and services. As a result, the rate of unemployment does not fall. This anticipation of the effects of the Fed's policy on the economy ends up undermining the Fed's ability to stabilize prices.

NAIRU: The Record

Until at least the mid-1990s, NAIRU became an accepted economic fact of life for neo-Keynesians and rational-expectations theorists. They believed that the Phillips curve is something we just have to live with. The only debate on the issue was the actual NAIRU rate. The consensus was that, at least for the United States, the rate of unemployment associated with NAIRU approximated 6 percent. The

historical perspective

NEED FOR STABILIZATION? THE 20TH-CENTURY CYCLICAL RECORD

Have you ever gone on roller coaster rides that were not only scary but dangerous as well? Did you think that some climbs were a bit too high and some descents a bit too steep for comfort? If you were to redesign the ride, would you moderate some of its twists and turns?

That's what governments do—at least some of them, some of the time—to the roller coaster rides of employment, output, and prices. It's always a roller coaster ride, to be sure, but the idea is to redesign the "ride" in such a way as to tone down the scary and dangerous parts.

Look at the cyclical record over the 20th century. It's been a long ride, and some of it has been rather bumpy. Look at the peak-to-trough descent from 1929 to 1933. Dangerous? Scan the other periods of descent. Most don't run deeper than a year; some stretch to two. But how many months in the downturn and trough phases of the cycle should the government tolerate before intervening?

Just as folks like you and me may differ on how scary and dangerous a roller coaster ride is and how to redesign one for greater safety, so too do economists differ on just how scary and dangerous a business cycle ride may be and how and when to redesign its structure to secure greater stability.

PEAK (quarter)	TROUGH (quarter)	CYCLE: PEAK FROM PREVIOUS PEAK (months)
1902 (IV)	1904 (IV)	39
1907 (II)	1908 (II)	56
1910 (I)	1912 (IV)	32
1913 (I)	1914 (IV)	36
1918 (III)	1919 (I)	67
1920 (I)	1921 (III)	17
1923 (II)	1924 (III)	40
1926 (III)	1927 (IV)	41
1929 (III)	1933 (I)	34
1937 (II)	1938 (II)	93
1945 (I)	1945 (IV)	93
1948 (IV)	1949 (IV)	45
1953 (II)	1954 (II)	56
1957 (III)	1958 (II)	49
1960 (II)	1961 (I)	32
1969 (IV)	1970 (IV)	116
1973 (IV)	1975 (I)	47
1980 (I)	1980 (III)	74
1981 (III)	1982 (IV)	18
1990 (III)	1991 (I)	108
2001 (I)	2001 (IV)	128

feeling was that any rate below 6 percent would generate inflationary havoc in the economy. The Fed fixed on that rate and built its monetary policy around it. Even Alan Blinder, the most liberal voice at the Fed—vice chairman from 1994–96—accepted the Fed's 6 percent position. Most policy advisers on the Clinton team bought into that rate as well.

With all this conventional wisdom shoring up the 6 percent NAIRU rate, it was more than a surprise—*shell shock* may be a better term—when empirical data on rates of inflation and unemployment for the 1990s came in. The data not only undermined the validity of the 6 percent rate, but also seemed to undermine the idea of NAIRU itself.

What the 1990s data showed was that during that high-economic-performance decade, *both the economy's rate of unemployment and rate of inflation fell.* Look again at Exhibit 1.

This was simply not supposed to happen. If the rate of unemployment falls from 5.4 percent in 1996 to 4.9 percent in 1997, how can the rate of inflation fall from 2.9 percent to 2.3 percent? Why didn't the patterns of economic activity that rational-expectations people predicted would develop materialize? What went wrong?

One explanation that made sense to some economists was that the world had changed since the early 1990s. The change was triggered by the reach of globalization and by the massive employment of information technology. These events contributed to a burst of productivity that blunted inflationary pressures. Rates of employment increased without generating higher rates of inflation. The Phillips curve trade-offs disappeared.

SUPPLY-SIDE ECONOMICS

Keynesian countercyclical policy focused on what the government can or cannot do to change aggregate demand. Changes in aggregate demand were the principal vehicle for changing real GDP and employment. Phillips curve analysis—by neo-Keynesians and rational-expectations economists—took issue with the simplicity of the Keynesian prescriptions, but they too focused on what government spending can or cannot do.

An altogether different view on stabilization policy emerged in the early 1980s. The analytic focus of **supply-side economics** shifted from aggregate demand to aggregate supply. The idea was that changes in real GDP can best be achieved by changing the environment that suppliers live in. To supply-siders, whatever makes the suppliers happy tends to make the economy better.

> **Supply-side economics**
> The school of thought that emphasizes the possibility of achieving full employment without inflation. It argues that through tax reductions, spending cuts, and deregulation, government creates the proper incentives for the private sector to increase aggregate supply.

What makes suppliers happy? The supply-side economists' happiness checklist includes lower taxes, less government regulation, less government spending, and less union power in wage determination. In short, everything that promotes profit. It was this view that attracted President Reagan to supply-side economics. He believed, as supply-siders do, that not only suppliers benefit when these checklist items are addressed, but also everyone else whose job depends upon successful businesses. During the 1980s, supply-side policy became popularized as "Reaganomics." The idea was that it was possible to lower rates of inflation along with rates of unemployment—an old Keynesian idea—but by working on the supply side of the economy.

Lower Tax Rates

Supply-side economists emphasize the importance of reducing tax rates. They accept the Keynesian idea that lower tax rates will increase consumer demand, but they believe a more important consequence is the added incentive it provides suppliers. For example, lower corporate tax rates increase after-tax profit, which induces suppliers to increase aggregate supply. Lower income tax rates encourage more people to work longer, adding as well to aggregate supply.

Their argument was carried a step further by economist Arthur Laffer, who insisted that high tax rates not only check the expansion of real GDP and employment, but end up producing less tax revenues. His explanation for this unusual outcome is illustrated in Exhibit 12.

applied perspective

THE PHILLIPS CURVE IS ALIVE AND WELL AT THE IMF

The Wall Street Journal reported in May 2008 that the International Monetary Fund—an organization created to provide loans of foreign currencies to countries facing balance of payments problems—had changed course, advocating now policies designed to curb inflation rather than the pro-employment policies it had been promoting up to now. Not that curbing inflation and promoting employment are not *both* desirable. But to economists at the IMF, both cannot be achieved concurrently. It boils down to choice. Either the IMF chooses to fight inflation regardless of its effect on employment or it advocates buttressing employment at the expense of price stability. In other words, the IMF embraces the Phillips curve ideology.

The key issue in its May 2008 statement of policy change was the interest rate. Worried about rising fuel and food prices, the IMF pressed the central banks of developing nations and especially those of Russia, Saudi Arabia, China and Eastern Europe to raise their rates of interest.

John Lipsky, IMF's deputy managing director, minced no words: "Macroeconomic policies need to be tightened in response to generalized inflationary pressures." That message was a dramatic turnabout from the one he had sent out just two months earlier when he urged IMF members to develop policies that stimulate economic growth and employment. The

concern just that short time ago was the spreading the housing crisis "virus" that seemed to leave no economy untouched, causing economic hardships and weakening labor markets. So why the sudden change of the IMF mind? After all, the housing crisis had not abated. Mr. Lipsky was forthright: Inflation risks were now more worrisome than an economic slowdown.

Nor was he alone in shifting priorities. The European Central Bank president, Jean Claude Trichet, too, acknowledged the unavoidable Phillips Curve trade-off. And Michael Saunders, a British economist with Citigroup concurred: "The only way to get inflation back to target is through a deeper slowdown."

There were dissenters. Carnegie Mellon's Allan Metzer, a perennial critic of the IMF, called the advice dead wrong. The IMF policy of raising interest rates now would weaken aggregate demand and increase the chances of a downturn. "It's not the business of central banks to try to create recession. It's the business of central banks to head off recessions."

Whatever the policies of the IMF, one thing stands clear: All parties to the debate acknowledge that the Phillips curve trade-off is our economic reality. Rates of inflation and rates of unemployment are inversely related. To pursue one goal is to give up on the other. Take your choice.

Tax revenues are measured along the horizontal axis, tax rates along the vertical axis. Consider the most extreme position first. If tax rates were 100 percent, no one would work. GDP is $0, and of course, income tax revenue is $0 as well. If the tax rate is lowered to 75 percent, some people would work, GDP grows, and the tax revenue that GDP generates is $800 billion. If the rate is reduced further, say to 50 percent, GDP increases and tax revenue is $1,300 billion. The Laffer curve shows that a tax rate of 30 percent provides suppliers with incentive to produce a GDP large enough to generate a maximum $1,500 billion tax revenue. A lower tax rate, say, at 20 percent, will increase GDP but end up lowering tax revenue.

Laffer's message was clear. Our tax rate is so high that it stifles incentive and produces less than the maximum tax revenue. By lowering the tax rate, he argued—the key factor in supply-side economics—GDP and tax revenue could grow.

Laffer's argument had considerable weight in President Reagan's decision to change the tax structure. In 1981, Congress passed the Kemp-Roth tax cut, which lowered tax rates. The highest marginal tax rate was cut from 70 to 50 percent. In 1986, the Tax Reform Act followed Kemp-Roth's lead, reducing the number of tax brackets to three and cutting the top marginal rate to 31 percent. The two other marginal tax rates were set at 28 and 15 percent.

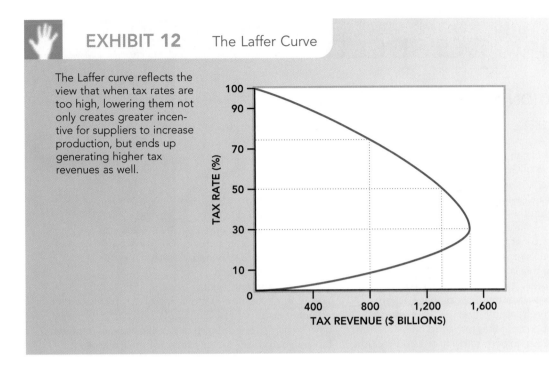

EXHIBIT 12   The Laffer Curve

The Laffer curve reflects the view that when tax rates are too high, lowering them not only creates greater incentive for suppliers to increase production, but ends up generating higher tax revenues as well.

The result? Not very positive. Tax revenues did not increase, contributing to the exceptionally large budget deficits of the 1980s.

The supply-siders' clout ended with the Reagan presidency. Still the view that tax rates are too high on personal and corporate incomes exists in the White House and Congress, but no meaningful attempt was made since the mid-1980s to follow through on this aspect of supply-side thinking. The most likely target for rate reductions are at corporate levels, the idea being that higher net corporate profit will encourage production.

Less Government Regulation

To supply-siders, the myriad of government regulations affects almost every industry in the economy, reducing productivity and undermining industrial efficiency. Although most regulations are designed to protect consumers, workers, and the environment, they also represent a substantial added cost to suppliers. They stifle creativity and trigger higher prices.

Although supply-siders acknowledge the need for some regulation, they insist that the cure has become worse than the disease. They argue for substantial deregulation of the economy. They had some success during the Reagan years, especially in banking, energy, and transportation.

Less Government Spending

Supply-siders believe that the government's reliance on its own spending to create employment not only is not a quick fix but is a major contributor to the unemployment problem. Because government typically ends up spending more than it receives in tax revenues, budget deficits grow. These deficits are financed by the sale of government securities—that is, government borrowing—which

global perspective

GLOBALIZATION AND SUPPLY-SIDE ECONOMICS

The idea and practice of globalization is certainly as old as the compass. Adam Smith's comment that "the discovery of America and that of a passage to the East Indies by the Cape of Good Hope are the two greatest and most important events recorded in history" may seem more than a slight exaggeration, but he was certainly on to something. Smith understood that the colossal expansion of markets made British goods and goods from every other country more affordable and more accessible to everyone, everywhere.

That was then; this is now. However imaginative Smith may have been, he could never have visualized the extent and impact of the technological advances associated with the transportation, communication, and information industries that reshaped our economic world since the 1980s. Exports and imports now include the exports and imports on a massive scale of people, financial capital, physical plants, technology, and ideas. It is no longer a matter of enlarging the size of the market, as Smith saw it, but of shrinking the economic world we live in.

How does supply-side economics fit into this new world? Supply-side economists have long advocated a minimalist role for government. What is most important, they believed, was for government to create the most supplier-friendly kind of economic environment: low corporate taxes, lean government spending, and inconsequential regulation of business. They foster lower costs and higher profit. These are supply-side prescriptions for stabilizing the economy at low levels of inflation and high levels of employment.

But globalization now provides suppliers with these supplier-friendly environments, with or without a supplier-friendly government at home. American businesses, for example, can and do relocate their production facilities abroad, in countries where labor union activity is negligible, where environmentalist concerns are virtually disregarded, where taxes are minimal, and where government regulation is, in effect, non-existent. Many U.S. businesses, attracted by these foreign supply-side conveniences, have simply cut-and-run; many others remain in place but outsource substantial pieces of their business activity abroad.

© CORBIS

This could be the start of something big.

To the extent that globalization matters, it has undermined—at least for some industries and for the short run—the benefits that supply-side economists have championed. What makes suppliers happy now ends up making some workers sad. While globalization may keep national inflation rates in check and increase real GDPs, it *may* also simultaneously contribute to higher rates of unemployment.

Note the emphasis on the final *may*. There is good reason to believe that in the long run, most American workers will enjoy the substantial benefits accruing from globalization. But in the shorter run—and that's where we all live—making suppliers happy may not always generate all that supply-siders promised.

Crowding out
A fall in private investment spending caused by an increase in government spending.

Why would less government spending result in a lower rate of unemployment?

undermines private sector investment in two ways. First, government competes in the securities market with firms trying to sell their own securities, **crowding out** these firms from the source of funds. Second, the increase in government borrowing drives up the interest rate, crowding out private investment once again. This crowding-out phenomenon checks the rate of economic growth.

Supply-siders argue that if the government reduces its spending, more investment capital will be made available at lower rates of interest to private sector suppliers. Combined with lower tax rates and less government regulation, lower government spending produces lower rates of inflation and unemployment. Exhibit 13 illustrates their view.

The shift in the aggregate supply curve from AS to AS_1 that results from supply-side stabilization policy causes a decrease in the price level, from $P = 110$ to $P = 100$, and an increase in GDP, from \$900 billion to \$1,000 billion, cutting the rate of unemployment.

EXHIBIT 13   Supply-Side Effects on Unemployment and Inflation

If aggregate supply shifts to the right from AS to AS_1, real GDP increases from $900 billion to $1,000 billion, while the price level falls from $P = 110$ to $P = 100$.

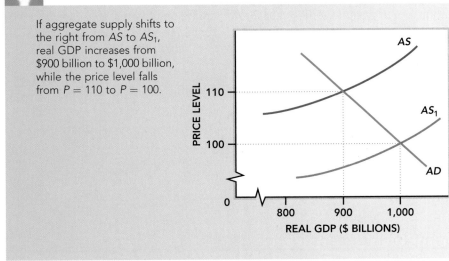

IS THERE A MACRO CONSENSUS?

The question of who is right on stabilization policy has as many answers as there are economists with views on stabilization. Macroeconomic models—classical, Keynesian, neo-Keynesian (the short-run and long-run Phillips curve varieties), rational expectations, and supply-side—all generate outcomes that differ and, depending on one's economic ideology, can be compelling. In other words, not everyone agrees with any one "correct" stabilization policy.

Yet real-world events since the 1970s have brought macroeconomists together, notwithstanding the specific policy disagreements that make interesting bedfellows. For example, rational-expectations economists and neo-Keynesians share the same view concerning government's ability to change the economy's long-run employment position. They both demonstrate its futility. They see stabilization policy—what we can do with rates of inflation and unemployment—as constrained. Their observations are not entirely revolutionary. Classical economists came to the same conclusions, insisting that even well-intentioned government interference in the economy was not only futile but counterproductive.

Note what supply-siders and Keynesians agree and disagree on. They agree that with the correct approach to stabilization policy, it is possible to reduce both the rate of unemployment and the rate of inflation. But supply-siders and Keynesians disagree on the correct approach to stabilization. The Keynesians focus on changing aggregate demand; supply-siders focus on changing aggregate supply.

Even among Keynesians, there is disagreement about what government can and cannot do to promote employment, although they all share the belief that government has a positive role. Some Keynesians are convinced that government can create policy to increase employment without causing inflation. Others take a different view. They accept the validity of the Phillips curve, which requires us to make choices between employment and inflation. And among those economists, what policies the government should pursue is still a matter of some disagreement.

AUTOMATIC STABILIZERS

Wouldn't it be wonderful if we had an economic stabilization thermostat built into our economy that would *automatically* create employment when the economy's rate of unemployment grew to unacceptable levels and *automatically* cut inflation when the rate of inflation became too high? It would mute much of the activist-nonactivist debate and would set aside many of the ideological differences and much of the controversial, discretionary decision making by government and the Fed that stabilization policy demands. But is it possible? Can anyone really design automatic economic stabilizers?

To some extent, that's what our economy already has. We have built into our system **automatic stabilizers** that kick in at the right times to moderate the ups and downs of business cycles. One of the principal stabilizers is the unemployment insurance system. The other is our income and corporate tax structure. How do they work?

Automatic stabilizers
Structures in the economy that tend to add to aggregate demand when the economy is in recession, and subtract from aggregate demand when the economy is inflationary. Unemployment insurance payments and benefits and the progressive income tax are two such automatic stabilizers.

Unemployment Insurance

When people work, they contribute part of their earnings *indirectly* to an unemployment insurance program. Although employers, not workers, actually pay the insurance, employers are reimbursed, at least in part, by paying workers lower wages. That is, workers would probably earn higher wage rates if employers were not obligated to pay the insurance. The point is that while workers are working at jobs, part of their income is siphoned off by employer-employee contributions to the unemployment insurance program.

On the other hand, when workers are unemployed, they receive income payments in the form of unemployment insurance benefits from that program. This simple and practical spreading of workers' incomes more evenly over the business cycle not only makes life more tolerable for affected workers but acts as an automatic stabilizer in the economy.

Consider the prosperity phase of a business cycle. With unemployment approaching the natural rate and wage rates rising along with the price level, the one thing you don't want to encourage is more consumer spending. But that's just what happens when wages increase. Unemployment insurance payments (which leave less take-home dollars in paychecks than would otherwise be the case) come to the rescue. With less income, people spend less, which modifies somewhat the upward pressure on prices.

On the other hand, in the recession phase of the cycle, the unemployment insurance program automatically pumps more spending into the economy. People out of work find their earning power considerably diminished, but those who are eligible for unemployment benefits now have some spending power. In this respect, spending does not decrease as much as it would without the unemployment insurance benefits. This ultimately means fewer workers lose their jobs, which translates into less unemployment than would otherwise have occurred.

check your understanding

How does unemployment insurance work to moderate the ups and downs of the business cycle?

Personal and Corporate Income Taxes

Our personal income tax structure has a built-in stabilizing feature as well. The tax structure is progressive, meaning that as income increases, the percentage of income paid to taxes increases. How does it work? When incomes and real GDP increase during a prosperity phase, taxes increase at an even higher rate, leaving less disposable income in the hands of people. With less income, people spend less. That's good news because less spending dampens the inflationary pressure on the economy.

on the net

Visit the Internal Revenue Service (http://www.irs.gov/) to learn more about the federal tax system.

During a recession, when income and real GDP are falling, less is collected in taxes. Disposable income and spending do not fall as fast. That's good news as well, because the less spending falls, the less real GDP will fall, and, consequently, fewer workers will lose their jobs. This means unemployment will not increase as much as it would in the absence of these automatic stabilizers.

Our corporate income tax structure operates the same way. In fact, economists consider the corporate profit tax to be the most countercyclical of all automatic stabilizers. In the prosperity phases of the cycle, corporate profits tend to increase faster than any other income form. In recessions, they tend to decrease faster. As a result, corporations pay considerably more taxes in inflationary periods than in recessions.

CHAPTER REVIEW

1. Since economists have different temperaments and ideologies and work with imperfect information, they don't always agree on how an economy behaves or what appropriate policy should be. Liberal economists tend to advocate greater government intervention in the economy, while conservative economists are more disposed to advocate a laissez-faire approach.

2. The five schools of macroeconomic thought related to the analysis of employment and inflation are the classical, Keynesian, neo-Keynesian, rational expectations, and supply-side.

3. Classical economists believe that because markets are basically competitive and prices flexible, unemployment exists only in the short run. In the long run, all prices, including the price of labor, will adjust to equilibrium, eliminating unemployment. Their policy is to wait out the adjustment, that is, to do nothing. Inflation simply represents too much money chasing too few goods. Classical policy is to fix the rate of growth in the money supply to the rate of growth of real GDP.

4. Keynesian economists argue that markets are not competitive and prices are downward inflexible. Under these conditions, a fall in aggregate demand leads to lower real GDP, not a lower price level. Unemployment, then, can persist—in the short and long run—as long as aggregate demand is insufficient to absorb everyone willing and able to work. This idea supports the view that government should fine-tune the economy, creating an aggregate demand sufficient to generate full employment. Inflation becomes a problem only when aggregate demand creates a macroequilibrium level beyond full-employment real GDP. The solution: reduce government spending to reduce aggregate demand. The Full Employment Act of 1946 reflects the thinking of the Keynesian school.

5. The coexistence of inflation and unemployment—referred to as stagflation—in the 1970s led to the creation of the neo-Keynesian school. Its principal tool of analysis was the Phillips curve, which showed the inverse relationship between rates of inflation and unemployment. Unions' market power and strategic resource supply shocks explain how the Phillips curve works. For example, if government policy reduces unemployment, it relaxes the unions' concerns about jobs and allows them to focus on wage increases. If successful, these wage increases, which result in inflation, cut into firms' profits, so the firms cut back on production and, consequently, employment. The result: Government's effort to decrease unemployment succeeds in the short run but not in the long run. In the process, inflation occurs.

6. Rational-expectations economists believe that government cannot even succeed in reducing unemployment in the short run. They reason that unions learn that wages are eroded by inflation and bargain not just to make up for lost real wages but for anticipated losses that will occur if government tries to reduce unemployment. The result: Firms suffer wage increases (which raises prices in general) that include accounting for future inflation so that firms do not increase production or employment at all. In the process, inflation occurs.

7. Supply-side economists believe that economic policy should focus on the supply side—that is, on ways of shifting the aggregate supply curve to the right. Lower taxes, less government spending, and less government regulation, they argue, are the appropriate policies to deal with issues of economic growth, unemployment, and inflation.

8. Is there a macro consensus? Not really, even though areas of agreement among economists associated with the different schools do exist.

Keynesians and supply-siders agree that some form of stabilization policy can reduce unemployment and inflation, but they disagree on what that policy ought to be. Rational-expectations economists and neo-Keynesians are far less willing to accept the view that, in the long run, any stabilization policy works.

9. To some extent, the economy has automatic stabilizers built into the system. They are the unemployment insurance and progressive income tax systems. During periods of prosperity, people's after-tax incomes are reduced by the contributions they make to the unemployment insurance program and by the progressiveness of the income tax. These reductions tend to dampen the upward momentum of the prosperity phase of the business cycle. During periods of recession, people receive unemployment insurance payments and pay taxes on a lower percentage of their income, both of which tend to counteract the downward momentum of the recessionary phase of the cycle.

KEY TERMS

Stabilization policy
Classical economics
Keynesian economics
Phillips curve

Neo-Keynesian economics
Rational expectations
Non-accelerating inflation rate of
   unemployment (NAIRU)

Supply-side economics
Crowding out
Automatic stabilizers

QUESTIONS

1. There are five mainstream schools of economic thinking on issues relating to what government can or cannot do with respect to stabilizing the economy. What are these schools and how do they differ on issues concerning unemployment and inflation?

2. The Theoretical Perspective "Crossing Ideological Boundaries" notes that "pragmatism often prevails over economic ideology." What does that mean and what proof does it offer?

3. Keynesian economists were fine-tuning the economy during the 1960s but found their policies ineffectual in the 1970s. Why?

4. "The key to any economic stabilization is managing aggregate demand." Keynesians and neo-Keynesians would agree with that statement, even though they see quite different outcomes stemming from such management. Discuss.

5. To supply-siders, the key to any economic stabilization is managing aggregate supply. What kinds of policy do they advocate, and what outcomes do they expect to achieve?

6. In 1958, A. W. Phillips published his celebrated article introducing the Phillips curve. It changed the way economists think about stabilization policy. Why?

7. "Unions make it difficult for government to reduce the rate of unemployment." Discuss the logic underscoring this view and show how it relates to the Phillips curve.

8. "In periods of inflation, any attempt by the Fed to increase real GDP through increases in the money supply ends up increasing only the rate of inflation." What school of economists makes this point? How do they make their argument?

9. "To rational-expectations economists, it makes no difference whether we think in terms of the short run or the long run: Government cannot reduce the rate of unemployment, period." Explain.

10. "The Fed should just increase the money supply at the same rate that the full-employment economy grows, and the government should desist from any stabilizing urges." What school of thought would make such a suggestion, and how do economists of that school justify that prescription?

11. "To *some* extent, automatic stabilizers work." What are they supposed to do, and why do they work?

12. What is the Laffer curve? What impact did it have on government policy?

13. Explain why unemployment insurance is a good example of an automatic stabilizer.

14. In some instances, government spending may trigger a "crowding out" outcome that undermines the reason for the government spending. What is "crowding out" and how can government spending cause it?

WHAT'S WRONG WITH THIS GRAPH?

The Phillips Curve

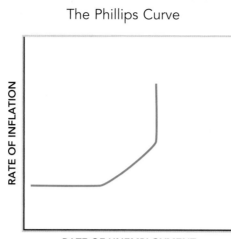

RATE OF INFLATION (y-axis)

RATE OF UNEMPLOYMENT (x-axis)

Economic Consultants

Economic Research and Analysis by Students for Professionals

Mindy Manolakes worked in a North Carolina textile factory before she became president of the Union of Needletrades, Industrial and Textile Employees' (UNITE) Southern District. She and other key people in UNITE's national office have been debating whether to propose a 10 percent wage increase for all unionized garment workers. Mindy supports the increase, justifying it by arguing that years of inflation have eroded the real incomes of workers. Other union leaders are hesitant because they fear that the wage demand may induce textile firms to leave the country. They cite the recent migrations of textile factories to Lima, Peru. Mindy suggests that UNITE hire Economic Consultants to evaluate the effects of a 10 percent wage increase. You are asked to prepare a report for UNITE that addresses the following issues:

© Image 100/Royalty-Free/CORBIS

1. What effects might the 10 percent increase in wages have on textile prices and the competitiveness of the American textile industry worldwide?
2. What effect might the 10 percent increase in wages have on textile employment in the United States and on inducing the migration of textile plants out of the United States?

3. What kind of support can UNITE expect from federal and state governments?

You may find the following resources helpful as you prepare your report for Mindy and UNITE:

- **Union of Needletrades, Industrial and Textile Employees (UNITE)** (http://www.unitehere.org/)—UNITE provides news and information about union activities.
- **LabourStart** (http://www.labourstart.org/)—LabourStart is a collection of labor and union news from around the world.
- **UnionWeb** (http://www.unionweb.org/)—UnionWeb provides links to resources by and about unions.
- **Thomas: Legislative Information on the Internet** (http://thomas.loc.gov/)—Thomas, named after Thomas Jefferson, is a service of the Library of Congress that provides news and information about congressional activities.
- **Bureau of Labor Statistics** (http://www.bls.gov/)—The Bureau of Labor Statistics provides data and information about employment and inflation.

practicetest

1. The Full Employment Act of 1946 and the Humphrey-Hawkins Act of 1978
   a. assigned responsibility to government to achieve full or near full employment.
   b. imposed penalties on businesses that hired illegal immigrants.
   c. made inflation the primary policy issue of government.
   d. legislated minimum wages to create full employment.
   e. created civil rights in the American workplace.

2. Classical economists attribute inflation to which of the following?
   a. Growth in the money supply
   b. Low levels of unemployment
   c. Money supply growth that exceeds the growth in real output
   d. Shocks to aggregate supply in the economy
   e. Shifts in the economy's aggregate demand curve

3. Keynesian economists reject many of the solutions to problems presented by classical economists because
   a. they believe that prices are not flexible.
   b. classical economists rely too heavily on expectations to derive useful policies.
   c. inflation is a worse problem than unemployment.
   d. they believe that the long-run Phillips curve is vertical.
   e. they believe that tax reductions and spending cuts are the most efficient way to achieve macroeconomic goals.

4. Inflation was not viewed as a serious problem by Keynesians in the 1930s because
   a. government intervention could easily reduce inflation.
   b. they believed that the market forces would eventually lower inflation.
   c. real GDP was above the full-employment level.
   d. when the aggregate demand curve shifts to the right, inflation decreases.
   e. proposed increases in aggregate demand would be insufficient to cause inflation.

5. The Phillips curve illustrates that
   a. as inflation rises, the rate of unemployment falls.
   b. as inflation rises, the rate of unemployment rises.
   c. as real GDP rises, the price level in the economy falls.

   d. as wages rise, real GDP rises.
   e. as real GDP rises, the rate of unemployment falls.

6. Unlike the Keynesian school, the neo-Keynesian school explains
   a. why inflation is not a problem.
   b. why markets do not automatically adjust to equilibrium.
   c. why inflation and unemployment coexist.
   d. why prices tend to be inflexible downward.
   e. how expectations affect individual behavior.

7. Rational-expectations economists argue that
   a. inflation and unemployment are avoidable.
   b. if policies are anticipated, they magnify the impact on the economy.
   c. people typically do not understand how policy affects them.
   d. government can do nothing to reduce unemployment.
   e. government can control either inflation or unemployment, but not both at the same time.

8. Which school of economics advocates spending cuts and lower tax rates as a means of achieving macroeconomic goals?
   a. Keynesian economists
   b. Classical economists
   c. Rational-expectations economists
   d. Neo-Keynesian economists
   e. Supply-side economists

9. Which of the following groups of economists are the strongest advocates for government intervention to reduce unemployment?
   a. Classical economists
   b. Keynesian economists
   c. Supply-side economists
   d. Neo-Keynesian economists
   e. Rational-expectations economists

10. The progressive income tax structure is considered an automatic stabilizer because as income increases, taxes
    a. increase by a smaller amount, which promotes spending.
    b. increase by a larger amount, which restrains spending.
    c. increase by a lower rate, which promotes spending.
    d. increase by a higher rate, which restrains spending.
    e. decrease, which restrains spending.

14

GOVERNMENT SPENDING

There will *always* be public debate about whether government spends too much or too little, about whether it taxes too much or too little, and about whether the kinds of things it does and the way it goes about collecting revenues to pay for what it does represent the best that government can or should do.

Perhaps the first question we should ask is, *Why is government spending at all?* Why, for example, is government in the business of providing interstate roads, street lights, education, national defense, and public parks? We have already seen in our analysis of countercyclical fiscal policy the usefulness of government spending to achieve target employment and GDP levels. Government spending is a vital part of aggregate demand. But is government spending strictly a matter of countercyclical fiscal policy?

THIS CHAPTER INTRODUCES YOU
TO THE ECONOMIC PRINCIPLES
ASSOCIATED WITH:

- Public goods
- Merit goods
- Transfer payments

© PictureArts/CORBIS

It would seem unreasonable to argue that the only reason government builds city streets is because the dollars spent on street construction generate—through the income multiplier—desired levels of GDP and employment. Think about it. Wouldn't we need city streets even if the economy were at full-employment GDP? But why rely on government to provide the streets? Why don't we rely on the market to produce the city streets, just as we rely on it to produce automobiles?

GOVERNMENT SPENDING AND PUBLIC GOODS

Automakers produce automobiles because people demand them. People demand them because the personal benefits they derive from an automobile are greater than the personal costs they incur buying it. That's also why raincoats, strawberries, and CDs are produced. In each case, people compare the benefits they derive against the costs they incur. Look at your own collection of household items. Didn't you calculate, perhaps subconsciously, benefits and costs before making each purchase? Why, then, can't you make the same kind of personal cost-benefit calculation for city street lights?

Hard to even imagine such a calculation, isn't it? After all, no matter how much you may personally benefit from a city street lighting system, the cost is far beyond your personal means. If each of us relied exclusively on the market to determine what to buy, we would all end up with lots of strawberries and no city street lights.

How, then, do we get city street lights, sewage systems, and police protection? By replacing the market with government. How does it work?

Consider the small community of Logan Square, with a population of 20,000. Suppose that a network of street lighting would cost the community $40 million. And suppose that the personal benefit each of the 20,000 people derives from the network is $5,000. The community's total benefit, then, is $100 million, or 2½ times its cost of production. In other words, the street lighting project is economically sound. But how do you get it built?

Suppose Doug Dubson, the mayor of Logan Square, calls a town meeting to discuss the economic costs and benefits of the project. He asks each resident to contribute $2,000. The community accepts the mayor's estimate of a $5,000 personal benefit. But Denise Miller, a Logan Square psychiatrist, has another idea. She figures that if everyone *except her* contributes $2,000, the street lights will be built anyway and she will still be able to use them. She doesn't feel too guilty about not contributing because she reasons that even if she uses the street lights, it's not at her neighbors' expense. They each still end up deriving a $5,000 benefit. What Denise doesn't count on, however, is that everyone has the same idea. The result is that nobody makes a $2,000 contribution, and, consequently, no street lights are built.

Frustrated, the mayor calls a second meeting. This time, he brings along Paul Budin, an economic consultant, who explains the difference between a **public good**, such as a city street light, and a private good, such as an automobile. Public goods, he points out, have two distinct features: nonexclusiveness and nonrivalry.

When you buy an automobile, he explains, the benefits it provides are exclusively yours, if you wish. You can prevent others from gaining any benefit simply by denying them access to the automobile. It's the same with your raincoat. When you wear it, others can't. You're dry, they're wet.

This exclusive character of a good is absent in public goods. Once the city street lights are installed and the current turned on, you cannot deny anyone

Public good
A good whose benefits are not diminished even when additional people consume it and whose benefits cannot be withheld from anyone.

on the street the benefits of the lighting. The exclusiveness of the good—the lighting—is lacking. It makes no difference who owns the good or who actually paid for it; once it is provided, no one can be excluded from deriving benefit.

Private goods are also rival goods. As you eat through a banana, there's less and less of it left. If others were expecting to eat it too, they're out of luck. In this sense, your consumption of the banana rivals theirs.

Not so with public goods. Consider the city street lights again. You can use the lighting as much as you want without others being denied its use. If others crowd the street to enjoy a late evening stroll, you won't notice the lights dimming. In other words, their benefit doesn't rival yours.

The nonexclusivity and nonrival properties of public goods, Paul Budin explains, mean that Logan Square will never get city street lights if people rely on markets, because there is no way to exclude anyone who has not paid for the lighting from deriving equal benefits. Each individual therefore waits for everybody else to pay for them. If Logan Square wants city street lights, it must bypass the market. That bypass is government spending. We rely on government to provide the street lights and to tax the community accordingly.

GOVERNMENT SPENDING AND MERIT GOODS

Don't you wish there was more goodwill among people? After all, goodwill is good! The truth is that we can actually generate more goodwill among ourselves if we behave more kindly to one another. But we don't.

Some goods are like goodwill. We would be much better off—at least some people think so—if we had more of them, but we don't. Economists call them **merit goods**. The reason we don't have as much of them as some people think we ought to is that market demand and supply generate less. How, then, do we get more? If the market doesn't produce the quantities some people think we should have, in many instances, government comes to the rescue.

Consider higher education. The private market is quite capable of generating the quantity of colleges and universities to educate students at demand-and-supply-determined prices. So what's the problem? It's simply this: *The government doesn't like the quantities and the prices that the market generates for higher education.* It places higher value or merit on higher education than people's individual choices declare in the private market. The result: Government produces higher education in the form of state universities and community colleges and sells the higher education at below-market prices *even though there's a flourishing private market for the good.*

What other merit goods does government produce or subsidize? You're probably familiar with many of them. For example, the government's National Endowment for the Arts subsidizes experimental film, art, and music that would otherwise never see the light of day. The National Institutes of Health produce merit goods in the form of research in medicine and medicine-related fields. Public libraries, art galleries, symphony orchestras, and museums are typically merit goods subsidized by government. In radio and television, the government's NPR and PBS networks provide programming that would otherwise not be aired by competing private networks, such as CBS and NBC.

How many private goods individuals buy on the market and how many public and merit goods they buy through the system of government spending and taxation are a matter of individual choice. That's what the ballot box allows each person in Logan Square to do: elect a mayor to represent the levels and character of government spending he or she wants.

Merit good
A good that market demand and supply do not produce enough of, in some people's opinion.

check your ✓
understanding

Why does government produce merit goods?

on the

The National Endowment for the Arts (http://arts.endow.gov/), the National Institutes of Health (http://www.nih.gov/), National Public Radio (http://www.npr.org/), and the Public Broadcasting Service (http://www.pbs.org/) all produce merit goods.

GOVERNMENT SPENDING AND TRANSFER PAYMENTS

Not all government spending is designed to satisfy our need for public and merit goods or to be used as a tool of countercyclical fiscal policy. Some government spending simply transfers income from some people—government taxes them—to other people—government pays them. These transfer payments are typically in the form of government services, price subsidies, and cash payments. They are intended to moderate the harshness of poverty among low-income people and, in some cases, to moderate the economic distress suffered by groups, such as farmers, whose income source has been undermined by adverse changes in market conditions.

Government is also in the business of administering Social Security, an obligatory social insurance program. The program provides benefits to retired people, spouses of people in the program who have died, and disabled people. Every working person who contributes to Social Security—contributions are matched by employers—receives Social Security benefits.

The contributions are held in a specifically earmarked trust fund. Social Security contributions and benefits are transfer payments. Income is transferred from the young (who typically pay into the trust fund more than they receive from it) to the elderly (who typically receive more from the trust fund than they pay into it), even though the payers themselves regard their own contributions to the trust fund more as personal savings than as part of a transfer payment system.

on the net
Social Security contributions and benefits (http://www.ssa.gov/) are examples of government transfer payments.

GOVERNMENT SPENDING AND THE PUBLIC DEBT

Each year, government makes interest payments to people who own the public debt. The debt is in the form of Treasury bills, notes, and bonds and is held not only by individuals, but by banks, corporations, the Federal Reserve, other government agencies, and foreigners. A more detailed analysis of the government's debt is offered in the next chapter.

on the net
Government helps provide for national security through the National Guard (http://www.ngb.army.mil/).

HOW MUCH DOES GOVERNMENT SPEND?

Exhibit 1 shows total government spending for 2007.

Slightly less than half of total government spending is in the form of purchases of goods and services. At the federal level, purchases made up only 30 percent of spending, while transfer payments and interest accounted for 55.6 percent. The federal government also provided state and local governments

EXHIBIT 1   Federal, State, and Local Government Spending: 2007 ($ Billions)

	FEDERAL	STATE AND LOCAL	TOTAL
PURCHASES	$ 856.1	$1,355.9	$2,212.0
TRANSFER PAYMENTS	1,290.4	430.8	1,721.3
NET INTEREST	312.6	98.5	411.1
GRANTS-IN-AID	376.3	—	376.3
OTHER	45.1	7.2	52.3
TOTAL	$2,880.5	$1,892.4	$4,772.9

Source: *Survey of Current Business* (Washington, D.C.: U.S. Department of Commerce, September 2008).

EXHIBIT 2   Government Spending in 2007, by Function ($ Billions)

	FEDERAL	STATE AND LOCAL
SECURITY, NATIONAL DEFENSE	$ 583.9	$ —
SECURITY, CIVILIAN PROTECTION	44.4	244.7
EDUCATION	72.1	663.9
TRANSPORTATION	31.8	108.3
NATURAL RESOURCES	20.9	14.3
ENERGY	14.3	—
SPACE	16.9	—
AGRICULTURE	24.2	6.0
INCOME SUPPORT, SOCIAL SECURITY, AND WELFARE	880.7	144.3
HEALTH AND HOSPITALS	718.2	391.2
HOUSING AND COMMUNITY SERVICES	52.5	15.7
NET INTEREST	312.6	98.5
CENTRAL EXECUTIVE, LEGISLATIVE, AND JUDICIAL ACTIVITIES	73.2	155.9
OTHERS	34.8	49.6
TOTAL	$2,880.5	$1,892.4

Source: *Survey of Current Business* (Washington, D.C.: U.S. Department of Commerce, September 2008).

with $376.3 billion of grants. As much as 71.6 percent of state and local spending is for purchases of goods and services. What do federal, state, and local governments buy? Exhibit 2 details government spending by function.

Security

Some public and merit goods that government provides seem to be almost beyond public controversy. One of these is national security. How many people do you know who contest our need for a reliable national defense? How many people advocate leaving defense preparedness to individual purchases in the marketplace? There appears to be a wide consensus that national security properly belongs in the federal government's domain.

Some of our security is managed by other levels of government. Local governments, for example, provide police protection to safeguard our communities. State police cast a wider security net. Our National Guard is administered by state governments and is sometimes called upon to assist local police.

How Much Security Is Enough?   But how much security is enough? Can we ever be *too* well protected? How many times have you heard someone say about our police, "They're always around except when you need them!" If there's any substance to the charge, it may signal a need for more police. But how many more? Do you want them around everywhere, all the time?

Doesn't our personal security also depend upon what we do with security offenders? What kinds of correction facilities—local jails, state prisons, federal penitentiaries—should we build? What should we do with offenders once they are incarcerated? Should we try to rehabilitate them? That could be expensive. Perhaps the least-expensive policy is to hang them immediately after sentencing! Ridiculous? Society has done it for centuries. Many countries still do it. Remember: *Whatever form and level of security we choose, determined by whatever sets of values we hold, carries a price tag that can be compared with those for alternative security systems.*

EXHIBIT 3   Government Spending ($ Billions) on Security: 2007

	FEDERAL	STATE AND LOCAL	TOTAL
NATIONAL DEFENSE	$583.9	$ —	$583.9
POLICE	31.1	93.4	124.5
PRISONS	5.4	72.4	77.8
LAW COURTS	7.5	40.9	48.4
FIRE	0.5	38.0	38.5
TOTAL	$628.4	$244.7	$873.1

Source: *Survey of Current Business* (Washington, D.C.: U.S. Department of Commerce, September 2008).

How would *you* go about deciding how much to spend on what? That's what Congress and the White House must do. That's also what state and local governments must do.

How Much Security Do We Buy? Exhibit 3 details the $873.1 billion spent in 2007 on security by federal, state, and local governments. As you see, our $583.9 billion national defense spending is our major security item, although its share of total federal spending has declined steadily and significantly over the past quarter century. (In 1970, that share was 41.8 percent; in 2007, it was 20.3 percent.) Not surprisingly, 85 percent of all 2007 government spending on police, fire, and corrections was done at the state and local levels.

Education

Government funding of elementary and high school education has deep roots in our society. It is one of Thomas Jefferson's cherished legacies.

How much government spends each year on education is partly determined by school enrollments and the quality of education we demand. The costs associated with a quality education depend on teacher training, the length of the school term, class size, and physical facilities, such as space and classroom equipment. Think back to your own elementary and high school days. If you were on the school board then, what changes would you have made? How would those changes have affected government spending?

What's our track record on funding public education? Over the period 1980–2007, the annual rate of increase in government spending on elementary, secondary, and higher education, measured in constant dollars, was approximately 3 percent, slightly above the percentage rate of increase in real GDP.

As we see in Exhibit 4, the lion's share of the 2007 government spending on education—90.3 percent—was done by state and local governments.

EXHIBIT 4   Federal, State, and Local Government Spending on Education: 2007 ($ Billions)

	FEDERAL	STATE AND LOCAL	TOTAL
ELEMENTARY AND SECONDARY	$33.3	$510.4	$543.7
COLLEGES AND UNIVERSITIES	22.7	103.3	126.0
OTHER	15.2	50.3	65.5
TOTAL	$71.2	$663.9	$735.2

Source: *Survey of Current Business* (Washington, D.C.: U.S. Department of Commerce, September 2008).

appliedperspective

© Royalty-Free/Corbis

Willing and able

NO CHILD LEFT BEHIND

In 2001, Congress passed the No Child Left Behind (NCLB) Act, which puts more muscle into its much earlier legislation, the Elementary and Secondary Education Act of 1965. There were and certainly are no illusions about what the NCLB Act could accomplish. It was never considered by its advocates to be "the solution" to the troubling problems of sliding academic performance of students and teachers. Everyone acknowledges the importance of home environment as a major contributor to students' inability to achieve minimally acceptable outcomes. And few deny that many teachers in many classrooms are both ill-equipped and underfunded.

But where do you start? The NCLB Act was essentially designed to tackle three items in the federal government's school reform agenda: teacher quality, accountability, and corrective stratagems to ensure quality instruction wherever needed.

Concerning teacher quality, the NCLB Act requires that (1) new teachers must have a bachelor's degree, (2) elementary school teachers must pass a state test demonstrating knowledge of mathematics and other skills pertinent to the basic school curriculum, and (3) middle and high school teachers must pass a state test in each academic subject they teach as well as have an undergraduate major in that discipline or course work equivalent to it. These requirements and others have been viewed by the National Education Association as a frontal attack on the union.

Yet, the accountability item is far more controversial. The NCLB Act is very prescriptive with regard to how proficiency assessments will be made, allowing very little flexibility. Student performance will be measured to ensure adequate yearly progress (AYP). The NCLB Act's end product includes higher scholastic scores and narrowing the gap between average and minority students' outcomes.

If schools fail to perform, corrective action becomes mandatory. Schools that do not meet AYP requirements for two consecutive years will be identified as "in need of improvement" and must offer parents the option of sending their children to another district school. Those that are chronic laggards must take corrective actions that involve restructuring the school's internal organization, including dismissing relevant staff, shifting key administrative authority to outside expert advisers, revamping the curriculum, and in some cases, extending the length of the school day.

Revamping the curriculum influences not only what teachers teach but how they teach it. The NCLB Act mandates "scientifically based research" teaching methods that advocates of the NCLB Act insist have been tested and proved to work. These imposed methods often conflict with methods devised and preferred by the teachers themselves. Resistance to these intrusions is understandably passionate.

In the main, the NCLB Act directives are regarded by many teachers, particularly those in jeopardy, as horrific and damaging to the teaching environment. Advocates of the NCLB Act acknowledge that they are harsh but consider them absolutely necessary.

Funding is always an issue. So is the issue of federal interference with what has traditionally been a local matter. Opponents of the NCLB Act argue that it is unfair and unwise to mandate these changes without providing the necessary funds to do a credible job. And there is much substance to that charge. But how much funding is enough? And is the federal government responsive to it?

Consider the comparative data: Federal funding for elementary and secondary education grew at an annual rate of 7.0 percent during 1995–2000, that is, during the five years prior to the NCLB Act. That growth rate increased to 13.3 percent during the 2000–2004 years. By contrast, GDP for 2000–2004 grew at 4.6 percent.

Transportation, Natural Resources, and Space

Interstate highways, county roads, city streets, canals, bridges, sewage systems, street lighting, city playgrounds, national parks, and zoos are just a few in a long list of public goods that government has assumed responsibility for over the years. Some are traditional public goods, with long histories; others are of more recent vintage, such as space exploration and securing strategic reserves of crude oil.

Transportation It's probably just as hard to imagine an interstate that is privately owned as it is to imagine our economy without the interstate. But like government spending on security and education, the question with highways and streets always is, How much spending is appropriate?

The answer is never without controversy. As small communities grow into large metropolitan suburbs, and as our incomes permit us to become increasingly mobile, we need to build and maintain more city streets, more bridges, more expressways, more bypasses, and more county, state, and interstate highways.

Approximately $140.1 billion was spent on transportation in 2007, with the lion's share being handled by state and local governments. The highway system alone accounted for 78 percent of transportation spending. No surprise, is it? Is there a road you on that isn't under repair or doesn't need repair?

Natural Resources And what about government spending on conservation and natural resources? Although such spending is minor—$30.9 billion—compared to that on security, education, and transportation, the same question confronts us concerning natural resources: How much is appropriate?

How much should we spend caring for our national, state, and county parks; wildlife preserves; and government forests, minerals, and agriculture lands? How much for promoting such projects as land reclamation, irrigation, drainage, and flood control?

There are competing interests that press for different levels of spending on our environment. Environmental groups such as the Sierra Club are actively engaged in promoting greater public concern and raising money to preserve our natural resources. They are opposed by people who are more interested in committing our resources to economic development. The issue, in the short run, is whether we can afford not to develop these resources. The long-run issue, according to conservation groups, is whether we might not all lose out if we allow them to be developed.

Space If 500 years ago government spending had not included exploration, Christopher Columbus might never have ventured beyond the coastal waters of southern Europe. But King Ferdinand and Queen Isabella did finance Columbus's expedition, and the rest, as they say, is history.

Perhaps some tax-paying Spaniards then complained that such spending was a poor investment and that there were countless competitive demands being made on the Crown that were more productive. It would be hard to discredit their claims even today.

Twentieth-century space exploration faces the same kinds of charges, and those supporting our space missions and moon landings rely on the same spirit of adventure that put Columbus on our shores. But whether the opportunity costs associated with space exploration make it a worthwhile investment or not, it is clear to both advocates and opponents of space exploration that if we are to have a space program, government is the appropriate provider. Once again, the question is how much spending. In 2007, it was $16.3 billion.

Agriculture and Public Assistance

What common denominator is there for government spending on security, education, transportation, natural resources, energy, and space? For each, the target population is everyone. Government does not intentionally target its spending on these items to satisfy any one segment of the population. National defense is intended to defend everyone. Interstate highways are built and maintained for everyone. Elementary and high school education is free and open, and even our community colleges and land-grant universities are open to those who meet the requirements.

Of course, not everyone takes advantage of these public and merit goods to the same degree. Families without children, for example, do not benefit from

on the net The Sierra Club (http://www.sierraclub.org/) promotes greater public spending on our natural resources.

applied perspective

SPACE EXPLORATIONS

The moon is not made of green cheese nor are there martians on planet Mars. We know that because we were there. We also know a great deal more about the rest of our galaxy and about our own planet Earth. Space explorations during the past half century opened up worlds of knowledge, mystery, and images of physical beauty, the likes of which no person could have dreamed of only decades before.

On May 5, 1961, the first U.S. spaceflight took Alan Shepard into a 15-minute, 28-second suborbital burst into space. It was one of six Mercury space flights; the third, manned by John Glenn, was our first orbital one, lasting about five hours while he circled the globe three times.

The 12 *Gemini* spaceflights that followed were designed to subject two-man crews to longer durations in space, to achieve rendezvous and docking with other orbital vehicles, to perfect methods of reentry and landing, and to acquire information concerning the effects of weightlessness on crews.

The 22 *Apollo* missions that followed the *Gemini* series were designed to land humans on the moon and bring them back to Earth. Six missions—*Apollos* 11, 12, 14, 15, 16, and 17—achieved this spectacular goal.

NASA shuttle missions began in 1981. The shuttle is a vehicle capable of taking off from Earth with crew and cargo, performing its mission while in orbit, then gliding softly to a runway landing on Earth to be used again. The accompanying table lists NASA's shuttle series—*Columbia*, *Challenger*, *Discovery*, *Atlantis*, and *Endeavor*— and their loggings.

If you haven't already glanced at the table, venture a guess at how many miles the shuttle series logged. Now check with the record. If you guessed 500 million, you ought try out for Alex Trebek's *Jeopardy*. Note as well the number of flights, orbits, and days in flight.

It's hard not to think about Christopher Columbus, Vasco da Gama, Ferdinand Magellan, Amerigo Vespucci, Meriwether Lewis, and William Clark when you think about astronauts Neil Armstrong, Virgil Grisson, Ronald McNair, Walter Schirra, and Judith Resnick. It's also not hard to think about governments' decisions over the centuries to invest in reaching out beyond known horizons.

© 2007 JupiterImages Corporation

To Pluto, planet or no planet.

SHUTTLE	FLIGHT DAYS	ORBITS	DISTANCE MILES	FLIGHTS	LONGEST FLIGHT DAYS	CREWS
COLUMBIA	300.74	4,808	125,204,911	28	17.66	160
CHALLENGER	62.41	995	41,527,416	10	8.23	60
DISCOVERY	268.62	4,229	176,657,672	32	13.89	199
ATLANTIS	220.40	3,468	144,694,078	26	12.89	161
ENDEAVOR	206.60	3,259	136,910,237	19	13.86	130
TOTAL	1,058.77	16,759	435,800,333	115	17.66	800

elementary education in the same way that families with children do. And some people benefit more from an interstate highway than do others. There are people who feel more secure with more people in jail. But no one is intentionally shortchanged.

But not all government spending is so universal. Some spending is exclusive and targeted to specific segments of the population and takes the form of goods and services or direct cash payments.

What's the rationale underlying such exclusion? Why is government in the transfer payment business, providing some people with goods, services, and cash, and not others? Perhaps the two most important principles governing such targeted spending are equity and stability.

What should we do about people who simply can't afford the bare necessities of life? Economic equity has always been a concern. Private philanthropy, which at one time was the only institution to address the problems of the destitute, now shares that responsibility with government.

check your understanding

Why is some government spending targeted to specific populations?

What should we do about people who are not destitute but are adversely affected by technological change? In some cases, the economic stability of a community or of an entire region is significantly shaken. In many of these cases, government has chosen to supplement the incomes of the people who are adversely affected.

Agriculture

Consider, for example, the government's $29.2 billion spending on agriculture. It's essentially a transfer payment. Money is taken from the general population in the form of taxes and transferred to the farm population in the form of subsidies. But why should the government transfer your money to farmers? Why not simply allow the market to solve the problem of chronic farm surpluses the way excess supplies are reduced or eliminated in other markets? Aside from the obvious—the political muscle of the farm population—the government also worries that the market consequences would undermine the stability of not only the farm economy, but the national economy as well.

Public Assistance

The transfer payment that seems to be the lightning rod for media attention and political controversy is public assistance—the government's **welfare** program. The raison d'être of welfare is to moderate the economic hardships facing the poor, the elderly, and the disabled. This is accomplished by supplementing their incomes with government-provided goods and services, direct cash payments, or both.

In 2007, the federal government spent $142.3 billion on welfare and related social services, while state and local governments added another $122.1 billion.

Who is eligible for cash-payment welfare? Until recently, eligibility was linked to single-parent families (the Aid to Families with Dependent Children program, AFDC) and to the sick or disabled (the Supplemental Security Income program, SSI). Eligibility to either one meant entitlement, with no time limit specified. Opponents of public assistance argued that cash payments and welfare programs such as food stamps and Medicaid undermined the recipients' motivation to become independent and responsible. Advocates for welfare dismissed as nonsense the idea that people prefer to live on welfare rather than work to earn a living wage.

The mid-1990s political debate on welfare resulted in Congress legislating the Personal Responsibility and Work Opportunity Reconciliation Act of 1996. This act created Temporary Assistance for Needy Families, which effectively abolished what had been the two principal components of our cash-aid welfare system: AFDC and Emergency Assistance to Families with Children. This major change was followed by the Balanced Budget Act of 1997, which added a welfare-to-work grant program to assist families moving from welfare to work.

The basic idea behind these welfare changes was to eliminate entitlement. No individual or family is entitled to receive welfare. Under this new welfare scheme, the federal government provides state governments with capped block grants to administer state-run welfare programs, but welfare recipients must participate in work activities within two years of receiving welfare or risk losing it. The government also imposed a time limit on welfare. Although families may be eligible for welfare on more than one occasion, eligibility per family runs out after five years of benefits.

The government's new welfare package still contains two critical carryovers from the old system: the food stamp program and Medicaid.

What are food stamps? Welfare recipients receive **food stamps** that are accepted as money at most retail stores and supermarkets. Because these stamps are earmarked for the purchase of only some goods (and not others), the government influences, at least minimally, the welfare recipients' diets. The criteria for food stamp eligibility remain as they were before: income (or lack of it) and size of family. In 2007, the food stamp program amounted to $30.4 billion.

Welfare
Government-provided assistance—cash payments and goods and services—to the poor, the elderly, and the disabled. Eligibility is based principally on income and size of family.

on the
net
The Social Security Administration (http://www.ssa.gov./) provides information on recent federal public assistance legislation (http://www.ssa.gov/legislation/).

Food stamp program
An aid program that provides low-income people with stamps that can be redeemed for food and related items.

The single most significant service item in the welfare package $303.8 billion in 2007—is still **Medicaid**, a federally subsidized, state-administered program that pays the medical and hospital costs of welfare recipients and other low-income people. Medicaid covers fee-for-service payments to private physicians as well as hospitalization, nursing-home expenses, and skilled nursing care at home.

Medicaid
A health care program administered through Social Security that is applicable to low-income and disabled people.

Social Insurance

Since the 1930s, the government has taken on the functions of an insurance agent, collecting premiums from those who participate in its insurance program and paying out benefits to claimants. These premiums and benefits appear as government taxes and spending—in fact, that's what they are commonly called—but the truth of the matter is that government is principally the agency handling the insurance dollars.

Why is government in the insurance business, and what does it insure? Government is in the business because it is responding to an insurance need that, it feels, is not being adequately served by private insurance. What does it insure? In a nutshell, government insures families against incurring sizable income reductions when they retire or when they are disabled or unemployed during their working life. As you can imagine, most people who pay into the government-managed insurance program hope that they do not have to make claims for disability or unemployment.

Social Security
The core of the government-managed insurance program was established in 1935 when Congress passed the Social Security Act. **Social Security** provides old age and survivor insurance. Payments to the insured or to their surviving dependents were originally intended to supplement incomes, not to be the major source of income. Disability insurance was added to Social Security in 1956, and health insurance—Medicare—was added in 1965.

Social Security
A social insurance program that provides benefits, subject to eligibility, to the elderly, the disabled, and their dependents.

Social Security is first and foremost a pension system. There are a host of private pension systems in the marketplace, but none compares with the size and inclusiveness of Social Security. It was designed to provide income security upon retirement to people who would not otherwise have that form of security. Social Security differs from private pension systems in a number of respects.

First, it is compulsory. Wage earners must belong whether they like it or not. Second, Social Security transfers income across income and age groups. How so? Premiums, paid in the form of Social Security taxes, are based on ability to pay. That is, high-wage earners pay more into the system than low-wage earners. But benefits received depend not only on how much a person has paid into the system but also on the number of surviving dependents. As a result, low-wage earners tend to receive more retirement benefits, relative to their contributions, than do high-wage workers. Age is also a factor. Most people today retire with more benefits than Social Security offered, say, a generation ago. But what they paid into the system years ago was determined by what benefits were provided then. In other words, in each year, younger workers paying Social Security taxes subsidize those in retirement.

Third, Social Security is a pay-as-you-go system that is financed through a pay-roll tax, half of which is paid by the worker and the other half by the employer. The revenues from this Social Security tax go into a trust fund from which benefits are paid out. In some years, government receives less in Social Security taxes than it pays out in Social Security benefits, in which case it makes up the difference by drawing from its trust fund. In other years, more money comes in than goes out, allowing government to build up the fund.

Unemployment Insurance
Unemployment insurance was introduced as a provision of the Social Security Act in 1935. Its main purpose is to provide temporary income support for unemployed workers. How much the

Unemployment insurance
A program of income support for eligible workers who are temporarily unemployed.

applied perspective

© Picture Arts/CORBIS

ARE THE SOCIAL SECURITY AND MEDICARE SYSTEMS IN JEOPARDY?

There are about as many opinions among economists concerning the viability of Social Security and Medicare as there are economists willing to talk about it. The overriding issue is whether the aging of our population will eventually place on those taxpayers who finance Social Security and Medicare a burden so intolerable that the modus operandi of these entitlement programs will simply become unworkable.

Consider the problem. Just a few generations ago, the ratio of working people to retirees was sufficiently high to support what was then a not-too-demanding standard of living for those in retirement. That has changed. The ratio has fallen considerably, and the standard of living of those in retirement and enjoying the fruits of Social Security and Medicare has risen dramatically. If the ratio of working people to retirees keeps falling—and it will with the baby boomers soon reaching retirement age—who's left in the workplace to pay the needed Social Security taxes?

That's what unnerves a lot of economists who look at the accompanying exhibit. It shows the projected increases in the claims on the economy by the entitlement programs between 1996 and 2035. As you can see, the projected growth of Medicare claims far outstrips that of Social Security. Not really surprising. After all, there is a direct and positive relationship between age and health care demands, and with new and more life-securing technologies available in medicine, the sky seems the limit on how much a society can invest in caring for the health needs of its senior population.

How do you deal with the implications of the exhibit? Are the Social Security and Medicare systems in jeopardy? If reform is inevitable, what kind of reform will be both politically and economically sound?

Social Security is financed largely by taxes on workers' income, and promised Social Security benefits are legislated by Congress. The problem of insufficient future tax revenues to cover promised benefits can be handled in a number of ways.

First, simply raise the Social Security tax by an amount necessary to meet the promised benefits. But legislating tax increases in this political climate is politically unhealthy, and there appears to be very little support for this option. Second, reduce future benefits by a sufficient amount so that future retirees will not exhaust the projected Social Security tax revenues. This option, too, invites strong political backlash and has few staunch

supporters. Third, increase the number of years of earnings used to determine benefits. This is a disguised way of reducing benefits. Fourth, change the law to allow the Social Security system to invest some of the trust funds in the private sector, where the rates of return on investment are considerably higher than the rates currently earned by the fund's investment in long-term government bonds.

I can deal with the pain—but not the pain of financial obligation that it imposes on my children.

Current and Projected Levels of Entitlement Program Operations as a Percentage of GDP

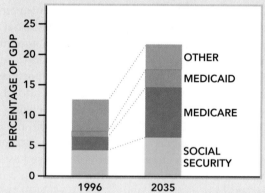

Source: Congressional Budget Office, *Long-Term Budgetary Pressures and Policy Options* (Washington, D.C.: Congress of the United States, March 1997), Executive Summary, Table 2.

While each of these reform options will work, each is perceived by some economists as a decisive backward step in providing an acceptable standard of living for our senior citizens.

. . . .

MORE ON THE NET

For different perspectives on Social Security reform, review the Cato Institute Project on Social Security Privatization (http://www.socialsecurity.org/) and the National Committee to Preserve Social Security and Medicare (http://www.ncpssm.org/).

unemployed worker receives each week and the number of weeks the unemployed worker is allowed to receive benefits varies from state to state.

Medicare In 1965, the government added a health care insurance program, **Medicare**, to the Social Security system. Its purpose is to reduce the financial burden of illness on the elderly. The criterion for eligibility is uncomplicated: Medicare covers everyone 65 years of age or older.

Like Social Security's pension program, Medicare's funding is anchored in a trust fund. In any year, workers pay into the Medical Insurance Trust Fund through a payroll tax system that provides the money needed to cover payments to Medicare recipients in that year.

What does Medicare provide? Subject to deductibles and caps, Medicare covers hospitalization, skilled nursing care at home, outpatient care, and physician fees.

Because Medicare is focused primarily on the elderly, who continue to be a growing percentage of our population, and because new, expensive, state-of-the-art technologies are increasingly becoming part of health care, Medicare's trust fund may soon be added to the list of endangered species. How long Medicare can continue to function as a health insurance program without radically changing its structure of revenues and benefits is a problem that ranks among the most critical government faces today.

How Do Our Social Security Payments Compare to Those Elsewhere?

Are our Social Security payments out of line? That is to say, is our commitment to Social Security in 2006 frightfully expensive or pitifully low? Or is it just about right? How can we assess the role of Social Security in our economy? Perhaps one way is to compare what we do to what other democratic market economies do. Exhibit 5 does just that.

What do you make of this exhibit? Whatever else can be said about our commitment to Social Security, it does not appear to be too large. The 12.0 percent of GDP is below the percentages for most similar democratic market economies. Perhaps it should give us some comfort to know we're not off the deep end.

Interest

The government borrows, accumulates debt, and each year pays interest on that debt. In 2007 the public debt reached $9.0 trillion, and $411.1 billion was spent by government on interest payments. Both the size of the debt and the annual interest payments it creates grew considerably in the 1980s.

Medicare
A health care program administered through Social Security that is applicable to everyone over 65 years old.

on the net
The Centers for Medicare and Medicaid Services, a federal agency within the Department of Health and Human Services, provides information on Medicare and Medicaid (http://www.cms.hhs.gov/).

on the net
The Bureau of the Public Debt (http://www.publicdebt.treas.gov/), among other services, provides the amount of the federal government's debt, to the penny.

EXHIBIT 5 Social Security Expenditures as a Percentage of GDP for Selected Economies: 2006

COUNTRY	PERCENTAGE OF GDP
JAPAN	17.7
UNITED STATES	12.0
CANADA	8.7
ITALY	20.0
NETHERLANDS	20.1
GERMANY	25.8
FRANCE	23.4

Source: International Monetary Fund: *Government Financial Statistics Yearbook, 2007.*

IS THE LEVEL OF GOVERNMENT SPENDING TOO HIGH?

Looking back over each of these government spending items, it becomes difficult to advocate wholesale cuts in government spending. Just where would you start? What parts of what programs are expendable?

Every government dollar spent has a purpose. Moreover, every government program has a strong support system buttressed by a determined constituency. It is always possible for government to spend money foolishly, and sometimes that seems to be what it does, but what indicators should we use to gauge whether government spending—federal and state and local—is too big or too small?

The Growth of Government Spending

Government spending in 2007 was $4,772.9 billion, 60 percent of which was handled in Washington, D.C. How has it grown? Exhibit 6 traces the historical record of total government spending from 1970 to 2007, adjusted for inflation.

If your impression is that government spending just keeps going up and up, you're absolutely right! Total government spending, measured in 2000 dollars, tripled over the 37-year period. But that's only part of the picture. After all, our GDP was going up and up as well. Looking at the government's slice of the increasing GDP pie, then, may give us an entirely different perspective on government spending. Throughout the 1970–2007 period, government's slice was no more than a few percent away from a third of the GDP pie.

Government Spending in Other Economies

Is a third of the GDP pie too big a slice? After all, we do need our police protection, schools, and highways. How much is enough? While we are all entitled to our own opinion, it may still be worthwhile to compare our slice to those in other economies. That's what we see in Exhibit 7. We allocate a smaller portion of our GDP to government than almost any other nation shown in Exhibit 7.

GOVERNMENT SPENDING AND RESOURCE ALLOCATION

As we showed in Exhibit 1, some of government spending takes the form of public and merit goods—government purchases of goods and services—and some takes the form of transfer payments.

The distinction is important. When government provides a highway, it takes steel, concrete, heavy equipment, labor, and other resources away from the production of private goods. That is, a reallocation of the economy's resources

EXHIBIT 6   Government Spending: 1970–2007 ($ Billions, 2000)

	TOTAL	FEDERAL	STATE AND LOCAL	TOTAL/ GDP
1970	$1,280.0	$ 785.5	$ 442.5	32.6
1980	1,692.7	1,083.4	609.3	32.8
1990	2,431.0	1,535.9	895.1	34.2
2007	4,065.5	2,453.6	1,611.9	36.8

Source: *Economic Report of the President*, (Washington, D.C.: U.S. Department of Commerce, 2008).

EXHIBIT 7   Government Spending as a Percentage of GDP: 1981–2003

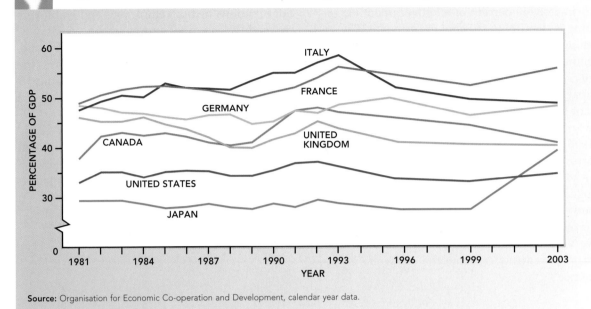

Source: Organisation for Economic Co-operation and Development, calendar year data.

occurs. Assuming full employment, the highway we enjoy comes at the expense of private goods consumption.

What about the government's transfer payments? Do they involve the same kind of opportunity cost? Not exactly. Consider the government's welfare programs. Government spending on food stamps, for example, does not represent government purchases of goods and services. Government simply engineers a transfer of private goods and services from one group in the economy, the taxpayers, to another, the welfare recipients.

What do welfare recipients do with the transfer payments? They don't buy highways. Their purchases of private goods and services substitute for the taxpayers' purchase of private goods and services. Although these two different groups of people may buy different private goods, the allocation of GDP between private and public goods and services is unaffected.

In other words, the character of government's intervention in the allocation process depends on the character of government spending. How significant a share of GDP is in the form of government purchases? Big? Bigness lies in the eyes of the beholder.

CHAPTER REVIEW

1. Government spending serves multiple purposes. On occasion, spending is used as an instrument of countercyclical policy. Government spending also provides public and merit goods as well as transfer payments.

2. Public goods are nonexclusive and nonrival. *Nonexclusive* means that once the good is provided, no one can be excluded from deriving its benefits. *Nonrival* means that one person's use of the good does not diminish the good for other people's use.

3. Merit goods are goods provided by the market, although not in quantities or at prices that government prefers. As a result, the government produces the goods and sells them at subsidized prices.

4. Transfer payments represent a redistribution of income from taxpayers to specific groups, such as welfare recipients (receiving public assistance), the unemployed (receiving unemployment insurance payments), people in retirement (receiving Social Security payments), and farm producers (receiving government subsidies).

5. Approximately 50 percent of all government spending is in the form of government purchases of public and merit goods. Another 35.5 percent is in the form of transfer payments. The

remaining 14.5 percent of spending is for interest, federal grants-in-aid, and other items.

6. Approximately 60 percent of all government spending is done by the federal government. The remaining 40 percent represents state and local government spending.

7. Security, education, and transportation are the principal public and merit good items that government buys, accounting for approximately 35 percent of total government spending.

8. The 1996 Personal Responsibility and Work Opportunity Reconciliation Act reformed our public assistance program. Welfare recipients no longer have a right to welfare and must work to receive welfare aid. Also, the government put a limit on the number of years a family can receive welfare benefits. Food stamps and Medicaid are carryovers from the old welfare program.

9. Social Security is the government's social insurance program. It takes the form of a trust fund. Contributions by both employees and employers are made to the fund, and payments are drawn from it to provide for retirement, disability, and unemployment benefits. The fund also pays for Medicare, which provides health care for the elderly.

10. Government spending during the period 1970–2001 was relatively stable at 30 percent of GDP.

11. Consumer sovereignty is affected by government spending. Excluding transfer payments—since they still end up as purchasing power dictated by consumer sovereignty—government decides what goods and services will be produced for approximately 15 percent of GDP.

KEY TERMS

Public good
Merit good
Welfare

Food stamp program
Medicaid
Social Security

Unemployment insurance
Medicare

QUESTIONS

1. While people may disagree about how much government spending is appropriate and what programs ought to be funded, most people accept the idea that there are legitimate purposes for government spending. What are these purposes?

2. Police protection and public housing are two of many goods that government provides. One is considered a public good, the other a merit good. Which is which and why?

3. What are the most important spending items of the federal government? Of state and local governments?

4. Explain why each of the following is either a private good or a public good: traffic lights, in-line skates, a city park, a chicken salad sandwich, a tennis racket, national defense, a coastal lighthouse.

5. What is a transfer payment? Why does the government engage in such transfers?

6. Why is some of the federal government's spending on agriculture considered a transfer payment?

7. What are the principal 1996 changes made to our welfare program?

8. What is the principal difference between Medicare and Medicaid?

9. If government decides, it can reduce defense spending and even spending on education to a penny, but it can't do that with Social Security. Why not? (*Hint:* Distinguish between a trust fund and discretionary government spending.)

10. Is the level of government spending too high? How has it grown? How does it compare to government spending in other industrial economies?

11. Imagine two government budgets, each $100. The first allocates $50 to the provision of public goods and $50 to transfer payments. The other allocates $75 to the provision of public goods and $25 to transfer payments. If GDP were $500, explain why the two budgets would generate different positions on a production possibilities curve, with private good production measured on the vertical axis and public goods production on the horizontal. Graph the two curves.

Economic Consultants

Economic Research and Analysis by Students for Professionals

The National Education Association (NEA) is an organization with over 2 million members who work at every level of education. JoAnn Weber, a high school teacher and local volunteer for the NEA, often meets with parents and school officials to discuss education funding in the United States. Recently, a group of parents expressed concerns that, first, federal government spending on education was too low, and, second, that recent political efforts to cut federal spending have had an adverse impact on education funding.

© Image 100/Royalty-Free/CORBIS

JoAnn is unsure how to answer these concerns, and she has asked Economic Consultants to provide her with information. Prepare a report for JoAnn that addresses the following issues:

1. How much does the federal government spend on education?
2. In recent years, has federal spending on education increased or decreased? By how much?
3. Does U.S. education spending, as a percentage of GDP, compare favorably or unfavorably with that of other nations?

You may find the following resources helpful as you prepare this report for JoAnn:

- **National Education Association (NEA)** (http://www.nea.org/)—The NEA provides information about its programs and activities.

- **Organisation for Economic Co-Operation and Development (OECD)** (http://www.oecd.org/els/)—The Education, Employment, Labor and Social Affairs Department of the OECD provides international data and information on education spending.

- **National Center for Education Statistics (NCES)** (http://nces.ed.gov/)—The NCES is the primary federal entity for collecting and analyzing data related to education in the United States and other nations.

- *Education Indicators: An International Perspective* (http://nces.ed.gov/surveys/international/intlindicators/)—*Education Indicators: An International Perspective,* an NCES report, provides comparative data and analysis on education spending by the United States and other nations.

- **U.S. Department of Education** (http://www.ed.gov/)—The U.S. Department of Education provides information on its offices and programs, education initiatives, and reports and publications.

1. When the federal government shifts $100 from interstate construction to transfer payments,
   a. its impact on the economy's resource allocation decreases.
   b. its impact on the economy's resource allocation increases.
   c. its impact on the economy's resource allocation remains unchanged.
   d. it raises GDP by $100.
   e. it decreases GDP by $100.
2. Which of the following is an example of a merit good?
   a. National defense
   b. Private education
   c. Public education
   d. Professional sports
   e. Amateur sports
3. What are the properties of a public good?
   a. Government spending and government use
   b. Rivalry and exclusivity
   c. Nonrivalry and nonexclusivity
   d. Merit and security of the population
   e. Merit and government use
4. When the government receives income from one group and gives it to another group, it engages in an activity associated with
   a. countercyclical fiscal policy.
   b. transfer payments.
   c. the transformation of public into merit goods.
   d. public goods equality.
   e. merit distribution of income.
5. The largest share of state and local spending is for
   a. transfer payments.
   b. purchases.
   c. countercyclical policy.
   d. civilian protection.
   e. interest on the state and local debt.
6. Spending on public education is
   a. the largest single use of federal spending.

   b. the largest single use of state and local spending.
   c. divided equally among federal and state and local governments.
   d. exclusively the responsibility of state and local governments.
   e. exclusively the responsibility of the federal government.
7. As a percentage of GDP, spending on national defense
   a. has remained relatively constant since 1970.
   b. has risen dramatically since 1970.
   c. has fallen since 1970.
   d. is approximately 75 percent of federal spending.
   e. is approximately 75 percent of all government spending.
8. The major change in welfare legislation in the mid-1990s concerned the
   a. decrease in eligibility among welfare recipients.
   b. elimination of entitlement to welfare.
   c. exclusion of undocumented immigrants.
   d. shift from cash to in-kind assistance.
   e. shift from in-kind to cash assistance.
9. Social Security includes
   a. Medicaid.
   b. Medicare.
   c. Aid to Families with Dependent Children.
   d. public assistance.
   e. all of the above.
10. Government spending as a percentage of GDP in the United States
    a. has fallen considerably since 1970.
    b. has risen considerably since 1970.
    c. is higher than the percentages for European economies.
    d. is lower than the percentages for European economies.
    e. is similar to the average percentage for European economies.

FINANCING GOVERNMENT: TAXES AND DEBT

THIS CHAPTER INTRODUCES YOU TO THE ECONOMIC PRINCIPLES ASSOCIATED WITH:

- Commandeering resources
- Commandeering money (taxes)
- Regressive, proportional, and progressive tax structures
- Social Security taxes
- Government securities and public debt
- Internally and externally financing the public debt

Many years ago, one of our nation's most beloved comedians, Jack Benny, used to entertain millions on Sunday night prime-time radio. He always played the penny-pincher, obsessed with the fear of parting with money. In one of his celebrated skits, a holdup man approaches him and says, "Your money or your life." There is a long pause. The holdup man says, "Well?" And Benny replies, "Wait a minute, I'm thinking."

Change the scene and the question slightly. Ask, "Your taxes or your life," and many Americans, it seems, would be hard-pressed to decide. Exaggeration? Of course. But taxes are about as unpleasant a thought as any. We are repelled by the idea of increasing taxes, and we typically vote accordingly. As any politician who has gone through the campaign mill will tell you, the one thing you must promise never, never to do is raise taxes.

And that's strange indeed. After all, few people question our need for national defense or for most of the items that

have become an integral part of our government sector. We are an intelligent people, yet we often seem to forget the obvious: There's no such thing as a free lunch.

It doesn't take much thinking, even for the village idiot, to figure out that if we demand a penny's worth of public goods, then we're going to have to tax ourselves a penny. If we raise the demand to $100 billion of public goods, then our taxes increase accordingly.

OPPORTUNITY COSTS AND TAXES

Put this one-to-one relationship between public goods and taxes in real terms. Consider a public goods demand in the form of a fighter aircraft. How do we go about getting it, and what must we give up to get it? To produce a fighter aircraft, we are obliged to give up something else that could have been produced with the resources used to produce the aircraft. That is to say, to produce a public good, *we tax our ability to produce other goods.* The opportunity cost of providing the aircraft is illustrated in the production possibilities curve of Exhibit 1.

Producing the first airplane means giving up 500 houses. The economy's output shifts from point *a* to point *b* on the production possibilities curve. Simple enough? But how do you get people to give up 500 houses? That is, how is it physically done? Even if people are willing to sacrifice houses for the airplane, how does government go about designing a mechanism that shifts resources from home building to aircraft making?

COMMANDEERING RESOURCES

The most direct method a government can use to acquire resources is simply to commandeer them. In fact, that's precisely the way governments for centuries have acquired resources. That's how pharaohs built their pyramids. That's how armies have often been recruited.

In the economy of Exhibit 1, the government can just go out to the construction sites, round up a number of construction workers, transport them to the aircraft factories, and set them to work. The result is fewer houses and more airplanes.

Exaggeration? It was customary throughout the Middle Ages for governments to construct road systems by just that kind of commandeering. During our

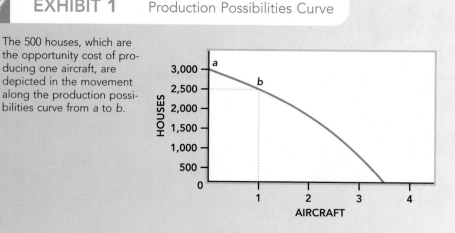

EXHIBIT 1   Production Possibilities Curve

The 500 houses, which are the opportunity cost of producing one aircraft, are depicted in the movement along the production possibilities curve from *a* to *b*.

Civil War, draft animals, wagons, and food were sometimes commandeered by both southern and northern armies from unlucky farmsteads that happened to be located close to a war zone.

Even modern democratic governments haven't completely abandoned this practice of commandeering resources. After all, isn't the military draft simply another form of commandeering labor? Army wage rates are not related to the draftees' opportunity costs. Although we switched from the draft system to an all-volunteer army, some European armies are still recruited through a draft.

Military service aside, there are good reasons why the practice of commandeering has been virtually forsaken by democratic governments as a method of procuring resources. It can be capricious and unpopular, but above all else, it is terribly inefficient. Suppose government decides to produce that aircraft. Should it really draft construction workers to make it? Do they have the skills? Would *you* fly it?

THE TAX SYSTEM

The tax system is an alternative way of shifting resources from the private sector to government. In this system, *government commandeers money, not resources.* Government uses the money in the marketplace to buy what it needs.

There's no need now for the government to run after construction workers or aeronautical engineers. It taxes money away from the general population and *buys* fighter aircraft. Who produces it? An aircraft company, of course. Why shouldn't it? It gets paid by government. The aeronautical engineers, along with everyone else associated with building the airplane, are hired by the company at wage rates that match or better their opportunity costs.

Since people end up—after taxes are imposed—with smaller after-tax incomes, their demand curves for private goods, such as houses, decrease. This is how resources used in the production of private goods are transferred through the government to the aircraft company.

How much money should government tax away from the people? You might suppose that it depends upon how many airplanes or other public goods and services it intends to buy. But sometimes, cause and effect get reversed. Government buys only what its tax revenues allow.

THERE'S MORE THAN ONE WAY TO LEVY TAXES

Suppose the government decides to spend $100 billion and plans to finance the $100 billion expenditure by taxation. How does it go about taxing? Taxes are not voluntary contributions. The government has to be particularly careful about the method it uses to raise the $100 billion. It has several options.

The Poll (or Head) Tax

The government can levy a fixed tax, sometimes called a **poll tax**, on every adult in the population. If tax equity—the fairness of the tax—is an issue, the poll tax presents a serious problem. If everyone is taxed the same absolute amount, say, $500, then poorer people end up paying a higher percentage of their income. Economists describe such a tax as **regressive**. The poor pay proportionally more.

But who are the poor? If the government had little or no information about people's personal incomes, then the poll tax might be the most equitable way of

Poll tax
A tax of a specific absolute sum levied on every person or every household.

Regressive income tax
A tax whose impact varies inversely with the income of the person taxed. Poor people have a higher percentage of their income taxed than do rich people.

distributing the tax burden. You can see why a poll tax would be an attractive option in some less-developed economies where income data are virtually unknown.

The Income Tax

In most modern economies, however, governments have access to income data. They can tax these incomes in as many ways as their imagination allows, but two options stand out as the most used.

The Proportional Income Tax System The government can levy a flat-rate tax on personal income, that is, tax a fixed percentage of all incomes. Unlike a poll tax, the rich and poor don't end up paying the same amount. Now the rich obviously pay more. In the **proportional income tax** system, equity is described as paying the *same proportion* of income to taxes.

Consider, for example, two people who work but earn very different incomes. Sandy Roos, an oncology nurse, earns $25,000. Her next-door neighbor, Gary Behrman, is a psychologist earning $50,000. If the flat-tax rate is 20 percent, then the government collects a total of $15,000. Gary, who ends up paying twice the tax Sandy pays, would probably prefer the poll tax. If you were in his shoes, wouldn't you? What about Sandy?

	Income	Tax Rate	Tax Bill
Gary	$50,000	20%	$10,000
Sandy	$25,000	20%	$ 5,000

The Progressive Income Tax System Sandy would probably complain about the flat-tax rate. She would argue that a flat-tax rate, although better than a poll tax, is unfair because the tax burden still falls more heavily upon the poor than upon the rich.

She believes that she suffers a greater loss in giving up 20 percent of her income than Gary does in giving up 20 percent of his. After all, he makes twice her income. She thinks that the enjoyment she derives from the $5,000 she gives up is greater than the enjoyment Gary gives up paying his $10,000 tax.

Of course, it is impossible to make interpersonal comparisons of enjoyment. How can she possibly know how he feels about giving up $10,000? But her reasoning is entirely plausible, isn't it?

At least some governments think so. Instead of taxing a flat rate across incomes, they design a **progressive income tax** structure in which the tax rate on higher incomes increases progressively. For example, the government could tax everyone's first $25,000 at 20 percent, everyone's second $25,000 at 40 percent, everyone's third $25,000 at 50 percent, and all income beyond $75,000 at 60 percent. As you see, the marginal tax rate is steeper in the higher income brackets.

What does Gary Behrman pay under such a progressive tax system? He pays 20 percent on his first $25,000, or $5,000, plus 40 percent, or $10,000, on his second $25,000. His total tax is now $15,000, $5,000 more than he paid before. Sandy's tax remains unchanged at $5,000.

	Income	Tax Rate	Tax Bill
Gary	1st $25,000	20%	$ 5,000
	2nd $25,000	40%	$10,000
			$15,000
Sandy	1st $25,000	20%	$ 5,000

Proportional income tax A tax that is a fixed percentage of income, regardless of the level of income.

Progressive income tax A tax whose rate varies directly with the income of the person taxed. Rich people pay a higher tax rate—a larger percentage of their income is taxed—than do poor people.

Gary now ends up paying three times the tax Sandy pays. Through this progressive tax system, based on ability to pay, the government hopes to achieve a more equitable sharing of the tax burden. It calculates that Gary's loss of enjoyment in giving up $15,000 now approximates the enjoyment loss incurred by Sandy.

Of course, the government can introduce exemptions and allow deductions from all sorts of taxable income. But as you would guess, there will always be some grumbling among some people no matter what exemptions and deductions are allowed and no matter what the tax rates are at various income brackets.

The Corporate Income Tax

In most modern democratic economies, governments also tax the income of corporations. They could levy a progressive **corporate income tax**, using the same rationale that justifies imposing a progressive income tax, but there's a complicating factor here. Shareholders of corporations receive income in the form of dividends and since their personal incomes are certainly not identical, the burden of the corporate income tax—whatever its progressivity—would fall unevenly among corporate shareholders.

Corporate income tax
A tax levied on a corporation's income before dividends are distributed to stockholders.

The Property Tax

Why limit taxes to income and profit? Why not tax wealth? Why shouldn't the government also impose a tax on part or all of a person's wealth?

Taxing wealth could involve the government in the rather messy business of taxing personal belongings, such as furniture, carpets, and household appliances. Or the government could tax financial assets, such as savings deposits, bonds, stocks, and certificates of deposit, which would be much easier to evaluate. The government could also tax real estate.

The most commonly taxed wealth holdings are residential, commercial, and industrial properties. Typically, the **property tax** is a flat-rate tax applied to the property's assessed value. In this sense it becomes a proportional wealth tax. That is, people who live in mansions on hilltops pay more than people who live in mobile homes. But how much more? The proportionality of the tax depends on accurate assessments of property values. Most states give residents over a certain age a break on their property taxes. Forty states provide either property tax credits or homestead exemptions that limit the value of assessed property subject to tax.

What about financial wealth? Don't we pay taxes on our savings accounts? No! The government typically taxes the *income earned* on savings, which is taxed as personal income, but not the accounts themselves.

Property tax
A tax levied on the value of physical assets such as land, or financial assets such as stock and bonds.

Unit tax
A fixed tax in the form of cents or dollars per unit, levied on a good or service.

Sales tax
A tax levied in the form of a specific percentage of the value of the good or service.

Customs duty
A sales tax applied to a foreign good or service.

Excise tax
Any tax levied on a good or service, such as a unit tax, a sales tax, or a customs duty.

Excise Taxes

Aside from taxing personal income, corporate profits, and physical and financial property, the government can levy taxes on specific goods and services that people consume. It has several options.

It can levy (1) a **unit tax**—an amount of money per item; (2) a **sales tax**—a percentage of the sales price on every item sold; or (3) a **customs duty**—a sales tax applied to foreign goods imported into the economy. All of these are different kinds of **excise tax**.

In any form, an excise tax is regressive. For example, if you fill up your gas tank in New Hampshire, the 24-cents-per-gallon unit tax on the 20 gallons

applied perspective

ARE WE REALLY PAYING HIGH TAXES?

Nobody likes to pay taxes, although we grudgingly accept the idea that we have to (just as we have to go to the dentist). But it's one thing to be taxed, and quite another to be weighted down with taxes. And that's the complaint we commonly hear. Don't we? In fact, it would be difficult to find anybody in the United States who would not buy into the proposition that we are, as a nation, heavily overtaxed and that this taxation will yet be the ruin of us all.

Tax Revenues, by Country (Percentage of GDP)

	PERCENTAGE OF GDP
JAPAN	30.5
AUSTRALIA	33.6
UNITED STATES	34.3
UNITED KINGDOM	40.6
CANADA	43.4
GERMANY	45.1
NETHERLANDS	46.4
ITALY	46.7
BELGIUM	49.5
NORWAY	50.0
FRANCE	51.1
DENMARK	56.8
SWEDEN	62.7

Source: OECD.

Even a comparative analysis with economies similar to our own of tax revenue share of GDP—which shows us as a relatively lightly taxed people—would not really matter. Aversion to taxes is, in many cases, visceral. Still, it may be worthwhile to make comparisons, because they are so striking. Look at the accompanying table.

Look at taxation as a percentage of GDP. Whereas taxes represent 34.3 percent of GDP in the United States, it is over 50 percent in Sweden and Denmark, and over 40 percent in most other Western European economies. While the high percentages in Scandinavia might be attributed to the social democratic governments there, the same cannot be argued for the United Kingdom and Germany. The data are unambiguous. Comparatively speaking, we simply do not pay high taxes.

MORE ON THE NET

Visit a few organizations that advocate tax reform, such as Americans for Tax Reform (http://www.atr.org/) and Citizens for Tax Justice (http://www.ctj.org/). Do these organizations believe U.S. citizens are taxed too heavily? Too lightly? Why?

check your understanding

Why are excise taxes regressive?

purchased yields the government $4.80. Dorothy Shelly-Vickers's Porsche at the next pump takes 20 gallons as well, and Dorothy pays the same $4.80 tax. But the $4.80 tax Dorothy pays probably represents a smaller percentage of her income than it does of yours.

If you are impressed with the $60,000 Porsche and decide to buy one yourself, the 20 percent customs duty paid by the Porsche dealer and passed on to you, plus the 10 percent sales tax you pay on the $60,000 purchase, nets the government $18,000. The tax is regressive, unrelated to income, but the government probably figures that a new Porsche owner can afford that level of taxation.

The equity issue may not be very disturbing in the matter of Porsches—after all, few of the poor own one—but sales taxes on bread, milk, medicine, and other basics of life do add up, and their burden tends to fall more heavily upon the poor. Governments typically exercise moral judgment in levying excise taxes. Some exclude from taxation such items as milk, medicine, and books and place a relatively high rate on items such as cigarettes and alcohol. Discriminatory? Of course.

While sales taxes vary from state to state, from 0 percent—Alaska, Delaware, Montana, New Hampshire, Oregon—to 7.25 percent in California, not all goods are taxed at the same state rate. The Illinois sales tax, for example, has a two-rate structure: one percent for qualifying foods, drugs, and medical appliances, and 6.25 percent for general merchandise goods. Many agricultural-based states impose lower sales tax rates on farm vehicles and equipment: 1 percent in Mississippi and North Carolina, 1.5 percent in Alabama, 2.5 percent in Minnesota, and 3 percent in Florida.

Like a poll tax, an excise tax is relatively easy to impose. It doesn't require the government to know much about your income, your corporation's profit, or your property assets. When you buy milk, you pay a tax. When you smoke, you pay a tax. It's as simple as that. For some governments in some economies, it's about the only tax they can administer.

Estate (or Inheritance, or Death) Tax

People acquire income and property over the course of their working life, and at the time of their death, these accumulated holdings, that is, the deceased's estate, are passed on to individuals—typically members of the family—as an inheritance. And here's where the federal government steps in. It levies a tax on the value of the estate prior to its disbursement among the inheritors so that the income and wealth holdings of the individual inheritors have no bearing on the tax.

These taxes can range anywhere from 0 to 100 percent of the estate's value, all this at the government's pleasure. Also, the government can, if it wishes, exempt part of the estate from taxation. For example, the government may choose to impose a 25 percent tax on only that part of the estate's value that exceeds $100,000. In other words, it exempts the first $100,000 from any taxation.

As you can imagine, there are ferocious political battles concerning percentages and exemptions even though 98 percent of all estates today end up paying no estate tax. The most recent legislation—The Economic Growth and Tax Relief Reconciliation Act of 2001—created a planned phasing out scheme that takes the estate tax to zero by 2010. But the respite is short-lived. After 2010, the tax exemption is scheduled to bounce back to $1 million.

A glance at recent history: The Economic Recovery Act of 1981 set exemptions at $225,000, The Tax Reform Act of 1986 bumped it up to $600,000, and the Taxpayer Relief Act of 1997 raised it further to $1 million. It is now at $1 million, to be raised to $1.75 million in 2009, repealed entirely in 2010, then scheduled to be reimposed thereafter. But the Congressional battle over its future continues. There is legislation already in Congress that proposes making the full repeal of the estate tax permanent.

THE SOCIAL SECURITY TAX

How your $1,000 of income tax or your $10 sales tax on shoes is used by the government is left to government discretion. It can use these taxes to purchase an aircraft or an interstate highway. It can use them to retire the national debt. There is no connection between the source of the tax and the purpose it's applied to.

However, unlike corporate and personal income taxes as well as property, estate, gift, and excise taxes, Social Security contributions, commonly referred to as Social Security taxes, are earmarked funds. That is, they are used specifically

applied perspective

WHAT THEY'RE SAYING ABOUT THE ESTATE TAX

You would think, wouldn't you, that the rich and famous—mostly the rich—would oppose the estate tax, while those of lesser economic means would be in favor of one, and a stiff one at that. But that's not entirely the case. Well-known "zillionaires" such as William Buffet, Steven Rockefeller, George Soros, and actor Paul Newman, among many others, advocate for the estate tax and at levels that matter.

Bill Gates, Sr., one such advocate, explains: "The reason the estate tax makes so much sense is that there is a direct relationship between the net worth people have when they pass on and where they live. The government that protects their business activities, the traditions that enable them to rely on certain things happening, that's what creates capital and enables net worth to increase."

William Buffet argues that inherited wealth undermines the free market system: "Without the estate tax, you will in effect have an aristocracy of wealth, which means you pass down the ability to command the resources of the nation based on heredity rather than merit." He uses a sports analogy to press his point: "Choosing the 2020 Olympic team by picking the eldest sons of the gold-medal winners in the 2000 Olympics" has no less merit than allowing the sons and daughters of the wealthy to lead in the economics competition. George Soros adds a twist that reflects his own philanthropic concerns: "Abolishing the estate tax would remove one of the main incentives for charitable giving."

Steel magnate Andrew Carnegie worried that inherited wealth destroys the work ethic of the inheritors: "Great Sums bequeathed often work more for the injury than the good of the recipients. It is not the welfare of the children, but family pride, which inspires these legacies."

Advocates of the estate tax date back to pre-revolutionary America. Thomas Paine's *Common Sense* (1776) takes issue with the idea of heredity and succession. His primary target was British monarchy but it applied to economics as well. The idea of any heredity was "as absurd as a hereditary mathematician, or a hereditary wise man; and as ridiculous as a hereditary poet." But in the same year, Adam Smith's *Wealth of Nations* (1776) expressed a very different view on estate taxes, which he argued served to diminish the national wealth.

Does Oprah Winfrey's view resonate with you? She may never have read Adam Smith, but she offers a companion viewpoint: "It's irritating that once I die, 55 percent of my money goes to the U.S. government. You know why that's irritating? Because you would have already paid nearly 50 percent." Whether her numbers add up or not is beside the point. Winfrey, like Adam Smith centuries before, links individual effort with reward.

How do *most* people feel about the estate tax? The Tax Foundation's *2006 Special Report: Annual Survey of U.S. Attitudes on Taxes and Wealth* is clear about one thing—there is strong support to repeal the estate tax permanently. When asked the question: "Do you personally favor or oppose completely eliminating the estate tax—that is, the tax on property left by people who die?" the response was 68 percent in favor of the repeal, 19 percent opposed, and 14 percent not sure.

From generation to generation.

© CORBIS

---

to finance the benefits that the Social Security system is obligated to pay. The system provides retirement income, survivors' income, income to the disabled, and hospital insurance.

The government is simply the Social Security system's collection and disbursement agency. Funds are collected by the government from workers and businesses, and government pays out the benefits.

In any one year, the Social Security taxes collected by the government do not necessarily equal the Social Security payments that the government makes. What happens when there is a surplus? The funds are invested in government bonds, which pay interest to the Social Security system.

Although the government acts as the system's agency, it is not simply a conduit of funds. It decides not only on the amount and quality of benefits paid out, but on the form of revenues collected.

ACTUALLY, EVERYTHING IS TAXABLE!

When you think about it, there is probably nothing that can't be taxed. Even love and marriage. Don't we pay marriage license fees? Of course, not everything is. In fact, what gets taxed is surprisingly limited and varies among the forms of government doing the taxing. The federal government, for example, relies almost exclusively on personal income, corporate income, and excise taxes. It collects revenue from its estate and gift taxes, but these are rather minor sums.

Even among the sources it taxes, the federal government is still selective. Not all personal income or corporate income is subject to taxation. The government allows deductions, exemptions, credits, and write-offs that reduce the tax base. Matters of fairness, incentives to work, incentives to save, and incentives to invest influence what government decides.

Some state governments, too, tax personal and corporate income. Among those that do, the variations in rates, progressivity, and what actually gets taxed are great. States also levy their own excise taxes. Local governments rely heavily on property taxes.

Because the federal government taxes two of the most productive revenue sources—personal and corporate income—it shares some of its tax revenues with both state and local governments. Local governments also receive some funding from their state governments.

THE U.S. TAX STRUCTURE

What does the U.S. tax structure look like? Exhibit 2 describes the federal income tax structure.

Note how the marginal tax rate increases from bracket to bracket, from 10 percent at the lower end to 35 percent at the upper end. Progressive? This six-bracket structure, legislated in the 2006 tax reform, replaced a tax structure whose brackets had higher rates. This 2006 structure represents a remarkable change, particularly when compared to the 1959 structure for joint incomes, which had seven income brackets and an upper marginal tax rate of 91 percent.

EXHIBIT 2   2006 Tax Rate Schedule for Married Persons Filing Jointly

INCOME BRACKET	PERCENTAGE OF INCOME TAXED
$0 TO $7,000	10
$7,001 TO $28,400	15
$28,401 TO $68,800	25
$68,801 TO $143,500	28
$143,501 TO $311,950	33
$311,951 AND OVER	35

Source: Internal Revenue Service, *Instructions for Form 1040* (Washington, D.C.: Department of the Treasury, 2006).

applied perspective

WHAT A DIFFERENCE A HALF CENTURY MAKES!

It's one thing to say that there were more tax brackets in the past and that the marginal tax rate then—the rate paid on income earned within specific income brackets—increased to percentages that absorbed almost all the income earned within the bracket and quite another thing to see the actual number of income brackets and tax rates.

That's what you see in the accompanying table. It is the Internal Revenue Service's 1954 1040 form that relates marginal tax rates for each of the 24 income brackets. Progressive? You better believe it. Consider this: If you had earned $250,000 in 1954, did it really pay for you to work for that last $50,000? You would have given the federal government $45,500 of it. Does it seem worthwhile? While people complained about taxes then—who doesn't, even now—people were as complying then as they are today. It's a testament, isn't it, to our civility. But imagine the uproar if we were to reinstate the 1954 brackets and rates!

Individual Federal Income Tax: Income Levels and Tax Rates for 1954

INCOME RANGE	TAX RATE	INCOME RANGE	TAX RATE
UP TO 2,000	20	26,001–32,000	62
2,001–4,000	22	32,001–38,000	65
4,001–6,000	26	38,001–44,000	69
6,001–8,000	30	44,001–50,000	72
8,001–10,000	34	50,001–60,000	75
10,001–12,000	38	60,001–70,000	78
12,001–14,000	43	70,001–80,000	81
14,001–16,000	47	80,001–90,000	84
16,001–18,000	50	90,001–100,000	87
18,001–20,000	53	100,001–150,000	89
20,001–22,000	56	150,001–200,000	90
22,001–26,000	59	200,001 OR MORE	91

FEDERAL, STATE, AND LOCAL TAX REVENUES

The revenues generated by taxes for federal, state, and local governments are shown in Exhibit 3.

As you can see and perhaps could have guessed, the single most important tax is the income tax. The lion's share of the income tax goes to the federal government and accounts for almost half of the federal tax revenues. The income tax is also an important source of revenue for state governments. Local governments rely almost exclusively upon the property tax for their self-generating revenues. The state and local governments also receive revenues in the form of grants-in-aid from the federal government.

TAXES, SPENDING, AND DEFICITS

on the net

The Bureau of the Public Debt (http://www. publicdebt.treas.gov/) provides the latest statistics on the public debt, as well as information on Treasury bonds and notes.

The $202.2 billion in federal budget deficit—measured in constant 2000 dollars—in 2007 continues a steady stream of deficit budgets that were interrupted only by the four years of surpluses 1998–2001. Exhibit 4 shows that while deficits dominated the 27-year period 1990–2007, there seemed to be no discernible pattern, nor was there a pattern for the surplus/deficits as a percent of GDP. If we took 1960 as our starting point, we would find that deficits occurred in every year leading up to 1990.

✋ **EXHIBIT 3**   Federal, State, and Local Government Revenues: 2007 ($ Billions)

	FEDERAL	STATE AND LOCAL
TAX REVENUES	**$2,651.2**	**$1,902.8**
INCOME TAX	1,167.3	325.4
CORPORATE INCOME	365.4	60.9
SALES, EXCISE, CUSTOMS	97.7	436.5
PROPERTY	—	390.9
FEDERAL REVENUE SHARING	—	376.8
SOCIAL SECURITY CONTRIBUTIONS	942.3	22.8
OTHER	78.5	289.5

Source: *Survey of Current Business* (Washington, D.C.: U.S. Department of Commerce, August 2008).

✋ **EXHIBIT 4**   Federal Government's Surpluses and Deficits and as Percent of GDP: 1990–2007 (in constant 2000$)

	SURPLUS/ DEFICIT	PERCENT OF GDP		SURPLUS/ DEFICIT	PERCENT OF GDP
1990	−280.4	−3.9	1999	128.9	1.4
1991	−327.3	−4.5	2000	236.2	2.4
1992	−341.2	−4.7	2001	125.3	1.3
1993	−292.3	−3.9	2002	−151.3	−1.5
1994	−228.2	−2.9	2003	−352.8	−3.5
1995	−179.8	−2.2	2004	−374.8	−3.6
1996	−115.2	−1.4	2005	−279.1	−2.6
1997	− 23.0	−0.3	2006	−210.0	−1.9
1998	72.1	0.8	2007	−202.2	−1.8

Source: *Statistical Abstract of the United States: 2008* (Washington, D.C.: U.S. Department of Commerce, 2008).

So the question begs: How has the government managed to stay solvent while incurring these long and sizable deficits year after year? *By borrowing.*

FINANCING GOVERNMENT SPENDING THROUGH DEBT

When the federal government discovers that its revenues fall short of its planned spending, it instructs the Treasury Department to do precisely what private companies do when they need funds beyond their own resources to finance investment projects—print up interest-bearing IOUs and peddle them on the market.

Every $100 IOU that the Treasury sells transfers $100 to the government from the person who buys it. Why would anyone want to hold the Treasury's IOU? Because it yields interest. Besides, buying a Treasury IOU is not risky business. The U.S. government has never welshed on its IOUs.

interdisciplinary perspective

DON'T MESS WITH THE IRS: AL CAPONE'S ULTIMATE MISTAKE

Crime doesn't pay? If the crime is racketeering, intimidation, brutality, or execution-style murder, it may pay. But it probably doesn't if the crime is tax evasion. In the one case, you're only up against the FBI, the police, and the courts. In the other, you're up against the Internal Revenue Service (IRS). Forget it! It's no contest.

Al Capone, the most notorious mobster of the 1920s and 1930s, figured that out only too late. He got away with multiple murders, high-stakes bootlegging, and wholesale racketeering. But his *real* troubles began when the IRS went after him.

The key to Capone's eventual demise was a 1927 Supreme Court decision against a small-time bootlegger named Manny Sullivan. The court ruled that although reporting and paying income tax on illegally derived revenues was self-incriminating, that did not make it unconstitutional. That ruling sent the tax-evading Manny Sullivan to prison. It also gave IRS's Elmer Ivey the idea. He put together a special intelligence unit of the IRS to nail Al Capone for tax evasion.

Capone's "activities" were legendary and engaged in with virtual impunity. He had a highly disciplined and corporate-styled criminal enterprise. He bought enough of the Chicago police force and the Chicago mayor to assure himself minimal harassment, if any at all. *But he didn't pay his full share of income tax.*

The IRS went to work. It knew this: When Capone wanted to be conspicuously absent from an impending Chicago crime or when he simply wanted to relax with his family—wife Mea and son Sonny—he would retreat to his palatial estate in Palm Island, Florida. That estate, to the IRS, was evidence that Capone had "earned" considerably more income than he admitted to. As well, the IRS came into possession of several of Capone's financial ledgers that detailed his enormous unreported incomes.

© CORBIS

Reminder: Pay your taxes.

The accumulated evidence of Capone's unreported income was overwhelming. In October 1931, he was convicted of tax evasion and sentenced to serve 11 years at Alcatraz, a federal prison. There, his health declined rapidly. He suffered dementia, a characteristic of late-stage syphilis.

Not all tax evaders are as notorious as Al Capone. Although there are many who had some celebrity status—such as Vice-President Spiro Agnew, who was convicted of tax evasion in the 1970s—most are folks like you and me. But we are many! Some evasions are relatively large, while others are small-time, but the unreported incomes year after year add up to considerable losses of government revenue. Punishments are typically fines, although many tax evaders do end up in prison.

The accompanying table details the tax loss for the end years 1981 and 1992.

According to the IRS, individuals account for $94 billion of the $127 billion tax loss in 1992, while corporations account for the remaining $33 billion. Approximately half of the $127 billion represents unreported income. The other half of the tax loss results from less offensive taxpayer behavior, such as errors in calculation and overstated deductions.

MORE ON THE NET

Review other IRS statistics at http://www.irs.gov/. Click on "Tax Stats" at the bottom of the page.

Relative Magnitude of Tax Evasion: 1981–92 ($ Billions, 1992)

	1981	1992
TOTAL TAX LOSS	$76	$127
AS PERCENT OF INCOME TAX COLLECTED	23.3	22.0
AS PERCENT OF GDP	1.6	2.0
ANNUAL GROWTH RATE OF TAX LOSS		6.1

Who buys them? Individuals like you, commercial banks—actually anyone interested in a secure, interest-bearing investment—and even the Federal Reserve. Look at Exhibit 5.

Wouldn't you think that foreigners, looking for a good way to earn interest, would also consider buying the Treasury IOUs? If enough IOUs are sold, the

EXHIBIT 5   Ownership of the U.S. Public Debt: 2007 (Percentage of Total)

OWNER	PERCENTAGE OF TOTAL
FEDERAL AGENCIES AND TRUST FUNDS	44.4
FEDERAL RESERVE	8.0
COMMERCIAL BANKS	1.4
MONEY MARKET FUNDS	3.9
INSURANCE COMPANIES	1.5
STATE AND LOCAL GOVERNMENTS, INDIVIDUALS	5.7
PENSION FUNDS	4.1
FOREIGNERS	25.5
OTHERS*	5.5

*Savings and loan associations, nonprofit institutions, credit unions, mutual savings banks, corporate pension trust funds, certain U.S. Treasury deposit accounts, and federally sponsored agencies.

Source: *Federal Reserve Bulletin* (Washington, D.C., August 2008).

Treasury covers the deficit created by the difference between government's spending and taxes.

But solving one problem creates another. Now the government is involved in **public debt**. After all, Treasury IOUs in the hands of others are financial claims against the government. How can the government pay these claims? One way is to raise taxes and use the revenues to redeem the IOUs. But it was insufficient taxes to cover spending that caused the deficit in the first place. The other way is to sell new IOUs to pay off the old ones.

Public debt
The total value of government securities—Treasury bills, notes, and bonds—held by individuals, businesses, other government agencies, and the Federal Reserve.

Treasury Bonds, Bills, and Notes

Government sells a variety of debt forms, principally to satisfy the tastes of debt holders. People who prefer not to tie up their money in long-term debt holdings can buy Treasury bills that mature in 3 months, 6 months, or 12 months. These bills are offered in minimum amounts of $10,000 and in multiples of $5,000 above the minimum, which makes them inaccessible to some people.

Longer-term debt is available in the form of Treasury notes and bonds. Because they are sold in denominations as low as $1,000, they are more accessible than Treasury bills. Notes carry maturities of 2 to 10 years. Treasury bonds have a maturity of 30 years.

All Treasury securities (bonds, notes, and bills) are marketable debt. That is, anyone holding a Treasury security who decides to sell it before maturity can offer it for sale on the market.

TRACKING GOVERNMENT DEBT

The federal government has been in the business of supplementing tax revenues with sales of Treasury securities for many, many years. Federal debt more than doubled during the 1930s, reflecting the extraordinarily large deficits incurred during the Great Depression. It increased fivefold during the 1940s, largely due to expenditures associated with World War II. It took a long hard climb thereafter. Exhibit 6 records a half-century of federal indebtedness, from 1945 to 2005.

EXHIBIT 6   The Federal Debt

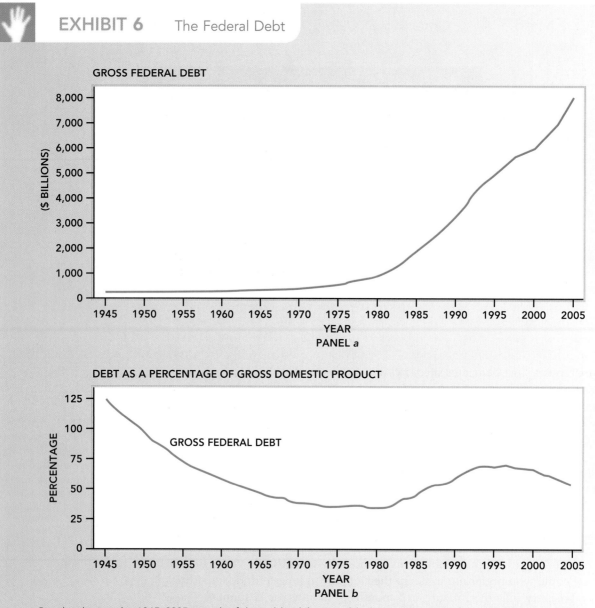

Panel *a* depicts the 1945–2005 growth of the public debt. Panel *b* depicts the ratio of the public debt to GDP. If the economy's growth rate is greater than the growth rate of public debt, the debt-to-GDP ratio falls, even though the absolute level of the public debt may increase.

Source: *Statistical Abstract of the United States, 2006* (Washington, D.C.: U.S. Department of Commerce, 2006).

In panel *a*, the sharp rise in the 1970s mirrors the sharp rise in annual federal deficits, which occurred largely because the OPEC-induced recession took its toll on tax revenues. Federal debt more than doubled. The combination of the tax reforms of 1981 and 1986 (which reduced tax rates) and the recessions of the early 1980s and early 1990s doubled the debt once again.

Looking at Ratios, Not Dollars

But how horrendous is the debt? It is frightening when looked at in terms of absolute dollars, but perhaps less frightening when viewed as a percentage of GDP. Look at Exhibit 6, panel *b*.

EXHIBIT 7   Gross Public Debt as a Percent of GDP for Selected Economies: 2007

Most OECD economies have debt-GDP ratios similar to or greater than the ratio for the United States.

AUSTRALIA	15.4	ITALY	104.0
BELGIUM	84.9	NETHERLANDS	46.2
CANADA	68.5	SWEDEN	41.2
FRANCE	64.0	JAPAN	195.5
GERMANY	63.1	UNITED KINGDOM	43.0

Source: *The 2008 World Factbook, 2008.*

During the first half of the 1940s, the ratio rocketed above 100 percent and then drifted steadily downward to approximately 40 percent in the 1980s, before climbing again during the 1980s to reach 65.7 percent in 2005.

Is $8,371.2 billion too large? Is 65.7 percent of GDP worrisome? Exhibit 7 records the debt ratios for other democratic market economies.

Just because other economies' debt ratios are similar to our own does not necessarily mean our debt ratio or theirs isn't a problem. But it is perhaps noteworthy that our ratios are not out of line. In Italy, the ratio of public sector debt to GDP is 104. Canada's ratio of public debt to GDP in 2007 was 68.5 percent. As you can see in Exhibit 7, the ratios for France, Germany, and the Netherlands match fairly closely the ratio in the United States.

DOES DEBT ENDANGER FUTURE GENERATIONS?

One of the most commonly held views about government debt is that "we can live in debt today, but only at tomorrow's expense." That is, by incurring debt now, we bequeath a debt problem to our children. That's a tough charge to make. And it seems to make a certain amount of sense. After all, *someone* has to pay! If the debtors don't, won't their children have to?

Let's pursue the debt burden argument by examining what happens to debt and the debt burden when a government finances a one-year war by selling bonds. We'll simplify the argument by supposing that prior to the war, GDP was $1,000. Let's assume also an economy initially with no taxes, no government spending, and no private savings. People simply consumed all of the $1,000 GDP.

Now, responding to external aggression, the government chooses not to tax but instead to finance the defense of the nation by selling Treasury bonds totaling $100 at 10 percent interest. In other words, it chooses to incur public debt.

Let's compare the prewar and wartime conditions:

Prewar	Wartime
GDP = $1,000	GDP = $1,000
Consumption = 1,000	Consumption = 900
Government = 0	Government = 100

Before the war, the people produced and consumed the $1,000 GDP. Things change when the war comes. During the war year, the government sells $100 worth of bonds to *its people*. Now the people, exchanging $100 for the bonds, can consume only $900. What did government do with the $100? It spent it on the purchase of ships, tanks, aircraft, and armed forces.

global perspective

Universal response on tax day.

HATRED OF TAX COLLECTION IS THE WAY OF THE WORLD

In Russia, tax collectors have been known to wear commando uniforms and carry weapons. In China, only suckers pay taxes. In Sweden, the government and your employer do your taxes for you. Perhaps the only thing universal about taxes is that no one likes to pay them.

"We are too heavily taxed," gripes securities industry executive Peter Walker in London. "People who have more money have more places to hide it," grumbles Harry Brum, a 36-year-old elevator repairman in Stuttgart, Germany. "They pay less in taxes than those of us who earn an average income."

For all its faults, the U.S. tax system is one of the world's most efficient. About 83 percent of taxes owed come into the U.S. Internal Revenue Service voluntarily, a figure that is the envy of most other nations. IRS audits and investigations bring in an additional 3 percent, leaving 14 percent of U.S. taxes owed uncollected every year. The IRS spends 50 cents to collect $100 in taxes. British tax collectors spend $1.72 to collect $100; Japanese, $1.00; Canadians, $1.13.

FRANCE: Everyone pays a 20.6 percent value-added tax on most goods and services; food and other essentials are taxed at 5.5 percent. Then the government takes money out of paychecks to cover the state health service and social security. The French also pay income taxes ranging from 10.5 percent to 54 percent, but there are so many deductions that half of France's households pay no income tax at all.

French tax collectors also are more sympathetic than their IRS counterparts: They'll negotiate lower tax payments and waive penalties for taxpayers who lose their jobs or face other hardships.

RUSSIA: Collecting taxes was a dangerous business in post-Soviet era Russia. Hundreds of Russian tax collectors were assaulted; some even murdered. During the Yeltsin administration (1991–1999), tax cheating was widespread, as was corruption among the tax cops. In a desperate effort to bolster its finances, the Russian government then launched a major effort to encourage taxpayers to file their income taxes. It also tried to frighten evaders by parading a tax police brigade, decked out in commando uniforms and heavily armed.

Vladimir Putin, elected to Russia's presidency in 2000, inherited Yeltsin's tax legacy, too. Among other accomplishments, Putin reformed Russia's antiquated tax system by introducing the flat tax system. While this revolutionary tax change may make it easier for Russian taxpayers to calculate their tax burden, it doesn't necessarily change the way the Russian taxpayers practice tax paying or even view their obligation to pay taxes.

CHINA: Virtually no one pays income tax voluntarily. Those who do almost always understate their earnings. Chinese citizens are supposed to go to the local tax bureau by the 7th of each month to pay taxes for the previous month. Only income over 800 yuan a month, slightly less than $100, is taxable. There is a graduated scale starting at 5 percent of income and rising to 45 percent.

The government newspapers are always extolling the virtues of model citizens who pay their taxes voluntarily, but any individual or business owner who does so is viewed as a fool. The few peasants who earn enough to pay taxes are in a tougher situation. In some places, they must pay their taxes in grain.

Until about five years ago, the government didn't view individual incomes as a significant source of revenue because incomes were so low. The government has begun to get more zealous about collecting taxes, but it still generally targets state companies, private businesses, and joint ventures. Chinese business owners typically evade taxes by keeping only a token amount of money in their "principal bank account." By law, they are not allowed to have more than one account for their businesses, but that law is widely ignored.

GERMANY: The federal government has been tied up all year trying to reform the tax system and cut the income tax. The reform effort has failed for now, except for a cut in the so-called "solidarity tax" on income paid by all taxpayers to help bring eastern Germany's infrastructure and economy up to par with the western part of the country.

Meanwhile, German taxpayers complain that their tax system unfairly favors the wealthy. "People who earn a lot of money should be sharing the burden," says Erika Geldner, 63, a retired secretary who lives in Esslingen, near Stuttgart.

SWEDEN: Most citizens don't have to worry about filing their taxes. Businesses deduct the tax from the employees' wages and send it into the government. Banks send the government information about citizens' accounts. The government calculates citizens' tax bills. Once a year, in the spring, it sends a notice saying whether money is owed or a refund is due. If citizens accept it, the form is signed and sent back. Or they can try to claim some special deductions (for job-related expenses, for instance). But they had better be ready to document them with receipts.

The new system had a rocky start. The government made some well-publicized gaffes, miscalculating some people's taxes. But now it seems to be working well. "The reform has been very popular," says Lars Mathlein, an official who specializes in finance and economics at the Swedish embassy in Washington,

D.C. In fact, a congressional commission in the United States, looking for ways to improve the IRS, suggested that the Swedish system, and a similar one in Denmark, might be worth a look.

Source: Adapted from Paul Wiseman, "Hatred of Tax Collection Is the Way of the World," *USA Today*, November 5, 1997, p. 18A. Copyright 1997, USA TODAY. Reprinted with permission.

Now let's compare the postwar condition to the blissful prewar status:

Prewar		Postwar	
GDP =	$1,000	GDP =	$1,000
Consumption =	1,000	Tax =	−10
Government =	0	GDP − Tax =	$ 990
		Interest =	+10
		Consumption =	$1,000
		Government =	0

It's really not terribly complicated. After the war, GDP remains at $1,000—the quantity of resources remains the same—and the government no longer sells Treasury bonds. But there is $100 worth of bonds *already sold,* and the government is obligated to pay the promised 10 percent interest on its $100 debt. That is, government's postwar annual interest payments are $10.

Where does it get the revenue to pay the interest? Suppose it chooses to tax. Now the people, producing and earning $1,000 GDP, can't keep it all. Every year, they pay a $10 tax to government, leaving them with $990. Government now has the money to pay its $10 interest obligation. People who hold the bonds receive the $10 as interest payments; that $10, coupled with the $990, ends up as $1,000 available to the people for consumption.

What about production? Government spending returns to $0—no need for ships, tanks, or aircraft—so that the economy is producing precisely what it did before the war.

Let's suppose 25 years pass. The government still taxes and pays $10 annually. Suppose also that the people who bought the $100 worth of Treasury bonds 25 years ago have died and bequeathed the bonds to their children. Should the children be thankful? *For what?*

Although their parents left them bonds that yield $10 each year, they left them also the obligation to pay taxes. After all, dead people cannot pay taxes. Are the children any poorer because they must assume the tax obligation? No. What they pay in taxes, they receive in interest payments. Perhaps they are richer on one account: Their parents were wise enough to secure their future by choosing to produce less consumption and more defense back in the war years.

Are There No Problems with Incurring Debt?

Do you feel as if you've been had? That somehow a sleight of hand has taken place? First you see it, then you don't. Not at all. There's no magic, no tricks, no illusions. The debt, held by the people themselves, neither adds to nor subtracts from national production or consumption. But that neutrality doesn't rule out complications.

check your understanding

Why is an internally financed public debt not a burden to future generations?

Not Everyone Holds the Debt Although the nation neither gains nor loses, individuals may. For example, not everyone holds the debt. If the bondholders are only the rich, then they alone receive the interest payments. Depending on how many bonds they hold, they may end up receiving more in interest than they pay in taxes. On the other hand, because they hold fewer bonds, poorer people may end up paying more in taxes than they receive in interest. Under these conditions, the debt can indeed be a burden to some. The progressiveness of the income tax and the presence of the corporate income tax might mitigate somewhat the inequity of the burden.

Government is particularly conscious of this burden effect and has kept a watchful eye on who holds what bonds. For example, it has at times instructed commercial banks to reduce their total debt by divesting some of their bond holdings. That's also why the Treasury created the relatively low-priced **savings bond**. It allows more people to buy and hold government debt.

Debt Promotes Overconsumption The debt can also distort our choices of consumption and saving. How? Many people who hold bonds tend to consume more out of their income than they should because they *think* they are wealthier than they really are. They mistakenly view the bonds as their personal assets and as the government's liabilities, without realizing that in the end the government's liabilities are actually their own. They don't realize that the source of the interest they receive is the taxes they must pay. By regarding their bond holdings as part of their savings, they feel they can afford to spend more on consumption. That is, by holding bonds, they end up undersaving and overconsuming.

Debt Can Create Inflation Debt complications can develop if government chooses to finance its debt interest obligations not by taxing people or by issuing and selling more bonds directly to people, but by issuing bonds that are purchased by the Federal Reserve. Since the Fed pays for the bonds by creating an equivalent deposit in the Treasury's account at the Fed, the economy's money supply increases, which may cause prices to rise.

Crowding Out Private Investment If, to sell its bonds, the government raises the interest rate on the bonds it offers, it forces private businesses, who must stay competitive as suppliers of bonds in the bond market, to raise the rates they offer on their corporate bonds. That is, financing government spending by government debt makes it more costly for private industry to finance its own investment. As a result, government debt may end up crowding out private investment and slowing economic growth in the private sector.

Some economists who acknowledge this crowding-out phenomenon do not necessarily subscribe to the idea that crowding out undermines overall economic growth. After all—to exaggerate their point—is it really detrimental to economic growth if private investments in gambling casinos are crowded out by debt-financed government spending on public schools? The effects of crowding out, then, aren't so much a matter of who crowds out whom as they are of measuring the relative contributions to economic growth made by the specific private and public investments.

External Debt Is a Different Matter

Suppose that foreigners, not the people living and working in the economy, buy the government bonds. For example, suppose that Saudi Arabians, attracted by the Treasury's high interest rates, buy a large share of the bonds issued by the U.S. government.

Savings bond
A nonmarketable Treasury bond that is the most commonly held form of public debt.

How does debt promote consumption?

How does crowding out slow the growth process in the private sector?

To simplify, we assume GDP = $1,000 for both the U.S. and the Saudi economies, and that the $100 U.S. government bond issue is bought entirely by the Saudis.

Year of Bond Purchase

United States	Saudi Arabia
GDP = $1,000	GDP = $1,000
Government = + 100	Bond = – 100
Consumption = $1,100	Consumption = $ 900

Thereafter

United States	Saudi Arabia
GDP = $1,000	GDP = $1,000
Tax = – 10	Interest = + 10
Consumption = $ 990	Consumption = $1,010

What happens to national consumption in each country during the year of the bond purchase? Suppose that the U.S. war effort involves the purchase of $100 of Saudi oil, which is financed by selling $100 worth of bonds to Saudi Arabia. During the war period, U.S. civilian and war consumption increases to $1,100. Americans consume their own $1,000 GDP and the additional $100 Saudi oil, which is recorded as government spending, G = $100. The Saudis, now holding the U.S. debt, consume $100 less. Their consumption falls to $900 in the year that they buy the U.S. bonds.

Thereafter, the burdens shift. In subsequent years, GDP remains $1,000 in each country, but the U.S. government taxes its people $10 to make its annual debt payments to the Saudis. That reduces American consumption to $990. On the other hand, the $10 interest paid to the Saudis allows them to claim $10 of U.S. production, increasing their consumption to $1,010.

What happens after 25 years? The new generation is still debt-obligated. American children grow up and are taxed to pay the grown-up Saudi children who inherited the $100 worth of bonds. In other words, if government debt is an **external debt**, that is, held outside the country, the debt burden can be passed on to future generations. Of course, the U.S. government can always buy back its own bonds.

External debt
Public debt held by foreigners.

ARE DEFICITS AND DEBT INEVITABLE?

Aside from whether or not budget deficits and the public debt burden are really troublesome, what can the government do to reduce deficit and debt levels? Basically, there are only two ways for the government to tackle the problem. It can increase taxes or reduce spending. Everyone in government is aware of these options. But knowing isn't doing. Putting either of these alternatives into action is the difficult part.

Tax Reforms of the 1980s

Let's look at the tax-design efforts associated with deficit and debt reduction. In 1981 President Ronald Reagan came to the White House with a tax-cutting agenda in mind. He was intent on revising the basic income tax structure by reducing tax brackets and marginal tax rates and by eliminating tax loopholes. This, he hoped, would be coupled with a cut in government spending. He expected the combination to reduce the government's deficit and debt.

Congress responded positively, at least with respect to taxes, by legislating the Economic Recovery Tax Act of 1981 (the Kemp-Roth Act), which cut marginal tax rates. It was less forthcoming on government spending. At the time, the economy was in recession, and the idea of leaving more money in the hands of people by cutting tax rates was not only politically popular but made good countercyclical fiscal policy.

President Reagan was convinced that the tax reform would not only stimulate the economy through the demand side—raise aggregate demand—but also stimulate the economy through the supply side—encourage investments and production. He believed the tax rates were too high and acted as a disincentive to production. Supply-side advocates pushed the argument for tax reduction further, asserting that such tax cuts would end up creating more tax revenues. Their arithmetic was elementary. Lower tax rates mean expanded production, employment, and income. More income adds up to more tax revenues.

The Tax Reform Act of 1986 completed the Reagan tax agenda. It lowered the marginal tax rates further, reduced the number of tax brackets, eliminated many tax loopholes, and made changes in deductions, exemptions, and capital gains.

Both the 1981 and 1986 tax reforms were integral parts of the president's political agenda, which was to disengage the government from the economic life of the nation.

Supply-side expectations notwithstanding, the Reagan tax reforms did not do much to increase tax revenues during the 1980s. At the same time, government spending continued to grow. That combination of tax cuts and government spending growth produced in the 1980s the largest annual deficits in the history of the republic. As a result, the public debt increased dramatically.

The size of the debt and deficits alarmed most in Congress and summoned for many a call to action. Government spending, in an environment of tax reform, simply had to be cut. Everyone in Congress seemed prepared to cut spending as long as the cuts were not made in their own districts. The outcome was obvious; spending continued to grow.

A frustrated Congress passed the Gramm-Rudman-Hollings Act in 1985 that required automatic cuts of the same percent on every budgetary item according to a timetable that eventually reduces the deficit to zero. Much hope was placed on Gramm-Rudman-Hollings, but it didn't work. Soon after passage, efforts were made by some to exclude defense from the chopping block. Others sought preferential treatment for social welfare items. Restraint failed. The timetable was extended in 1987 and again in 1991, but nothing could save Gramm-Rudman-Hollings. The tax reforms, unaccompanied by a curb on government spending appetite, was doomed to generate deficits.

Change was only an election away. President Clinton's 1992–2000 agenda, to the dismay of many of his early supporters, shifted focus to "growing down" federal deficits and public debt and that shift precluded any significant tax reforms or spending sprees. He vetoed tax reforms proposed by the Republican-held Congress. Presidential discipline and the luck of being in office during an unprecedented economic growth spurt did what prior administrations couldn't. By 2000, debt was actually falling and the federal budget was generating surpluses.

The Tax Reform of 2003

If tax reform was pushed to the side during the 1990s, it became center stage once again when George W. Bush became president in 2000. With an economy spinning into a downturn phase of the cycle, he proposed an immediate tax cut as part of his "stimulus package," and began to design an accompanying Reagan-like tax reform.

Bush's Jobs and Growth Tax Relief Reconciliation Act became law in 2003. As a tax reform package, it contains many tax-saving provisions, including a child credit, changes in standard deductions, elimination of discrimination of married

on the net

Visit the House (http://www.house.gov/) and the Senate (http://www.senate.gov/). What initiatives do you see Congress promoting to reduce the federal deficit?

couples filing jointly, and so on. But the key features of Bush's 2003 tax reform were reductions in tax rates, dividends, and capital gains.

Marginal rates in income brackets were cut from 27 percent to 25; from 30 percent to 28; from 33 percent to 31; and from 35 percent to 33. Capital gains tax was cut from 20 percent to 15. The capital gains tax rate for lower-income taxpayers drops to zero in 2008 The cuts in capital gains apply as well to taxes on dividend distributions by both foreign and domestic companies.

With the recession lingering through Bush's first three years in office and with the events following 9/11 and the war in Iraq, his tax cuts and tax reform faced the inevitable return to budget deficits. In 2005, the federal deficit was $426.6 billion.

on the net

Try your hand at balancing the federal budget (**http://www.budgetsim.org/nbs/**). Did you finish with a surplus or a deficit?

CHAPTER REVIEW

1. In pre-modern economies, when government required resources to create public goods such as a road or an army, it commandeered them. In modern economies, when government requires resources to create public goods such as a road or an army, it commandeers money through taxes and uses the money to buy the required resources.

2. Taxes are either regressive, progressive, or proportional. A regressive tax is one in which the poor pay a higher tax rate, that is, a higher percentage of their income to taxes. A poll tax and a sales tax are examples of regressive taxes. A progressive tax is one in which the poor pay a lower tax rate, that is, a lower percentage of their income to taxes. An income tax is an example of a progressive tax. A proportional tax is one in which everyone, rich and poor, pays the same tax rate, that is, the same percentage of his or her income to taxes. A property tax is an example of a proportional tax.

3. Social Security contributions (taxes) are levied on employees and their employers and are earmarked to finance the benefits that the Social Security system is obligated to provide.

4. The federal income tax structure is progressive. The marginal rates in its 6 tax brackets range from 10 to 35 percent. It is the largest source of revenue for the federal government.

5. Deficits arise when tax revenues are insufficient to finance government spending. The government creates and sells Treasury securities to finance its deficits. The securities are attractive to buyers because they are relatively secure and bear a competitive rate of interest.

6. The federal debt, representing the accumulation of federal deficits, has risen steadily since the 1930s and quite sharply since the 1970s. While debt rose through the 4 decades preceding the 1980s, the corresponding debt-to-GDP ratio actually fell. It rose with the debt during the 1980s and 1990s.

7. An internally financed debt does not necessarily burden future generations. It can, however, create problems of inequity, overconsumption, and crowding out of private investment. An externally financed debt, on the other hand, can burden future generations.

8. The tax reform acts of 1981 and 1986 reduced tax revenues. Government spending, however, continued to rise. The Gramm-Rudman-Hollings Act of 1985 attempted to curb the soaring deficits created in the 1980s. Deficit levels began to fall in the 1990s, and the prolonged prosperity, which provided higher tax revenues, combined with more conservative government spending appetites (led by cuts in defense and welfare) cut the deficit to zero in 1997.

9. The Bush Tax Reform of 2003 cut rates on personal income, capital gains, and dividends.

KEY TERMS

Poll tax	Property tax	Public debt
Regressive income tax	Unit tax	Savings bond
Proportional income tax	Sales tax	External debt
Progressive income tax	Customs duty	
Corporate income tax	Excise tax	

QUESTIONS

1. What were the principal reasons for the tax reforms of 1981, 1986, and 2003? What were the unintended consequences of these reforms?
2. If the issue is equity, how can you justify a head tax on income, a proportional tax on income, and a progressive tax on income?
3. Unlike direct income taxes and sales taxes, social security taxes are earmarked. What does that mean?
4. How does an excise tax differ from an income tax?
5. What is the federal government's most important source of tax revenue? What are the state and local governments' most important sources of tax revenue?
6. What are Treasury securities? Who owns them?
7. What is the relationship between Treasury securities and the public debt?
8. What is the relationship between the public debt and the debt-to-GDP ratio? How does the U.S. debt ratio compare to the ratios in other democratic market economies?
9. Explain why some economists believe the burden of a public debt cannot be shifted onto future generations.
10. Some economists believe that the public debt may be detrimental to the economy's growth. Explain.
11. If the U.S. government is indebted $200, and if $100 is in the form of an externally held public debt, while another $100 is an internally held public debt, the impacts of these two different debts on the U.S. economy differ. Explain.

Economic Consultants

Economic Research and Analysis by Students for Professionals

Kristen Hersh plans to run in 2004 for the presidency of the United States. Kristen, a successful businesswoman, worked as a campaign strategist for Steve Forbes's failed run for president in 1996. During the 1996 campaign, Kristen observed that Forbes's primary message, to simplify the federal tax structure, was well received, and his primary initiative, the flat tax, was popular with some voters. As a result, Kristen intends to establish a political platform around tax reform.

Kristen has hired economic consultants to explain to her the economic issues surrounding the tax reform debate. Prepare a report for Kristen that addresses the following issues:

© Image 100/Royalty-Free/CORBIS

1. What are the major positions in the debate over tax reform?
2. What is a flat tax, and what are the pros and cons of this system of taxation?
3. What initiatives are underway in government to reform the tax system?

You may find the following resources helpful as you prepare this report for Kristen:

- **Internal Revenue Service (IRS)** (http://www.irs.gov/)—The IRS provides news and information about federal taxes.
- **EconDebate Online: Tax Reform** (http://www.swcollege.com/bef/policy_debates/tax_reform.html)—EconDebate Online provides links to and commentary on primary and secondary resources addressing the tax reform debate.
- **Americans for Tax Reform (ATR)** (http://www.atr.org/)—The ATR works with hundreds of organizations active at the federal, state, and local levels on issues that pertain to taxes.
- **Citizens for Tax Justice** (http://www.ctj.org/)—Citizens for Tax Justice is a research and advocacy organization addressing taxation at the federal, state, and local levels.
- **Citizens for an Alternative Tax System (CATS)** (http://www.cats.org/)—CATS is a national grassroots public interest group established to abolish the federal income tax system and replace it with a national retail sales tax.
- **Joint Economic Committee Taxation Page** (http://www.house.gov/jec/)—The U.S. Congress's Joint Economic Committee maintains a page addressing issues of taxation.
- **1040.com** (http://www.1040.com/)—1040.com provides tax information and resources.

1. The 7.5 percent sales tax on gasoline in South Dakota is an example of a
   a. progressive tax.
   b. proportional tax.
   c. regressive tax.
   d. unit tax.
   e. flat tax.

2. Picture a production possibilities curve with public goods on the vertical axis and private goods on the horizontal. The tax that people pay to produce a unit of public good represents the
   a. amount of goods each person pays to government.
   b. quantity of goods government receives from the population.
   c. opportunity cost of producing a unit of public goods.
   d. opportunity cost of producing a unit of private goods.
   e. shift of resources from public to private goods production.

3. A poll tax is a
   a. tax on those exercising their voting privileges.
   b. fixed tax levied equally on all taxpayers.
   c. fixed rate of taxation on all taxpayers.
   d. fixed tax on all taxpayers, but the amount of tax varies with the taxpayer's income.
   e. prepaid tax, that is, a tax paid before income is received.

4. The federal government's most important source of tax revenue is
   a. sales tax.
   b. property tax.
   c. corporate tax.
   d. custom duties.
   e. income tax.

5. A proportional tax means that each taxpayer pays
   a. the same amount of tax.
   b. the same percentage of his or her income to taxes.
   c. a tax rate proportional to his or her income; that is, the higher the income, the higher the tax rate.
   d. a tax rate proportional to his or her income; that is, the higher the income, the lower the tax rate on the higher income.
   e. a tax proportional to his or her share of the public goods provided.

6. The tax reform of 2003
   a. reduced the tax rate paid by people in the top tax bracket exclusively.
   b. reduced the tax rate paid by people in the lowest income tax bracket exclusively.
   c. reduced to zero the tax rates on income less than $25,000.
   d. reduced the tax rate paid by people in low tax brackets and raised the tax rate paid by people in high tax brackets.
   e. reduced the tax rate paid by people in all tax brackets, although not proportionately.

7. An income tax structure is progressive when
   a. the average tax rate increases as income increases.
   b. the tax rate on each tax bracket is the same.
   c. the amount of tax paid by the rich is greater than the amount paid by the poor.
   d. the tax base is not reduced by exemptions and deductions.
   e. taxpayers earning the same income pay the same income tax.

8. The Social Security tax is
   a. a regressive tax.
   b. a proportional tax.
   c. the largest source of state and local tax revenues.
   d. an earmarked tax.
   e. a poll tax.

9. An alternative way government can finance its spending, aside from taxing, is by
   a. selling government securities, which creates public debt.
   b. selling government securities, which reduces the government's deficit.
   c. creating surplus budgets.
   d. reducing its public debt.
   e. invoking the Gramm-Rudman-Hollings Act.

10. Does an internally financed public debt endanger future generations?
    a. Yes, because someone has to pay it off at some future time.
    b. Yes, because the interest will eventually overtake the debt, and the interest is what future generations will have to pay.
    c. Yes, because inflation increases the debt, making it impossible for one generation to pay it off.
    d. No, because future generations not only pay interest on the debt, but also receive an equivalent value in interest payments.
    e. No, because inflation erodes the value of the debt, which means that future generations are not endangered.

PART 5
The World Economy

Chat Economics. Tune into the conversation. It's about *your* course. Just change the names, and it's *your* campus, *your* classroom, *your* professor, *your* classmates, and *you.*

Professor Gottheil and his student, Chris Stefan, a senior majoring in international economics, meet up with each other walking across campus. Gottheil had just assigned the chapters on international trade and exchange rates for next week's discussion. Chris opens the conversation.

....

CHRIS: Professor Gottheil, I don't know if you recognize me, but I'm in your 10 o'clock class.

GOTTHEIL: You're Chris Stefan, and you sit in the second row.

CHRIS: That's right! If it's not too much of an imposition, could I chat with you while we're walking?

GOTTHEIL: No imposition at all. What's on your mind?

CHRIS: I've already read the chapters on international trade and exchange rates, and I'm really confused. I mean . . . really confused. Mainly about exchange rates. But I'm also sort of puzzled about the way you arranged the chapters in the text.

GOTTHEIL: You mean the chapter organization? What's wrong?

CHRIS: Well, throughout the semester you kept mentioning that we live in a global economy. You kept stressing the term *global*, and how important international trade is in our lives. Many of the examples you use in the text are international, yet we don't really get to international trade and exchange rates until now, toward the end of the course! Why did we wait so long? I mean, don't these chapters belong up front in the textbook because they're so important?

GOTTHEIL: OK, I see your point. You're right about how important these chapters are. But what we really have to understand before we can appreciate the value of international economics are the basic principles of economics, which are what you've been reading about up to now. Once you know the principles, you can apply them everywhere and to all things. Look, we buy bananas from Honduras, and that's called international trade. But is there something special about this trade? Not really. In terms of understanding how economics works, buying bananas from Honduras is no different

from buying oranges from California. If you understand how supply and demand for oranges determines the prices of oranges, you really understand all there is to know about international trade and international prices. It's the exact same economics, just carried across international borders. That's why we can leave international trade and exchange rates until now.

CHRIS: You say understanding the market for oranges is the same as understanding the market for bananas, but is it? It doesn't seem that simple to me. Where do exchange rates fit in? I can understand buying oranges for dollars, but what baffles me is the market for other people's money, like buying so many pesos for a dollar or so many dollars for a peso. That's a different kind of thing, isn't it?

GOTTHEIL: Not really. Let me try to unconfuse you by explaining exchange rates in a very different context. Just forget all about oranges, bananas, dollars, and pesos for now.

CHRIS: OK.

GOTTHEIL: Suppose there are two night spots on campus featuring live entertainment. Let's call them Mabel's and the Blind Pig. And suppose both Mabel's and the Blind Pig sell sets of tickets—say, 10 tickets to a set. Students buy these packets of tickets—let's pick an easy number, say, 100 Mabel's sets and 100 Blind Pig. Are you with me so far?

CHRIS: Sure. There are 200 sets of tickets sold to students and these tickets—2,000 of them—buy admission to live entertainment events. Right?

GOTTHEIL: Right. You can't get in without a ticket. Well, suppose the Breeders are booked to play at Mabel's, and a lot of people holding tickets to the Blind Pig want to see the Breeders. And suppose the

continued on next page

ChatEconomics

Flaming Lips are booked to play at the Blind Pig, and a lot of other students holding Mabel's tickets want to see the Flaming Lips. What do you think would happen?

CHRIS: Well, if I had a Blind Pig ticket but wanted to go to the Breeders concert at Mabel's, I would try to trade my Blind Pig ticket to someone who had Mabel's tickets but wanted to see the Flaming Lips concert at the Blind Pig.

GOTTHEIL: That makes good sense. And suppose there were 10 like you who wanted to trade Blind Pig tickets for Mabel's tickets, and 10 others who had Mabel's tickets looking for Blind Pig tickets. You would be able to exchange 1 for 1 and satisfy all 20 students. Right?

CHRIS: That's right.

GOTTHEIL: But let's suppose there were 10 like you looking for Mabel's tickets, but only 5 like the other students looking for Blind Pig tickets. Then what? How would you get a Mabel's ticket?

CHRIS: If I really wanted to see the Breeders at Mabel's, I would offer 2, maybe even 3 of my Blind Pig tickets for a single Mabel's.

GOTTHEIL: What if others like you offered 3 Blind Pig tickets, too. You may still not get 1.

CHRIS: That's right. But if I offered 4, maybe someone who had a Mabel's ticket would say, "Hey, I could get to see 4 Blind Pig concerts if I give up the Breeders concert at Mabel's. That's a good deal—I'll do it."

GOTTHEIL: Well that's right, Chris. And that's all there is to exchange rates. Nothing more complicated, and you already understand how it works. Just substitute the United States and Mexico for the two night spots, and substitute U.S. dollars and Mexican pesos for the two kinds of tickets. If you're in the United States and you want to buy something from Mexico, you have to first get Mexican "tickets." We call their tickets Mexico's currency, which is the peso. What we have to give up to get those pesos depends on how many of our own "tickets"—called dollars—Mexicans want, and that depends on how much they want to buy from us. If we want to buy more from Mexicans than they want to buy from us, just like you had to give up more Blind Pig tickets for the Mabel's ticket, we will have to give up more dollars for pesos. These dollars for pesos determine the exchange rate, and the reason why there's a market for other people's money is because we want things from each other.

CHRIS: You know, I think I actually have a better feel for international trade and exchange rates now. I'll try to keep Mabel's and the Blind Pig in mind when I read the chapters again.

To understand how the world economy works, keep in mind the principles you have learned so far. You can apply these principles everywhere and to all things, including the next few chapters.

INTERNATIONAL TRADE

If you can't be a highway then just be a trail
If you can't be a sun be a star
It isn't by size that you win or you fail
Be the best at whatever you are.

Not bad advice, is it? These are the closing lines of Douglas Malloch's (1877–1938) inspirational poem, "Be the Best at Whatever You are." Imagine him counseling a classroom of enthusiastic 10-year olds. If you were one of them listening to him, you would probably feel pretty good about who you are, wouldn't you? And that's lovely. His words are words of wisdom.

But can you imagine Douglas Malloch talking this way to the entire state of Illinois, saying something like: "Look, your fondest wish may be to be the financial heart of the United States, but you're not New York. You may wish to grow the largest and tastiest artichokes, but you're not California. You may even fantasize about oceans of crude oil lying just beneath your prairie grass, but you're not Oklahoma. Yet here's the good news: Your Illinois acres are blessed with the right nutrients to grow magnificent corn. No other state, no

THIS CHAPTER INTRODUCES YOU
TO THE ECONOMIC PRINCIPLES
ASSOCIATED WITH:

- Absolute advantage
- Comparative advantage
- Free trade
- Tariffs
- Quotas
- Customs unions
- Free trade areas

© CORBIS

matter how hard it may pray, can match your corn productivity. My advice then: Be *the* great state of corn producers!"

And there's even more good news: If Illinois heeds the poet's advice, it will end up having more corn, more artichokes, more oil, and more of other goods than if it had chosen not to specialize in corn. Being the best at whatever you are benefits all. In the same way, Oklahoma will benefit if it specializes in oil. Just be the best at whatever you are!

To explain why it's a win-win outcome for any two trading economies, let's analyze the Illinois economy and compare what people there end up producing and consuming before and after economic specialization. We'll also show that what works for Illinois works as well for Oklahoma, for Mexico, and for the rest of the world.

INTRASTATE TRADE

Illinois Corn for Illinois Oil

Imagine the Illinois economy sealed off from the rest of the world. And suppose that working people in Illinois are either corn farmers or oil producers. In other words, Illinois is a two-goods economy. Let's also suppose that labor is the only resource used to produce goods and that it takes 1 hour of labor to produce either a bushel of corn or a barrel of oil. And to round out the supposes, let's suppose that there are 200 labor hours.

Exhibit 1 portrays Illinois's production possibilities. If the straight-line curve looks unfamiliar to you—a production possibilities curve typically balloons out from the origin—it is because we assume away the law of increasing costs.

How many barrels and bushels does Illinois produce? Look at point *a*. It shows that if Illinois devotes all of its 200 hours of labor to corn production, it produces 200 bushels of corn and 0 barrels of oil. On the other hand, if it puts its 200 hours to oil production, it produces 200 barrels of oil and 0 bushels of corn, point *b*. It can also choose any combination of corn and oil, such as 100 bushels of corn and 100 barrels of oil, point *c*. Let's suppose the choice is point *c*.

If corn farmers want to trade corn for oil, or oil producers want to trade oil for corn, how do they do it? How do they arrive at mutually acceptable prices? For example, how many bushels of corn would an Illinois oil producer expect to get trading a barrel of oil? What about the corn farmer? How many barrels of oil would he get for his bushel? If they produce and sell in competitive markets, the relative prices of oil and corn reflect the relative costs of producing oil and corn.

Given their cost equivalents, a bushel trades for a barrel. That is, if a corn farmer is willing to trade 10 bushels of corn, she can expect to get 10 barrels of oil for them.

Oklahoma Corn for Oklahoma Oil

Let's now look at Oklahoma and suppose, as we did for Illinois, that the Oklahoma economy has 200 hours of labor and is sealed off from the rest of the world. Let's also suppose that Oklahomans, like the folks in Illinois, produce

EXHIBIT 1   Illinois Production Possibilities Curve

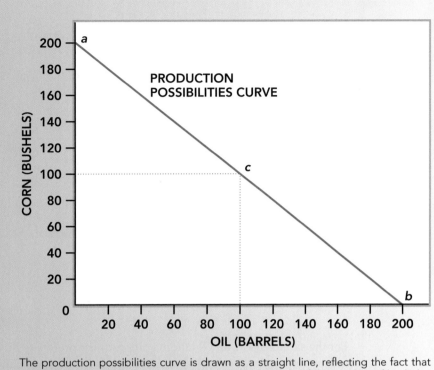

The production possibilities curve is drawn as a straight line, reflecting the fact that the opportunity cost is one barrel per bushel regardless of the number of bushels or barrels produced. The economy can use its 200 hours of labor to produce any combination of oil and corn, such as 100 bushels of corn and 100 barrels of oil, shown at point c.

corn and oil, but the labor costs involved in producing corn and oil are different. It takes not 1, but 4 hours of Oklahoma labor to produce a bushel of corn. Their oil fields, however, are another matter. They are gushers. It takes only 20 minutes of labor to fill up a barrel.

Exhibit 2 represents Oklahoma's production possibilities. Look at point *a*. If Oklahoma devotes its 200 labor hours to corn, it gets 50 bushels of corn and 0 barrels of oil. If it devotes the 200 labor hours to oil, it gets 600 barrels of oil and 0 bushels of corn, point *b*. Suppose it chooses point *c*, 100 labor-hours producing 25 bushels of corn and 100 labor-hours producing 300 barrels of oil. Since corn and oil exchange according to their relative costs, 1 bushel of corn trades for 12 barrels of oil.

INTERSTATE TRADE

Let's now relax the assumption of sealed-off economies and suppose that people in Illinois can trade with people in Oklahoma, and vice-versa. Imagine yourself as an Illinois corn farmer looking for oil. Here are your options. You can stay in Illinois and trade—at Illinois prices—your bushel of corn for a barrel of oil, or you can take your bushel of corn to Oklahoma and there—at Oklahoma prices—get 12 barrels of oil. No difficulty deciding what to do, right?

EXHIBIT 2   Oklahoma Production Possibilities Curve

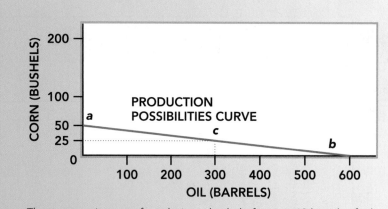

The opportunity cost of producing a bushel of corn is 12 barrels of oil. The economy can use its 200 hours of labor to produce any combination of the two, such as 300 barrels of oil and 25 bushels of corn, shown at point *c*.

For the same reason, an Oklahoma oil producer prefers to buy corn in Illinois. Instead of getting ¹⁄₁₂ of a bushel of corn for his barrel in Oklahoma, he gets an entire bushel of corn trading in Illinois.

It's no secret what would happen if Illinois and Oklahoma engage in **free trade**. Oklahoma oil producers would quickly drive Illinois oilers out of business. Think about it. How can any Illinois oiler who has to pay 1 hour of labor for each barrel compete against a producer who can fill a barrel in 20 minutes?

What about corn producers? Here, the tables are turned. Oklahoma farmers wouldn't stand a chance. By the time they could put a bushel of corn together, the Illinois farmer would have 4 in the bin.

Free trade
International trade that is not encumbered by protectionist government policies such as tariffs and quotas.

The Case for Geographic Specialization

The case for geographic specialization, producing corn in Illinois and oil in Oklahoma, is simple enough: Everybody benefits. We all end up with more corn *and* more oil.

How can we show the benefits? Suppose people in Illinois use their 200 labor-hours to produce corn exclusively, and people in Oklahoma use their 200 labor-hours to produce oil exclusively. How much better off would they be with this kind of geographic specialization? Exhibit 3 compares their combined productions before and after specialization and free trade.

The results of specialization are dramatic. Illinois workers now produce 200 bushels of corn, or 60 percent more than the amount that two states, with the same number of labor-hours expended, had produced before free trade.

The oil yields are also impressive. The 200 hours of labor expended in Oklahoma produce 600 barrels, or 50 percent more than the amount the two states, with the same number of labor-hours expended, had produced before free trade.

What set of relative prices—barrels in terms of bushels—would they end up with? The price should fall somewhere between 1 barrel per bushel prevailing in Illinois and 12 barrels per bushel prevailing in Oklahoma.

EXHIBIT 3   Corn and Oil Production in Illinois and Oklahoma, before and after Free Trade (Bushels and Barrels)

	NO TRADE		FREE TRADE	
	CORN	OIL	CORN	OIL
ILLINOIS	100	100	200	0
OKLAHOMA	25	300	0	600
TOTAL	125	400	200	600

EXHIBIT 4   Corn and Oil Consumption in Illinois and Oklahoma, before and after Free Trade (Bushels and Barrels)

	NO TRADE (PRODUCTION = CONSUMPTION)		FREE TRADE (PRODUCTION)		FREE TRADE (CONSUMPTION)	
	CORN	OIL	CORN	OIL	CORN	OIL
ILLINOIS	100	100	200	0	100	300
OKLAHOMA	25	300	0	600	100	300

Let's suppose the price is 3 barrels per bushel. Exhibit 4 shows the gains that trade offers to both Illinois and Oklahoma.

Look at Oklahoma's consumption. People there produce 600 barrels of oil, keep 300 barrels for themselves, and sell the remaining 300 barrels to Illinois for 100 bushels of corn. They now have four times their pre-trade corn consumption.

What about people in Illinois? Having bought 300 barrels of oil from Oklahoma with 100 of their 200 bushels of corn, they have 100 bushels of corn left. Look at their improved condition. They have 200 more barrels than their pre-trade consumption. In other words, everybody gains!

Impressive? That's why we consume Oklahoma oil, Illinois corn, Washington apples, Michigan automobiles, Georgia peaches, Idaho potatoes, Florida grapefruit, Hawaii pineapples, Ohio steel, Pennsylvania coal, Oregon lumber, New York banking, North Carolina furniture, Iowa hogs, Louisiana sugar, Wyoming cattle, Vermont maple syrup, and California wine.

check your understanding

Why would an Oklahoma oil producer buy Illinois corn?

Nobody Loses?

Are we all always winners? Does nobody lose? Why, then, do we find some people objecting vigorously to free trade? Well, imagine how you would feel if, as an Illinois oil producer, you suddenly discovered an Oklahoma oil producer selling oil in your backyard.

You wouldn't be overjoyed, would you? In fact, you probably couldn't survive the competition. Of course, there's always a place for you farming corn. Still, it isn't entirely painless to give up doing what you know best, oil rigs, and turn to corn farming.

You can count on some oilers trying to prevent Oklahoma oil from coming into Illinois. How could they do that? By exercising political muscle on their Illinois legislators. Nothing really new, is it? That's the primary reason we have protective tariffs.

Of course, if everything else fails, you could always get on a Greyhound bus bound for Tulsa. That's assuming Oklahoma places no restrictions on interstate immigration.

INTERNATIONAL TRADE

The same economic argument that promotes interstate free trade should promote international free trade. After all, why should national boundaries have any bearing on the economic benefits that people derive from free trade?

Suppose, for example, that it takes only 10 minutes to produce a barrel of oil in Mexico. That's half the labor cost of an Oklahoma barrel. Suppose also that it takes Mexican farmers one hour to produce a bushel of corn.

The conditions are ripe, now, for exploiting the full benefits of **international specialization** and trade. United States corn for Mexican oil. Why not? *Everybody ends up with more corn and more oil.*

International specialization
The use of a country's resources to produce specific goods and services, allowing other countries to focus on the production of other goods and services.

Let's pursue the argument. Exhibit 5 details the before-and-after conditions of international free trade. Before free trade, the United States split its 400 labor-hours evenly, with 200 hours devoted to oil and 200 to corn production. Mexico did the same with its 400 labor-hours.

U.S. oilers now face the same problem Illinois oilers did before interstate trade. How can U.S. oilers survive against a more efficient Mexican competitor?

Look at the relative prices of corn and oil in the United States and Mexico. U.S. farmers could get 3 barrels of oil for their bushel of corn. However, if they sold their bushel of corn on the Mexican market at Mexican prices, they could take home 6 barrels of oil!

Mexican oilers will immediately discover the advantages of international free trade as well. Why should they sell their oil for Mexican corn? The relative prices in Mexico—6 barrels to 1 bushel—will give the Mexican oiler only ⅙ bushel of corn for his barrel. By selling the Mexican barrel north of the border at U.S. prices,

✋ EXHIBIT 5   Corn and Oil Production in the United States and Mexico, before and after Free Trade (Bushels and Barrels)

	NO TRADE		FREE TRADE	
	CORN	OIL	CORN	OIL
UNITED STATES	200	600	400	0
MEXICO	200	1,200	0	2,400
TOTAL	400	1,800	400	2,400

EXHIBIT 6   Corn and Oil Consumption in the United States and Mexico, before and after Free Trade (Bushels and Barrels)

	NO TRADE (PRODUCTION = CONSUMPTION)		FREE TRADE (PRODUCTION)		FREE TRADE (CONSUMPTION)	
	CORN	OIL	CORN	OIL	CORN	OIL
UNITED STATES	200	600	400	0	200	800
MEXICO	200	1,200	0	2,400	200	1,600

the Mexican takes home ⅓ bushel of corn. That's twice the quantity of corn that could be obtained in Mexico.

International competition will drive both the United States and Mexico to specialize. The United States becomes the corn producer; Mexico becomes the oil producer.

As we see in Exhibit 5, total production increases from 400 bushels of corn and 1,800 barrels of oil to 400 bushels of corn and 2,400 barrels of oil. That's a net gain of 600 barrels of oil.

What set of prices—barrels in terms of bushels—would prevail on the international market? Clearly, it has to be at least 3 barrels per bushel, otherwise U.S. farmers would do better buying oil at home. It also has to be no more than 6 barrels per bushel, because Mexican oilers can purchase a bushel of corn in Mexico for 6 barrels.

Exhibit 6 shows what happens to the consumption of corn and oil in the United States and Mexico before and after free trade when price is 4 barrels per bushel.

The United States produces 400 bushels of corn, keeps half, and exports the remaining 200 bushels to Mexico in exchange for 800 barrels of oil. Free trade has increased U.S. oil consumption by 800 − 600 = 200 barrels.

What about Mexico? Having bought 200 bushels of corn from the United States with 800 barrels of oil, it is left with 2,400 − 800 = 1,600 barrels, which is 400 barrels more than it had before. Both the United States and Mexico have gained.

ABSOLUTE AND COMPARATIVE ADVANTAGE

Some trading economies are considered perfect trading partners because each can produce one of the goods with fewer resources than the other, that is, using less labor.

Economists describe economics engaged in such trade as having an **absolute advantage**. In our illustration of interstate trade, Illinois has an absolute advantage in growing corn, and Oklahoma has an absolute advantage in producing oil. It's easy to think of real-world absolute advantage cases. What about trade of Japan's automobiles for Egypt's cotton? Do you suppose each country has an absolute advantage? Or Colombian coffee for U.S. steel? Or Czech glass for Russian caviar? Or Israeli oranges for Icelandic fish? Or Dutch tulips for Danish furniture?

Absolute advantage
A country's ability to produce a good using fewer resources than the country it trades with.

Comparative Advantage

Absolute advantage, however, is not always the condition under which nations trade. In fact, absolute advantage is not present when the United States trades corn for Mexican oil (see Exhibit 5 again).

There, Mexico uses fewer resources than the United States to produce oil—10 minutes per barrel versus 20 minutes per barrel—but the same quantity of resources as the United States to produce corn—both one hour per bushel. The United States had no absolute advantage in trading with Mexico. Yet Mexico still gains by specializing in oil.

Why? Why should Mexico bother importing corn from the United States when it can grow its own corn at home using the same quantity of labor that Americans use? The reason is that even though the absolute cost of producing corn in Mexico is the same as it is in the United States, the *opportunity cost of producing corn in Mexico is higher*. Consider this: The one hour of labor used to produce corn in Mexico could be used to produce 12 barrels of oil. That is, Mexico gives up 12 barrels of oil to get that 1 bushel of corn. In the United States, Americans give up only 3 barrels of oil to produce a bushel of corn. In other words, the opportunity cost of producing corn in the United States is considerably lower. This lower opportunity cost is defined by economists as a **comparative advantage** for the United States.

The United States has a comparative advantage—a lower opportunity cost—in producing corn, and Mexico has a comparative advantage—a lower opportunity cost—in producing oil. Both countries gain if each specializes in producing the good that affords it a comparative advantage. Even if Mexico had an absolute advantage over the United States in both corn and oil production, it would still benefit Mexico to abandon producing the good that has the higher opportunity cost.

How Much Is Gained from Free Trade Depends on Price

Look at Exhibit 7. Suppose price is 4 barrels per bushel. Look at Mexico's consumption of oil and corn before and after trade. Mexico, specializing in oil, keeps 1,600 of the 2,400 barrels it produces and trades the remaining 800 barrels to the United States for corn. It ends up, then, with 200 bushels of corn. This 1,600 barrels and 200 bushels compares favorably to the 1,200 barrels and 200 bushels Mexico would have consumed if it did not trade with the United States.

Suppose, however, that the price is set at 5 barrels per bushel instead of 4. The gains from trade are now distributed somewhat differently. At 5 barrels per bushel, the United States, still producing 400 bushels of corn, keeps half

check your understanding

Why would Mexico import U.S. corn when it can produce the corn using the same labor-hours?

Comparative advantage
A country's ability to produce a good at a lower opportunity cost than the country with which it trades.

✋ **EXHIBIT 7**   Corn and Oil Consumption in the United States and Mexico, Under Conditions of No Trade and Free Trade

	NO TRADE		FREE TRADE			
			4 BARRELS/BUSHEL		5 BARRELS/BUSHEL	
	CORN	OIL	CORN	OIL	CORN	OIL
UNITED STATES	200	600	200	800	200	1,000
MEXICO	200	1,200	200	1,600	200	1,400

and exports the remaining 200 bushels to Mexico for 1,000 barrels of oil. That's 1,000 − 800 = 200 barrels more than it got from Mexico when the price was 4 barrels per bushel.

What about Mexico? Having bought 200 bushels of corn from the United States with 1,000 barrels of oil, it is left with 1,400 barrels, which is still more oil than it consumed before free trade. That is, the shift in price from 4 to 5 barrels per bushel shifts the gains from free trade to the United States. If the price increases to 6 barrels per bushel, the gains from trade would shift *completely* to the United States.

Political power sometimes influences international prices and therefore the distribution of gains among the trading nations. During the era of European colonialism in the 17th through 19th centuries, lopsided gains were common-place. Trade between the colonies and the European colonial powers was often politically engineered, giving the Europeans exclusive rights to markets and at prices designed to shift most of the gains to them.

Today, it's not so much political power as the market power of supply and demand that determines international prices. An increase in world demand for corn, for example, will have more influence in shifting prices from $2 to $3 per bushel than all the speeches in the Mexican Assembly or the U.S. Congress.

CALCULATING TERMS OF TRADE

Many of the less-developed countries (LDCs) of Asia, Africa, and Latin America are behind the proverbial eight ball when it comes to international prices and gains from trade. Why? LDC exports, which are typically agricultural, trade on highly competitive markets. Their principal **imports** from the industrially advanced economies, on the other hand, are manufactured goods traded in markets that tend to be far less competitive. As a result, new technologies in agriculture and shifts in demand for agricultural exports over the years have depressed the LDCs' **export** prices, while new technologies in manufacturing and changing demands for manufacturing imports have raised the LDCs' import prices.

The Dilemma of the Less-Developed Countries

Exhibit 8 illustrates the problem facing the less-developed economies. It shows what happens to the prices of Japanese motorcycles and Bolivian tin when demands and supplies for these goods change over time. Let's look at 1980 and 2000.

In panel *a*, a strong increase in demand combines with a moderate increase in supply to raise the price of motorcycles from $6,000 to $7,500. (These are hypo-thetical numbers, of course.) In panel *b*, a moderate increase in demand combines with a strong increase in supply to decrease the price of tin from $6,000 to $5,000 a ton. Back in 1980, Bolivians bought a motorcycle with a ton of tin. Not so in 2000. Now, it takes 1.9 tons of tin to buy that same motorcycle.

Economists express Bolivia's deteriorating international trade position with Japan in the **terms of trade** equation:

$$\frac{\text{index of export prices}}{\text{index of import prices}} \times 100$$

Using Bolivia's tin export prices to represent the index of its export prices in general, and using Japan's motorcycle prices to represent the index of the price of goods Bolivia imports, then the terms of trade for Bolivia in 1980 was

$$\frac{\$6,000}{\$6,000} \times 100 = 100.$$

Imports
Goods and services bought by people in one country that are produced in other countries.

Exports
Goods and services produced by people in one country that are sold in other countries.

Terms of trade
The amount of a good or service (export) that must be given up to buy a unit of another good or service (import). A country's terms of trade are measured by the ratio of the country's export prices to its import prices.

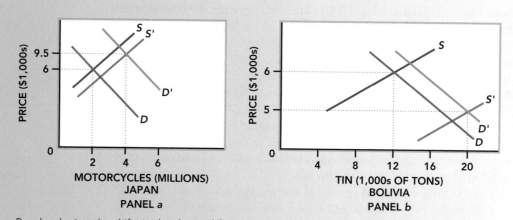

EXHIBIT 8   Japanese Motorcycle and Bolivian Tin Exports

Panel *a* depicts the shifts in the demand for and supply of Japanese motorcycles. The robust demand shift, from *D* to *D'*, combines with the moderate supply shift, from *S* to *S'*, to raise the price of motorcycles from $6,000 to $7,500. Panel *b* depicts the shifts in the demand for and supply of Bolivian tin. The moderate demand shift, from *D* to *D'*, combines with the robust supply shift, from *S* to *S'*, to reduce price from $6,000 to $5,000 per ton.

Look what happens in 2000. Bolivia's terms of trade deteriorates to

$$\frac{\$5,000}{\$9,500} \times 100 = 53.$$

Bolivia's exports end up with only 53 percent of their former purchasing power. Of course, the Japanese are delighted. The gains from international trade move in their favor. And there isn't much Bolivia can do about it. It simply obeys the dictates of the markets. Should Bolivia give up trading with Japan? Certainly not! Bolivia is still better off trading than not trading. After all, the opportunity cost of producing a motorcycle in Bolivia is, more likely than not, greater than the 1.9 tons of tin it must now pay for the Japanese motorcycle.

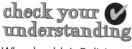

Why shouldn't Bolivia stop trading when its terms of trade worsens?

Looking at Real-World Numbers

What do real-world LDC terms of trade look like? Two features seem to dominate: year-to-year volatility and for many LDCs, steadily worsening terms of trade. The data in Exhibit 9 show a worsening condition for ten LDCs over

EXHIBIT 9   LDC Terms of Trade for 2002 (1980 = 100)

PAKISTAN	88	COLOMBIA	71
NIGERIA	28	EGYPT	53
ECUADOR	36	ALGERIA	31
ZAMBIA	79	PERU	50
CENTRAL AFRICAN REP.	78	BURUNDI	58

Source: *Human Development Report*, Oxford University Press, 2005.

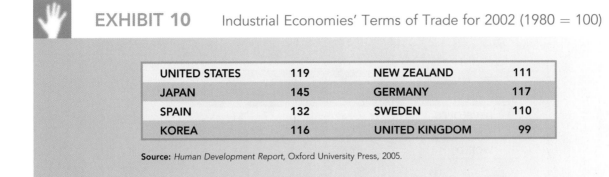

EXHIBIT 10   Industrial Economies' Terms of Trade for 2002 (1980 = 100)

UNITED STATES	119	NEW ZEALAND	111
JAPAN	145	GERMANY	117
SPAIN	132	SWEDEN	110
KOREA	116	UNITED KINGDOM	99

Source: *Human Development Report*, Oxford University Press, 2005.

the period 1980–2002. In Peru, for example, a unit of exports in 2002 buys 50 percent of the imports it was able to buy in 1980. For Pakistan, a unit of its exports in 2000 buys a little less than 90 percent of what that unit bought in 1980.

On the other hand, look at Exhibit 10. Most of the terms of trade data associated with the industrial economies show that a unit of their exports buys more imports in 2002 than it did in 1980.

WHO TRADES WITH WHOM? TRACKING INTERNATIONAL TRADE

Small wonder that the world's economies are engaged in massive exchanges of almost every kind of familiar and exotic good. We find food processors from France, television sets from Japan, wool sweaters from Scotland, processed meat from Australia, microchips from Israel, cheese from Switzerland, coffee from Brazil, tin from Bolivia, anchovies from Portugal, shirts from China, and shoes from Italy in almost every one of our metropolitan and small-town markets.

They are found as well in markets all over the world. No surprise also that the United States is a major world trading partner. Our imports provide vital markets to many exporting countries. Our exports rank among the highly competitive goods and services sold on international markets.

More and more, the world's economies are becoming linked into one unified market network. In 2008, more than 15 percent of the world's GDP made its way onto the international market in the form of exports. That compares to less than 3 percent of the world's GDP in 1970. As communications and transportation technologies become even more advanced and accessible, we should expect that exports and imports in the 21st century will account for even higher percentages of the world's production.

The one striking observation we can draw from international trade statistics is that the big ones play with the big ones and even the little ones want to play with the big ones. Look at Exhibit 11.

Approximately two-thirds of world exports in 2007 were exported to the industrially developed countries. The less-developed countries accounted for the remaining one-third. The major markets for the exports of the developed economies were themselves. They absorbed 70 percent of their own exports. They also absorbed 53 percent of LDC exports.

The Major Leagues

There's no doubt which of the developed economies play in the major leagues. Exhibit 12 lists them in order of their 2007 trade volumes.

on the

The World Trade Organization (WTO) (http://www.wto.org/), an international body addressing trade among nations, provides data and analysis on international trade.

on the

The World Factbook (http://www.cia.gov/cia/publications/factbook/), compiled by the U.S. Central Intelligence Agency, provides detailed economic information, including exports and imports, on all of the nations of the world.

EXHIBIT 11   Percentage Distribution of Exports to Developed, LDCs, and Other Economies: 2007

	EXPORTS TO	
EXPORTER	DEVELOPED	LDCs
DEVELOPED	69	31
LDCs	51	49
WORLD	61	39

Source: *Direction of Trade Statistics, Yearbook 2008* (Washington, D.C.: International Monetary Fund, 2008).

EXHIBIT 12   2007 Exports and Imports of the Major Developed Economies ($ Billions)

	EXPORTS	IMPORTS		EXPORTS	IMPORTS
UNITED STATES	$1,163	$2,017	NETHERLANDS	$552	$492
GERMANY	1,327	1,059	ITALY	492	504
JAPAN	711	619	BELGIUM	431	414
FRANCE	553	615	CANADA	415	381
BRITAIN	432	635	SPAIN	240	373

Source: *Direction of Trade Statistics, Yearbook 2008* (Washington, D.C.: International Monetary Fund, June 2008).

The United States dominates the list. Its $3,180 billion trade volume is followed by Germany's $2,386 billion. But, as you see, all 10 countries have annual trade volumes in excess of $500 billion. That puts them in a league by themselves.

WHO DOES THE UNITED STATES TRADE WITH?

The U.S. Department of Commerce, International Trade Administration (http://www.trade.gov/), provides foreign trade data by country and trade sector.

There is so much heated discussion over our trade relations with China that sometimes we forget that two of our very major trading partners are located just across our own borders, Canada on our north and Mexico south across the Rio Grande.

Proximity is important. Look at Exhibit 13. Trade between Canada and the United States represents the largest trade flow between any two countries in the world. Mexico ranks as our second largest trading partner. U.S. exports to Canada and Mexico were greater than the combined U.S. exports to all the other countries shown in Exhibit 13.

No wonder many Canadians are upset about our benign neglect of them. Important as they are to us, however, we are much more important to them. The United States alone bought 84.1 percent of Canada's 2005 exports to the world. U.S. markets also bought as much as 73.3 percent of Mexico's exports.

Their import packages, too, carry a clear U.S. stamp. U.S. exports to Canada added up to 55 percent of their total 2007 imports, and U.S. exports to Mexico

✋ **EXHIBIT 13**   2007 U.S. Trade with Its Major Trading Partners ($ Billions)

	U.S. EXPORTS TO	U.S. IMPORTS FROM		U.S. EXPORTS TO	U.S. IMPORTS FROM
CANADA	$248	$318	BRITAIN	$50	$58
CHINA	65	340	KOREA	35	49
MEXICO	137	213	FRANCE	29	43
JAPAN	63	149	NETHERLANDS	33	19
GERMANY	50	97	ITALY	14	37

Source: *Direction of Trade Statistics, Yearbook 2008* (Washington, D.C.: International Monetary Fund, June 2008).

accounted for 56 percent of its 2007 total imports. For both neighboring economies, that's an enormous one-country dependence.

The singular importance of the United States to Canada and Mexico is striking when compared to their next-best markets. For example, Canada's $328 billion in exports to the United States was followed by its $9 billion exports to Japan. Mexico's $194 billion exports to the United States towered over its $15 billion exports to Canada.

DO WE NEED PROTECTION AGAINST FREE TRADE?

No one, not even those who lobby Congress for protection against free trade, deny the economic benefits that free trade offers. The evidence is overwhelming. The arguments against free trade, then, are made strictly as *exceptions to the rule*. They address particular circumstances.

Ask U.S. oil producers how much they benefit when we allow Mexican oil into U.S. markets. The economic pain *they* suffer is, unquestionably, real. Although in general, the nation gains from free trade—tens of millions of U.S. oil consumers now pay less for oil—some individuals do get hurt.

How do we weigh the widespread general gains against the particular losses? Should we simply ignore the downside of free trade, or is that pushing a good thing too far? For example, should we sacrifice gains to protect injured parties? *All* injured parties?

A number of classic arguments have been made against *indiscriminate* free trade. These have had considerable effect not only in persuading Congress to limit trade in specific industries of our economy, but also in persuading other governments to do precisely the same in their economies, and for the same reasons.

The National Security Argument

Suppose France's Mirage is a less costly, more effective fighter aircraft than our own F-16. Should we close down our F-16 factories and import Mirages? Although this move might create gains from trade for both the United States and France, we do not want to rely on France for our national survival. Most of the major industrial economies of the world produce their own security systems, even though most understand that they forfeit the gains that would result from international specialization. Production of weapons, munitions, missiles, tanks, submarines, aircraft carriers, cannons, and radar equipment are obvious candidates for protection against free trade on national security grounds.

Some goods, however, are less obvious, and that's when abuse begins. It's not terribly difficult, particularly for industry lobbyists, to draw some connection between any industry and national security.

The national security argument against free trade has a long and active history. As early as 1815, the British Parliament enacted a series of corn laws that established tariffs on grain imports from Europe. Although corn law advocates insisted that England must never be beholden to Europeans for their food supply, their main objective was to protect the English landlord class (and their rents) from the cheaper European grain.

What worked then, works today. Our agricultural industries, too, have invoked the national security argument to protect markets from cheaper imports.

In fact, almost everything can be brought under the umbrella of the national security argument. In times of national crisis, can we really rely on foreign supplies of sheet metal? What about photographic equipment, surveying instruments, lumber, pharmaceuticals, steel fabrication, optical equipment, orthopedic equipment, radio communication systems, and petrochemicals? Shouldn't they, too, qualify for protection on national security grounds?

The Infant Industries Argument

Learning curves—time required to gain expertise—apply to new industries just as they do to people. Because of that, it's sometimes unfair to expect a fledgling industry at home to survive free trade competition from its older, more-experienced foreign competitors. It needs more time.

Protecting infant industries from foreign competition, then, has some validity, because without such protection, many promising industries just wouldn't get started. It's perhaps worthwhile for a country to suffer the higher prices of its own less-efficient new industries in the short run because it expects to gain from greater efficiency and lower prices in the long run.

But how long is the long run? When is an industry's infancy period over? There's the problem. The comforts of protection, once experienced by the infant industry, are difficult to forgo. Many, having run the learning curve many times over, are still as inefficient as they were the day protection was granted. Others remain protected under new guises. Our steel industry, for example, was protected as an infant industry over a century ago and is still protected today. It's an argument that can too easily be abused.

The Cheap Foreign Labor Argument

Perhaps the most frequently invoked battle cry against indiscriminate free trade is the injustice of having to compete in markets against foreign firms that employ cheap labor. How can the U.S. textile industry, for example, employing highly paid unionized labor, compete against textiles imported from Jamaica, China, Brazil, Mexico, the Philippines, and Malaysia? Those countries, even if unions exist at all, still pay wage rates considerably below U.S. levels. Some argue that the U.S. textile industry can't compete, and the consequences are declining wages rates, real incomes, employment, and standards of living at home.

You may wonder if that is really so. The cheap foreign labor argument ignores the fact that higher levels of productivity (output per hour) typically accompany the higher wage rates in the United States, so that the wage cost per unit of U.S. manufactured goods is not necessarily higher than the wage cost associated with the foreign good.

If raincoats produced in China are less costly because of cheap labor than the raincoats produced in New York, shouldn't we take advantage of the lower cost? After all, isn't that precisely why we engage in specialization? Rather than lowering our standard of living, trade with low-wage economies increases the real goods we are able to purchase, so that our living standards should actually improve.

Of course, the widespread gains consumers enjoy from such trade are not universally shared. Some people end up losing. Some firms, for example, cannot survive the competition. People lose jobs and don't always find new ones. Entrepreneurs fail, and many never recover. Stockholders lose their investment, and many never invest again.

The Diversity-of-Industry Argument

Some economies have become so highly specialized in one or two production activities that these alone account for a major share of national product and, typically, an even greater share of exports. Think, for example, of Saudi Arabia and oil, or Honduras and bananas. When the prices of their few specialized exports are relatively high, their economies perform well. When prices fall, however, their economies suffer.

Since these prices reflect the swings of demand and supply in the international market, in many cases the fate of highly specialized economies is out of their hands. Moreover, if the swings are erratic, these economies also tend to become unpredictable and unstable.

No one wants to live in an unstable world. Good enough reason to diversify industrial production, isn't it? That's where protection comes in.

Many less-developed countries argue for such protection. They understand the costs involved in abandoning specialization but still prefer the greater economic stability that the protection affords. In their case, it may make sense. However, it is hardly the argument that industries in the United States can make for protection. The United States and Western European economies are already sufficiently diversified.

The Antidumping Argument

Some industries seeking protection insist that it is not lack of absolute or comparative advantage on the international market that does them in, but rather the sinister strategies of their foreign competition. Why sinister? Because their foreign competitors dump goods on the market, *priced below cost*, to knock them out of the game. Once the competition is eliminated, these sinister producers—now monopolists—will use their monopoly power to raise prices to levels even higher than they were before. That's pretty cheeky, isn't it?

Our Congress thought so, and made **dumping** on our markets illegal. The problem is, how do we go about proving that low-cost foreign goods are priced below cost? One way is to compare the export prices of the foreign producer to the prices it charges in its own domestic market. That's not always easy to do, and sometimes the comparisons are rigged to support inefficient producers in the United States.

check your understanding

What is the major flaw in the cheap foreign labor argument supporting protection?

Dumping
Exporting a good or service at a price below its cost of production.

The Retaliation Argument

Should we allow other countries free access to our markets if they restrict our exports in theirs? That's rather unfair, isn't it? Yet that's precisely the trading conditions we confront with many of our trading partners. Perhaps the most glaring case of such lopsided access is our trading experience with Japan. Our complaints to them about their restrictive practices seem to fall on deaf ears.

Many U.S. producers, frustrated by Japanese protection of their own domestic markets, call for retaliation. If the Japanese won't allow us free entry into their markets, they argue, we should simply deny them free entry into ours. Since we are a major market for their exports, the retaliation may "encourage" them to rethink their protection strategies.

It may in fact work. With greater access to their markets, our own export and even import volumes would most likely increase, benefiting both us and the Japanese. It may make sense, then, to threaten retaliation—and even in some cases to carry out the threat.

But suppose retaliation doesn't work. If it leaves us with less, not greater trade, it makes no sense at all. After all, even with restricted access to their markets, we still benefit by importing Japanese goods. Otherwise, we wouldn't import them.

THE ECONOMICS OF TRADE PROTECTION

How do we restrict imports? Basically, with tariffs and quotas. What are they, and how do they work?

Tariffs

Tariff
A tax on an imported good.

A **tariff** is a government-imposed tax on imports. It can be levied as a percentage of the import's value or as a specific tax per unit of import. Like any other tax, it becomes government revenue. Although U.S. importers pay the tariff to U.S. customs when importing foreign goods, they typically shift at least part of it onto the consumer by raising prices. To the consumer, the tariff is invisible. After all, do you really know what percentage of the price you pay for an Italian bike is the tariff on the bike and what percentage represents the price the Italian bike producer actually receives?

How can a U.S. tariff on bikes protect U.S. producers? Let's suppose that bike manufacturers in the United States cannot produce a bike as efficiently as manufacturers in Italy. Suppose the Italians price their bikes in U.S. markets at $200, which is $250 less than the $450 price for U.S. bikes on the U.S. market.

Without a tariff, the U.S. manufacturers are in serious trouble. How can they compete with the cheaper Italian bike? But suppose Congress, persuaded by any one of the protectionist arguments, imposes a 100 percent tariff, that is, a $200 add-on to the price of Italian bikes. Exhibit 14 shows what happens to the price and quantity of bikes bought and sold under conditions of no foreign trade, unrestricted foreign trade, and tariff-restricted foreign trade.

The supply curve, S_{US}, represents the quantities of bikes that U.S. producers are willing to supply at various prices. The demand curve represents U.S. demand for bikes. If the market were completely insulated from foreign competition, U.S. manufacturers would be busy producing 3 million bikes and selling them at a price of $450.

on the net

The U.S. International Trade Commission (http://www.usitc.gov/), the Office of the U.S. Trade Representative (http://www.ustr.gov/), and the U.S. Department of State issue reports on foreign trade barriers and unfair practices.

KEY EXHIBIT 14   Tariff-Restricted Trade

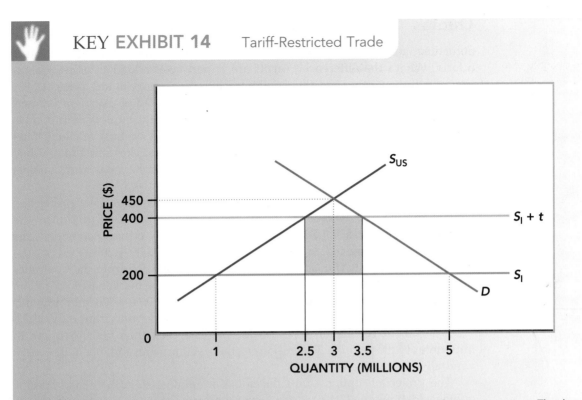

The supply curve, S_{US}, records the quantity of bikes U.S. producers are willing to supply at varying prices. The demand curve records the quantity of bikes Americans are willing to buy at varying prices. With no foreign suppliers, 3 million would be bought and sold at an equilibrium price of $450.

S_I records the willingness of Italian bike producers to supply any quantity at $200. When Italian suppliers are allowed to enter the U.S. market, equilibrium price and the quantities of bikes demanded and supplied in the United States change dramatically. Price falls from $450 to $200 and the quantity demanded increases to 5 million; 1 million supplied by U.S. producers and 4 million imported from Italy.

If the U.S. government imposes a 100 percent tariff on bikes, the Italian supply curve in the United States becomes $S_I + t$. At a price of $400, 3.5 million bikes are demanded: 2.5 million supplied by U.S. producers and 1 million imported from Italy. The shaded area shows the U.S. government's tariff revenue.

Let's now introduce free trade. Suppose Italian producers are willing to supply any quantity of bikes at a $200 price. The Italian supply curve on the U.S. market is shown as S_I. How does that supply affect U.S. manufacturers?

At a $200 price, U.S. consumers increase their quantity demanded from 3 to 5 million bikes. Only 1 million of the 5 million, however, would be supplied by U.S. manufacturers. That is, the U.S. firms lose 2 million of their former sales to Italian competitors and now have only 20 percent of this new, flourishing market. We now import 4 million Italian bikes. You can imagine how the U.S. bike manufacturers would react.

Suppose a 100 percent tariff, t, is applied to bikes. The Italian supply curve shifts to $S_I + t$, and the price of Italian bikes in the U.S. market increases to $400. At this higher price, the quantity demanded by U.S. consumers falls from 5 to 3.5 million. U.S. firms produce 2.5 million, and importers of Italian bikes provide the other million.

In other words, the tariff gives the U.S. bike industry a new lease on life, but only at the expense of the U.S. consumer. What about government? It ends up with a revenue of $200 × 1 million = $200 million, the shaded rectangle in Exhibit 14.

Quotas

Quota
A limit on the quantity of a specific good that can be imported.

Sometimes governments prefer to restrict imports by imposing a **quota** instead of a tariff. What's the difference? Tariffs are import taxes added to prices; quotas limit the amount of a good that is allowed into the country at any price.

The outcomes are different. Let's suppose that instead of placing a 100 percent tariff on Italian bike imports, the government limits the number of imports to 500,000 units. Picture the scene. U.S. importers would be busy making long-distance calls to Rome to buy up the 500,000 Italian bikes. These are brought into the U.S. market at the free trade price of $200 each. What happens now? Look at Exhibit 15.

The supply curve is horizontal until we reach 1.5 million bikes, reflecting 500,000 supplied by Italian producers and 1 million that U.S. producers are willing to supply at $200. At higher prices, the supply curve becomes S', the horizontal sum of the U.S. supply curve, S, and the 500,000 quota.

There we have it. The U.S. producers suffer a slight fall from the quantities they would sell if there were no Italian competitors in the market, from 3 million to 2.75 million. Quota protection raises the price from $200 to $420, although it is still less than the $450 that would prevail without competition from Italy.

What about the Italian bike producers? They sell their 500,000 quota to importers at $200 per bike. The importers, then, end up with a $420 − $200 = $220 windfall on each bike.

The protection options with the quota are almost countless. Each specific quota yields a unique U.S. production and market price. As with the tariff, there's no magic number that defines every quota. It could be any number, depending on the objectives of the government and U.S. producers.

EXHIBIT 15   Quota-Restricted Trade

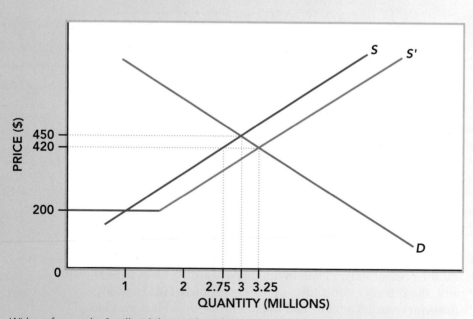

With no free trade, 3 million bikes are bought and sold in the United States at an equilibrium price of $450. If the U.S. government sets an import quota of 500,000 bikes, the relevant supply curve becomes S' (which is $S + 500,000$). The equilibrium price falls to $420, and 3.25 million bikes are bought and sold, of which 2.75 million are produced by U.S. suppliers.

Other Nontariff Barriers

Tariffs and quotas are not the only mechanisms that can be used by domestic producers and by government to reduce imports. The government can also pass a law that specifies highly restrictive health and safety standards that imports must meet. For example, the government can insist that all Italian bikes be dismantled and reassembled by U.S. bike inspectors—at a cost, say, of $75 per bike—to guarantee safety.

That's not a particularly creative idea. The Japanese once prohibited ski imports because, they maintained, only Japanese skis were suitable for Japanese snow. The Germans disallowed foreign-brewed beer on grounds of health and safety. U.S. beef imports were shut out of European markets because U.S. cattle were fed with government-approved hormones.

In some cases, import barriers are self-imposed by foreign exporters who agree to "voluntarily" limit the quantity of their exports. For example, Japanese automakers voluntarily agreed to limit auto exports to the United States. They understood the alternatives: Volunteer or face higher tariffs or lower quotas.

NEGOTIATING TARIFF STRUCTURES

Whatever tariff structure a nation chooses, it would seem only fair that the structure, once established between two trading partners, should apply to all other countries as well. For example, if the United States and France agree to a mutual reduction, from 40 to 25 percent, in their tariffs on imported wine, then a third country, say Portugal, should be allowed to sell its wine in the United States and France at the same 25 percent tariff rate. Otherwise, international trade would be marked by country-to-country discrimination.

This idea of tariff **reciprocity** became the guiding principle industrial nations adopted after World War II in establishing rules of international trade. The aim was to increase the free movement of goods across national boundaries, and to do so nondiscriminately.

Reciprocity
An agreement between countries in which trading privileges granted by one to the others are the same as those granted to it by the others.

GATT and WTO

The **General Agreement on Tariffs and Trade (GATT)** served as a framework for this multilateral trade objective, and nations came together under its auspices to negotiate trade policies. Organized in the aftermath of World War II with 22 industrial nations, GATT grew to over 100 member nations, representing over 80 percent of all international trade. GATT's objective was to reduce tariffs worldwide. It promoted the *most-favored-nation clause* and sought to apply it universally.

The U.S. role in GATT reflected its interest in freer world trade. GATT's success is recorded in three sequential rounds of negotiations: The Kennedy Round (1962–1967), which reduced tariffs by 40 percent; the Tokyo Round (1973–1979), which cut tariffs by an additional 30 percent; and the Uruguay Round (1986–1993), which cut them again by 40 percent and tackled nontariff issues such as intellectual property.

Many of the less-developed nations complained about GATT's unsympathetic ear. How could they comply with tariff reductions when their principal concern was economic development? They needed tariff protection to jumpstart industrialization. GATT got the message: The less-developed nations could still enjoy the tariff reductions agreed upon by the industrial nations without having to reciprocate.

General Agreement on Tariffs and Trade (GATT)
A trade agreement to negotiate reductions in tariffs and other trade barriers and to provide equal and nondiscriminating treatment among members of the agreement. Around 100 countries are members of GATT.

global perspective

U2 CAN BE IRISH!

It's the mid-1990s. Picture yourself CEO of a major U.S. based multinational. You peek over the European Union's tariff walls to feast your eyes on its enormous single market—350 million consumers—and dream of having zero-tariff access to them! But you're an American, not a European, firm and not entitled to the European Union's intra-Union free trade. The export goods you produce face a common E.U. tariff. Can access to that European market become a reality?

It can, and for some foreign-based multinationals, it has. The story behind acquiring zero-tariff access begins in 1973 with Ireland joining the European Economic Community (EEC), the forerunner to the E.U. As an E.U. member, the Irish economy is an integral part of that large and growing E.U. single market. It could export to and import from other E.U. economies tariff free.

So how does Ireland's membership in the E.U. serve you? The answer is simple enough: *Become Irish!* Can you really do that? Yes, and with Irish blessings.

Consider this: Although Irish goods and services have zero-tariff access to the E.U. market, having such access doesn't necessarily mean that Ireland could take advantage of it. Compared to the giant economies of the E.U., Ireland's economy was quite small and underdeveloped. The Irish worry was that with open E.U. access to E.U. markets, other E.U. countries' goods would swamp the small Irish domestic market. Rather than profiting from being part of the E.U. market, Ireland could end up with a smaller export market and ruined domestic industries. What the Irish needed was precisely what they didn't have: domestic firms that could compete successfully with European firms on the European continent. But how could Ireland get them? The answer was inescapable. If it couldn't "grow" them domestically—and it couldn't—then it would have to import them. These imports—perhaps your own multinational—would enter Ireland in the form of foreign direct investment.

The strategy Ireland pursued was dubbed "industrialization by invitation," an appeal to foreign multinationals to locate in Ireland. Irish enticement was twofold: It offered an attractive corporate profit tax—considerably below that of other E.U. economies—and, because of Ireland's E.U. membership, zero-tariff access to the E.U. market. After all, foreign

multinationals with production facilities in Ireland would be producing in those facilities *Irish-made* goods and services, which, because they were Irish, would be entitled to enter the wider E.U. market tariff free. Other attributes, such as Ireland's English-speaking, highly educated, and skilled labor force, helped.

James Joyce (1882–1941), the most valued export Ireland ever produced.

The strategy, after some refinements, was enormously successful. By 1999, foreign direct investment in Ireland—much of it U.S.-based multinational investment—accounted for 88 percent of Ireland's total capital formation and generated fully 20 percent of its GNP.

For both the foreign multinationals in Ireland and for Ireland, it was clearly a mutually beneficial alliance. While no foreign direct investment was discouraged, the "industrialization by invitation" strategy targeted the computer, pharmaceutical, and chemical industries. These were regarded as generating high value-added output and providing high productivity jobs for its working population.

The targeted strategy succeeded. Named foreign multinationals took advantage of the Irish offer. In 1997, these foreign-owned software multinationals accounted for 88 percent of industry revenues and 91 percent of Ireland's software exports.

In less than a decade, these multinationals and others who took advantage of Ireland's "locate in Ireland" offer made Ireland an economy to be reckoned with in the intra-E.U. market.

The attractiveness of the E.U. market grows. Twelve additional European economies joined the European Union since 2004, expanding its market strength from 350 million to 500 million consumers and Turkey, with its 70 million population, looms large in the E.U. background as a likely entrant. The stakes, already high, are growing higher for U.S. firms to find ways of circumventing E.U. tariffs. The Irish 1990s experience may be for many U.S.-based multinationals a proven strategy for their future in Europe.

In 1995, as an outcome of the Uruguay Round, GATT became the **World Trade Organization (WTO)**. The key difference between GATT and the WTO was in dispute settlement procedures. Compliance with GATT rulings was not mandatory, and while its achievements in global tariff reductions were remarkable, it was less successful in resolving nation-to-nation disputes over compliance to agreed-upon concessions. The WTO became more aggressive on this issue, insisting on compliance with its rulings and accepting, as its charge, the *settlement* of disputes. Its record at being effective is incredible, settling more trade-related disputes in its first years than GATT did in 50.

Customs Unions

In 1958, the six West European economies of France, Germany, Italy, Holland, Belgium, and Luxembourg established a **customs union**—the **European Economic Community (EEC)**—whose special trade arrangements allowed for complete free trade within the union and a common tariff schedule against the rest of the world. That's precisely the economic arrangement that exists between Vermont and California, isn't it? In the 1970s, Denmark, England, and Ireland joined the community. In the 1980s, the EEC expanded again to include Greece, Spain, and Portugal. The 1992 Treaty of Maastricht officially changed the name of the EEC to the **European Union (E.U.)**, whose agenda now included not only economic but also political integration among its member nations. Iceland, Finland, Sweden, and Austria joined the E.U. in the 1990s, and the Czech Republic, Estonia, Hungary, Latvia, Lithuania, Poland, Slovakia, Cyprus, and Malta followed in 2004. Bulgaria and Romania joined in 2007.

The objectives of the E.U. raise fundamental questions that concern the reciprocity principle underlying the WTO agreements. For example, if the United States lowers its tariff against French wine, according to WTO instruction it must also lower its tariff against wine imported from other countries.

The United States is disadvantaged, however, when it comes to competing with French wine in Britain. While French wine comes into Britain tariff-free, California wine faces a common E.U. tariff. That's not fair, say California wineries. The French respond that California wine comes in tariff-free to Vermont; French wine doesn't. It's the same, *n'est-ce pas?* Not exactly. California trade with Vermont is strictly domestic; trade between France and England is still international. *WTO's rules apply only to international trade.*

Free Trade Areas

A variant of the customs union is the **free trade area**. The single difference between it and the customs union, such as the E.U., is that the free trade area permits free trade among members, but each is allowed to establish its own tariff policy with respect to nonmembers. In other words, the free trade area permits each member greater independence in trade policy making.

The North American Free Trade Agreement

By far the most significant trade agreement concluded by the United States is with Canada and Mexico. In 1989 both the U.S. Congress and the Canadian House of Commons enacted the **North American Free Trade Agreement (NAFTA)**. Mexico joined NAFTA in 1993, making it the largest free trade area in the world, matching the total production of goods and services of the E.U.

NAFTA called for the elimination of all tariffs, quotas, and other trade barriers within 10 years. Although over 75 percent of Canadian-U.S. trade was

---

World Trade Organization (WTO)
The successor to GATT. The WTO is the only global international organization dealing with the rules of trade between nations. It promotes free trade. Once negotiated and signed by member nations, WTO agreements are ratified by member nations' parliaments.

on the net

Review GATT (http://www.ciesin.org/TG/PI/TRADE/gatt.html) in its entirety.

Customs union
A set of countries that agree to free trade among themselves and a common trade policy with all other countries.

European Economic Community (EEC)
A customs union consisting of France, Italy, Belgium, Holland, Luxembourg, Germany, Britain, Ireland, Denmark, Greece, Spain, Portugal, Iceland, Finland, Sweden, and Austria.

European Union (E.U.)
An organization of European nations committed to economic and political integration without abandoning individual national sovereignty.

Free trade area
A set of countries that agree to free trade among themselves but are free to pursue independent trade policies with other countries.

North American Free Trade Agreement (NAFTA)
A free trade area consisting of Canada, the United States, and Mexico.

tariff-free even before NAFTA, the expansions in both U.S. and Canadian markets that NAFTA was expected to create made the agreement a very significant economic event for both countries. Canadians gained a considerable advantage vis-à-vis other exporting countries in a market ten times the size of their own. On the other hand, the United States, having faced tariff rates in Canada higher than those Canadians faced in the United States prior to NAFTA, gained more when both cut their rates to zero.

Still, NAFTA was not engineered without some political controversy. Although some debate concerning its merits took place in the United States, NAFTA was a major political issue in Canada. The U.S. economy has always been regarded by Canadians as a potentially threatening colossus. Some Canadians feared that free access to each other's markets would result in U.S. production overwhelming their own. But their voices were muted by the logic of comparative advantage. It proved too much for Canadians to ignore.

Mexico's entry into NAFTA generated a somewhat more unsettling promise for the future. Although the expansion of all three markets—Canada, Mexico, and the United States—is seen by all three as an outcome of Mexico's membership in NAFTA, a disquieting note is voiced in the United States and Canada. The issue is low-wage Mexican labor. With tariffs completely eliminated, many worry that low-wage Mexican labor will lure firms, particularly labor-intensive ones, out of Canada and the United States to Mexico. Polluting firms that are forced to adhere to tough Canadian and U.S. environmental regulations will also be attracted to Mexico, where pollution regulations are fewer and poorly enforced.

Advocates of NAFTA respond with compelling arguments of their own. The economic development of Mexico, which NAFTA will assist, provides not only markets for Canadians and Americans, but employment opportunities for Mexicans. In other words, NAFTA can help reduce the illegal immigration flow across the Rio Grande. And the low-wage jobs that Americans and Canadians will lose are precisely the jobs that should be lost in the United States and Canada. The greater production in Canada and the United States that Mexico-included NAFTA generates should be able to reemploy those Canadian and American job-losers in higher-paying jobs.

TRACKING TARIFFS SINCE 1860

Some people see a half glass of water as being half empty, while others view the same glass as half filled. It's just a matter of how you look at things. The same idea applies when we assess tariffs and trade performance. Look at Exhibit 16.

Just a cursory glance shows that whatever our view about whether tariffs are too high or too low, they have clearly dropped dramatically during the past 75 years.

As you can see, our tariff history shows some erratic behavior. In earlier years, our international trade policy was clearly protectionist. During the period 1870 to 1900, the average tariff rate on imports was over 25 percent. But note how the average tariff rate on all imports steadily declined during the next two decades.

The skyrocketing of rates during the 1920s and early 1930s appears as an exception, the direct result of the highly protectionist Fordney-McCumber Tariff Act of 1922 and the Smoot-Hawley Tariff Act of 1930. The Reciprocal Trade Agreement Act of 1934 reversed the upward movement in rates, and by 1950, rates were back to pre-1920 levels. Since 1970, the rates have fallen below 10 percent and continue to decline.

Are our tariff rates still too high? The average U.S. tariff, 2000, was 4.0 percent, which compares to Canada's 3.9 percent, Australia's 5.8 percent, Japan's 4.5 percent, and Mexico's 16.2 percent.

EXHIBIT 16   Average U.S. Tariff Rates on Imports

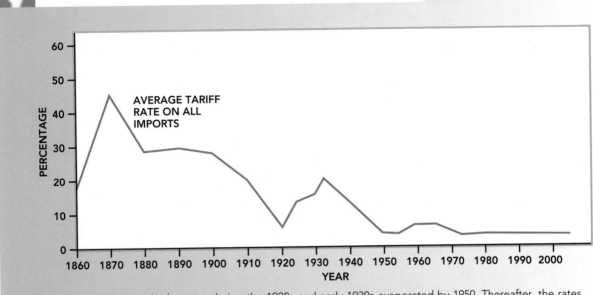

The dramatic increase in the rates during the 1920s and early 1930s evaporated by 1950. Thereafter, the rates steadily declined and by 1970 were less than 10 percent.

Source: *Economic Report of the President*, January 1989 (Washington, D.C.: U.S. Government Printing Office, 1989), p. 152, and *Economic Report of the President*, January 2006 (Washington, D.C.: U.S. Government Printing Office, 2006), p. 154.

THE REGRESSIVE CHARACTER OF TARIFFS

While the 4 percent average tariff rate for goods entering the United States would seem not to be particularly burdensome to American consumers, it is—to emphasize—*an average rate*, and therein lies the problem. Some tariff rates are higher than the average, and others are lower. And some of the highs can be substantially higher.

How burdensome a particular tariff rate is to a U.S. consumer depends essentially on three circumstances: whether the consumer buys the good, what percentage of his or her total consumption is spent on that good, and the income level of the consumer. For some Americans, these circumstances can weigh heavily on their fortunes.

Consider: Some of the highest tariff rates in the United States are placed on textiles, footwear, and apparel items. Like death and taxes, these goods are virtually impossible to avoid. And because these high-tariff goods make up a higher percent of the consumption package of low-income Americans compared with their richer neighbors, the tariff burden on them is more severe. That is, calculated as a percent of income, the tariff burden increases as income decreases. It is in this sense that the tariffs on goods such as textiles, apparel, and footwear are regarded as regressive.

But the regressive character of these tariffs is compounded in yet another way. Among the high-tariff items of textiles, apparel, and footwear, the cheaper varieties within these categories carry the highest tariff rates. For example, lower-priced sneakers—selling at $3 to $6 per pair—are subject to a 32 percent tariff rate, while the more expensive $100 track shoes are subject to a 20 percent tariff rate.

global perspective

Translated: Good luck.

THE CHINA CONNECTION: PROBLEM OR PROMISE?

On October 1, 1949, after two decades of civil and international warfare, Mao Zedong, a communist revolutionary, seized power in China and established the People's Republic of China. For the next 28 years until his death, Mao succeeded in converting this vast semi-feudal society and economy of over a billion people into a state-dominated system, which, in retrospect, was not only politically and culturally cruel but also not terribly successful in improving the economic lot of its people.

With the death of Mao in 1976 came the death of China's policy of economic isolation. China slowly rediscovered the principles of comparative advantage and for the next three decades not only maintained an astonishing rate of economic growth but made its presence known in almost every one of the world's markets, particularly those in the United States.

China's decision to compete in world markets was the single most important decision it could make to revitalize its economic life. It meant not only gearing its own production to export markets but also allowing foreigners—mainly from Japan, Korea, and Taiwan—to invest and own factories in China. In 1979, China's exports were 5 percent of its GDP. By 2005, they were 36 percent.

China's cheap and abundant labor made it a fierce competitor in low-tech markets, where labor is a significant factor of production. Textiles and apparel are naturals. Between 1995 and 2005, U.S. imports from China increased fivefold. In 1995, the U.S. trade deficit with China—imports minus exports—was $20 billion. By 2005, it grew to $202 billion, accounting for almost 30 percent of the total U.S. 2005 trade imbalance.

Producers and workers in our textile and apparel industries think this China connection is a serious problem and have been agitating, with some success, in getting Congress to put the brakes on Chinese imports. They have a point. These low-tech Chinese imports have devastated their industries. On the other hand, U.S. consumers have enjoyed the lower prices that come with these Chinese imports. As much as 80 percent of Wal-Mart's merchandise is made in China.

Noteworthy, China's sights are not trained solely on low-tech export markets. According to the OECD, China has overtaken the United States as the world's largest exporter of information and communications technology goods. Here's where their foreign investors fit in. Roughly 60 percent of China's high-tech exports are produced by foreign-invested enterprises in China and the percentages rise with the level of high-tech technology.

Is China merely an export platform, a convenient low-cost base for the world's high-tech multinationals, or is it instead an up-and-coming, honest-to-goodness high-tech competitor in its own right? Hint: Think of Japan's Sony and Korea's Samsung. U.S. high-tech firms as well as its low-tech firms must learn to compete with a determined China. But that's what free trade is all about.

There's another impressive upside to our China connection. While Chinese exports to the United States increased fivefold during 1995–2005, U.S. exports to China increased 3.6-fold. That's a classic example of a free trade win-win outcome. In 1995, China ranked 13th among the leading U.S. export markets and moved up to rank 2 in 2007. Simply put, China's exports invigorate our own. To economists, that's very good reason to believe that the promise of our China connection outweighs the problem.

Why? There is no conspiracy here against the poor. Rather, it is that the push toward freer trade tends to work more slowly in labor-intensive industries where union strength is stronger. To keep imports out, pressure is placed by organized labor and by domestic producers on raising or maintaining high tariffs. Over the long run, the successes of their efforts end up creating quite disparate tariff rates. In other words, while the *average* tariff rates have fallen dramatically over the past half century—as we see in Exhibit 16—they have fallen less dramatically, if at all, for those goods that are relatively more important to low-income people.

CHAPTER REVIEW

1. The prices of goods in competitive markets reflect their costs of production. Any differences in the costs of producing a specific good in any two countries—or within regions of a country—present opportunities for geographic specialization that, when taken, result in more total goods produced.

2. If the United States can produce a good using fewer resources than, say, Canada, then the United States is said to have an absolute advantage over Canada in producing that good.

3. If the United States can produce a good whose opportunity cost is lower than the opportunity cost of producing the good in, say, Canada, then the United States is said to have a comparative advantage over Canada in producing that good.

4. In a two-country, two-goods world, specialization will create absolute, comparative, or both types of advantages for both countries, and goods will exchange at prices that fall within the relative price range—or relative labor costs—in each of the countries. The gains each country derives from international trade depend upon the prices at which the two goods trade for each other.

5. While both countries gain from specialization and free trade, people in each country who produce goods that have been displaced by the more efficient producer in the other country end up losing, at least in the short run.

6. The quantity of Canadian goods the United States gets when trading a unit of its own goods with Canada depends on the prices of the goods it exports and imports. The terms of trade for the United States measure the ratio of its export prices to its import prices and reflect the purchasing power of a U.S. unit of goods.

7. Because the less-developed economies specialize and trade in agricultural goods while industrially advanced economies specialize and trade in manufactured goods, and because changes in relative prices tend to favor manufactured goods, changes in terms of trade typically work to the disadvantage of less-developed economies.

8. The industrially advanced economies do most of the world's trading, and their trading is mostly with each other.

9. The major trading partners of the United States are Canada, Japan, and Mexico, and the United States is even more important to them as a trading partner than they are to us.

10. Advocates of limitations to free trade cite the following reasons for exceptions to free trade: national security, infant industries, cheap foreign labor, diversity of industry, antidumping, and retaliation against countries limiting our exports to them.

11. Tariffs and quotas are used to limit free trade. A tariff is a tax on imported goods that, by raising its price, makes domestic goods more competitive. A quota, by limiting the quantity of imported goods, creates a larger market share for domestic goods than tariffs do.

12. The General Agreement on Tariffs and Trade (GATT), now known as the World Trade Organization (WTO), seeks to lower tariffs. A tariff concession offered one member must be offered to all. WTO members offer LDCs lower tariffs than are granted to industrial countries, without demanding reciprocity.

13. A customs union, such as the European Economic Community, allows free trade among member countries and a common trade policy with all other countries. A free trade area allows free trade among member countries but grants each member country the right to pursue independent trade policies with other countries.

KEY TERMS

Free trade
International specialization
Absolute advantage
Comparative advantage
Imports
Exports
Terms of trade

Dumping
Tariff
Quota
Reciprocity
General Agreement on Tariffs and Trade (GATT)
World Trade Organization (WTO)

Customs union
European Economic Community (EEC)
European Union (E.U.)
Free trade area
North American Free Trade Agreement (NAFTA)

QUESTIONS

1. The World Trade Organization (WTO) has often been on the front pages of our newspapers. What is its history and what is it designed to do?
2. Consider two trading partners: Canada and Ireland. Suppose someone told you that in the production of corn, Canada has an absolute advantage, but in the production of sheep, Ireland has a comparative advantage. What does Canada's absolute advantage tell you? What does Ireland's comparative advantage tell you?
3. Admitting all exceptions to the rule, the rule is that free trade benefits all nations. Make the case.
4. Using 1990 as the base year (= 100), Bolivia's terms of trade in 2003 were 60. Explain what that means for Bolivia in 2003.
5. The world's nations were "up in arms" in late 2003 when the United States insisted on maintaining its tariff on imported steel. It has since rescinded that tariff. But what are tariffs? How does a tariff on steel affect the price?
6. Many Detroit autoworkers do not buy the argument that everybody gains in international trade. What's their point?
7. Suppose France can produce surface-to-surface missiles more efficiently than we can, while we are able to produce artichokes more efficiently than they can. Should we specialize in artichokes, trading them for French missiles? Make the pro and con arguments.
8. The Irish complain that they never got a chance to make automobiles because the English, their major trading partner, are more experienced and therefore more efficient at it. Would-be Irish automakers ask their government to impose a tariff on foreign automobiles to help them get started. Can you make the case supporting their complaint and request?
9. Who are the major trading nations of the world? Who are the major trading partners of the United States?
10. The European Union started out as a customs union of six nations, but that is not what it is today. What is it today?
11. One of the most important ideas promoting free trade was GATT's "most-favored-nation" clause. Explain.
12. NAFTA is a free trade agreement among the United States, Canada, and Mexico. How does it differ from the trade agreement that binds the European Union?
13. Is the United States a nation that believes in and promotes free trade? Trace the history of U.S. tariffs to make your point.

PRACTICE PROBLEMS

1. The U.S. demand for, U.S. supply of, and Japanese supply of VCRs are shown in the following schedule.

| PRICE | UNITED STATES | | JAPAN |
	QUANTITY DEMANDED	QUANTITY SUPPLIED	QUANTITY SUPPLIED
$100	500	100	100
200	400	200	200
300	300	300	300
400	200	400	400
500	100	500	500

If Japanese VCRs are prohibited from entering the United States, what will be the equilibrium price and quantity bought and sold by Americans in the VCR market in the United States?

2. Suppose the United States allowed Japan free trade privileges in the U.S. market. What would happen to the equilibrium price and total quantity of VCRs bought and sold in the U.S. market?
3. Suppose the United States imposed a $100 tariff on each Japanese VCR imported. What would happen to the equilibrium price and total quantity bought and sold in the United States?
4. Graph the situations described in practice problems 1–3.
5. England and France can produce both wine and cloth. The English use 80 labor-hours to produce

a unit of cloth and 40 labor-hours to produce a unit of wine. The French use 100 labor-hours to produce a unit of cloth.

	CLOTH	WINE
ENGLAND	80	40
FRANCE	100	

Fill in the blank cell—labor-hours to produce a unit of French wine—to show France's absolute advantage in producing wine. Explain.

6. Fill in the blank cell—labor-hours to produce a unit of French wine—to show France's comparative advantage in producing cloth. Explain.

7. Fill in the blank cell—labor-hours to produce a unit of French wine—to show no advantage to either France or England in trading with each other. Explain.

WHAT'S WRONG WITH THIS GRAPH?

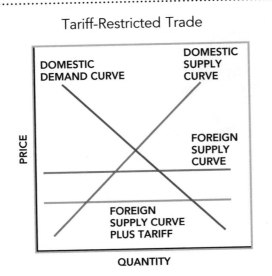

Tariff-Restricted Trade

QUANTITY

PRICE

Economic Consultants

Economic Research and Analysis by Students for Professionals

Viva, a U.S. bicycle firm, designs and manufactures racing bicycles, favorites of world-class riders in the United States. Given the increased success of bicycle racing in the United States, many European riders have expressed interest in buying Viva bikes. However, Viva bikes currently are sold only in the United States, although Viva's owners want to expand their distribution into Europe, particularly into France, Italy, and Germany.

Viva's owners have hired Economic Consultants to examine what barriers exist to selling Viva bikes in France, Italy, and Germany. Prepare a report for Viva that addresses the following issues:

© Image 100/Royalty-Free/CORBIS

1. What barriers, if any, exist to exporting bikes into France, Italy, and Germany?
2. What government agencies exist to assist firms in exporting their products?

You may find the following resources helpful as you prepare this report for Viva:

- **The World Factbook** (http://www.cia.gov/cia/publications/factbook/)—The World Factbook provides information on trade with France, Italy, and Germany.
- **U.S. International Trade Commission (ITC)** (www.ita.doc.gov/td/tic/)—The ITC issues reports on foreign trade barriers and unfair practices.

- **U.S. Department of State** (http://www.state.gov/e/eeb/rls/rpts/eptp/)—The U.S. State Department publishes *Country Reports on Economic Policy and Trade Practices*, which is based on information supplied by U.S. embassies and analyzed and reviewed by the Department of State in consultation with other U.S. government agencies.
- **Bureau of Export Administration** (http://www.bis.doc.gov/)—The Bureau of Export Administration administers export control policies, issues export licenses, and prosecutes violators.
- **International Trade Administration (ITA)** (http://www.ita.doc.gov/) The ITA provides export assistance and information by country and by industry. Of note is the Trade Information Center (http://www.ita.doc.gov/tic/).
- **Export-Import Bank of the United States (Ex-Im Bank)** (http://www.exim.gov/)—The Ex-Im Bank is an independent U.S. government agency that helps finance the overseas sales of U.S. goods and services.

1. While tea is the beverage of choice in both China and the United Kingdom, the Chinese have an absolute advantage over the United Kingdom in producing tea, which means that
   a. China can produce more tea than the United Kingdom.
   b. price of tea is higher in China than in the United Kingdom.
   c. price of tea is higher in the United Kingdom than in China.
   d. fewer resources are used to produce tea in China than in the United Kingdom.
   e. opportunity cost of producing tea in China is lower than in the United Kingdom.

2. If Cuba has a comparative advantage over Canada in the production of sugar, it means that
   a. Cuba can produce more sugar than Canada.
   b. the price of sugar is higher in Cuba than it is in Canada.
   c. the price of sugar is higher in Canada than it is in Cuba.
   d. fewer resources are used to produce sugar in Cuba than in Canada.
   e. the opportunity cost of producing sugar is lower in Cuba than in Canada.

3. The table that follows shows the production and consumption of wheat and sugar in Canada and Cuba under conditions of no trade. When free trade occurs, the entire gains from such trade shift completely to Canada when the price of sacks per bushel is
   a. 3 sacks per bushel.
   b. 4 sacks per bushel.
   c. 5 sacks per bushel.
   d. 6 sacks per bushel.
   e. 7 sacks per bushel.

	WHEAT (BUSHELS)	SUGAR (SACKS)
CANADA	200	600
CUBA	200	1,200

4. The terms of trade are said to worsen for Cuba when
   a. its volume of exports increases more than its volume of imports.
   b. its volume of imports increases more than its volume of exports.
   c. its export prices increase more than its import prices.
   d. its import prices increase more than its export prices.
   e. it minimizes its gains from trade.

5. The most important trading partner of the United States is
   a. Germany.
   b. the United Kingdom.
   c. Japan.
   d. Mexico.
   e. Canada.

6. Which of the following arguments against free trade is based on the idea that industries should be protected through their learning-curve stage of development?
   a. Cheap foreign labor
   b. Diversity of industry
   c. Infant industry
   d. Antidumping
   e. Retaliation

7. When the United States imposes a tariff against Canadian leather goods, it
   a. limits its imports of Canadian leather goods to a specific quantity.
   b. fixes a percentage rate on the price of the imported goods, which creates a revenue that becomes a subsidy for domestic leather producers.
   c. fixes a percentage rate on the price of the imported goods, which creates a revenue for the U.S. government.
   d. disallows the importation of Canadian leather goods unless Canadians allow an equal value of U.S. leather goods into Canada.
   e. disallows the importation of Canadian leather goods.

8. The main objective of the World Trade Organization (WTO) is to
   a. promote free trade worldwide.
   b. create a universal tariff system.
   c. provide agricultural subsidies mainly to developing economies.
   d. convert tariff barriers to nontariff barriers.
   e. organize all nations into one unified customs union.

9. The members of the North American Free Trade Agreement (NAFTA) are
   a. Canada and the United States.
   b. Canada, Mexico, and the United States.
   c. Japan and the United States.

d. the European Community, Canada, Mexico, and the United States.

e. Canada, Mexico, North West Territories (NWT), Greenland, and the United States.

10. A customs union is several countries that agree to free trade

a. among themselves and a common trade policy with other countries.

b. among themselves and allow each to determine its own policy with other countries.

c. among themselves and with every other country.

d. with other countries, fixing common tariffs among themselves.

e. with other countries, fixing common quotas among themselves.

KEY **EXHIBIT 1**   Foreign Exchange Market

Keep this in mind when you think about exchange rates: Americans demand yaps to buy South Pacific goods, and South Pacific islanders supply yaps to buy U.S. goods.

The demand curve for yaps, *D*, depicts the demand for yaps at varying rates of exchange, that is, number of dollars required to buy a yap. At $2 per yap, the quantity of yaps demanded is 40,000. At $3 per yap—the yap is now more expensive, that is, people have to give more dollars to buy a yap—the quantity of yaps demanded falls to 30,000.

The supply curve of yaps, *S*, depicts the supply of yaps at varying rates of exchange, dollars for yaps. At $6 per yap—1 yap buys a $6 U.S. good—the quantity of yaps supplied by people holding yaps and wanting to buy dollars is 60,000. At $1 per yap—1 yap now buys only a $1 U.S. good—the quantity of yaps supplied by people holding yaps and wanting to buy dollars is 10,000.

At $1 per yap, a 50,000 − 10,000 = 40,000 excess demand for yaps emerges, driving up the exchange rate. The market reaches equilibrium at $3 per yap, where the quantity of yaps demanded and supplied is 30,000.

The Demand Curve for Yaps

If the exchange rate was not $3 but, say, only $1 per yap, then the 4 yap teakwood carving would be considerably less expensive *in terms of dollars*. And because it's cheaper, we would buy more carvings. That's simply the law of demand, isn't it? But to buy more carvings, we would need more yaps. In Exhibit 1, the quantity demanded of yaps increases from 30,000 to 50,000 when the exchange rate drops from $3 to $1 per yap. That's why the demand curve for yaps is downward sloping.

What about the craftsman? Whether the exchange rate is $3 or $1 per yap, that is, whether we end up paying $12 or $4 for the carving, he still ends up with 4 yaps. How does he feel about the exchange rate? If he had any say in the matter, he would probably prefer the $1 per yap. Why? Because at $1 per yap, we buy more of his carvings.

check your ✔
understanding

Why do we buy more foreign goods when the exchange rate—dollars for yaps—decreases?

The Supply Curve of Yaps

What about the supply curve of yaps in Exhibit 1? The South Pacific islanders supply yaps—exchange them for dollars—to buy our goods. Suppose a South Pacific islander on vacation in New York spots a graphite fishing rod in a window at Macy's. It sells for $60. He immediately translates the price into yaps. After all, that's the currency he's familiar with. At $3 per yap, that rod costs him 20 yaps. Not a bad buy. But at $1 per yap, the rod's price jumps to 60 yaps. It makes a difference.

Why is the supply curve of
a foreign currency upward
sloping?

That's why the supply curve of yaps is upward sloping. At $3 per yap, South
Pacific island people find U.S. goods relatively inexpensive *in terms of yaps* and
end up buying more goods. To buy more, they supply yaps for dollars. That's
what we see in Exhibit 1. The quantity supplied of yaps increases from 30,000 to
60,000 as the exchange rate increases from $3 to $6 per yap.

Shifts in the Demand Curve for Yaps

Changes in the dollars-for-yaps exchange rate cause people demanding yaps to
change the quantity of yaps demanded, which is shown as a movement along the
demand curve for yaps in the foreign exchange market. But what causes the
demand curve itself to shift?

Changes in Income Imagine what would happen to our demand for yaps if
our incomes increased by, say, 20 percent. With more dollars in our pockets, we
end up buying more goods. Suppose among the more goods we buy are teakwood carvings from the South Pacific islands. To buy more teakwood imports,
we need more yaps. Look at Exhibit 2.

Our demand curve for yaps shifts to the right. As a result, the equilibrium
exchange rate increases from $3 to $5 per yap, and the quantity of yaps
demanded and supplied on the foreign exchange market increases from 30,000 to
50,000.

Changes in Taste What about changes in taste? If teakwood carvings catch
on, the increased demand for the carvings creates an increase in the demand for
yaps as well.

On the other hand, suppose our tastes change from wood carvings to Irish
cut glass. What happens to our demand for yaps? The fall in demand for teakwood carvings shifts our demand for yaps to the left, depressing the exchange
rate to below $3 per yap.

Changes in Interest Rates A fall in the interest rate in the United States or
a rise in the interest rate in the South Pacific island will affect the demand for
yaps as well. For example, suppose you were looking through the pages of the

---

EXHIBIT 2   Effect of an Increase in the Demand for Yaps on the Dollars-for-Yaps
Rate of Exchange

The demand curve for yaps
shifts from D_1 to D_2, reflecting an increase in demand
for yap-priced imports.
At the old equilibrium
exchange rate of $3 per yap,
a new 70,000 − 30,000 =
40,000 excess demand for
yaps emerges, driving the
equilibrium exchange rate
from $3 to $5 per yap, where
the quantity of yaps
demanded and supplied is
50,000.

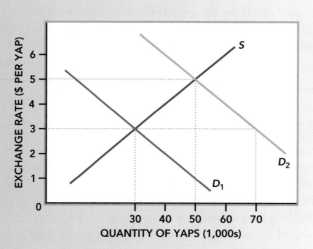

EXHIBIT 3   Effect of an Increase in the Supply of Yaps on the Dollars-for-Yaps Rate of Exchange

The supply curve of yaps shifts from S_1 to S_2, reflecting an increase in demand for dollar-priced imports. At the old equilibrium exchange rate of $3 per yap, a new $50,000 - 30,000 = 20,000$ excess supply of yaps emerges, driving the equilibrium exchange rate from $3 to $2 per yap, where the quantity of yaps demanded and supplied is 40,000.

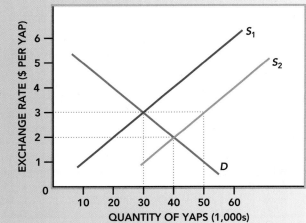

Wall Street Journal and came upon an announcement that the Teakwood Carvings Company, a South Pacific island firm, wants to expand its plant capacity and expects to finance the expansion by offering bonds, in denominations of 10,000 and 20,000 yaps, at a 10 percent rate of interest. If the rate of interest offered by U.S. companies on their corporate bonds is 6 percent, the 4 percent rate spread makes the South Pacific bond rather attractive. Wouldn't you be tempted to buy a 10,000-yap bond?

But how do you go about buying the bond? You first must exchange your dollars for 10,000 yaps and with the purchased yaps, buy the 10,000-yap bond. That shifts the demand curve for yaps to the right, as in Exhibit 2.

Shifts in the Supply Curve of Yaps

Just as changes in U.S. incomes, tastes, and interest rates shift the demand curve for yaps, changes in South Pacific incomes, tastes, and interest rates shift the supply curve of yaps. After all, South Pacific islanders are very much like us.

If their incomes increase, wouldn't you expect that they, too, would buy more goods, which might include imports from the United States? Their increase in demand for U.S. goods results in an increase in their demand for U.S. dollars. They buy dollars by supplying yaps; that is, the supply curve for yaps shifts to the right. The effect of this supply shift on the dollars-for-yaps rate of exchange is depicted in Exhibit 3.

The equilibrium exchange rate decreases from $3 to $2 per yap, and the quantity of yaps demanded and supplied on the foreign exchange market increases from 30,000 to 40,000. And if the interest rate on the island falls, wouldn't that fall encourage islanders to look elsewhere for possible investments? They may end up buying U.S. bonds, which creates a demand for U.S. dollars and a supply of yaps.

FLOATING EXCHANGE RATES

Imagine a world of economies, all importing and exporting goods from each other, investing in each other's capital markets, and demanding and supplying each other's currencies to carry out these many international transactions. That

appliedperspective

TOURISTS AT THE MALL

Imagine having a Canadian cousin George from Calgary, Alberta, who came to visit you in the summer of 2006, bringing with him 300 Canadian dollars that his mother gave him to buy gifts for the Calgary family. Suppose he shopped in your neighborhood mall and the gift shops there were willing to exchange his Canadian dollars for U.S. dollars at the 2006 exchange rate. He would end up buying gifts worth 268 U.S. dollars. Not knowing much about free-floating exchange rates, he would be a little disappointed. Why? Because his mother told him that when she visited your folks back in 1960, she was able to use her 300 Canadian dollars to buy as much as 300 U.S. dollars' worth of gifts. What could possibly explain the difference?

Suppose also that at the mall, George and you met a Japanese tourist from Tokyo who also was gift shopping for family back home. You notice that she exchanges 35,100 Japanese yen for 300 U.S. dollars and makes the same purchases your cousin does. While you are all waiting for gift wrapping, she tells you a surprising story. Her mother was here back in 1960

and she, too, bought 300 U.S. dollars' worth of gifts. But her mother had to exchange 107,400 Japanese yen for those gifts! What could possibly explain the difference?

If tourists from Korea, Britain, and India were at the mall, what stories would they tell about buying U.S. gifts with won, pounds, and rupees in 1960 and 2006?

But how much is that in Canadian dollars?

....

MORE ON THE NET

The Board of Governors of the Federal Reserve Board publishes current and historical exchange rates (http://www.federalreserve.gov/releases/H10/).

Source: End-of-year exchange rates from International Monetary Fund, *International Financial Statistics* (Washington, D.C.).

Exchange Rates of Selected Countries (Currency Units Per U.S. Dollar)

YEAR	CANADIAN DOLLAR	JAPANESE YEN	AUSTRALIAN DOLLAR	INDIAN RUPEE	KOREAN WON	BRITISH POUND
1960	1.00	358	1.12	4.76	65	.36
1970	1.01	358	1.12	7.57	317	.42
1980	1.19	203	1.18	7.93	660	.42
1990	1.16	134	0.77	18.10	716	.52
2008	1.07	110	1.13	41.90	1,029.3	.52

Floating exchange rate An exchange rate determined strictly by the demands and supplies for a nation's currency.

would create a multiplicity of exchange rates, each one reflecting the specific demand and supply condition for its own national currency.

Such an array of exchange rates would be **floating**, that is, in a continuous state of flux, adjusting always to the changing demand and supply conditions in the international market for goods and capital.

Depreciation and Appreciation

The market forces that determine floating exchange rates are really no different from the market forces that determine the prices of goods such as umbrellas, microwave popcorn, and houses. Yet, curiously, many people seem to be more than just a little confused about the significance of a change in exchange rates.

CBS Evening News's Katie Couric and her media friends report regularly on how the U.S. dollar has fared against other currencies during the week. For example, in reporting the dollar's **appreciation**, meaning we pay fewer dollars for a yap, or the dollar's **depreciation**, meaning we pay more dollars for a yap, they typically go one step further by referring to the appreciation as a *strengthening* of the dollar and to the depreciation as a *weakening* of the dollar.

In other contexts, the words *strength* and *weakness* convey moral attributes. Do they convey the same in foreign exchange markets? Is a weak dollar bad? Not if we're interested in exporting U.S. goods. After all, Italians, who are getting more dollars for their lire, buy more U.S. goods. That makes our exporters happy. It also contributes to employment in the United States.

On the other hand, if we're interested in consuming imports, then a strong dollar isn't bad. Why? We can buy Italian imports more cheaply.

Arbitrage Creates Mutually Consistent Exchange Rates

Suppose you pick up a copy of *USA Today* and read the following set of exchange rates: (1) 2 U.S. dollars per British pound, (2) 2,000 Korean won per British pound, and (3) 1,500 won per U.S. dollar. You go over it again to make sure you have read it correctly. No mistake. What would you do?

Wouldn't it be profitable for you to take $100 to the foreign exchange market and buy 150,000 won? With those 150,000 won, you could then buy 75 British pounds. You take the 75 British pounds and buy 150 U.S. dollars. Look what you've done. You started with $100 and ended up with $150. That's **arbitrage**.

Can you do this forever? Not really. Because others, too, will probably have noticed the chance for arbitrage; together the total buying and selling of currencies will change the demand and supply curves in the foreign exchange market, making all exchange rates mutually consistent with each other.

Problems with Floating Exchange Rates

Sometimes free-floating exchange rates are not desirable. Suppose we are importers of wood carvings and strike a deal with a South Pacific island producer to buy 1,000 pieces at 4 yaps each, with the exchange rate at $3 per yap. We expect, then, to pay $12,000. Six months later when the 1,000 wood carvings are delivered, we send a check for $12,000 only to be told that it is now insufficient. Why? Because in the six months between the contract agreement and the delivery, the exchange rate changed from $3 to $5 per yap. The 4,000 yaps we promised to pay, expecting that they would cost $12,000, now cost $20,000. There goes our profit and more.

Of course, the exchange rate could have gone the other way. For example, it could have fallen to $2 per yap. We would then end up with a windfall. Instead of paying $12,000 for the 1,000 carvings, we would have to pay only $8,000.

But our business is importing, not gambling. Floating exchange rates add an element of uncertainty to international trade, making it a less reliable venture than simple domestic trade.

Fixing Exchange Rates

Can we avoid that kind of uncertainty? After all, shifts in demand and supply curves that change equilibrium levels of exchange rates simply reflect our changing preferences. Do we really want to interfere with these preferences?

Perhaps the way out of the dilemma is to *fix* exchange rates—to no longer allow them to float—in such a way that uncertainty is reduced to zero, but at the same time allow demand and supply conditions on the market to dictate the quantities of imports and exports.

Appreciation
A rise in the price of a nation's currency relative to foreign currencies.

Depreciation
A fall in the price of a nation's currency relative to foreign currencies.

Arbitrage
The practice of buying a foreign currency in one market at a low price and selling it in another at a higher price.

check your understanding

What disadvantage can a free-floating exchange rate create?

EXHIBIT 4   Trade Under Free and Fixed Exchange Rates

Panel a depicts changes in the equilibrium exchange rate—dollars per yap—caused by shifts in the demand curve. In panel b, the U.S. government fixes the exchange rate at $3 per yap and supports that rate regardless of changes in the U.S. demand for yaps.

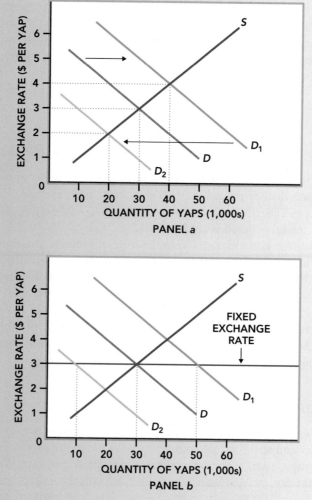

Fixed exchange rate
A rate determined by government and then maintained through the process of buying and selling quantities of its own currency on the foreign exchange market.

How can this be done? Look at Exhibit 4. Panel a depicts what happens to the exchange rate over three years of changing demands for island goods when the rate is allowed to float. Look at the first year. Demand, D, and supply, S, generate an exchange rate of $3 per yap. The quantity demanded and supplied is 30,000 yaps.

Suppose in the second year an increase in demand for South Pacific island goods shifts the demand for yaps to the right, to D_1. The exchange rate increases to $4 per yap, and the quantity demanded and supplied increases to 40,000 yaps.

Now suppose in the third year the demand for island goods decreases. This time, the demand curve for yaps shifts to the left, to D_2. The exchange rate falls to $2 per yap, and the quantity demanded and supplied decreases to 20,000 yaps.

These roller-coaster exchange rates are precisely what we want to avoid. If the rate can drop from $4 to $2 per yap in one year, what's in store for us next year? Not a very comfortable world if you're an importer or exporter calculating profits and losses on constantly fluctuating exchange rates. But what can we do?

Let's bring government into the market. The government announces that it is replacing the floating exchange rate system with a **fixed exchange rate**. All trade will take place at the government's fixed rate of exchange. Follow the effects of

globalperspective

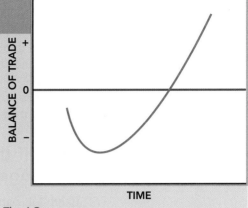

TIME

The J-Curve.

BEGGAR-THY-NEIGHBOR

Every sports fan knows that in every game, at crucial moments, everybody stands up to get a better view of the play, thereby ensuring that nobody actually ends up getting that better view. This observable fact illustrates the concept of "fallacy-of-composition," the idea that what would seem to work for one, doesn't work for anyone if everyone thinks they're the one. And there's no way of overcoming it. It's frustrating for all but unavoidable, even though everyone knows that *no one gains when everyone tries to gain at someone else's expense.*

It's like that as well in the game of currency devaluation. Economists refer to outcomes associated with currency devaluation as beggar-thy-neighbor. Each government knows that by devaluing its currency vis-à-vis other countries currencies, it stands a good chance of improving its balance of trade position. But to the extent that it improves that position, it worsens the balance of trade positions of those economies it trades with. Hence, the nomenclature: beggar-thy-neighbor.

How it works is rather simple. Consider, by way of illustration, a decision taken by the Indonesian government to devalue its currency, the rupiah. Once devalued, it takes more rupiahs to buy a unit of foreign currency. The consequence: Indonesian imports now become more expensive because Indonesian importers must shell out more rupiahs to purchase the foreign currencies needed to buy the foreign goods it wants. At the same time, the devalued rupiah means that other countries use fewer of their own currencies to purchase rupiahs they need to buy the Indonesian exports. Mission accomplished! Indonesian imports decrease and exports increase, improving Indonesia's balance of trade.

The J-curve, shown here, depicts the theoretical shift in the balance of trade following devaluation. It shows a worsening of the country's balance of trade in the short run, reflecting a possible contraction of output and employment before the full steam of devaluation takes effect. Once it kicks in, the country's balance of trade position steadily improves.

End of story? Not by a long shot. You probably see the problem right off, don't you? Beggar-thy-neighbor is a workable policy for Indonesia only as long as other countries don't opt for beggar-thy-neighbor policies of their own.

But what if Indonesia's major trading partners—Japan, China, and Thailand—pursue their own beggar-thy-neighbor policies to overcome their worsening balance of trade positions caused by Indonesia's devaluation policy? The J-curve makes sense only if trading partners don't retaliate. If Japan, China, and Thailand devalue their yen, yuan, and baht, the J-curve for Indonesia evaporates. In fact, there's no improvement in anyone's balance of trade positions and no beggar-thy-neighbor victims.

So why bother? Because the lure of a beggar-thy-neighbor policy is sometimes too irresistible for some government not to pursue. As we noted earlier, that's why we all stand up at sporting events.

government intervention in Exhibit 4, panel *b*. Suppose the government fixes the exchange rate at $3 per yap. How can it keep it fixed when our demand for imports from the South Pacific island changes?

The first year is no problem. The economy's exports and imports themselves create a set of demand and supply conditions on the exchange rate market that, by chance, drives the rate precisely to the government's fixed rate. The quantity demanded and supplied is 30,000 yaps, and the market clears.

In the second year, demand for South Pacific island goods increases, raising our demand for yaps to D_1. Look what happens. At that rate, the quantity demanded becomes 50,000 yaps. However, only 30,000 are supplied. The market now generates an excess demand of 20,000.

How can the government handle the 20,000-yap excess demand pressure on the foreign exchange market? It does so *by coming up with its own supply of yaps.* It goes into the foreign exchange market to exchange its own 20,000 yaps for $60,000. It absorbs the entire excess demand for yaps, relieving pressure on the exchange rate. Of course, to play such a role, the government must have sufficient **foreign exchange reserves**.

Look at panel *b*'s third year. A fall in demand for South Pacific island goods shifts the demand curve for yaps to the left, to D_2. At \$3 per yap, only 10,000 yaps are demanded but 30,000 are supplied, creating now an excess supply of 20,000 yaps. This time, the government intervenes by supplying \$60,000 of its own dollar reserves to buy up the 20,000 excess supply of yaps. We're back where we started. The government has replenished its foreign exchange reserves.

What If the Government Runs Out of Foreign Exchange Reserves?

Exhibit 4, panel *b*, is carefully drawn to allow the third year's excess supply of yaps to replenish the shortage created by the excess demand for yaps in the second year. Unfortunately, life isn't always that convenient. The economy's foreign exchange reserves can build up far beyond sufficient levels or can be drawn down to dangerously low levels.

Suppose the excess demand for yaps, shown for only panel *b*'s second year, persists year after year. How long can the government keep digging into its foreign exchange reserves before it comes up empty? And what can it do if it confronts that predicament?

Adjusting the Exchange Rate Perhaps the simplest remedy is **devaluation** to adjust the fixed exchange rate at a higher level. For example, if the government fixed the exchange rate at \$5 instead of \$3 per yap, our exports would rise, our imports would fall, and excess demand for yaps would disappear. The drain on the government's foreign exchange reserves would cease.

Imposing Import Controls A second option is to impose **import controls** by tariff and quota adjustments. By either raising tariffs or lowering quotas, the government can limit imports. Either way, it can shift the economy's demand curve for yaps as far to the left as it needs to bring the quantity of yaps demanded and supplied into line at \$3 per yap.

Imposing Exchange Controls Another way of accomplishing the same goal is for the government to introduce **exchange controls**. It can require exporters earning yaps to turn them over to the government in exchange for dollars at the \$3 per yap rate. In this way, government ends up with all the yaps in the economy. It then rations them out among importers, keeping the quantity of yaps demanded and supplied in balance.

Borrowing Foreign Currencies Finally, the government can go to the **International Monetary Fund (IMF)** or into the foreign exchange market and borrow yaps to cover the country's excess demand for yaps. Sometimes borrowing is the most reasonable option. In periods of crisis, such as wars or famines, the government cannot afford to cut basic imports, nor can it easily increase exports. To stabilize the economy, its best option may be borrowing. The IMF was created in 1944 to provide temporary loans of foreign currencies to countries that borrow to stabilize their own currency. The loan is actually a purchase-and-resale agreement in which the borrowing country sells its own currency to the IMF for the foreign currencies, agreeing to reverse the transaction at a later date.

But if not held in check, borrowing can lead to problems. Just as doctors who prescribe narcotics to overcome postoperative pain always worry about addiction, so must governments who borrow foreign currencies to overcome economic

---

Foreign exchange reserves
The stock of foreign currencies a government holds.

Devaluation
Government policy that lowers the nation's exchange rate; its currency instantly is worth less in the foreign exchange market.

Import controls
Tariffs and quotas used by government to limit a nation's imports.

Exchange controls
A system in which government, as the sole depository of foreign currencies, exercises complete control over how these currencies can be used.

International Monetary Fund (IMF)
An international organization formed to make loans of foreign currencies to countries facing balance of payments problems.

check your understanding

What does the IMF do?

crises worry about becoming addicted to the habit. Borrowing, and the interest payments that accompany it, can too quickly lock an economy into unmanageable international debt.

BALANCE OF PAYMENTS

An economy's **balance of payments** account provides a statement of the economy's financial transactions with the rest of the world. For example, the U.S. balance of payments account for 2005, shown in Exhibit 5, records the dollars that flowed into the U.S. economy in 2005 from the rest of the world and the dollars that flowed out of the United States to the rest of the world. These flows influence the demand and supply for foreign exchange.

Balance on Current Account

The **balance on current account** summarizes U.S. trade in goods and services, net investment income, and unilateral transfers that occur during the current year. Exports of goods and services and income receipts on investments abroad represent dollar inflows (+) from the rest of the world. Imports of goods and services and income payments to the rest of the world represent dollar outflows (−).

Merchandise Exports   Look at line 1 in Exhibit 5. The single most important source of dollar inflow was the $1,148.5 billion that foreigners paid for our merchandise exports. How do exports contribute to the dollar inflow?

Suppose Dennis Wiziecki, a British engineer from Liverpool, wants to buy a $50,000 Hummer manufactured in Mishawaka, Indiana. He first needs to get his hands on $50,000. After all, that's the currency General Motors wants. How does he get the dollars? By trading his own British pounds for U.S. dollars in the foreign exchange market. That is, the Hummer export from the United States creates the demand for U.S. dollars. Dennis buys the $50,000 with his British pounds, then transfers the $50,000 to General Motors in the United States. That's a $50,000 inflow into the U.S. balance of current account.

on the net
Visit the International Monetary Fund (http://www.imf.org/).

Balance of payments
An itemized account of a nation's foreign economic transactions.

Balance on current account
A category that itemizes a nation's imports and exports of goods and services, income receipts and payments on investment, and unilateral transfers.

on the net
The Bureau of Economic Analysis publishes U.S. balance of payments data (http://www.bea.gov/bea/di/home/bop.htm).

EXHIBIT 5   The U.S. Balance of Payments Account: 2007 ($ Billions)

CURRENT ACCOUNT	
1. MERCHANDISE EXPORTS	1,148.5
2. MERCHANDISE IMPORTS	−1,967.9
3. BALANCE OF TRADE	−819.4
4. EXPORT OF SERVICES	497.3
5. IMPORT OF SERVICES	−378.1
6. INCOME RECEIPTS ON INVESTMENTS	817.8
7. INCOME PAYMENTS ON INVESTMENTS	−726.0
8. UNILATERAL TRANSFERS	−112.7
9. BALANCE ON CURRENT ACCOUNT	−731.2
CAPITAL ACCOUNT	
10. CHANGE IN U.S. ASSETS ABROAD	−1,289.9
11. CHANGE IN FOREIGN ASSETS IN U.S.	2,057.7
12. STATISTICAL DISCREPANCY	36.6
13. BALANCE ON CAPITAL ACCOUNT	731.2

Source: *Survey of Current Business* (Washington, D.C.: U.S. Department of Commerce, August 2006).

Merchandise Imports Line 2 records the $1.967.9 billion outflow from the United States to the rest of the world. That's a lot of dollars going out. Of course, it represents a lot of imports coming in.

How do imports translate into dollar outflow? Well, suppose Carolyn Hatch, a New York tea importer, decides to buy 500 pounds of Darjeeling tea from India. She learns that the Indian tea exporter wants 50 rupees per pound. That adds up to 25,000 rupees. Carolyn obtains 25,000 rupees by going into the foreign exchange market. There, she supplies U.S. dollars in exchange for Indian rupees. This simple transaction represents a U.S. dollar outflow.

Balance of Trade The focus of much discussion and debate on the balance of payments is fixed on the **balance of trade** account, that is, the value of exports minus the value of imports, shown in line 3. The terms we use to describe the balance reveal how we view it. For example, when exports are greater than imports, we describe the balance as *favorable*. When imports are greater than exports, the balance is described as *unfavorable*.

In 2007, the value of the goods we exported was $819.4 billion less than the value of the imports of foreign goods we bought. As Exhibit 6 shows, the United States has been running negative balances of trade for some time.

Negative balances are seen by American industrial workers as a factor that undermines their economic well-being. If the bumper-to-bumper traffic in Cleveland is a stream of imported Toyotas and Hondas, Detroit becomes a wasteland.

How do you switch from an unfavorable to a favorable balance of trade? Depreciate the exchange rate? Impose import quotas? Increase tariffs? Considerable pressure from American exporters and labor unions is continually being brought to bear on the Congress and the administration.

Export of Services Another source of U.S. dollar inflow into the current account was the $497.3 billion export of services, shown in line 4 of Exhibit 5. When Mary Constantine, an account executive in one of Italy's leading advertising agencies, flew from Rome to New York on Delta, she had to purchase the $900 ticket with U.S. dollars. After all, that's the currency Delta demands. To make life more convenient for its passengers, Delta may accept her euros and itself go into the foreign exchange market, exchanging them for $900.

What about exports carried out of the United States by foreigners? For example, when Ryan Walter, a Dubliner, spends his vacation in Cincinnati, that vacation is equivalent to our exporting goods and services to Ireland. If he stays at the Cincinnati Hyatt Hotel, isn't that equivalent to an export of our services? He supplies euros and demands U.S. dollars for the hotel service.

Import of Services What about the $378.1 billion of imported services, shown in line 5? Remember Mary Constantine's flight to New York on Delta? Now suppose, at the same time, Jonathan Richman, a welder from Kenosha, Wisconsin, decides to visit Canada. He buys a deluxe package tour that includes round-trip fares, hotels, and sightseeing trips to Montreal. Just as Delta demanded U.S. currency, Air Canada and Canadian hotels demand Canadian dollars. The travel agent handling the tour takes Jonathan's U.S. dollars to the foreign exchange market and there trades them for the needed Canadian dollars. Jonathan's trip, then, represents an outflow of U.S. dollars.

Income Receipts on Investments Many U.S. companies have investments abroad that earn income. For example, United Fruit, a U.S. food conglomerate with investments in Honduran banana plantations, earns income each year selling bananas to the rest of the world. Part of the income earned remains in

---

Balance of trade
The difference between the value of a nation's merchandise exports and its merchandise imports.

on the
The *United States Foreign Trade Data* (http://www.ita.doc.gov/td/industry/otea/usfth/), published by the International Trade Administration, includes monthly analysis of U.S. trade balances.

EXHIBIT 6   U.S. Balance of Trade, 1960–2007

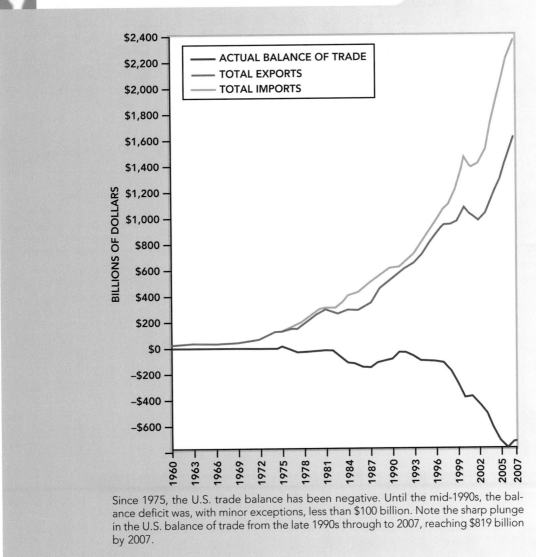

Since 1975, the U.S. trade balance has been negative. Until the mid-1990s, the balance deficit was, with minor exceptions, less than $100 billion. Note the sharp plunge in the U.S. balance of trade from the late 1990s through to 2007, reaching $819 billion by 2007.

Source: U.S. Census Bureau, Foreign Trade Statistics.

the Honduras as additional investment, and part ends up in the United States as income receipts. The $817.8 billion, shown in line 6, is the sum of the income receipts of U.S. investments in the rest of the world.

Income Payments on Investments   In the same way that U.S. investments abroad create annual income that flows into the United States, so do foreign investments in the United States generate income that flows out of our economy. The Japanese investment in an Ohio Honda plant, for example, generates income that is repatriated to Japan. In 2007, such income payments, or outflows, amounted to $726.0 billion.

Unilateral Transfers   The final item in the current account is **unilateral transfers**. These are both private and government income transfers that we make to governments or to people abroad—typically family members living there—or receive from people living abroad. In 2007, net outflow of unilateral transfers amounted to $112.7 billion.

Unilateral transfers
Transfers of currency made by individuals, businesses, or government of one nation to individuals, businesses, or governments in other nations, with no designated return.

globalperspective

© CORBIS

Nothing free floating about these guys.

CHINA'S ARTIFICIALLY PEGGED YUAN

There's a strong consensus among district attorneys that the most reliable form of evidence in prosecuting a case is circumstantial. Eyewitness accounts are too often undependable. In this sense, logic trumps observation.

In the case of the Chinese yuan, the circumstantial evidence seems to be quite convincing that China pursues a foreign exchange policy vis-à-vis the dollar that manipulates a trade balance outcome with the United States. And this not only violates the spirit of the World Trade Organization (WTO) to which China joined in 2001 but provokes the United States to counter China's artificially fixed exchange rate with a series of tariffs directed at China's exports to the United States.

The circumstantial evidence is presented in the accompanying table.

If there is anything striking about the table, it's the relative inflexibility of the yuan during the past decade while the trade deficit soars. For seven years—1999–2005—the exchange rate remains fixed at 8.27 yuans per dollar, and this despite the fact that the U.S. trade deficit with China increases threefold, from $68.67 billion to $201.45 billion. It suggests that something fishy (or artificial) is going on here. If market forces were at

work, even imperfectly, the Chinese yuan would have appreciated. No less noteworthy is the five-year period 1990–1994, during which the deficit almost triples while the exchange rate actually depreciates significantly.

The evidence points to government manipulation. China not only relies on comparative advantage to promote exports but appears as well to have sustained its export drive by engaging in exchange-rate fixing.

The United States is notably irked by this long-term rate fixing, and threats of tariff retaliation are as bipartisan in the Congress as are the economic interests to which it serves. Even the WTO gets into the act. Article XV, paragraph 4, of the General Agreement on Tariffs and Trade bars signatories—of which China is one—from using "exchange-rate action" to "frustrate" the intent of the Agreement. It seems likely that if U.S. producers continue to be undermined by China's exchange-rate policy, the tariff threats against China will turn out to be an unpleasant reality. The "threat" seems to have worked. The rate fell from 8.27 yuan per dollar in 2006 to 7.5 in 2007.

Yuan per Dollar and U.S. Trade Deficit with China, 1990–2007

YEAR	YUAN PER $	TRADE DEFICIT	YEAR	YUAN PER $	TRADE DEFICIT
2007	7.50	256.20	1998	8.31	56.92
2006	8.07	232.50	1997	8.32	49.69
2005	8.27	201.45	1996	8.34	39.52
2004	8.27	161.93	1995	8.46	33.78
2003	8.27	124.06	1994	8.72	29.50
2002	8.27	103.06	1993	5.76	22.77
2001	8.27	89.09	1992	5.45	18.30
2000	8.27	83.33	1991	5.23	12.69
1999	8.27	68.67	1990	4.73	10.43

What are private transfers? Suppose you decide to study at Oxford, England, and your parents send you $100 monthly. That represents a unilateral transfer of dollars. It's described as unilateral because it flows in only one direction—in this case, out of the United States. What do you do with $100? March right down to an Oxford bank to exchange it for British pounds. After all, the local restaurant takes British pounds, not U.S. dollars.

Foreign students studying in the United States create private unilateral dollar transfers that flow in the opposite direction, that is, into the United States. There are thousands of students from the rest of the world on U.S. campuses who exchange their own currencies for U.S. dollars.

The economic and military aid that the U.S. government provides other governments is an example of a government unilateral transfer. Although such aid represents a dollar outflow, the recipient countries typically use the aid to purchase U.S. goods (adding to our exports).

Balance on Current Account   Line 9 sums up the inflows (+) and outflows (−) on the U.S. current account, which in 2007 amounted to −$731.2 billion.

Balance on Capital Account

What about capital account entries? These entries refer to the flow of capital into and out of the United States that takes place when people buy and sell real and financial assets across borders.

Changes in U.S. Assets Abroad   When a U.S. natural-fiber broom company decides to take advantage of the low labor costs in Mexico to build a factory on the outskirts of Mexico City, it needs pesos to construct the plant, buy and install the machinery, and hire workers. How does the company get the pesos? By supplying dollars on the foreign exchange market (an outflow of dollars). In the end, U.S. assets abroad, in the form of a new broom factory in Mexico, increase.

You don't have to be a broom company to own assets abroad. Individuals can buy assets abroad as well. For example, suppose Gary Adelman, a university professor, chanced upon a prospectus at his broker's office describing a new stock issue by an Israeli medical equipment company and bought 50,000 shekels worth of the stock. His assets now include a piece of the Israeli company. But to get that asset, he created an outflow of dollars.

In 2007 the outflow of dollars from the United States that ended up as changes in U.S. assets abroad amounted to $1,289.9 billion, shown in line 10 of Exhibit 5.

Changes in Foreign Assets in the United States   Just as Gary Adelman can buy assets abroad, so can foreigners buy U.S. assets. Imagine a Saudi sheik, sitting in his living room in Mecca reading the *Wall Street Journal*. He reads that the U.S. government has put a new issue of its bonds on the market at a 6 percent rate of interest. He decides to buy $10 million of them. But how? He needs U.S. dollars to make the purchase. His broker goes into the foreign exchange market, supplying the sheik's Saudi riyals and demanding 10 million U.S. dollars. The bond is a U.S. asset.

Foreigners buying any U.S. asset—such as Japanese automakers building an Ohio automobile factory—provide an inflow of dollars. In 2007 changes in foreign assets in the United States amounted to $2,057.7 billion (line 11). As you see, changes in foreign assets in the United States in 2005 were higher than changes in U.S. assets abroad.

Balance on Capital Account   Subtracting capital inflows from capital outflows and introducing a $36.6 billion statistical discrepancy produces a $731.2 billion **balance on capital account**, shown in line 12. As you see, it equals the negative $731.2 billion in the current account.

WHAT IS A BALANCE OF PAYMENTS PROBLEM?

Do U.S. dollar inflows and outflows always cancel each other out? Is it by chance or is there some kind of magic at work bringing these dollar flows into balance? And if current and capital accounts always balance, how can we possibly end up with a balance of payments problem?

Balance on capital account
A category that itemizes changes in the foreign asset holdings of a nation and that nation's asset holdings abroad.

global perspective

A new giant in the world of currency.

THE EUROPEAN UNION'S EURO

If you had looked at the exchange rates listed in the *Wall Street Journal* on July 14, 1998, you would have discovered that one U.S. dollar bought 2,094 Italian lire. One U.S. dollar also bought 2.11 German marks. These exchange rates—the U.S. dollar for specific European currencies—disappeared on January 1, 2002 when 11 of the 15 countries of the European Union discarded their national currencies in favor of a common currency, the euro.

Making the shift to the euro were Austria, Belgium, Finland, France, Germany, Ireland, Italy, Luxembourg, the Netherlands, Portugal, and Spain.

Why the shift? The euro represents a major commitment to the idea of a "State of Europe." It virtually undermines the ability of any one country within the European Union to pursue independently its own national economic interests. By giving up the French franc, for example, France cannot control the money supply in France. Nor is it able to control its exchange rate—to devalue or appreciate—to promote French trade. While the French no doubt will continue to celebrate Bastille Day, its adoption of the euro necessarily altered for the French the meaning of French political independence.

Layered upon the central bank of France, the central bank of Italy, the central bank of the Netherlands, and so on is a new European central bank. The advantage: People, trade, and investment are able to move throughout the European Union as easily as people, trade, and investment move through the 50 states of the United States. And just as the economic strength of the United States is greater than the sum of its parts, so is the economic strength of Europe greater than the sum of its parts. The euro is indispensable in putting the European parts together. Global economic power—vis-à-vis other national or regional economies, and the United States in particular—is the sought-after European Union goal.

Even though the combined countries of the European Union rival the United States in population, GDP, volume of trade, and banking, most of the people and institutions involved in global economic activity—importers, exporters, international lenders, international borrowers, commercial and central banks—rely on and use the currency that other global participants are using. That currency is still the U.S. dollar. Like the English language, people use the dollar internationally because, at this time and in this world, most everyone else is using it.

MORE ON THE NET

Find out more about the euro, including what the banknotes and coins look like, at http://www.euro.ecb.int/.

The problem associated with the balance of payments is how the balance is obtained. Consider, for example, what happens when the outflow of dollars to pay for our imports exceeds the inflow of dollars earned by our exports. Some source of financing has to be found to cover the difference. Foreigners don't export for the love of it. And currencies don't just materialize out of thin air.

How, then, do we cover? There are three alternatives. First, we can dip into our foreign currency reserves. For example, if we import more from Japan than we export to Japan, we can use our yen reserves to cover the difference. Second, the Japanese may decide to buy some of our assets, such as the Sears Tower in Chicago. Their supply of yen to buy the dollars needed for the Sears Tower purchase may be just the yen we need to cover the difference between our imports from and exports to them. Third, we can go into the foreign exchange market or to the IMF to borrow the needed yen. Each alternative serves to bring dollar inflows and outflows into balance.

But that's also how we get into trouble! How deep are our currency reserves? How many assets do we really want to sell off? How many foreign currency loans can we take out before foreigners close the door?

Do Trade Imbalances Always Create Problems?

Governments are not always concerned about trade imbalances, even when their economies import considerably more than they export. Why not? Because if an economy's principal imports are in the form of industrial and agricultural machinery, the government may expect that by building up the economy with these imports, the economy will *eventually* expand its export markets. That is, the government believes that imports, properly selected, can contribute to future exports and, therefore, *future* dollar inflows.

Foolhardy? Not really. No one would call a farmer foolhardy for scattering seed during spring sowing. The late summer harvest is expected to more than make up for the cost of seed. If imports modernize the economy's productive capacity and improve its competitiveness in world markets, then greater export sales would make the earlier balance of payments problem a gamble well worth taking.

The problem with such a strategy is that it doesn't always work. There is simply no way of guaranteeing that imports intended to develop the productive base of the economy today translate into exports tomorrow. Too often, governments are too optimistic about their export prospects. They view the future through rose-colored glasses. In the end, what was thought to be a calculated risk becomes a real problem.

In many cases, an economy's deficit on current account may not reflect any government strategy at all, not even a failed one. It may simply record the economy's lackluster export performance, at least compared to its import appetites. But why lackluster, and why the appetite?

HOW DEFICITS ON CURRENT ACCOUNT DEVELOP

The Trouble with Being Popular

It's sometimes hard to stay out of trouble when you're too popular. That may be precisely why the United States sometimes gets into balance of payment difficulties. Paradoxically, it is the strength and stability of the U.S. economy compared to other economies that creates the problem. That's the way many economists explain the sharp reversal from favorable balances on current account to deficit ones during the mid-1980s.

Foreigners shopping around the world for attractive investment opportunities found them right here in the United States. In very few other economies did they find such inviting combinations of investment security and reasonable rates of return. Not surprisingly, then, foreigners invested in the U.S. economy, supplying their own currencies on the foreign exchange market and demanding U.S. dollars.

But consider what this popular demand for U.S. dollars does to the U.S. exchange rate. It drives it up. *We now find foreign goods relatively inexpensive in terms of dollars, while foreigners find our goods increasingly expensive in terms of their currencies.* As a result, we import more and export less. If foreigners persist in viewing our economy as a popular domicile for their investments, we may end up with chronic deficits on current account.

The High Cost of High Interest Rates

We can arrive at the same deficit on current account when our interest rates climb above those prevailing in other economies. Canadians, for example, compare interest rates offered at home and abroad and choose those yielding the highest rates. Many individuals, regardless of nationality, invest in securities offering the highest rates. The rising U.S. interest rates in the 1980s shifted the demand curve for the U.S. dollar to the right, driving up the exchange rate on the U.S. dollar. As a result, it made imports more attractive, our exports less attractive.

In this same way, domestically driven monetary policy can inadvertently affect the balance on current account. If the Fed, fighting inflation in the economy, raises its discount rate, it may trigger an increase in interest rates. If the interest rates in the United States climb above foreign rates, the demand for U.S. dollars will increase, appreciating the U.S. dollar, and in this way contributing to the deficit on current account.

The High Cost of Budgetary Deficits

Keeping in mind this link between exchange rates and interest rates, imagine what happens to the deficit on current account when the government, pursuing a purely domestic fiscal policy, finances its deficit budget by selling government securities. If it offers a relatively high interest rate to attract buyers, wouldn't foreigners be just as receptive to the securities offer as Americans?

Budgetary deficits can affect exchange rates and, consequently, balances on current account.

The High Cost of Low Productivity

There's little that the government can do—even correcting for troublemaking monetary and fiscal policies—if the economy's level of productivity, compared to the levels of productivity in other economies, is low and falling. Maintaining export markets becomes increasingly difficult for industries that cannot compete with foreign prices and quality. In fact, when confronted by stiff foreign competition, domestic producers have difficulty holding on to their own domestic markets.

In an economy characterized by low productivity, there are no quick-fix solutions. Unless its industries make the effort to match foreign competition by adopting successful technologies or by creating a more productive culture within its management and labor force, the economy's balance on current account position will steadily worsen.

How serious can a trade imbalance become? How much can an economy borrow or how much of its assets can it sell to finance chronic deficits on current account before pressure builds up to force changes in its exchange rate? Ultimately, depreciation of its rate must occur, making its exports cheaper and its imports more expensive. But unless a low-productivity economy confronts the problem of its low-level productivity, even exchange rate adjustments won't work in the long run.

INTERNATIONAL DEBT

It isn't only the very low-income, low-productivity, less-developed economies that make their way to lending institutions. In many cases, it is economies with higher incomes, among them relatively high performers that still find themselves strapped to substantial **international debt**. It doesn't matter whether an economy is borrowing to survive or borrowing to sustain high-gear development—both are still borrowing. If the high-gear economy jams, it can create international debt havoc.

A large volume of international debt in economies, such as Argentina's $140 billion, is not the only, or even the best, measure of the debt's burden on an economy. A small or moderate amount of international debt can become a very

International debt
The total amount of outstanding IOUs a nation is obligated to repay other nations and international organizations.

EXHIBIT 7   Debt Service of Selected Countries, as a Percentage of Exports: 2003

ARGENTINA	34.7	TURKEY	20.3
LEBANON	81.5	BRAZIL	38.1
SIERRA LEONE	10.9	MOROCCO	25.7
INDIA	18.1	PAKISTAN	16.8
NICARAGUA	11.7	URUGUAY	23.1

Source: United Nations Development Programme, *Human Development Report 2005* (New York: Oxford University Press, 2005).

heavy burden on a developing economy if the interest payments on the debt account for a large percentage of the economy's export revenues.

Exhibit 7 records the **debt service** (the ratio of interest payments on the debt to the economy's exports) for 10 less-developed debtor economies.

Once debt accumulates, it is sometimes difficult to pay off, or even keep under control. Imagine yourself in debt to a credit agency, with the interest payments you make each month on the debt eating up as much as 30 percent of your monthly take-home pay. Not much room to maneuver, is there? Look at Argentina's debt service in 2003. It represents 34.7 percent of Argentina's 2003 exports. Unless Argentina changes the character of its balance of payments, that debt service may become increasingly unmanageable.

Debt service
Interest payments on international debt as a percentage of a nation's merchandise exports.

WILL IT ALL WORK OUT RIGHT IN THE LONG RUN?

David Hume, an 18th-century political philosopher, explained why Spain's demise as an economic superpower was inevitable. Hume argued that Spain lost its ability to compete successfully in world markets because it was so successful in amassing great quantities of gold, then the international currency, from the New World. The more gold Spain acquired, the less able it was to maintain its export markets.

Hume understood why. He saw the relationship between money, prices, exchange rates, and exports. As money, in the form of gold, flowed into Spain, it drove up Spanish prices, making foreign imports less expensive in Spain and Spanish exports more expensive abroad. As a result, Spain's balance on current account became negative, with gold now flowing out of the country. It was as unavoidable as the common cold.

We can apply that same logic to our modern economies. In spite of what they try to do, economies with negative balances on current account will find their exchange rates falling. And unless these rates are propped up by government intervention, they will fall to stem the currency outflows. As long as a negative balance exists, the exchange rate will keep on falling. Eventually, the rate will reach the level appropriate to a zero balance on current account. It takes only time.

This automatic correction mechanism, however, may also push the economy into lower living standards. Some people may be pleased when the economy's exchange rate generates a zero trade balance, but it is somewhat less pleasing if the economy cannot afford to provide the majority of its population with the necessities of life.

In many cases, that is indeed what results. If the Zambian kwacha, for example, is driven so low relative to the U.S. dollar that the Zambian people lose the ability to import needed food, then whatever the equilibrium level of the exchange rate, Zambia's standard of living falls. Equilibrium levels of exchange rates, perhaps inevitable, do not guarantee a desirable outcome.

on the net
The World Bank (http://www.worldbank.org/) maintains data on international debt.

applied perspective

The debt's crushing! Help!

FORGIVING LDC DEBT

Some people with limited incomes and unlimited appetites borrow to satisfy their insatiable appetites. Too often, the borrowing becomes habitual. And that can be very dangerous business. The borrowing, of course, is not interest-free; very quickly, the interest payments the borrowers are obliged to make get to be as burdensome as, if not more burdensome than, the debt repayment itself. So they borrow again to cover their interest and debt obligations and the debt numbers spiral upward. How long does it take before their debt situation becomes utterly hopeless?

What would you do if you were one of these people? Work harder to increase your income? Curb your appetite? How about going to your creditors on bended knees to ask for debt forgiveness. After all, they may know, as you do, that forgiveness or not, you're not going to repay the debt *ever* because you simply can't.

Many developing (or not so developing) countries are in precisely that situation. With limited GDPs and unlimited appetites, they plunge into international borrowing that eventually puts them in that hopeless situation. What can they do about it? What can their creditors—commercial banks, Western governments, the World Bank, and the International Monetary Fund (IMF)—do about it?

Can these developing countries really "work harder" to increase their GDPs? Not if, as it is for many, their resources and energies are diverted to war activity or to curbing internal conflicts. And even if they were to "work harder" on their economies, most are agriculturally based and because agricultural prices are typically weak on world markets, their GDP growth performance can't be anything but unimpressive. Adding to their woes is the fact that industrial world economies, receptive to special interests at home, are reluctant to open their markets to LDC agricultural exports.

What about curbing their appetites? Theoretically, LDC borrowing was designed to develop productive capacity. But in fact, too much of their debt was siphoned off by corrupt government leaders—in many cases, nonelected, military dictatorships (Suharto, Marcos, Samoza, Noriega, and Banzer, to name a few)— and stored away in Swiss, Bahamian, and Cyprus banks. Debt that did find its way into development projects was often mismanaged or used to support politically showcased, grandiose development schemes that had

minimal if any impact on the economies of these nations. The development success stories were simply too few. The result was that for most of the debtor nations, the debt created more problems than it solved.

Most of the more than 2 trillion of LDC debt is owed by 33 countries, 90 percent of them African. None of them are able to repay. What's left to do?

The issue of forgiveness is on the table. Creditor nations and institutions, such as the United States and the IMF, are disposed to forgive many for much of their debt, *but with strings attached*. The IMF wants assurances that the debtor nations "get their houses in order." By that it means cutting spending to stabilize their currencies; slashing social spending on education, health, and social services; cutting government employment and payrolls; converting inefficient small-scale farming to large-scale export crop farming; and privatizing public industries. The IMF formula is traumatic: Living standards must get worse for many in the indebted world—particularly the middle class and poor—before they can get better.

The IMF positions has been challenged not only by the indebted countries, but also by the World Bank and creditor governments such as the United States. The United States favors debt relief only if the debtor countries apply the savings toward primary health and education. Nongovernmental organizations (NGOs) such as Oxfam America support that position and emphasize poverty reduction as well.

There appears to be little disagreement among the debtor and creditor nations concerning the basic problem and solution: The major percentage of the debt is beyond repayment, and creditor forgiveness of the debt is the only viable policy option.

··

MORE ON THE NET

Find out about the International Monetary Fund at http://www.imf.org/. The World Bank Group's home page is at http://www.worldbank.org/, and Oxfam America is at http://www.oxfamamerica.org/.

But what's to be done? Is there anything the less-developed economies like Zambia can do to correct their international trade and debt problems? Perhaps the starting point is first to understand why their economies look the way they do. That's the task we set for ourselves in the next chapter.

CHAPTER REVIEW

1. The U.S. demand curve for European euros is downward sloping. When the price of the euro—dollars for euro—is relatively high, a 10-euro bottle of French wine for an American is relatively expensive in terms of the dollars needed to pay for the wine. When the dollars-for-euro exchange rate falls, that same 10-euro bottle of wine for the American is now less expensive in terms of dollars. Because wine now costs fewer dollars, the quantity demanded by the American increases. This increase in quantity demanded of wine creates the increase in quantity demanded of euros.

2. The French supply curve of euros is upward sloping. When the price of the euro—dollars for euros—is relatively high, a $10 CD for the French is relatively inexpensive in terms of the euros needed to pay for the CD. When the dollars-for-euros exchange rate falls, that same $10 CD for the French is now more expensive in terms of euros. Because the CD now costs more euros, the quantity demanded by the French decreases. This fall in quantity demanded of CDs creates the decrease in quantity supplied of euros.

3. The demand curve for European euros—reflecting U.S. demand for French goods—and the supply curve of euros—reflecting French demand for U.S. goods—create on the foreign exchange market the equilibrium exchange rate of dollars for euros (or euros for dollars).

4. Shifts in the demand and supply curves for euros—occasioned by changes in income, tastes, and interest rates—change the equilibrium exchange rate. Appreciation of the dollar means we pay fewer dollars for euros, while depreciation of the dollar means we pay more dollars for euros.

5. To decrease the volatility of its exchange rate, a government may impose a fixed exchange rate. This may require the government to intervene in the foreign exchange market, using its foreign exchange reserves to buy and sell foreign currencies in sufficient quantities to eliminate any excess demand or supply generated on the foreign exchange market.

6. When the fixed exchange rate becomes difficult to maintain, the government can resort to policies such as devaluation, import controls, exchange controls, or borrowing foreign currencies.

7. An economy's balance of payments account describes its financial transactions with the rest of the world. The current account adds up exports and imports of merchandise and services, income payments and receipts on investments, and unilateral transfers. The capital account shows the sum of changes in the value of overseas assets and the value of foreign assets in the economy. The difference between merchandise exports and merchandise imports is the balance of trade. When imports exceed exports, there is an unfavorable balance of trade.

8. Exports of services occur when foreigners purchase U.S. services. When Americans travel overseas, they create service imports. When we earn income on our investments overseas, an inflow of dollars from the rest of the world is created. Similarly, when foreign companies operating in the United States earn profits, dollars flow abroad. Unilateral transfers are payments by individuals that are sent abroad and exchanged for a foreign currency.

9. The capital account line for changes in U.S. assets abroad shows the extent to which firms in the United States have invested overseas. These investments create an outflow of dollars. Foreign firms' investments in the United States show up as changes in foreign assets in the United States. Such investments create an inflow of dollars.

10. If the outflow of dollars to pay for imports exceeds the inflow of dollars to pay for exports, then the difference must be financed. Four financing options exist. Reserves of foreign currency can be drawn down. Domestic assets can be sold. Government securities can be sold. Or a country can go into foreign exchange markets and borrow the difference.

11. It may make sense for a country to import more than it exports if the kinds of goods being imported contribute to future gains in productivity.

12. International debt can become a problem for a developing country if interest payments on the debt take a large percentage of export revenues. The debt service is the percentage of a country's exports that interest payments on the debt represent.

KEY TERMS

Foreign exchange market
Exchange rate
Floating exchange rate
Appreciation
Depreciation
Arbitrage
Fixed exchange rate

Foreign exchange reserves
Devaluation
Import controls
Exchange controls
International Monetary Fund (IMF)
Balance of payments
Balance on current account

Balance of trade
Unilateral transfers
Balance on capital account
International debt
Debt service

QUESTIONS

1. Each nation has its own currency. Americans have the dollar, Italians have the euro, and the British have the pound. So how do they trade?

2. Think about the United States and Japan. Suppose the exchange rate, yen per dollar, falls from 125 yen to 100 yen. How would that affect trade between the United States and Japan?

3. What circumstances would shift the demand curve for U.S. dollars on the foreign exchange market to the right?

4. What circumstances would shift the supply of U.S. dollars on the foreign exchange market to the right?

5. How can the government fix an exchange rate? Can the government fix it at any level, for any length of time? Discuss the limitations that a government faces in maintaining a fixed rate.

6. What control mechanisms can a government introduce to support its exchange rate policy?

7. What are the major categories and items in a balance of payments account?

8. How would each of the following affect the U.S. balance of payments account?

a. Every month, a Bangladeshi professor at the University of Utah sends $200 to his family living in Bangladesh.

b. A Japanese businessperson in Nagasaki buys 100 shares of General Motors stock.

c. The U.S. government sells 20 Patriot missiles to the Israeli government.

d. The U.S. government gives the Russian government 50 million tons of wheat, priced at $3 per ton, in the form of a unilateral transfer.

9. In some cases, a balance of payments problem really isn't a problem at all. Yet in other cases, it could signal a fundamental problem in the economy. Explain.

10. Some economists argue that our budgetary deficits contribute to our balance of payments problems. How do they make their case?

11. Balance of payments problems and long-term international debt plague the less-developed economies. The two issues are related. Explain.

PRACTICE PROBLEMS

1. The only information given for the following table is that the equilibrium exchange rate is 4 Israeli shekels per U.S. dollar.

SHEKELS PER U.S. DOLLAR	QUANTITY DEMANDED (SHEKELS)	QUANTITY SUPPLIED (SHEKELS)
6		
5		
4		
3		
2		

Fill in the blank cells, constructing quantity demanded and quantity supplied schedules so that the equilibrium exchange rate occurs at 4 shekels per dollar.

2. Change the numbers in the table in practice problem 1 so that the equilibrium exchange rate is 5 shekels per U.S. dollar. What explanation can you offer for such changes?

3. Suppose the following data represent Israel's international transactions (in shekels). What

is Israel's balance of trade? What is its balance on current account? What is its balance on capital account?

ITEM	SHEKELS
MERCHANDISE EXPORTS	10
CHANGE IN FOREIGN ASSETS IN ISRAEL	2
EXPORT OF SERVICES	5
INCOME RECEIPTS ON INVESTMENT	3
ITEM	SHEKELS
MERCHANDISE IMPORTS	−8
CHANGE IN ASSETS ABROAD	−5
IMPORT OF SERVICES	−4
INCOME PAYMENTS ON INVESTMENT	−2
UNILATERAL TRANSFERS	−1

4. How would each of the following events affect the quantity demanded and quantity supplied schedules in practice problem 1? Indicate whether the numbers in the schedules would increase or decrease and the resulting increase or decrease in the equilibrium exchange rate. Then show how each event would affect the numbers in each of the categories in practice problem 3.
   a. A U.S. manufacturer moves a factory from New Jersey to Israel.
   b. Hilton builds a new 150-room hotel in Jerusalem.
   c. The United States removes its tariff on oranges from Israel.
   d. Israeli citizens working in the United States send part of their income back to Israel.

WHAT'S WRONG WITH THIS GRAPH?

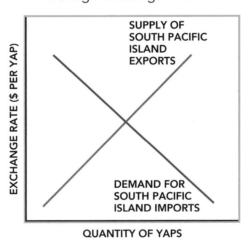

Foreign Exchange Market

Economic Consultants

Economic Research and Analysis by Students for Professionals

David Tietlebaum recently opened Excursions Around the World, a travel agency that conducts tours in over 50 countries. Before opening Excursions Around the World, David worked as a tour guide in Europe and, in this role, had experience with different currencies and exchange rates. However, as owner of Excursions Around the World, David must be able to explain to customers how exchange rates work and, in particular, what the value of their own currency is in relation to the currency of the country, or countries, these customers want to visit.

© Image 100/Royalty-Free/CORBIS

David has hired Economic Consultants to prepare a brochure that customers may read to familiarize themselves with foreign currencies and the dynamics of exchange rates. Prepare a brochure for Excursions Around the World that addresses the following issues:

1. What information is available about foreign currencies?
2. In basic terms, how do exchange rates work? What do customers traveling in foreign countries need to consider about exchanging currencies?
3. Where can customers find current information about exchange rates?

You may find the following resources helpful as you prepare this brochure for Excursions Around the World:

- **Currency News** (http://biz.yahoo.com/reports/currency.html)—Yahoo! Finance provides the latest news, taken from Reuters, concerning currencies.
- **The Interactive Currency Table** (http://www.xe.com/ict/) and **Universal Currency Converter** (http://www.xe.com/ucc/)—The Interactive Currency Table and the Universal Currency Converter, maintained by Xenon Laboratories, automatically provide exchange rate values and foreign exchange rate conversions.
- **Pacific Exchange Rate Service** (http://fx.sauder.ubc.ca/)—This service provides access to current and historic daily exchange rates. Also provided is a list of all the currencies of the world and the countries' exchange rate arrangements.
- **Federal Reserve Statistical Release, Foreign Exchange Rates** (http://www.federalreserve.gov/releases/H10/)—The Federal Reserve releases, every Monday, official foreign exchange rates.

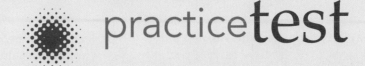

1. The *Times of London* reported that the demand for U.K. pounds in 2003 shifted to the right. What could have caused the shift?
   a. Americans bought more U.K. goods.
   b. More American goods were bought in the United Kingdom.
   c. Incomes in the United Kingdom increased.
   d. Incomes in the United Kingdom decreased.
   e. American incomes decreased.

2. If the supply curve for euros shifts to the left, then
   a. the demand curve for euros will shift to the right.
   b. the equilibrium exchange rate of euros for other currencies will rise.
   c. there will be more euros in equilibrium held in world markets.
   d. the equilibrium exchange rate of euros for other currencies will fall.
   e. the demand curve for euros will shift to the left.

3. If the United States fixes the exchange rate of Indian rupees per dollar at 45 rupees per dollar, then to maintain it at that rate
   a. Indian and American exporters and importers must agree to keep their mutual trade in balance.
   b. Indian and American exporters and importers must agree not to trade at any other exchange rate.
   c. The U.S. government must do the exporting and importing for the United States.
   d. both the U.S. and Indian governments must do the exporting and importing for their respective countries.
   e. the U.S. government must buy and sell U.S. dollars on the foreign exchange market.

4. If there is an appreciation in the dollar relative to the Japanese yen, then
   a. more dollars are needed for Americans to buy Japanese goods.
   b. Americans get fewer yen per dollar on the foreign exchange market.
   c. American goods become cheaper for the Japanese to buy than before.
   d. American goods become more expensive for the Japanese to buy than before.

   e. the supply curve of the yen will shift to the right.

5. Which of the following groups would benefit from a depreciation in the euro relative to the Canadian dollar?
   a. Exporters of Canadian goods
   b. Exporters of European Union goods
   c. Consumers of Canadian goods in Germany
   d. Consumers of European Union goods in Germany
   e. Importers of Canadian goods

6. One problem with floating exchange rates is that they
   a. do not take into account shifts in the demand for a nation's currency.
   b. do not take into account shifts in the supply of a nation's currency.
   c. add uncertainty to international trade.
   d. decrease price variability in world markets.
   e. eliminate the possibility of arbitrage in foreign exchange markets.

7. If Costa Rica uses import controls to maintain its foreign exchange reserves, it means that the Costa Rican government
   a. uses international borrowing to finance its imports.
   b. sells foreign exchange reserves to finance its imports.
   c. imposes tariffs and quotas to limit its imports.
   d. devalues the Costa Rican peso to limit its imports.
   e. appreciates the Costa Rican peso to limit its imports.

8. All of the following except one are included in a nation's balance on current account. Which one?
   a. Foreign exchange reserves
   b. Unilateral transfers
   c. Export of services
   d. Income receipts on investments
   e. Income payments on investments

9. Which of the following is an example of a unilateral transfer?
   a. The United States borrows dollars from Italy in the foreign exchange market.
   b. Spain purchases oil from Venezuela.

c. Norway pays dividends on bonds issued to Chinese citizens.
d. A French citizen working in the United States sends money home to her family.
e. Colombia imports shoes from Italy.

10. Interest payments on a country's international debt are referred to as
a. debt service.

b. loan payments.
c. currency devaluation.
d. trade imbalances.
e. income payments on investments.

THE ECONOMIC PROBLEMS OF LESS-DEVELOPED ECONOMIES

In July 1846, Henry David Thoreau was sentenced to jail in Concord, Massachusetts for having refused to pay a $1.50 poll tax. He believed that paying the tax would signal tacit approval of the county's acceptance of slavery. His dear friend Ralph Waldo Emerson was reputed to have visited the county jail and asked: "Henry, what are you doing in here?" Thoreau replied, "Waldo, the question is what are you doing *out there*?"

This Thoreau-Emerson exchange is meant to show that part of understanding a problem might be found in addressing the right question. One obvious question that comes to mind concerning economic growth and development of the world's **less developed countries—the LDCs—** must be: What causes nations to grow? Adam Smith's *Wealth of Nations* and the voluminous growth literature that followed attempted to explain precisely that; why some nations, with only minor and short-lived interruptions, can grow year after year. Perhaps another fruitful approach to an understanding of the nature and causes of economic growth and development may involve restructuring the question to explain not success but failure; that is, asking why some economies *have not grown and seemingly cannot create an environment that fosters economic growth*.

That was the approach economist Paul Collier took in his insightful 2007 volume *The Bottom Billion*. He noted that most LDCs of the world have been rather successful in generating higher standards of living for their populations during the past half century. And while that's pretty good news, it's not the entire news.

Less-developed countries (LDCs)
The economies of Asia, Africa, and Latin America.

Consider this: Of the 2.5 billion world population in 1950, one fifth was comparatively rich while the remaining four-fifths lived in poverty, most barely subsisting. Prospects for a better future then for those impoverished seemed rather remote. Yet only 50 years later, a new and very different view of LDC economic achievement and possibilities—more positive and more promising—was offered, and with much evidence to support it. By 2000, the world's population had increased to six billion; and along with the one billion in the rich world, there were now four billion living in rapidly growing economies where standards of living had improved dramatically.

The bad news concerns those left behind. Collier's numbers show that there are still one billion people living in failed LDCs and for them the future remains as bleak as it ever was. These are the *bottom billion.*

Exhibit 1 puts into graphic form the 'good-news, bad-news' LDC record, by region. It shows, for 1960–1998, regional convergence toward or divergence away from a moving target: the average annual per capita GDP for high-income OECD. OECD refers to the 30-member Organization for Economic Co-operation and Development and its high-income economies are mainly Western Europe and the U.S.

What do we see? The horizontal OECD line is the bar that allows us to measure how well other regional economies have done vis-à-vis OECD. It's a bar much to be admired. After all, the average annual rate of per capita GDP growth in the high-income OECD

EXHIBIT 1   Regional Average GDP per capita as a Ratio of OECD Economies

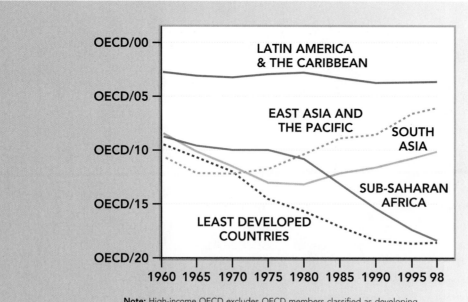

Note: High-income OECD excludes OECD members classified as developing countries and those in Eastern Europe and the CIS. See the Classification of countries

Source: Human Development Report Office calculations based on World Bank 2001g.

countries over the 1960–1998 years was a rather impressive 2.2 percent.

As Exhibit 1 shows, the Latin American and Caribbean track record is no less impressive. Its average per capita GDP was one-third to one-half of OECD's in 1960 and managed to maintain that performance ratio through to 1998. That is to say, its own per capita GDP matched that 2.2 percent rate.

But look at the set of regions whose per capita GDPs in 1960 clustered around one-tenth the OECD level. For them, a very different picture emerges. The East Asian and Pacific region drew to within one-sixth of OECD's 1998 level. Good reason, then, isn't it, for economists to dub that region the "Asian Tigers." South Asia's performance relative to OECD's, on the other hand, was mixed, declining until 1975 and recovering to one-tenth of OECD in 1998. On the whole, then, its track record was rather successful as well. The conspicuous problem clearly is Sub-Sahara Africa and the Least Developed Countries. Their relative positioning deteriorated from one-tenth of OECD performance to almost one-twentieth.

The problem with the failed economies of Sub-Sahara Africa and the Least Developed Countries is more troubling than simply the widening gap between their achievement and those of other LDCs. For many, it is also a problem of them being unable to keep up with their own past performances. Exhibit 2 tells that depressing story.

EXHIBIT 2 GDP per Capita, Annual Growth Rates, and Year of Highest Value for Selected Regions and Countries (1975–2005)

	GDP PER CAPITA (US$ 2005)	ANNUAL GROWTH RATE (1975–2005)	YEAR OF HIGHEST VALUE
UNITED STATES	$41,890	2.0	
OECD	29,860	2.0	
LEAST DEVELOPED	424	0.9	
SUB-SAHARA	845	−0.5	
ZIMBABWE	259	−0.5	1998
DJIBOUTI	894	−2.7	1990
COTE D'IVOIRE	900	−2.1	1978
CONGO (DEM REPUBLIC OF)	123	−4.9	1975
CENTRAL AFRICAN REPUBLIC	339	−1.5	1977
ETHIOPIA	157	−0.2	2005
SIERRA LEONE	216	−2.1	1982
HAITI	500	−2.2	1980
NICARAGUA	954	−2.1	1977

Source: *Human Development Report 2007/2008*, Palgrave McMillan, New York, 2007, pp. 278-80.

Not only are the Exhibit 2 countries confined to triple-digit levels of per capita GDP—Ethiopia's as low as $157—but these already troublesome levels have been falling for the past 30 years.

If you were living in Sierra Leone and for the umpteenth time heard your grandparents talk about the 'good ole days' of some twenty years ago, you shouldn't roll your eyes. While those days may never have been 'good' in the sense that we know 'good'—look at U.S. per capita GDP—they were certainly better. Think about it: Sierra Leone's highest per capita GDP was in 1982. It's been downhill ever since. That's what the negative growth rates of column 3 imply.

No surprise then that these LDCs would make up the better part of the *bottom billion*. And the question is: What makes them different? What explains their failure?

DEVELOPMENT TRAPS

If you were a mouse, you would have little trouble appreciating the difference between an obstacle and a trap. Obstacles are something you could overcome with a little effort and a touch of imagination. Traps, on the other hand, are lock downs; ensnaring its victims and denying options. They can be physical, institutional, cultural, or even psychological. For the *bottom billion* LDCs, a set of development traps have been in place to frustrate their attempts at breaking free to join the parade of other economies that are on growth paths generating rising standards of living.

Let's look at some of these traps and at development strategies designed to weaken their grips.

The Demographic Trap

How successful or unsuccessful an economy is in raising its per capita GDP depends not only on how well it generates economic growth, but also on how well it contains population growth. If population grows faster than GDP growth, per capita GDP falls. It's simple but devastating arithmetic.

Therein lies an LDC double-whammy. While GDP growth has been somewhat less than impressive in many LDCs, population growth has been *too* impressive. And the problem is that for some of these LDCs, population growth is not only near impossible to manage, but even considered desirable.

The rate of population growth is written as

$$\frac{birth\ rate - death\ rate}{100}$$

check your understanding

Why have LDC birth rates outdistanced death rates over the past 50 years?

When birth rates exceed death rates population increases. Over the past half century, the combination of improvements in public health, such as cleaner water and sanitation and the increased availability to the LDCs of basic medical technology, such as vaccines and antibiotics have cut LDC death rates quickly and substantially. On the other hand, LDC birth rates depend on ethnic, religious, and cultural institutions and customs, such as the prestige attached to having large families, the status of women, the age of marriage, and attitudes toward contraception and family planning. And these deeply engrained societal institutions and customs are less given to quick-fix solutions. The result is that over the past

EXHIBIT 3   Annual Population Growth Rate and Percent of Population Under Age 15: 1975–2005 and 2005

	ANNUAL POPULATION GROWTH RATE (1975–2005)	PERCENT POPULATION UNDER AGE 15 (2005)
UNITED STATES	1.0	19.4
OECD	0.8	20.8
LEAST DEVELOPED	2.5	41.5
SUB-SAHARA	2.8	43.6
ZIMBABWE	2.5	39.5
DJIBOUTI	4.3	38.5
COTE D'IVOIRE	3.5	41.7
CONGO (DEM REPUBLIC OF)	2.8	47.2
CENTRAL AFRICAN REPUBLIC	2.4	42.7
ETHIOPIA	2.8	41.0
SIERRA LEONE	2.1	42.8
HAITI	2.0	38.0
NICARAGUA	2.2	37.9

Source: *Human Development Report 2007/2008*, Palgrave McMillan, New York, 2007.

few generations, the fast falling death rates trumped the much slower falling birth rates so that these LDC population growth rates surged.

Look at the population data in Exhibit 3. Some of the LDCs have population growth rates greater than 2.5 percent per year. This means that their GDP growth rates must be at least 2.5 percent per year just to sustain their already low-level per capita GDPs. Look at Djibouti or Cote d'Ivoire or at the 2.8 percent for all of Sub-Sahara Africa. It's a tough situation and the prospects don't look any brighter.

After all, these high population growth rates also create an age distribution profile that loads the population in the under-15-years-old group. The consequences, in terms of struggling out of this demographic trap, are dire. Look at the contrast between the age distributions in these LDCs and those of the U.S. and OECD.

Imagine being the chief economist advising the government of Ethiopia. What kind of policy would you advise? How would you go about changing those Exhibit 3 numbers?

Almost half the population of Ethiopia is under 15 years old. Most of them—particularly those under 10 years of age—although consuming meagerly, still consume more than they are able to produce. Because they represent so large a proportion of Ethiopia's population, these many-mouths-to-feed Ethiopians undercut Ethiopia's ability to shift resources from the production of consumption goods to the production of capital goods. Economists refer to this condition as the vicious circle of poverty: People are poor because they can't invest in capital goods, and they can't invest in capital goods because they are poor. The problem is illustrated in the production possibilities curve of Exhibit 4.

check your understanding

What is meant by the vicious circle of poverty?

EXHIBIT 4   The Vicious Circle of Poverty

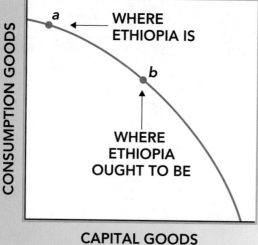

If Ethiopia is going to get onto an economic growth path, it will have to move down along its production possibilities curve from point *a* to a production possibilities position that affords it greater capital goods production, such as point *b*. That may be difficult with population growth at 2.8 percent per year.

Point *a* signals the predicament. The demands of Ethiopia's growing population force it to devote its meager resources almost exclusively to the production of consumption goods, impeding the development of its capital goods production. Point *b* is where it prefers to be. But how do you get there with a fast-growing population? Is Ethiopia, or any of the other economically troubled LDCs, willing to adopt a population policy similar to the one initiated in China in the 1970s, which limits families to one child? Unlikely.

The Political Instability Trap

These millions of young people, too, have become fodder for the rash of civil wars that have plagued and continue to plague these *bottom billion* LDCs. The list is extensive, as you see in Exhibit 5.

These are vicious wars of human and material attrition, with disastrous economic costs. On average, these civil wars decrease by 2.2 percent the economies' annual growth rates during periods of conflict so that their rates of economic growth are, in most cases, pounded into negative percentages and, of course, even more negative rates of per capita growth. When the civil war subsides—the root causes typically remain unchanged—GDP ends up being as much as 15 percent less than it would have been otherwise. In the Congo, for example, Paul Collier estimates that it would take 50 years of peace at Congo's present growth rate just to reach the GDP level it had obtained in 1960! And the probability that these LDC civil wars will reignite is 15 times greater than the chance of a civil war occurring in other LDCs.

EXHIBIT 5   Civil Wars in Sub-Sahara Africas

ANGOLA	1974–89; 95–97; 1998–2002	LIBERIA	1989–96; 1999–2003
BURUNDI	1998–91; 1993–2005	RWANDA	1990–94
CHAD	2005–PRESENT	SIERRA LEONE	1991–2002
CONGO	1996–97; 1998–2003	SOMALIA	1991–PRESENT
COTE D'IVOIRE	1999–2000; 2002–PRESENT	SUDAN	1995–72; 1983–PRESENT
GUINEA-BISSAU	1998–99	UGANDA	1987–PRESENT

global perspective

It's the finish line that counts.

THE BETS ARE ON INDIA

Yogi Berra, the oft-quoted ex-New York Yankees' catcher, famed for having said such things as "You can observe a lot by just watching," or "If you come to a fork in the road, take it," also is reputed to have said "This is like déjà vu all over again."

And it sure seems that way when economists debate the long-run economic prospects of China and India. The debate is astonishingly reminiscent of the debates that occurred decades before when economists were debating the long-run economic prospects of the United States and Soviet Russia.

The Russian rate of GDP growth during the 1960s was estimated to have been twice the American rate, and the concerns expressed by U.S. economists then were twofold: How long will it take the Russians to catch up to us, and what does that striking differential in GDP growth rates tell us about the efficacy of our economic system compared to theirs?

Some economists were downright pessimistic. Others, while acknowledging the scores of economic successes made by the Russians, still put their money on the United States. The power of the free market and the daringness of private enterprise, they argued, will ultimately trump whatever accomplishments the Russian state-controlled and planned economic system may generate. And they were right. In 1991, the already faltering and stumbling archaic Russian economic system collapsed entirely.

The same kind of debate rages on now concerning China and India. The Chinese rate of GDP growth over the 15-year period 1990–2005 was 13 percent per year, about twice the rate of India's 6.2 percent per year. And the issues concern the efficacy of China's totalitarian, state-directed, top-down economic performance versus the democratic, free market, bottom-up

kind of economic system that characterizes India's performance. Together, India and China make up 40 percent of the world's population. They are both big players among our world's economies. How each will fare not only matters to their own people but may signal to many of the world's other developing economies which mode of economic system is the preferred.

Although China's progress is both undeniable and impressive, it relies heavily on its foreign investment, mainly from Korea, Japan, and Taiwan. It is unclear to what extent modern technology has permeated beyond this foreign shell. It is unclear as well how China will manage the inevitable flow of its massive rural population into its cities. The prospect of substantial unemployment and the political fallout it may create looms large and real.

India, on the other hand, although striving along in lower gear, has bred a domestic entrepreneurship that has already spun off world-class, cutting-edge, knowledge-based industries. In addition, India has already done an amazing job of absorbing its excess rural population into its cities. It has been plodding away, decade after decade, building a domestic infrastructure platform for the kinds of economic transformations needed to secure its industrialization. Like the tortoise in Aesop's fable, India may be less swift than the Chinese hare, but in the long-run, two-economies race, the smart bettors are putting their money on India.

But *why* these scores of civil wars? They seem not to be associated with the histories of colonialism, nor with income inequality, nor with repression of minorities, as you might think. What does appear to matter are the relatively high proportion of young, uneducated men—think again of the demographic trap—an imbalance between ethnic groups, and LDCs with an abundance of highly-valued natural resources, such as oil and diamonds whose economic rents provide power-seeking factions both incentive and finances to initiate political rebellion. Climbing out of this kind of violence trap requires, in many cases, a transformation of the country's demographic and ethnic arrangements and an attempt at diversifying production. These are formidable challenges.

But even in the absence of destructive civil wars, political instabilities in the form of nonviolent but frequent and erratic government changeovers may be sufficient to curb the enthusiasm of people and government to strike out on new and bold long-term development activities that are sorely needed to position the economy on an attractive growth path.

After all, can you imagine how difficult and chancy it would be to plan *any* economic future if you thought that the government—with its laws, commitments, and promises—can be overthrown overnight and that the character of the political system might radically change with that overthrow?

Laws become meaningless when governments that displace each other too frequently and by force are inclined to set aside past government commitments and, at times, even basic property rights. Such political discontinuities must interfere with routine economic decision making, increasing people's uncertainty everywhere in the economy.

For example, how can anyone rely on a military junta or on a revolutionary party government whose political support among the people is always questionable and whose legitimacy can be contested only in disruptive ways? How can such a regime provide confidence in anyone's economic future when its own time horizon is, by past experience, short?

In many LDC economies, juntas, single-party regimes, and puppet-like monarchies are precisely the kinds of governments that hold power. Generals in government are soon deposed by their colonels, and one revolutionary party is undone by another, with each new regime always claiming power on behalf of the people. For many, secret police and political prisoners are commonplace.

While some changes in regime may represent new faces in old uniforms or new revolutionary parties replacing old ones, many incoming regimes actually do go about undoing much in the economy.

How then can endangered LDCs gain political stability? It's certainly not by the act of writing it into a constitution. Political stability—or something approximating it—is an acquired state of political toleration, a product of societal tradition. Evolving into that tradition is never an uncomplicated matter and for many of the *bottom billion* LDCs, it remains an elusive goal.

The Natural Resource Trap

If you're good at what you do and the pay-off for doing it is rather attractive, then it makes good sense for you to keep doing it. That's precisely the advice economists offer trading countries, basing that advice on the principles of absolute and comparative advantage. By specializing, they insist, everyone gains in the long run.

Well, maybe. A number of economists are no less impressed with what they call the contagion of "Dutch Disease" so named because the discovery and export of natural gas in 1960s Netherlands, they argue, was responsible for the erosion of its manufacturing base. And with it, the employment it supported. After all, it just seems easier to rely on the export of a natural resource to provide the foreign currencies needed to import goods than to rely on exports that require sizeable and skilled labor as well as a constant need to protect that competitive edge in the world market gained only by forever creating new technologies and products. It's never a sure thing.

In the longer run, then, a country's reliance on a natural resource, such as oil, coffee, or diamonds, may, by sheer neglect of other options, "crowd out" just those productive activities that are necessary to develop higher levels of production, employment, and income.

The evidence, they insist, is on their side. It was resource-poor economies like Mexico, South Korea, Singapore, Malaysia, and Hong Kong that, by having to focus on labor-intensive manufacturing, catapulted from low-level LDC performers into high income-generating economies. As well, this no-other-option focus on people as their springboard to economic development allowed for their eventual progression from low-tech to high-tech production and export.

In other words, not having a good thing sometimes is a good thing. This natural resource trap traps for yet another reason. Because the earnings from natural resource production are relatively quick and readily obtainable, the resource-reliant LDCs are prey to political bribery, corruption, and patronage, conditions likely to subvert democracy. It becomes then for these natural-resource *bottom billion* LDCs, the survival of the fattest rather than the survival of the fittest.

The Absence of Infrastructure Trap

While overcoming noneconomic traps is critical to any effort at development, several economic traps pose equally insurmountable problems. Among them is the conspicuous absence of economic **infrastructure**.

What is infrastructure? When we think about how our own economy works, we tend to take for granted the money and banking system that provides the major investment loans to our nation's businesses; the educational system that turns out the incredible varieties of skills and basic research that actually run our nation's production lines; the extensive transportation and communications system—interstate roads, railroads, airports, canals, telephones, Internet sites, postal systems, television stations—that links almost every piece of our geography into one market; the energy system that powers our factories; and, of course, the market system itself, which brings our nation's goods and services into our households.

Although the basic systems that make up our economic infrastructure were either completely absent or underdeveloped when the United States became a republic, they are now so common to us that we tend to overlook the fact that without them our national productive capacity would suddenly and dramatically collapse.

Imagine transplanting a modern Detroit automobile plant to Chad, an African country southwest of Egypt. Even if U.S. technicians were sent along to put it in place, this major piece of private direct investment would probably do the Chadians little good.

Why? Because physical plants themselves cannot create output. The manufacture of automobiles requires, at the least, a variety of skilled workers, engineers, accountants, salespeople, plant managers, and maintenance crews. Just who in Chad would be qualified? But that's just the beginning.

Infrastructure
The basic institutions and public facilities upon which an economy's development depends.

on the net

Review *The World Fact-book* profile of Chad (www.cia.gov/library/publications/the-world-factbook/geos/cd/html).

globalperspective

© Royalty-Free/CORBIS

To be replaced by the Internet. But when?

INTERNET AND INFRASTRUCTURE

The Internet represents basic infrastructure. It is as indispensable a prerequisite to economic development as are roads, electric power, housing, education, and health. The Internet provides a platform for firms in the developing world to leapfrog from the traditional to the most advanced technologies, allowing them to compete successfully with the industrial economies in producing high-value-added goods and services. It can do this by lowering costs of transportation and communication, making previously inaccessible markets of the industrial world accessible to them. It may even reverse the chronic worsening of terms of trade for the developing economies.

As attractive as these prospects may seem, they remain for many countries in the developing world only tantalizing potential and for some no more than fantasies. The reality they face is an extraordinary Internet gap between themselves and the rest of the world. This gap is shown in the accompanying table.

Narrowing the Internet access gap may be exceedingly difficult for many of the developing economies. It requires considerable capital outlay and the availability of highly skilled labor, both typically in short supply. In 1996, the average cost of Internet access in Africa was over $60 per month, more than most Africans' total monthly income. That is why it may seem more reasonable for developing countries to stay focused on the lesser skill-demanding, labor-intensive technologies. But such a short-sighted view will only keep the Internet gap shown in the table wide open. A new version of the vicious circle of poverty results: The developing country can't access the Internet because it is poor, and it is poor because it cannot access the Internet.

Still, prospects may not be as bleak as they appear to be. After all, the costs of accessing the Internet continue to fall—thanks to incredible and continuing technological changes in the computer industry—and these costs may soon make access affordable for many in the developing countries. Note that the Internet access shown in the table for the developing countries, while considerably less than access for the developed countries, is still not zero. In Kenya, telecommunication microwave towers are

beginning to dot the landscape. Some access is even filtering down to the education process, where it must take root: A senior school in Kampala, Uganda, has a virtual exchange program, via the Internet, with a comparable high school in Jackson Hole, Wyoming. All roads have beginnings.

Internet Hosts per 10,000 Population and Personal Computers per 1,000 Population for Selected Countries

	INTERNET HOSTS	PERSONAL COMPUTERS
ALGERIA	0.0	4.2
ARGENTINA	27.8	44.3
BOLIVIA	0.5	7.5
BRAZIL	18.5	30.1
EGYPT	0.3	9.1
INDIA	0.2	2.7
INDONESIA	0.7	8.2
KENYA	0.2	2.5
MOROCCO	0.3	2.5
NICARAGUA	2.2	7.8
PAKISTAN	0.2	3.9
PERU	3.1	18.1
ZIMBABWE	0.9	3.0
UNITED STATES	1,122.6	458.6
CANADA	365.7	330.0
ISRAEL	160.4	217.2
FRANCE	82.6	207.8

Source: The World Bank Group, 2000. "Internet hosts" refers to the number of computers with active Internet protocol (IP) addresses connected to the Internet.

Who would do the financing? Chadians have always financed the purchase of seed for their few acres or a new milk cow with funds drawn from their own savings or from a moneylender, but neither the moneylender nor the saver is capable of financing an automobile plant. The Chadian banking system is still embryonic.

The plant, of course, requires some energy source. What good is the plant and its state-of-the-art machinery if there is no electricity to power it? Chad simply doesn't have the megawatts. But suppose it did—what's the point of the plant if there are no decent roads in the country?

Obviously, we've only scratched the surface of the problem. Even with a road system, the plant would still require an accessible service station industry, with ready stocks of fuel, spare parts, repair equipment, and, most important, people with completely different sets of skills, to make it work. It gets rather complicated, doesn't it?

Where do all these skilled people come from? Without a modern educational system, the answer is nowhere. Too few colleges in Chad graduate engineers, accountants, and doctors. Its literacy rate is critically low. Peasants farming in traditional ways rely upon experience, not education.

To educate people involves not only the monumental task of acquiring compliance—a population willing to send its children to school—but the funds needed to build the schools and to staff them. Where do these funds come from?

As you can see, the automobile plant would quickly rust unless it were accompanied by an expansive set of direct and indirect investments. That's all but impossible. Chadians have neither the material nor the human resources to undertake such a tremendous development departure. Chad's poverty trap seems rather formidable, doesn't it?

PURSUING STRATEGIES OF DEVELOPMENT

If you were asked to map out a grand strategy for economic development in Chad or any of the other *bottom billion* LDCs, just where would you begin? Economists have struggled with this vexing challenge and have come up with essentially two competing strategies. Both focus on the task of breaking the vicious circle of underdevelopment that traps the LDCs into national poverty.

The vicious circle of underdevelopment refers to LDCs that are poor because of the underdeveloped state of their economies, a state of underdevelopment that persists because they are poor. It's both logical and frustrating. The only way to cut into that self-sustaining trap is by massive doses of infrastructure and accompanying investments. But how? Is there a particular order or sequence of investing that works? Who does what investing? What role does government play? Should the private sector do it alone?

The Big Push

One idea that has found a receptive audience among development economists is the **big-push** strategy. It argues that because each potential investment's success depends upon there being a market for its output, none of the potential projects ever get realized because none have ready markets.

How do you create ready markets for, say, 1,000 potential investment projects when none exist? By investing in the 1,000 projects *all at once*. That's the idea behind the big push.

For example, a tire plant would have no chance of succeeding unless it had an automobile plant to serve. Investing in both tire and automobile plants provides the ready market for the tire plant. Investing in road construction provides the beginnings of a market for automobiles and trucks. After all, the tire plant needs trucks to move its raw materials in and its tires out to market—impossible without a road system, possible with one. The road construction project itself needs trucks to move its equipment and materials. That, too, becomes a market for the auto plant.

Big push
The development strategy that relies on an integrated network of government-sponsored and -financed investments introduced into the economy all at once.

Investments in steel and concrete production now become feasible because each can see a new, ready market. Steel is the primary raw material in automobile production. It is also needed in the construction of the physical plants. Concrete's major market emerges with road construction.

You can see the connections to investments in the mining industries, can't you? Iron ore, if available, is used in the production of steel. If ore is produced, it finds a ready market in steel, which in turn becomes a market for automobiles and trucks.

How Big Must a Big Push Be?
The bigger the total all-at-once investment commitment, the easier it is to generate ready, attractive markets for each project. And that's the trick.

The big-push strategy triggers a dynamic swelling of investments in the economy that serves to break through the vicious circle of underdevelopment. There is a critical minimum level required for a big push to set the strategy in motion. The initial projects must be carefully chosen to take advantage of the economy's human and material resources and synchronized to form interlocking markets. And each of the selected projects must be large enough to absorb the other outputs.

Is there an upper bound to a big push? The problem with grandiose big-push schemes is not only their cost, but the inevitability of confronting bottlenecks that can stall an otherwise well-planned strategy. Among the first of the serious bottlenecks confronted is the shortage of technical expertise and skilled production-line workers.

Breakdowns in production lines are common to all economies, but if the skills and materials needed to maintain the lines are too few and spread too thinly across too many big-push projects, the big push becomes distorting and itself distorted.

It sometimes pays to think in more modest and reasonable terms rather than pursue a big-push strategy, and to curb an ambitious development appetite to guarantee proper digestion.

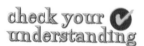

check your understanding

Why is government the logical choice to execute the big push?

Who Does the Pushing?
Big-push advocates argue that such an interlocking set of infrastructure and development investments can be undertaken only by government. Why government? Because the fruits borne from these big-push investments are forthcoming only in the very long run. Who else but government has a time horizon lengthy enough to wait upon these fruits?

Make sense? Rely on government? Think about it. There may be something very wrong with this idea, especially if the governments doing the developing are themselves caught up in political instability traps, such as civil wars, quick and frequent changeovers, or in-government corruption and bribery. In other words, reliance on government may be part of the development problem, not its solution, particularly since the expected gains from any big push effort most likely emerge well beyond the life spans of the governments-in-power. The LDC record on this is not too promising.

But the alternatives are few if any.

Entrepreneurs in the private sector cannot be expected to invest long term in an economy with limited investment promise. After all, it is unreasonable to expect them to think that by the time their output is ready for market, there will be a market. What assurances do they have? How are they supposed to know that others are thinking the same thoughts? And if they wait upon others to start, nothing starts.

But once the government-sponsored big push gets underway, the private sector is indeed expected to participate. Entrepreneurs do so not because they want to develop the economy, but because they now discover a stream of new, profitable opportunities that the big-push strategy has created.

Who Finances the Big Push? Big-push strategies, depending on their aggressiveness, require enormous national commitments that can sometimes tax an economy beyond its capabilities. Government funds the push because no one else can.

How? Primarily through taxes. But levying even more taxes on an already impoverished people not only is painful but can be destabilizing. Because government's ability to tax incomes is restricted by its lack of effective tax collecting at the source, LDC governments typically rely on sales taxes on consumer goods and on customs duties. The results tend to be regressive. Egypt's attempt in the 1970s to cut government subsidies on food led to riots in Cairo that almost brought the government down.

These want-of-basic-food riots erupt periodically. The latest, in 2008, caused by the unavailability of subsidized foods, such as bread, rice, sugar and cooking oil, led to violent protests against the Egyptian government.

The Unbalanced Development Strategy

A competing strategy to the big push relies essentially upon entrepreneurs doing the major part of investing in and supervising the development. While this uncoordinated or unbalanced development strategy still counts on some initial government undertakings, unlike the big push, these undertakings are limited to infrastructure. The rest—the bulk of the development—is private enterprise. How does it work?

The strategy is based on the idea that every private investment has a set of **forward and backward linkages**. A forward link connects the goods produced by a firm to demands for those goods made by other firms. For example, the existence of a new bottling plant generates demands by beverage firms for those bottles. The backward linkage describes the relationship between that bottler and its suppliers. For example, the existence of the new bottling plant creates demands for its raw materials, such as glass and plastics.

Forward linkages
Investments in one industry that create opportunities for profitable investments in other industries, using the goods produced in the first as inputs.

Backward linkages
Investments in one industry that create demands for inputs, inducing investment in other industries to produce those inputs.

Linkages in Sri Lanka Imagine the Sri Lankan government thinking about a strategy to get its development process started. Suppose Sri Lanka, a world supplier of raw tea has no tea processing plant nor container-packaging capacity. Its tea is shipped in bulk to industrial economies—England, primarily—and there is processed and packaged.

Suppose now the Sri Lankan government decides that tea is a trigger industry in its development program. It invests in a processing plant that prepares the raw tea for domestic and export markets. While the plant goes into construction, a number of Sri Lankans take note.

It becomes clear to a sharp Sri Lankan entrepreneur that the tea processing plant will need container and packaging supplies. He seizes the opportunity and gets into the container business. Note: government itself need not worry about this kind of undertaking. It knows that private entrepreneurship will take advantage of this new enterprise possibility. That is to say, backward linkages will come into being on their own.

Now let's suppose that the newly-created container/packaging plant has the capacity to generate more output than the newly-created processed tea plant can use. It becomes inventive, diversifying its container/packaging products to satisfy all kinds of domestic demands. In other words, the first-round imbalance between the tea processing plant's specific demand for packaging and the packaging plant's ability to supply greater quantities allows for new private enterprise ventures.

After all, other packaging-using Sri Lankan firms now need not buy expensive foreign imports when there's a new and cheaper domestic supply available. And for firms in which packaging is a major input, it's a profit-margin bonus.

That is to say, other domestic firms, now confident in accessing this new and cheaper domestic supply, may be induced, *on their own reckoning*, to expand production. These expansions will likely generate yet another round of forward and backward linkages.

The mutually reinforcing imbalances caused by new supplies creating new demands—forward linkages—and these new demands creating new and different supplies—backward linkages—play off against each other, forming a dynamic chain reaction of economic development.

The attraction of such a development strategy is that it places minimal stress on government. It requires neither a grandiose design nor a grandiose taxing scheme.

Who Does the Investing? The key to success in the unbalanced strategy is the role played by entrepreneurs. The idea is that, there are always creative, energetic people who, presented with a chance at enterprise, will take it.

Who Does the Funding? While government triggers the process by putting into place some of the economy's key infrastructure investments, the primary source of development finance is the private sector. Entrepreneurs themselves are expected either to invest their own savings in their own businesses or to find the funding in the banking system.

It is precisely the demands for private business loans that create the *rationale* for commercial banking. If domestic banks aren't available, foreign banks, lured by the new prospects, will come in. It's just a matter of time before Sri Lankan entrepreneurs get into the banking business.

FOREIGN DIRECT INVESTMENT AND FOREIGN ECONOMIC AID

The trouble with being a *bottom billion* LDC is that the demands for consumption goods—just meeting the basic nutritional needs of the vast majority of the population—use up pretty much the meager resources available. Perhaps there's an ample supply of unskilled labor and maybe even sufficient acreage, but the relative scarcities of managerial talent, of differentiated technical skills, of capital equipment, and of modern technology often puts an ambitious development program out of a LDC's immediate reach.

After all, it takes time to build up an arsenal of appropriate resources needed to trigger that development. And whatever the chosen strategy—big-push or creating imbalances of forward and backward linkages—there are development traps of all kinds that get in the way.

How then can foreign intervention contribute? Whether the interventions come in the form of direct investment or as economic aid, or perhaps both, the net result is breaking through traps and barriers that traditionally stall a development effort.

applied perspective

TRACING LINKAGES: THE CANNED PINEAPPLE INDUSTRY IN INDONESIA

Linkages exist in the most unsuspecting places. A case in point is the canned pineapple industry in Indonesia. Agricultural economist Prayogo Hadi, of Indonesia's Ministry of Agriculture, studied the stream of linkages associated with canned pineapple production in Lampung and West Java. Among those he found were several linking the large canning firms to small non-canning producers and traders and to marketing chains that provide market accessibility for many small producers.

The canned pineapple industry has strong backward and forward linkages with other sectors in the economy and at various levels in the vertical structure of the industry. At the upstream level—the production stage of the pineapple fruit—the wide acreage of a pineapple plantation requires substantial amounts of fertilizers, pesticides, herbicides, and equipment from both the industrial and trade sectors. This direct production stage uses a substantial workforce that requires little or no formal education as well as a significant labor increment involved in the trucking of large harvests from farm to canning factories.

At the intermediate linkage level—the processing stage of canned pineapple—the transformation activities necessitate machinery, equipment, oils, fuels, electricity, packing materials (cans), syrup ingredients,

and so on. Another important linkage is found in the cattle-farming industry, where pineapple pulp, a waste product generated by the pineapple industry, is used for fodder. At the downstream level—the export market stage—the canned pineapple demands substantial services in shipping, telecommunication, and banking.

Loaded with vitamin C and economic activity.

© Steve Lupton/CORBIS

The link with cattle farming is symbiotic. GGPC established a subsidiary company called Great Giant Livestock Company (GGLC) in 1990. Its principal operation has been cattle fattening, using imported feeder steers from Australia to produce better-quality beef. The linkage lies with the use of available and abundant pineapple pulp produced from pineapple-canning factories as cattle feed, while the substantial amount of manure produced from cattle fattening is used for fertilizing the company's pineapple plantations. This dual linkage—pineapple canning and cattle—has less of a negative impact on Indonesia's sensitive environment.

Foreign Direct Investment

Think of a cruise vacation. The nice thing about taking a cruise is that it's a complete package: transportation, lodging, food, entertainment all rolled into one. Foreign direct investment is something like that. A foreign company, perhaps Nike, decides to build a plant in Haiti. Nike provides the capital to construct the physical plant, to procure raw material inventories, and to install the equipment which probably represents the latest in shoe-making technology. Nike also brings in a team of professionals—managers, designers, dyers, cutters, assemblers, shipping experts, accountants, lawyers, and even medical staff—to get the plant up and running. Nike also hires and trains Haitians to jobs that didn't exist in Haiti before.

When production delays occur, the Nike crowd puts the Nike know-how to work. All the while, Haitians learn the modern art of shoe-making. In time, much of the foreign crew is replaced by a Haitian crew. And there are investment spin offs. Backward and forward linkages develop. All this happens without the Haitian government or Haitian individuals having to invest one Haitian gourde (one dollar equals 40 gourdes) in the venture.

Multiply the Nike practice by a hundred or by thousands and the resources that were impossible for Haiti to commit to development are now—almost magically—making the Haitian economy grow. In this way, some of the development traps that have plagued Haiti weakened.

Foreign Economic Aid

While this kind of foreign direct investment is essentially a private sector activity, foreign economic aid—loans and grants—is government to government. How is the aid used? In the best of times, it is assigned to infrastructure development, such as roads construction, housing projects, health facilities, and education. In the worst of times, but for good reason, it is channeled to LDC government agencies to supplement insufficient food stocks. For many of the donor and recipient governments, avoiding famine and starvation must trump economic development.

The development loans are typically made to LDC governments at below-market rates of interest. The downside is that the accumulating interest payment obligations often add a troubling financial burden to an already capital-thin LDC. Grant aid, on the other hand, are outright gifts. Over the course of the past half-century, more and more of the economic aid given to the LDCs by the United States has been in the form of grants.

While foreign direct investment and economic aid are useful, the idea and practice of LDC economic development must, in the end, be of their own choosing and enterprise. At best, this form of foreign intervention has been a catalyst for many of the economic aid-receiving LDCs to jump-start their development programs. However, for the *bottom billion* LDCs, that jump-start has yet to take place in earnest.

CHAPTER REVIEW

1. In the 1950s, 80 percent of the world's 2.5 billion population lived in poverty. By 2000, 5 billion of the world's 6 billion population were enjoying relatively high and increasing standards of life. But that still left one billion trapped in poverty. Oxford economist Paul Collier refers to these unfortunates as the *bottom billion*. Most live in Sub-Sahara Africa.

2. Many of the less-developed countries—LDCs—are caught in traps that can be physical, institutional, cultural, and even psychological. These traps prevent the LDCs from moving forward onto self-sustaining economic development paths.

3. The demographic trap reflects the fact that in many LDCs, population growth outpaces economic growth so that per capita GDP growth rates are often negative. The problem is chronic because it has been easier for a LDC to cut death rates than to cut birth rates. Improvements in public health, such as access to safe water and the availability of medical technology, such as antibiotics, have dramatically reduced death rates. Birth rates, however, reflect, cultural and religious values, both less given to change.

4. The political instability trap—civil wars, frequent and erratic government changeovers, government corruption and bribery—contribute to an environment that undermines a LDC's ability to engage in a sustained development effort.

5. The natural resource trap occurs because natural resource exports can more easily generate

revenues to finance imports than can other exports and this is incentive enough for many LDCs to focus excessively on their natural resource endowment. But this focus eventually comes at the expense of developing a more diversified economy that, in the long run, would generate higher rates of GDP growth and employment.

6. The absence in many LDCs of basic infrastructure, such as communication and transportation systems, housing, health facilities, and education disallows private investments from taking root. And because many LDCs do not have the resources needed to develop the infrastructure, they are trapped in non-development poverty.

7. There are many competing development strategies for the LDCs. The big-push strategy emphasizes investment in many projects all at once to create both productive capacity and

markets for the production. Government plays a dominant role as coordinator, planner, and financier of the strategy.

8. An alternative approach to development is the unbalanced strategy, which relies less heavily on government. Here, initial private sector development in key areas of the economy creates backward and forward linkages to new projects that had been unthinkable before these key investments. These linkages provide opportunities and incentives for private firms to invest, creating even more opportunities and incentives.

9. Foreign direct investment allows an LDC to create capital goods production without having to sacrifice consumption goods production. Foreign economic aid can do the same.

KEY TERMS

Less-developed countries (LDCs)   Big push   Backward linkages
Infrastructure   Forward linkages

QUESTIONS

1. While countries with relatively low per capita GDP have been with us from time immemorial, there has been for many an encouraging change in their economic fortunes during the past 50 years. Still, there remains a set of countries that have not experienced much change. Discuss.

2. Describe the circumstances that create the demographic trap.

3. Describe the circumstances that create the political instability trap.

4. Describe the circumstances that create the natural resource trap.

5. Describe the circumstances that create the absence of infrastructure trap.

6. Distinguish between the impact on a recipient LDC of foreign direct investment and foreign economic aid.

7. Describe the economic logic associated with the big-push development strategy. What are its pitfalls?

8. Describe the economic logic associated with the unbalanced development strategy. What are its pitfalls?

9. Show the effect of foreign direct investment on an economy's production possibilities curve.

10. Professor Miguel Ramirez asks his students at Trinity College to respond to the following problem: "If LDCs cannot generate sufficient capital to engage in development, then perhaps the richer nations of the world can provide capital in the form of foreign economic assistance. What has been the record of such assistance? What effect would it have on the LDCs?"

11. What are backward and forward linkages, and how do they contribute to a country's economic development?

Economic Consultants

Economic Research and Analysis by Students for Professionals

South African businesspeople and government officials have formed an organization, Economic Development in South Africa (EDSA), to map a strategy for economic development in post-apartheid South Africa. EDSA understands the need for direct foreign investment and foreign aid, but individuals within EDSA are worried that such strategies may make South Africa overdependent on foreign powers. EDSA also understands the need for controlled growth and investment, but the group is unsure about the best strategy to pursue to ensure stable growth.

EDSA has hired Economic Consultants to present to its members the pros and cons of different economic development strategies. Prepare a report for EDSA that addresses the following issues:

© Image 100/Royalty-Free/CORBIS

1. What basic strategies should South Africa pursue for economic development, particularly in terms of foreign investment?
2. What problems arise with different economic development strategies? How can South Africa avoid uncontrolled growth and investment?
3. What groups and organizations specialize in direct foreign investment and foreign aid?

You may find the following resources helpful as you prepare this report for EDSA:

- **PRAXIS: Resources for Social and Economic Development** (http://www.sp2.upenn.edu/~restes/praxis.html)—PRAXIS provides a library of links to resources on international and comparative social development.
- **World Bank** (http://www.worldbank.org/)—The World Bank provides news, publications, and country and regional economic reports.
- **World Bank Institute** (http://www.worldbank.org/wbi/home.html)—The World Bank Institute promotes awareness of development strategies through publications and educational initiatives.
- *Finance and Development* (http://www.imf.org/external/pubs/ft/fandd/2008/09/index.htm)—*Finance and Development* is a joint quarterly publication of the International Monetary Fund and the World Bank.

practicetest

1. The vicious circle of poverty associated with LDCs refers to
   a. their ability to borrow but inability to pay their debts.
   b. their traditional sector becoming modern only to revert back to traditionalism.
   c. their misuse of capital goods over and over again.
   d. their being poor because they choose population growth over economic growth.
   e. their being poor because they cannot devote resources to capital goods production because they are poor.

2. During the past 50 years, the world's population experienced
   a. substantial increases in per capita GDP for 20 percent while the remaining 80 percent remained in abject poverty
   b. substantial increases in per capita GDP for 50 percent while the remaining 50 percent remained in abject poverty
   c. declining per capita GDP
   d. substantial increases in per capita GDP for 4 billion while the remaining one billion remained in abject poverty
   e. substantial increases in per capita GDP for one billion while the remaining 4 billion remained in abject poverty

3. Compare and explain changes in LDC birth and death rates over the past 50 years.
   a. Birth rates fell faster than death rates because modern contraceptive became commonplace
   b. Birth rates fell faster than death rates because of massive emigration of young child-bearing people.
   c. Death rates fell faster than birth rates because modern medical technology, such as antibiotics cut death rates quickly and substantially while birth rates, reflecting cultural and religious values, fell much more slowly.
   d. Death rates fell faster than birth rates largely because of the AIDS epidemic in Sub-Sahara Africa.
   e. Birth and death rates have changed little in the past century, both reflecting LDC's unwillingness to engage in economic development.

4. One of the major factors contributing to the political instability trap that inhibits the economic development of *bottom billion* LDCs is
   a. the prevalence of civil wars
   b. excessive competition among political parties
   c. their choice of domestic monarchies to replace colonial political rule
   d. the low-level turnout for national elections
   e. the illiteracy of voters

5. One of the major factors contributing to the demographic trap that inhibits the economic development of *bottom billion* LDCs is
   a. late marriages, resulting in fewer children and a smaller labor force
   b. birth rates exceeding death rates
   c. death rates exceeding birth rates
   d. massive immigration
   e. massive emigration

6. The difference between economic aid given in the form of loans from aid given in the form of grants is that
   a. loans are for development use, grants for supplementing food needs
   b. grants are for development use, loans for supplementing food needs
   c. loans may result in high interest payment obligations, grants are outright gifts
   d. grants may result in high interest payment obligations, loans are outright gifts
   e. loans are for civilian use, grants are for military use

7. The big-push strategy proposes all-at-one-time multiple investments because
   a. they provide markets for each other.
   b. they create forward, rather than backward, linkages.
   c. they involve a smaller initial investment than do alternative strategies.
   d. unsuccessful projects would be canceled by successful ones.
   e. foreign governments are more inclined to finance this strategy.

8. The unbalanced development strategy
   a. relies on government to finance each stage of the strategy.
   b. creates forward, but not backward, linkages, which trigger top-down development.
   c. creates backward, but not forward, linkages, which trigger bottom-up development.

d. creates forward and backward linkages, which play off each other to create the development.
e. involves an imbalance between the roles played by LDCs and foreign entrepreneurs.

9. Forward linkages are investments in industries that create
   a. investment opportunities for other industries, using the goods produced in the first as inputs.
   b. demands for inputs, inducing investments in other industries to produce those inputs.
   c. future demands for investments in the same industries.

d. future supplies of investment in the same industries.
e. top-down development.

10. Economic aid from the United States to the LDCs
   a. is mainly given as loans, not grants.
   b. represents a higher percentage of its GDP compared to other donor countries.
   c. is greater than the economic aid given annually by other donor countries.
   d. is mainly for military purchases of U.S. weaponry by LDCs.
   e. is mainly allocated to sub-Saharan Africa.

practicetests

ANSWER KEY

Chapter 1
1. b
2. d
3. e
4. e
5. c
6. d
7. c
8. d
9. a
10. b

Chapter 2
1. a
2. c
3. a
4. c
5. b
6. b
7. b
8. c
9. e

Chapter 3
1. b
2. a
3. d
4. a
5. a
6. b
7. e
8. d
9. e
10. e

Chapter 4
1. d
2. d
3. e
4. a
5. e
6. a
7. b
8. d
9. b
10. d

Chapter 5
1. a
2. d
3. e
4. d
5. a
6. c
7. e
8. a
9. c
10. c

Chapter 6
1. d
2. d
3. a
4. e
5. d
6. e
7. b
8. c
9. d
10. e

Chapter 7
1. c
2. c
3. c
4. a
5. b
6. e
7. a
8. a
9. a
10. d

Chapter 8
1. a
2. b
3. b
4. a
5. d
6. e
7. b
8. a
9. c
10. a

Chapter 9
1. d
2. e
3. c
4. a
5. b
6. b
7. d
8. a
9. b
10. a

Chapter 10
1. c
2. c
3. a
4. b
5. e
6. d
7. a
8. e
9. b
10. e

Chapter 11
1. b
2. a
3. c
4. a
5. b
6. b
7. e
8. b
9. a
10. d

Chapter 12
1. c
2. e
3. a
4. d
5. e
6. c
7. d
8. e
9. a
10. a

Chapter 13
1. a
2. c
3. a
4. e
5. a
6. c
7. d
8. e
9. b
10. d

Chapter 14
1. a
2. c
3. c
4. b
5. b
6. b
7. c
8. b
9. b
10. d

Chapter 15
1. c
2. c
3. b
4. e
5. b
6. e
7. a
8. d
9. a
10. d

Chapter 16

1. d	6. c
2. e	7. c
3. d	8. a
4. d	9. b
5. e	10. a

Chapter 17

1. a	6. c
2. b	7. c
3. e	8. a
4. d	9. d
5. b	10. a

Chapter 18

1. e	6. d
2. d	7. a
3. c	8. d
4. a	9. a
5. b	10. c

Glossary

A

Absolute advantage A country's ability to produce a good using fewer resources than the country it trades with. (Chapters 2 and 31)

Absolute income hypothesis As national income increases, consumption spending increases, but by diminishing amounts. That is, as national income increases, the MPC decreases. (Chapter 21)

Accelerator The relationship between the level of investment and the change in the level of national income. (Chapter 24)

Actual investment Investment spending that producers actually make—that is, intended investment (investment spending that producers intend to undertake), plus or minus unintended changes in inventories. (Chapter 22)

Administrative lag The time interval between deciding on an appropriate policy and the execution of that policy. (Chapter 24)

Aggregate demand The total quantity of goods and services demanded by households, firms, foreigners, and government at varying price levels. (Chapter 19)

Aggregate expenditure Spending by consumers on consumption goods, spending by businesses on investment goods, spending by government, and spending by foreigners on net exports. (Chapter 22)

Aggregate expenditure curve (AE) A curve that shows the quantity of aggregate expenditures at different levels of national income or GDP. (Chapter 22)

Aggregate supply The total quantity of goods and services that firms in the economy are willing to supply at varying price levels. (Chapter 19)

Antitrust policy Laws that foster market competition by prohibiting monopolies and oligopolies from exercising excessive market power. (Chapter 13)

Appreciation A rise in the price of a nation's currency relative to foreign currencies. (Chapter 32)

Arbitrage The practice of buying a foreign currency in one market at a low price and selling it in another at a higher price. (Chapter 32)

Asymmetric information A situation in which one side of the market—buyer or seller—has more information about the good than does the other side—buyer or seller. (Chapter 14)

Automatic stabilizers Structures in the economy that tend to add to aggregate demand when the economy is in recession, and subtract from aggregate demand when the economy is inflationary. Unemployment insurance payments and benefits and the progressive income tax are two such automatic stabilizers. (Chapter 28)

Autonomous consumption Consumption spending that is independent of level of income. (Chapter 21)

Autonomous investment Investment that is independent of the level of income. (Chapter 21)

Average fixed cost (AFC) Total fixed cost divided by the quantity of goods produced. *AFC* steadily declines as more of a good is produced. (Chapter 8)

Average revenue (AR) Total revenue divided by the quantity of goods or services sold. (Chapter 9)

Average total cost (ATC) Total cost divided by the quantity of goods produced. *ATC* declines, reaches a minimum, then increases as more of a good is produced. (Chapter 8)

Average variable cost (AVC) Total variable cost divided by the quantity of goods produced. *AVC* declines, reaches a minimum, then increases as more of a good is produced. (Chapter 8)

B

Backward linkages Investments in one industry that create demands for inputs, inducing investment in other industries to produce those inputs. (Chapter 33)

Balance on capital account A category that itemizes changes in the foreign asset holdings of a nation and that nation's asset holdings abroad. (Chapter 32)

Balance on current account A category that itemizes a nation's imports and exports of goods and services, income receipts and payments on investment, and unilateral transfers. (Chapter 32)

Balance of payments An itemized account of a nation's foreign economic transactions. (Chapter 32)

Balance sheet The bank's statement of liabilities (what it owes) and assets (what it owns). (Chapter 26)

Balance of trade The difference between the value of a nation's merchandise exports and its merchandise imports. (Chapter 32)

Balanced budget Government spending equals tax revenues. (Chapter 23)

Balanced budget multiplier The effect on the equilibrium level of national income of an equal change in government spending and taxes. The balanced budget multiplier is 1. (Chapter 23)

Balanced oligopoly An oligopoly in which the sales of the leading firms are distributed fairly evenly among them. (Chapter 12)

Bank note A promissory note, issued by a bank, pledging to redeem the note for a specific amount of gold or silver. The terms of redemption are specified on the note. (Chapter 27)

Barter The exchange of one good for another, without the use of money. (Chapter 25)

Base year The reference year with which prices in other years are compared in a price index. (Chapter 19)

Big push The development strategy that relies on an integrated network of government-sponsored and -financed investments introduced into the economy all at once. (Chapter 33)

Brand loyalty The willingness of consumers to continue buying a good at a price higher than the price of its close substitutes. (Chapter 10)

Brand multiplication Variations on essentially one good that a firm produces in order to increase its market share. (Chapter 12)

Budget deficit Government spending exceeds tax revenues. (Chapter 23)

Budget surplus Tax revenues exceed government spending. (Chapter 23)

Business cycle Alternating periods of growth and decline in an economy's GDP. (Chapter 19)

C

Capital Manufactured goods used to make and market other goods and services. (Chapter 2)

Capital deepening A rise in the ratio of capital to labor. (Chapter 24)

Capital depreciation The value of existing capital stock used up in the process of producing goods and services. (Chapter 20)

Capital equipment The machinery a firm uses in production. (Chapter 17)

Capital-labor ratio The ratio of capital to labor, reflecting the quantity of capital used by each laborer in production. (Chapter 24)

Capital-output ratio The ratio of capital stock to GDP. (Chapter 24)

Cartel A group of firms that collude to limit competition in a market by negotiating and accepting agreed-upon price and market shares. (Chapter 12)

Cash assistance Government assistance in the form of cash. (Chapter 18)

Ceteris paribus The Latin phrase meaning "everything else being equal." (Chapter 1)

Change in demand A change in quantity demanded of a good that is caused by factors other than a change in the price of that good. (Chapter 3)

Change in quantity demanded A change in the quantity demanded of a good that is caused solely by a change in the price of that good. (Chapter 3)

Change in supply A change in quantity supplied of a good that is caused by factors other than a change in the price of that good. (Chapter 3)

Circular flow of goods, services, and resources The movement of goods and services from firms to households, and of resources from households to firms. (Chapter 20)

Circular flow model A model of how the economy's resources, money, goods, and services flow between households and firms through resource and product markets. (Chapter 1)

Circular flow of money The movement of income in the form of resource payments from firms to households, and of income in the form of revenue from households to firms. (Chapter 20)

Classical economics The school of thought that emphasizes the natural tendency for an economy to move toward equilibrium at full employment without inflation. It argues against government intervention. (Chapter 28)

Closed shop An arrangement in which a firm may hire only union labor. (Chapter 16)

Collective bargaining Negotiation between a labor union and a firm employing unionized labor, to create a contract concerning wage rates, hours worked, and working conditions. (Chapter 16)

Collusion The practice of firms to negotiate price and market share decisions that limit competition in a market. (Chapter 12)

Comparative advantage A country's ability to produce a good at a lower opportunity cost than the country with which it trades. (Chapters 2 and 31)

Complementary goods Goods that are generally used together. When the price of one increases, the demand for the other decreases. (Chapter 3)

Concentration ratio A measure of market power. It is the ratio of total sales of the leading firms in an industry (usually four) to the industry's total sales. (Chapter 12)

Conglomerate merger A merger between firms in unrelated industries. (Chapter 12)

Constant returns to scale Costs per unit of production are the same for any level of production. Changes in plant size do not affect the firm's average total cost. (Chapter 8)

Consumer price index (CPI) A measure comparing the prices of consumer goods and services that a household typically purchases to the prices of those goods and services purchased in a base year. (Chapter 19)

Consumer sovereignty The ability of consumers to exercise complete control over what goods and services the economy produces (or doesn't produce) by choosing what goods and services to buy (or not buy). (Chapter 1)

Consumer surplus The difference between the maximum amount a person would be willing to pay for a good or service and the amount the person actually pays. (Chapter 5)

Consumption function The relationship between consumption and income. (Chapter 21)

Contestable market A market in which prices in highly concentrated industries are moderated by the potential threat of firms entering the market. (Chapter 13)

Corporate bond A corporate IOU. The corporation borrows capital for a specified period of time in exchange for this promise to repay the loan along with an agreed-upon rate of interest. (Chapter 7)

Corporate governance Corporate governance is concerned with the rules governing the structure of the corporation and the exercise of power and control of the corporation by shareholders, directors, and management. (Chapter 7)

Corporate income tax A tax levied on a corporation's income before dividends are distributed to stockholders. (Chapter 30)

Corporation A firm whose legal identity is separate from the people who own shares of its stock. The liability of each stockowner is limited only to what he or she has invested in the firm. (Chapter 7)

Cost-push inflation Inflation caused primarily by a decrease in aggregate supply. (Chapter 19)

Countercyclical fiscal policy Fiscal policy designed to moderate the severity of the business cycle. (Chapter 24)

Countercyclical monetary policy Policy directives used by the Fed to moderate swings in the business cycle. (Chapter 27)

Countervailing power The exercise of market power by an economic bloc is ultimately counteracted by the market power of a competing bloc, so that no bloc exercises undue market power. (Chapter 13)

Craft union A union representing workers of a single occupation, regardless of the industry in which the workers are employed. (Chapter 16)

Creative destruction Effective competition that exists not among firms within highly concentrated industries but between the highly concentrated industries themselves. Such competition ensures competitive prices. (Chapter 13)

Cross elasticity The ratio of a percentage change in demand of one good to a percentage change in the price of another good. (Chapter 4)

Crowding out A fall in private investment spending caused by an increase in government spending. (Chapter 28)

Currency Coins and paper money. (Chapter 25)

Customs duty A sales tax applied to a foreign good or service. (Chapter 30)

Customs union A set of countries that agree to free trade among themselves and a common trade policy with all other countries. (Chapter 31)

Cyclical unemployment Unemployment associated with the downturn and recession phases of the business cycle. (Chapter 23)

D

Debt service Interest payments on international debt as a percentage of a nation's merchandise exports. (Chapter 32)

Demand curve A curve that depicts the relationship between price and quantity demanded. (Chapter 3)

Demand-pull inflation Inflation caused primarily by an increase in aggregate demand. (Chapter 19)

Demand schedule A schedule showing the specific quantity of a good or service that people are willing and able to buy at different prices. (Chapter 3)

Depreciation A fall in the price of a nation's currency relative to foreign currencies. (Chapter 32)

Depression Severe recession. (Chapter 19)

Deregulation The process of converting a regulated firm into an unregulated firm. (Chapter 13)

Devaluation Government policy that lowers the nation's exchange rate; its currency instantly is worth less in the foreign exchange market. (Chapter 32)

Differential land rent Rent arising from differences in the cost of providing land. (Chapter 17)

Discount rate The interest rate the Fed charges banks that borrow reserves from it. (Chapter 27)

Discouraged workers Unemployed people who give up looking for work after experiencing persistent rejection in their attempts to find work. (Chapter 23)

Diseconomies of scale Increases in the firm's average total cost brought about by the disadvantages associated with bureaucracy and the inefficiencies that eventually emerge with increases in the firm's operations. (Chapter 8)

Disposable personal income Personal income minus direct taxes. (Chapter 20)

Dividend That part of a corporation's net income that is paid out to its stockholders. (Chapter 7)

Downsizing Implementing a firm's decision to decrease its plant size to produce in the most efficient manner its current volume of output. (Chapter 8)

Downturn A phase in the business cycle in which real GDP declines, inflation moderates, and unemployment emerges. (Chapter 19)

Dumping Exporting a good or service at a price below its cost of production. (Chapter 31)

Durable goods Goods expected to last at least a year. (Chapter 20)

E

Econometrics The use of statistics to quantify and test economic models. (Chapter 1)

Economic efficiency The maximum possible production of goods and services generated by the fullest employment of the economy's resources. (Chapter 2)

Economic growth An increase in real GDP, typically expressed as an annual rate of real GDP growth. (Chapter 24)

Economic model An abstraction of an economic reality. It can be expressed pictorially, graphically, algebraically, or in words. (Chapter 1)

Economic profit A firm's total revenue minus its total explicit and implicit costs. (Chapter 11)

Economics The study of how people work together to transform resources into goods and services to satisfy their most pressing wants, and how they distribute these goods and services among themselves. (Chapter 1)

Economies of scale Decreases in the firm's average total cost brought about by increased specialization and efficiencies in production realized through increases in the scale of the firm's operations. (Chapter 8)

Efficiency wages A wage higher than the market's equilibrium rate; a firm will pay this wage in the expectation that the higher wage will reduce the firm's labor turnover and increase labor productivity. (Chapter 15)

Elasticity A term economists use to describe sensitivity. (Chapter 4)

Engel's law The observation that income elasticities of demand for food are less than 1.0. (Chapter 4)

Entrepreneur A person who alone assumes the risks and uncertainties of a business. (Chapter 2)

Equation of exchange $MV = PQ$. The quantity of money times its velocity equals the quantity of goods and services produced times their prices. (Chapter 25)

Equilibrium level of national income $C + I_i = C + S$, where saving equals intended investment. (Chapter 22)

Equilibrium price The price that equates quantity demanded to quantity supplied. If any disturbance from that price occurs, excess demand or excess supply emerges to drive the price back to equilibrium. (Chapter 3)

European Economic Community (EEC) A customs union consisting of France, Italy, Belgium, Holland, Luxembourg, Germany, Britain, Ireland, Denmark, Greece, Spain, Portugal, Iceland, Finland, Sweden, and Austria. (Chapter 31)

European Union (E.U.) An organization of European nations committed to economic and political integration without abandoning individual national sovereignty. (Chapter 31)

Excess demand The difference, at a particular price, between quantity demanded and quantity supplied, quantity demanded being the greater. (Chapter 3)

Excess reserves The quantity of reserves held by a bank in excess of the legally required amount. (Chapter 26)

Excess supply The difference, at a particular price, between quantity supplied and quantity demanded, quantity supplied being the greater. (Chapter 3)

Exchange controls A system in which government, as the sole depository of foreign currencies, exercises complete control over how these currencies can be used. (Chapter 32)

Exchange rate The number of units of foreign currency that can be purchased with one unit of domestic currency. (Chapter 32)

Excise tax Any tax levied on a good or service, such as a unit tax, a sales tax, or a customs duty. (Chapter 30)

Expenditure approach A method of calculating GDP that adds all expenditures made for final goods and services by households, firms, and government. (Chapter 20)

Exports Goods and services produced by people in one country that are sold in other countries. (Chapter 31)

External debt Public debt held by foreigners. (Chapter 30)

Externalities Unintended costs or benefits that are imposed on unsuspecting people and that result from economic activity initiated by others. Unintended costs are called negative externalities, and unintended benefits are called positive externalities. (Chapter 14)

F

Factor of production Any resource used in a production process. Resources are grouped into labor, land, capital, and entrepreneurship. (Chapter 2)

Farm Security and Rural Investment Act of 2002 The Act represents a retreat from the direction taken by the Freedom to Farm Act of 1996, which sought to create a market-determined farm program. The 2002 Act provides farmers with three types of subsidies: direct, countercyclical, and loan deficiency payments. (Chapter 6)

Federal Deposit Insurance Corporation (FDIC) A government insurance agency that provides depositors in FDIC-participating banks 100 percent coverage on their first $100,000 of deposits. (Chapter 26)

Federal funds market The market in which banks lend and borrow reserves from each other for very short periods of time, usually overnight. (Chapter 27)

Federal funds rate The interest rate on loans made by banks in the federal funds market. (Chapter 27)

Federal Open Market Committee The Fed's principal decision-making body, charged with executing the Fed's open market operations. (Chapter 27)

Federal Reserve System (the Fed) The central bank of the United States. (Chapter 27)

Fiat money Paper money that is not backed by or convertible into any good. (Chapter 25)

Final goods Goods purchased for final use, not for resale. (Chapter 20)

Financial intermediaries Firms that accept deposits from savers and use those deposits to make loans to borrowers. (Chapter 26)

Firm An economic unit that produces goods and services in the expectation of selling them to households, other firms, or government. (Chapter 1)

Fiscal policy Government spending and taxation policy to achieve macroeconomic goals of full employment without inflation. (Chapter 23)

Fixed cost Cost to the firm that does not vary with the quantity of goods produced. The cost is incurred even when the firm does not produce. (Chapter 8)

Fixed exchange rate A rate determined by government and then maintained through the process of buying and selling quantities of its own currency on the foreign exchange market. (Chapter 32)

Floating exchange rate An exchange rate determined strictly by the demands and supplies for a nation's currency. (Chapter 32)

Food Stamp program An aid program that provides low-income people with stamps that can be redeemed for food and related items. (Chapter 29)

Foreign exchange market A market in which currencies of different nations are bought and sold. (Chapter 32)

Foreign exchange reserves The stock of foreign currencies a government holds. (Chapter 32)

Forward linkages Investments in one industry that create opportunities for profitable investments in other industries, using the goods produced in the first as inputs. (Chapter 33)

Fractional reserve system A banking system that provides people immediate access to their deposits but allows banks to hold only a fraction of those deposits in reserve. (Chapter 26)

Free rider Someone who consumes a good or service without paying for it. Typically, the good or service consumed is in the form of a positive externality. (Chapter 14)

Free trade International trade that is not encumbered by protectionist government policies such as tariffs and quotas. (Chapter 31)

Free trade area A set of countries that agree to free trade among themselves but are free to pursue independent trade policies with other countries. (Chapter 31)

Freedom to Farm Act of 1996 Legislation enacted by Congress that phases in, over a seven-year transitional period, the complete dismantling of the government's farm price support and crop restriction systems. (Chapter 6)

Frictional unemployment Relatively brief periods of unemployment caused by people deciding to voluntarily quit work in order to seek more attractive employment. (Chapter 23)

Full employment An employment level at which the actual rate of employment in the economy is equal to the economy's natural rate of unemployment. (Chapter 23)

G

Game theory A theory of strategy ascribed to firms' behavior in oligopoly. The firms' behavior is mutually interdependent. (Chapter 12)

GDP deflator A measure comparing the prices of all goods and services produced in the economy during a given year to the prices of those goods and services purchased in a base year. (Chapter 19)

General Agreement on Tariffs and Trade (GATT) A trade agreement to negotiate reductions in tariffs and other trade barriers and to provide equal and nondiscriminating treatment among members of the agreement. (Chapter 31)

Gini coefficient A numerical measure of the degree of income inequality in an economy. It ranges from zero, depicting perfect equality, to one, depicting perfect inequality. (Chapter 18)

Government failure The failure of the government to buy the quantity of public goods that generates maximum efficiency. (Chapter 14)

Government purchases All goods and services bought by government. (Chapter 20)

Gross domestic product (GDP) Total value of all final goods and services, measured in current market prices, produced in the economy during a year. (Chapter 19)

Gross national product (GNP) The market value of all final goods and services in an economy produced by resources owned by people of that economy, regardless of where the resources are located. (Chapter 20)

Gross private domestic investment The purchase by firms of plant, equipment, and inventory goods. (Chapter 20)

H

Herfindahl-Hirschman index (HHI) A measure of industry concentration, calculated as the sum of the squares of the market shares held by each of the firms in the industry. (Chapter 12)

Horizontal merger A merger between firms producing the same good in the same industry. (Chapter 12)

Household An economic unit of one or more persons, living under one roof, that has a source of income and uses it in whatever way it deems fit. (Chapter 1)

I

Import controls Tariffs and quotas used by government to limit a nation's imports. (Chapter 32)

Imports Goods and services bought by people in one country that are produced in other countries. (Chapter 31)

Income approach A method of calculating GDP that adds all the incomes earned in the production of final goods and services. (Chapter 20)

Income curve or **45° line** A line, drawn at a 45° angle, showing all points at which the distance to the horizontal axis equals the distance to the vertical axis. (Chapter 21)

Income elastic A 1 percent change in income generates a greater than 1 percent change in demand. (Chapter 4)

Income elasticity The ratio of the percentage change in demand to the percentage change in income. (Chapter 4)

Income inelastic A 1 percent change in income generates a less than 1 percent change in demand. (Chapter 4)

Income multiplier The multiple by which income changes as a result of a change in aggregate expenditure. (Chapter 22)

Industrial union A union representing all workers in a single industry, regardless of each worker's skill or craft. (Chapter 16)

Industry A collection of firms producing the same good. (Chapter 10)

Inferior goods Goods for which demand decreases when people's incomes increase. (Chapter 4)

Inflation An increase in the price level. (Chapter 19)

Inflationary gap The amount by which aggregate expenditure exceeds the aggregate expenditure level needed to generate equilibrium national income at full employment without inflation. (Chapter 23)

Infrastructure The basic institutions and public facilities upon which an economy's development depends. (Chapter 33)

In-kind assistance Government assistance in the form of direct goods and services, such as Medicaid or food stamps. (Chapter 18)

Innovation An idea that eventually takes the form of new, applied technology. (Chapter 2)

Intended investment Investment spending that producers intend to undertake. (Chapter 21)

Interest rate The price of loanable funds, expressed as an annual percentage return on a dollar of loanable funds. (Chapter 17)

Intermediate goods Goods used to produce other goods. (Chapter 20)

International debt The total amount of outstanding IOUs a nation is obligated to repay other nations and international organizations. (Chapter 32)

International Monetary Fund (IMF) An international organization formed to make loans of foreign currencies to countries facing balance of payments problems. (Chapter 32)

International specialization The use of a country's resources to produce specific goods and services, allowing other countries to focus on the production of other goods and services. (Chapter 31)

Interpersonal comparison of utility A comparison of the marginal utilities that different people derive from a good or a dollar. (Chapter 5)

Inventory investment Stocks of finished goods and raw materials that firms keep in reserve to facilitate production and sales. (Chapter 20)

Invisible hand Adam Smith's concept of the market, which, as if it were a hand, guides firms that seek only to satisfy their own self-interest to produce precisely those goods and services that consumers want. (Chapter 1)

J

Joint venture A business arrangement in which two or more firms undertake a specific economic activity together. (Chapter 12)

K

Keynesian economics The school of thought that emphasizes the possibility that an economy can be in equilibrium at less than full employment (or with inflation). It argues that with government intervention, equilibrium at full employment without inflation can be achieved by managing aggregate demand. (Chapter 28)

Kinked demand curve The demand curve facing a firm in oligopoly; the curve is more elastic when the firm raises price than when it lowers price. (Chapter 12)

L

Labor The physical and intellectual effort of people engaged in producing goods and services. (Chapter 2)

Labor force People who are gainfully employed or actively seeking employment. (Chapter 23)

Labor productivity The output per laborer per hour; the quantity of GDP produced per worker, typically measured in quantity of GDP per hour of labor. (Chapters 8 and 24)

Labor specialization The division of labor into specialized activities that allow individuals to be more productive. (Chapter 2)

Labor union An association of workers, each of whom transfers the right to negotiate wage rates, work hours, and working conditions to the association. In this way, the union presents itself as a single seller of labor on the labor market. (Chapter 16)

Laissez-faire Government policy of nonintervention in market outcomes. Translated, it means "leave it be." (Chapter 13)

Land A natural-state resource such as real estate, grasses and forests, and metals and minerals. (Chapter 2)

Land rent A payment to landowners for the use of land. (Chapter 17)

Law of demand The inverse relationship between price and quantity demanded of a good or service, *ceteris paribus*. (Chapter 3)

Law of diminishing marginal utility As more of a good is consumed, the utility a person derives from each additional unit diminishes. (Chapter 5)

Law of diminishing returns As more and more units of one factor of production are added to the production process while other factors remain unchanged, output will increase, but by smaller and smaller increments. (Chapter 15)

Law of increasing costs The opportunity cost of producing a good increases as more of the good is produced. The law is based on the fact that not all resources are suited to the production of all goods and that the order of use of a resource in producing a good goes from the most productive resource unit to the least. (Chapter 2)

Legal reserve requirement The percentage of demand deposits banks and other financial intermediaries are required to keep in cash reserves. (Chapter 26)

Less-developed countries (LDCs) The economies of Asia, Africa, and Latin America. (Chapter 33)

Life-cycle hypothesis Typically, a person's MPC is relatively high during young adulthood, decreases during the middle-age years, and increases when the person is near or in retirement. (Chapter 21)

Life-cycle wealth Wealth in the form of nonmonetary assets, such as a house, automobiles, and clothing. (Chapter 18)

Liquidity The degree to which an asset can easily be exchanged for money. (Chapter 25)

Loanable funds market The market in which the demand for and supply of loanable funds determines the rate of interest. (Chapter 17)

Loanable funds Money that a firm employs to purchase the physical plant, equipment, and raw materials used in production. (Chapter 17)

Location rent Rent arising from differences in land distances from the marketplace. (Chapter 17)

Long run The time interval during which producers are able to change the quantity of all the resources they use to produce goods and services. In the long run, all costs are variable. (Chapters 3 and 8)

Lorenz curve A curve depicting an economy's income distribution. It records the percentage of total income that a specific part of the population—typically represented by quintiles, ranging from the poorest to richest—receives. (Chapter 18)

Loss minimization Faced with the certainty of incurring losses, the firm's goal is to incur the lowest loss possible from its production and sale of goods and services. (Chapter 9)

M

M1 money The most immediate form of money. It includes currency, demand deposits, and traveler's checks. (Chapter 25)

M2 money M1 money plus less-immediate forms of money, such as savings accounts, money market mutual fund accounts, money market deposit accounts, repurchase agreements, and small-denomination time deposits. (Chapter 25)

Macroeconomics A subarea of economics that analyzes the behavior of the economy as a whole. (Chapter 1)

Macroequilibrium The level of real GDP and the price level that equate the aggregate quantity demanded and the aggregate quantity supplied. (Chapter 19)

Margin requirement The maximum percentage of the cost of a stock that can be borrowed from a bank or any other financial institution, with the stock offered as collateral. (Chapter 27)

Marginal cost (MC) The change in total cost generated by a change in the quantity of a good produced. Typically, *MC* is used to measure the additional cost incurred by adding one more unit of output to production. (Chapter 8)

Marginal cost pricing A regulatory agency's policy of pricing a good or service produced by a regulated firm at the firm's marginal cost, $P = MC$. (Chapter 13)

Marginal labor cost The change in a firm's total cost that results from adding one more worker to production. (Chapter 15 and 16)

Marginal physical product The change in output that results from adding one more unit of a resource, such as labor, to production. *MPP* is expressed in physical units, such as tons of coal, bushels of wheat, or number of automobiles. (Chapter 15)

Marginal propensity to consume (MPC) The ratio of the change in consumption spending to a given change in income. (Chapter 21)

Marginal propensity to save (MPS) The change in saving induced by a change in income. (Chapter 21)

Marginal revenue (MR) The change in total revenue generated by the sale of one additional unit of goods or services. (Chapter 9)

Marginal revenue product The change in total revenue that results from adding one more unit of a resource, such as labor, to production. *MRP*, which is expressed in dollars, is equal to *MPP* multiplied by the price of the good. (Chapter 15)

Marginal revenue product of capital The change in total revenue that results from adding one more dollar of loanable funds to production. (Chapter 17)

Marginal utility The change in total utility a person derives from consuming an additional unit of a good. (Chapter 5)

Market-day supply A market situation in which the quantity of a good supplied is fixed, regardless of price. (Chapter 3)

Market demand The sum of all individual demands in a market. (Chapter 3)

Market failure The failure of the market to achieve an optimal allocation of the economy's resources. The failure results from the market's inability to take externalities into account. (Chapter 14)

Market power A firm's ability to select and control market price and output. (Chapter 12)

Market share The percentage of total market sales produced by a particular firm in a market. (Chapter 10)

Market structure A set of market characteristics such as number of firms, ease of firm entry, and substitutability of goods. (Chapter 10)

Median income The midpoint of a society's income distribution, above and below which an equal number of individuals (or families) belong. (Chapter 18)

Medicaid A health care program administered through Social Security that is applicable to low-income and disabled people. (Chapter 29)

Medicare A health care program administered through Social Security that is applicable to everyone over 65 years old. (Chapter 29)

Merit good A good that market demand and supply do not produce enough of, in some people's opinion. (Chapter 29)

Microeconomics A subarea of economics that analyzes individuals as consumers and producers, and specific firms and industries. It focuses especially on the market behavior of firms and households. (Chapter 1)

Money Any commonly accepted good that acts as a medium of exchange, a measure of value, and a store of value. (Chapter 25)

Money supply Typically, M1 money. The supply of currency, demand deposits, and traveler's checks used in transactions. (Chapter 25)

Monopolistic competition A market structure consisting of many firms producing goods that are close substitutes. Firm entry is possible but is less open and easy than in perfect competition. (Chapter 10)

Monopoly A market structure consisting of one firm producing a good that has no close substitutes. Firm entry is impossible. (Chapter 10)

Monopsony A labor market with only one buyer. (Chapter 16)

Moral hazard A situation in which individuals in a market—buyers or sellers—react to market signals by altering their behavior in ways that undermine the benefits others derive from the market. (Chapter 14)

MR = MC rule The guideline used by a firm to achieve profit maximization. (Chapter 9)

Multinational corporation A corporation whose production facilities are located in two or more countries. Typically, multinational corporate sales are also international. (Chapter 7)

MU/P equalization principle The idea that a person's total utility is maximized when the ratios of marginal utility to price for each of the goods consumed are equal. (Chapter 5)

Mutual interdependence Any price change made by one firm in the oligopoly affects the pricing behavior of all other firms in the oligopoly. (Chapter 10)

N

Nash equilibrium A set of pricing strategies adopted by firms in which none can improve its payoff outcome, given the price strategies of the other firm or firms. (Chapter 12)

National income The sum of all payments made to resource owners for the use of their resources. (Chapter 20)

Nationalization Government ownership of a firm or industry. Price and production decisions are made by an agency of the government. (Chapter 13)

Nationally chartered bank A commercial bank that receives its charter from the comptroller of the currency and is subject to federal law as well as the laws of the state in which it operates. (Chapter 27)

Natural monopoly The result of a combination of market demand and firm's costs such that only one firm is able to produce profitably in a market. (Chapter 10)

Natural rate of unemployment The rate of unemployment caused by frictional plus structural unemployment in the economy. (Chapter 23)

Natural resources The lands, water, metals, minerals, animals, and other gifts of nature that are available for producing goods and services. (Chapter 1)

Negative income tax Government cash payments to the poor—an income tax in reverse—that is linked to the income levels of the poor. The cash payments decrease as income levels increase. The payments are designed to provide a minimum level of income to the poor. (Chapter 18)

Neo-Keynesian economics The school of thought that emphasizes the possibility that an economy can be in equilibrium at less than full employment with inflation. It argues that by managing aggregate demand, government can achieve the most acceptable combination of unemployment and inflation. (Chapter 28)

Net exports An economy's exports to other economies, minus its imports from other economies. (Chapter 20)

Nominal GDP GDP measured in terms of current market prices—that is, the price level at the time of measurement not adjusted for inflation. (Chapter 19)

Non-accelerating inflation rate of unemployment (NAIRU) Any rate equal to or higher than this rate will not cause the inflation rate to increase. Any rate lower than this rate will cause the inflation rate to increase. (Chapter 28)

Noncompeting labor markets Markets whose requirement for specific skills necessarily excludes workers who do not have the required skills. (Chapter 15)

Nondurable goods Goods expected to last less than a year. (Chapter 20)

Normal good A good whose demand increases or decreases when people's incomes increase or decrease. (Chapter 3)

Normal profit The entrepreneur's opportunity cost. It is equal to or greater than the income an entrepreneur could receive employing his or her resources elsewhere. Normal profit is included in the firm's costs. (Chapter 11)

Normative economics A subset of economics founded on value judgments and leading to assertions of what ought to be. (Chapter 1)

North American Free Trade Agreement (NAFTA) A free trade area consisting of Canada, the United States, and Mexico. (Chapter 31)

O

Oligopoly A market structure consisting of only a few firms producing goods that are close substitutes. (Chapter 10)

Open market operations The buying and selling of government bonds by the Federal Open Market Committee. (Chapter 27)

Opportunity cost The quantity of other goods that must be given up to obtain a good. (Chapter 2)

Outsourcing The practice of a firm contracting out or delegating part or parts of its production process to external sources, often located in foreign countries. (Chapter 8)

P

The paradox of thrift The more people try to save, the more income falls, leaving them with no more and perhaps with even less savings. (Chapter 22)

Parity price ratio The relationship between prices received by farmers and prices paid by farmers. (Chapter 6)

Partnership A firm owned by two or more people who each bear the responsibilities and unlimited liabilities of the firm. (Chapter 7)

Patent A monopoly right on the use of a specific new technology or on the production of a new good. The monopoly right is awarded to and safeguarded by the government to the firm who introduces the new technology or good. (Chapters 10 and 13)

Payoff matrix A table that matches the sets of gains (or losses) for competing firms when they choose, independently, various pricing options. (Chapter 12)

Peak The top of a business cycle. (Chapter 19)

Perfect competition A market structure consisting of a large number of firms producing goods that are perfect substitutes. Firm entry is open, easy. (Chapter 10)

Permanent income Permanent income is the regular income a person expects to earn annually. It may differ by some unexpected gain or loss from the actual income earned. (Chapter 21)

Permanent income hypothesis A person's consumption spending is related to his or her permanent income. (Chapter 21)

Per se A judicial standard or criterion by which a firm's size within an industry is considered sufficient evidence for the court to rule against it in an antitrust suit. (Chapter 13)

Personal consumption expenditures All goods and services bought by households. (Chapter 20)

Personal income National income, plus income received but not earned, minus income earned but not received. (Chapter 20)

Phillips curve A graph showing the inverse relationship between the economy's rate of unemployment and rate of inflation. (Chapter 28)

Poll tax A tax of a specific absolute sum levied on every person or every household. (Chapter 30)

Positive economics A subset of economics that analyzes the way the economy actually operates. (Chapter 1)

Potential money multiplier The increase in the money supply that is potentially generated by a change in demand deposits. (Chapter 26)

Poverty threshold The level of income below which families are considered to be poor. (Chapter 18)

Present value The value today of the stream of expected future annual income a property generates. The method of computing present value is to divide the annual income generated, R, by the rate of interest, r. That is, $PV = R/r$. (Chapter 17)

Price ceiling A maximum price set by government below the market-generated equilibrium price. (Chapter 6)

Price discrimination The practice of offering a specific good or service at different prices to different segments of the market. (Chapter 12)

Price elastic Quality of the range of a demand curve where elasticities of demand are greater than 1.0. (Chapter 4)

Price elasticity of demand The ratio of the percentage change in quantity demanded to a percentage change in price. Its numerical value expresses the percentage change in quantity demanded generated by a 1 percent change in price. (Chapter 4)

Price elasticity of supply The ratio of the percentage change in quantity supplied to the percentage change in price. (Chapter 4)

Price floor A minimum price set by government above the market-generated equilibrium price. (Chapter 6)

Price inelastic Quality of the range of a demand curve where elasticities of demand are less than 1.0. (Chapter 4)

Price leadership A firm whose price decisions are tacitly accepted and followed by other firms in the industry. (Chapter 12)

Price level A measure of prices in one year expressed in relation to prices in a base year. (Chapter 19)

Price-maker A firm conscious of the fact that its own activity in the market affects price. The firm has the ability to choose among combinations of price and output. (Chapter 11)

Price-taker A firm that views market price as a given and considers any activity on its own part as having no influence on that price. (Chapter 11)

Principal-agent problem A problem that arises when either demander or supplier in a labor market exercises an undisclosed personal interest or motive that undermines the efficacy of the market. (Chapter 15)

Producer surplus The difference between the minimum price a producer would be willing to accept for supplying a good or service and the market price. (Chapter 5)

Product differentiation The physical or perceived differences among goods in a market that make them close, but not perfect, substitutes for each other. (Chapter 10)

Production possibilities The various combinations of goods that can be produced in an economy when it uses its available resources and technology efficiently. (Chapter 2)

Profit Income earned by entrepreneurs. (Chapters 9 and 17)

Profit maximization The primary goal of a firm: To achieve the most profit possible from its production and sale of goods or services. (Chapter 9)

Progressive income tax A tax whose rate varies directly with the income of the person taxed. Rich people pay a higher tax rate—a larger percentage of their income is taxed—than do poor people. (Chapter 30)

Property rights The right to own a good or service and the right to receive the benefits that the use of the good or service provides. (Chapter 14)

Property tax A tax levied on the value of physical assets such as land, or financial assets such as stocks and bonds. (Chapter 30)

Proportional income tax A tax that is a fixed percentage of income, regardless of the level of income. (Chapter 30)

Prosperity A phase in the business cycle marked by a relatively high level of real GDP, full employment, and inflation. (Chapter 19)

Public choice The theory of collective decision making. (Chapter 14)

Public debt The total value of government securities—Treasury bills, notes, and bonds—held by individuals, businesses, other government agencies, and the Federal Reserve. (Chapter 30)

Public good A good whose benefits are not diminished even when additional people consume it and whose benefits cannot be withheld from anyone. (Chapters 14 and 29)

Q

Quantity theory of money $P = MV/Q$. The equation specifying the direct relationship between the money supply and prices. (Chapter 25)

Quota A limit on the quantity of a specific good that can be imported. (Chapter 31)

R

Rational expectations The school of thought that emphasizes the impossibility of government reducing the economy's rate of unemployment by managing aggregate demand. It argues that because people anticipate the consequences of announced government policy and incorporate these anticipated consequences into their present decision making, they end up undermining the policy. (Chapter 28)

Ration coupon A coupon issued by the government, entitling the holder to purchase a specific quantity of a good at or below the price ceiling. (Chapter 6)

Real GDP GDP adjusted for changes in the price level. (Chapter 19)

Recession A phase in the business cycle in which the decline in the economy's real GDP persists for at least a half-year. A recession is marked by relatively high unemployment. (Chapter 19)

Recessionary gap The amount by which aggregate expenditure falls short of the level needed to generate equilibrium national income at full employment without inflation. (Chapter 23)

Reciprocity An agreement between countries in which trading privileges granted by one to the others are the same as those granted to it by the others. (Chapter 31)

Recovery A phase in the business cycle, following a recession, in which real GDP increases and unemployment declines. (Chapter 19)

Regressive income tax A tax whose impact varies inversely with the income of the person taxed. Poor people have a higher percentage of their income taxed than do rich people. (Chapter 30)

Regulation Although ownership of the regulated firm remains in private hands, pricing and production decisions of the firm are monitored by a regulatory agency directly responsible to the government. (Chapter 13)

Relative income hypothesis As national income increases, consumption spending increases as well, always by the same amount. That is, as national income increases, *MPC* remains constant. (Chapter 21)

Relevant market The set of goods whose cross elasticities with others in the set are relatively high and whose cross elasticities with goods outside the set are relatively low. (Chapter 10)

Rent The difference between what a productive resource receives as payment for its use in production and the cost of bringing that resource into production. (Chapter 17)

Rent control Government-set price ceilings on rent. (Chapter 6)

Reserve requirement The minimum amount of reserves the Fed requires a bank to hold, based on a percentage of the bank's total deposit liabilities. (Chapter 27)

Return to monopsony power The difference between the *MRP* and the wage rate of the last worker hired, multiplied by the number of workers hired. (Chapter 16)

Rightsizing Implementing a firm's decision to adjust its plant size to produce in the most efficient manner its current volume of output. (Chapter 8)

Rule of reason A judicial standard or criterion by which a firm's size within an industry is insufficient evidence for the court to rule against it in an antitrust suit. Evidence must show that the firm actually used its size to violate antitrust laws. (Chapter 13)

S

Sales tax A tax levied in the form of a specific percentage of the value of the good or service. (Chapter 30)

Saving That part of national income not spent on consumption. (Chapter 21)

Savings bond A nonmarketable Treasury bond that is the most commonly held form of public debt. (Chapter 30)

Scarcity The perpetual state of insufficiency of resources to satisfy people's unlimited wants. (Chapter 1)

Services Productive activities that are instantaneously consumed. (Chapter 20)

Short run The time interval during which producers are able to change the quantity of some but not all the resources they use to produce goods and services. (Chapters 3 and 8)

Shutdown The cessation of the firm's activity. The firm's loss minimization occurs at zero output. (Chapter 9)

Social cost The cost to society of producing a good. This cost includes both the private costs associated with the good's production and the externalities cost generated by its production. (Chapter 14)

Social Security A social insurance program that provides benefits, subject to eligibility, to the elderly, the disabled, and their dependents. (Chapter 29)

Sole proprietorship A firm owned by one person who alone bears the responsibilities and unlimited liabilities of the firm. (Chapter 7)

Special-interest lobby A group organized to influence people in government concerning the costs and benefits of particular public goods. (Chapter 14)

Stabilization policy The use of countercyclical monetary and fiscal policy by the government and the Fed to stabilize the economy. (Chapter 28)

Stagflation A period of stagnating real GDP, inflation, and relatively high levels of unemployment. (Chapter 19)

Stakeholder Someone who has a personal and consequential interest in the viability of the firm. (Chapter 9)

State-chartered bank A commercial bank that receives its charter or license to function from a state government and is subject to the laws of that state. (Chapter 27)

Stock Ownership in a corporation, represented by shares that are claims on the firm's assets and earnings. (Chapter 7)

Stockholder (shareholder) A person owning stock in a corporation, that is, a share of a corporation. (Chapter 7)

Strike The withholding of labor by a union when the collective bargaining process fails to produce a contract that is acceptable to the union. (Chapter 16)

Structural unemployment Unemployment that results from fundamental technological changes in production, or from the substitution of new goods for customary ones. (Chapter 23)

Substitute goods Goods that can replace each other. When the price of one increases, the demand for the other increases. (Chapter 3)

Supply curve A curve that depicts the relationship between price and quantity supplied. (Chapter 3)

Supply schedule A schedule showing the specific quantity of a good or service that suppliers are willing and able to provide at different prices. (Chapter 3)

Supply-side economics The school of thought that emphasizes the possibility of achieving full employment without inflation. It argues that through tax reductions, spending cuts, and deregulation, government creates the proper incentives for the private sector to increase aggregate supply. (Chapter 28)

T

Tariff A tax on an imported good. (Chapter 31)

Tax multiplier The multiple by which the equilibrium level of national income changes when a dollar change in taxes occurs. The multiple depends upon the marginal propensity to consume. The equation for the tax multiplier is $-MPC/(1 - MPC)$. (Chapter 23)

Terms of trade The amount of a good or service (export) that must be given up to buy a unit of another good or service (import). A country's terms of trade are measured by the ratio of the country's export prices to its import prices. (Chapter 31)

Third parties People upon whom externalities are imposed. (Chapter 14)

Tit-for-tat A pricing strategy in game theory in which a firm chooses a price and will change its price to match whatever price the competing firm chooses. (Chapter 12)

Total cost (TC) Cost to the firm that includes both fixed and variable costs. (Chapter 8)

Total labor cost Quantity of labor employed multiplied by the wage rate. (Chapter 15)

Total revenue (TR) The price of a good multiplied by the number of units sold. (Chapters 4 and 9)

Total utility The total number of utils a person derives from consuming a specific quantity of a good. (Chapter 5)

Transactions demand for money The quantity of money demanded by households and businesses to transact their buying and selling of goods and services. (Chapter 25)

Transfer payments Income received but not earned. (Chapter 20)

Transitory income The unexpected gain or loss of income that a person experiences. It is the difference between a person's regular and actual income in any year. (Chapter 21)

Trough The bottom of a business cycle. (Chapter 19)

U

Unbalanced oligopoly An oligopoly in which the sales of the leading firms are distributed unevenly among them. (Chapter 12)

Underemployed resources The less-than-full utilization of a resource's productive capabilities. (Chapter 2)

Underemployed workers Workers employed in jobs that do not utilize their productive talents or experience. (Chapter 23)

Underground economy The unreported or illegal production of goods and services in the economy that is not counted in GDP. (Chapter 20)

Unemployment insurance A program of income support for eligible workers who are temporarily unemployed. (Chapter 29)

Unilateral transfers Transfers of currency made by individuals, businesses, or government of one nation to individuals, businesses, or governments in other nations, with no designated return. (Chapter 32)

Union shop An arrangement in which a firm may hire nonunion labor, but every nonunion worker hired must join the union within a specified period of time. (Chapter 16)

Unit elastic Price elasticity is equal to 1.0. In this range, price cuts or increases do not change total revenue. (Chapter 4)

Unit tax A fixed tax in the form of cents or dollars per unit, levied on a good or service. (Chapter 30)

Unlimited liability Personal responsibility of the owners for all debts incurred by sole proprietorships or partnerships. The owners' personal wealth is subject to appropriation to pay off the firm's debt. (Chapter 7)

Unwanted inventories Goods produced for consumption that remain unsold. (Chapter 22)

Util A hypothetical unit used to measure how much utility a person obtains from consuming a good. (Chapter 5)

Utility The satisfaction or enjoyment a person obtains from consuming a good. (Chapter 5)

V

Value added The difference between the value of a good that a firm produces and the value of the goods the firm uses to produce it. (Chapter 20)

Variable cost Cost that varies with the quantity of goods produced. Variable costs include such items as wages and raw materials. (Chapter 8)

Velocity of money The average number of times per year each dollar is used to transact an exchange. (Chapter 25)

Vertical merger A merger between firms that have a supplier-purchaser relationship. (Chapter 12)

Vicious circle of poverty A country is poor because it does not produce capital goods. It does not produce capital goods because it is poor. (Chapter 2)

W

Wage rate The price of labor. Typically, the wage rate is calculated in dollars per hour. (Chapter 15)

Wage-related rent The difference between what a resource receives and what it takes to bring the supply of that resource to market. (Chapter 17)

Wealth The accumulated assets owned by individuals. (Chapter 18)

Welfare Government-provided assistance—cash payments and goods and services—to the poor, the elderly, and the disabled. Eligibility is based principally on income and size of family. (Chapter 29)

World Trade Organization (WTO) The successor to GATT. The WTO is the only global international organization dealing with the rules of trade between nations. It promotes free trade. Once negotiated and signed by member nations, WTO agreements are ratified by member nations' parliaments. (Chapter 31)

Index